Mary Moody Emerson and the Origins of Transcendentalism

Mary Moody Emerson and the Origins of Transcendentalism

A Family History

PHYLLIS COLE

New York Oxford

Oxford University Press

1998

In memory of my parents—
"the twofold cord, then fourfold"

Oxford University Press

Oxford New York
Athens Auckland Bangkok Bogota Bombay Buenos Aires
Calcutta Cape Town Dar es Salaam Delhi Florence Hong Kong
Istanbul Karachi Kuala Lumpur Madras Madrid Melbourne
Mexico City Nairobi Paris Singapore Taipei Tokyo Toronto Warsaw

and associated companies in
Berlin Ibadan

Published by Oxford University Press, Inc.
198 Madison Avenue, New York, NY 10016

Oxford is a registered trademark of Oxford University Press

Library of Congress Cataloging-in-Publication Data
Cole, Phyllis.
Mary Moody Emerson and the origins of transcendentalism : a family history /
by Phyllis Cole.
p. cm.
Includes index.
ISBN 978-0-19-515200-5
1. Emerson, Mary Moody, 1774–1863. 2. Intellectuals—New England—
Biography. 3. Women intellectuals—New England—Biography.
4. Transcendentalism. 5. New England—Intellectual life—19th
century. 6. United States—Intellectual life—1783–1865.
7. Emerson, Ralph Waldo, 1803–1882. 8. Emerson, Mary Moody,
1774–1863—Influence. 9. Emerson family. I. Title.
F8.C67 1997
974'.03—dc21 97–1413

Printed in the United States of America
on acid-free paper

Preface

This book began as a study of Ralph Waldo Emerson's ancestral family, which extended into the Puritan past through a series of ministerial fathers. But early on, a woman who could claim no official pulpit or authority took center stage from her famous nephew. Mary Moody Emerson proved the key to a longer Emerson family tradition, for she actively celebrated the memory of her grandparents and taught the young to revere such enthusiastic piety. This is a biography of enthusiasm, conveyed in the intimate setting of a family from the Great Awakening of the eighteenth century through the Romantic revolution and millennial reform of the nineteenth.

Mary Emerson deserves our attention as much more than a conveyor of the past, however. She spoke in her own intellectually complex, personally feisty voice, diverting old religion into new and unconventional form in hundreds of letters and a diary ("Almanack") of more than half a century's duration. A full generation before Ralph Waldo Emerson's early manifestos, her Almanack was claiming a life of solitude and an experience of God through nature and the imagination. Her letters then formed the matrix of his thought, both early in life and through the years of his landmark literary utterance. Waldo Emerson valued this writing highly and partially acknowledged his debt to it, but until recently his biographers and critics have not cared to follow his lead back to her manuscripts. It took the women's studies revolution to provide that energy. I felt its momentum in 1981, reading Mary's letters at Harvard's Houghton Library, when I opened a box of uncatalogued family papers and discovered the reportedly lost manuscript of her Almanack.

Unfolding the significance of Mary's private writing has taken time. Women's studies scholarship is first of all archaeology, then discovery of a female context for interpretation, then reassessment of two-gender human culture. My lucky dig at Houghton led to texts with rich enough implication to take me through all these kinds of work. From the central point of Mary Moody Emerson's life and writing, I have been able to draw lines to both female and male worlds, to lives silent in history and to America's major, male-identified literary tradition. Just alongside the canon lies unexplored territory.

Putting a little-known, self-educated woman at the center affects the form as well as the content of this book. I have certainly not wanted to speak, like many biographers of the famous essayist, about "Emerson" and "Aunt Mary," but instead I refer to all the multiple Emersons by their first names, where necessary designating family relationship to her. In quoting the words of an intellectual woman whose spelling shows both absence of formal education and sheer willfulness, I place corrected spellings in brackets only where needed for clarity of meaning. Otherwise Mary's spelling remains intact as a crucial aspect of her style; I ask the reader's collaboration in construing such forms as "it's" as a possessive pronoun and "w'h" for "which," as well as her key terms "nessacary," "independance," and "imajanation."

My work has been enabled by a wide range of new scholarship by others. A boom in studies of Ralph Waldo Emerson has greatly expanded the available body of his writing, as the *Sermons, Topical Notebooks*, and *Poetry Notebooks* have emerged and Eleanor M. Tilton's new edition of *Letters* reached completion. Tracing the influence of Mary's words on her nephew would have been severely limited without these resources. My sense of Mary's importance was confirmed and extended by Evelyn Barish's investigation into Waldo's early relationship with her. Most of all, a first reading of Mary's letters expanded immeasurably when Nancy Craig Simmons began editing them; her generous sharing of typescripts at every stage of work has provided the letter texts for this book, even where I am not quoting directly from her *Selected Letters of Mary Moody Emerson*. Meanwhile, the women's studies work that offered early energy has burgeoned. I have gained perspectives on Mary from historians of women's friendship, education, and political life; from literary scholars recovering the "Other American Renaissance" of women's writing, especially in the informal genres of letter and diary; and from theological and historical studies of women and religion.

I am grateful for the generous institutional support that made this project possible. My work began with a fellowship from the National Endowment for the Humanities and a base at the Charles Warren Center for American History at Harvard University. The Rockefeller Foundation funded a year in the Women's Studies in Religion Program of Harvard Divinity School, and the Ellis Phillips Foundation extended that rich experience for an additional semester. In years when I worked independently, the Wellesley College Center for Research on Women offered me a place as a visiting research scholar. Since coming to Penn State, I have twice received support from research development grants and twice from the Institute for the Arts and Humanistic Studies. A summer stipend from the National Endowment for the Humanities brought to a close the work the

NEH had also allowed me to begin. I want especially to thank, among many supporters in these places, Peggy McIntosh, Connie Buchanan, and Madlyn Hanes.

Library support and assistance have likewise been extensive. At Houghton, Rodney Dennis shared the pleasure of my early research, and Leslie Morris has wonderfully facilitated completion. Marcia E. Moss offered her personal interest and wide knowledge of Concord history at the Concord Free Public Library. At Penn State Delaware County Campus, Ṣara Whildin, Susan Ware, and Jean Sphar have energetically sought out needed books and information. I wish to thank as well the staffs of the Andover-Harvard Theological Library, the Schlesinger Library, the Massachusetts Historical Society Library, and the American Antiquarian Society Library. Finally, thanks are due to three assistants who shared my early work in these libraries—Kathryn Stanis and Ann Brennan through funding from the Wellesley Center, Laurie Ledeen through her own generosity.

I am grateful to the Houghton Library, Harvard University, and the Ralph Waldo Emerson Memorial Association for permission to quote from Emerson family papers. Other manuscript materials are quoted by the courtesy of the Concord Free Public Library, Schlesinger Library, Harvard University Archives, Andover-Harvard Theological Library, Massachusetts Historical Society, and American Antiquarian Society. For permission to quote papers in their private possession, I would like to thank David Emerson, Miriam Sylvester Monroe, Beatrice B. Parker, and Joan W. Goodwin.

These investigations have been personal and immediate, as well as scholarly. I had the good fortune to live in Concord, Massachusetts, while doing research—where a neighbor recalled Dr. Edward Emerson from her early childhood, where local churches responded with interest, and where program directors like Ann McGrath, Jane Gordon, and Stuart Weeks offered opportunities to speak. Most heartfelt thanks are due to the Muse-Orlinoff family for their unceasing hospitality during my at-least-annual returns to Concord since 1989, as well as to Pat Padden for his photographic skill. Mary Moody Emerson has also led me to other towns, and there, too, I have enjoyed companionship and hospitality. Especially memorable were Margaret Sawyer's introduction to Mary's world in Waterford, Maine; Philip Woodwell's glad reception in York; and a foray into the neighborhoods of Brooklyn with Jennifer Adams Poser.

At Oxford University Press, three editors have ably supported this project—William Sisler in its early stages, Elizabeth Maguire as I completed drafting the manuscript, and T. Susan Chang in bringing the book to press.

My greatest debt is to the colleagues who have also become friends through this work. Joel Porte first taught me about Waldo Emerson and unhesitatingly published my new thoughts on Mary. I met Bob Gross while first planning my Emerson family history, and now he and I are exchanging book manuscripts as we both approach publication. Bob never hesitated to share his latest discovery, and he was equally eager to know my results. Likewise, Joel Myerson offered his voluminous transcript of the Emerson brothers' letters, as well as his wide professional expertise and interest in sharing food and conversation. Bob Richardson expressed excitement about my work and respected my claim to it; he also urged the importance of Waldo's "MME" journals. Paula Blanchard graciously shared her knowledge of New England literature and the art of biography, George Huntston Williams his long immersion in Protestant church history. Megan Marshall drew me into the Biography Group, offered plentiful moral support, and dispatched relevant news from her research on the Peabody sisters. Likewise, Joan Goodwin has given generously from her knowledge and transcripts of Sarah Alden Bradford Ripley and the Ripley family. Nancy Simmons and I have been each other's strongest supporters and toughest critics through years of puzzling over the prose of Mary Moody Emerson. Her visits north have always been occasions, and we have assisted each other's work on every level. Once I corrected her location of the town of Byfield, but then she read my manuscript and corrected my spelling of that same Massachusetts town.

Through these years of slow growth, the Cole family has also grown up. My daughters, Sarah and Rachel, have long since surpassed Mary Moody Emerson's reputed height of four feet three inches, but still their mother labors at her word processor. I want to thank them for their patience and interest. The greatest commitment, however, has come from my husband, Bob, who immediately recognized Mary's metaphysical insight, gave me perspectives on her history from the mental health community, and never doubted that I would at last finish the book.

Media, Pennsylvania
September 1996

P. C.

Contents

Emerson Genealogies

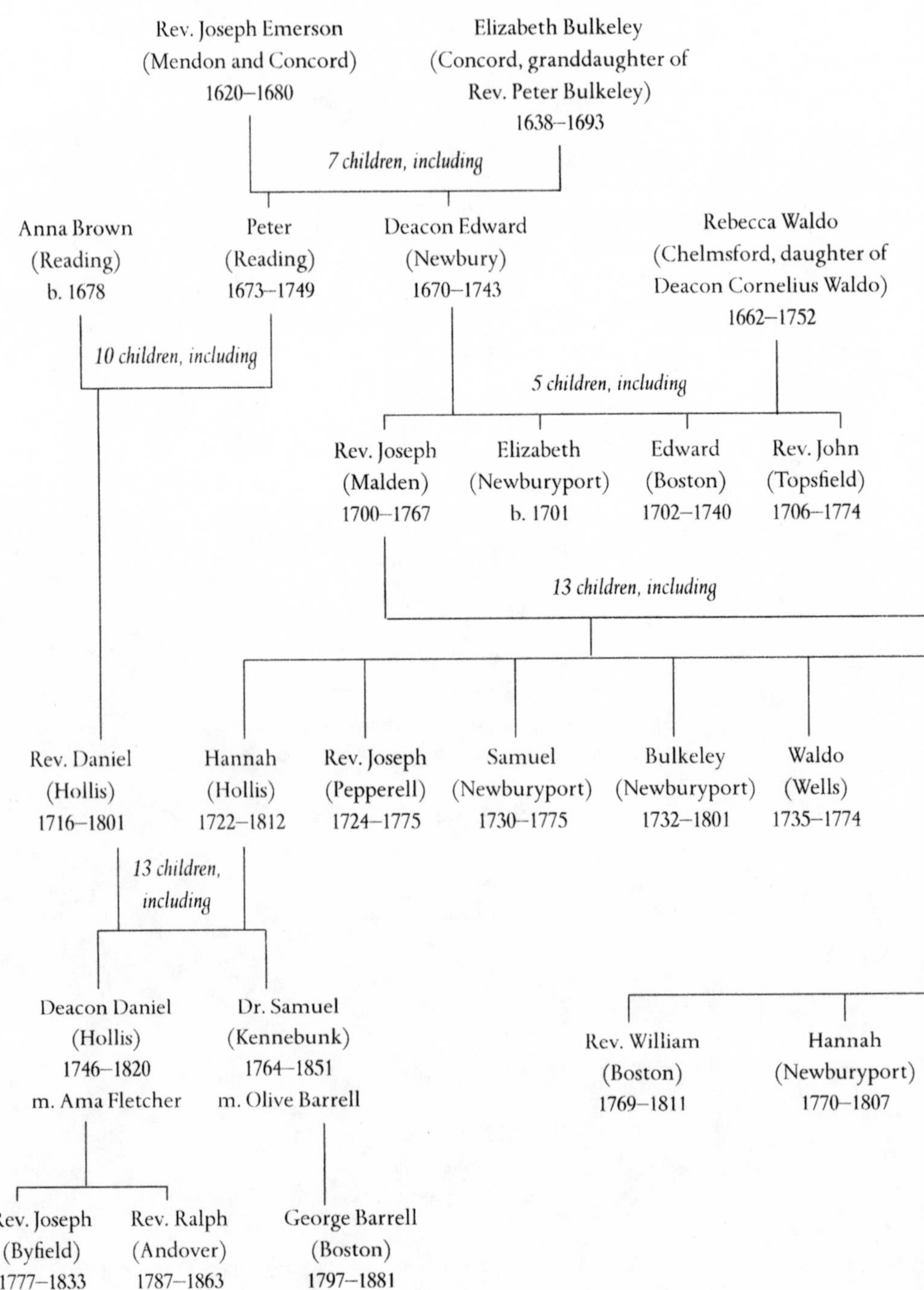

Eighteenth Century

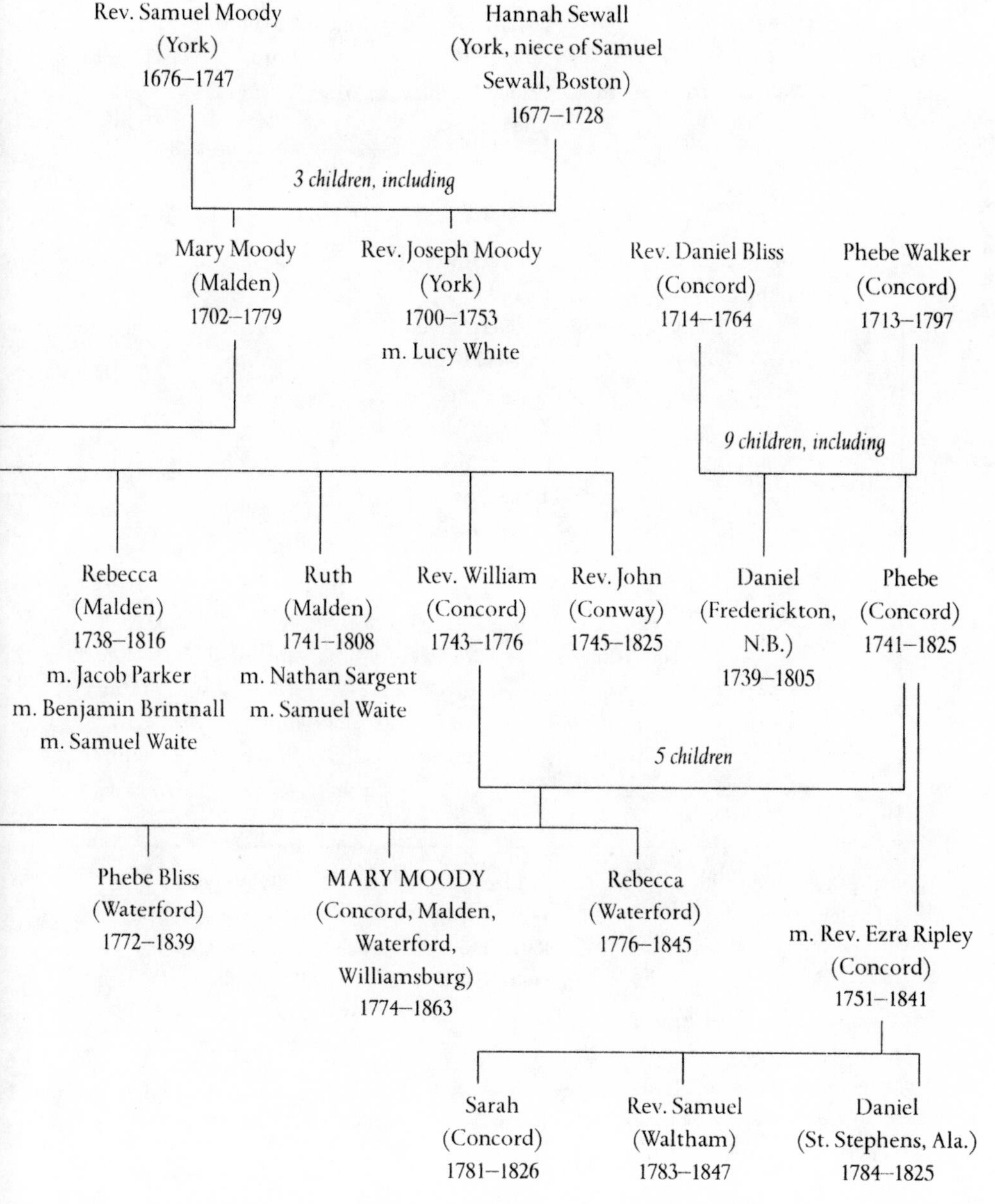

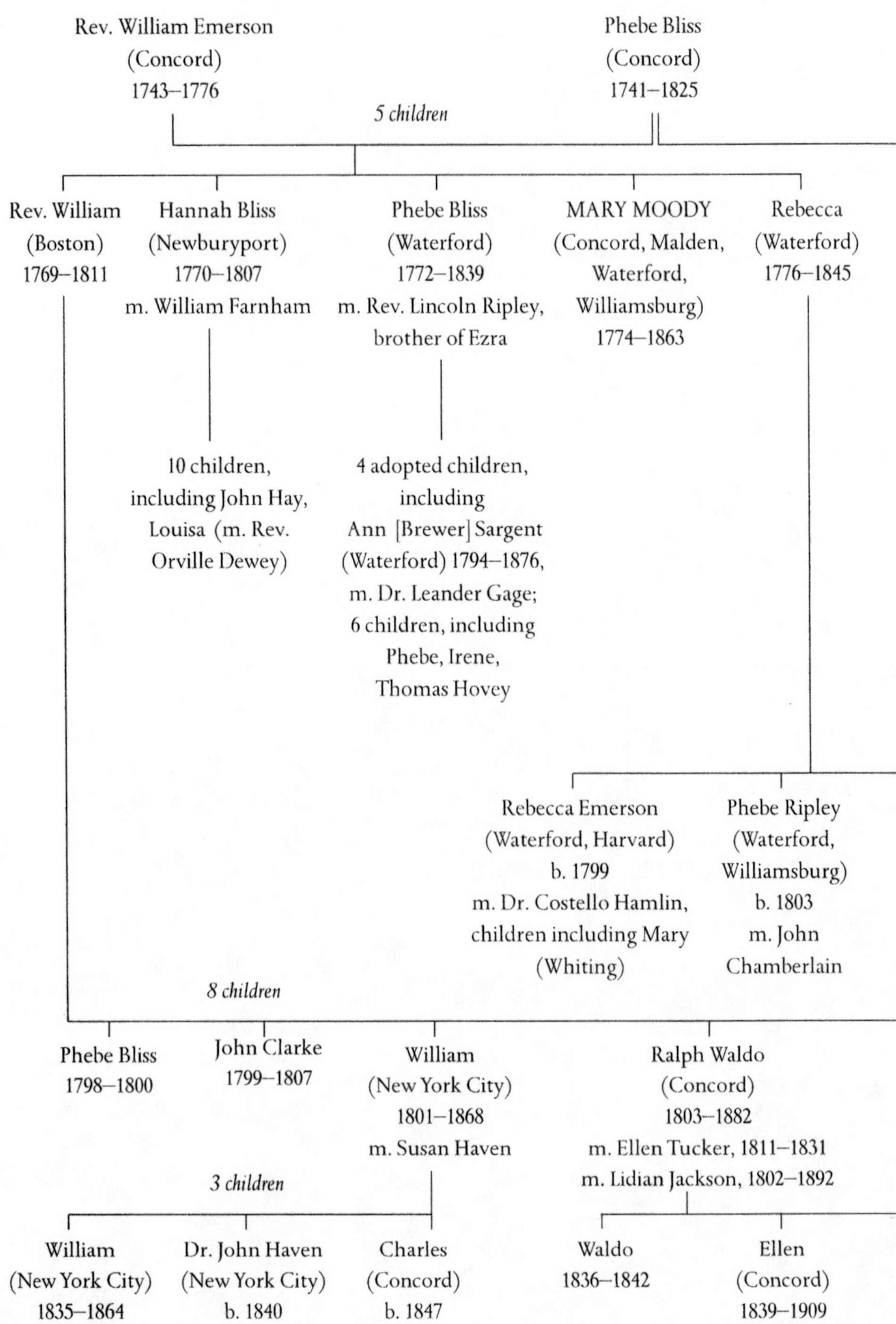
Rev. William Emerson
(Concord)
1743–1776
Phebe Bliss
(Concord)
1741–1825
5 children
Rev. William
(Boston)
1769–1811
Hannah Bliss
(Newburyport)
1770–1807
m. William Farnham
Phebe Bliss
(Waterford)
1772–1839
m. Rev. Lincoln Ripley,
brother of Ezra
MARY MOODY
(Concord, Malden,
Waterford,
Williamsburg)
1774–1863
Rebecca
(Waterford)
1776–1845
10 children,
including John Hay,
Louisa (m. Rev.
Orville Dewey)
4 adopted children,
including
Ann [Brewer] Sargent
(Waterford) 1794–1876,
m. Dr. Leander Gage;
6 children, including
Phebe, Irene,
Thomas Hovey
Rebecca Emerson
(Waterford, Harvard)
b. 1799
m. Dr. Costello Hamlin,
children including Mary
(Whiting)
Phebe Ripley
(Waterford,
Williamsburg)
b. 1803
m. John
Chamberlain
8 children
Phebe Bliss
1798–1800
John Clarke
1799–1807
William
(New York City)
1801–1868
m. Susan Haven
Ralph Waldo
(Concord)
1803–1882
m. Ellen Tucker, 1811–1831
m. Lidian Jackson, 1802–1892
3 children
William
(New York City)
1835–1864
Dr. John Haven
(New York City)
b. 1840
Charles
(Concord)
b. 1847
Waldo
1836–1842
Ellen
(Concord)
1839–1909

Nineteenth Century

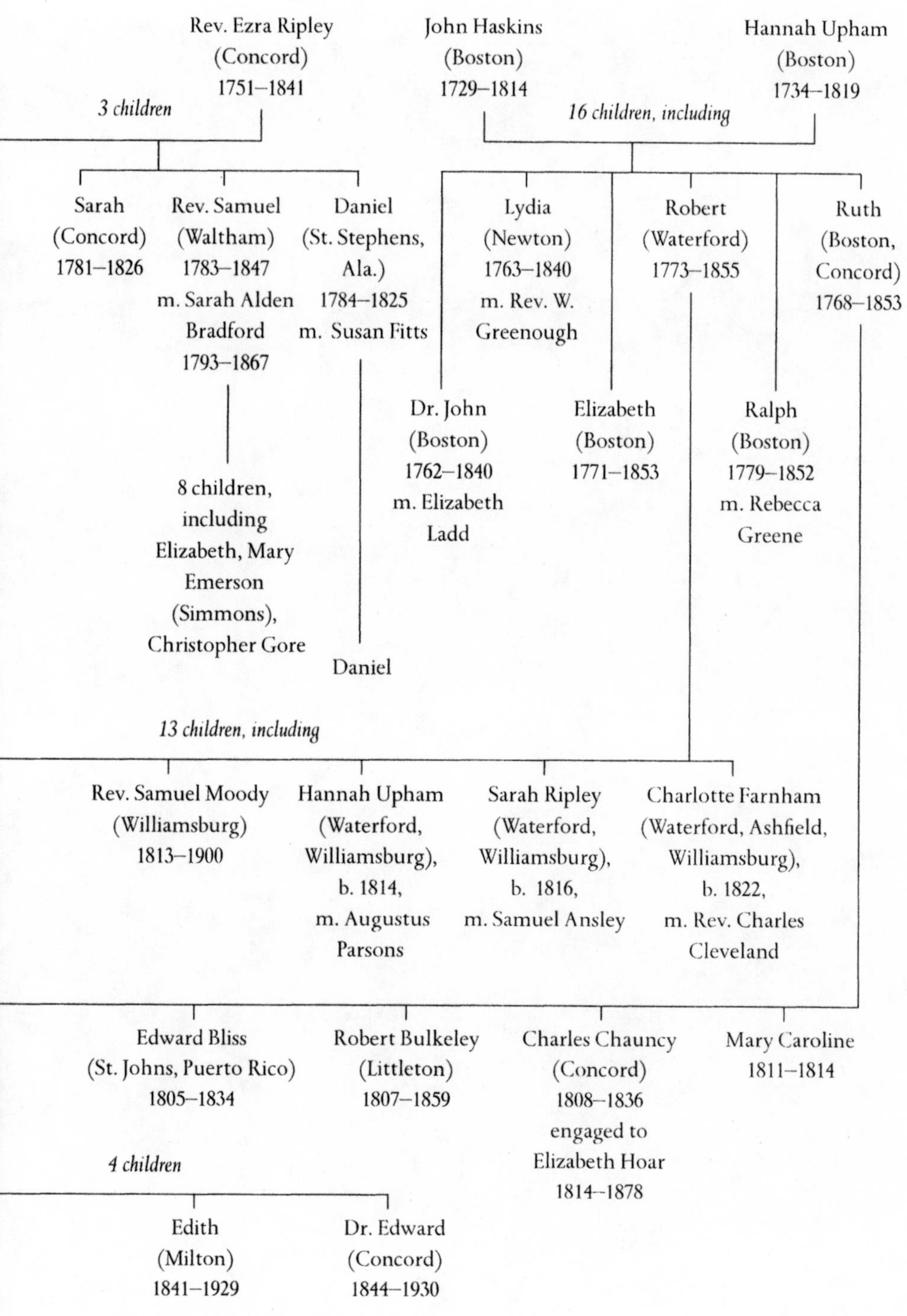

Mary Moody Emerson and the Origins of Transcendentalism

Introduction

Where were thine own intellect if others had not lived?

Mary Moody Emerson, quoted by
Ralph Waldo Emerson (*Works* 10:405)

Among the last completely new lectures that Ralph Waldo Emerson delivered was a biographical portrait of his own aunt Mary Moody Emerson. He called it "Amita," Latin for "aunt," and first read it to the New England Women's Club on March 1, 1869, when he was nearly sixty-five and she had been dead for six years. "Amita" was neither a traditional eulogy nor a personal reminiscence, for the speaker declined even to speak of his subject by name. "As I do not wish to embarrass her memory or your thought by unnecessary details, I shall leave geography names and dates as vague as is becoming," he explained to the audience, going on to call Mary only by her Latin title.[1] Genteel reticence shielded this woman's life from public view.

But such concealment allowed him to present his "heroine" by reading from a most private form of writing, her diary, simply framing it with a sketch of the life. Through sketch and reading he had a bold aim, to offer Mary Moody Emerson's life as cultural history:

> It is a representative life, such as could hardly have appeared out of New England; of an age now past, and of which I think no types survive. Perhaps I deceive myself and overestimate its interest. It has to me a value like that which many readers find in Madam Guyon, in Rahel, in Eugénie de Guérin, but it is purely original and hardly admits of a duplicate. Then it is a fruit of Calvinism and New England, and marks the precise time when the power of the old creed yielded to the influence of modern science and humanity."[2]

To Ralph Waldo Emerson a "representative life" was not average but exemplary, a "type" of its age. He had called an earlier book of biographical essays

Representative Men, but in it considered only famous male Europeans. Now he placed "Amita" in the company of three renowned French and German women of sensibility, claiming a kindred interest for her within New England culture. Indeed, through his very effort to treat "Amita" as a type in native history, he implicitly brought her significance back to himself. By 1869 he had long been famous for enunciating the new "science and humanity" known as Transcendentalism; *he* represented the culture to which New England's creed had yielded. By implication, "Amita" was his own forerunner.

As Waldo Emerson went on to narrate Mary's life, however, he did not press for either historical meanings or personal implications. Instead, his story held poignant human interest, describing "a country girl, poor, solitary,—a 'goody' as she called herself,—growing from youth to age amid slender opportunities and usually very humble company." She was born to higher status as the daughter of Concord's patriot minister; in adulthood, Waldo recalled, she told Lafayette that she had been " 'in arms' at the Concord fight." But her father died early in the Revolution, and her childhood unfolded amidst the loneliness and poverty of an aunt's household in Malden. She returned to Concord in adolescence, but as an adult chose more loneliness, now in the picturesque natural setting of a farm near the White Mountains in Maine. Waldo surmised that her decision not to marry amounted to a religious vow, but, in addition, this was a woman of difficult temperament who "could keep step with no human being." She actively, even jokingly, courted death; eventually she wore a shroud as her everyday garment when death refused to come. Yet Mary loved youth and success, beauty and genius. Notable people were her friends throughout life, and she "gave high counsels. It was the privilege of certain boys to have this immeasurably high standard indicated to their childhood; a blessing which nothing else in education could supply."[3] In this covert self-reference Waldo came closest to autobiography.

Images from myth and literature, rather than the specific record of New England's creeds, evoked her religious type. This was a Greek oracle, "our Delphian," a "Cassandra" who "uttered, to a frivolous, skeptical time the arcana of the Gods." "What a subject is her mind and life for the finest novel!" Waldo exclaimed, though spelling out no prophetic message for his Cassandra or significance to her novel-like plot. He found that reading Dante recalled her "eloquent theology" but offered no account of these religious ideas. Nor did he go beyond listing her favorite authors: among them the British poets Milton, Young, Coleridge, Byron; the ancient philosophers Plato, Aristotle, Plotinus; two widely divergent New England theologians, Edwards and Channing; and one woman writer, Germaine de Staël.[4] How this impressive reading might chart a woman's course from old Calvinism to new humanity, how the reading was registered in the writing, even how a "goody" in Malden or up-country Maine had obtained and understood such books at all—these matters all went unelaborated.

Waldo did let Mary speak for herself, though in a highly selective way corresponding to her role as "oracle," in language "happy, but inimitable, unattainable by talent, as if caught from some dream." Some of the diary and letter excerpts that he read certainly hinted at affinity with the British Romantics on her reading list, as well as with Emersonian Transcendentalism. In one, recalling her youthful effort to "wake up the soul amid the dreary scenes of monotonous Sabbaths," she asserted that nature "looked like a pulpit"; telling of social isolation in another, she found it a "mystic dream" and opportunity for "solitude with the Being who makes the powers of life!" Waldo's narrative had presented solitude as the sad result of a childhood with aging relatives, driving Mary to "find Nature her companion and solace."[5] The quotations from her writing, however, claimed religious ecstasy and dissenting vision in these resources—vision that might well be taken as evidence that for her the Calvinist creed had passed.

Such an elusive portrait left a great deal for members of Waldo's audience to construe on their own, but some members of the New England Women's Club could well do so from separate knowledge of "Amita." Well over a hundred people, more than had so far enrolled as members of the year-old organization, filled Boston's Chickering Hall that evening to consider (as the minutes recorded) "a New England woman of rare gifts and originality of character." These people all knew Ralph Waldo Emerson as a writer, many knew him personally, and quite a few recalled Mary Moody Emerson. The membership list included Waldo's own wife, daughters, and half cousin Elizabeth Ripley, as well as such cultural kindred as Elizabeth Peabody, Julia Ward Howe, Ednah Dow Cheney, Annie Fields, and Louisa May Alcott.[6] In such a gathering, of course, the subject's true identity was transparent.

One member of the audience, Harriet Hanson Robinson, left a record of responses to the event in her diary. She misunderstood the title to be "Ermita": not knowing Latin, she probably transcribed the lecturer's Yankee accent as it sounded, making the "aunt" into a pseudo-Latin, female "hermit." But that was an apt misunderstanding, since what impressed Robinson about this woman was her otherworldly asceticism. Robinson herself had seen Mary in a shroud on the streets of Concord. She also remembered the figure whom Hawthorne had fictionalized in "The Minister's Black Veil": "There seems to be a streak of oddity & eccentricity in that family—or is it genius? Some think her to have been descended from the famously odd parson Handkerchief Moody, who always wore a veil over his face."[7] Her guess hit home: the parson was in fact Mary's great-uncle, though neither Mary nor Waldo emphasized their relation to him.

If Robinson could speculate at a distance about the Emersons, moreover, Elizabeth Peabody offered decisive judgments based on long acquaintance. A week after the lecture she recalled to Robinson Waldo's private words about Mary. His aunt's life, he had once said, was "of more importance than that Greece and Rome should have been." "Emerson," Peabody concluded, "derived much of his character from his aunt—he has improved the talent, hers was buried."[8]

In fact, Peabody had already published an account of Mary Moody Emerson's talent and its burial. Six years earlier, an obituary essay by Peabody had proposed an edition of Mary's writing, declared her a "wonderfully intellectual woman," and straightforwardly named her allegiances. The Arian theology of Samuel Clarke and Richard Price had provided her foundation, Peabody recalled, "yet it seemed to us that she valued any dogmas for others, rather than for herself, conscious as she was of that power of thinking, which, as she once said of adequate conversation, 'makes the soul.'" Furthermore, Peabody's Mary had been politically engaged, finding in the antislavery movement a "counterpart of her religious devotion, a flaming fire." Rather than mythologizing Mary, Peabody found her a real and admirable, if unconventional, woman. "She had a great heart, although she was not tender, like most women. . . . She was not without sentiment—the union of thought with feeling; but it was so far removed from what we call sentimental, that she impressed some persons as having no affection." Finally, Peabody spoke from a woman's perspective of Mary's influence on "illustrious nephews," naming its cost, as well as its accomplishment: "To [their] early nurture and education she gave not merely the mental but the physical energies of the meridian of her life—no small sacrifice in a person of her peculiar turn of mind."[9]

Peabody did not step onto the lecture podium and offer a rebuttal to Waldo Emerson in 1869, but through her essay on Mary we can let the female audience have a voice. This was a proto-feminist gathering: before the spring ended, many members of the culturally oriented Women's Club had joined in founding the more political American Woman's Suffrage Association. Just as Waldo publicly characterized his female relative in March, so he addressed the Suffrage Association in May; no other famous male writer of nineteenth-century America so willingly offered his public presence to organizations of women. Yet he presented conciliating, conservative messages both times, telling his second audience that women, embodying affection as men embodied intellect, should value their special gift of religious grace because "a man likes to have his wife possess piety."[10] If he wanted that spring to celebrate the memory of "Amita" as a figure of the New England past, jointly valued by these women and himself, he surely sought as well to contain whatever was too disruptive in her unhusbanded, Cassandra-like prophecies or too painful in her story.

In contrast, Peabody's tribute to Mary Moody Emerson, though it enjoyed considerably less prominence than Waldo's, anticipated themes that twentieth-century feminists would perceive anew. Young Virginia Woolf, reviewing the new edition of Waldo Emerson's *Journals* in 1910, immediately recognized Mary as most powerful among the women who had surrounded his childhood. The review paraphrased Waldo himself on Mary's conflict between old faith and new ideas, a conflict too intense to withhold from others, but then Woolf commented, "Unlike [her nephews], she was only self-taught, and her fervour boiled within her, scalding those she loved best." Decades later, Tillie Olsen benefited from Woolf's full analysis of the creative life and domestic constriction of women—and read Ralph Waldo Emerson's essay on his aunt—before presenting her first impassioned address on women's "Silences." She commented, "Emily Dickinson freed herself, denying all the duties expected of a woman of her social position except the closest family ones, and she was fortunate to have a sister, and servants, to share these. How much is revealed of the differing circumstances and fate of their own as-great capacities, in the diaries (and lives) of those female bloodkin of great writers: Dorothy Wordsworth, Alice James, Aunt Mary Moody Emerson."[11] The difficult achievement of self-education, the loss of creative energy amidst domestic obligation, the substitution of diary-writing for publication: these were subjects that many members of the New England Women's Club, as well as subsequent feminist critics, could have recognized in "Amita."

THE AIM OF MY BOOK is to reconstruct the lives of Mary Moody Emerson and her family in ways suggested but not fulfilled by her nephew's memorial and the comments surrounding it. This is the study of a private woman writer, within New England's evolving intellectual culture; of Emersonian Transcendentalism, as brought forth by soul-making conversation between aunt and nephew; of the multigenerational Emerson family, as experienced by an unmarried and solitary woman within it. Our sense of Mary has been almost entirely embedded in the tradition of Emerson studies ever since Waldo's lecture; today a scholar in pursuit of her will find the manuscript letters and diary that he quoted amidst the "Emerson Family Papers" rather than in a women's archive. But there is an advantage in that context. In addition to extricating a woman's experience from the male tradition that preserved it, I have sought to turn the tables and reenvision the tradition from her vantage point. To generations of biographers and critics, Mary has been seen as Waldo's "eccentric" aunt;[12] my goal is to revalue her at the center of the larger circle.

Living from 1774 to 1863, from Revolution to Civil War, Mary was a daughter of the early American Republic, knowing both its rising expectations and its chaos through the peculiar fortunes of her Massachusetts clerical family. Both an intense religious life and an obsession with writing grew out of this experience. While Mary's life has "representative" value within its generation, her writing itself represents and reflects upon her life. The letters and diary amount to an extended autobiography and essay, originating from decades for which we have few substantial women's voices.[13]

These texts are powerful as language and idea, though daunting as a result of both intrinsic complexity and vagary of form. The Almanack is far from a complete and openly readable text; as Mary comments within its pages, "This poor old memoir is as disconnected and collected in loose leaves as its Author."[14] She wrote it on letter paper, whatever she had available, not in bound books as Waldo did his journals. Her method was to sew these pages together into pamphlets, piecing together a book and an authorial self. Even this hand-crafted unity, however, was seriously reduced by the nomadic circumstances of Mary's life, by her habit of lending pieces to friends, and eventually by the 1872 fire at the Emersons' house in Concord.

The Almanack survives as a partial and damaged text, but very much a book of the self in relation to God. At once a spiritual diary in the Puritan tradition and a commonplace book, ingesting theology and literature in vehement peronal pursuit of divine knowledge, Mary's Almanack is possibly New England's last great Puritan diary. It is surely the longest and richest by a woman, directly manifesting the "union of thought with feeling" that Peabody saw in Mary.[15]

She wrote it primarily for herself and God; when Waldo asked for some of its pages too eagerly in 1830, Mary exploded, "I send you an Almanack! 'Catch me'—soberly—I will not till you return the others. They are my *home*—the only images of having existed." But at the same time she included within it notes to "any Nephew who may read this" and often looked ahead to future influence on an aspiring youth or an aged seeker of sympathy. Though sure that Waldo would not want "the trouble of looking over many a womanish whim or theology he dont believe in," adamant that "not a scrap is to see print as many deceased persons have had their papers," she did at last arrange to have others inherit the Almanack.[16]

She wanted her words preserved because, though insistently private, Mary's diary and letters were the work of a stifled author. At the age of thirty, in 1804, she had begun to publish epistolary essays under the pseudonym "Constance" in her brother William's literary magazine, the *Monthly Anthology*. His censure of her supposed errors seems to have contributed significantly to the experiment's demise. Even more, though, Mary clearly felt that censure internally, never admitting in the Almanack or in letters before, during, or after her appearance in print that she harbored any ambition to publish at all. "At reading the lives of women eminent for piety learning influence &c," she wrote, "I feel a secret exulting that I am eminent for nonadvantages in life. I am glad I have nothing, as I can't have much." In the logic of this sentence, her first choice was to have much. Proudly unwilling, however, to adopt the conciliating gestures that allowed women's appearance in print, she channeled her "secret exulting" into private forms of writing with an energy that stormed against external and internal barriers. "I want influence—agency—," she confessed to her Almanack in 1817. "I know not what to do oftentimes—offer my every sense & faculty to God—trusting Him for their disposal, waiting for His sending for me."[17]

When seen as a whole, Mary's writing amounts to an early and groundbreaking woman's text of American Romanticism, powerful both for its positive vision and for its record of conflict and self-silencing. During her nephew's infancy in 1804 and 1805, a period that he later described as New England's "Month-of-March," she lived and wrote a celebration of the solitary imagination and of nature as analogous to God, valuing both explicitly as a woman's resources. "You ask, how can the faculty of imagination benefit us as immortal beings?" she asked her female correspondent in the *Monthly Anthology*. "Whither, Cornelia, can we go without it? How blind, how deaf, how dumb, and inanimate without this sensitive pioneer!" Four decades later, Mary had repudiated authorship but still wrote copiously to explain her rationale for silence, and she did so by claiming fellowship with a female nature "so eloquent that she refuses to take the voice of any interpreter." In the aftermath of Ralph Waldo Emerson's *Nature*, Mary's words evoked not his book but her own lifelong experience of hearing nature's voice.[18]

Indeed, her language of solitude, nature, and imagination directly nurtured the more renowned generation that followed hers. Mary deflected personal ambition onto protégés of both sexes. From "Cornelia" to Elizabeth Peabody, writing women elicited her own writing. Through correspondence with her nephew Waldo, however, Mary became a direct source of Transcendentalism. Just as William Wordsworth wrote some of the founding texts of British Romanticism through silent partnership with his diary-writing sister Dorothy, so Ralph Waldo Emerson appropriated and assimilated his aunt's language from youth through old age.[19] Mary's authority surpassed Dorothy Wordsworth's, though, because she held generational priority and actively served as her kinsman's mentor.

Waldo's late lecture "Amita" was just one outcropping in the intertextual field between these two writers, an account that omitted most of his own most telling thoughts and quotations over the years. At the age of eighteen, he began copying whole letters into his journal as the work of "Tnamurya" (anagram for "Aunt Mary"); he begged and transcribed her Almanack as much as she would allow. By 1826 he looked upon the whole of her "living wit" as a personal legacy. Even after their correspondence abated, his journal continued to reflect upon her. Years later, largely after 1850, he filled one thick "MME" notebook with passages from her letters and three more with Almanack excerpts.[20]

The results for his own writing were enormous. He found in Mary so powerful an influence that he could neither speak of it in detail (veering from the "Greece and Rome" hyperbole to silence) nor ever be entirely free of her presence. The lecture "Amita" partially paid a very old debt. In 1837, at the height of early confidence as a prophet of nature, Waldo recorded Mary's name in his journal among his seven most vital "benefactors," but he admitted that he would rather take gifts of thought from others "as we take apples off a tree without any thanks."[21] He had already picked many apples from Mary's tree; nor was his harvest at that point complete.

The history of one sentence suggests the quality of their relationship through time. About 1859 Waldo revised a line of Mary's directly into his essay "Culture" for *The Conduct of Life.* "Solitude, the safeguard of mediocrity," he wrote, "is, to genius, the stern friend, the cold, obscure shelter where moult the wings which bear it farther than suns and stars." Mary had first written this counsel to him in 1824, when he was twenty-one years old. The original sentence illustrates her image-clotted language, nonstandard spelling, and awkwardly parenthetical syntax, but even more the visionary individualism that she pressed upon him: "Solitude w'h to people, not talented to deviate from the beaten track (w'h is the safe gaurd of mediocrity) without offending, is to learning & talents the only sure labyrinth (tho' sometimes gloomy) to form the eagle wings w'h will bear one farther than suns and stars." Waldo transcribed Mary's letter into his journal soon after receiving it in 1824. Almost thirty years later, the passage reappeared in his notebook "MME 1" and was indexed for use under the heading "Solitude." Then, while struggling to complete his last major book, he revised it in the published work of 1860 without quotation marks or attribution.[22] One sentence might seem inconsequential, but this one defines his essential stance of solitary, transcendent genius. It echoes across the decades separating his origins from his closing reflections. Even in the proclamation of self-reliance, Waldo never wholly outgrew or left behind this "benefactor."

MY AIM HERE IS not, however, simply to reverse the traditional judgment of literary reputations and claim Mary Moody Emerson rather than Ralph Waldo Emerson as the true genius and prototype of Transcendentalism. Mary is too cryptic, fragmentary, and damaged as a writer to bear the full weight of such claims; in addition, the field of writing by aunt and nephew itself suggests a wider story and tradition, a story about the intergenerational family as a culture, where books and parlors, public and private affairs, speech and silence, male and female literally cohabited. Waldo and Mary are better understood in kinship to each other than separately, but so does their bond need to be seen within the larger history that contained them both.

As a study of Mary Moody Emerson and her family, this book begins not with Mary's generation, but with her grandparents and great-grandparents. I will trace a family tradition of piety that, adopting Waldo's terms, extended literally from the old creed to the new humanity, with Mary Moody Emerson both its transmitter and its transformer. Living out an unorthodox religious consciousness that was the "fruit of Calvinism," Mary found revelatory power in herself and in nature, but simultaneously revered the more orthodox heritage of her ancestors. She personally knew representatives of five generations, two before and two after herself, so in her late eighties could retell stories that she had heard in childhood. This oral tradition reached deep into the Puritan past. "Samuel Moody of York—he was Father Moody—married Hannah Sewall," she told Waldo's daughter Ellen in 1861, "so you are cousins to the Sewalls, and it's a good name; they used to make a great deal of the relationship."[23] Lineage and kinship were live values despite the passage of 163 years since the marriage of Mary's great-grandparents Samuel Moody and Hannah Sewall.

The lineage defined itself as a succession of Massachusetts clergymen. Like Mehitable Rossiter in Harriet Beecher Stowe's *Old Town Folks*, Mary had "the savor of ministerial stock . . . strong about her." Family—and the prominent, learned profession of its men—was a major source of status and identity for women as well. About 1838 Mary listed in her Almanack the thirty-one Emersons who had graduated from Harvard College between 1656 and 1828. "How much of poetry in this catalogue of the Cambridge Emersons—," she exclaimed.[24] Such "poetry" was not directly her own. She used the Latin names symbolizing their position as male scholars: Latin that she had never studied, at the college and for the pulpit that excluded her.

Within the Emerson family, however, Mary wielded a power competing with Harvard and the Massachusetts Standing Order of Ministers. About the same year as her praise of "the Cambridge Emersons," Waldo commented in his journal that Mary's family lore had saved him from the "levitical education" of Harvard. "I cannot hear the young men whose theological instruction is exclusively owed to Cambridge & to public institution," he wrote, "without feeling how much happier was my star which rained on me influences of ancestral religion. The depth of the religious sentiment which I knew in my Aunt Mary imbuing all her genius & derived to her from such hoarded family traditions, from so many godly lives & godly deaths of sainted kindred at Concord, Malden, and York, was itself a culture, an education." He followed his entry with the line from Proverbs, "Where there is no vision, the people perish."

What Mary gave to Waldo, as to Waldo's daughter a generation later, was a culture of Puritan vision through ancestral stories. "I heard with awe her tales," Waldo recalled, then summoned up a few: of two grandfathers on their death-beds, one calling to open the door for the Angel of Death, the other mutely stretching up his hands to witness Christ's presence; of Father Moody's unstinting charity and "commanding administration of his holy office"; of another who "whilst his house was burning, stood apart with some of his church & sang 'There is a house not made with hands.' " Waldo's lecture "Amita" omitted not only the substance of Mary's intellectual life and the extent of her influence on him, but also his own vivid memories of her telling about heroes of the old creed. Both his journals and her letters to him (as Woolf recognized) reverberated with this heroism, and his thoughts about Mary were deeply intertwined with the value of a more distant past. In 1841, recording his interest in writing a family memoir, he saw Mary as its center: "I doubt if the interior & spiritual history of New England could be truelier told than through the exhibition of family history such as this, the picture of this group of M.M.E. and the boys, mainly Charles."[25]

In Waldo's imagining of this "interior history," Mary was the "devout genius" standing between the ancestral heritage and his own generation. His famous rhetorical gesture in *Nature* of abandoning "the sepulchres of the fathers" for "an original relation to the universe" suppressed his own interest in ancestors. Mary loomed behind this interest, and in youth he tried to shake it off. "It is my own humor to despise pedigree," he wrote in 1825. "I was educated to prize it. The kind Aunt whose cares instructed my youth (& whom may God reward) told me of the virtues of her & mine ancestors. . . . But . . . my business is with the living." Just three years later, however, he was keeping a special notebook called "Genealogy," with the inscription "Bonus sanguis non mentitur" ("Good blood does not lie") alongside six generations of fathers and sons down to himself.[26]

This study of aunt and nephew, then, begins with genealogy and the "interior or spiritual history of New England" that it contains. But, following Mary's leads, my interest will not be limited to a pedigree of descent from founding fathers. Though Waldo's record of her family stories was entirely patriarchal, containing no women except Mary the storyteller, her own writing and speaking always remembered women as well as men. All of the stories that Ellen Emerson recorded in 1861 primarily concerned wives and offspring of the sainted clergymen in Waldo's journal entry. Ellen recorded as well the women's way of recollection that Mary shared with her—the cherishing of a family name, a monogrammed porringer, a "little old-fashioned worked case" of letters inherited from female elders. Ancestral graves and epitaphs moved Mary intensely.

As she told Ellen, she once took her Concord-bred brother William to visit their grandfather Joseph's grave in Malden. "Your Father went with us," she recalled. "He was a little boy then, and skipped about among the graves." For Mary, if not for her nephew, ancestry was overtly important, a matter deserving conscious reflection.[27]

The way back to ancestry lay with women in Mary's mind by particular reason of circumstance: whereas she knew grandfathers through stories and epitaphs, she knew grandmothers and aunts directly. In this family line over three generations, husbands had died before wives, leaving widows to support offspring and preserve tradition. There would have been no family tradition to pass on to "the boys" without the living memory of women, including others before Mary. She learned about the patriarchs from their widows and daughters, and she passed these stories on to younger generations.

As a "representative life" of New England, Mary Moody Emerson reveals her past and present in ways that studies of nephew Waldo alone have not uncovered. But his lecture "Amita"—never itself critically examined—at least points the way toward such revelations. He gave a second reading of it in 1872 at Annie Fields's salon, where one member of the audience was the fledgling novelist Henry James. Ellen Emerson noted that James "took an interest in the character of Aunt Mary." Some years later, James reviewed Cabot's *Memoir* of Ralph Waldo Emerson and expressed disappointment not to hear more about her: "We want to see her from head to foot, with her frame and her background; having (for we happen to have it), an impression that she was a very remarkable specimen of the transatlantic Puritan stock, a spirit that would have dared the devil.[28]

Any biographer would kindle to such a request. Mary can never be visible from head to foot; there is no surviving portrait or photograph to help us visualize her, and there are few physical descriptions. But how she got a spirit from Puritan ancestors to dare the devil: there the record is discernible.

I

THE FAMILY

1 Fathers and Sons of the Awakening

There, in that old house, was born one who was connected with my condition, Rev. D.[aniel] Bliss. Would he had dropt his fiery mantle on my cold spirit!

Almanack, March 7, 1830, in Springfield, quoted in "MME 2," 10

Bulkeley, Waldo, Moody, Bliss: these names, all preserved in the small circle of "M.M.E. and the boys," were a roll call of generations and intermarriages stretching back to the Puritans' Great Migration of the 1630s. Each had come into the family when a woman who bore it married a man named Emerson. But the name recalled her father more than herself, in what amounted to an alliance of New England ministers, a double distilling of clerical vintage.

The Emerson, Waldo, and Moody families came to Ipswich, Massachusetts, in the first generation of Puritan settlement, soon extending their reach from Boston Bay to the lower Maine coast and the inland towns of Essex and Middlesex Counties. None of the three original settlers was a minister, but in the second generation Joseph Emerson became one and married the granddaughter of Concord's Peter Bulkeley, a founding churchman of colony-wide authority and aristocratic status. From that point on, at least one Emerson son in every generation joined the religious leadership and married one of its daughters. In the third generation Edward Emerson, deacon in Newbury, married Rebecca Waldo, daughter of a deacon and wealthy landholder in Chelmsford. Their son Joseph Emerson was ordained in the Malden church and wed to Mary Moody, daughter of the eminent minister Samuel Moody of York. In turn, their son William married Phebe Bliss, daughter of his predecessor Daniel Bliss in the Concord pulpit. Mary Moody Emerson, three sisters, and a brother were born to William and Phebe of Concord [1] Six generations after the founding of Massachusetts, they had through multiple channels inherited the expectation and status of church leadership.

Mary did not recall all of her ancestors equally, however; nor did the family's oral memory reach back with certitude to Puritan beginnings.[2] The saintly ministers of Concord, Malden, and York whose lives she celebrated—father William, grandfathers Joseph Emerson and Daniel Bliss, and great-grandfather Samuel Moody—were men of the eighteenth century. Knowing none of them directly, but hearing their past deeds glorified by women kin, Mary sought all the more vehemently for their holiness, as if she were a female Elisha assuming the "fiery mantle" of prophetic Elijah. In 1830 she wrote that she could never be a Calvinist but found it "possible to love such a God as Calvinism in it's early days represented." A few years later she added, "My Ancestors if they had the same feeble flexible texture of mind [that we have] were fortified by a profound faith in a solemn & terrific theology."[3]

From the Edwardses to the Emersons

The theology in question was preeminently Jonathan Edwards's, and the "early days" those of the colonies' First Great Awakening. In 1734 a harvest of revivals spread from Edwards's Northampton to adjoining towns in the Connecticut Valley of western Massachusetts; then six years later George Whitefield, the British "Grand Itinerant," preached to unprecedented crowds in city and country, churches and outdoor spaces throughout the colonies, profoundly stirring the religious establishment. Each minister had to decide whether the resulting conversions were an authentic work of the Holy Spirit or an overturning of order. Those who supported Awakening were called "New Lights," and those opposed, "Old Lights." Quickly a division of the New England church opened, never again to close.[4]

As their descendants well knew, Samuel Moody, Joseph Emerson, and Daniel Bliss had all been New Lights. Mary perpetuated their memory with more than simple devotion, for in her own generation the New England churches still hotly contested the value of the First Great Awakening. Her brother William, writing the history of First Church Boston, claimed unswerving allegiance to order like his predecessor Charles Chauncy, who had led the opposition to revival. With some irony William added that its supporters had included "Mesrs. Moodey of York, Emerson of Malden, and Bliss of Concord. The first was the great-grandfather, the two last grandfathers of the writer of this tract." William and Mary at least agreed on the facts of family history, if not their interpretation. She attempted to instruct him by sending a genealogical record defining her own standard of greatness. "Why," he responded in defense, "should you contrive . . . to mortify your poor brother that his name is never to be splendid?"[5] Neither sibling exercised memory impartially. Whereas William walked away from the very ancestors who were Mary's heroes, Mary suppressed darker figures on the record. Apparently she spoke not a word of her mother's brother Daniel Bliss Jr., a renegade from his father's example, nor of her grandmother's brother Joseph Moody, who gained a dubious fame for covering his face from the world with a handkerchief.

Mary's vision of the past, however, had a culturally powerful result, for it deeply influenced her nephew Ralph Waldo Emerson. To take her inherited memory and influence seriously is to see nineteenth-century Transcendentalism in significant relation to native religious tradition: not only as a rebellion against Unitarian rationalism of the kind that Waldo associated with Harvard but also as a recasting of older and more spirit-filled ways of faith.

In his classic essay "From Edwards to Emerson," Perry Miller claimed the continuity of a visionary and ecstatic mode in New England religious thought, from its original Puritanism through Jonathan Edwards in the eighteenth century to Ralph Waldo Emerson in the nineteenth. His thesis has proven both influential and controversial, its connecting links elusive. The complicating factor is the division of New England Puritanism that began in the First Great Awakening. Edwards and his New Light followers, so the historians conclude, defended "affections" as the center of religious experience from their base in the Connecticut Valley, while in Massachusetts Bay the Old Lights of Boston and Harvard argued instead for a religion of reason and virtue. Boston-born Emerson, though rebelling against the reasonable religion of his father and college by celebrating visionary feeling, seemed to stand on the other side of a cultural divide from the theologically orthodox Edwards tradition. Even Perry Miller responded to critics by disclaiming the "mystical pretension" of direct descent from Edwards to Emerson, as if ideas could migrate from the Connecticut Valley to the Harvard Divinity School.[6]

If other agencies of social memory than the pulpit and seminary are taken into account, however, no journeys across Massachusetts become necessary to link Ralph Waldo Emerson and the evangelical past. The family was also a conveyor of culture, as Waldo affirmed; and with the family saints that Mary was "so swift to remember" came a pietism that through life called him to solitude amidst the crowd of his modern friends: "Not praise, not men's acceptance of our doing, but the Spirit's holy errand through us, absorbed the thought."[7]

Eighteenth-century records confirm the allegiance to spirit-driven religion that such memories suggest. The Emersons and their in-laws—an identifiable, not mystical, social unit of eastern Massachusetts with a strong Harvard affiliation—sided with Edwards and Whitefield even as Harvard was turning against both. In 1743, when the pro-Awakening clergy met in Boston to draft a "Testimony" supporting Whitefield's work, Samuel Moody led the gathering in prayer and signed the document along with Joseph Emerson of Malden, Daniel Bliss of Concord, and several of their kinsmen. Moreover, though Moody had died by the time Jonathan Edwards began publishing his theological works by subscription, Daniel Bliss and *two* Joseph Emersons—Senior and Junior—all signed in supporting his *Life of Brainerd, Freedom of the Will*, and *Doctrine of Original Sin*.[8] The marriage and family ties among these men seem to have followed from common cause and shored it up as well.

Joseph Emerson Jr., elder brother to William of Concord, lived out the family's Awakening loyalties with particular immediacy. As a sixteen-year-old sophomore at Harvard in September 1740, he joined the throng on Boston Common to hear newly arrived George Whitefield's first sermon "from those words in Corrin[thians] *all old things having past away all things become new.*" In short time Joseph experienced conversion, became an itinerant preacher while still at Harvard, and graduated in 1743 the very week of the pro-Whitefield testimony. Five years later, now ordained, he set out to visit the Edwards family of Northampton. And the goal was marriage: his hosts seemed "the most agreeable family I was ever acquainted with," Joseph reported, and Esther Edwards "a very desirable person to whom I purpose by divine leave to make my addresses."[9] Ideas (to paraphrase Miller) may not have traveled independently across Massachusetts, but young men on horseback could. In fact, Esther protested that she was too young for marriage, and both eventually wed elsewhere. If Joseph had succeeded in wooing Esther Edwards, there might have been a line of cousins to Mary Moody Emerson with the historically interesting double-barreled name Edwards Emerson.

Like Edwards, the New Light Emersons and their kin both belonged to an established ministerial dynasty and worked urgently to convert the wider society. Even before the Awakenings of 1734 and 1740, Samuel Moody and Joseph Emerson were among those preaching zealously for conversion, endorsed in these efforts by the Mathers of Boston. In 1701, Moody's first published sermon was an impassioned plea to "Vain Youth" of the sort that later would bring New England towns to experiences of revival. "What is the very Cream and Quintessence of all Flesh-pleasing delights," he asked, "in comparison of that Spiritual, Heavenly Joy, which at times, and commonly at our first Conversion, diffuseth itself all over the Renewed Soul?" A generation later, Joseph Emerson eloquently unfolded the text "Seek ye the Lord while He may be found." All hearers, he insisted, were eligible for the "unspeakable Felicity" that his words held forth. "Hence we are counsell'd . . . to apply ourselves to Christ for that precious Eyesalve, which will cure us of our Blindness."[10]

Such a line springs from the page for readers of Ralph Waldo Emerson's plea to "look at the world with new eyes," as Moody's earlier evocation of heavenly joy recalls that later young man "glad to the brink of fear." But both sermons offer the pleasure of holiness within a rhetoric that more closely anticipates Edwards's "Sinners in the Hands of an Angry God." In Samuel Moody's words, once the soul is "launched into the boundless and bottomless Ocean of Eternity, where God shall Rain Fire and Brimstone," it can never return. As Joseph Emerson warned, "God is angry with the Wicked every day, If he turn not, he will whet his Sword, He hath bent his Bow and made it ready, to shoot the Arrows of his Indignation." "Now" is the time to seek, he concluded, now in "God's Season of Astonishing Grace." Moody and Emerson alike were calling forth a highly pitched tension between hope and terror, the keynote of conversionist preaching. "Realize it to your selves, when alone," Moody proclaimed, "that there is a Heaven of unconceivable Glory above, and a Hell of unutterable Torment below."[11]

When Edwards and Whitefield appeared, Moody, Emerson, and their younger colleague Bliss offered support out of a new light that was really the old Puritan hunger for unmediated experience of divinity and the millennial anticipation of Christ's Second Coming. All held in common a belief that they were experiencing the last days predicted in Revelation, before God's judgment brought in a glorious new kingdom for the saints. In 1727 Joseph Emerson urged the seeking of God to a people "on whom the ends of the world are come." "But is anything too hard for Immanuel?" Moody asked Emerson the same year. "He has said He will not Quench ye smoking Flax—Isn't ye Time near for great Things?" Eight years later, with Edwards's revival in its first flush, Samuel and Joseph Moody and Joseph Emerson jointly wrote an unelaborated report for the Boston newspaper: a nineteen-year-old Kittery woman, taking three loaves of Indian bread out of the oven, had found two white and the third "turned exactly the colour of a Blood Pudding." The younger and the older clergymen assumed that readers would understand the meaning of this event.[12] All were searching for providential signs, even in the humblest places, of the imminent change that God would bring forth.

Following Mary's memories of her male ancestors back to the contemporary record, we discover distinct and complex experiences in three different New England towns, each searching for awakening and millennial change. In each the minister was a patriarch, father of both town and family, attempting to transform the community as well as transfer his own vocation to a son.

The Moodies of York

Samuel Moody, as his great-granddaughter Mary Moody Emerson often said, practiced a "commanding administration of his holy office" on the coastal frontier. In 1698, straight from Harvard College and marriage to Hannah Sewall, he became chaplain of the York garrison, where his predecessor had been massacred by Indians six years earlier. For the next forty-nine years, their house would be fortified and his parishioners armed even at church. Called "Father Moody" with awe, he preached in an aggressive, extemporaneous style, often rebuking individuals from the pulpit. Mary told Waldo a century later that when a member took offense and started to walk out, he cried, "Come back, you graceless sinner, come back!" Similar oral traditions remained after him in York itself. "Fire, fire!" he called out to an inattentive congregation. When someone demanded where, he roared, "In Hell, for sleepy sinners." The charismatic, almost magical, power ascribed to him seemed to justify such verbal assaults. Malden parishioners remembered his guest sermon for a fast day, appealing to God for deliverance from a plague of canker worms. His text was "I will rebuke the devourer for your sakes"; and when the congregation emerged from the "prophetic fire" of his preaching, they saw insects lying dead all around them.[13]

Not all of Moody's authority, however, came from oral power over folk audiences. From the beginning, he took his place in the Massachusetts ministerial establishment, though stationed in the colony's northern province. Moody drew young Harvard men like Joseph Emerson to teach and preach under him at

York, and he represented the Puritan way in mission work among the Baptists and Quakers of Rhode Island. The Mather-endorsed sermon of 1701 and a dozen subsequent works made him Maine's first published writer, and his cousin by marriage Samuel Sewall served as a Boston courier when visiting York on judicial circuits. Sewall respected Moody in turn, giving his *Children of the Covenant* to Increase Mather and three copies of *The Vain Youth Summoned*—along with a pound of chocolate—to his own son.[14]

Moody's printed sermons refined his blunt extemporaneous style into a skillful, highly charged rhetoric. Drawing the line between God's sovereignty and human agency in *Children of the Covenant*, he found God "as willing to feed [the soul] with his Flesh and Blood as ever Tender Mother was to draw out her full & aking Breast to her hungry, Crying Child." He exhorted parents to "give the Lord no Rest . . . till ye have obtained Converting Grace for your Dear Children. . . . If thy Child were in *Turkish* Slavery, or Condemned for Treason against his Prince, wouldest thou not make all the Interest possible to be made for his Ransom, or Pardon?" In his Boston election sermon of 1721, Moody called upon legislators to depend absolutely on Christ, presupposing their own sinfulness "as to the Fact, the Fault, the Filth, the Folly, the Fruit and the Fountain of it." With his insistence on human degeneracy and the need to know grace directly, Moody anticipated the Awakening spirit more powerfully than any other election preacher of the decade.[15] To do so he ranged from the plain style to an elaborate language of feeling.

As patriarch of church and family, Samuel Moody likewise acted upon feeling with warmth and generosity. Refusing the customary settlement of a ministerial salary, he left house and income entirely up to his parishioners' charity. As Mary later told Waldo, they "gave alms profusely & the barrel of meal wasted not." Her grandmother Mary, Samuel's daughter, told stories of his faith in God's provision that were eventually recorded in the periodical press. When there was nothing for dinner, Samuel had his wife set the table, and a neighbor brought a dinner already cooked. When the wood had run out, a passing Quaker could take his broken sled no farther and delivered its contents—a full load of wood—to the Moodies. Samuel expressed love of family as openly as faith in God, declaring himself "ravished" at the birth of his daughter Mary's latest child.[16] He was a man of passion in relation to God and kindred both.

Yet in the most arresting single document of the Moodies' life, the diary of Samuel and Hannah's son Joseph from 1720 to 1724, the only paternal passions appear to be wrath and provocation of fear. "At noon my father grew very angry," wrote the young schoolmaster at twenty-three, "at first, perhaps, in my absence, for a cause known only to him; for I did ask whether I should dismiss the pupils, but I cannot be charged with having been negligent this week, and I spoke too angrily to my father." Joseph noted similar currents of fear and anger around Samuel's preaching, and others apparently agreed: one parishioner walked out of church in wrath, and another took offense at his reproof of wifely disobedience. "Mother is afraid these occasions may cause trouble," Joseph commented darkly.[17]

Joseph Moody doubly concealed his words from readers, writing in Latin with a letter-substitution code. Only recently deciphered, the diary reveals a volatile emotional life. Serving as a ministerial candidate and lay preacher himself in these years, Joseph had deeply internalized his father's pleas for conversion from the slavery of sin. But in the four years of his diary, instead of progress toward conversion, Joseph recorded many forbidden behaviors and feelings: "too hilarious and talkative" an appearance in social scenes, "hostility toward God and toward his work," secret pleasure when Samuel could not reach Malden for the Sabbath, envy at brother-in-law Joseph's preaching, lustful feelings toward a variety of women, many occasions of "self-defiling." Amidst such outbursts, the background was an almost-daily record of apathy and despair: "Sat. 2 [June 1722] Wind fresh S. . . . Extreme insensibility took complete possession of me. . . . Nevertheless divine Jesus, . . . wilt Thou not, through thy Spirit, come to the aid of my worst of souls?"[18]

Though many Puritan diarists lamented their lack of grace and excess of worldly sensation, Joseph felt these with an extremity anticipating his overt mental collapse seventeen years later. Indeed, the diary shows not only his own incipient swings between mania and depression but also his parents' kindred afflictions. "In the evening," Joseph wrote just a month before the election sermon in 1721, "Father considered himself to be in the worst state of health, and said he had for a long time been weary of his life." Two years later he was even more explicit about Hannah Sewall Moody's condition: "My mother is afflicted by a kind of mental disorder. I was affected to the point of tears." After two days she had recovered from her intense headache and at last could speak coherently, but only after twelve days did she significantly overcome her "black bile." To the eighteenth century, black bile was the bodily humor responsible for melancholy, the temperament most conducive to madness. To the late twentieth century, such melancholy is depression, physiological and genetic in origin.[19] The Moody family of York—as though spontaneously acting out the allegory of its name—appears to have suffered such illness in both sporadic and permanently disabling forms.

Temperamental excess on both sides raised the common Puritan drama of a father's severity and a son's humility to crisis proportion in the pages of Joseph's diary. "I do not honor him, as I ought, in my mind," Joseph confessed. When Samuel returned from preaching his election sermon in June 1721 and told how the spirit had worked through him on the youth, Joseph only feigned pleasure. This trip inadvertently opened a major confrontation between father and son, because Samuel brought back from Boston his in-law Sewall's elegant, recently orphaned granddaughter, Mary Hirst. Within months Joseph was sharing evenings and affectionate conversations with Mary, even though formally engaged by his parents to Lucy White of Gloucester. By early fall Mary Hirst had been converted as he was not, and he wrote out her confession of faith. "I can scarcely keep myself from loving [Mary]," he admitted. So he gathered courage to present the dilemma to Samuel. "I discussed with my father last night, and with Hirst today, the question of my giving up Lucy—much too freely. . . . I said hardly anything of a religious nature, but a great deal incautiously about marrying my cousin. Father did not approve."[20]

More remarkable than Samuel's disapproval is the speed with which Joseph's only exercise of personal will subsided into sullen obedience. Though harboring fond thoughts for Mary, he followed Samuel's orders and gave her spiritual advice about "the way of modesty," hid his jealousy when Captain Pepperell came courting, and with no particular enthusiasm prepared to marry Lucy White. The four-year diary ends with him en route to Gloucester for this event in 1724. Joseph summed up more than one evening's quarrel when he wrote, "I cannot bear the reprehension of my father." Ironically, his lack of autonomous will even stood in the way of what his father most wanted for him, the experience of conversion. Though Calvinist belief required submission and self-accusation, some sense of individual worth was also needed for new life in Christ to be possible.[21] Through a finally unknowable combination of predisposition and paternal severity, Joseph never stopped seeing himself as the "worst of souls."

Joseph still served with apparent competence in the double role of town clerk and assistant to his father until, in 1732, he was ordained as the minister to York's Second Parish. Four years later, his by now beloved wife, Lucy, died in childbirth, leaving in his care several children between the ages of three and ten. Then, in the autumn of 1738, Joseph appeared before his congregation on a Sabbath morning wearing a white handkerchief over his face, falling rapidly thereafter into severe and disabling sorrow. The only reference to his illness in surviving family papers hints at the degree of concern: in Malden fifteen-year-old Joseph Emerson Jr. noted in his diary that his parents had visited York expressly to see their beloved friend and brother but found him "very Malancholy." George Whitefield described the situation evocatively in the fall of 1740 but was allowed no visual impressions at all: "Mr. [Samuel] Moody has a son, a Minister who was once full of Faith and Joy in the Holy Ghost, . . . but for these Two Years Last Past has walked in Darkness and seen no light. He has an inexpressible gloominess upon his soul, and cannot apply any of the Promises to himself. I was informed that he was at the Meeting but dared not see me."[22]

Tradition offers several explanations for this religious depression. Hawthorne, noting Joseph Moody's case in a footnote to "The Minister's Black Veil," probably followed the Maine historian Timothy Alden in ascribing his behavior to guilt over the accidental shooting of a friend in childhood. Others have pointed to grief over his wife's death, the pressure of work, and his possibly unwilling assumption of the ministerial vocation. While no definitive answers are possible, certain themes in the legendary accounts of Joseph's illness certainly fit the character that he manifested in his earlier diary. As he wanted his thoughts doubly hidden then, now he allowed no face-to-face meeting with the world at all, addressing other people only from behind the handkerchief or with his back to them. As he then struggled unsuccessfully to assert an adult self in the world, now he acted out (to the world's shocked attention) an extreme of Calvinist willlessness. A descendant wrote that Joseph excused himself from preaching by saying he was "nothing but a *shadow.*" At last a friend suggested that he serve as "a *mouth* for his friends to express their *desires through* to God," and so he adopted an intermediary role, praying publicly as the voice of others. Significantly, he often enacted the voice of his own father. From Samuel's pulpit he would remark, "If Mr. Moody were present, he would preach from the following text," then expound it with words ostensibly not his own.[23]

Even Samuel Moody claimed a position of humility when George Whitefield swept New England in the fall of 1740. As the evangelist later recalled to a York congregation, father Moody declared himself unworthy to sit by the pulpit and planted himself in mid-aisle to judge the preaching. As Whitefield was then just twenty-six and Moody an elder statesman of the church, the young man clearly looked with some surprise at the reversal of authority that he had wrought. Samuel promised a hundred new converts, and Whitefield brought the congregation to tears with his words of consolation. Perhaps only Joseph felt left out of the release that Whitefield offered. Remaining "only a shadow" at the meeting was his paradoxical claiming of separate identity, whereas his father maintained lowliness with exuberant self-display. Four years later, Samuel greeted Whitefield's landing from England in York harbor: "Sir, you are first welcome to *America*; secondly, to *New-England*; thirdly, to all the faithful ministers of *New-England*; fourthly, to all the good people of *New-England*; fifthly, to all the good people of York; and sixthly and lastly, to me, dear Sir, less than the least of all."[24]

Such lowliness allowed Samuel a vigorous role in support of the Awakening, both in York and in New England more broadly. He led the 1743 convention in prayer and at least once preached to crowds on Boston Common himself. With the help of Whitefield's evangelizing—and Joseph's echoic voice as well—Samuel left the largest church in Maine at his death in 1747, with 317 members in full communion. On the Awakening's crucial political issues he was moderate, unwilling to preach without permission in another minister's parish, slow to praise or blame the bands of saints seeking to separate from established churches. His personal style, however, knew less moderation. Coming upon two men arguing in the streets of Boston about the Awakening, he rashly struck the apparent opposer with his cane, then just as profusely apologized when he found he had mistaken their positions.[25]

Nor was Samuel Moody's militancy limited to an occasional caning of the opposition. His down east region maintained the boundary between Puritan Boston and the perceived Antichrist of French Catholic Canada, and at the age of sixty-nine he epitomized a new political zeal by serving as chaplain to Sir William Pepperell in the storming of Louisburg. Pepperell had grown up in York and married Joseph Moody's once-beloved Mary Hirst; by the early 1740s, as colonel of the York militia, he had also been converted by Whitefield. When the General Court raised three thousand volunteers under his command, Pepperell asked Father Moody to accompany him. Declaring his axe "*the Sword of the Lord and of Gideon*," Moody cut down the papist cross and images at the Cape Breton chapel, then introduced Protestant preaching from the text "Enter into his gates with thanksgiving." A half century of ministry amidst the threat of French and Indian warfare culminated in his prophetlike sense of this victory. Back in York a year later in 1746, conducting a fast day as the French fleet sailed to resupply Canada, he prayed like Isaiah against Israel's foe: "Put a hook in his nose, and a bridle in his lips. . . . Send a storm upon them, and sink them in the deep."[26] Such vanquishing of the enemy would surely bring in the "great Things" of God that Moody had long awaited.

His son Joseph had a hand in prophecy, too. When Samuel sailed for Louisburg with Pepperell in 1745, Joseph supplied the York pulpit and conducted a day of fasting on behalf of the expedition. Two hours into his prayer he turned from pleading with God to thanksgiving, that "it was done, it was delivered, it was ours." After the troops returned and compared dates, they determined that the surrender of Louisburg had taken place just at the hour when Joseph was praying. In York from that point on, Joseph's selflessness was taken as telepathic power.[27]

Mary Moody Emerson and her nephew Waldo remembered Samuel Moody most of all for his powerful, spirit-driven language. Hearing the Methodist preacher Edward Taylor for the first time in 1835, Waldo wrote that he "explains at once what Whitefield & Fox & Father Moody were to their audiences, by the total infusion of his own soul into his assembly, & consequent absolute dominion over them." Neither spoke of Joseph, though both doubtless knew of his notoriety in New England folk history. In 1842 Mary remarked that she was reading Hawthorne's *Twice Told Tales* without pleasure, possibly registering dislike for its footnoted reference to Joseph. A decade later she insisted that Waldo return her history of the Moodies;[28] as this was probably Charles C. P. Moody's book of family biographies, she therefore knew the best single gathering of lore about Joseph. That she never mentioned her great-uncle suggests how grievous his mental illness had been in Emerson family memory.

Joseph, though never wholly recovered or assured of grace, still had his own peculiar authority as an Awakening preacher. In 1744 Whitefield visited Joseph in York. Rather than offer counsel, the evangelist saw this man to "resemble Holy Job" and listened silently. "He often said, 'Look and learn, look and learn,' " reported Whitefield. "Oh that I may remember his advice, . . . for how know I what may befall me ere I die?" Joseph also had the last word with Samuel. As Father Moody died in 1747, Joseph reached around his father's body and exclaimed, "*And Joseph shall put his hands upon thine eyes,*" so likening himself to the patriarch Jacob's covenant-keeping son. Finally, Joseph managed a gentle deflation of the eminent Jonathan Edwards two years later. Joseph had been asked to pray at an ordination and, if Edwards did not arrive in time, preach in his place. As he lengthened out thanks for this great man, Edwards entered the pulpit silently. Discovering "Brother Edwards" at the end of the prayer, Joseph greeted him: "I didn't intend to flatter you to your face; but there's one thing I'll tell you: they say that your wife is a going to heaven, by a shorter road than yourself."[29] Such words did not necessarily gain dominion, but they told their own socially awkward, aphoristic truth.

The Emersons of Malden

Joseph Emerson, friend of Joseph Moody's and his senior by just a month, had a much calmer experience of growing up in New England's Puritan culture. Cotton Mather called him a "Pattern of Early Piety" because he had prayed in place of his father at family devotions before the age of eight, to the edification of all present. The year after graduating from Harvard, though not yet eighteen, Emerson began preaching; and he pursued a ministerial vocation and a wife at once while teaching in York. "Cousin Moodey tells me of Mr. J. Emmerson's Courting his Daughter," the tireless news recorder Samuel Sewall wrote in his diary of 1718. This was active and affectionate courtship by the young themselves, though conveniently cementing alliance with a professional mentor and receiving a father's blessing as well. When Joseph and Mary Moody Emerson were married in December 1721, right in the middle of Joseph Moody's courtship crisis, one father preached and the other performed the service.[30] Emerson had internalized his parents' desires and acted on them with what apparently felt like independence, both in the experience of grace and in the pursuit of love.

Joseph Emerson differed temperamentally from his father-in-law, Samuel Moody, choosing a style of ministry based upon reading and reflection. "He was the greatest student in the country," granddaughter Mary recalled, "and left a library considerable for those days. He was a reader of the Iliad, and said he should be sorry to think that the men and cities he had read of never existed." According to Mary he was "always shut up" in the study. He could preach fervently but read his sermons from shorthand notes after long preparation. Moody once tried Emerson's method, got lost in the text he had prepared, and exploded: "Emerson must be Emerson, and Moody must be Moody. I feel as if my head was in a bag."[31]

While both ministers spoke to their congregations as people "on whom the ends of the world are come," Joseph Emerson looked more for a kingdom of new peace in Malden than for holy war. While his character differed from Samuel Moody's, so did Malden's situation differ from York's. Just five years after Joseph's ordination, a conflict erupted in Malden over the site of its meetinghouse that would drag rancorously through the remaining forty years of his life, despite three separate General Court decisions. Malden had never been a frontier town. Settling in 1649 across from Charlestown on the northern bank of the Mystic River, its residents had always been just two ferry rides from Boston. Or they could as quickly travel the Salem Road east to the established towns of Essex County. Land was "exceeding streight" in Malden, as a 1739 petition conceded, and its people notorious for their "Disposition . . . to find matter of Offence."[32]

Changing the location of a meetinghouse could cause offense because, in every pragmatic and symbolic sense, it was the town's heart. From "Bell Rock," the old site, parishioners were summoned to hear Joseph's sermons, attend town meetings, and live their lives together. When parishioners voted in 1727 for a new house a mere quarter of a mile farther north, they were recognizing a shift in the town's center to the crossing of the Salem and Charlestown roads. But the more southerly citizens of "Mystic Side" felt resentful at being fully owned by neither Malden nor Charlestown. Over that quarter mile the southern quarter waged war, seceding from Joseph Emerson's parish, then trying to gain access to the taxes and lands that provided his salary. Amidst great animosity, Joseph remained steady and evenhanded. The move north cannot have been convenient for him. His parsonage remained at Bell Rock, the old site, and ministers never came out ahead in such battles; as Samuel Moody wrote, "You'll be desired to Preach in ye new House, which if you do or do not, a very great Part of your People will be dissatisfied."[33]

Ralph Waldo Emerson, reading his great-grandfather Joseph's diary in 1847, admired "the useful egotism of our puritan clergy." From his perspective it seemed that the minister of earlier days regularly transformed personal experience into public insight:

> If he keeps school, marries, begets children, if his house burns, if his children have the measles, if he is thrown from his horse, if he buys a negro, & Dinah misbehaves, if he buys or sells his chaise, all his adventures are fumigated with prayer & praise, he improves it next Sunday on the new circumstance and the willing flock are contented with this consecration of one man's adventures for the benefit of them all, inasmuch as that one is on the right level & therefore a fair representative.[34]

Waldo surely overidealized the colonial clergyman's power, probably never reading Joseph's sermons and only assuming that his ancestor had moralized the diary's events into them. In particular, Waldo seems to have reckoned without the meetinghouse controversy. The early diary in his hands stopped just short of that crisis, and Mary seems to have effaced the memory of her grandparents' struggle within their town.

The surviving record of sermons suggests that Joseph did not address Malden primarily with personal reference. Nor did he actively work out a settlement of the town's problems, leaving that work to the courts. Instead, he interpreted the conflict as a sign of God's displeasure, attempting to create new community by penitence and conversion. Just four months after the vote to relocate in 1727 came an earthquake, and this evidence of divine judgment at least temporarily produced revival. On a fast day Joseph prayed for an end to the "Spirit of Division and Contention," and forty people joined the church in two months. When the South Church formally called its own minister in 1735, Joseph exhorted his congregation to make affliction serve their souls' well-being, like Samson bringing "Meat out of the Eater" and honey from the carcass of a lion. One theme he brought to the experience of Awakening in 1740 was a dread of all "rash and disorderly" proceedings.[35]

Another, however, was yearning for the tranquillity that came only in ecstatic transformation by grace. When an epidemic of "throat distemper"—probably diphtheria—ravaged the families of Malden in 1738, Joseph used the last words of twenty-year-old Abigail Upham as an appeal from the grave for all to convert.

Urging the youth in his congregation to accept Christ as brother, friend, prince, and husband, Joseph nearly dissolved the Calvinist mysteries of election: "If you love CHRIST, you are certainly beloved of him." Even more, he portrayed this love as otherworldly, erotic, and feminine. "He loves you," Joseph assured his congregation, "and is gone before to prepare a glorious Mansion for you in the heavenly Places. . . . O the Rivers of Pleasures, and Fulness of Joys that you shall in a little time be satisfy'd, be ravish'd withal! . . . To see him Face to Face!"[36]

Whitefield preached three times in Malden at Joseph's invitation, not only in 1740 but also in 1744 and 1745, when the nearby forces of Harvard College and Charles Chauncy had gathered in opposition. Joseph proved "singularly steady and zealous in the late revival of Religion," commented the evangelist. Disinclined to preach in other parishes, Joseph urged his congregation to make use of God's extraordinary grace. "Stand fast therefore," he urged them, "in this Liberty of yours wherewith Christ has made you free. . . . Glory not in men. . . . But try the Spirits; bring every Doctrine to the Touch-Stone. . . . Oh, let us not be high minded, but fear."[37]

Trying the spirits proved to be a delicate matter; and as a New Light active in both the Boston and Essex ministerial associations, Joseph played a leading role in judging difficult cases. In 1742 he preached Boston's Thursday lecture the week that a court found Whitefield's unruly disciple James Davenport insane for declaring all of the city's ministers unconverted. As a text Joseph chose Jesus' defense of John the Baptist, ending with the line "Yet wisdom is justified of all her children." Stopping short of declaring Davenport a modern John the Baptist, he still declared the Awakening a prophecy in the desert and urged his congregation to seize religion despite extremists in either direction. In his eyes, complacency was more dangerous than zeal. "Have we not," he asked the Boston ministers, "some of us call'd some Things we have observ'd in Others by the Names of *Enthusiasm* and *Madness*, which if we duly examine will appear to be agreeable to *right Reason*, and that our Brethren were never more *themselves*, than when we were ready to think that they acted *beside themselves*?"[38]

The fate of moderates is to be pulled in opposing directions, and so apparently was Joseph Emerson. Preaching at the ordination of his son Joseph, he painted a rather dark picture of ministry in the midst of Awakening. He admitted:

> Some will fault a Minister for harping (as they term it) so long upon Election, upon Regeneration, and other Doctrines of Grace, and will represent him as an Antinomian. . . . Others again it may be, will fault him because he preaches up Holiness and Morality; and tho' he does it in a Gospel Strain, . . . yet they'll cry out upon him, that he's an Arminian, and is grown legal, and dead, and formal in his Preaching.[39]

The polarities that Joseph was rejecting here—"Antinomian" assurance of grace and refusal of social obligation, "Arminian" moralism at the expense of the spirit—were not equally attractive to him. The essential Emersonian position, for Joseph as for his descendants Mary and Waldo, verged on Antinomianism in its affirmation of the soul's union with divinity but insisted upon returning from that union to the duties of the world. Joseph defined the work of ministers as a powerful exercise of patience amidst peevish people. The sin of melancholy, he admitted, was all too apt to seize a minister and "take off his chariot wheels." In order for him to act in duty to his congregation, he would have to find courage in Christ. Joseph, unlike Davenport, had never been willing to condemn unconverted ministers. But his sermon made the ministry sound too arduous for any but the converted, any but "one that has himself seen the Excellency, and tasted the Sweetness, . . . one that is a real and zealous Friend of the Bridegroom."[40]

Amidst upheavals of town and church politics, the extended family was Joseph's most significant community. He brought his own parents to live in Malden, remained in touch with his brothers and sister, and regularly exchanged visits with his in-laws in York. Most of all, Joseph and Mary themselves produced thirteen children, eleven of whom lived to adulthood and remained associated with each other in an extended family network. Their offspring would eventually include three ministers and two ministers' wives, and Joseph seems consciously to have planned for such a posterity. "Am thinking of writing my sermons at length for children and relations," he wrote in 1738, when eldest son Joseph was only fourteen and much younger son William not yet born.[41] As a minister he was a "father" of Malden, reckoned among the elite and responsible for sanctifying the social order, but his most genuine relationships extended up and down the coast from Boston to York, back to the family's past and forward to its future.

The family of which Joseph was patriarch held together despite having no land, the resource of patriarchal power that his farming neighbors most valued. Unlike Samuel Moody, he got a stipulated salary from his parish but still owned no house or property in Malden. The "ministry house" built in 1724 still stands today across from Bell Rock, but after Joseph's death it went to his successor and belonged no more to the Emersons. Mary spoke fervently of the resulting family value: "They all believed in poverty, and would have nothing to do with uncle John of Topsfield, who had a grant of land, and was rich. My grandfather prayed every night that none of his descendants might ever be rich." Such a memory was only partially accurate; diaries of father and son from the late 1730s show the family in close touch with both John and his much richer Boston merchant brother, Edward, who died soon thereafter with an estate of more than eleven thousand pounds. Through the Waldo family they had strong business affiliations, and three of Joseph's four sons who did not receive Harvard educations became entrepreneurs. But Mary still recalled an important preference for all exercises of mind and soul over the settled state of worldly ownership; she preached this value herself in telling how Joseph watched the burning of his first house and sang, "There is a house not made with hands."[42]

Joseph expressed both his devotion to kin and his resistance to material wealth in reflections of 1735 on buying a shay; Waldo later cherished these entries and transcribed them from the aged diary. After the shay overturned, frightening the horse and endangering his wife, Joseph asked, "Have I done well to get me a shay? Have I not been proud or too fond of this convenience? Do I exercise the faith in the Divine care and protection that I ought to do? Should I not be more in my study and less fond of diversion? Do I not withhold more than is meet from pious and charitable uses?" Finally he "disposed of [the] shay to Rev. Mr. White"—the dubious consequences for Mr. White notwithstanding.[43] If he "believed in poverty," it was the poverty not of stark economic need but of conscience resisting the temptations of status.

Conscience surely was omnipresent in Joseph and Mary's family, not only in their own behavior but also in their manner of raising children. In a landless, bookish family, deference had to come from within. "The children sat upon a settle, with lessons or catechism," Mary recalled, "the biggest at one end, the next in size at the other end, and the little one in the middle." Father Joseph recorded the precociously pious sayings of his son Samuel, so suggesting the wider content of lessons received on the settle. At the age of six the boy could tell his mother the meaning of second birth: not to be born in the way of his newest brother, but to "rise again." He also asked "whether if wicked People should go to hell, & come out again, whether they would then be wicked." Evil was real to this child. He spoke uneasily of the boys in Boston who threw stones and called his cousin "Dog"; he dreamed "that the Devil tempted me to Sin, and said to me, do do Samuel, but I would not, & said what makes you keep asking me so many Questions[?]"[44]

Eldest son Joseph recorded a similarly acute conscience in its adolescent phase, filling his diary with pleas for divine help. "I find striving to destroy my poor soul," he wrote at fifteen. "O, Lord give me grace to resist Temtations which are very Stroung. . . . I must relie upon *Christ* alone for Salvation and not on my own Works which are as Rottan Rags." Death and judgment loomed near, with throat distemper only a house away from the parsonage. All the youth in town came to one friend's funeral: "I hope it will do me a great deal of good I desire it may do so & I do not know but that I shall be in my grave by the time a Weak is at an End."[45]

Unlike his Uncle Moody, however, young Joseph could follow the cultural script that allowed release from such anxiety, especially after Whitefield arrived in Massachusetts. The conversion with which his early diary ends soon fostered a militancy common among young men of the Awakening. In 1745 Joseph sailed to Louisburg with Pepperell's forces, a copy of Whitefield's sermons in hand. Present to hear Grandfather Moody's victory sermon, he came back to be ordained in the new northern Middlesex town named for Pepperell. A close colleague was his father's cousin Daniel Emerson, who had in the same years forsaken youthful immorality at Harvard, followed Whitefield in his travels, married the Malden family's eldest daughter, Hannah, and settled just over the New Hampshire border in Hollis. Young Joseph and his brother-in-law Daniel shared both the garrisoned circumstances of frontier life and the role of exhorting armies bent on defeating the French. For six months in 1755, Daniel joined an expedition to Crown Point; Joseph now stayed in Pepperell but sent forth townsmen to fight in "the Cause of God, the Cause of Religion, the Cause of Liberty."[46]

Having overcome the internal conflicts of youth, Joseph and Daniel looked primarily to enemies outside consciousness.

From the records of all these Emerson sons we can surmise a great deal about the childhood of their younger brother William as well. Born the year of the Whitefield testimony, he had multiple elders throughout youth. By his fifth year, brother Joseph and brother-in-law Daniel both had churches within a day's journey of Malden, and William came of age with their military enthusiasm in clear view. Such generational overlaps were common in large colonial families like the Emersons, but in this case they drew William early into a network of vocational, political, and theological allegiance that would eventually bring him to the Concord ministry. In some ways William resisted the ways of his conscientious household. Amidst later antagonisms, he was accused of having "fooled away his time" at college, and his own sisters told Mary what a humorist and mimic he had been. Father Joseph, having dedicated this child to the ministry after a failure of resources to educate four middle sons, did not approve such a carefree attitude. When William was cocking hay one afternoon, his father looked out the window and called, "Billy! Billy! that is a waste of your time. Go back to your precious books." Happily his mother intervened, saying, "No, it does him good to work a little. He has books enough."[47]

Mary remembered this resistant streak in her father with pleasure but also linked it to an inwardness that she called "ardent unselfism." Among her stories to Waldo was one that he so identified with as to record under the title "Autobiography":

> My great grandfather was Rev. Joseph Emerson of Malden, son of [Edward] Emerson, Esq. of Newburyport. I used often to hear that when William, son of Joseph, was yet a boy walking before his father to church, on a Sunday, his father checked him, "William, you walk as if the earth was not good enough for you." "I did not know it, sir," he replied with the utmost humility. This is one of the household anecdotes in which I have found a relationship.[48]

Father Joseph charged William with a pride that was not worldly, like the owning of a shay, but very much a danger of otherworldliness. If a sin, such pride was also familiar to this abstracted, heaven-bent, peace-loving father himself. But William deflected Joseph's criticism with the mild defense that he was too preoccupied to notice being proud, thus converting pride to humility, self-absorption to "unselfism." The point of this story to which Waldo "found a relationship" two generations later was that William had intuitively, without torments of conscience or violent battles, discovered grace.

The Blisses of Concord

While Mary celebrated Great-grandfather Moody's authority and Grandfather Emerson's scholarly devotion, she saved her highest praise for Grandfather Bliss.

"Have you read his epitaph on his monument there in the old burying-ground on the hill?" she asked Ellen. "You must. My father wrote it. There you can read all about him. He was a flame of fire! All enthusiasm!" Waldo agreed in his "Historical Discourse" for Concord's two hundredth anniversary, preferring Bliss the "favorer of religious excitement" to the "lovers of order and moderation" in Concord who had brought charges against him.[49] "Enthusiasm"—originally a term of condemnation by Old Light critics—was explicitly celebrated by Daniel Bliss's descendants.

Samuel Moody and the Emersons, even William the epitaph-writer, found Bliss a difficult ally in the ranks of New Light ministry. It was their work as moderates to reconcile his excitement and the critics' love of order. He was a purist and a true believer. Fourteen years younger than Joseph Emerson, Bliss grew up in Springfield—the heart of Edwards's Connecticut Valley—and graduated from Yale College in 1732. "[I had] parents yt did while in mine infancy devote me to GOD," he declared on joining the Springfield church, "and by times taught me to read his sacred word, and by times enformed me of death and of my corrupt nature by Adams sin." These parents were of pious farming stock rather than the ministerial elite. A Bliss forebear had, like the Bulkeleys, Emersons, Waldos, and Moodies, taken part in the Puritans' Great Migration to Massachusetts Bay, but had accompanied Thomas Hooker's exodus to Hartford and eventually migrated up the Connecticut River to Springfield.[50]

The first in his immediate family line to attend college, Daniel avoided the establishment at Yale, instead getting to know James Davenport and the unordained exhorter David Ferris. Though in the course of the 1730s he turned eastward to take a second degree at Harvard and a parish in Concord, Bliss brought with him both Connecticut Valley orthodoxy and a sympathy for its charismatic critics. Two-thirds of the Concord congregation voted in favor of calling Bliss: clearly his style of Calvinistic piety had genuine support just west of Boston. But they also met fierce opposition. Dissenters raised enough resistance to require an arbitrating council of neighboring ministers before ordination could take place,[51] so signaling the tenor of church life in Concord for the next quarter century.

Seventeen months later, in the fall of 1740, twenty-five-year-old Bliss and his Connecticut-born wife, Phebe Walker, settled into their parsonage just in time to receive George Whitefield as a guest and revivalist. In Concord Whitefield met a congenial preacher and receptive people. He spoke "to some thousands in the open air" until his "hearers were melted down." Then the two ministers rejoiced through the night. "Brother Bliss . . . broke into tears," Whitefield reported, "and we had reason to cry out it was good for us to be here." To Whitefield and his supporters such a high emotional pitch was the work of God, but to those already disaffected it was new cause for opposition. Fewer than fifteen hundred people lived in Concord, so the thousands "melted down" must have thronged to it from far afield. And if massive outdoor revival affronted order, the minister's behavior rankled more. More than two weeks passed, according to Bliss's own diary, before he returned to Concord from Connecticut "whereto I went with the Rev. Mr. Whitfield." The particular covenant of a minister to his people and village did not, in the eyes of his critics, allow such wandering.[52]

Soon Bliss put this new energy to work at home; over the next two years, church membership jumped from eighty-three to nearly two hundred. Meanwhile, the forces of resistance also gathered to a head, especially after Bliss challenged the statements of spiritual experience offered by two applicants. Like Jonathan Edwards, he supported revival but controlled it by strictly requiring that members be able to witness the workings of grace in their lives. Church membership was a significant measure of status in a New England village, however, and citizens in Concord and Northampton alike resisted their ministers' strait gate to it. By 1742 "aggrieved brethren" brought a list of charges against Bliss before a ministerial council from the area, and soon Concord became a widely known case of revival-induced dissension. The council decided between Bliss and his critics just as the outsider James Davenport was being judged by the Boston courts. Bliss was vindicated the same day that Joseph Emerson preached his Thursday lecture in Boston; Emerson may even have referred to his Concord colleague, as well as to Davenport, when he urged toleration of zeal in the prophetic cause of Awakening.[53]

Little toleration ensued, as both Old and New Lights, in Concord and all New England, moved toward confrontation a year later. Charles Chauncy, leader of the Old Lights from Boston's First Church, frowned upon Bliss's air of personally promoting Christ's cause. "Tis high time," Chauncy wrote to a friend, "his influence to do mischief should be lessened." Toward that end, he asked for a full account of Bliss's damaging the character of his friend's daughter, to use "as a rod to keep hold over him to keep him in order." There is no evidence that Chauncy went ahead with this attempt at blackmail. But he clearly had close contacts in Bliss's own parish; seventeen laymen from Concord subscribed to his *Seasonable Thoughts*—the definitive condemnation of Awakening—in 1743.[54]

That June two councils met in Concord. The aggrieved group found all complaints against Bliss justified and urged the formation of a separate Old Light church. The New Lights met simultaneously, with Samuel Moody as moderator, but their response was not to support Bliss so unequivocally as the other side condemned. Mobilizing toward the pro-Awakening Testimony of July, they postponed final judgment until a mutual council could be agreed upon. As Moody and the others went on to Boston to draft the Testimony, they drew lines so as to both include and control those among them like Bliss. Those signing the document declared the revival a product of divine influence but also decried "Irregularities and Extravagancies . . . contrary to Gospel Order." That September, when the council voted to support Bliss, it still found his unguarded words excessive and exhorted "for the future carefully to observe the testimony and advice of the late convention which he hath signed."[55]

We are forced to judge Bliss's controversial preaching mostly as reported by hostile witnesses, since he left only one printed sermon and a few shorthand notes. "He began in a low, moderate strain," an Old Light from Hopkinton wrote to the *Boston Evening Post,*

> and went on for some time in the same manner; but towards the close of his sermon, he began to raise his voice, and to use many extravagant gestures, and then began a considerable groaning amongst the auditors, which as soon as he perceived, he raised his voice still higher, and then the congregation were in the utmost confusion. Some crying out in the most doleful accents, some howling, some laughing, and others singing, and Mr. Bliss still roaring to them to come to Christ,—they answering,—"I will, I will, I'm coming, I'm coming."[56]

To Bliss, on the contrary, it seemed that his enemies were the source of excitement. "Oh they Shrieked they Cryed they Groaned so that I was obliged to cease Speaking," he wrote at the height of revival. "Oh what shall I do? All ministers almost seem against me."[57]

Perhaps even more than clamor, his critics also accused Bliss of proud and censorious behavior that belied his own demands for self-effacement. According to one charge, he had prayed for himself as "a poor vile worm of the dust, . . . allowed as Mediator between God and this people." None but Christ was allowed that role. According to another charge he had stood in judgment of his townspeople's prosperity, claiming "that it was as great a Sin for a Man to get an Estate by honest Labour if he had not a Single Aim at the Glory of God, as to get it by gaming at Cards and Dice." The farmers of Concord did not want their daily virtue and devotion to property condemned. To make matters worse, according to the memory of one Old Light descendant, Bliss appeared in the town's first chaise, inviting detractors to remark that the minister was imitating royalty.[58] His colleague Emerson had succumbed to the same temptation of owning a chaise but accused *himself* of pride for it; Bliss apparently let the accusations fall around him. Ministerial status meant a great deal to this son of humble background.

Bliss himself, however, could respond to such charges with greater complexity of thought than the detractors wanted to hear. He had never called labor itself a sin, he insisted, but only proposed that a husbandman living for the world and a gambler were "both enemies to God, self-lovers, self-seekers, and idolaters. That the one doth not take more sinful ways in carrying on his designs against God, I never thought of affirming." To the charge of pretension to Christlike power he answered, "In the prayer you speak of, Jesus Christ was acknowledged as the only Mediator between God and man; at which time, I was filled with wonder, that such a sinful and worthless worm as I am, was allowed to represent Christ, in any manner, even so far as to be bringing the petitions and thank-offerings to the people."[59]

This testimony to the wonder of serving Christ was the example of "true piety" that Waldo later quoted in his history of Concord. Much more does Bliss's single printed sermon show him responding to the awe of inwardly experiencing divinity. Its title declared "The Gospel Hidden from Them That Are Lost"; and in it Bliss as usual cleaved between the saved and the unsaved, proclaiming mere righteousness to no avail. But here he also invoked, as no doubt his extemporaneous sermons often did, the experience of sanctity that bound together the converts of his congregation. To "new Creatures," Bliss wrote, "old things are Past away.... They are become Light in the Lord, Children of the Day and of the Light." Bliss did not, like Joseph Emerson, urge his congregation to seek God's love; but he could ask them what they had witnessed. "Is the Day Star risen in any of your Hearts?... Have you seen a Glory in the Gospel?" Insofar as Bliss's voice is recoverable, it has no trace of political mission in it, even though wars with the French raged through most of his ministry. His message and experience centered on the "divine Beauty and Glory" working within.[60] Bliss seems to have known bliss as surely as the Moodies suffered moodiness. When Mary stood in front of his Springfield birthplace in 1830 and wished for his "fiery mantle" to descend, she was seeking after that inmost, finally unseekable, glory of Protestant religious experience.

So did many New Englanders of his own generation look for that gift through Bliss. By 1745 the aggrieved of Concord had consolidated forces and withdrawn from his church, succeeding in Massachusetts's first Old Light separation. But amidst separation, Bliss continued to draw the faithful to him. With fewer supporters in eastern Massachusetts, Whitefield brought friends from Boston to Concord, celebrating the Sabbath "with great sweetness and freedom to large and very affected audiences." The early pace of revival was not sustained, but established loyalty to Bliss and Whitefield persisted. Whitefield visited Concord a final time in the spring of 1764, insisting that Bliss preach instead of himself. "If I had studied my whole life, I could not have produced such a sermon," he said of his host.[61] This was the highest possible compliment by the acknowledged master of evangelical eloquence. Bliss never preached again, but within weeks afterward he died of consumption.

As many as he converted, however, Bliss seems not to have converted his own children. His radical evangelizing undercut the position accepted by Moody and Emerson, that "Children of the Covenant" had, if not sainthood by inheritance, at least a special likelihood of election. His revivals even allowed youths to rebel by declaring themselves holier than their elders. According to his critic in Hopkinton, he so excited the town's children that they stood up in church and contradicted the minister. How would the actual offspring of this contentious holy man react but by resisting his inquiries into their state of grace? No adolescent diaries survive to tell the story. But the church records for his years of ministry offer their own negative testimony: not a single one of the seven Bliss children is listed as a member, though four had reached their late teens or twenties by the year of his death.[62]

The eldest son, Daniel, born a year before Whitefield's first visit to Concord, openly resisted his father's example. Sent to study for the ministry at Harvard in 1756, he gravitated instead toward oratory and the classics. By the time of his father's death, Daniel was reading for a law career. But the memorable rebellion, as told by townsman Joseph Hosmer many years later, took place in Concord when young Daniel was fifteen, not yet a college student. Even then Daniel had such magnetism and outspoken views that all the young people looked upon him as their guide. So there was an impressive confrontation when he was called before the church to be disciplined for an unidentified offense, Hosmer recounted:

> He answered the questions asked him satisfactorily, and proved his entire innocence of the accusation brought against him. He then boldly turned upon his accusers and questioned their right to interfere in a matter which should lie between God and his own conscience. It is not he said by subscribing to this or that creed or by believing in this or that dogma, that a man may hope to scale and win the gates of Heaven, but he firmly believed that it was the character we built up here that must determine our condition hereafter.[63]

Hosmer does not specify that Daniel Bliss Sr. was his son's accuser; indeed, for unexplained reasons, the whole scene seems to have taken place in the Old Light West Church, where Hosmer and his family were members. But the story makes clear that Daniel's radicalism was Arminian, absolutely opposite to his father's dismissals of mere human "character" storming the gates of heaven. "It was as if a thunderbolt had fallen in that Church on that pleasant summer day," Hosmer recalled. "He annihilated conversion, and no falling from a State of Grace, and all the isms in which his Father in his lifetime had delighted." Even the West Church members, who had spurned Father Bliss for a decade and a half, were horrified by young Daniel's unapologetic stance. "But the young men and young women," Hosmer remembered, "carried his burning words home and pondered them in their hearts." Hosmer himself was clearly among these. Looking back from old age, he saw Daniel Jr. as "the John the Baptist of Unitarianism."[64]

Such a story testifies to how personally disruptive an experience the Awakening could be. A generation-long division in Concord, focused on father Daniel Bliss, turned to confront him publicly in the person of his own son. Ingrained habits of deference to the fathers of both family and town fell visibly at this moment. Father and son Moody, despite their painful relationship, could at least unite in zealous prayers against the common French enemy. Father Emerson and his sons had Malden's unending quarrel for their daily setting, but as a result they united in playing the part of moderates and reconcilers. When father Daniel Bliss died in 1764, neither his town nor his family was united.

Perhaps Bliss's truer heir was his successor, William Emerson, who began ministering in Concord twenty months later, married eldest Bliss daughter Phebe, and sought to reconcile the town's factions. A third of the church voted against calling him, just as they had against Bliss in 1738. But a new peacemaking process had already begun before he arrived. Explicitly to settle difficulties before his ordination, the church voted to receive all willing members of the now-defunct West Church. In this period of transition after the death of Bliss, William's brother-in-law Daniel Emerson of Hollis was chosen to moderate the

Concord church. An agent solicited William's candidacy after hearing that "Billy Emerson was a converted man," quite possibly receiving this New Light recommendation from Daniel Emerson. William had already come to know Concord and the Blisses by proximity to his own nearby brother and brother-in-law; and the 1766 ordination further solidified their three-way alliance, with both Daniel and Joseph Jr. joining the presiding council of ministers. Father Joseph preached from Chronicles, where David recommends his son Solomon to Israel as one chosen by God.[65]

The peacemaking in Concord did not go well or smoothly. One former officer of the West Church, a prominent landowner and physician named Joseph Lee, applied for full membership immediately upon William's ordination, but was challenged by members for "opresing ye fatherless and widoes in long Delays in Settling his accompts and making Large and exorbetent Demands for his Services." Whereas Daniel Bliss had demanded proof of grace from candidates for membership, the congregation now excluded Lee for sheer meanness. But even though the theological niceties of the 1740s had blurred, the lines of division were identical. Lee had opposed Emerson's ordination from the start, and in turn the New Light heart of Concord's church now opposed Lee. "Mr. Lee's affair in agitation," William recorded only a month after being installed. Six more years of church councils and antagonism would follow.[66]

William's diary, however, reveals that in the meantime he himself was searching for a middle ground between the inherited polarities of Arminian and Calvinist piety. Whereas his brother Joseph had encountered Whitefield's revival at college, William attended Harvard as it turned decisively toward liberal and rational religion, a new positive assertion of the "Old Light." He found considerable room for its beliefs. Twice William recorded traveling to Cambridge for Dudleian lectures "upon Natural Religion." Likewise, he attended a lecture in Boston by his elders' antagonist Charles Chauncy. Despite being branded illiberal in the unhappy affair of Joseph Lee, he looked for piety in many guises. On a trip through Concord, Ezra Stiles of Connecticut noted Emerson's principle of toleration toward any who claimed belief: "He don't like Covenants, i.e. thinks all Professors in full Communion."[67]

William had moved significantly away from Daniel Bliss's precedent, though without the confrontations of Daniel's own son. His surviving early sermons, carefully written out in full, sometimes espoused conversion in the manner of the Awakening. In 1765 he found Paul's trembling before God a model for all sinners, especially those "the most strenuous and rigid, in the Performance of all religious duties." The human will, William argued, must "lay down the Weapons of the Rebellion and . . . enlist under his Banner, who is the Captain," so allowing human understanding and affection to "ripen into a holy heavenly habit and Temper of soul." This was good Edwardsian theology, very much in line with father Joseph's moderate sermons in Malden. But William's new form of moderation, the expression of his own Harvard years, is better heard in a sermon of the previous year on immortality. Arguing the worth of the soul when weighed against the world, William expounded its immateriality and excellence as the glory of God's creation:

> And this doctrine has been looked upon as a very rational, and indubitable Thing not only among those that have been favored with the Light of Revelation, and the Oracles of God, but also among those that have had nothing but the Light of Nature, even Pagans and Mahometans have discovered an Apprehension of a future and eternal State. . . . The Phylosoph Plato, has very largely wrote upon the immortality of the Soul, who flourished about 400 years before Christ, and among many Arguments to prove the Truth of his Proposition, urges this, that if it were not so, wicked men would certainly have the advantage of Righteous Men.[68]

When William considered the mind's "Light of Nature" in Plato as argument for immortality, he was presenting an "internal natural religion" important to Arminian thinking. In this view the mind itself, even without the work of Christ's grace, was its own best evidence of God. William carefully adjusted such a claim to the needs of Calvinism. "O! that we may all be excited from a Consideration of the worth of our Soul," he concluded, "to make it our chief Concern to Secure our Salvation. . . . See to it, my Brethren, that your Evidences are clear for Heaven." Steering between the free-willers and the will-less, he warned that none could buy heaven through performance of duty, yet he urged the utmost effort to arrive there. William also sidestepped these divisive issues by dwelling on heaven itself in terms available to both heirs and opposers of the Awakening: heaven "where our Souls . . . shall be always delighted with such ravishing Pleasures as shall be agreeable to their immortal natures, through Jesus Christ."[69]

George Whitefield narrowly missed Concord on his 1770 tour of New England, dying suddenly in Newburyport right after visits to both York and Malden. By now Samuel and Joseph Moody had died long since, as had Daniel Bliss Sr. and Joseph Emerson Sr. more recently. But all their congregations remained eager for the evangelist's words. In York Whitefield told how Moody had welcomed him thirty years before; in Malden he blessed Emerson's successor, Peter Thacher, as a "young Elijah," drawing so many people to the meetinghouse that he had to make his way into the pulpit by a ladder through the back window. In Concord, Bliss's successor and son-in-law, William Emerson, preached a memorial sermon for Whitefield, whom all had been "in expectation of seeing in this Desk, but the Sabbath before last."[70]

The memorial was William's New Light masterpiece, reminding a people who had "seen the Face and heard the voice of that Servant of God" that grace was still available for their improvement. Yet William spoke not at all of grace in opposition to work or will, nor did he declare the gospel hidden from anyone. His sermon, on the text "Enter thou into the Joy of thy Lord," was all heavenly vision, celebrating the saint's joy on entering the presence of God. Though William reserved that meeting for eternity, he also emphasized the immediate glimpses that God allowed: "Tis a full heart-ravished View of his glorious beatific Father, that constitutes the Joy of Heaven. . . . The nearer we are to God the more joyful and happy because God is the Centre of the Soul's Happiness. . . . Now my hearers, ye who have been so happy as to experience the sensible presence of the blessed God, know that tis high Joy on Earth, that is the most lively Emblem of Heaven."[71]

In this sermon William articulated a prevision of heaven closely akin to his grandson Waldo's inherited memory of him, as a young man walking the earth with his mind in the beyond. The mortal capacity for heavenly joy was a major element in the family heritage with which Waldo later "found a relationship." In his "Historical Discourse," naming those decisively present in Concord's history, he included not only William Emerson and Daniel Bliss but also George Whitefield, "whose silver voice melted his great congregation into tears." He wrote this lecture at his grandparents' house, the "Old Manse," with its attic full of family papers and a portrait of Whitefield still hanging in the upstairs hallway. "Hail to the quiet fields of my fathers," he had written in his journal ten months earlier, upon arriving at the Manse to devote full attention to writing. "Not wholly unattended by supernatural friendship let me come hither."[72]

2

Mothers and Daughters of the Awakening

> My Grandmother [Bliss] came afterwards to live at the Manse with my Mother. I took care of her in her last sickness. I was over twenty years old. She used to say to me "Cleave to God, Mary, cleave to God."
>
> Mary to Ellen Emerson, 1861, in "Stories of Our Ancestors"

Though a lineage of fathers and sons linked Ralph Waldo Emerson to the Great Awakening, he also stood at a great remove from all his male forebears and their religious loyalties. As he spoke of Concord history in 1835 at the age of thirty-two, his father had been dead for twenty-four years and his grandfather for fifty-nine. There had been no ongoing succession of patriarchs inspiring or provoking their sons as in the eighteenth century, and Waldo could select his "fathers" after the needs of his own imagination. But the female lineage had been, if not untroubled, at least continuous. The aunt who instructed Waldo in "ancestral religion"—indeed was present with him in 1835—had herself been instructed by female elders in Concord and Malden. Who were they? Mary's own words offer the best clues, as does her birthplace, the Manse.

Household Stuff

Concord's famous "Old Manse," the ministry house of William and Phebe Bliss Emerson, was new in the fall of 1770 as followers mourned the death of George Whitefield. "When my Father and Mother were married," Mary recalled nearly a century later, "they lived at first still in Grandmother Bliss's house while the Manse was building. . . . They all lived together there, they made one happy family together." In fact, William and Phebe lived at the Blisses' house a full four years before moving to their own house, and William's diary suggests some desire for privacy and autonomy from the start. "Divided into two families," he recorded in 1767, less than a year after the wedding. "Divided up the household

Stuff and Furniture." Even after Phebe Emerson moved her inherited furniture a mile away to the new house, however, daughter and mother continued in the close bonds of an extended family.[1] Eventually, as Mary told Ellen, Phebe Bliss came to live at the Manse herself. She and her eldest daughter shared not only names but also their lifelong domestic spaces and relationships.

A significant amount of the furniture that daughter Phebe received from her mother in 1767 is still visible at the Manse today. The sign that greets approaching tourists tells why: this house was "occupied by Mrs. William Emerson and her descendants for 169 years." Though a series of descendants redecorated and modernized it, they cherished family heirlooms as well. They even referred sentimentally to the "old manse" by the late 1820s, a decade and a half before tenant Nathaniel Hawthorne made the house's name and antiquated furnishings famous. Among all of New England's historic houses, the Concord Manse is the only pre-Revolutionary ministerial house with a portion of its original domestic goods intact.[2]

As such, it offers a doorway into the world of Mary Moody Emerson's mother and grandmothers, into "woman's sphere" as experienced by eighteenth-century New England ministers' wives and daughters. Standing in the dining room, one can easily feel transported back to that earlier time. In the corner stands a case clock that William recorded buying for twenty dollars at the Boston Vendues in 1767. Two generations later, Mary wrote a meditation on this clock as an emblem of time, invoking its presence before the grief of widows and its obedience to "the relentless hand of female order."[3] It is still running today. And if the clock and its winding represent domesticity through generations, the dining room chairs near it embody that "female order" more literally. New when Phebe and Daniel Bliss married, hand-carved with the pointed horse-bone feet and gracefully curved backs of Queen Anne design, the chairs came from one of Boston's master craftsmen and declared their owners' place in an elite, city-based culture.[4] Over almost ninety years in two different Concord houses, amidst the successive upheavals of Awakening, Revolution, and Unitarian-Calvinist controversy, Phebe Bliss and Phebe Emerson did their particular work as ministers' wives by serving dinners and teas to guests seated on these chairs.

Hawthorne declared the Manse haunted, claiming to have found the identity of its ghost in a tattered portrait of Daniel Bliss. But he was hypothesizing a ghost who had never even lived in this house. If the Manse is to have a ghost at all, it should arguably be a composite female one, the figure of generations of women who really occupied and identified their lives with its spaces. Phebe Bliss, Phebe Emerson, and their kinswomen are ghosts at the Manse because, though undeniably present in its life, they remain nearly invisible on the historical record surrounding them. The invisibility of premodern women is wide and systemic, but it can be realized most keenly through individual cases, archives where they might be found and are not. The surviving collection of "Emerson Family Papers," though preserving Mary Moody Emerson's prodigious output of diaries and letters, includes just three pages of writing by women from the earlier generations of this articulate, record-keeping clan, short messages from Hannah Moody to her daughter Mary, from the elder Phebe Bliss to the younger, and from Elizabeth Emerson to her brother Joseph of Malden.[5]

These, along with a scattering of signatures on legal documents and comments in the men's letters, are enough to establish the Moody, Emerson, and Bliss women in the literate minority of their sex. A skillfully embroidered sampler by daughter Phebe Bliss, "age 8 years," attests uncommunicatively to her knowledge of the alphabet. Still, the greater written fluency of kinsmen absorbed all of these women's identities. For three generations, Harvard-educated in-laws wrote to each other about the welfare of women who made them each other's relatives. "Dear Love to my only daughter," wrote Samuel Moody to Joseph Emerson in 1727; "my writing to you is as if I wrote to her." "Read to her Psalm 73:24–26," Joseph advised son-in-law Daniel after his daughter Hannah had lost a child. "I have but a moment's time," Daniel Bliss Jr. wrote to William Emerson, "to ask you . . . how dear Mrs. Emerson does, and to reprimand you in some small degree for not giving me a particular account of her in your last." Nor did dear Mrs. Emerson (any of them) apparently resist this culturally assigned silence. William even encouraged the reluctant Phebe to return his "epistolary visits" during their engagement. "When you write," he suggested, "don't stand about ye Manner of expressing your Thoughts, but write just as you converse."[6] Her letters were not kept, however. Phebe, who preserved William's letters in a hand-worked case, is as likely as her husband to have discarded her own writing.

As a result, no sharply individualized portraits of character or intellectual allegiance are discernible for the mothers and daughters who preceded and directly nurtured Mary. However, the Manse's composite ghost can still be invoked.

"Remember it was my Mother's fault," Mary told Ellen, "that the Manse was cut up into so many small rooms. My Father built it just according to her ideas, and she used to say 'she was tired of great barns of rooms,' so he had all the rooms made little boxes to please her."[7] The rooms of the Manse do not seem particularly boxlike, but Mary's story hints at what the Blisses' establishment must have been. Called the "Block House" because it originally served as a garrison during King Philip's War, the house may well have had rooms like "great barns." Furthermore, it stood at the center of communal life, between cemetery and courthouse on the Milldam, just a hundred yards from the Concord meetinghouse.[8] Young Phebe's "fault" may have been a desire for seclusion, both by choosing more family-sized rooms and by moving away from the town center. William, having grown up at Malden's equally public and contentious Bell Rock, might have found reason to agree. For whatever reasons, they bought land and built their new house a full mile from the meetinghouse, amidst farming land alongside the quiet Concord River.

Yet the Manse was also a large house, a New England saltbox with a gambrel roof added to accommodate a third story. Probably built in this ample form even in 1770, it was expected to serve more than a nuclear family of two young parents and one baby. If Phebe Emerson wanted seclusion and privacy, she had to find them amidst a complex and essentially public domestic economy. Even at a mile's remove, the Manse extended the work of the meetinghouse, with two parlors in front, a modestly imposing entry hall, the minister's study behind, four bedrooms on the second floor, and more sleeping space on the third. William and Phebe's 1776 inventory of household goods tells more of life in these rooms. Guests who sat on the Queen Anne chairs also shared with the family six full-sized bedsteads and twenty cream-colored, English-imported plates. On the walls were two looking glasses, two "Pictures on Canvas," and three more "under Glass," "—decorations bepeaking genteel status. The Emersons aimed at gentility on a low budget. In 1776 they owned the frame of a chair but had not yet had it upholstered. Several items listed as "old" were probably hand-me-downs from the Blisses.[9] Through this frugality, however, they sought space and elegance for those who came to their door. When ministers' associations met, they did so in each other's homes; one of the upper chambers in the Manse was eventually called the "Prophet's Chamber" because so many traveling clergy had stayed there.

This hospitality expanded the arduous domestic labor required of every colonial housewife. Phebe Emerson's descendants later remembered her as a "real lady" who "sat in her chair and from it ruled the home," and her early household benefited from the labor of indentured servant Ruth Hunt, slave Frank, and frequently her mother's slave Phillis. But in pre-Revolutionary days country ministers' wives were not ladies of the kind Phebe eventually became; instead, she worked actively alongside her servants and kin. The inventory captures this productivity. Mistresses and servants together were responsible for both the house and its immediate yard full of geese and hens; for processing the corn and potatoes that William raised; for either producing soap, candles, and salt beef or trading for these with women of the town. They spun and churned; they employed an array of brass kettles and skimmers and skewers, which made an art of open-hearth cooking.[10]

Ministerial houses and their ceremonies especially required abundant cooking. Holidays in the Puritan tradition were fasts or thanksgivings, economies or abundances of food, and so part of women's responsibility. The restored hearth in Phebe's kitchen today may date from the Manse's earliest years. It is exceptionally large and efficient. The recess to the right holds a vast copper kettle that could keep water hot in quantity; the "beehive oven" to the left is deep, suggesting prodigious quantities of everyday and ceremonial baking. Mary's stories set both of her grandmothers at their hearths and producing food. "Darter," great-grandfather Edward Emerson had said to grandmother Mary, "your puddings is somewhat hard,—but not often." Grandmother Bliss was laboring intensely in her kitchen when she heard of the death by drowning of her daughter Hannah:

> It was court week in Concord and a great holiday, and they were all in the kitchen together making preparations. My Grandmother Bliss was making the

> pastry and the others were cooking, when my Father came into the kitchen, walked up to my Grandmother and said "Madam, prepare for heavy tidings." She took her hands, all flour, out of the pan and knelt right down on the kitchen floor. Then she stood up and said "I am ready." And he told her that Hannah's lover had tried to ford the Connecticut at the wrong place, and the river was high, and the current had drawn her right out of the chaise and swept her away.[11]

All the women in the Block House kitchen—mother, daughters, and servants—together must have mourned this loss from their circle.

The domestic circle was not closed within an individual house or village, at least for women of genteel family. As Hannah met her end amidst courtship and socializing in the Connecticut Valley, so did her older sister Phebe pay visits often and happily. The one surviving note from mother to daughter was called forth by such a separation: "I wish you to be wise for your Soul to be discrete Prudent & well behaved in Every Respect," Phebe Bliss urged. Young Phebe and William courted amidst many chaise rides to neighboring houses and towns; even before marriage she began meeting the Emersons and befriending new female kin. "Set out with Miss Bliss for the Eastern Provinces," William recorded in May of 1766. They stayed at Malden first, then went up the coast to Newburyport, York, and brother Waldo Emerson's in Kennebunk. When William returned to Kennebunk without Phebe, having left her to rest in Falmouth, consternation followed. "My Sister [in-law], when I arrived, with Tears in her Eyes wondered at my Conduct, & tells me I'm not half so welcome as if you were in the Company," he wrote back to her. The women in both families made new bonds through a marriage. When the Pepperell and Hollis Emersons visited Concord, wives came as well as husbands; when William and Phebe visited his family, her sister Patty often joined them.[12] For the husbands, kinship supported and enabled professional identity; for the wives, it offered the widest community in a constricted world.

William's diary refers especially often to visits with his mother and sisters Ruth and Rebecca, the two Emerson children just above him in age and the only ones still living in Malden. "My Honored Mother & Sister Becke" visited Phebe in a dangerous illness; sometimes just Becke and Ruth would come, joining William in a sleigh ride around the town square. So did the busy young minister find time in 1769, amidst dining in Boston and lecturing in Malden, to paper Becke's room at Bell Rock.[13]

By then the Malden Emerson women dwelt only tenuously in their ministerial house. Joseph had quietly expired at the end of a Sabbath in 1767, after asking the children for their mother's whereabouts: "When [she] came," Mary recounted, "they told her, and she went at once, and found him dead." Joseph's sudden end left his widow and daughters a great deal to contend with. Over the next three years, they stayed at the Bell Rock house and boarded prospective ministers. Ten candidates for the ministry came and went before eighteen-year-old Peter Thacher accepted Malden's offer in 1770; apparently, congregational quarrels and a niggardly salary kept others, including William's younger brother John, from accepting the position. Grandmother Emerson had to petition from 1768 to 1774 to be paid her due, the parish granting reimbursement for Joseph's funeral nine months later than promised and voting not to allow her whole account in 1770, instead appointing a committee of five to discuss whether she should be paid for feeding the candidates' horses as well as the candidates.[14] This congregation drove a hard bargain.

As usual, the family proved her truer community. Joseph's estate provided for his widow as well as eleven children, but economic and personal support went primarily to Mary Moody Emerson from the younger generation. William found his "poor Mother in a very weak State" and invited her back to Concord. His brother Waldo, an affluent merchant in Kennebunk, provided a house that he owned through his Malden-born wife. This "Madam Emerson house" was smaller than their former parsonage but was closer to the meetinghouse and center of town. Waldo's prosperity had eased what might have been a meager life for Grandmother Mary. Furthermore, Peter Thacher, having taken over the parsonage, proved a close friend: his 1772 diary shows frequent dining and evening visits between the two houses.[15]

Unlike William Emerson in Concord, however, Thacher did not marry the daughter of his predecessor. Half a generation younger than Ruth and Rebecca, the minister chose a wife elsewhere and only invited the two women to join them socially. At twenty-nine and thirty-two, respectively, with limited opportunities and resources, Ruth and Rebecca were settling into single life in Malden, which meant not independence but availability for the needs of others. Rebecca made clothing for the town poor; both cared for their aging mother, occasionally with Phebe Emerson's help; and they seem to have taken turns in the work of Phebe's household in Concord.[16] By rights they, too, should be included among the Manse's ghostly female presences.

As wives, widows, and single women, the mothers and daughters associated with the Manse experienced varieties of the same dependence on their families. Within marriage a woman had no legal will or ownership of her own; under the British common law of coverture her identity was submerged, or "covered," by her husband's. As much as the Queen Anne chairs belonged to the domestic world of mother and daughter Phebe, they were property of Daniel Bliss and William Emerson. As widows, or "relicts," grandmothers Bliss and Emerson did become owners of the goods willed to them by their husbands, even administered the family estates; but they relied on the stipulations of these wills and the generosity of male offspring to provide the actual means of living. There were few resources for economic autonomy. Mary remembered the heroic story of widowed Aunt Elizabeth of Newburyport, Joseph Emerson's sister, who "was reduced to making gingerbread to sell—but calling in children to give it away finished her last resource."[17] Nor were unmarried women able to do much more on their own. When Ruth and Rebecca joined Phebe in Concord, they were expanding their female community but also working to live in the primary way offered to them.

Hidden Manna

Bound to home and family, the Moody, Emerson, and Bliss women knew their most public eminence in the meetinghouse and the domain of religion. Ministers' wives were called "Madam," a title reserved for only the highest few in each town's scale of wealth and power.[18] Traditional congregations leveled family rank by emphasizing gender, listing members and seating churchgoers in separate male and female sections. At Malden's meetinghouse, remembered as "the old Puritan all over" in its unpainted plainness, women and younger men climbed to the gallery by separate stairs and sat firmly divided by a railing. But if the Puritan custom was followed consistently, Madam Mary Moody Emerson did not join the other women upstairs. For the minister's wife and the widow of his predecessor was reserved the best seat in the house—high, isolated, alongside the pulpit, and facing the congregation. In Concord, Phebe Bliss and Phebe Emerson would have shared that seat as they listened to William preach. In Hollis, Hannah Emerson sat so close to Daniel's pulpit that, growing deaf in later years, she could place her hearing trumpet a few inches from his mouth. When even that method failed, she devoutly read the sermon text in silence, then expounded her own points about it to the family at home.[19] A lifetime's proximity to the clergy had enabled her to preach inwardly.

Nonetheless, Mary, Phebe, and Hannah counted as laity in the church's order. Like all other women and men, they brought their experience of grace to the minister and, when accepted into membership by a vote of the congregation, visibly enacted their election by monthly presence at the communion table. Having one's own father or husband hear the experience and serve the communion may have heightened or burdened that privilege but did not fundamentally alter it. As a community of the redeemed, the Puritan church offered women a powerful spiritual equality and their most public visibility. In one sermon William spoke of the "hidden manna" of communion as "agreeable to every taste, whether old or young, Male or Female." Here no identity was "covered": women joined the company of saints with or without husbands.[20]

Paradoxically, they did not also become voting members of the covenanted church but were excluded from it more fundamentally than from the rights of secular society. Defined as political noncitizens by the circumstance of wifehood, they were noncitizens of the church by absolute reason of female gender. Single women or widows could at least sign a will; but when in 1749 the Concord church made and signed its public covenant, no women signed—single, married, or widowed. Indeed, the ceremony for covenant renewal further dramatized the difference between men and women: "The Chh solemnly Expressed their renewed Vows & Engagements to the Lord, the male Members standing & lifting up the Hand & the female standing the Time of Reading." Women made no gesture of will or capacity for action but merely assented. Nor did such customs change easily. In 1776 William Emerson exactly followed Daniel Bliss's form in both the signing procedure and the ceremony, despite the opposition to exclusionary covenants that he had professed. His wife, sister Ruth, mother, and mother-in-law were all present for this ceremony—then adjourned to the dinner they had prepared at the Blisses' house.[21]

Women's subordination in the New England church, distinct from legal subordination though socially interlocking with it, derived ultimately from the Bible. Paul had declared that in Christ there was "neither Jew nor Greek, . . . neither bond nor free, . . . neither male nor female"; yet he also instructed the church in Corinth, "Let your women keep silence in the churches." To Timothy he elaborated, "For Adam was first formed, then Eve. And Adam was not deceived, but the woman being deceived was in the transgression." According to Paul women had been second in creation but first in sin; and even though in Christ sex would be obliterated, the earthly church still followed God's will by denying women public voice. Increase Mather cited both Corinthians and Timothy to justify the Puritans' exclusion of women not only from preaching but also from the foundational lay privilege of forming the covenant. Only men, he concluded, could be "constituent" members of the church, "entrusted with the Keys of the Kingdom of Heaven"; if the brethren should all die in a particular congregation, the sisters would "immediately Cease to be Church members." His son Cotton Mather neatly, though with no intention of promoting change, described the resulting situation of a Puritan woman, that she was "desirous to eat and to *drink*, where she may not *speak*."[22]

Phebe Bliss and Phebe Emerson signaled both privilege and disenfranchisement as they rose without vote or gesture in the ministerial pew to hear the covenant read. A few African-American bondsmen numbered among Concord church members; Lyn and Boston, labeled "Negroes" on the list of signers, had fully affirmed the 1749 covenant.[23] Possessing no last names or rights to their labor, these men occupied the lowest rung of a hierarchy in which the ministerial women stood high. Yet by Puritan logic Lyn and Boston constituted the church as the women did not. Only in communion was the promise of eventual equality for women and men, slave and free made visible.

Women's exclusion from voting membership in the church was all the more contradictory internally since Judeo-Christian tradition represented every human partner to divine covenant as a woman. When Phebe Bliss urged, "Cleave to God, Mary," she echoed Concord's own covenant: "We promise & engage by the Help of divine Grace to cleave to God in Christ as our chief Good." In the King James Bible, "cleave" described the union of Hebrew nation to God but also the union into one flesh of husband and wife.[24] According to the ancient language, God was the husband and humanity the wife, so that a woman's earthly life corresponded more completely than a man's to her divine "spousal." In Malden, Joseph Emerson could invite both men and women to conversion in the courtship language of Canticles: "I charge you, O Daughters of Jerusalem, if you find my Beloved, that ye tell him, I am sick of Love." Yet he only pushed beyond biblical metaphor to a biographical instance of bridehood to Christ when the person in question was actually a woman: "she lov'd the LORD JESUS . . . *superlatively*, above *Father* or *Mother, Brother* or *Sister*. . . . She could and did say with the Psalmist, 'As the Hart panteth after the Water Brooks, so panteth my Soul after GOD.' "[25]

Regardless of their near absence from historical records and their silence in the churches, women were numerically and symbolically central as Puritan believers, seen to possess a special aptitude for the grace that all were called to experience. Throughout New England's history, women, both single and married, had joined in larger numbers than men—five women for every three men at the time of Daniel Bliss's ordination in Concord, exactly matching one historian's estimates for the wider colonial church.[26] The ministers often recognized their own disadvantage compared with the sanctity of women in their churches and households. Joseph Moody not only declared to Jonathan Edwards that his wife, Sarah, was going to heaven by the shorter road; he himself, recording the frustrations of an unconverted state, saw women "especially endowed with grace," wished for the same fervor, and felt reassured that they were at least making progress under *his* ministry. His sister appeared similarly to her husband, Joseph Emerson. "I have reason to be concerned," Emerson wrote in his diary of 1737, "that I am no more affected with Spiritual Things. My Wife in a serious & spiritual frame when she wak'd in ye Night, uttered herself to this Purpose, I'm well assured that Spiritual Blessings are sweeter to me, and I have a greater desire after them, than after [worldly things]."[27]

These women never told publicly of their blessedness, but after death it was epitomized by others in the truncated, emblematic forms of memorial art. "CONSORT to the Rev. Samuel Moody," begins the epitaph on Hannah Moody's gravestone in York: every surviving epitaph of the Emerson-related women tells first of that vital affiliation, often naming daughterhood to the clergy as well as wifehood. But Hannah's then goes on to the even more important tribute, "Early and Thorough CONVERT." The second title rather than the first extends into an eye-stopping catalogue of virtue: "Eminent for Holiness, Prayerfulness, Watchfulness, Zeal, Prudence, Sincerity, Humility, Meekness, Patience, Weanedness from the World, Self-Denial, Publick-Spiritedness, Diligence, Faithfulness & Charity."[28] Hannah's fifteen virtues earn her the title "Eminent," a title pointing toward the eschatological communion of saints but resulting in conspicuous elevation before the world as well.

Such a visual memorial told not biography or personality—certainly not Hannah's worries about alienated parishioners or experiences of melancholy—but instead a set of roles and values that she sought to follow. Her triumph was to become in death a text that others could read and imitate. In Malden's cemetery we read of Hannah's daughter Mary Moody Emerson: "By her Piety and devotion, her zeal and charity her spirituality and holiness she adorned ye christian profession she lived the life of the righteous and died ripe for glory." The best an individual could do was to "adorn ye christian profession"—render more visible an ideal transcending personal circumstance. The epitaph of Mary's daughter Hannah Emerson in Hollis directly claims her as a model for others: "She lived a pattern of filial obedience, respect, and affection; . . . She lived the life of a true Disciple of Christ." In life as well as death, a woman felt the privilege or obligation to be a "pattern," imitating the ultimate pattern of Christ and so offering a Christlike example to children, servants, and neighbors.[29]

Though Phebe Bliss has no epitaph in Concord, we cannot assume a lesser regard for her eminence, for a contemporary portrait brings to more individual life those titles "consort" and "convert." Drawn in crayon sometime during Phebe's middle years (her hair is still dark), it makes a symmetrical pair with an oil portrait of Daniel Bliss. Husband and wife are inclined slightly toward each other, both dressed austerely in black, though with contrasting and more elegant white details: Daniel's clerical bands and wig are matched by Phebe's cap and the facing of her gown. Her hair and breast are covered and unadorned; in her person there is none of the gentility suggested by her taste in furniture. But along with such asceticism comes authority. Like her husband, Phebe holds an open book, the Word, and looks up from it as though seeking to address the viewer. This is Phebe the New Light saint, as vigorous and penetrating of eye as her husband, represented with an emblem of sanctity rather than domesticity in hand. At the height of revival in 1742, Daniel sent love to a New Light colleague and his wife from "our Sister Phebe my Dear fellow Helper in the Lord." The portrait also tells of that equalizing partnership, of a ministerial wife as "fellow Helper" and not subordinate.[30]

When Phebe Bliss died in 1797, thirty-three years after Daniel, she had not forgotten the intensities of the Awakening. Among her last possessions was a portrait of George Whitefield, possibly the one hanging in the Manse today. But her partnership with Daniel had by now yielded in significance to the individual example of her life. In the form of a hand-inscribed memorial, accompanied by a simply drawn mourning emblem of urn and willow, enclosed in a lady's pocket-sized purse, an epitaph expanded on Phebe's qualities:

> Died at Concord on the 2nd, and was respectfully entombed on the 5th inst. Mrs. Phebe Bliss, the pious relict of the rev. Daniel Bliss, former minister of that town deceased, in the 85 year of her age. She had been a tender and solicitous wife; a fond and provident parent; a firm and faithful friend. But the prominent feature in her character, and that, for which her memory will ever be embalmed, was a love of holiness. Repentance and humility towards God, and faith and confidence in Christ, seemed to possess her whole soul. Her love and gratitude to an unseen savior were ardent; His words and promises were her study and hope; his disciples were her best friends; his table was her richest repast; his prayerfulness and resignation were her example; his cross was her chief glory; his resurrection was her greatest joy and triumph. Blessed are the dead who die in the Lord: for they rest from their labors, and their works do follow them.[31]

This expansive tribute comes close to the heart of Puritan women's piety in its sense of Phebe's reading of Scripture, partaking of communion, and exercising faith with her "whole soul." Furthermore, it underlines the preeminence of an abstract, encompassing "love of holiness," even beyond the roles of wife, parent, and friend that she had also successfully fulfilled.

Mary had her own more pointed language for declaring grandmother Phebe Bliss's sainthood superior to her wifehood: "She was a woman such as I have read about, but, except her, I have never seen one. A perfect Christian. She was a woman who never fell before affliction. My Mother often reproached her with want of feeling because she went to church while her husband lay dead in the house. But she was rapt in another world! She knew nothing of this world."[32] In Mary's version of family history, Phebe Bliss differed from her daughter Phebe Emerson in a piety rendering even her marriage to Daniel a mere matter of the world. Mary would have agreed in honoring Grandmother Bliss as a "solicitous wife" and "pious relict," but she found her perfection to lie in individual rapture of spirit.

Throughout life, Mary took part in the culture of idealizing and memorializing faith. She knew the cemeteries of Malden and Concord intimately and understood their lesson. "When we contemplate the graves of the departed," she wrote from Malden in 1804, "the ideas of their pleasures and honors never incites emulation, but their virtues do." Later in life she willed to her niece Hannah the portraits of her grandparents, probably copies of the Bliss pair, that she had long cherished, and in her Almanack recorded a childhood memory of the Malden house with Grandmother Emerson's portrait in it. Almost surely she owned one of the pocket epitaphs to Phebe Bliss, for eventually a member of the family copied its words into Waldo's "Genealogy" notebook. The presence of Phebe's portrait in Waldo's Concord household, like the copying of the epitaph, suggests that Mary passed on to him her reverence for this female ancestor, the inmost figure in her "interior history of New England." But most of all, Grandmother Bliss headed a tradition that Mary conveyed to other women, as when she saluted an adopted niece, "*Phebe*, (a name almost sacred to my early remembrance from my Granmother Bliss whose saintly life will never be effaced from me)."[33] Mary's mind had been permanently formed by the "pattern" that her grandmother offered.

Awakenings

In Mary's characterization of Phebe Bliss, the Emerson women's heritage of Great Awakening piety becomes most immediate and audible. Daniel Bliss's "Dear fellow Helper in the Lord" was also Mary's ideal Christian. But Mary had other immediate life contacts with the Awakening's mothers and daughters as well. Her two most important nurturers in Malden, Grandmother Mary and Aunt Ruth, had jointly lived out its entire history. Three years before Whitefield's arrival, the elder Mary was her husband's model of a soul "affected with Spiritual Things." Ruth, born three months after the evangelist first preached in Malden, was reported as a young woman to be attending Whitefield's latest sermons in

Medford. Still later, Ruth impressed her niece Mary, and Mary remembered, "that Providence and Prayer were all in all."[34] These meager scraps of evidence point to the certainty that all the Bliss and Emerson women heard New Light preaching often and intensely, from both Whitefield and their own kinsmen.

The context in which they experienced the Awakening can best be felt, in the absence of their own testimony, from the men's record of other women in their parishes. A series of episodes in York, Malden, and Concord suggests the possibilities and limits of women's authority of grace within an urgent culture of conversion. As ministers, the men sought a balance between endorsement and control of their female converts. In the spring of 1735, when Joseph Emerson and the two Moodies bore witness to a woman's discovery of a millennial sign in her loaf of blood-colored bread, they were declaring females capable of receiving messages from God. They may also have been fending off alternative readings of the event as witchcraft or sanction for independent prophecy.[35]

A more terrifying female-centered drama drew in both Samuel and Joseph Moody during these same months. An Indian servant, inaptly named Patience Boston, had been in the York jail all winter, charged with murder for pushing her master's eight-year-old son into a well. But she was also a Christian convert, daughter of the Indian Church of Nauset on Cape Cod. Years of rage and guilt churned within her so that she could not cease from "crying out in a most terrible manner" from her jail cell. From her raging, Samuel and Joseph Moody shaped a call to revival, eventually publishing the "astonishing Relation of a bloody Malefactor's Conversion, . . . taken from her Mouth while she was in Prison, and . . . publickly read to her on the Lecture a few Hours before her Execution." The relation, following her own words as closely as they could be transcribed, told a life of violence, from fire setting and drunkenness to abuse of her husband and desire to kill her child. When the child died, she claimed to have killed him—and finally killed another child so as to be "guilty of Murder indeed." But conversion came when, having owned the murder, she could look for forgiveness, and so was hanged at the age of twenty-three in July 1735 with full ministerial testimony to a "marvellous Work of sovereign and superabundant Grace."[36]

Samuel Moody and Patience Boston worked almost in dialogue at this grim ceremony, played out before a larger and no doubt rougher audience than had ever entered York meetinghouse. Samuel preached and read the narrative; then Patience addressed the crowd herself, praying for her surviving child, warning young people against the sins of lying and drunkenness. After she lapsed into confusion, Samuel picked up again and urged "that hundreds there present if they did not begin to seek God in earnest that Night, would perish forever." Patience claimed a voice that the Bible would forbid her, and Samuel also assumed a role beyond the usual limits of Puritan ministry by declaring this woman's sins forgiven.[37] Her penitence and its effect on the crowd augmented his ministerial power, and that in turn set her sad life's story before the hearing and reading public.

An unlikely partner to Patience Boston's brink-of-execution testimony is the

"Message . . . from the Dead" that twenty-one-year-old Abigail Upham addressed to Malden, but both were printed by Boston publishing houses in 1738 and sponsored by the Moody-Emerson ministerial clan. As she died of throat distemper, this devout young woman had very little to repent, but she had so much to say that she very nearly reversed the relationship of pastor and laity. "She was desirous," Joseph reported, "that the Minister would use all the Arguments he could think of, to move young ones to come to Christ." But then she presented her own arguments—about Christ's willingness, her personal struggles against hardness of heart, her advice that others begin seeking "Now! Now! Now! They must not any longer drive it off. Let them know, says she, what Comfort I now feel."[38]

Abigail addressed the women who watched at her bedside without intermediary, and from their accounts Joseph transcribed her words. Having asked for prayers that Christ might be revealed before her death, she awoke the next morning to declare, "I have seen Christ, and he smil'd upon me: and now I am going." When her neighbor asked where she was going, Abigail responded with her vision of the heavenly Jerusalem: "I see . . . the LAMB upon a Throne sparkling, and the Streets of the heavenly City pav'd with Gold, and there they are singing Hallelujahs to GOD and the Lamb."[39] Neither Abigail Upham's vision, her assurance of election, nor her assertive speech was entirely conventional Puritan piety, but in the extraordinary situation of townwide grieving, Joseph Emerson both allowed and celebrated them all.

As with Patience Boston, Upham spoke in print only from beyond the grave, when the tradition of funeral and execution sermons gave permission. There was also a stirring of revivalistic fervor, however, in the coincidence in timing of these two published female exhortations. Just a year before, in 1737, Jonathan Edwards had written of Northampton's Abigail Hutchinson in his first history of the Connecticut Valley revivals. This woman had died "swallowed up with a sense of the glory of God's truth and other perfections," determined to evangelize neighbors from her deathbed.[40] Joseph Emerson's portrait of another Abigail could well be a response in kind to Edwards, as in another vein the Moodies' publication of Patience Boston in 1738 (three years after her death) appears a contribution to the literature of extraordinary grace.

All these episodes suggest how ready women's grace was to transcend the limits placed upon it by the institutional church, long before a more visible growth of women's activism and expression in the nineteenth century. Historians have not called the First Great Awakening, like the Second, a women's revival. In fact, enough men followed Edwards and Whitefield to raise the proportion of their membership in churches like Concord's. But even if the gender balance shifted slightly toward men, still the majority of Concord's new converts were women, both at the Awakening's height and thereafter.[41] The church's perennial appeals for women could only have been heightened in the new revival. In the controversial literature of this upheaval, gender issues surely played a role. In 1742 Jonathan Edwards described his own wife Sarah's religious exaltation as a centerpiece to his *Thoughts Concerning the Revival*, but this time concealed both her name and her gender. A woman still living—and his own wife—could not be publicized. Still, the word about Sarah's piety must have been out in New England evangelical circles. By telling Edwards that "they say" Sarah's piety was above his, Joseph Moody was revealing a level of religious culture that did not appear in print.[42]

Edwards was circumspect about his wife's piety amidst fierce criticism from Old Lights, who quickly associated "enthusiasm" with women. Davenport, it was said, had gone into "the women's side" at one church, singing and praying until all were in hysterics. "Our presses are for ever teeming with books, and our women with bastards," charged Anglican Timothy Cutler.[43] Revival, in the critics' view, made women noisy and promiscuous. Charles Chauncy, responding directly to Edwards in *Seasonable Thoughts*, raised the specter of female enthusiasm in another form. The book's entire thirty-page preface recited the history of seventeenth-century antinomian heretic Anne Hutchinson, who had declared her direct illumination by the Holy Spirit and her freedom from the directives of merely "legal" preachers. According to Chauncy, "the like spirit and errors" were "prevailing *now* as they did *then*." By implication Jonathan Edwards was—or at least would produce—another Anne Hutchinson.[44]

No enthusiastic Anne Hutchinson arose from the Moody, Emerson, or Bliss churches, but the Concord case of Hannah Melvin certainly spoke to Old Light fears of revival-induced disobedience by women. Melvin joined the church as a girl of twelve in 1759, the daughter of poor parents who had never joined the church or baptized their children. This was no "child of the covenant" but an autonomous preadolescent saint, newly included by Bliss in his challenge to the Concord social order. Looking back at this conversion experience from her forties, Melvin claimed that she had "received a spark of grace, . . . that she could never lose it, and that it would revive again before she should die, otherwise she should go distracted."[45] Such doctrines had come straight from Bliss, who preached that grace was both the only way to salvation and irreversible once received. But subsequent behavior opened her to charges of both claiming direct communication with God and resisting authority on the strength of that inspiration.

We cannot know how Daniel Bliss would have judged his own convert; instead, Bliss's two successors, William Emerson and Ezra Ripley, inherited the burden of Hannah Melvin's "disorderly walking." In 1775 William admonished Melvin before the church, naming the sins of an antisocial woman of spirit: going about "from House to House," "refusing to labor with your Hands, & to eat of your own Bread," "Slandering the character of Several Persons . . . as an idle Person Tattler & a busy-body." At the heart of her fall, however, was sexual sin. "You have, to yr Shame & Confusion, be it spoken," William addressed her, "been fully & evidently prov'd guilty of a Scandalous Breach of ye 7th Commandment, and that at a Time, when you were under a disgraceful Confinement, and ought to have been mourning & weeping before God, on Acct. of yr Sins, yt bro't you to the loathsome prison." For a self-avowed saint to offend with her body was to violate the very fabric of community, both in Concord and in heaven. "You have . . . crucify'd ye Son of God afresh—struck at ye very Vitals of ye Chh, & cruelly wounded ye Sacred Body, of which you yourself are a Part." To awaken her short of total reprobation, William pronounced, Melvin would be deprived of the right to take communion, "shut . . . out from a Seat at His Table."[46]

None of the awe before God's power that seized York in the Patience Boston case came to Concord in this unhappy affair. Unlike the Indian servant in her confinement for much worse crimes, Melvin denied all charges, refused all penitence, and included the minister among her targets of slander. A single woman apparently living apart from her parents by the time of this admonition, Melvin only hardened her resistance and isolation afterward. William's successor, Ezra Ripley, repeated the ceremony of warning in 1783, then finally excommunicated her in 1791 before the assembled congregation. "S[ai]d Hannah was present in ye gallery, but had so often solemnly declared that she would not attend, that her presence excited suspicion of an intention to make disturbance, & ergo, she was not called upon or noticed as present." Looking back on the case, Ripley used terms that Charles Chauncy could only have approved: "She supposed herself converted, to use her phrase. . . . It is a lamentable truth, that she gave no evidence of repentance while she lived. Let this warn us not to depend upon any religious impressions or experiences that are not followed by a good and godly life."[47] If Phebe Bliss's sainthood lived on as a legacy of the Awakening into the 1790s, so did Hannah Melvin's disorder. In her youth Mary surely knew both, learning to fear the charge of deviance, as well as emulate the greatness that could result from a woman's experience of conversion.

It is small wonder that women of ministerial family, even when pious, were rarely enthusiasts themselves. The same clerical judgment that proceeded from pulpits also controlled homes and the "pattern" that they made visible. A minister's wife was expected to complement her husband, in subordinate partnership to fulfill all roles that were not his own. Her access to grace provided one possible fulfillment of his striving, whether for himself or for his congregation. But there was another aspect of partnership that especially compromised spiritual intensity: when a husband spent his time praying and studying rather than bargaining in the marketplace, a wife became responsible for "seculars." Sarah Edwards may have enjoyed a short road to heaven, but she was praised by Jonathan's biographer for relieving him of all the "multiplied toils and anxieties" of his earthly life—and this with "becoming deference." Hannah Moody, praised after death for fifteen virtues, apparently spent her life representing the needs of the world in her marriage. She would complain to Samuel of the emptying larder, woodpile, or purse, and *his* ardent prayer would fill their needs. Once he gáve away her only pair of shoes to a poor woman, assuring her that the Lord would provide another before night. That very morning a neighbor brought over a pair that were too small for his wife.[48] The story does not report whether the new pair fit Hannah.

In terms of women's experience, this assignment to practical business spelled conflict. The religious culture expected a woman to come early and thoroughly to grace but not to act upon it with authority or autonomy. Mary's two grandmothers seem to have balanced between heaven and earth rather differently, perhaps neither without tension. Grandmother Emerson devoted herself to marriage and family. Telling of Joseph's long hours in the study, Mary added, "My Grandmother brought up all the children, without disturbing *him*."[49] But Grandmother Emerson also told stories about her own parents' conflicts over firewood and shoes, perhaps revealing an undercurrent of wifely resentment. Grandmother Bliss declared herself wed more fundamentally to God than to man, going to church while Daniel "lay dead in the house." The reproach her daughter Phebe voiced, however, may also have reflected a side of her own mentality: she herself had advised this daughter to be discrete and prudent less than two years earlier. Phebe Bliss could not have maintained her position in a suspicious, conflict-ridden Concord by acting otherwise herself.

The shadowy record of Phebe Bliss Emerson, Mary's mother, shows no sign of indiscretion, from the dutiful sewing of her eight-year-old's sampler to her elderly role as "lady" of the Manse. Religious and personal assurance, however, seems to have come with difficulty to her. At the time of marrying William, she felt both frail of body and despondent of spirit. "Well my Phebe Bird," he wrote soon after, "be happy: let Peace and Quiet, Contentment and Serenity & Ease possess your Mind." Praying for God's grace to make her a "Pattern of Patience," he alluded to undefined physical afflictions that stood in the way of spiritual peace as well. A week after William recorded her improved health, in October 1767, he also recorded, "Received my Wife into Full Communion." He added no comment about peace or conversion.[50]

Phebe, born in 1741 amidst the white heat of her father's converting work, six years older than her troublesome contemporary Hannah Melvin, seems to have joined the church more as an expected step in life than out of any trans forming experience. No public or private memorials to her piety survive whatsoever. Close in age and affection to her brother Daniel, she lacked his rebelliousness but possibly shared his rejection of their father's "isms."[51] She reproached her mother for failing to mourn father Daniel properly, but she was surely not "rapt in another world" to the extent that both parents were.

The greatest commonality of religious experience among all these women of clerical family, with or without personal assurance, was the nurturing of children into the covenant. In this area of life, spiritual vocation and supplying of family need came together. Phebe Bliss Emerson may not have experienced conversion in the way that her father required, but she went on to raise her son William through "blameless childhood" into the ministry, so fulfilling the expectation of Blisses and Emersons alike.[52] She did not serve as a pattern for her daughter Mary's piety. But other women in the extended family took on that work.

Spending most of her childhood in Malden, Mary was Grandmother Emerson's child, recipient of her care both directly and indirectly through Aunt Ruth. As Mary herself reported, Grandmother Emerson had always done more than keep her thirteen children from disturbing Joseph. Whenever she found out that an additional baby was coming, "she gave thanks that another immortal soul was created."[53] The elder Mary found a direct catechetical role with her children, asking how they understood the new birth and later praying for their vocations. When father Joseph urged William to leave the hayfield for his books, she even confronted her husband over the best way to prepare for the ministry. If she thought of each child as "another immortal soul," her namesake granddaughter Mary was the fourteenth and last soul that she instructed.

After that childhood experience, Mary returned to Concord as a young adult and encountered Grandmother Bliss's fervor, engaging in direct and private conversation apart from her mother's interference. For finally unknowable reasons, Phebe Bliss had made no converts of her own children nor replicated her New Light zeal in daughter Phebe. So perhaps she found her life's most successful converting work in granddaughter Mary, as nearing death at the Manse she urged that the young woman "cleave to God."

In Arms at the Concord Fight

> Hail happy day—tho' the revolution gave me to slavery of poverty & ignorance & long orphanship,—yet it gave my fellow men liberty—my Country threw the gage.
>
> Almanack, July 4, 1826

Mary Moody Emerson served as a keeper of her extended family's history because its enthusiasm and eminence sustained her life. She knew this family, however, amidst estrangement, disruption, and intensity of need for its resources. Women taught her its glorious past firsthand, but only after the loss of her first home and parents, and throughout life she traced both glory and loss directly to the American Revolution.

Her pun to Lafayette—that she had been " 'in arms' at the Concord Fight"—connected Mary's earliest days with both a mother's nurture and a father's militancy. On April 19, 1775, she had literally been in Phebe's arms as an infant of eight months, while at a meadow's distance William exhorted the Minutemen to arms against the British at North Bridge. Often, however, her retrospections about early childhood recalled that moment only as the beginning of chaos and deprivation. A few years after meeting Lafayette, Mary again relived the past in her Almanack. "My God how glorious is the story of our war," she exclaimed. "It thrills it absorbs. I see the streets of my native Town, I hear the fire, I see the smoke—God of battles protect the injured, give new force." But then followed a welter of grievous emotions: "I see my father—I forget him—my infancy, begun how grandly—how sunken now. . . . Happy the man who finds an early bed of honor."[1]

As Mary went on to reflect, her own long life had been far less grand than her father's short one. "The first gleams of hope of enterprise are dearer than fruition. Soul of man made for immortal races sickens at possession." In her life's experience the Revolution had possessed only negative fruits: "Ah, it was the possession of headless families—of poverty—of protracted sufferings w'h quench the light even of such a noble struggle—w'h doom the helpless orphan to find liberty & all that makes life valuable sunk in the beloved grave." Her Almanack entry on the fiftieth anniversary of independence put the matter even more starkly: her "fellow men" had claimed liberty by throwing down their challenge to the British; but since her father's death, she herself had lived outside that liberty in "orphanship," a condition declared marginal even by the odd form of her word for it. Sometimes grandiose and self-pitying in the personal story that she told in fragments throughout life, Mary also rose to an almost mythic self-characterization. Her father's fight for independence was hers as well, for it had resulted in an unsought independence that was the condition of her life.[2]

Days of Adversity

Mary was born in Concord on August 25, 1774, fourth child of William and Phebe Bliss Emerson. Around her family and town the Revolution was also coming to birth that year, and William rode out often to keep in touch with the course of events. Writing back to Phebe from Boston in April, he declared unabated love after seven years' marriage, alluded with "Propriety & Dissimulation" to their love's increase through Phebe's pregnancy, then shifted abruptly to politics in the wake of Britain's port closure. "This Town, has a Face upon it, I never saw before," he reported. "Ye Torys . . . vainly imagined that Parliament would have found out in their wisdom a Punishment for ye Friends of their Country that would not have so nearly concerned 'em also; but (thanks be to God) they are as deeply plunged as we." William described the city's "*best*" sort in terms that revealed his own allegiance: "Far from being discouraged or fainting in this Day of Adversity, [they] do Hope in GOD, do already believe that he will appear for them—& that Peace & Prosperity, civil & secular Rights & Privileges will be restored to ye Town & Country & that we shall see good Days according to the Time we have seen Evil."[3]

By 1774 William spoke as a committed patriot minister, interpreting the oppressive acts of Parliament as God's way of testing his people. William had been called to this political religion by a lifetime of hearing about grandfather Moody's zeal against the French and cousin Daniel's service at Crown Point. His fifty-year-old brother, Joseph, who had carried such militancy from Louisburg through the Stamp Act crisis of the 1760s to this day, was his closest ally. "My Father and my Uncle Joseph of Pepperell were very active and instrumental in bringing on the Revolutionary War," Mary recalled. "They thought it was very wrong to drink tea." Both led their towns in pledging that year, along with the Boston Committee of Correspondence, not to consume any British-imported goods.[4]

The extended family was hardly unanimous in politics, however. In Malden, Grandmother Mary Moody Emerson would have nothing to do with boycotting tea. She "once made some when she thought her son Joseph was away," namesake Mary said, "and he came in and found her drinking it! He was very much displeased. His Mother was hurt. She never got over it that he wasn't willing that his Mother should take tea when she needed it." This was a dispute of generation more than gender. Across the countryside, younger women were refusing tea and learning again to spin their families' cloth in support of the protest.[5] At seventy-two and often ill, however, Grandmother Emerson recoiled from both the hardship and her sons' principled intolerance.

In Concord, intrafamily difference ran deeper, so much so that both William's letters and Mary's retrospective stories are loudly silent about it. While Phebe was hearing of William's satisfaction at the chagrin of Tories, her own beloved brother Daniel was leading the pro-Crown forces of Concord. Though family papers barely mention him, the public record tells his story clearly. Upon returning from Worcester County to practice law in 1772, Daniel had immediately been chosen among the town's leading citizens to draft its first response to the Boston Committee of Correspondence. He alone declined to support Concord's modest statement of rights. Soon he found an indirect way to satirize the Whigs' labeling of their ills as "slavery," writing an epitaph for John Jack, a former slave and Awakening convert who had been Daniel's client:

Tho' born in a land of slavery
He was born free.
Tho' he lived in a land of liberty,
He lived a slave.
Till by his honest, tho' stolen, labor,
He acquired the source of slavery,
Which gave him his freedom;
Tho' not long before
Death, the grand tyrant,
Gave him his final emancipation,
And set him on a footing with kings.[6]

Daniel had been a dissenter since his early defense of character in the West Church; now he turned his skill in irony and antithesis to showing how slavery gave the lie to the professed American ideal of liberty. Sympathizers with the Crown recognized a good hit, and eventually the verse appeared in a London newspaper. It can be read even today at Concord's Hill Burial Ground.

By the year of Mary's birth, Uncle Daniel had been appointed justice of the peace for Middlesex County and lived in town, upholding General Gage and Parliament at the bench as father William was attacking both from the pulpit. No records suggest whether the Bliss and Emerson houses kept up the social contact that they once had enjoyed. Certainly their worlds crossed at Grandmother Bliss's Block House, just a stone's throw from Daniel's residence on Walden Street. Phebe Emerson gave birth to Mary a month before the Blisses also had a fourth child, named Isabella after her mother; and church records show that William baptized both babies soon after their births.[7] There must have been tension among the kin gathered for these ceremonies.

Indeed, the short weeks between Mary's and Isabella's births saw a cleft open between the two families that would never be closed. On August 30, 1774, when Mary was six days old, Concord made its first move toward political leadership by inviting 150 delegates from across Middlesex County to plan resistance to the Crown's Coercive Acts. Daniel Bliss took the opportunity to make another dramatic public pronouncement. When a speaker cautiously advanced the wisdom of collecting arms, Daniel rose and demanded, "For what purpose?" "To protect ourselves if necessary," called a voice from the crowd. "From what," Daniel countered, "from the power of the British nation?" Then he turned his scorn to the entire gathering:

> Once raise a hand against an English soldier and every ship the winds waft to these shores will come laden with armed men, your taxes will be doubled, every petty colonial officer will have its salary doubled, new offices will be created, and in six months you will be a crushed, conquered, humiliated people, every man within the hearing of my voice tonight will place his hand on his mouth, and lay his mouth in the dust and cry "Peccavi."[8]

One young man from Worcester remembered this as the most eloquent speech he had ever heard: "There was something so thrilling in his words and manner . . . that when I looked upon the audience it seemed to me that they were as pale as dead men." But Daniel's words did not hold the day for long. From the opposite side of the courthouse chamber rose a Concord cabinetmaker, Joseph Hosmer, who resisted Daniel's prophecies with a modest cogency that broke the spell. Daniel was hardly pleased. "Who is this man?" he asked impatiently. "Hosmer, a mechanic," came the answer. A Crown-appointed justice of the peace did not expect confrontation from a common man in his own courtroom. But before that winter was over, Hosmer would be lieutenant of the newly formed Minutemen, and all Tories would be pushed to the margin of the community. The mob would even force Dr. Joseph Lee, William's old antagonist in church politics, to apologize for reporting Concord's mobilization to the British just after the County Convention. Daniel held more respect than Lee, receiving at least for the moment the townspeople's censure but not rage. As Hosmer family tradition put it, "They had hoped their beautiful young orator would have adopted their counsels. They were sadly disappointed." Daniel mourned his loss of authority over them, too. "Time was . . . when the young men of this town followed wherever I led," he said. "Now a child of twelve has more influence than I."[9]

In the rapid unfolding of events, William won all the influence that Daniel lost, making his pulpit an instrument of mobilization. By October the Provincial Congress was convening in Concord, and when the courthouse proved too small for its members, he offered the meetinghouse. In return, the Congress appointed him chaplain, and he opened two sessions a day with politically resonant prayers. By January, William was preaching explicitly to recruit Minutemen; Mary afterward recalled the family tradition that he freed his own indentured servant to fill up a space in the ranks. Two companies were complete that March when, after a review of arms, he preached on "the Character of the Christian Soldier." And with William's meetinghouse now serving political and military ends, the Manse necessarily met the accompanying need for bed, board, and extended discussion. The Provincial Congress returned a week later, and his father's old ally John Dexter represented Malden, staying with William and Phebe. "Refreshing News from home," William recorded, "great Appearance of a Change in the State of our public Affairs."[10]

As political affairs divided William from brother-in-law Daniel Bliss, they forged new links to Malden. There the young minister Peter Thacher, a mere twenty-two to William's thirty-one, was claiming political influence by even bolder means. By spring he had joined Malden's Committee of Correspondence and thereafter would take on direct political leadership. Madam Mary Moody Emerson surely got no comfort from her minister if she complained about her sons' position on tea, though she counted both of the leading Malden patriots as friends and counselors. Crises of political change and family loss were compounding for the Malden women in these months. William's brother Waldo, the merchant who provided their mother's major financial support, had died a year before; and now early in 1775 came news that brother Samuel—he whose childish piety had won parental notice—had succumbed to illness in Newburyport. The Concord Emersons were often on the road to William's first home. "Went to Malden in a double sleigh with Mrs. E, Miss Patty [Bliss] & the baby [Mary] & [four-year-old] Hannah," he recorded.[11] Changes of state and family intertwined in the conversation that these visits allowed.

Meanwhile, Concord had become a seat of resistance for the whole province, and within it forces were coming into realignment. William's church renewed its offer of reunion to members of the old West Church, whose members no longer cared so vehemently to defend the Tory Joseph Lee. At the same time, William distanced his church from the divisive Awakening by admonishing Reverend Bliss's convert Hannah Melvin for "disorderly walking." Both William and the parish recorded this public humiliation, the latter in full and official detail that shows its importance beyond the ordinary discipline of New England churches. A disruptive and "unclean" woman served as a scapegoat in the community. None of Hannah's sins was explicitly political, but in a fearful time slandering the minister and going about as a "Tattler & busy-body" would not be tolerated. As she was admonished in February, Concord became one of the province's two depositories of military stores, with field pieces, mortars, and provisions for fifteen thousand soldiers secreted in its houses.[12] Tension ran high.

Hannah Melvin's false holiness preoccupied the town at a time when the more genuine menace, Tory informers, could not so easily be resisted. On March 9, an unnamed spy successfully penetrated the town's defenses and sent word to General Gage detailing the amount and location of hidden stockpiles. Daniel Bliss did not necessarily provide information to this agent; others in town shared his Tory principles, if less openly. But when two members of Gage's staff arrived in town on March 20 for further information, they asked a woman the way to the Bliss house. Just as they began to converse with Bliss, the woman came in crying that the crowd had threatened her with tar and feathers. Soon a further message arrived for Daniel himself, that "they should not let him out of town alive that morning."[13] His immunity from the town's rage was over. Daniel took his time in leaving Concord, first finishing both his dinner and his description of the military stores. Then he accepted the offer of an armed escort, bade Isabella and their children farewell, and pointed out the Lexington Road as the safest exit from town. He never returned, but sent his Tory brother Samuel to collect a doubtlessly anxious family soon after.

The wider family circle—perhaps never at peace internally—would not be united again. Challenged by the British to prove the provincial will to fight, Daniel pointed out his window in Concord to brother Thomas Theodore Bliss and said, "There goes a man who will fight you in blood up to his knees." Town tradition preserves comments by Daniel and William that imply the extent of their animosity toward each other. Like a Greek tragic hero, Daniel declared, "Whom the Gods would destroy, him they first make mad," whereas William warned in dark biblical prophecy, "Verily our enemies are of our own household." William's words had come from the book of Micah, part of his text for a fast-day sermon preached short days before Daniel's departure: "Trust ye not in a friend, put ye not confidence in a guide; keep the doors of thy mouth from her that lieth in thy bosom. For the son dishonoureth the father, the daughter riseth up against her mother, the daughter-in-law against her mother-in-law; a man's enemies *are* the men of his own house."[14] The congregation apparently heard the personal reference in this description of a terrible breakdown in human trust. No comments survive about Phebe Bliss Emerson, caught between the opposing loyalties of her male kin.

William recorded what happened next with much greater exhilaration and fullness of detail. "Battle at Concord and Lexington," he wrote in his diary for April 19—then the same night filled a blank leaf with an account headed "Fight at the North Bridge." The impulse to narrate and interpret this event would long continue in the Emerson family, from William's first-anniversary oration to his grandson Waldo's and great-grandson Edward's reimaginings, from the oral traditions of women to the public performances of men.[15] The Emersons claimed April 19 as their particular moment of national centrality.

So the story must be told as much as possible in the terms of family memory, distant and proximate. "This Morning between 1 & 2 O'clock," William wrote that evening, "we were alarmed by the ringing of ye Bell, and upon Examination found that ye Troops, to ye No. of 800, had stole their March from Boston . . . & were at Lexington Meeting House." Townsmen ascended the hill across from the meetinghouse, and there in the dawning light saw the British only a quarter of a mile away, "glittering in Arms, advancing . . . with the greatest Celerity."[16]

The Minutemen had to decide quickly how to respond. Some, William wrote, urged an immediate stand despite the odds against them, but others preferred to wait for recruits from nearby towns. Town historian Lemuel Shattuck, interviewing veterans in the 1830s, found that William himself had been the hot-headed man who called out, "If we die, let us die here." Edward Emerson added two generations later, "Fortunately some of the old Indian-fighters had a better plan." But Edward also recorded a story of the chaplain's way with his militia. Walking along behind their line, William laid his hand on the shoulder of a young man trembling at the sight of British bayonets: "Don't be afraid, Harry; God is on our side." With that the man took heart, fought the British, and lived to tell his neighbors of William's words.[17]

By retreating from immediate battle the Minutemen also relocated their confrontation to the road across William and Phebe's field from the Manse. The militia watched and moved as British troops seized the Town House, destroyed the ball they found, and sent troops by way of North Bridge to seize more military stores. Redcoats and Minutemen now faced each other across the bridge visible from the Emersons' house. Inside, Phebe with her small children—Mary "in arms"—felt the keenest distress. As granddaughter Sarah Haskins Ansley later wrote, "The first news that grandmother had, of what was going on in the morning of the 19th of April, was from the black man Frank, who rushed up into her room with his axe in his hand saying, 'The Red Coats have come!' She fainted: she was always delicate."[18]

Phebe could not have been so innocent of the morning's events as this story implies. She had been receiving political news from William for years and just a month earlier had known the strife culminating in her brother's flight. But the story epitomizes the family's memory of Phebe as physically frail, personally unassertive, and desirous of seclusion from the public world. Coincidence had brought that world to her. Such "delicate" femininity was far from universal in Concord. Goods had been stored in thirty private homes, and female keepers of domestic space were generally their protectors. A servant at the tavern protested that one room was her own chamber and so saved the papers of the provincial treasurer; another hid the church's communion silver in a soap barrel, then decoyed the soldiers from entering her home by feeding them at the door.[19] Women could find strategic advantage in their traditionally subordinate roles. But the patriot minister's wife—perhaps ambivalent in her political allegiance anyway—does not seem to have joined the public resistance.

As a result, William felt torn between the needs of his household and militia, and in any case a minister could not join in the actual battle. While the Minutemen crossed North Bridge, he stayed on the nearer side by the Manse, watching as they tried to recross the bridge, were met by British warning shots and a volley of fire, then in return "fired the shot heard round the world." By William's own testimony, he was close enough to recognize the two Minutemen who died: "Davis and Hosmer,—the only Friends that fell within our Boundaries," he orated a year later, "I saw them fall in Front of Battle."[20]

William's location during the Concord Fight mattered to his descendants because, at least by the late nineteenth century, they felt a need to defend his bravery. Phebe's second husband, Ezra Ripley, had unwittingly implied that William withdrew from danger, witnessing the battle "from the windows of his house near the battle field." So great-grandson Edward pursued the question and got a clarification from his elderly aunt Phebe Haskins Chamberlain, who had in turn heard of the day's events from her grandmother Phebe. "It is a great mistake that our grandfather remained in the house," she wrote. "Grandmamma told me herself that she felt hurt because he did not stay more with her, and once when he was feeding the women and children with bread and cheese she knocked on the window and said to him that she thought she needed him as much as the others. The lane in front of the house was nearly filled with people who came to the minister's house for protection." In grandmother Phebe's memory, only *she* sat by the window, watching both her husband and the larger scene. To her eyes it appeared that "he had been holding back our men from firing, but at the last he same as gave permission."[21] Though no doubt overestimating her husband's authority over the Minutemen, she still reported events as an eyewitness.

Phebe's report most of all confirms her own timidity in crisis. She offered neither food nor sanctuary to the townspeople who thronged to her house for help, as a minister's wife might have done. So her husband, rather than either going inside or directly joining the pursuit of redcoats, did the women's work of feeding others. In the memorial oration of a year later, he remembered "Women and Children" in terms that confusedly combine the experiences of his wife and the women outside: "Mythinks I view the mournful Sight, the frightened Mother, encompassed round with all her little Brood fast clinging to her Clothes, all speaking at once impatient for an answer, asking the Cause of all this dreadful Tumult! 'No more, my Loves' says she, 'No more, let's run; our Father save! nor dare we stop or linger here or we shall all be killed.' "[22] Neither he nor Phebe appears to have expected heroism from women amidst a military alarm.

Mary kept nearly total silence about her mother, never mentioning Phebe's conduct on April 19 beyond the oblique reference to maternal "arms." She overwhelmingly preferred the masculine example of her father, both to undergird her own identity and to teach others. How, she exclaimed to young nephew Waldo, could he be more excited by Cicero than by his own "noble & heroick Ancestor"? Aunt and nephew together construed that heroism as a matter much more of words and vision than of literal engagement in arms. Discovering his grandfather's diary while preparing the "Historical Discourse" in 1835, Waldo quoted its understated comment at the end of April 1775: "This Month remarkable for the greatest Events taking Place in the present Age." "He, at least, saw clearly the pregnant consequences of the 19th April," Waldo concluded. Mary likewise revered William for what he saw and how he spoke. One of her moments of greatest satisfaction came when she passed the Concord meetinghouse in a stagecoach and overheard a stranger tell his companions, "There I first heard eloquence."[23]

Zealous Whig Sermons

The content and style of William's Revolutionary eloquence can be discerned from even the fragmentary record that survives.[24] Not only did he mobilize Concord, but also, for another sixteen months after April 19, 1775, he joined in the nation-building that followed. Recent scholars have disputed the relative importance of diverse religious and political origins in producing the civil religion that brought the colonies to action: whether the Boston-centered Whig pamphlets, with their rhetoric of liberty and slavery; the enthusiasm of the Great Awakening and its promise of millennial fulfillment in a union of believers; or the religious militancy engendered by wars with the French.[25] William Emerson offers a case in which all of these influences focused and ignited. Holding to a New Light family tradition of preaching, and one that early turned to military ends, he was also a Boston man, directly attuned to the new political radicalism. "Arise my injured Countrymen," he urged the Minutemen in 1775, "and plead even with the Sword, the Firelock and the Bayonet, . . . the Birthright of Englishmen the dearly purchased Legacy left you by your never to be forgotten Ancestors, and if God does not help, it will be because your Sins testify against you, otherwise you may be assured."[26] He was calling for spiritual awakening, but assurance now sanctioned the people's claim by arms to their English political rights.

Place and time lent William's sermon to the Minutemen dramatic resonance; he was not merely reacting to events but anticipating and shaping them. "Gentlemen:" he addressed Concord's officers five weeks before the battle, "In all Probability you will be called to real Service. The clouds hang thick over our Heads." But his rhetorical emphases were hardly unique, instead taking their strength from a shared sermonic language that read American political events as a fulfillment of the history of Israel. As his brother Joseph had celebrated the repeal of the Stamp Act in 1766 as a deliverance from Babylonian captivity, so now William anticipated battle with Abijah, the king of Judah who assured his army that "God is with us for our Captain." Joseph's sermon had stood directly in Whig tradition, outlining a history of British liberty from the Spanish Armada to the recent ministry's plot against constitution and people. By 1775 William had long since taken this legacy as his own. Even as he castigated British politicians, William also agreed with Joseph in claiming "cordial Affection and true Loyalty to our rightful Sovereign" in the act of resistance to Parliament's tyranny. "And now," he protested,

> because we, the Descendants of such worthy Ancestors, are not willing, nay, dare not be guilty of such Edomitish Prophanity as to sell, or rather tamely resign our glorious Birthright into the bloody fangs of hungry Courtiers and greedy Placemen, we are unjustly . . . charged with Rebellion and Sedition; when perhaps there never was any Part of the British Dominions since Civil Government was invented, that ever less deserved so reproachful a Character.[27]

William rather than his brother the Whitefield convert, however, had the richer biblical imagination. While Joseph just alluded to the type of Babylon and went on to his political litany, William lingered over the particular scriptural analogy of the text, where Abijah calls Judah's army to resist ten aggressor tribes. As in the current conflict with England, Judah was facing civil war in a spirit of covenant loyalty. William's language repeatedly invoked the biblical promise of covenantal freedom: as he imagined the selling of a birthright as "Edomitish prophanity," befitting the children of Esau rather than God's chosen Jacob, so he characterized New England's ancestors according to the biblical type of flight from Egyptian slavery. Echoing a Pauline phrase that would twice provide his main text later in the summer, he urged the Christian soldier to "put on the whole Armor of God."[28] Such biblical symbols had multiple meanings and persuasive emotional depth: "slavery" evoked both Israel's ancient bondage and the Coercive Acts, "whole Armor" the blessing of grace as well as a recruit's new skill in firearms.

This sermon mediated an anxious and unprecedented passage into action, warning that an "ungovernable mutinous Spirit . . . would be one of the most dark and melancholy Omens upon the Face of our present Military Preparations that could pass before us!" Rather than envisioning new possibilities, William lamented the present day as "the most dark and gloomy that ever New England saw." The steady theme of Calvinist sermons meeting political crisis was apocalyptic judgment; William took the Minutemen toward April 19 through rituals of penitence encouraging reliance on God. The same week came his fast-day sermon from Micah, evoking the threat of social anarchy in family enmity. He did conclude his military sermon with the hopeful prospect of God's kingdom, but only in the "better world" of heaven "where Peace and Righteousness will forever dwell—when Wars shall cease, when Men shall beat up their Swords into Ploughshares and their Spears into Pruning hooks."[29] While not quite banishing prospects of a new earthly order from his reading of the crisis, he was making no prophecies.

Even though William anticipated battle hesitantly, however, the energy and motion following from it led directly to a new rhetoric of vision. Two days after the battle at North Bridge, he took part in a prayer service for seven hundred Minutemen, pouring into Concord from across Massachusetts, then went to Cambridge and Malden. In Cambridge a new Continental Army was gathering. Brother Joseph arrived a day before William, claiming the honor among all the clergy of preaching first to soldiers on the Common. Soon Peter Thacher also came with the Minutemen of Malden, whom (as Mary later remembered from Aunt Ruth) he had gathered under the town tree by their house. The Cambridge camp repeatedly drew William and his colleagues in the patriot clergy. By the end of May, he had also heard Harvard's President Samuel Langdon preach the annual election sermon to Congress in Watertown, hailing the "ever memorable day" in Lexington and Concord as the moment of rupture with the king. The skirmish at his door had been appropriated as a rationale for autonomy, with only the "Eternal King" as guide.[30]

Praying with soldiers on the Common, William himself moved toward new consciousness. "New Lords, new Laws," he wrote home in approbation of the order brought by Virginia Generals Washington and Lee. But order was also rising out of the army itself. Walking among the camps, he noticed the variety of dwellings created by the citizens of different colonies, some thrown up of boards and sailcloth, others "curiously wrought with doors & windows, done with Wreaths and Withes in manner of a Basket." Such diversity, he reflected to Phebe, seemed "upon ye Whole rather a Beauty than a Blemish to ye Army."[31]

Indeed, these neighboring encampments, beautifully formed by previously unacquainted native craftsmen, represented his larger sense of the potential American nation. On July 20, 1775, would come the first Continental Fast, proclaimed by Congress in Philadelphia to forge a new national unity in prayer. William anticipated preaching for it with excitement and trepidation. "Mrs. Emerson," he wrote, "I'm not a little concerned what I shall do on ye approaching Fast. The people will expect something out of ye common Course, & I shall have nothing to entertain them with. What shall I do?" How he took his church beyond the common course can be surmised from his text, a fully messianic prophecy from Isaiah: "And it shall be for a sign and for a witness unto the Lord . . . for they shall cry unto the lord because of their oppressors, and he shall send them a Saviour, and a great one, and he shall deliver them."[32] If William had long read colonial politics in relation to Israel's covenant-keeping God, he could now anticipate the coming fulfillment of that relationship in a new kingdom of the redeemed.

In the midst of such growing confidence, the fall and winter brought new losses and responsibilities. In October, brother Joseph Emerson died of a lingering illness contracted at the Cambridge camp, bringing to three the list of premature deaths among the Malden brothers. But William's colleague Peter Thacher now became chaplain to the Provincial Council; and William himself, through acquaintance with President Langdon, brought Harvard College to Concord for the duration of the siege of Boston. By the new year and the British army's evacuation, he was addressing Concord citizens and Harvard faculty alike at the meetinghouse, from texts that rang with commitment to a cause well under way: "And shall God not avenge his elect?" (Luke 18:7); "Be ye not again entangled in ye Yoke of Bondage" (Galatians 5:1). One hostile observer, Harvard official Caleb Gannett, found the first "a most zealous Whig sermon"; undeterred by naysayers, William repeated it to his late brother's congregation in Pepperell. He also listened as others preached; just before the departure of British troops in March, he again visited the army in Cambridge, then went on to Malden for Thacher's fast-day preaching. Almost surely he was present as well that week when Thacher memorialized the Boston Massacre to an audience of exiles in Watertown. "With transport, my countrymen," Thacher concluded, "let us look forward to the bright day, which shall hail us a free and independent state." The audience's responding tears and demands for instant publication testify that many in eastern Massachusetts were ready to hail a "bright day" ahead and define it as separation from England.[33]

William's memorial to the Concord Fight in April 1776 sought by its own rhetorical power to bring the congregation—still including exiles from Harvard and Boston—abreast of these rapid changes: "The God of Heaven has wrought for us. Let his be all the Praise, and all the Glory. . . . It has been a Year of Wonders—a year of the Right Hand of God." But even as he preached the traditional language of praise to God, he localized and secularized God's wonders. Like Thacher's performance the previous month, this was an "Oration" instead of a thanksgiving sermon, expounding no biblical text. Instead, William departed directly from the shared experiences of his townspeople, in the speaking voice of a representative witness as much as a minister. He himself had heard the "alarming Signal" and seen Davis and Hosmer die. His language rather floridly echoed Homer and Milton as well as the Bible: a British shaft dropped harmless as "Priam's Spear of Old," and a barbarous shout sounded "as if the infernal Doors were burst, and all their kindred Crew had broke their adamantine chains." Caleb Gannett, William's most vocal critic, found it "a flat insipid thing, . . . & performed in a miserable manner."[34] But by blending classical and scriptural language, epic sweep and first-person intimacy, William rather than Gannett was reaching toward a new republican oratory.

As it celebrated the Concord Fight and hailed the British evacuation, William's oration was his declaration of national independence. An electric union of equals had resulted from the enemy's approach to Concord, he recalled, so that even in aged men "a short youth boiled up within their Veins, and strung their Nerves anew!" Speaking for nation as well as town, he found that "the brawny arm of tyranny" had struck a fire that might otherwise have lain inactive. All Americans, even the aged, were sons now released from filial love by the ruler's misdeeds. Britain, he proclaimed, "has taught us Lessons we should ne'er have learnt—has taught us our own Strength, and how to live without her." Such an education could not be regretted or undone. "O Brittain how art thou fallen!" William proclaimed. "For thy King is a Child and thy Princes through unbounded avarice and inhuman pride have robbed thee of thy brightest Glory."[35]

William affirmed, moreover, that the newly independent "American Israel" would be God's heavenly kingdom on earth:

> Oh! When once the rising World shakes off this dreadful Yoke, then mythinks, we may hail America as the Glory of all lands. . . . Then may we look for the full and Complete Accomplishment of all the inspired Sages have said of civil Peace and Liberty, that never have been fulfilled heretofore,— . . . that the Wolf also shall dwell with the Lamb and the Leopard shall lie down with the Kid,—that Nation shall no more rise up against Nation,—that Swords shall be beat into Ploughshares and Spears into Pruning Hooks,—that Satan shall be bound . . . ,—that our Land shall be Immanuel Land and the Prince of Peace assume his rightful Power and sway the glorious Sceptre over all Nature and his Dominions extend from Sea to Sea and from Shore to Shore.[36]

William's peroration presented this vision with no attendant gestures of self-abasement or calls to revival. At this moment the revival had occurred, and the anticipation of future glory alone held his imagination. If a new classicism and humanism, as well as an unprecedented political circumstance, informed his millennial design, however, he was still his Calvinist father's and grandfather's heir in this language. "But is anything too hard for Immanuel?" Moody had asked Emerson fifty years earlier. "Isn't ye Time near for great Things?"[37] William was taking the vision of a transformed society always inherent in Awakening thought and declaring its time come at last.

Neither had the anxiety and God-dependence inherent in this New Light heritage really disappeared by the spring of 1776. William could turn epic poet of the American future on the anniversary of the Concord Fight, but he articulated other needs and assurances from Sunday to Sunday. The optimism of the April 19 oration had no place in his communion sermon of two months later, when his attention turned to God's manna as "angel food" in "the Wilderness of this World, in this Valley of Baca, which is as destitute and barren of spiritual Provision suited to the Nourishment of the Soul as the Wilderness thro' which the Israelites pass'd was of natural Food." Such food, said William, fed a world of evil and rebellion, and whoever partook would never thirst after the "Vanities of Time."[38] In the language befitting a sacramental occasion, William's Israel was still in the desert, suffering from its own rebelliousness. God's presence could be discerned only in signs from beyond the world, not the "Immanuel Land" of an imminent public order.

Furthermore, William never stopped preaching sermons enforcing the order required of fallen humanity. The very overturnings of hierarchy that he seemed to sanction in the oration could also be disturbing in their more local manifestations. Local cases of self-interest, he warned that February, compelled him to teach the Golden Rule as the first and simplest principle of human conduct. He did not interpret this rule as one of democratic reciprocity, but explained that God intended every person "to be treated according to the Office and Condition in which a wise Providence has placed him." William was defending the deferential society that he had always known. "The high and low, rich and poor, bond and free, are not so by Nature," he asserted, as though beginning an argument for the right of revolution. His sentence, however, went another direction: "but [they are so] by the wise and sovereign Disposition and Permission of Providence. HE who has a sole Right to set up one, and pull down another, makes this Difference in the Character and Condition of Men."[39]

As William prepared in July 1776 to leave Concord as a chaplain in the army, after both the wondrous events of the spring and the Declaration of Independence in Philadelphia, he and his people affirmed their bonds through the traditional ceremony of covenant renewal. Here was neither justification of independence nor vision of the coming kingdom but a vow to "walk together as a well-order'd Chh of Christ . . . , obeying them that have ye Rule over us watching over one another in Love." Concord was not repudiating the Revolution they themselves had helped to begin; far from it, they were meeting the crisis of the Revolution in this language of communal obligation. William changed the ritualistic words he inherited from Daniel Bliss only by darkening them, adding to the confession a plea to "return unto ye Lord from whom we have ungratefully Revolted," pressing for a particular resolution "against some crying Sins of ye present corrupt & degenerate Day."[40] The sins he listed did not include the social and economic self-serving indicted earlier. Instead, they were private sins of the heart, intemperance and uncleanness, pride and vanity, profanation of the Lord's Day—a list suggesting inner unease more than public breakdown.

The one social disorder explicitly named was in that sphere closest to home and heart, the "Neglect of Family Government." He and his male church members (the women silently assenting) confessed guilt "in not resolutely restraining our Children & Servants, from taking those Sinful Liberties that ruin their Morals & subvert all Order and Government." Family government was the intersection point between private morals and public order; and here "liberties" (a different word from Whig "Liberty") had especially to be resisted. In the metaphors of the April oration, a union of sons could repudiate their unworthy father, but neither William nor the men of his congregation wished to surrender their own patriarchal privileges.

Just how much he insisted on the traditional ways of deference comes to life in his daughter Mary's story of early childhood. "I remember my Father's punishing me once," she recalled. "I was two years old and when I came into his study I wouldn't make my curtsey . . . [so] he whipped me. Mother came in and asked why he had punished me. He said 'Because she wouldn't make her duty on coming into the room.' 'What! Whip a child two years old for that!' My Father said 'My dear, since you have interfered I must whip her again,' and he did." The old English custom of requiring a child to signal "duty" with a bow or curtsy still survived in New England culture, and William saw it as the earliest lesson to enforce. More was at stake than the curtsy itself. By punishing her refusal, he was breaking her inborn will, so driving out original sin and preparing her soul for grace.[41] Despite William's own resistance to the "brawny arm of tyranny," children had no new dispensation at the Emersons' house in 1776. Nor could a wife "interfere." Women were not classed with children and servants in the language of covenant, but neither were they equal partners in the affirming or enforcing of "Family Government."

Both William's ardent affection and his desire for patriarchal control can be felt in the fourteen letters he wrote after riding away to Fort Ticonderoga on August 16. In a time of separation and uncertainty, his words again evoked covenantal order. "I can't but hope," he wrote to Phebe from Acton, "that You at home, and I abroad, shall reap the Benefit of our kind Friends interceedings for us at the Throne of Grace, especially when we keep in the Way of Duty. I trust that I am while I pursue my Journey, & that You are, while You rely upon the love of a kind watchful Providence for yourself, and for our dear little Ones, & the whole Family."[42] "Duty" was not merely a ceremony enforced upon childhood but an encompassing way of life.

Asking Phebe to deliver "Salutations and Directions" to members of the family at both the Manse and the Block House, William spelled out a list of duties as they befitted age, gender, and station. Eldest son Billy, age seven, must "read a Chapter in the Family [Bible] (whenever his Mamma is able to bear it), every Morning, except when there is somebody else can do it better." In his father's absence, if prematurely, Billy was man of the family. Hannah, age six, "*must* mind what is said to her and everybody will love her." At first William wrote "or nobody will love her," but he crossed out the threat and substituted more encouraging words. Phebe, not yet four, "must learn her Book." Neither Mary nor newborn Rebecca received directions, though both were named within the embrace of parental love ten days later. But the list of family members did include Ruth, the indentured servant, told "to be careful, active, and *complying*"; Frank, the slave, who must "cutt up the Wood if he has Time and take care of the Hay in the Barn, and the Flax on the Grass and the Corn in the Field, that they be kept out of Harm's Way"; and every resident at "the other House" as well. His own deference—as well as desire to instruct—determined the language of his greeting to Phebe Bliss: "My Duty to our honoured Mamma and pray her never to distrust a kind and watchful Providence for herself, nor for her Children either at home or abroad."[43]

The vocation taking William away from home was to inspire and correct soldiers as he had in Concord and Cambridge. But Ticonderoga fell far short of his expectations. His letters to Phebe do not refer to a single instance of public prayer or preaching in his few weeks as an army chaplain; instead, he consumed dinners with colleagues, looked for direction from General Gates, and watched the descent of rain and sickness. "Instead of much influence he found he had none," Waldo wrote later of his grandfather. Listening to the sound of hammers and idle talk on a Sabbath morning, William decided that in the army he had found "stronger Proofs than I've heretofore (without myself) perceived, of the Depravity of human Nature!" The experience prompted more introspection than condemnatory anger. Was his own uneasiness at violation of the Sabbath mere custom? "I want to be ascertained in my own Mind why this is the Language of my Heart, as I think it truly is."[44]

To William's pietistic mind, no public order present or future could be relied upon apart from heart-assurance of filiation to the divine. It was his last source of reliance. Within a week after this Sabbath reflection, he had contracted the "mongrell Feaver" common to the camp; on September 18 he applied for a discharge from the army, so unwittingly cutting off the pension that Phebe would have received if he had declared a furlough; by September 23 he had reached Rutland, Vermont, on his ride home, too sick to go farther. He died there on October 21 at the home of Rutland's minister, Benajah Root. In a last, shakily written letter to Phebe from Rutland, William resigned himself and his family to a "Covenant-keeping God." Still trying to instruct and encourage, he also gave up personal control: "My dear, strive for Patience, let not a murmuring Thought, and sure not a murmuring Word drop from your Lips. Pray against Anxiety—don't distrust God's making Provision for you."[45]

Headless Families

In 1826, when family members asked Mary to help compose an epitaph for Concord's monument to William Emerson, she suggested the following: "Truth charity and enthusiasm distinguished him from the dawn till the close of life; exalted by profound peity. He passed the ordeal of affliction uninjured. He loved his office and filled it with the eloquence of the soul. He loved his family and was to it as a good Angel. He loved our blessed revolution better and would minister to it he said, tho' it should cost his life." Mary idealized her father's patriotic ministry as a perfect consummation of piety, but her obsession was the death that it had exacted. She claimed to remember standing in the doorway of the Manse at two and watching her father ride away. A Concord plowman later told her that, before turning his horse's head at the bend in the road, William had paused and given a long look back at the house. She felt sure he knew that he would never come back. "I shall never cease to think of my father," she wrote amidst planning for the monument, and a quarter of a century later still declared herself a "long mourner."[46]

Grief became a central force in her subjective life, but not hers alone. After William's death, the Emersons became a family of mourners, whether in open or more hidden forms. Mary was educated in bereavement by Aunt Ruth, William's next older and fondest sister. His widow, Phebe, often cried in secret over the case of William's letters. On her deathbed in 1825, as Mary reported, Phebe asked that her husband of more than four decades not be summoned to the final moment: "Don't call Dr. Ripley his boots squeak so, Mr. Emerson used to step so softly, his boots never squeaked." As a young man, eldest son William found and exhumed his father's body, so setting a pattern of pilgrimages to the unmarked grave in Rutland that other Emersons would follow. In 1795, his memory awakened by the demise of a contemporary, young William recalled as the gloomiest day in his life "the Lordsday on which intelligence was brought of my father's death." Past and present collapsed into one lament: "The world seems half dead, and the surviving half seem to stalk about like ghosts."[47]

Mary felt that sense of loss and disorientation more painfully than her brother, however, because father William's death separated her from home for the remainder of childhood. The Concord Manse, she wrote as an adult, held "invariably gloomy associations of my infant exile, by the death of a peculiarly benevolent & affectionate Parent." When she sought to distance herself from family members, the terms of expression were even more absolute: "I have no claims—never, never had any since I was [two] years old—*never mentioned any*."[48] For life Mary saw herself with resentment and defiance as a have-not in a world of American and Emersonian haves, simply because she was raised in the Malden rather than the Concord branch of her family.

Viewed within the circumstances of 1776, this "exile" was far from cruel abandonment; instead, it was a means of coping by women who had always worked together. Waldo later claimed that William himself had carried infant Mary to his mother in Malden before leaving for the army. But more immediate records show that the choice was her mother's. William clearly referred to Mary ("Polly") among his five children in a letter from Ticonderoga, but two years later Phebe's estate records named the cost of "Boarding Cloathing Schooling Doctoring and Nursing . . . four Children."[49]

The family around Phebe was now made up of women without men. Her mother, already in 1776 a widow for twelve years, had lost her influential Tory son to Canada, and three other sons soon joined opposing armies. In Malden, Grandmother Mary had experienced the death of four sons in thirty months, after a husband's death nine years earlier; and daughters Rebecca and Ruth remained unmarried. Phebe could still turn in both directions for help. Her mother's slave Phillis, according to later stories, rocked newborn baby Rebecca along with her own child. As for little Mary, as she herself later put it, "My Aunt Ruthy adopted me, and took me over to Malden." Ruth had visited in Concord through the summer of 1776 and probably taken charge of the children while Phebe was pregnant and lying in. There was no absolute necessity for Mary's being the one child chosen by her. In 1775 four-year-old Hannah had spent a month in Malden and might have returned now. Possibly Mary went because she had reached the difficult age of two with a will imperfectly bent to obedience. More likely, Mary's name set her future by virtue of its bond to the Malden family. In elder years, one of her most precious mementos was a silver porringer with "E" over "I + M" on the handle. "My grandmother left it to me for my name," she explained.[50]

The three family households operated on a par financially in the early war years. All had secure dwelling places, but none a steady source of income.[51] Concord's town meeting soon proposed to "take the Difficult Circumstances that Mrs. Emerson is left in into Consideration and in some way and manner Grant her relief." Over the next years, however, sustenance would come largely through the women's own efforts, as meanwhile the new paper money printed by Continental Congress plunged to worthlessness. "If all our Men are drawn off and we should be attacked," Abigail Adams wrote her husband that same dark fall of 1776, "you will find a race of Amazons in America."[52] None of the Bliss and Emerson women seem to have been Amazons, nor even patriots of Abigail Adams's acuity. But they shared with her a will to survive amidst the wider upheavals of wartime.

The woman in this family most prepared to earn money was Phebe Bliss, who operated a boardinghouse at her garrison-sized dwelling on the Milldam. She had probably taken in boarders ever since her husband's death brought a series of ministerial candidates to the door. During Harvard College's year in Concord, one paid guest had been William's critic Caleb Gannet, who as college purveyor could acquire scarce goods during the siege of Boston. Scarcity continued to plague the boardinghouse, ending her ability to house three imprisoned British officers in 1778. One left with regret, since he found Mrs. Bliss "the genteelest woman I have met with in New England," and her treatment of his illness equal to any a family member would receive.[53]

For a woman later remembered as "rapt in another world," Phebe Bliss managed dwindling resources with determination. She even defended her son Daniel's interests. When Tory property was confiscated, the Committee of Correspondence complained of difficulty getting anything away from her. She finally had to deliver up all that was left in Daniel and Isabella's house, but this was valued at only twenty-eight pounds total and included no luxury goods. Phebe probably delayed responding until the rest could be sent on to them. Furthermore, she gave the committee enough trouble that it allowed her to keep Daniel's barn in return for surrendering other claims. But these were small victories. Daniel was gone and would not return, gradually communicating less and less with his mother. In 1783 he wrote to General Knox of the Continental Army asking for transmittal of a letter to her with four coins in hard money. "Perhaps She may much need it," Daniel wrote. "I have not heard from her these some years past."[54]

Phebe Emerson's experience from 1776 to 1780 is implied by the spare language and numbers of probate accounts. Administering William's estate with the help of a court-appointed adviser—and son Billy as "humble amanuensis"—Phebe learned harsh lessons about income and debt. In her 1778 report, £232 had been spent of the £327 left by William, £171 for debts he incurred. Two years later the remainder was gone and debts still mounting. Money had been needed for settling William's accounts with the army and for hiring a worker to repair the barn; by this time Frank had gone to the army and freedom, and there was no manservant at either house. Meanwhile, no income came from the army and very little in any other form—eleven pounds by 1778, forty pounds by 1780 through real estate sales.[55] Phebe ("always delicate") does not seem to have followed her mother by trying to run a boardinghouse.

She did have one boarder in 1778, however, and as it turned out she needed no other. Ezra Ripley, William's successor in the Concord ministry, had first known the Emersons three years earlier when he had been a Harvard student in Concord. Ezra and Phebe married in November 1780. Town legend, perhaps apocryphal, is that some opposed the marriage because she was a full ten years older than Ezra. He threatened to refuse his ceremonial blessing on other couples unless he could marry the woman he wanted.[56] Ministers had special prerogatives when it came to marriage.

Her later tears and dying words suggest that Phebe felt less affection for her second husband than her first. Still, this marriage secured the future on both sides. Ezra wed the Concord ministry itself in marrying Phebe, and the Emerson Manse became his for more than sixty years. After four difficult years, Phebe returned to wifely dependence on a minister and his salary. Ezra later recalled the difficulties that surrounded his early ministry because of wartime inflation; among them must have been the debts that he and Phebe began with. Only by teaching and doing manual labor had he gotten through this time. However, he acknowledged that "a particular event in Providence and the long credit given him by one benevolent trader" made life easier.[57] One need only look at the Manse today to see the results of that good fortune. Ezra and Phebe may have felt the pinch of inflation, but they were also able the year of their marriage to choose new, English-imported wallpapers for the parlor and hallway of a house merely ten years old.[58] On the wall of the "Prophet's Chamber" is young William Emerson's inscription from earlier that year, "Began Greek, Jan. 26, 1780." The continuity of learning and gentility was assured at the Manse.

Neither providence nor credit proved so generous in Malden, this contentious, unhappy town still racked by a meetinghouse controversy that lingered from the early years of Joseph Emerson's ministry. Even the Revolution, which in Concord had overcome the divisions of Daniel Bliss's time, failed to create unity in Malden. The parish that had haggled over Madam Emerson's account as a ministerial widow would hardly become more generous amidst new financial hardship. So the Emerson women, bereft of four sons and brothers, met the winter of 1776 and 1777 with uncertain sustenance from either family or town. Marriage again proved a way out of difficulty. In February, Rebecca became the wife of Jacob Parker, a widower of sixty-nine and longtime member of her father's church. Parker's reputation as a housewright was solid. For years he had made Malden's coffins, repaired the meetinghouse, and served the town as "inspector of timbers"; he even offered Rebecca a house with the largest chimney and oven in town.[59] In pragmatic terms she had done well enough. But this was neither a romantic match nor the social equivalent of Phebe's marriage to Ezra Ripley; it was an alternative to entering her forties as a single woman in wartime.

Soon the Emerson women were using both of their houses to make money. Off and on for the next few years, Rebecca conducted a dame school in hers, the probable site of Mary's earliest lessons in reading. In addition, during the winter of Rebecca's marriage, mother and sisters together opened a shop for household goods in their house at the center of town.[60] Like Grandmother Bliss with her boardinghouse in Concord, they were turning domestic space to the most entrepreneurial advantage possible.

The best evidence of the Emersons' vulnerability in Malden, however, is that their shop not only faltered like the Concord boardinghouse but almost immediately became a target of community hostility. In March, two members of the Committee of Correspondence brought charges that the Emerson and Parker houses were violating a recently passed "Act to Prevent Monopoly and Oppression," hoarding wool and linen that the army needed. Probably Madam Emerson was guilty as charged; the constable reported searching her house and purchasing at the state price forty-three yards of checked wool and twenty-five of tow-cloth. The Committee of Correspondence was convicting her of the same economic self-interest that her son William had decried in Concord a year earlier. In fact, all authorities condemned hoarding, and so many people practiced it in every town that by the end of 1777 the new law was declared unenforceable. In Concord, the only person formally charged was a newcomer to town; in Malden, the sole charge fell on the Emersons. Malden was acting in astonishing disregard for the habits of deference long holding together New England society. For decades, Joseph Emerson had ministered amidst contention without incurring personal blame, but now the shopkeeping widow and her daughters invited attack. Neither of the selectmen who reported the violation belonged to the

Emersons' congregation, and one of them had come from a family of leaders in the breakaway South Church.[61] Possibly decades of ill will lay behind this public humiliation.

Just three weeks later, seventy-five-year-old Grandmother Mary made her will. Its careful apportioning of resources and pious reference to "the certainty of death" have new resonance with the hoarding incident as background. The will also suggests the social and material surroundings of young Mary's childhood. Madam Emerson's executors were John Dexter and Peter Thacher, friends of unimpeachable patriotism and high social station. They had proved powerless to stop the cloth seizure, but at least they could promise now to support her family's interests. The Emersons' remaining affluence is also revealed in the silk, velvet gowns, and silver buckles that Grandmother Mary divided among numerous daughters and granddaughters. Little Mary received four pounds as sole representative of William's family. Rebecca and Ruth were chief legatees: each got half of their mother's "plate"; Rebecca a gold necklace, the best apparel, and fifteen pounds; Ruth sole use of the house along with the "household stuff" and family chaise.[62] (Joseph Emerson's qualms about owning such a proud conveyance had apparently been overcome long since.) What the will could not provide was any way to sustain the style of life that such goods suggested. In other circumstances they might have helped bring an elite marriage; now they could either be sold for debt or kept for pride.

Circumstances worse than genteel poverty were soon to follow. Late in 1778 an epidemic of smallpox broke out in Malden, and soon eight people died, among them both Rebecca's husband, Jacob Parker, and Grandmother Mary herself. Death once again visited the child Mary's immediate world. Furthermore, says the town historian as though it were a simple matter of record, the smallpox was "brought by Mrs. Rebecca Parker." Rebecca was apparently the first person infected, the link between two infected houses, and by implication the source of all other cases. That any one person "brought" smallpox to Malden could not have been certain. After the heavily infected British army left Boston in 1776, all surrounding towns had done their best to prevent the disease from crossing bays and rivers toward them; as town meeting records reveal, Malden citizens were proposing to meet ubiquitous disease by building a smallpox hospital four months before the outbreak. However, the town fixed blame on Rebecca. Even though her own husband and mother died, with ill grace "Mrs. Parker recovered."[63]

Possibly Rebecca invited blame by acting in odd or antisocial ways even before 1778; possibly she could not bear the multiple shocks of loss and ostracism. In either case, the record is clear that from the early 1780s to her death in 1816 Rebecca was judged insane. She appeared responsible enough to be declared sole executrix of Parker's estate—and attractive enough in person or worldly goods to marry another widower, Deacon Benjamin Brintnall, just a year later. But by 1782 Parker's adult son was complaining in court that Rebecca had refused to settle with him; in 1784 she and Brintnall were being visited by Peter Thacher "on account of their family difficultyes"; and by 1790 the selectmen, though disclaiming all desire to meddle, pronounced Rebecca unsuited to execute an estate "by Reason of her former troubles ill state of Health and a disordered mind which we think has and doth Render her very incapable to transact Business of that sort."[64] Her illness was of long standing by then, and community opinion had turned decisively against her.

The events beginning in 1778–79, disastrous for Rebecca, also touched those around her. One can especially imagine Ruth's burdens: the death of a mother, the sole care of a four-year-old niece, the care of a troubled sister, and the increased isolation in Malden. The onset of Rebecca's mental illness may also have confirmed to the Emersons an ongoing family inheritance. Ruth and Rebecca's uncle had been Joseph Moody, disabled by an insanity possibly linked in turn to both parents' episodic troubles. By the 1780s, Joseph's son Samuel Moody, the successful founder of Dummer Academy in Byfield, was being relieved of his position on account of irrationality and delusional behavior. Rebecca is the only one of Grandmother Mary Moody Emerson's many children known to have suffered from mental illness. But genealogical records add that two children of Rebecca's brother Edward died "non compos mentis" and that brother John had a son who spent twenty years as "a chained maniac before his parents' eyes." Later in life, Mary raised the possibility of hereditary insanity in her family only to deny that her ancestors had ever been "tainted" by it. "Some of my Cousins have been so—and an Aunt—but it was an embicillity rather in *those*."[65] However such fearful realities were to be named, she had witnessed and heard about them from an early age.

Furthermore, as illness increased, so did economic distress: as Mary later commented, Aunt Ruth was soon "reduced by connection in marriage." Ruth married townsman Nathan Sargent in the midst of the smallpox crisis, a month after Parker's death and a month before her mother's. Sargent probably seemed a good partner in difficulty, this widowed "gentleman" of forty-four and commissioned captain in the Continental Army. Having led a troop of Malden soldiers at Ticonderoga and guarded Burgoyne at Prospect Hill, Sargent was a respected figure and associate of Thacher's in wartime Malden. Like Ruth, however, he was slipping downhill economically. Taxed as a prosperous man in 1770, he had asked the town to forgive his taxes just three years later. When he married Ruth, they became joint tenants of the six heirs to Madam Emerson's house; clearly Sargent had neither a house of his own nor money to buy the Emersons', as the will had specified that Ruth's future husband might do. By 1783 they had begun a complex set of legal transactions, selling to Thacher first their share of the house and then their goods, only to continue using them by his grace. The minister—who had begun his career in Malden dining with both Captain Sargent and Miss Ruth—now owned them both. Mary called Nathan a "shiftless, easy man" and Ruth her "poor, unpractical aunt."[66]

The real trouble with Mary's stay in Malden was its longevity. In 1776 three households of women had shared hardship and child-rearing responsibilities, but by 1780 Phebe Bliss Emerson Ripley and Ruth Emerson Sargent stood on very different ground. As her brother William began Greek, Mary was divided from him not only by gender but also by widening social and economic difference. No contemporary or retrospective account explains why Phebe did not reclaim her daughter when she married Ezra Ripley. Beginning at almost forty to have a second set of children, she apparently could let one child go. On the other hand, childless Ruth, as Waldo later said, "became strongly attached to Mary, and persuaded the family to give the child up to her as a daughter, on some terms embracing the care of her future interests."[67] By a finally unknowable combination of disregard on Phebe's part and need on Ruth's, Mary stayed in Malden.

She habitually spoke of the result in tragic terms. Losing one's mother to a new baby and one's infantile will to discipline made the third year a time of vulnerability for many children in New England Puritan culture, and Mary seems to have been permanently scarred by the simultaneous loss of her father and home.[68] But the more fully remembered trauma was her grandmother's death and its attendant disasters in her fifth year. One retrospective account of stages in life began by naming her "early remembrance at 5 respecting trouble." "Trouble" was Mary's one-word story of childhood, opaque as to particulars even while declaring its centrality. The unarticulated memories within this word concern events beginning the year of the smallpox epidemic. A more evocative Almanack meditation, written on a Sabbath morning in 1841, does not tell of those experiences but moves instead inside its writer's early childhood consciousness. "How well this hum[m]ing fly brings back emotions of a certain Sab. Morn," Mary wrote,

> when I was perhaps 4 years old and every chair & old bit of furniture on w'h the sun glanced thro' a small eastern window. That consciousness of sober rich tranquility has never been lost to memory, & returns when the contented vagrant serenades my lonely chamber—not more alone than in childhood and youth. . . . I already see the cold beams of the sun glowing thro' the leafless arms of the trees on my grandmother's portrait—and feel the still nameless tone of feeling w'h will unite the infinite to the finite—tho' no chain of dialectics will be the medium.[69]

This memory passage reaches back even before "Trouble" to its emotional opposite, a "sober rich tranquility" that Mary associates with her grandmother. The first departure from Concord must not have been an irreparable loss, for her description of a humming fly, worn furniture, and winter sunshine presents the Malden home as benign and secure. But in the remembered scene, Mary is alone, the grandmother oddly distanced as she presides over her house. Sun shines coldly "thro' the leafless arms of the trees" onto her *portrait*, which in turn overlooks the tranquil room. Mary seems to be recalling her grandmother as both present and absent, both nurturing and dead. It is as though she remembers an early experience of love but cannot attach an actual face to it, only the face of the portrait that survived death. This is both a rich scene and a cold one;

and it evokes a "nameless" feeling of loss as well as pleasure in the remembering adult. In turn, however, that feeling unites "the infinite to the finite," the heavenly grandmother to the mourning child.

Mary expressed no comparable satisfaction in Aunt Ruth, her longest and most genuine parent. Ruth's 1808 gravestone declares, "She has left one who will always cherish her memory with filial love and gratitude," and that "one" can only be Mary. But Mary also blamed Ruth for her own sorrows. "No sum," she wrote amidst the final settlement of her father's estate in 1825, "can compensate the wants and ignorance which my dear Aunt's poverty induced." Calvinist piety did not keep Ruth from anger, anger directed at Mary when more genuine wrongdoers were out of reach. "Poor woman!" Mary commented. "Could her own temper in childhood or age have been subdued, how happy for herself, who had a warm heart; but for me would have prevented those early lessons of fortitude, which her caprices taught me to practise."[70] The tortured logic of this sentence, attributing Ruth's temper to providential design for Mary's good, is itself a Calvinist exercise in subduing anger; in fact, Mary must have learned both prematurely and painfully about Ruth's "caprices."

Life with Ruth and Nathan, as she looked back on it, was a "slavery of poverty & ignorance & long orphanship." Though in no literal sense an orphan, Mary testified that the result of growing up in Malden was "a lonesome solitude." As for "ignorance," the expected limits on learning for female children were surely narrowed still further by her family's reduced position. Waldo evoked her "slavery" and "poverty," doubtless from stories Mary herself told: "There was plenty of work for the little niece to do day by day, and not always bread enough in the house. One of her tasks, it appears, was to watch for the approach of the deputy-sheriff, who might come to confiscate the spoons or arrest the uncle for debt."[71] Silver spoons and debt, sometimes a lack of bread: these were the realities of declining status faced by a clerical family without clerical income. The spoons that once had declared elite position and served guests were also specie in the Revolution's last days; both debtors and debt collectors wanted them. Meanwhile, Ruth not only had no children but also had lost her onetime servants; Mary served in both ways.

Near the end of the Revolution, even its early patriot ministers admitted discouragement. "This day 6 yrs ye war began," Peter Thacher wrote in his diary on the anniversary of the Battle of Lexington and Concord in 1781. "God grant it may soon end!" Two years later, with peace concluded, he felt called to protest the hardships of the New England clergy. "Perhaps no set of men, whose hearts were so thoroughly engaged in [war with Great Britain] . . . have suffered more by it." In the recent paper money crisis, he claimed, the people had left their clerical leaders impoverished and despised. But if the ministers had lost status and authority, what of their dependents? Soon Thacher himself would recognize the problem by incorporating the Congregational Charitable Society for the Relief of Destitute Widows and Children of Deceased Ministers.[72] Already in 1783, subsidizing Ruth Sargent's household and arbitrating Rebecca Parker Brintnall's conflicts, he was exercising such charity.

Mary, one of Thacher's charity cases, grew up hating dependence in all forms. Even while celebrating the past history of her family, she sought to live from her own resources. For life Mary associated the triumph of the American Revolution with her martyred father and its failure with the "infant exile" her mother and aunt forced upon her. She often repudiated the weakness of women in favor of masculine heroism. But she could also recognize the sheer endurance of widows and orphans. "War! what do I think of it," she wrote in 1832 to her nephew Charles, who had recently read Channing's plea for peace:

> Why in your ear I think it is so much better than oppression that if it were ravaging the whole monarchial world it would be an omen of high & glorious import. Channing paints it's miseries—but does he know those of a worser war—private animosities—pinching bitter warfare of the human heart—the cruel oppression of the poor by the rich w'h corrupts old worlds. How much better are blood & conflagration. . . . What of a few days of agony—& what of a Vulture being the bier tomb & parson of a hero, compared to the long years of sti[c]king on a bed and wished away! Of the widows and orphans—Oh, I could give facts of the long drawn years of imprisoned minds & hearts, w'h uneducated orphans endure.[73]

Her archetypal war was the American Revolution, glorious when it battled oppression but bitter in enforcing new imprisonment on its survivors.

II

A WOMAN'S LIFE

4

Single Woman

> I never expected connections & matrimony. My taste was formed in romance & knew I was not destined to please. I love God & his creation as I never else could.
>
> Mary to Charles Chauncy Emerson, 1833
>
> (*Letters of MME*, p. 344)

An Emersonian self-reliance struggled to birth out of the family inheritance of piety and the immediate intensities of need—and it did so in a woman's life, in the generation of the early Republic. Mary Moody Emerson's temperament grew directly from her childhood losses. "Destitution is the muse of her genius," Waldo wrote in a brilliant epigram, "—Destitution and Death." But Mary also claimed compensation beyond these: "Decrees—predestination—place—purpose by whatever name I love thee in secret—the faith has been my father mother prized house & home when destitute of all. . . . More—there—there—lies the embryo of hope w'h will become vision."[1] Like her ancestors, Mary embraced a providential God of grace; but with a new insistence, her love of God also provided a heavenly and earthly home for the visionary self.

Mary wrote no sustained autobiography but told her story by epigram and allusion throughout the letters and Almanack. Sometimes stages of life are clear from her elliptical sentences. "My early remembrance at 5 respecting trouble," she wrote, "continued till at 17 I entered refined society at N.[ewbury]Port. After that I was obliged to go to Concord & learn duties w'h tried me."[2] Mary lived with Aunt Ruth in Malden until invited in adolescence to join first her newly married sister Hannah in Newburyport, then her mother and stepfather at the Concord Manse. As other comments reveal, however, by her midtwenties she had again chosen Malden over those more affluent households as the setting for adult life. Malden may have meant "trouble," but it also offered space for her own choices.

Probably before returning to Malden, Mary had posed for the silhouette portrait that is the only surviving visual representation of her. It reveals little about character but at least suggests her youthful appearance and style. Mary's bosom is revealed in profile, her hair swept attractively to the top of her head, with additional curls sketched in freehand. The silhouette presents a young lady of age and social condition for courtship, neither a kitchen drudge nor a hermit. Descriptions by others partially fill out the portrait. Her hair was blond, her complexion delicate, her eyes blue. She shared none of the lankiness or craggy features of Ralph Waldo Emerson. In the silhouette, Mary's nose and face appear of moderate proportion, attractively upturned. She was short, even by the standards of another century, though not enough to warrant comment by early contemporaries. Late in life she was once described by Frank Sanborn as standing only four foot three, but elsewhere he estimated a more normal five feet. Already in young womanhood her eye showed a gleam of steel, her tongue a ready word, and her manner an impulsive brashness. She never behaved quite conventionally. When stepfather Ezra Ripley asked her at nineteen whether she was happier to live now amidst relatives, she answered "that such things were no more to her than the color of her gown."[3]

This rejoinder tells of Mary's contempt for fashion, but even more of her resistance to authority and encumbering ties. At the same period of life she also determined that pleasing others was not her destiny, by which she meant that she would not marry. For her, this decision allowed the higher and more venturesome goal of loving God and creation. Such were the thoughts revolving behind the face of the silhouette, which she later referred to as her "pilgrim profile."[4]

Strange Power Within

Mary's intense faith began early in her Malden years, as though a spontaneous intuition. Instead of recording a conversion experience in adulthood, she speculated that one might experience grace from birth itself. "I must own that I premise [God's] electing love for me," she wrote. In her Almanack entry on the "trouble" of childhood, the point was to recall an early certainty that God would prevail against it:

> The first sermon I heard with attention, *probably*, was to prove the divine goodness. It surprised and pained! [I knew] the impossibility of the reverse. This "theodicy" depresses. The knowledge of children in mines and all the slavery & suffering of history (w'h I avoid) brings up a mystery a "cloud" but I never doubted the perfection of God's benevolence and *justice*. I *knew* that righteousness "was the habitation of his existence."[5]

Mary declined either to enumerate the stresses of her early years or to dwell in detail on any human suffering. But from childhood she "*knew*" that a benevolent God could not be indifferent to need, and on the strength of that knowledge could reject as unnecessary the minister's effort to argue logically for God's goodness.

Her statement of faith was extreme in both its exclusion of doubt and its accompanying sense of need. In many self-characterizations Mary appears an unnurtured and resourceless child apart from God: alone in an empty house with no grandmother, destitute of "father mother prized house & home." "The infant famished" was her metaphor for all suffering, and parents were unnamed except in negatives and passive constructions. "I, that I call I," she wrote, "have had no one to wake me since first put in the cradle—only half slumbers & painful consciousness of weariedness at times." With God as ally, she had fed and awakened herself in the absence of human caretakers. Moreover, Mary spoke in fixated memory of such a childhood, as though both her need and its satisfaction were unchanged realities decades later. "I've past the 25 [of August] with pleasure—," Mary recorded after her sixty-first birthday in 1835, "tis joy to know consciousness in childhood—the spirit in deepest ignorance of all but faith. What a glory to be possessed of *abstract* principles, to dive into the ocean, tho' fathomless, of Him who makes necessary existence." Past and present, ignorance and knowledge, conflate even in the tense of her verbs. "I never need meta[physics]," she added elsewhere, "for the first thought at orphanship or sorrow was God's will."[6]

Such extremity of self-characterization might be called both disturbed and heretical. By genetics and circumstance, Mary probably suffered a mild form of the mania that crippled certain of her relatives. Throughout life she sought out heightened states of being and lapsed back to "half slumbers" when deprived of that influx; she often felt pressed by inner urgency to declare herself before the world, then divorced from it or disgraced in its eyes. Likewise, her religious experience frequently bordered on the heresy that her ancestors had called Antinomianism, both in subjective certainty and in resistance to outward authority. But the record of her writing shows a much wider range than either of these excesses: a power of self-scrutiny far beyond the manic's, as well as humor, irony, and conscious rejection of Antinomianism.[7] Mary claimed intuitive knowledge of "abstract principles" akin to the philosophers', but she went on to read philosophy, as well as to learn from and share daily conversation with her contemporaries.

To make such a claim requires taking Mary's own words as vital self-representation and inner truth, but not literal report of life circumstance. If her childhood had lacked resources to the degree that she sometimes implied, she would have developed neither the ego strength to seek wisdom nor the engagement with other people sufficient to know her family's history. Her accounts mythologize even apparent matters of fact. Waldo wrote that Mary called herself a "country girl" and a "goody," as if she had been raised literally in rural isolation and humble station. In fact, the farm on which she lived amounted to three acres abutting the meetinghouse and tavern at Malden center, about six miles from Boston Common. Her choice of titles evokes lost clerical status rather than mere simplicity: Goody Mary was also the granddaughter of Madam Emerson. As she herself put it, "Pride and humility often hug."[8]

Likewise, she was indebted to others even for her early religious knowledge.

God's will—her own "first thought"—was also the doctrine of Aunt Ruth, who taught that "Providence and Prayer were all in all." Indeed, Mary's precocious faith in God's benevolence not only reflected a heritage from the past but also partook of a changing religious climate. As a child, she wrote, she was "never terrified," even while hearing "the full terrors of Calvinism." Perhaps Ruth taught these terrors, for at the meetinghouse next door Peter Thacher was departing from the orthodoxy that once had made him Whitefield's young prophet. Like Mary's own father before the Revolution, Thacher could moderate New Light doctrine without abandoning it. Her childhood faith that God was good and knowable may have reflected Thacher's easing of divine inscrutability. In 1784, when she was ten, Boston's affluent Brattle Street Church recognized both Thacher's shifting theology and his eminence by calling him away from Malden.[9]

At no one moment in Mary's life did the old creed suddenly yield to the new. But the conflict following Thacher's departure from Malden may have been crucial for her dawning religious awareness. A contingent of the church recoiled angrily from his drift into liberalism and his ambitious move to Boston. After accepting a thousand-dollar settlement from Brattle Street, they next hired Adoniram Judson, who had been trained at Yale in the new, doctrinally rigid school of Calvinist theology led by Samuel Hopkins. In turn, the Emersons' friend John Dexter led a protest against Judson. Now Malden's habitual squabbling took the form of argument about sermons attempting to "prove the divine goodness"; as a Hopkinsian, Judson would have insisted that God was good even though he declined to cure all sorrows—even (in the classic case) if he chose to damn newborn infants.[10] Mary, twelve years old the summer that Judson arrived, must have "heard with attention" in a new way, knowing God's righteousness without the minister's help.

By the age of twelve she also had begun reading, so laying the foundation for an independent life of mind and spirit. Formal schooling was meager. Mary probably had learned the rudiments from Aunt Rebecca's dame school, where the instruction (as another pupil remembered it) amounted to reading and spelling from the Psalter, then "shelling beans or some other useful and improving occupation." Even this instruction would have been interrupted or ended by the dame's mental aberrations. Yet Mary learned enough to decipher first the Bible, then the remnants of grandfather Joseph's library at Ruth's house.[11]

The earliest encouragement to read came from neither of her aunts but from an important third female elder named Martha Dexter, daughter-in-law of the theologically liberal John and mistress of a capacious, elm-shaded mansion in Malden. Later Mary recalled her as "the person . . . who first gave me a taste for books and the idea of a friend. A woman whose strong sense and taste rendered her interesting." These brief words point to an entire social world. Martha's husband, Richard, after imprisonment by the British for privateering, had come home to head his own fleet of vessels, adding new commercial income to the family's already considerable affluence. So in childhood, even while fearful of the deputy sheriff coming for the family spoons, Mary had access to one of Malden's most elegant houses. Her right to be there resulted from long family alliance, but Mary's affection for Mrs. Dexter went beyond such bonds. The gift of a "taste for books" sustained her life, and so did other lessons: that an elder woman could befriend instead of berate, that the female mind could develop sense and taste as well as resignation to divine will. Mary would live out all of these patterns. Once she signed a letter to Waldo "in continuation" like Richardson's Charles Grandison, expressing her wish for "some of those old novels w'h so delighted childhood."[12] Early in life she must have learned, probably through Martha Dexter, the eighteenth-century, novel-inspired manners of epistolary exchange.

About the same time, Mary beheld another model of reading womanhood, when seventeen-year-old Ruth Haskins, daughter of a Boston merchant family, came visiting her maternal grandmother in Malden. The village elders riveted their gaze on Ruth at church, and Mary, as she later reminisced, found her "first idol in the female line." To the fervor of Protestant piety Ruth Haskins added the advantage of the city's best schooling for girls. "She conversed on riligion from the heart & I loved every accent—of Young, Cowper & such like with calm & stedfast degree of confidence in her own genius." Later Waldo would name Young among Mary's favorite authors without acknowledging that her taste for such devotional poetry derived significantly from Ruth, his own mother.[13]

Possibly the friend who influenced Mary's adolescence most directly, however, was her brother William. When Mary turned eleven he was fifteen, studying at Harvard and visiting her after years of separation. Later she recalled that he had appeared as a live embodiment of their father's "beauty & popularity." She prophesied a great future for him, and they became confidants, with William even sharing news of his romantic entanglements. He and his future wife, Ruth Haskins, may have met for the first time in Malden under the doubly admiring eye of Mary; surely she basked in the recognition and encouragement that such a brother offered. "[He] was the first object of my enthusiastic love & admiration,—my only first natural protector," she summed up in tribute to his memory.[14]

William's confidences flattered, but his masculine air of knowledge was life and breath. He provided Mary a personal link to the otherwise inaccessible world of Harvard. She had read and reread a favorite book, discovered without cover or title page in the garret of Aunt Ruth's house. Now hearing her brother and his student friends speak of Milton, Mary asked to borrow his poems and discovered for the first time that her old book was Milton's *Paradise Lost*.[15] The anecdote of Mary's discovering Milton has often been told as a sign of her deprivation and maverick genius. But it reveals as well a cultural access unavailable to poorer women. Mary lived on the margin of New England's learned class, both feeling her exclusion from it and making the most of her opportunities. Clerical family gave her tattered remnants of literature and a brother at Harvard; from her pew in Malden meetinghouse she could glimpse a new generation of educated women reading and conversing from the heart. Young and

Milton, Ruth Haskins and William Emerson: books and people represented what she wanted, what she lacked. They aroused her to resentment but also to imitation.

For those who could seize its possibilities, a new age was dawning by the end of the decade. As recent graduate William Emerson noted in his diary on New Year's Day of 1790, "Never, perhaps, did a year open on America with more flattering prospects than the present. She beholds her admirable constitution firmly established; her agriculture rapidly improving; manufactures thriving; commerce reviving,—and her arts and sciences hasting to mature the growth of liberty and national happiness." A new optimism held the day, and William declared his own prospects "far from unpleasing."[16]

Mary hardly shared the open prospects that Harvard College and the new Constitution offered William. She was an adolescent girl without either education or citizenship. Yet the mood of possibility did not wholly bypass her; from old age she would look back on youth as a time "when freedom was alive and promises so splendid were realized." In the limited manner of poor female relations, Mary also began in January 1790 to enjoy new hopes: she restored ties to her family of birth by legally choosing Ezra Ripley as a guardian. Ripley was settling his stepchildren's future; and whether or not Mary had previously been considered one of her father's heirs, now, at fifteen, she was guaranteed her portion. Ezra Ripley arranged for young William to receive the full estate but also for his four sisters eventually to divide an equal sum among them. Nor were such arrangements made in a vacuum. The same year a letter of Ezra's mentioned "Polly"—still Mary's functioning name—as visiting the Manse and acquainted with the wider circle of her siblings.[17] The isolation of earlier childhood had already abated.

Possibly William had a hand in making Mary's needs known to Ezra, so winning her lifelong gratitude as a "protector." These needs seem to have intensified rather than eased in her adolescent years. If Ruth Sargent had ever promised to provide for Mary's future interests, she surely could not by 1790. Soon thereafter Nathan and Ruth signed a warranty deed deepening their dependence on Peter Thacher, still a benefactor from his Boston pastorate. In addition, that spring the Malden selectmen declared Rebecca Parker Brintnall mentally incompetent; as Waldo later recounted, her breakdown was causing "more and sadder work" for Mary and the Sargent household.[18]

Waldo did not, however, mention the additional burden that by now had fallen on Mary—Nathan Sargent's own progressive illness. His epitaph in Malden cemetery alone tells this story. "Stop thotful Passenger," the inscription urges, "and shed a tear over this grave; which shelters a man known to misfortune from his early days, misfortunes which he resisted with courage or submitted to with patience; together with a distressing disease, whose violence after many years destroyed his fortitude, and at length his life." Mary had the wearisome woman's work of nursing both this unidentified, violent condition and Aunt Rebecca's insanity. Her later grim sense of the human body "sti[c]king on a bed and wished away" resulted directly from such encounters: "the anatomy of one carcase ('pah! how it smells') answers for a thousand to him"—really her—"who can see." Only one reference to Nathan's illness survives in Mary's writing, but there it stands as the most dreadful circumstance of all that blighted her early years. Listing the places she had spent her life "running from," she gave final position to "Malden *itself* when my dear Uncle became broken."[19] By 1791, at seventeen, Mary fled Malden for Newburyport and "entered refined society" at her sister Hannah Emerson Farnham's house.

She fled to a wider life, however, as well as away from distress. Though no writing from her early Malden years survives, later memory passages offer glimpses of that time. Looking out over a nighttime field of fireflies four decades later, Mary reflected on the "strange power within" that had been hers from childhood:

> Who would doubt mental identity when the dim eye of age recognizes the same tranquil hues—the same bright visions w'h soothed the sorrows of childhood and youth? Then the fly held out its torch to please the sense—now it wakes the soul—and the soul turns over many a blank and blotted page before it comes to the leaf turned down on a luminous hour—to scenes when rustic ignorance itself dreamt of wisdom.[20]

Seeing memory itself as a book to reread, she found its brightest pages in the early visions that "ignorance" had of "wisdom." Leaving Malden at seventeen, such a dream must have been fresh and powerful.

Ironically, the incomplete social development of Mary's Malden years made this boldness possible. "In childhood & youth," she commented, "I did not know that I was not morally great as anybody." Even William's attitudes might have defined the limits as well as the opportunities before her. In 1790 he wrote a series of letters to the adolescent girls in his Roxbury grammar school that imply his advice to a sister as well. Conceding that "too little attention has ever been paid to female education," he instructed them to bypass external accomplishment for genuine knowledge. They should write, he especially emphasized, so as to acquire a concise style and create an aid to memory. But at the same time, William explained that female education should always befit a life of marriage and the home. Unless she was financially independent, no young lady should "attend solely to books, to the neglect of all knowledge in domestick economy." He called modesty a "beauteous plant . . . peculiarly amiable in your sex, who move in a sphere, where nothing of that bold, forward, and enterprizing disposition, necessary in man, is required to carry you through life." Only in the domain of religion, he conceded, might there be no limit to female intellect: "Here . . . we are all equally concerned."[21]

William was saying nothing unique in these letters, only repeating a widely shared ideology of womanhood in the new Republic, substituting for active citizenship a more indirect contribution to public good through the domestic sphere. Mary probably knew already of the schools springing up around her, a direct product of the new emphasis on female virtue serving family and society within the home. Roxbury was only one of the Massachusetts towns—though not yet Malden—opening its grammar schools to female students; and in Medford, just one town away, Yale-educated William Woodbridge had launched the first school for women in the area to merit the name "academy."[22] Just as circumstances in Malden became intolerable, so were the possibilities beyond it most irresistible. But, bringing to her pursuit of education an intensity born of need, Mary would never observe the limits that books, schools, and brother alike recommended for the educated woman. She would seek out the loopholes in his rhetoric—the independence that let a woman forgo home skills, the religion in which she and William could be "equally concerned."

In this ambition she was following a call from her brother not really intended for women. In his 1789 Phi Beta Kappa oration at Harvard, William uncannily anticipated his son Waldo's more famous one by sweeping away the need for ancient languages and Harvard educations: "The ghost of books, however, shall not continually haunt us. . . . Advert, ye rising candidates for glory, to the American sun, and those other shining orbs, that irradiate our Columbian world. Guided by their luminous example, embark for greatness. Follow, as they did, the light of native genius."[23] To his book-learned male audience, this would have been a call to wisdom beyond the printed page. To Mary, trying to get her hands on books, it might also have lent new glory to a path always open to New England women, fame in the sight of God through "native genius."

Newburyport and Concord

Mary lived with Hannah and William Farnham for only two years, but the world of Newburyport visible from their house was as elegant as any that Massachusetts had seen. This enclave of maritime trade, a seedbed of New England's Brahmin aristocracy, stood at its peak of prosperity during the last decade of the eighteenth century. In 1764 Newburyport had separated from the original farming town of Newbury and established its own parish and economy, with 350 houses stretching along the Merrimac River harbor. Mary's Uncle Bulkeley Emerson had served all the intervening years as the town's principal stationer, binding books and running the postal service at his shop near Market Square. He does not seem to have aided his Malden sisters, but probably maintained contact with the Concord family. By some means the Ripleys had ties in Newburyport, for in the summer of 1790 mother Phebe was visiting the Farnhams there, and three months later her daughter Hannah married their son William.[24]

Hannah was twenty years old and William thirty when they became mistress and master of the Farnham family house on High Street at Market. Like young William Emerson, Farnham taught grammar school, but within the year he would gain a lucrative post as collector of liquor taxes for the port. His style followed the new merchant aristocrats with whom he lived. In 1788 John Quincy Adams, studying law in Newburyport, had played quadrille with William Farnham and described his excellence in "the *science* of politeness": "he understands to perfection all the nice and subtle distinctions between confidence and assurance, between ease of behaviour and familiarity, between elegance and foppery, &c, a science in which I am very ignorant."[25]

It is hard to imagine a more daunting host to seventeen-year-old Mary, who possessed considerably fewer social graces than young Adams. She harbored dreams of wisdom, but the Farnhams immediately set her to work in the nursery. Giving birth to her first child in the summer of 1791 and a second seventeen months later, Hannah needed the assistance that a sister reared to care for others might give. Without doubt, Mary's earnestness met ridicule at their house: she later recalled Hannah's laughter at her incessant talk of "Death, Judgment, and Eternity." Mary's dealings with Farnham could only have been more strained. When Hannah died fourteen years and eight more children later, William Emerson would admit within the family that Farnham had lacked "the feeling of tenderness which should ever mark the character of a husband." The thought of Hannah's laborious married life, he confessed, was "nearly sufficient to sink us in the dust."[26] Mary spoke no direct word of William Farnham, true to her habit of minimal elaboration on "trouble."

Newburyport still brought Mary out both by resistance and by affinity. The household of a schoolmaster and neighborhood of a bookstore put reading at close range, and attending church with Farnham and Emerson relatives at the First Religious Society meant hearing liberal doctrine instead of Calvinism. Bulkeley Emerson's three daughters, in these years establishing a school for girls in Newburyport, later remembered Cousin Mary as "bookish, rather strong-minded, not nice in her habits." They educated students in needlework and grammar but stopped short of ciphering in fractions, declaring it sufficient for a lady to count her beaux and skeins of yarn. Closer to Mary's own temperament was fifteen-year-old Ann Bromfield, the gifted daughter of an eminent Newburyport family, who immediately became a friend. Mary's ties to Ann, as well as to the Farnhams, would endure. Nonetheless, by the age of nineteen she had again "fled—from Newburyport the best of sisters."[27]

In fleeing she returned at last to Concord, which had changed only in increments during the seventeen years of her absence. Ezra Ripley had emerged as an influential voice of conservatism in 1786, joining other town fathers in leading the suppression of debt-ridden farmers in Shays Rebellion. In 1791 the Concord church had voted to add a steeple to the meetinghouse and finally to carry out its excommunication of Hannah Melvin. Phebe Bliss had sold the Block House to a doctor, Isaac Hurd, and moved in with her daughter's family at the Manse. Three Ripley children now occupied the family home—Sarah, twelve; Samuel, ten; and Daniel, nine—as well as Mary's older and younger Emerson sisters, Phebe and Rebecca.[28] Though Mary had already visited the Manse in the past few years, now she entered a new social world.

In her laconic terms, this world meant the trial of "duties." On one occasion she claimed to have fled there from Hannah's house, but another time explained that Dr. Ripley had sent for her to "come home" when half sister Sarah went to school in Lincoln. Domestic work would have felt all the more burdensome if required by a younger sister's departure to pursue learning. No newborns or desperate illnesses required Mary's physical care to the extent that they had in two previous houses, but mother and grandmother alike were invalids keeping to their own chambers. The sense of being exploited—in Concord just as much as in Malden or Newburyport—remained with Mary for life. "Oh how quietly (as puss own self) did I use in early years to pass from Mother to Aunt from Sister to Sister," she recalled, "for all was without mentality & to keep souls & bodies together."[29]

Concord differed from Newburyport, though, because Mary's move to it was a homecoming after exile, calling forth her full expectation and resentment. Here she was looking for the key to her father's life and a personal birthright beyond the portion that Ezra Ripley had prepared for her. Inquiring into her happiness, Ezra had confidence in his own ability of remediation. But Mary was too defiant to fall back into the social order that extended from her stepfather's pulpit into the Concord community. "Be watchful of our rebellious passions," Ezra preached the year of Mary's arrival, in a sermon on "the benefit of affliction, and especially for young people."[30] Mary, though wishing as well to benefit from affliction, would do so precisely by acting rebellious and passionate.

Ripley's sermons do not reveal him to be harsh, but very much devoted to duty as the heart of religion. It is "the duty of parents to restrain children . . . by authority and discipline," he preached in his definitive series of the decade on "social virtues." To Ripley the new Republic's liberty had brought a threat of degeneration to the old ways of family government. Yet he spoke as a republican himself by emphasizing moderation in the exercise of authority. In his view, both parents headed the family, not just the father, and they needed to use corporal punishment only rarely. Imprudent or tyrannical authority would itself result in disobedience, he argued, so that wise parents should strive for a "rational, mild, and moral" style of governing.[31]

Mary, however, seems to have perceived Ezra as the tyrant he counseled Concord parents not to be. Waldo later recorded her memory that "Dr. Ripley . . . used to wake up the boy by slapping for the back of the body, he said, was made to whip." In public Waldo declared Ezra Ripley "just and charitable," but privately recalled being "educated in a certain suspicion & dislike of him from the tone in which M.M.E. spoke of him." Mary, more overtly than Waldo a generation later, had come to adulthood in rebellion against the paternal authority that her stepfather represented. "In your future course of life," she once told a niece who had been attending Ezra at the Manse, "remember to follow Duty rather than Inclination; a good rule, of which your Aunt Mary has always held the opposite."[32]

Mary expressed suspicion and dislike more readily toward Ezra than toward the elder who was perhaps her more fundamental target: mother Phebe, arranger of the infant exile and now amidst invalidity the actual supervisor of household duties. The reunion of daughter with mother appears in Mary's writing, contemporary or retrospective, only as a heavy silence. Her brother William's letters to Phebe in these same years show mutual affection, even mother-son favoritism. Mary, however, preserved all the formalities in her single surviving letter to

Phebe, addressing her as "honored parent," "my dear Mother," even "Madam." Phebe embodied the conventional female passivity against which Mary defined herself. The only discernible bond between them was mutual love of the deceased William.[33] Mary took satisfaction in that loyalty, if she did not therefore forgive her mother's limitations.

Still she was happier, though she would not admit as much, in having this family, since for the first time she lived amidst a household of siblings. Her personal loneliness and vulnerability now took sardonically humorous form. "The first use I made at 19 of the knowledge of imperishable matter," she recalled, "was, in gaity, to tell my sisters after all, *I* must have place to exist in."[34] But despite the tensions resulting from Mary's lack of "place," her years in Concord resulted in a world of friendship that she had only glimpsed in Malden.

Though the Almanack from these years does not survive, later Mary recalled that she had begun it by the age of twenty; she could then turn directly to her "own Journal of early days" and quote its words of admiration for brother William. She mocked as well as admired, however, when in 1793 she directly addressed William, who had recently been ordained as minister in the nearby town of Harvard: "What exalted seat may I humbly take to form one link of the descending chain that connects you with an epistler of *common size*? When mounted you the *demi*-throne?"[35] Again she was moderating anger at lowliness to humor. As "an epistler of common size"—female, ineligible for professional status, and at least a foot shorter than William—she had no intention of leaving him at rest on his throne. Meanwhile she spoke in a style far from "common," but self-consciously literary in its attempted elegance of diction and allusion to the "descending chain" of being. In her combative way, Mary was pursuing people and verbal power.

The young people of her new social group shared an eagerness for cultural sophistication and a predictable absorption in courtship. Never declaring any romantic interests of her own, Mary answered for all her female friends to William's query "if any of us girls are courted": "If the question extend to [the] circle of girls in Concord (or only to those of your own family), the same answer, No! will apply to the whole. . . . And what is more melancholy I see no prospect of such business, for . . . the grand question is, Is there money?" Meanwhile, she advised William on the merits of several young ladies. "L," Lucy Grosvenor of Harvard, "is even *finer* than you imagan," Mary exclaimed. "As follows—that the more compressed atmosphere of reason & sense might be too powerful for her fine wrought nerves, and alass! she *may evaporate* in the fumes of sensibility, & thus become extinct *in the world of reason*!" William expressed considerable sensibility himself with regard to this daughter of his predecessor in the Harvard ministry. When she suddenly died seventeen months later, he emotionally described the day of her funeral. Mary attended along with other Concord family members as William, much to the displeasure of some in this country town, lent his viol to a friend to accompany the church music.[36] Both sexes had "fine wrought nerves" in their network of siblings and friends.

Mary especially cultivated female friendship, with or without the company of William. Frequently she and her sisters rode with him to the fine houses of Harvard and Stow, meeting would-be sisters-in-law. Over several years she also made independent bonds to older and younger women of Concord, among them Rebecca Kettell Thoreau and Cynthia Dunbar, the future step-grandmother and mother of Henry David Thoreau. She became acquainted with Mary Wilder, Sarah Ripley's intimate friend through childhood and the stepdaughter of Dr. Hurd, at the Block House. Hardly a day passed without visits between the two houses, and as the younger girls moved through adolescence, Mary Wilder's grace and sprightliness made the Hurds' house a wider gathering place as well.[37]

But most visible in her letters of the 1790s is a web of friendship with the Haskins family of Boston. Mary's old idolatry of Ruth quickly grew to equal exchange from her new home, where the Emersons and Ripleys were already established in interfamily friendship with the Haskinses. As Mary wrote to Ruth in 1795, she also extended greetings for herself and sister Phebe to Ruth's sisters Mary and Elizabeth, just two of the thirteen living Haskins children. Later she particularly remembered Lydia Haskins, seven years older than herself, as a friend of "sound mind, warm heart & open hand"; the Manse today still owns a copy of Isaac Watts's *Guide to Prayer* inscribed in Mary's hand as a gift from "Miss Lydia Haskins whose invaluable friendship is one of the dearest treasures possessed by M. M. Emerson Concord 1795." The bonds of these women supported rather than conflicted with their marriage prospects. William took part in the Boston exchanges, too: in July 1795 he left his youngest sister, Rebecca, to visit at the Haskins house, and she stayed until December, when Mary welcomed her back to Concord from the world of fashion. Two marriages would come of these visits, not only William's to Ruth in 1796 but also Rebecca's to Robert Haskins a year later.[38]

Friends and siblings even encouraged Mary to seek an education. Later she complained of her "few months schooling at Concord," acknowledging that she had found her way at least briefly to its grammar school. But in 1795 she was also offered an opportunity to stay with Mr. and Mrs. Woodbridge—probably at the well-known academy in Medford—in an undefined arrangement that William felt "would be advantageous . . . in a literary way." She felt skeptical of it, for he wrote to sister Phebe that "Mary must refer her doubts . . . to those neverfailing judges of what is right, Misses Haskinses." Mary went but stayed less than a week. She wrote to William in December:

> I found by experience . . . what I had before reluctantly beleived, that without *money* or uncommon merit I had no right to expect much from uncommon professions of friendship. . . . I heartily rejoice that such disappointment[s] do not make me quarrel with myself or the prevailing constitution of the world. Humble at the knowledge of both I ought to be. I more over gain this religious knowledge by every days experience, that to be happy here & forever, I must be *meek and lowly in heart.*[39]

Though Mary felt resentment at unsought lowliness, increasingly it was also the stance that she chose as a safeguard against social disgrace, and potentially the means to more powerful self-education as well.

By the age of twenty-one, though lacking the skills in penmanship, arithmetic, and spelling that the Woodbridges could have provided, she had also advanced in knowledge far beyond what they taught. Books for her own use were available at close hand. Starting in 1795, all residents of Concord could borrow from the Charitable Library, and very soon women made up nearly half the readers—including Mary, her sisters, and Mary Wilder. Founded by Dr. Ripley with strong support from Dr. Hurd, the library brought challenging fare to Concord. From the lighter end of its reading list, Sarah Ripley could borrow the *Ladies Library*, an anthology of moral advice literature; but so could Mary obtain the *Meditations of Antoninus*, whose Stoic epigrams she would quote for decades thereafter.[40]

Mary's move from Malden had already shifted the context of her religious life, for Ezra Ripley and William Emerson, like their ministerial colleague in Newburyport, preached sermons that turned increasingly away from Calvinist theology and Awakening intensity. But in this broad access to books, the old creed continued yielding, because her reading was also theologically liberal. The Charitable Library did not own anything by Jonathan Edwards or his followers; instead, between the library and the family, Mary became immersed in the piety and theology of eighteenth-century England. Philip Doddridge's *Rise and Progress of Religion* and John Mason's *Self-Knowledge* were her staples; Samuel Clarke's *Discourse Concerning the Being and Attributes of God* was her passion. Mary probably began reading Anglican Clarke even the year of her arrival at the Manse, for he would have provided the post-Newtonian "knowledge of imperishable matter" that she turned against her sisters. Later Mary called Clarke her "first master" and reminded Ezra of their shared allegiance to his school. Her way into this daunting text was far from systematic, perhaps no more than to discover appealing passages. Though she returned several times to reading Clarke over the years, she always especially remembered one "sublime sentence" about the necessity of time and space as the mode of divine existence.[41] It was a vitally important concept both by endorsing a religion of rational proof and by understanding the physical universe as revelation of God. Clarke countered the subjective and biblically based piety of her childhood, providing a rationale for her devotion to a God of nature through the remainder of life.

More than a new set of ideas was at stake in Mary's reading, however; there was also a shift in the scene of religious instruction itself. Through a devotional life begun in the Malden garret and expanded at Uncle Bulkeley's bookshop in Newburyport, reading books had become more important than hearing sermons. The paradigmatic scene that her grandfather Bliss's portrait represented—authoritative minister with Bible in hand, addressing silent laity—had changed even within the family. Now the Emerson-Ripley ministers were encouraging piety by making books available, and Mary could read these books without their supervision. Ezra probably did not encourage her aspiration to understand Clarke, which was part of the Harvard curriculum; but she declined the manual of piety he offered in favor of his own theological bookshelf. Likewise, she could turn to poetry as an alternative to both sermons and Harvard courses: Young's *Night Thoughts*, the same work whose heart religion Ruth Haskins had expounded, was available at the Charitable Library, and along with *Paradise Lost* it won nearly scriptural authority in Mary's mind. Many other women shared this literate piety. Her friend Mary Wilder represented both their taste and its new confidence a few years later: "Next to the Bible, I rank the Poets. I am confident Milton, Cowper, Young, and Thomson excite more devotional feelings than all the controversial authors in Christendom."[42]

The same circle of literate friends—though not the library—also offered fiction. Current taste had moved on from Richardson, Mary's childhood favorite, to Ann Radcliffe. "Mary begins to read the 'Mysteries,' " William noted in 1797, referring to Radcliffe's gothic romance *The Mysteries of Udolpho*. Mary's response to this woman novelist does not survive, but her own copy of the novel and personalized claim to it do. Inside the front cover is William's nameplate, with the Emerson family's shield and motto "Fidem Servabo," "I will serve the faith"—then under his engraved name, "William Emerson," her own hand-inscribed addition, "To Mary Emerson."[43] The ministerial privilege of book ownership was being appropriated by new female readers, connecting them with new authors and heroines.

Mary and her friends thrilled to identify with the sufferings of Radcliffe's Emily St. Aubert, tormented by a corrupt uncle in a castle of ghostly murmurs and bloody stairs. Every evening Mary Wilder narrated the story by heart with such dramatic power that a young cousin, once in bed, could not banish the terrifying pictures from his imagination. With Mary Emerson the story's power lasted even longer. Half a century later, she wrote to her young confidante Elizabeth Hoar asking for a diagnosis of what seemed her "partial insanity in sleep." "I read whole pages of a tragical sort," she explained, "& after partly waking somthing carries it on wholly involuntary on my part, when I wish to learn its end hoping for some mitigation of the cruelties practised on a lovely young girl—not always the same & a stranger." Even Mary's dreams were of reading—reading of the gothic variety, with her own mind strongly identified with the fate of the heroine. When Mary wrote, "My taste was formed in romance," she referred to the fictional romance of Radcliffe and her followers.[44]

By reading gothic fiction, however, Mary knew that in another respect she was not like its heroines. Emily St. Aubert endured all trials and ended in peaceful, rational marriage to her young nobleman; by absorbing many such fictional plots, Mary knew she was not likewise destined to end her story in matrimony. Mary defined herself early as a single woman. Even as her youthful letters spoke of marriage as a good for others, she stood for opposing goods herself. "Of the aimiable Ruth I *must* write," Mary told William in 1795. "I have already told you that she is virtues self. . . . Added to this a natural good understanding and a uniform sense of propriety which characterizes her every action and enables her to make a proper estimate of every occurance." Mary recommended Ruth Haskins in the very terms of "aimiable" intellect that constituted William's own ideal of womanhood. At the same time, turning in midletter as though to address Ruth, Mary disparaged such virtue and by implication chose another ground for herself:

> Yet true it is, my dear Ruth, thou dost not possess *those energies,—those keen vibrations of soul* which seizes pleasure—which immortalizes moments and which give to life all the zest of enjoyment! But why should I regret this incapasity? If thou wert thus formed, thou wouldst be a very different being from what thou now art. The tear of commiseration which is now wont to fill thine eye would too often, e're it reached the lucid orb, be drenched in culturing some luxuriant flower which the fervid fancy creates at the sight of woe. The sigh of meekness and gratitude would frequently be suppressed by the anxious throb of vanity and the triumps of self exultation. A thousand unborn sensations would impede the gentle accents of benevolence, which now dwell on those lips that seem open but in the cause of virtue.[45]

Even while ostensibly celebrating the power of sympathy, Mary was revealing her own preference for "the triumps of self exultation." Ruth could marry because capable of the other-directed virtues of the female heart. Mary could not, she admitted slyly at the age of twenty-one.

Indeed, she vehemently declared the limitations of womanhood as men had defined it. The desire for approval had undone Ruth's sister Elizabeth—"How fatal does it prove to the real improvement of this ill-fated sex!" Mary exclaimed. She was acknowledging the inequality of the sexes, blaming women's intellectual deficit on an evil fate, and seeking "real improvement" through independence from men. Writing to William a few months later, she continued the thought with direct self-reference:

> I am aware that most of your sex would say my defection was merely the effect of that passion which in youth always seeks an object for its exercise. I promise you, my Brother, it is no such thing. My passions are not restless; besides I scorn to shelter the weakness that renders me insufficient to my own happiness, in the indulgence of a passion which for the most part, tends to enervate the female mind, and renders it avaric[i]ous of the smalest applause.[46]

William would define a woman's passion as appropriate only if subdued into love of his kind; Mary wanted to maximize passion by being self-sufficient. "To feel alone on earth was one of the highest emotions of youth," she wrote in retrospect.[47]

The extent of this aloneness resulted from Mary's particular circumstances, but she shared a desire for autonomy with other women of her generation. One of the Republic's promises was a new equality for women within marriage; a sermon which she later recalled from these years affirmed that woman had been taken from man's side rather than his head or foot, so meriting a position as "a faithful, bosom companion, truly a helpmeet." But Mary herself had grown up seeing the results of her two Malden aunts' difficult marriages, and in her twenties she felt a power of choice unavailable to them. Along with a growing minority of American women, she rejected the prospect of dependence on an unworthy man in favor of "single blessedness."[48]

Likewise, an undercurrent in Puritan religious belief justified her single-minded passion. Ruth Haskins surely belonged with the majority of young New England women who anticipated both earthly and heavenly marriage. "Come thou North wind," she wrote in her 1795 diary, "and blow thou South wind on my garden & cause the spices to flow out—that my Beloved may come in & eat his pleasant fruits—Come Lord Jesus come thou quickly." But Mary identified with a more ascetic and mystical experience of self-perfecting. While also seeing her religious commitments as "espousals," she imagined relationship to God with an abstraction that excluded any gardenlike settings, sensuous embraces, or earthly husband. "Nature," she wrote retrospectively, taught "from the solitary heart . . . to say, at first womanhood, Alive with God is enough,—'tis rapture."[49] Such language implies renunciation of other possible goods, of marriage and human company, but in exchange for the highest joy.

Along with younger sister Rebecca, Mary signaled her coming-of-age in November 1794 by the common ritual of joining the church. She probably delivered no statement of spiritual experience to her minister and stepfather. At just this moment, Ezra Ripley was initiating major reform in Concord, no longer requiring relations and confessions of potential church members, so bringing to fruition father William Emerson's vision of a church with "all Professors in full Communion." But the communal church mattered less in any case to Mary than her own form of testimony in letters to William and Ruth. In this earnest, declamatory prose she pronounced an exalted self-dedication to life with God. Human beings, Mary asserted, had fallen like the autumn leaves by the Manse, but could rise to immortal glory by exercising "persevering dilligence and activity to regain what is lost." In this conscious (and anti-Calvinist) aspiration to self-improvement, she spoke of her life as a "spiritual Journey" and vowed to do all she could to avoid losing ground in it. Knowing that the plot of her romance would not end in matrimony, she conceived of it as a quest instead.[50]

Her quest necessarily ended in heaven, the only glorious conclusion for a woman other than marriage. Mary has been notorious for her love of death ever since Waldo spoke of her wearing a shroud as a daily garment. Any such extreme acting out of her desire lay far in the future as she committed herself to God at "first womanhood." But eagerness for immortality was central to her early sensibility. "I hope I am not deceived in the sincerity of my obedience," she wrote, "or my views of Jesus Christ when I think of dying for I can think of death with some sattisfaction & much hope." Such a preoccupation was hardly surprising, given her lifelong exposure to death and the sermons and pious memoirs that followed it. Her own grandfather's endorsement of Abigail Upham's deathbed voice and vision was only one early expression of a printed and oral literature of female sainthood well established by the 1790s.[51]

That literature came to life in the example of Grandmother Phebe Bliss. Later recalling Phebe as "a perfect Christian," Mary added, "she was a woman such as I had read about, but, except her, I have never seen one." All of New England's praise of female excellence converged in this saint of the Manse. By the end of 1795, as Phebe actually approached death with Mary as nurse, the elder woman delivered lay sermons of spiritual instruction to young followers gathered in her chamber. Writing to Ruth Haskins in March 1796, Mary conveyed a message from Phebe to "press on toward the great mark of christian perfection." Could we not, Mary speculated to Ruth, "begin life with the same views with which the aged terminate it"? To do so would mean resisting inclination. "But let us rejoice & be thankfull that there *is a wisdom, . . .* so *pure and heavenly* that even the young possesor of *it* shall find a growing *indifference* to the pleasures of this life. . . . How animated do I feel, my dear Ruthe, at the bare mention of such an *indifference*." Such "indifference" recalled the New Light piety that women like Phebe Bliss and Sarah Edwards had known in the 1740s. Now it "animated" rather than deadened Mary's feeling in the 1790s, so that, like Phebe, Mary sought to be "rapt in another world."[52]

The sympathy across generations in Phebe Bliss's chamber at the Manse suggests that more was unchanged than changed for women in the post-Revolutionary world of Mary Emerson's youth. A new atmosphere of freedom, both political and theological, might be heard in the older woman's urging to "press on" for perfection. A greater female authority is evident in Mary's direct reporting of one woman's words to another; the endorsement of Ezra Ripley was neither required nor sought after. But Mary, like Phebe, vowed to live out a private and powerless eminence until its heavenly fulfillment. When Phebe Bliss at length died in July 1797, Elizabeth Haskins created memorials to Phebe's "love of holiness" that embodied both an older ideal of sainthood and a younger generation's culture of mourning. This otherworldliness signaled the world's meager offering of routes to accomplishment. Looking back on her youth at the Manse, Mary wrote to Elizabeth Hoar that there she had "past the best days of a life religious as far as my capasity addmitted." But her next thought told of subsequent defeat: "Could I have but died while a few simple pri[n]ceples absorbed."[53]

The Genius of the Christian Religion

Mary's settled life at the Concord Manse ended along with the work of caring for Phebe Bliss. During the months after, she stayed several weeks in Harvard with newly married Ruth and William, passed the winter at Newburyport, and by the fall of 1798 had resettled in Malden. The circumstances of her leaving Concord are far from clear. They "shirked me off," she wrote later, "without the least intimation that I was defective." She pondered what the defects might have been: folly, want of sympathy, "the stains of pride & passion." Possibly her pride had amounted to a fundamental flaw, "something constitutional w'h excited the ridicule of family & acquaintance."[54] Since the family had created the conditions of estrangement causing this defensive pride, their judgments would have wounded all the more deeply. Characteristically, even hints of ridicule or threats of being "shirked off" caused her to flee first.

Amidst feelings of rejection, however, she actively chose Malden as an adult home. Even in 1796 Mary had started, presumably with the inheritance of $151.21 from her father's estate, to acquire property there. For a nominal five shillings she ("Mary Emerson, single woman . . . of Concord") bought back Peter Thacher's shares in her grandmother's house, then leased them for the same sum to Ruth and Nathan Sargent—in effect becoming *their* landlord and guardian, though still with Thacher's generosity underwriting the project. For $133, nearly her whole fortune, she bought out the house share owned by Hannah and Daniel Emerson of Hollis; they must have asked the market price. And for both property and symbolic value, she bought a pew in the meetinghouse, scene of her grandfather's ministry and her own childhood dissent. Death again decreed Mary's timing: she arrived in Malden just as Nathan Sargent died in 1798. Now Ruth Sargent and her sister Rebecca, both widowed, were left to eke out a livelihood. Mary lived with them until 1802, when Ruth married her second husband, Malden tanner Samuel Waite; then Mary sold some rooms of the house to Samuel but continued to own her personal portion.[55]

She had achieved a modest economic autonomy within the family circle, preferring to be depended upon rather than dependent. By so doing, she seems also to have withdrawn from the marriage-minded social world of Concord. In a letter to William, Mary jokingly compared the two towns. Concord's "circle of the gay" made a woman of twenty-four wish to forget six of her years, whereas in Malden she had to accept an age that brought no respect:

> Here, your sex have the advantage of ours. Your vanity is seldom in danger of injury by the number of your years. You either welcome their approach as the means of your advancement, or find them the only security for respect. But poor woman had rather forfeit her title to superiority than her claims to youth, and is even tempted to adopt folly, [rather] than own wisdom, if she be called the child of experience.[56]

Surely all the world, not just Malden, gave men a privilege unavailable to women of advancing to respect as they reached maturity. A light tone, however, covered serious intentions. Even if lacking a profession in the world, Mary sought a way to "own wisdom" rather than regress to adolescence.

As she later remembered the decade from 1797 to 1807, she enjoyed some success in reaching this wisdom, combining the care of her "old folks" with continued religious concentration. In retrospect, even though Concord may have offered the days of highest feeling, Malden had an advantage in austerity, because there she "asked not [for] books," but was allowed "the quietism of faith & obedience." This memory suppresses a great deal of book reading and activity, evident in the letters and Almanacks of those years, but still suggests the almost monastic discipline that she sought in her childhood home. Renouncing the fame of women famous for piety and learning, she now declared, "I am glad I have nothing, as I can't have much."[57] Malden signaled a defeat of earlier hopes, but she embraced it as a vocation.

Mary's kin still expected her to marry, and family papers suggest that she turned down two proposals. In 1805, according to William's report, she was "combatting the attacks . . . of Cupid"; probably this was the moment later described by Waldo, when "she was addressed and offered marriage by a man of talents, education and good social position, whom she respected." In a note on his lecture manuscript, Waldo recorded the identity of this suitor as "a lawyer, (Mr. Austin of Charlestown)." Since William Austin, Charlestown's only lawyer of this generation and surname, married in 1806, he could not have been the suitor referred to in Mary's Almanack of a year later: "Jan. 30. I walked to Captain Dexter's. Sick. Promised never to put that ring on." There could have been no possibility of her marrying Captain Dexter: in 1807 the Emerson family's old ally Captain John was long dead, and his son Captain Richard married to her childhood mentor Martha Dexter.[58] So she must have walked to the Dexters' house to consult with her friends about some other, unidentified offer of a ring.

As shadowy as such records are, Mary's own response to the prospect of marriage comes through clearly, "sick" feelings and a permanent vow of noncompliance. Later in the spring of 1807, she converted her promise to a positive commitment: "Henceforth the picture I'll image shall be girded loins, a bright lamp, fervent devotion. My condition in life is singular, & presses me on the throne of my Master with peculiar strength."[59] She alluded to the Bible's lamp-carrying maidens who awaited the heavenly bridegroom, but by calling herself "singular" did not allow even for the company of other maidens around herself. Hers was a vow not only of celibacy but also of solitude. In the same way that she represented her child-self as nurtured only by God, she now represented her religious vocation without any surrounding community.

Even as Mary declared for religious individualism, however, she was simultaneously engaged with family, friends, church, and culture. Her protestations of simple asceticism were as much strategic as factual. In 1803 Mary wrote to Ezra Ripley about the theological sparring between Aunt Ruth and her new husband, Samuel Waite: "The religious skepticism of Mr. Waite affords her opportunity for the display of her controversial powers, and . . . [she] flatters herself that his universalism will be shaken by an attack the next sabbath, from Tutor Emerson, who Mr. Green tells us, called there this week to propose an exchange." But after this vivid and specific account she took no position herself. "I often think I might be a party," she continued to Ezra, "were the arguments about subjects on which I did not profess the profoundest ignorance."[60] Either she was withdrawing from dispute with her clerical stepfather or, more likely, sharing a joke with him about the wisdom of *professing* ignorance on theological subjects. She had been invading his library at the Manse for more than a decade, and he may have received an excess of budding opinion from her himself.

In fact, her survey of controversy in Malden can be read as a microcosm of stirrings in the New England church at the opening of the nineteenth century:

a Second Great Awakening had commenced both in and out of the Congregational Standing Order. Since Mary's flight from Malden in 1791, her grandfather's old parish had replaced its Hopkinsian minister Adoniram Judson and at last healed the ancient sectional divide, but almost immediately splintered again on sectarian lines. By 1803 a Baptist church had formed in opposition to the liberal doctrines of new, Harvard-trained Aaron Green; Methodist circuit riders were arriving; and Universalist opinion was encroaching from Gloucester. "Tutor Emerson," soon to shake down heterodoxy, was Mary's own second cousin Joseph, grandson of Daniel and Hannah Emerson of Hollis. But his view of New England's mainstream tradition was not at all what Aaron Green preached from the Malden pulpit. Though also a graduate of Harvard, Joseph Emerson adhered to Calvinism and responded with zeal to Timothy Dwight's call for national revival. Even within the Standing Order, orthodox and liberal ministers were moving toward confrontation.[61]

Mary's individualism was a way of responding to these differences of doctrine and loyalty. Having known both orthodoxy and liberalism, she belonged to both sides and neither. She had purchased a pew in Green's meetinghouse and, along with Ruth, attended church there, but felt no more obligation to concur with the sermon than she had as a child. "I could not be reverent tonight with poor Mr. G[reen]'s preaching—," she confided to her Almanack in 1804, "I sympathized with the joys of the vulgar—I trod on air—I danced to the music of my own imajanation." By listening to her own internal music rather than his words, she was experiencing an awakening-of-one while maintaining outward decorum in a liberalizing, rationalistic church. Possibly the Baptists or Methodists were the "vulgar" with whose joys she sympathized, for they expressed a New Light fervor that she valued. But she did not join them, containing her enthusiasm within silence. "It is well no one knows the frolick of my fancy," she continued, "for they would think me wild unless they knew me."[62]

Instead, through letters from Malden and travels among homes, Mary located her dance of imagination amidst a family that was rapidly moving into the ranks of the liberal establishment. In Concord, Ezra Ripley kept dissenters at bay by preaching everyday piety and social order; in Newburyport, William Farnham by now served as deacon to the First Religious Society. Unlike Concord, Newburyport had never healed the divisions of the First Great Awakening but lived in acrimoniously separate church cultures right up through the Second, with Mary's kin joining their affluent merchant-neighbors in the antievangelical party.[63] In both branches of the family, roots in the First Awakening were fading from memory.

In the town of Harvard, William Emerson most directly stood for liberalism amidst the burgeoning new faiths. He was not happy. "I have enemies, not personal ones," William wrote to Ezra in 1796, "who are but too firm & too active. From the various sects of religionists, that have been nurtured amid the caves & wilds of this town, there is a number of apostates, who worship they know not what, and who, to my great infelicity, bear a small proportion in the payment of my salary." Baptists, Universalists, and Methodists had all come early to Harvard, but he probably referred most of all to the "caves & wilds" of the town's northeast corner, where Ann Lee had arrived in 1781 and founded the central village of American Shakerism. By the 1790s Shaker ecstasies had yielded to community-building enough that the town no longer condoned persecution. William recorded visiting the Shaker village, and Ruth took her wool there for processing. But none of these sects paid taxes to support William's ministry, and the habit of dissent had fostered "apostates" who simply dodged all obligation.[64]

Mary idealized Harvard as a "shady retreat which might have been placed in the garden of Eden!" Perhaps it appealed to her religious ideals, as well as her desire for rural peace. No comments on the Shakers survive in her writing, and she stood too much within the elite clerical caste of Massachusetts to consider joining them; but she surely had opportunity through visits with William and Ruth to observe the Shaker practice of spiritual perfectionism through celibacy and separation from society, as well as their empowering of women. William himself expressed no interest in retreat—and certainly none in female prophets. Local Harvard tradition later recalled him as intractably at odds with all but a few wealthy landowners in his parish. Even church members took offense at his courtly manners and studied pulpit rhetoric.[65]

William's compelling interest was the new Republic's political and social order. As he ministered to rural Harvard, he dreamed of starting a church in Washington, D.C., with "no written confession of faith, no covenant, & no subscription whatever to articles as a term of communion." His actual opportunity for creedal freedom and public influence came instead in the form of an invitation to preach Boston's artillery election sermon in June 1799. For a full month William worked on his sermon, pacing between rooms in excitement. "Surely I am destined to frequent changes," he confided to his diary. A call from Boston's First Church was at stake in this guest oration; the day before his ceremonial sermon, he also preached "by particular desire at the old Brick," and after a week of visiting in Malden and Newburyport returned for a second Sabbath to Charles Chauncy's onetime pulpit. A day later the committee offered him the ministry, and William rode for Concord with the news.[66]

Such a momentous change from country parson to upholder of Boston culture signaled a new era in the New England church, as well as a personal ambition in William Emerson. Fifteen years earlier, Peter Thacher and the Brattle Street Church had first broken the expectation that a minister would serve one parish for life; now Thacher served as a model and go-between for William, visiting with his Revolutionary colleague's son both before and after the offer. Ministers, they were declaring, could bargain for professional advancement and power. With consternation and perhaps relief, Harvard accepted one thousand dollars from First Church and granted William's dismissal. He seized the new opportunity amidst illness and stress. "Feel poorly," he recorded three weeks before his installation that fall. "Am alarmed about my health. . . . Feel sore at my lungs." But he told of a powerful vindication in the terse record of October 20: "It is 23 years since my father died. Preached all day at the Old Brick."[67]

William's female kin shared the ensuing transformation in their way of life,

Ruth most directly, but with Mary and the unmarried Haskins sisters newly mobilized as well. Mary probably reflected her own preference more than Ruth's as she lamented the removal from Harvard's "scenes of tranquillity." After all Ruth, unlike any of the Emersons, had grown up in Boston. During the transition William stayed at the Haskins house in Boston, confined to bed and nursed by Ruth's sister Elizabeth, while Mary helped Ruth care for baby Phebe at the Manse in Concord. William urged Ruth by letter to let Mary know how important her presence was to their happiness; she apparently needed to be wooed back from Malden.[68] Rather than being "shirked off," Mary seems to have been much desired, if not completely understood, by both of them.

But Boston drew her even less than Concord. Twice in 1800 Mary visited the new parsonage, but that summer declined the request to keep house alone while Ruth made visits elsewhere. A prickly letter of 1802 suggests the confusion of feelings that city life elicited in Mary. Even while congratulating Ruth on her elegant dinner table and calmness amidst society's requirements, Mary herself refused to change. "At every retrospection, I have made of the time passed with you, I turn with disgust from the zeal with which I entered into the tributes of fashion & parade," she wrote, lamenting her "specious pretext of family honor" and habit of wounding Ruth's gentler sensibility.[69] Her pride swelled at the possibility of a splendid Emersonian presence in Boston, but at the same time she fled from such feelings. This letter to Ruth was a farewell until their reunion in heaven, though one by which she did not abide.

Meanwhile, other migrations also changed the map on which the five Emerson siblings would live out their lives. Lincoln Ripley—Ezra's brother and his junior by ten years—was ordained minister in Waterford, Maine, just fifteen days before William's installation at First Church. Ezra managed to officiate on both occasions. Lincoln had studied theology in Concord after graduating from Dartmouth College, and the February following ordination he returned to marry Mary's sister, twenty-nine-year-old Phebe Emerson. Mary attended the wedding and returned with William and Ruth to Boston, having seen the couple off to their new home on New England's northern frontier. As Lincoln later reminisced, he and Phebe reached Waterford in sleighing season and, the first winter in their new house, could reach outside between boards in their wall. By the following August, however, William found a five-day horseback ride to Waterford beneficial to health. Heading up the coast by the familiar stages of Newburyport and York, he then veered inland, around Lake Sebago and north along Long Lake to Waterford. He wrote back to Concord describing Lincoln and Phebe's house as a single story, commanding "a variegated view of a delightful pond at a small distance below the hill, & the neighboring highlands."[70] These highlands were the White Mountains, on whose borders the Ripleys had settled.

Waterford offered a deeper retreat than Harvard, Massachusetts, by far. But the Emersons and their in-laws were not going separate ways; instead, they created a network extending from city to frontier. Lincoln had been a missionary to Waterford every summer since its incorporation in 1797, representing the Congregational way amidst the rapid settlement of New England's hill country.

The arrival of his wife—"a lady of rare accomplishments and sweetness of character," as one town historian recalled—signaled the coming of additional civility. Family alliance and religious culture went with both of them; in the Waterford Congregational Church today is displayed a full pewter communion service, labeled as a gift from "some persons of Concord, Massachusetts, connections of the Rev. Lincoln Ripley and his wife Phebe Emerson." It symbolizes their style and polity against the less decorous evangelical faiths that vied with the Ripleys for tax dollars and church membership. In conditions that replicated what William had known in Harvard (some settlers came directly from it), Baptists and Methodists had already made headway by the time of Lincoln's ordination. "The opposition to Mr. Ripley diminishes," William reported optimistically the next summer, despite struggles at a recent town meeting.[71]

More family connections to Waterford soon followed. Mary made her first visit in the fall of 1800, and meanwhile, Robert and Rebecca Emerson Haskins planned a permanent departure for Maine. Just as the Ripleys extended the church establishment into new territory, so did the Haskins family represent Boston business interests in a growing commercial world. John Haskins, father to Ruth and Robert, had accrued a modest fortune in distilling and West Indies trading. Now son Thomas took charge of the family office and youngest son Ralph embarked as a supercargo in the China trade, while Robert, halfway between Ruth and Ralph in age, saw the potential profits of business on the frontier.[72]

In the course of 1801, he and Rebecca made their move to Waterford, arriving in the first chaise ever seen in town. The choice of conveyance said more about their origins than their knowledge of Maine roads. Following a route similar to William's, they managed to drive the chaise as far as Long Lake; then the horse had to be led for fifteen remaining miles, with a two-year-old in Rebecca's uneasy care and a newborn baby in a basket tied to the front of the lurching vehicle. Rebecca was a reluctant pioneer. "How do you like your new situation?" William asked in his teasing way. "Have the woods become familiar to you, and is the voice of the loon musical?" But then shifting to ministerial authority, he assured his sister that the troubles of life in Waterford could only prepare her to leave earth for heaven. "If we were placed exactly on that spot of our globe, on which we should choose to dwell, we should undoubtedly say, it is good for us to be here, and here let us ever abide."[73]

Again Mary was drawn into new family ventures, though for her domestic resourcefulness and good humor rather than her religious authority. "Is Mary with you, or with Phebe?" William went on to ask Rebecca. "As to her being with us at present, I am not selfish enough to wish it, since her company is so much more judiciously appropriated; for the desert of Waterford cannot be joyless to you, if Mary is there."[74] Eventually Mary would choose this wilderness as her own home, interpreting its landscape as a window on heaven rather than a preparatory trial. But she first arrived there as a helpful sister and only incidentally a religious pilgrim.

In the meantime, what solitude she could achieve amidst the judicious appropriations of her family remained in Malden. In actuality, a single woman could achieve only a partial autonomy either economically or psychologically. Neither Mary nor her family seems to have entertained the thought of her living apart from them or taking on work to support herself. But in the realm of religious imagination, in her partnership with God, she could project a much more powerful and independent being. As she wrote in 1804, a day after her interior dance at the Malden meetinghouse, "Were the genius of the [Christ]ian religion painted, her form would be full of majesty, her mein solemn, her aspect benign, and strongly impressed with joy & hope, her eyes raised to Heaven with tears for Zion and rays of glory descending to illuminate the earth at her intreaties!" Here Mary spoke neither in the first person nor in direct assertion of reality. She would not have claimed such authority or majesty for herself, and no one in fact had painted the "genius of the Christian religion" as female. But amidst the ferment of the Second Great Awakening, both evangelical and liberal women were widely claiming a moral authority in private prayer that they could not exercise directly as public citizens. Mary was creating an ideal emblem that transcended both isolation and division, in which a single female "genius"—unaccompanied by family, minister, or congregation—could entreat heaven with prophetic power on behalf of her New England Zion.[75]

Constance

> You ask, how can the faculty of imagination benefit us as immortal beings? Whither, Cornelia, can we go without it? How blind, how deaf, how inanimate without this sensitive pioneer!
>
> Mary Moody Emerson to Mary Wilder Van Schalkwyck in the *Monthly Anthology and Boston Review 1* (August 1804, p. 453)

Mary wrote rather than spoke her boldest thoughts. When she pictured a female genius of Christianity, no one could see it but herself; when she reported dancing to the music of her own "imajanation," no one heard her interrupt Mr. Green's sermon. A woman's private writing was hers to control, either to hide or to share. Letters addressed particular others and, even when passed on to additional readers, were encircled by the trust of friendship. Diaries enjoyed even greater privacy, as a silently articulate record whose writer and primary audience were one. While living, the writer controlled access by lending her work only to friends. Friends or family might decide after her death to quote these words in a memoir, breaking the code of privacy in the interest of broader instruction, but she could not then be called indiscreet for appearing in print.[1]

As a writer Mary lived with these inhibitions. She wrote for herself and friends, showing awareness that they might publish after her death even by disparaging such memoirs. The circumstances of her writing were widely shared—varying mainly by degree of leisure and affluence—in this early phase of women's authorship. To begin writing within her Malden house, Mary needed only a quill, ink, letter paper (for either letters or diary), and a modicum of quiet amidst the clamorous needs of elderly relatives. She read and wrote in the fire-keeping common room of her childhood, with uncle's and aunt's chairs nearby. Usually the "hours of ardent book, pen, &c" were interspersed among daily labors of "the needle, the flat-iron, the porridge pot." Writing held the higher priority: according to Waldo, she used her thimble twice for pressing wax on letters to once for sewing. She often wrote on the Sabbath or, as headings like "Night" and "5 a.m." show, while others slept. Mary's brother William revealed the likely source of her wakefulness when he commented that there was "no old toper in the province of Maine more attached to his brandy bottle than she . . . to the coffee pot." But her memoirist Waldo better appreciated the accomplishment: "Neither can any account be given of the fervid work in MME's manuscripts, but the vehement religion which would not let her sleep, nor sit, but write, write, night & day, year after year."[2]

In this fervor and persistence through a lifetime, Mary pushed the boundaries of women's private writing from within. Briefly and tentatively, she also joined women of her generation crossing from private into public writing. For over a year in 1804 and 1805, amidst labors of porridge making and diary writing, Mary appeared several times under the pseudonym "Constance" in Boston's first literary review, the *Monthly Anthology*, whose editorship William had recently taken on. Such an appearance in print would itself be relatively unremarkable, the gentlemanly *Anthology*'s token contribution by the fair sex. But in her letters as Constance to Mary Wilder Van Schalkwyck's Cornelia, Mary claimed for women's sensibility the later watchwords of Transcendentalism, "nature" and "imagination," in both cases filling out trains of thought begun in the pages of the Almanack. In the self-spelled private words of her diary as well as the corrected, stilted, nonetheless bold statements of Constance, Mary was a precursor of Romantic consciousness. Waldo referred to the period of his father's literary journal as "that early ignorant & transitional *Month-of-March*, in our New England culture."[3] However, he did not acknowledge his aunt's fervid writing, either public or private, as a significant dissenting voice in precisely that cultural setting.

The Vast Volume of Nature

The earliest surviving packet of Almanack manuscripts—probably written in 1801 and 1802—was far from Mary's first. At its end she hoped not to finish another "as I have again" before departing to the enjoyment of God.[4] Later allusions clarify what she meant in calling her diary an "Almanack": it was intended as a calendar of only life's most significant moments, "actions so pure as to be presented to the Infinite," and after it had continued through decades seemed "all time's chronicles of sun's rising & moon's waning." In charting her relation to the heavens, Mary played her own variation on the colonial almanac-diary: her father had kept his line-a-day record interleaved into blank pages of the *Ames Astronomical Diary, or Almanack*, a book that promised to tell, among other things, "Spring-tides; Judgments of the Weather; . . . Sun and Moon's rising and setting; . . . Eclipses." Mary's Almanack, however, gave her own perception of the heavens rather than leaving these to the formulas of a printed book. Moreover, she did not record the day's events in terse notes, but wrote a history of the spiritual self in freely expatiating form:

> I am weak but God is eternal immutable and full of love. This morning the woods were inchanting, the crescent was brilliant—near it was the morning

> star, the east was reddened, the air was mild. I was wrapt, I prostrated my self, I promised my truth, my charity and love should resemble those benign planets. They are now my contemporaries—they move in radiant regular orbs and often oh often reproach me with their order and splendor—and they too shall shine on my grave. . . . But when that star *falls from Heaven* I, even this feeble emanation of light shall then exist—be beginning new periods of glory forming new plans of extending, perpetuating my knowledge and union to the *Head of all principality & power*!! Heavens! can I ever again find time to wish, to waste or even to *mourn*[?][5]

Mary's Almanack was a latter-day Puritan diary of sanctification, recording the soul's progress in a language and sensibility of the Enlightenment sublime. Her "eternal immutable" God manifested himself in the reasonable order of the nighttime sky, and she responded in worshipful awe. The Almanack entry of 1801 really concerned human consciousness more than the stars: both seemed to her, in the language of Christian Platonism, emanations of divine light; but when the stars fell, human glory would only begin in union with God. A strain in her father William's sermons (if not diaries) had hinted at such a divine-human relationship when he argued from the "Phylosoph Plato" for the excellence of the human soul. But Mary experienced her own excellence and God's glory directly and internally, as often under nighttime skies as in church. Her Almanack was still attuned to Puritan ways, Sabbath an important time marker and setting within it, church-going often recorded. Rarely, however, did a preacher excite Mary's thought as she desired; never was a sermon's text named; and only once in the decade from 1801 to 1811 (then twice more in over forty years) did Mary record taking communion. In this record of religious life, authority, community, and sacrament were disappearing before the soul's direct perception of divinity. Already Mary had become, as she later called herself, a "deistical pietist."[6]

This religious expression still had powerful mediators in the poets and philosophers whom she had been reading now for over a decade. The Almanack is an intensely intellectual as well as devotional text. Amidst her patriarchs of reason and high feeling Mary felt severely inadequate:

> Young . . . who lived amid the world in ruin. . . . Seraphic Watts I name thee with reverence—! Newton a thousand souls of mine would be lost in thine—! Herculean Johnson! I have pitied thy soul in its last stage—illume the world of letters & intellect—but the humble uniform [Christ]ian passes thy lot! Addison, wise, learned & pious, with all thy faults, rest in peace! Beattie, respected, oh deeply respected philosopher! . . . Cowper, sad yet pious votary of devotion and poetry. . . . Compared to these I have *no mind*.[7]

The Almanack aimed precisely to acquire "mind" by inscribing responses to books, nature, and divinity. Conviction of sin and lack of intellectual training often led Mary to declare disability for the task, but then a recording of God's presence would prove enabling: "I'm dust guilt and weakness," she continued her entry. "*His mind shall rest in perfect peace whose heart is stayed in God.* I pronounce the name of God and all is lightened."[8]

Implicitly this "weakness" was a woman's as she read and wrote a place for herself in the male intellectual tradition. Although the conviction of grace allowed entry, she also lapsed back into "imbicillity" and needed to repeat the cycle again. Aunt Rebecca and her sickroom were especially the female realities—literally "non compos mentis"—that she fled: "Since sab. Aunt B[ecca] was bro't here sick. Ah mortifying sight, instinct, perhaps triumphs over reason, and every dignified respect for herself in her anxiety about recovery. . . . But it alarms me not. *I* shall delight to return to God." A few years later she was more graphic: "I took care of my weak folks with pleasure, but there are s[c]ents with bodies of ladies so disgusting to reason & refinement that to shrink is not anti-benevolent." Mary shrank by rising mentally. "How much easier it is," she confessed, "to adore the Creator in the glow of the star, than reverence Him in a poor deformed soul."[9]

In her stargazing Mary most directly followed Edward Young, whose *Night Thoughts* stood first on her list of greatness. Such a loyalty may have repressed experience of the female body and domestic condition, but it also amounts to a heroic effort of transcendence. In Young's book-length poem, an older man enjoins a worldly youth to recognize the permanent realities surrounding him; on nine separate nights he expounds the stars as a sign of God's omnipresence and argues the need for spiritual ascent through a human power proceeding at once from reason and imagination. The only woman in the poem, "Narcissa," takes no part in this scene of contemplation but ("soft, modest, melancholy, female, fair") has already died and so shown the way to heaven for male followers. Mary, however, massively appropriated the narrator's own perceptions and language into her own, both in the early Almanacks and for a lifetime thereafter. Characterizing Young as having "lived amid the world in ruin," she especially recalled "Night the Ninth and Last," in which the narrator envisioned the physical universe's final conflagration. Her Almanack passage on the stars' fall and her own eternal prospects echoed Young more directly than the Bible. Nearly half a century later, as Mary reported to a female friend, rereading Young's "9th" still "roused the old jaded imajanation": "I laid by the modern pages of philosophy &c to dwell in the glories of the nocturnal Muse & wished every young aspirant to know them."[10] She had no doubt about including herself and her correspondent among these aspirants.

Many other favorite texts supplemented Young, as her list reveals. She had only grudging praise to offer the Augustan taste of Addison and Johnson, but like her friend Mary Wilder she embraced the poets of sensibility who were their younger contemporaries. Cowper celebrated a life of solitary retirement and piety in *The Task*, Beatty the progress of a "visionary boy" from fancy to philosophy in *The Minstrel*. Likewise, she celebrated James Thomson, whose *Seasons* brought changing seasonal landscapes and starry skies within the poet's purview, ending in "Winter" with an apocalyptic vision of death and eternal spring; and along with Mark Akenside she embraced *The Pleasures of Imagination*.

Without distinguishing sharply between "imagination" and the lesser "fancy," as Coleridge would later do, Young and Akenside insisted that the imagination did not delude, but rather joined in the divine act of creation and united all other capacities of the human soul. Mary learned from them quickly. She almost always, even willfully, preferred the misspelling "imajanation," perhaps thereby making this favorite term more completely her own. She could also understand its significance philosophically and spell it right:

> It is to imagination that faculty of the mind w'h seems to unite the feelings of the heart to the exertions of intellect that we owe the soft[ene]d tints of past misfortunes and the liveliness of future hopes. . . . The peculiar gifts, the indefinable combinations of genius will never be the portion of vulgar souls (it seems) even in the ages of blessedness! They may grow expatiate and triumph in the devolving wonders of a God, but by analogy of all human education they will not acquire gifts different from the stamina—the constituent principles[—]which compose the soul.[11]

This was a powerfully self-vindicating concept, identifying her rhapsodies with "genius" rather than emotional excess, finding in them an ability to discover truth both on earth and in heaven.

By pursuing philosophical and theological truth in her private writing, Mary was violating convention just as surely as when she reported ecstatic, subjective experience. But she redoubled the offense by reading theology to justify ecstasy, appropriating the books that the Harvard faculty taught toward a different end than their own rationalism. "These tho'ts have passed my own mind in much the same connection," she wrote in November 1804 of a passage from Joseph Butler's *Analogy of Religion* on the compatibility of moral and physical laws in the universe. "Why, oh my God, are thy virtuous creatures ever unhappy? . . . It is because they comprehend nothing of the wonders which surround them in the vast vol[ume] of nature—in the divine book of Providence w'h nature unfolds, and which revelation writes with sunbeams!" Reading both Butler and Richard Price this year, thereby adding to a self-education begun with Samuel Clarke, Mary was deepening her grasp of Christian Platonism, whose images and ideas had also suffused *Night Thoughts.* Where Young spoke of eagle flights of soul, fountains of flowing light, and earthly sundials pointing to eternity, now Butler and Price presented a reasoned case for the correspondence of mental, natural, and divine attributes, providing Mary with a natural theology to support her response to God's "wonders."[12]

None of her preferred theologians endorsed imagination as did the poets, but they proved compatible by claiming reason as intuitive and God-given. Mary never confronted the presiding philosopher of the eighteenth century, John Locke, who saw human understanding as an aggregate of sense impressions. Instead, she learned from his successors and antagonists. Price had addressed Locke directly in claiming a much wider, deeper knowledge as inherent in the mind, studding his argument with lengthy quotations from the Cambridge Platonists, Plotinus, and Plato. Mary was able to move directly from the religious intuitions of her childhood to a Platonically grounded belief in intuition without ever being tempted by empiricism. Looking back from the 1820s, she described herself as "always hating Locke's real or supposed theory": "We are as conscious of certain moral truths, and an intuitive belief of the Supreme, as we are of our own existence."[13]

Mary began recording both the experience and the theory of this belief before her nephew Waldo was born, drawing upon the intellectual resources of her own generation and driven by personal hunger for knowledge. In the Almanack she filtered an inherited conviction of sin and assurance of grace through newer sciences of mind and nature. "The rapture of feeling I would part from," she wrote in what is perhaps the Almanack's earliest surviving sentence, "for days more devoted to higher discipline." Her diary recorded that effort at discipline. In this early entry, however, she also sounded an experiential authority in feeling: "But in dead of night—nearer morning, when the eastern stars glow . . . with a luster which penetrates the spirit with wonder and curiosity—then however awed, who can fear!"[14]

Constance and Cornelia

The context for this intellectual enterprise was a fledgling community of women readers and correspondents aware of new possibilities for women. In 1799 Mary was still turning to Ruth Haskins Emerson, her early model, for partnership in intellectual conversation. "Have you read Woolsencraft's works, about which we were so warmly disputing the last time I saw you?" she asked. Mary felt that if only Ruth would candidly read *A Vindication of the Rights of Woman*, her prejudices against the author would be removed and her virtue given new energy. Though Mary did not directly endorse Wollstonecraft's argument for women's social equality, she did favor the corollary proposal for education to eliminate "*that softness* in girls which lays a foundation for many future ills in thier lives." Ruth—settling into motherhood and the support of an ambitious husband—seems to have made no response to Mary's challenge, and this was the last letter ever to pass between them about any intellectual issue. Three years later, Mary asked Ruth to search for notes on the "future of [Christ]ian philosophy" that she had left in a book at their Boston house.[15] She did not invite Ruth to read or comment on them.

Not long after, Mary actively sought out a new epistolary partner in her half sister Sarah's old childhood friend Mary Wilder Van Schalkwyck. Like Mary herself, Van Schalkwyck had moved on from Radcliffe to Wollstonecraft since their days as neighbors in Concord. In a letter of 1803 she declared that though *The Rights of Women* threatened to undermine marriage, it still offered a better standard for women than the conventional advice to live as "mere baubles of an hour." Mary Van Schalkwyck and Mary Emerson talked more of Wollstonecraft upon meeting that week, for Van Schalkwyck thanked her for recommending the portrait of "perfect female character" in William Godwin's *St. Leon*.

Godwin was Wollstonecraft's husband and had idealized her in this novel. Both women could pursue virtue from authors widely rejected as radical in New England, as well as value the devotional feelings excited by Young and Cowper's poetry.[16] Van Schalkwyck was an intellectual and seeker as Ruth Haskins Emerson probably had never been.

In offering friendship to Van Schalkwyck, Mary Emerson must have been drawn by sympathy and sheer curiosity, as well as intellectual affinity, for this woman had just survived a tragedy as harrowing as any that their poems or romance novels could offer. She had sailed to Guadeloupe in September 1801 as the new wife of a French West Indian planter named Antoine Van Schalkwyck, who originally came to Concord in exile after the French Revolution. Married by Boston's new Catholic Bishop Cheverus, they embarked from Newburyport along with Mary Van Schalkwyck's brother, who sought both to help her with a convalescent husband and to launch a business career for himself. But within two months after landing, both husband and brother had died in a yellow fever epidemic, leaving Mary Van Schalkwyck to the uncertain protection of her husband's family during a slave insurrection. Only after ten months of yellow fever and violence, ending in escape by sedan chair past the liberated slaves' campfires, did she return to the safe harbors of Newburyport and Concord.[17]

Mary Van Schalkwyck was certainly the most interesting of Ezra Ripley's parishioners when, as a widow of twenty-two, she had him read during services the traditional prayer "that all the afflictive dispensations of Providence may be sanctified to her, for her spiritual good." Still maintaining her friendship with Bishop Cheverus, contemplating a residence at the Moravian community in Bethlehem, Pennsylvania, she spoke as a daughter of Puritanism but also a seeker of devotional feeling across the lines of parish and doctrine. Beautiful as well as shadowed by sorrow, she drew some of Harvard's most brilliant young graduates to the Block House in Concord.[18] Mary Emerson was operating within her own family's social world, but very much against her own claims of solitude and humility, to break so boldly into this circle. She offered real partnership, however, both in dark knowledge and in the will to transcend it intellectually.

The particular cure that Mary Emerson proposed was a strenuous one for both women—to begin a publishable exchange of letters, with Van Schalkwyck presenting the benefits of friendship so that she herself could respond with the case for "independency of mind." As Van Schalkwyck commented, the topic was somewhat ironic, since her own strongest argument for friendship was "the pleasant hours I lately passed with you, my dear Miss Emerson." At first, however, Van Schalkwyck declined the idea on grounds quite apart from its interest and merit. Though publishing translations from French under the pseudonym "Eugenia," she refused to present views of her own to the public even under a fictitious name. Nor would she submit to the judgment of the proposed go-between in this project, William Emerson, who "would censure me for presumption should I attempt a public disputation with his sister." The best she could offer was continued letters in private and a possibility that she might eventually "gain courage."[19]

Over the next sixteen months she did gain courage, exchanging essaylike letters with Mary on such topics as friendship and the novel; and in the meantime William became editor of his own literary journal, the *Monthly Anthology and Boston Review*. In July 1804 a first letter from Van Schalkwyck appeared in the *Anthology*, prefixed by elaborate gestures of modesty: "Should you be disposed to admit into your elegant publication the correspondence of two obscure females, who have hitherto written merely for their own amusement, and who still seek concealment, you will probably receive several letters from Constance and Cornelia." Though pseudonymous authorship was standard practice in this journal, no other submission began with such an explicit avowal of need for privacy, and none of the other pseudonyms was female. Still, the women's modesty cloaked ambition for an audience. In choosing the name "Constance," Mary Emerson may have recalled an older contemporary—"Constantia," Judith Sargent Murray, whose pseudonymous essays had appeared in the *Massachusetts Magazine* and only recently been collected into a book.[20] Murray's views of women's capacity and her sympathy for Wollstonecraft at least squared with the younger women's views, making her a fitting model for their project.

Constance and Cornelia had less rationalistic interests than Murray, however, as the opening exchange soon revealed. In her first letter, Cornelia recounted an experience of dreaming about a recently deceased friend. Trying mentally to follow this woman's progress into God's presence, she was awakened by heavy thunder and pulled back from the folly of such mental pastimes. "What is this strange propensity in our nature," Cornelia asked, "to turn from the contemplation of indubitable and essential truth, while we readily resign ourselves to imagination, and rove with delight in the boundless regions of possibility?"[21]

In the next month's *Anthology*, Constance answered with confidence that human wisdom would reach the "regions of possibility" only by exercising imagination. Women especially should seize this resource, she argued, because it was a "province . . . freely conceded us by the Proprietors of mental ground," one whose beauties "our lords" declined for themselves. Despite Young and Akenside's endorsement, imagination was widely associated with women assumed to lack the higher faculty of understanding. Boston's "lords" still lived in the Age of Reason and so could give away what was not reasonable. But she converted this depreciated mental activity to power, as a "sensitive pioneer" preventing the mind from becoming blind, deaf, or inanimate. "If, as philosophers tell us, the sublime abodes, where truth unveils her light and demonstrates her eternal counsels, cannot be ascended but by an almost endless chain of reasonings," she suggested, "we must be content to remain in the plains of ignorance. But if indulged the use of our less logical guide, we can climb the ladder of the pious patriarch in the company of angels."[22]

Her advice to climb Jacob's ladder toward divine truth powerfully challenged readers of the *Anthology* in two ways. Constance was engaging the possibility of female intellectual empowerment without compromise to domestic obligation; her woman-identified "we," as well as female personification of truth, might even be read to exclude the lords of reason from eligibility for this enlightenment. But the letter also provided a minority voice in the male discourse that dominated the *Anthology*; her endorsement of imagination and philosophical ascent was indebted to male authorities not generally favored in this periodical. To underscore one affinity, she separately (still under the signature Constance) contributed a passage from Richard Price's *Review of Morals* to this same issue of the *Anthology*.[23] She was appropriating his mode of transcendence for herself and her female readers, but she addressed men, too, if they cared to relinquish their exclusive hold on logic.

Four months later, Constance initiated a second exchange, now directly commenting on issues already present in the *Anthology*. Praising the essays of "Botanist," Harvard professor Benjamin Waterhouse, she went on to claim space for women in the temple of natural history that his work was helping to build. "And is it assuming too much," she asked, "to look forward with hope, that some of its pillars will be adorned with inscriptions of female achievement?" From ancient times to contemporary America, women had been among those who studied plants, and in so doing found means of both healing disease and understanding theology.[24]

She wanted especially to open theology to "every student of nature"—a more mystical and speculative natural theology than the empirically minded, Linnaean "Botanist" had held forth. Mary's reading of Butler's *Analogy of Religion*, recorded in her Almanack only a month before, probably influenced this thinking. From the "humblest shrub," she argued, the mind can trace laws of nature and therefore by "analogy . . . infer the operation of infinite wisdom in regions, which must remain unexplored by human knowledge." In her view, the mind joined divine wisdom in an organically unified creation:

> If the hyssop, which springs from the bosom of the barren rock, is related to every element of our earth, and the light of distant orbs, how infinitely extensive may be the relations of a being like man! A being, who, like the plant, is chained to the earth by his wants and necessities, but by his senses is connected to the universe, and by his reason and even his passions with a world beyond the precincts of sense.[25]

Once more her purpose was to open "wisdom"—as a goal of learning and a realm of divinity—to all; and she did so by affirming intuitive, natural powers of mind.

Under the name Constance, Mary even sought to influence the *Anthology*'s editorial direction. In March 1805, responding directly to William's earlier editorial about the figurative "son" he was fostering in this journal, Constance wrote to express fear "lest theological sentiments are to hold only a subordinate rank in the education of your ward." But by this time her epistolary partnership had already lost the energy and support it needed to continue this critique. In a last letter that February, Cornelia had mildly agreed with Constance's thoughts on nature, then shifted to Cowper, "the faithful poet of nature and of christianity." In order to get her response published, Mary resorted to pleading with William for the "indulgence" of a taste different from his own. Not until July did he print the piece, which expressed regret about Dr. Johnson's harsh biographies of Cowper and Young, and even then he appended a footnote informing his "fair correspondent" that the Young biography was by Herbert Croft rather than Johnson.[26] The two women's experiment in public letter writing ended with precisely the editorial censure that Van Schalkwyck had first predicted.

By that fall an Anthology Society had formed around William, bringing with it the requirement that each submission to the journal be read aloud to the all-male members over dinner, and probably neither William nor Mary Van Schalkwyck considered that form of scrutiny appropriate for the words of obscure females. Mary Emerson did not easily give up the effort to write for the public; remaining amidst her Almanack manuscripts is an additional piece from "Anthologian Correspondent"—either rejected or unsubmitted—defending the person and eloquence of British reformer Wilberforce against the attacks of columnist Sylva.[27] Still, Mary must also have felt the anxiety of facing censure, whether around the society's dinner table or on the printed page. Most noticeably, she never actually admitted in her Almanack, before, during, or after appearing as Constance, that she harbored any thought of publishing. The Almanack was a writer's journal keeping silence about its own intent.

Though her authorial child never grew to maturity, however, it has high retrospective significance in this "Month-of-March" publication. In eight years of the *Anthology*'s publication, only the most tentative openings from neoclassical to Romantic taste appeared from male contributors. Joseph S. Buckminster defended Gray's odes against the strictures of Dr. Johnson; Benjamin Welles declared the love of nature a "passion of the soul" and country pleasures even better than Cowper, Thomson, and Milton had promised. The poets from whom Mary learned were hardly unknown to these men of letters. Increasingly, as William wrote to Mary, "the literati of our as well as the literatee of your sex" were reading John Aikin's new editions of these British proto-Romantics. But no claims to knowledge of God were made even in Buckminster's defense of the sublime ode, no explicit analogy between human, natural, and divine realms in Welles's essay on nature. Mary's Platonized pietism—her metaphysics of correspondence, ascent, and self-transformation—had no parallel among the *Anthology*'s other contributors.[28]

Concessions to women were equally rare in its pages. Male writers occasionally reached toward a female reading audience by reviewing *Advice to Mothers*, and one even recognized mental equality in "such of our fair countrywomen, as honour these essays with perusal." They noticed Susanna Rowson's poetry, Suky Vickery's novel *Emily Hamilton*, Germaine de Staël's *Corinne*—and persistently championed the work of Boston Unitarian scholar Hannah Adams. The hierarchies of society and intellect central to their purpose, however, could result only in condescension and disparagement toward women. Ostensibly celebrating the presence in Boston of a "Bluestocking Club" where ladies might share literary conversation, one writer pointed out that there was no equal to Mrs. Montague among them, then commented of women in general that they were either "angels of light" or "active agents of misery and ruin." When Joseph Buckminster read an acrostic in honor of Hannah Adams at an Anthology Society dinner, the secretary recorded, "I believe [it] was rejected, for we were in such a roar of laughter, that no vote could easily be taken, or remembered."[29]

In this inhospitable climate very few women made actual contributions, and those who did presented the *Anthology*'s characteristically public and rationalistic themes. In 1809, reviewing the Scottish writer Anne Grant's *Letters from the Mountains*, Anna Cabot Lowell used most of her available space to quote a diatribe against Mary Wollstonecraft; a socially conservative woman's voice was decidedly welcome in these pages.[30] Constance and Cornelia stand out both for writing under the sign of female identity and for simultaneously questioning the limits of conventional womanhood.

Though their aspiration to public voice came to a swift end, moreover, the private writing and conversation that underlay it continued. The *Anthology* was right in acknowledging the growth of a "Bluestocking Club" in eastern Massachusetts, and within the limits of her solitary temperament Mary belonged to it. William's religious and intellectual world provided one source of contacts; Hannah Adams dined at his house, and probably she and Mary began a long if sporadic acquaintance there. More central were the friends she met in Newburyport through sister Hannah Farnham. Mary's eagerness to publish the essay defending Cowper and Young came after a conversation there with budding author Hannah Sawyer, and by the fall of 1806 she was reporting in letters on the Sawyer sisters as leaders of Newburyport's "beau monde." "I love & dislike—approve & shun [them]," she commented of their stylish manners. Old friend Ann Bromfield won fuller respect with renewed talk at the same time, and Mary recorded in her Almanack, "I hope a blessing will attend the acquaintance."[31]

Most of all, her network of intellectual women expanded through friendship with Van Schalkwyck. Though Mary was the venturous partner when it came to publishing, Van Schalkwyck promoted Mary's reputation in her own private, socially elite group. In 1804 Van Schalkwyck wrote to Ann Bromfield declaring Mary "one of the first of women" and asking for an opinion of her God-centered solitude. When Van Schalkwyck was later introduced by Bromfield to Anna and Susan Lowell, daughters of Boston judge John Lowell, she once again sang Mary's praises. "My dear Susan," Van Schalkwyck wrote, "you must know [Mary]. Ann already does, and admires. . . . A longer, or rather a *closer* intimacy, a more complete acquaintance with her heart, and all its generous, tender feelings, is necessary to ensure affections." Van Schalkwyck wanted Mary known in writing as well as in person; she sent Mary's sublime imagining of Niagara Falls to Susan Lowell and transcribed further passages with the intent of circulating them privately.[32]

These scattered reports hint at the membership of a women's literary group just outside Boston's Anthology Society. "Had I the eloquence of Ann Lowell," Van Schalkwyck wrote of Mary, "I would describe the influence of religion on the mind, the temper, and the life of this uncommon woman." Anna Cabot Lowell, author of the anti-Wollstonecraft essay, provided the standard of eloquence for all. A single woman six years older than Mary, a voluminous writer of letters and possibly of pseudonymous essays as well, Lowell coupled an opposition to women's rights with strong private activism on behalf of women. She solicited nine hundred private subscribers for the American publication of Anne Grant's *Letters from the Mountains*, sent the proceeds directly to the author, then went on to secure an annuity for Hannah Adams; further, she led a wide circle of female relatives and friends for years in discussing religious vocation. "Miss Ann Lowell is dead!" Mary exclaimed in her 1811 Almanack. "How sublime the future of such a mind! . . . I feel more my nothingness when surviving the eminent."[33] Lowell's social eminence and domestic ideology separated her from Mary, but without doubt their vocations, ideas, and conversational circles also overlapped.

They did so most immediately in the cultivation of feeling. Mary could overlook the conservatism of Grant's *Letters from the Mountains* and praise its "pretty flowers of literature," for, like her, this author was an admirer of Milton, Young, Cowper, and Thomson. So were many of the Boston bluestockings who subscribed to the book. Van Schalkwyck praised Cowper and echoed Thomson's "Autumn," then moved on to the newer literary taste for "Ossian" and Scott's "Lay of the Last Minstrel." Mary likewise tried her hand at Ossianic imitation and by 1809 was reading Scott. While the men of Boston's *Anthology* group were still advocating Pope and Johnson, their sisters read along the borders of Romanticism. They did so because they mutually valued what Anna Lowell, praising Bromfield, called a "deep sensibility and enthusiasm of feeling." This proto-Romantic vocabulary, which might seem an isolated case in Mary Emerson's usage, circulated in all directions among the friends. "I know enthusiasm has its attendant dangers," Van Schalkwyck wrote, "but, to me, they appear far less fatal than its cold reverse; and were happiness, even in this world, my object, I would prefer waking and weeping with enthusiastic Mary, at the foot of the cross, to being the icy-souled, the self-thought rational, enlightened Deist, or his dear friend and brother, the Socinian."[34] Van Schalkwyck could easily dismiss the delusive possibilities that previous generations had attached to the word "enthusiasm," embracing it as a saving warmth of religious feeling in a cold time.

This enthusiasm met severe constraints of social decorum, however, and aimed more for expression beyond the world than in it. Attachment to heaven became a strategy for rising above the sickrooms where all these devout women ministered. Mary Emerson, wrote Van Schalkwyck, showed herself the perfect "garde malade" in caring for bedridden Sarah Ripley, because she was able to supplement daily care with "sublime views of immortality." Books and ideas fundamentally gave hope of control over the body and its distress. "Unwilling that *matter* should for a moment triumph over *mind*," Van Schalkwyck wrote of Mary, "in proportion as the sufferings of the former increased, she endeavoured to interest the latter in reading or conversation." Ann Lowell would know the ultimate transcendence only after her release from disease. "Complaints of the lungs," Lowell wrote, "will, I know not how soon, call me from this world of shadows to bright realities."[35]

In these years, consumption was destroying not only Lowell but also Sarah Ripley, Mary Van Schalkwyck, and Hannah Emerson Farnham. In the spring of 1807, Mary and Sarah Ripley by turns attended Hannah's deathbed, while a circle of friends gathered as well in Newburyport. Hannah's attitude was exemplary. "I cannot think of that interesting woman without admiration," Van Schalkwyck wrote. "That in her situation resignation can be felt, is the triumph of Religion." In her Almanack Mary expressed inner stress amidst this caregiving. "I should have soared like the eagle & basked in the rays of light joy & serenity," she wrote, acknowledging that she had not achieved much real triumph of mind over matter.[36]

Indeed, her record of behavior and feeling during the months of Hannah's illness shows the limits of her participation in this convention-bound society. The women of Newburyport clearly saw romance developing when Mary made a friend and confidant of Daniel Appleton White, the young lawyer boarding at the Farnhams' house. "[He] became almost my sole companion," she wrote in her Almanack; "in the social table he occupied my attention & shortened my labors. Now thankfull that he did no more. To others he appeared to." Instead of following out the others' expectations, Mary extricated herself by arranging a meeting between Daniel and Mary Van Schalkwyck under Sarah Ripley's eye in Concord. Mary's two close friends became engaged in the first week of January 1807.[37] Playing the role of matchmaker, she both worked within the network of women and preserved her own distance.

Over the next few months Mary persistently cut ties, walking to the Dexters in Malden again to decline marriage, vowing to remain single like the maidens of the parable, and finally selling her portion of the house shared with Ruth and Samuel Waite. "My dear self has done well," she commented sardonically after several days of wrangling over money with Samuel. A more glorious future beckoned as she left Aunt Ruth after a decade in Malden. "I begin a new life—," she wrote in February 1807, "free—oh merciful God—from levity, pride, flattery, folly & weakness."[38] Mary did not elaborate upon the new life she planned in material or personal terms; in reality she met the needs of others and moved back to Hannah's sickroom in Newburyport. But whatever circumstances she had in mind, she sought amidst them to be unencumbered.

Feeling such inner demands for solitude and transcendence, Mary pushed her incipient Romantic sensibility, though shared with other women readers, to an extremity more akin to the male authors they were reading. She did not want to be Young's Narcissa but the solitary sky-viewer of *Night Thoughts*, not just an expectant of heaven but an immediate participant in its joys. According to later recollection, she read Wordsworth "before every or any body liked him," copying many pages from *Lyrical Ballads* into her Almanack. When Waldo offered her the same volume in 1829, she told Charles, "I saw them in 1805 and dont wish to again tell the Priest."[39] Unfortunately, her passages from Wordworth are among the many pages lost from the surviving Almanack manuscript. But what she saw is evoked in the line that she later reread and quoted: "there[']s nothing finite in solitude." Both the taste for Wordsworth and the seeking of transcendent solitude were Mary's unshared preoccupation in this year of writing as Constance.

A year later, on June 16, 1806, there was a total eclipse of the sun. "I flew to the woods to get beyond the din of human tongues," she wrote in her Almanack, "but before I arrived to the most sequestered spot the sun immerged. Alass I never so deeply regretted a loss—for never surely did the sublime in perception so fully appear." Yet the returning light was its own reward: "The appearance was unexpected so exquisite a light I cannot describe—the winds were hushed as if in awe—the birds screamed—the stars glowed—with what rapt devotion did I view my Maker's hand. Oh how forgotten are the vanities & sorrows of life at grand appearances! How easy death at clear views of God's works!" Mary found unexpected beauty after the climactic moment, vaulting upward and inward to the "sublime in perception." To her the eclipse was apocalypse, a "grand appearance" of God that lifted the vain and sorrowful self above earth. Exquisite light and sublime perception alike amounted to a mortal preview of heaven, possible only when the perceiver was in full retreat from "human tongues." A day later, with the experience still strongly in mind, she read from the Bible and Thomson's *Seasons*. "In communion with trees, with streams and stars and suns," she wrote, "man finds his own glory inscribed on every flower and in every beam."[40] Sharing her taste for the Bible and poetry with other women readers and writers, she also sought this glory on her own.

Mary Versus William

William Emerson also observed the solar eclipse of June 16, 1806, after sharing his interest in it with Mary over tea just a day before. But William spoke of neither solitude nor sublimity in his description of the event; instead, it was a landmark day in his Society for the Study of Natural Philosophy. "Have been with a congregation of astronomers in Mr. Bussey's garden," he wrote, "viewing the eclipse and making our remarks." This was an all-male group, significantly overlapping with the Anthology Society and including such Boston notables as John Lowell the younger, Josiah Quincy, and John Kirkland. The amateur scientists—mostly lawyers and ministers by profession—spent much of the day preparing equipment for the event, but they also mixed science with company and good food. "After the totality of the eclipse was over," William reported, "Mr. B[ussey] invited us into his house where [there] was a handsome collation &c."[41] While Mary savored the exquisite afterlight from her sequestered spot, William and his friends folded up their telescopes to dine.

Sister and brother were both children of the American Enlightenment—their grandparents would have beheld the eclipse with alarm as a sign of God's judgment. As Mary had commented the year before, however, their tastes differed fundamentally. In contrast to her valuing of sublime intuition, he sought out empirical truth within formally organized social groups. William's views had authority in Boston's "Month-of-March." She depended on him for information and influence, as well as supporting the career that renewed their father's and stood in place of her own. But Mary was also William's critic, as he was hers.

In 1806 William still worked from the same restless energy that seven years earlier had made him pace his Harvard parsonage and predict change. As he had won his Boston position then with a sermon on the value of a "whole community attending on the institutions of religion from a principle of piety," so ever since he had devoted this energy to building order. His aim was to extend clerical authority in the city's culture at large. So he edited the *Anthology* and wrote for the *Palladium* and *Polyanthos*, chief newspapers of Federalist Boston. He joined the new Massachusetts Historical Society and preached to the Charitable Society and the Boston Female Asylum. He demonstrated the workings of a battery to his natural philosophy society, though, as he ruefully noted, he "broke two of the phials." Copious dining and sociability went with all of these organizations, often in the Emersons' own dining room, where portraits of William's predecessors Charles Chauncy and John Clarke overlooked all company from the wall. After Thursday lecture, the time-honored weekly gathering of clergy at First Church, William would bring fellow ministers home to dinner; every Sunday evening the deacons and other friends enjoyed wine and spirits, arrayed in gleaming decanters on the sideboard. Ruth's book of recipes tells how to make a "plumb cake" involving twenty-eight pounds of flour, sixteen of currants, and seven dozen eggs.[42] Theirs was a perpetually open house.

Biographers of Ralph Waldo Emerson have portrayed William in a harsh light, often citing Waldo's memory that he was "a somewhat social gentleman, but severe to us children, who twice or thrice put me in mortal terror by forcing me into the salt water off some wharf or bathing house." In his letters, however, William emerges with geniality and emotion as well as authority. He lamented brother-in-law Farnham's lack of tenderness as a husband, and while his own letters to Ruth never fulfilled an initial promise to pour out "secret sighs & sorrows, . . . sentiments & affections," they spoke of personal news from within a confiding partnership. He often made a point with humor. Writing to eldest son John Clarke, at six living with the Ripleys in Maine, he reviewed the younger children's progress: at two and a half "Ralph is rather a dull scholar," and at four "William talks rather too much." The sentence about Ralph has often been taken out of context as evidence of father William's expectations of literacy in his children's toddlerhood, when in fact he was joking to a six-year-old about the immaturity of younger brothers. The same father, several years earlier, had written to Ruth that their fourteen-month-old daughter Phebe "makes great progress in her reading today," preferring "Mr. B's Magazine" above all others.[43]

Even jokes about reading, however, reveal William's interest in intellectual prowess, both for himself and for the eight Emerson children born between 1798 and 1811. William named two sons for his predecessors at First Church, John Clarke and Charles Chauncy, and his ambitions and methods as a father remained one with the other projects of his Boston career. As editor of the *Monthly Anthology*, he called the project his "infant hope" and laid out the education in languages, sciences, and politics that this figurative son should receive. Likewise with six actual sons, he expected cooperation in an ambitious program of improvement; as William wrote to mother Phebe in Concord, her grandchildren had to become "intelligent as well as moral beings . . . to take rank with professional characters and the upper classes in society."[44]

He attempted to mold them by offering rewards and conditions. "Papa will bring home cake for little boys who behave well at the dinner table," he reminded two-year-old Ralph Waldo. Firstborn John Clarke enjoyed a certain intimacy with William but also got the full burden of his expectations. "It will grieve me exceedingly to have you a blockhead," William wrote; "but it will excessively delight me to have you a bright scholar. . . . I hope you will be as bright as silver." By sharing his fear that John might be naughty, William drove the iron of conscience within. "Tell your mother to be very strict with you," he enjoined, in effect asking the child of six to take charge of his own discipline. Child-rearing practices change only incrementally between generations. William's grandfather had lined up his children on the settle by age rank, and his father had whipped two-year-old Mary for failing to curtsy in "duty." By contrast, William eased the old ceremonies of deference and exhorted to self-control. Waldo described his father's bathing regimen as a scene from ancient religion: "I still recall the fright with which, after some of this salt experience, I heard his voice one day, (as Adam that of the Lord God in the garden,) summoning us to a new bath, and I vainly endeavouring to hide myself."[45] But this father saw this harshness as preparation for a new age, not a replay of old judgments.

William approached the building of bodies and minds as a discipline of the senses. He owned Locke's *Essay on Human Understanding* and quoted David Hartley's view that "all our ideas originate in the vibrations of the nerves from external causes." Even his enthusiasm for ocean bathing arose from the Lockean theory that young bodies needed hardening. For such advice he would have had to search no farther than the *Anthology*'s review of *Advice to Mothers*, advocating British doctor William Buchan's program of fresh air and cold baths for children. William and Ruth sent John Clarke to Maine, though he was young and the November season inhospitable, hoping that his frailty and consumptive symptoms would be driven away. Five months later, Ruth expressed pleasure that the boy was hardy enough to play without mittens in the chilly Maine springtime. William practiced the same rigors on himself as on John. He rode to Waterford by horseback in 1806, pausing for doses of paregoric, systematically recording the theological position of each New Hampshire church, losing sleep in country inns to "strong tea, rats, fatigue and anxiety of mind." He tried to get John onto a horse for the return trip but progressed only one town from Waterford before hiring a chaise.[46]

Elegance of manner made William appear successful in the demanding social world of Federalist Boston. Fellow minister Charles Lowell, brother of John and Anna, saw him as "a handsome man, rather tall, with a fair complexion, his cheeks slightly tinted, his motions easy, graceful and gentlemanlike, his manners bland and pleasant." A daughter of Josiah and Eliza Quincy recalled instead the self-consciousness of this grace: "I think he was proud of his well-shaped leg," she told his granddaughter Ellen. "He wore knee-breeches and black silk stockings, and when he sat down he placed one ankle on the other knee, for that showed his leg to the best advantage." William's journal reveals the deliberation behind every gesture, less from pride than from determination to succeed. He thanked God for arriving in one of the world's best parishes, vowed to achieve dignity of manner, blamed his "inferiority" on neglect of order, and repeatedly wrote new schedules of daily accomplishment. "Nothing is more poignantly felt than contempt," he wrote in 1803. "It wounds; it galls; it lacerates; it destroys us."[47] William did not slip easily into the urban establishment but arrived with debt and anxiety to overcome.

Mary witnessed and worried. She claimed afterward to have seen William rarely in his years at First Church, and then with unhappy results because of her own "odd ways & disgust with society as it then was." But family correspondence suggests that brother and sister were often in touch, whether in Boston or on the larger circuit of family houses. Later she could answer Waldo's request for memories with probing judgment. "He went to [the] City believing he should disappoint society," Mary wrote, "—was out of health & alas for his clerical & domestic education, respected society too much & his whole being too little." Her argument with William was always fundamental and thoroughgoing. Bringing before him the standard of their forebears, she was urging a different rather than a lower ambition. "Notwithstanding all your pretensions to humility," he counterattacked, "you have in reality a plentiful share of family pride! Your relatives . . . must have a name in the world & must be called of men Rabbis and Fathers."[48] What she idealized was not simply fame, certainly not her own retirement from the world, but eloquence before it like their father's, proceeding from inner experience of God.

Their dispute was private, but on both sides it reflected the society around them. Current developments in religion and politics alike offered grounds of contention, and in her writings and exhortations to William the professedly reclusive Mary played a part. Contemporary Calvinism did not appeal either for herself or for her brother; instead, she urged excellence amidst the city's new liberal ministers. A week after his son Ralph Waldo was born in May 1803, William noted in his diary the ordination of William Ellery Channing at Federal Street Church. William asked Mary's opinion of this brilliant colleague and was surprised at the answer: "I said there was a cold vein in his face," she recalled. By 1803 William had achieved some seniority in the Boston clergy. After eulogizing Peter Thacher upon his sudden death a year earlier, he now greeted younger men—first Channing, then in 1805 Thacher's successor, Joseph Stevens Buckminster. William extended the right hand of fellowship at Buckminster's ordination but within a year was noting to Mary in a less collegial tone, "The celebrated Mr. Buckminster leaves for London next week." This most intellectual of colleagues, William's close collaborator in the Anthology Society, was winning a reputation that he quite transparently craved for himself. Mary's jaundiced memory of the man decades later still reflected her loyalty to William: "Alas, poor dear B.[uckminster], how didst thou fail in vanity I believe after returning from Europe the first time. . . . Mild & lowly—yet never able to touch (from what I've read) the deep recesses of the heart or to make one *think*."[49]

Of all the Boston clergy, Channing and Buckminster actually came closest to the theology and heart-piety that Mary sought for in her brother. Both won loyalty in her circle of intellectual women, Buckminster as the favorite when first ordained, then Channing because (in Van Schalkwyck's words) his eloquence proceeded from "an acquaintance with his own heart, and habitual intercourse with the Father of Light and Love." William remained unmentioned in these comparisons. Whatever capacity for sentiment he had once shown seems to have been banished in his resolution to serve public piety.[50]

William began editing the *Monthly Anthology*—and Mary submitting her letters as "Constance" to it—just in time for the first journalistic warfare between liberals and Calvinists. Brother and sister both, in varying degrees, had their say in print. In February 1805, when Harvard College chose Henry Ware as Hollis Professor of Divinity, Jedidiah Morse led the protest against this creation of an "Arminian College"; a month later, William joined the counterattack with a review of Morse's strictures on the Harvard appointment.[51] In that same issue Mary responded to William's earlier statement of hope for the *Anthology* by insisting on the need for Christian theology at its heart. Only Christ, she asserted, should serve as the model of human character, for only he conquered death:

> His body is nailed to a cross; . . . or, in the bold language of inspiration, *he is dead*; dead to a world of vanity, delusion, and sin. He passes, it is true, through courts and seminaries; but it is not in them he receives the rudiments of his education, or the form and complexion of his character. Strange as it may seem, he derives his birth and instructions from a world invisible and incorruptible. Thence he borrows his maxims of conduct, and there he is incorporated into the privileges of a being wholly spiritual, sublime, and immortal. In him we behold a hero.[52]

This portrait of Christ crucified in a world of sin might seem a direct contribution to Dr. Morse's cause, but Mary was speaking from a major position in liberal theology. The Christ of her portrait was divinely human—offering a heroic model to other humans, deriving instruction from God's "invisible and incorruptible" domain, but not himself a person of God. This Arian or anti-Trinitarian position characterized a good many leaders in the first generation of New England Unitarianism, including Channing. They derived it, as did Mary, largely from Clarke and Price. Mary refused to be called an Arminian, insisting that the human will was powerless to overcome sin without grace, but she eagerly embraced the title Arian.[53] In her seventies Mary would reread "Price on Morals" with surprise at finding there so many of her own first theological conclusions: her "old notion of the human mind," of a God inherent in the world but not one with it, and ("still greater wonder") her Arianism. "Never . . . read the book thro,' but always intending to," she added with disarming honesty.[54] Perhaps she had read only part of Price's treatise, but she had contributed both an excerpt from it and a portrait of the Arian Christ to the first months of the liberal church's newly public voice.

Mary claimed that William instead endorsed the Socinian position during his Boston years, believing in Christ only as a human teacher and not a savior at all. This doctrine is not obvious in his surviving sermons—it remained sufficiently radical that he may have kept it private. But she remembered her brother as "Priestlean altogether," and William's diary offers confirming evidence. There William both praised Joseph Priestley and recorded interest in his *History of the Corruptions of Christianity*, which argued that Jesus' humane teaching had been falsely hardened into a dogma of divinity. In Mary's view, these ideas had proved "fatal to [William's] young enthusiasm," for a Christianity without Christ's redemptive power had no center. If he had only left Priestley for Samuel Clarke and Locke for the "good sensible scotch school," and if he had not left Harvard for Boston, he "would have been a happier wiser man—somewhat resembling his ancestors who knew not the name of ambition—and his native elements expanded with patriotism & benevolence equal to his early aspirations."[55]

Her Almanack in these years dramatizes what an Arian Christ meant personally: not divinity but the means to it. She imagined relationship with Christ in physically immediate terms: "*Blood of Christ*. How I cling to that." But she wanted to receive Christ's power, not remain in supplication. "I need humility—that most firmly places me at my most revered Master's feet where I do most love—," she began one sentence; but then went on, "obedience raises me by his hand to walk on the waves with him." She dared envision a partnership with Christ that incorporated his heroic power: "Away with devout prayers, faith in a Mediator's responsibility—delight at tho't of death, & assurance of salvation because of the leading feature of Xianity. Nothing short of standing *Complete & perfect*—of imitating Jesus Christ in every part of his inimitable & sacred character shall henceforth be my object." Taking Christ as her model but not ultimate goal, she received atonement as a right to God's absolute presence, with all mediators left behind: "The first question I shall ask after drop[p]ing the flesh, if I behold any created being more immediately than my Father, *where is the throne*?"[56]

This vehemence and immediacy of relationship with the One God fitted wholly in neither liberal nor Calvinist thought in these years of their open rupture. She disliked the shift toward moral humanism that she saw in William. But the liberation of grace occupied Mary's thoughts much more than the technical nature of atonement, which increasingly became the ground for Calvinist theological argument. Frankly "bewildered" by the doctrine of imputation, which asserted Christ's suffering and death to be satisfaction of God's legal demand for justice, she concluded that the "paltry speculations of Philosophers & Divines" about God's means of grace signified nothing. But she never stopped pleading for God's intervention in her own life, her prayer as insistent as Jacob's wrestling with the angel, "Thou wilt thou must bless me! . . . I cannot let thee go without the grace to perform the part Thou assignest me."[57]

This direct use of Jacob's language, like her identification with Jesus walking the waves, exemplifies the intense subjectivity of her relation to the Bible. Leaving behind the individual text as proof of doctrine, she shared in the more "literary" use of scripture that Buckminster was embracing. "The collection of psalms," she wrote in 1806, "resembles the garden of Eden in its variety richness & magnificence. The citizen of the immortal Eden wanders from one luxuriant scene to another and [loses] himself in its beauties." Perhaps she had heard from Buckminster about Bishop Lowth's study of the Psalms and Prophets as sacred poetry, as well as about German scholar J. G. Michaelis's questioning of the New Testament canon. "I don't know what doubt means respecting the facts related in scriptures," she wrote the same year. "Were the bible fiction and I not shaken in the faith of God and his moral govt, I s[houl]d be happy & pious; after having been formed on the plan of the gospel rules I feel that while the first great Cause of beauty & holiness lives I shall be happy." Mary was responding to New England's earliest, liberal-sponsored discussions of higher biblical criticism by asserting through it an individual, intensely pietistic faith.[58]

The exercise of intuitive knowledge allowing this direct embrace of divinity—Mary's fusion of an impulse from New England's earlier pietism with a new language from the British poets and theologians—defined a position that her brother anathematized. Though William had published her defense of the imagination and her reading of nature's analogies as the harmless effusion of an "obscure female," he seems ever after to have honored her opinions with open warfare. William tried to suppress Mary's intellectual aspirations even as she continued writing as "Constance," not only by correcting errors but also by opposing her very search for higher knowledge. In the spring of 1805 William advised mother Phebe to discourage Mary from thirsting after the ancient languages and simply guide her to the Augustan poets readily available in the Manse's bookcase. A year later, with opposition perhaps having triggered new attacks by Mary, he broke into open expostulation. "I love you with all your faults," he began one letter, "yet these I do not love, and will not tolerate so long as there is any hope of your forsaking them." The faults were intellectual and stylistic as well as personal: illegible handwriting, worse spelling, censorious opinions, and "an obscure style of writing, consisting of bloated figures, far-fetched allusions, and turgid words." William protested that "plain christians" like himself attempted to be useful rather than to rise above mortality through the arrogant egotism of imagination:

> No man nor woman writes or talks well long, when the subject is self, dear self. . . . You must be sensible, that whenever from this quarter you have been reproved, they were wounds from the righteous, and you should have received them as an excellent oil, intended not to lacerate but to heal. . . . Do not henceforth accuse me wrongfully, nor misinterpret my actions, nor suffer your imagination, all fascinating and balloon like as it is, to carry you away from a correct judgement, whose voice, if you will but listen to it, you may constantly hear.[59]

Both defending his own wounded feelings and attacking in return, William still tried to play the impartial man of judgment with his sister. Mary seems to have been wholly unchastened by his critique: both her rapture at the eclipse and her biblical speculations, for instance, came later. But the game of "bagatelle" that (according to William) he and Mary were playing articulated a serious struggle to interpret the religious heritage that their father had left in the Revolution. Mary censured William's accommodation of the world as unworthy of their father's saving enthusiasm, upon which she was acting to maximize spiritual liberty. William believed that his position at First Parish, Boston, would begin to fulfill his father's unrealized goal of a new American order. Though their father had also sought to control liberty within hierarchies of order in town and family, including Mary's own resistance of "duty," the younger William saw the threat of disorder in much more fearsome and monolithic terms.

The difference between father and son was not just temperamental but central to their respective generations' situations. The younger William had come to Boston—a social world including President and Mrs. Adams—preaching institutional piety at a time when the French Revolution had "diffused death and manacles throughout all Europe." "Columbian warriors! Where are your swords?" he called out, as his father had to the Concord Minutemen; but now swords were drawn to preserve, not bring down, a system of rule. All that threatened order was by implication Jacobin to him and to the Federalist political society that he represented. By the Fourth of July in 1802, seventeen months after Jefferson's election as president, he already spoke of this order elegiacally. "Recall and prolong to your enraptured gaze the Age of Washington and of Adams," he urged his Boston audience. A whole vocabulary of negatives accompanied his conservative celebration: America was to have "no romantick notions," no "ferocious passions," no "garish projects of innovation" or "untried theories . . . learned in the closet." All these were the wild fancies of France, whose "twelve years of vicissitudes . . . defy the pen of description."[60]

In her anarchic individualism, full precisely of romantic notions, ferocious passions, and closet-hatched theories, Mary was at least a metaphoric Jacobin to William. Her writing of these years suppressed acknowledgment of public affairs, and his letters to her rarely mentioned politics. But the atmosphere of political antagonism was omnipresent around them, even breaking into open violence. One measure of it is the two Emersons' involvement with the Austin clan of Boston and Charlestown. Though a proprietor of William's Federalist-dominated First Church, Benjamin Austin stood high in the ranks of the state's Democratic party; and his second cousin William was the Charlestown lawyer of "talents, education and good social position" whom Waldo later identified as Mary's suitor.[61]

No trace of William Austin remains in family papers of these years. But in 1823 Mary, writing about earlier times, ended her recital of personal sacrifices with "what is dearest to woman the protection of a man of honor & talents, whose faith & politicks were not sound." Austin certainly fits that description. Already by 1805, the most likely year for their courtship, he must have expressed the radical Socinian opinions that reached print two years later in *The Human Character of Jesus Christ.* The year's current journalistic flap, however, concerned his book *Letters from London,* written to pillory the British while Austin studied law at Lincoln's Inn. Democrats loved the book, and Federalists—like William Emerson's friend John Gardiner in the *Anthology*—damned it. The next spring Austin waded into even deeper water by attacking Federalist Attorney General Simon Elliot in the press. Elliot's son James rode out to the Concord courthouse, where Austin was representing a client, to challenge him to a duel; Austin fought Elliot at a legal out-of-state site, was wounded, but survived to marry another woman in June.[62]

Sometime during 1805 and 1806, amidst the spiritual solitude of Mary's Almanack, the friendship with women in Concord and Newburyport, and the effort to sustain an identity as "Constance," Mary also met and declined this man of hotheaded Democratic opinion. Possibly she—who later would espouse "War" against all oppressors—shared his opinions in part. But such views still seemed unsound in the prevailing Federalist world that Mary's family and friends otherwise shared, and she sacrificed all political utterance, as well as "the protection of a man," turning inward and upward instead. Her vow of a single life may have come after real sacrifice.

William Emerson's involvement with the Austins also came in 1806, when an even more violent confrontation took place in the aftermath of separate, partisan festivities on the Fourth of July. Federalist lawyer Thomas Selfridge attacked Benjamin Austin's conduct of the affair, and another son sprang to defend his father's honor. Rather than inviting a duel, however, eighteen-year-old Harvard senior Charles Austin confronted Selfridge on State Street and beat him over the head with a heavy cane. Selfridge drew a pistol and shot his assailant pointblank. William Emerson had the difficult task of preaching at his young parishioner's funeral before a grieving family of unfriendly political persuasion and a congregation of three thousand.

Unlike the jury that acquitted Selfridge, William did not exonerate any parties in the dispute but lamented the murderous political atmosphere behind this needless death. "Folly hath been wrought," he preached. Drawing on a tradition of jeremiad much older than the year's political controversies, he pronounced the country ripening for judgment unless the people sought repentance: "I propose . . . that we bring hither the enemies of Christ, our habits of evil speaking, our inordinate ambition, our pride and malice, and slay them at his feet. . . . *In this frail, dying, guilty condition, cursed be our anger for it is fierce, and our wrath for it is cruel.*" In William's career of studied eloquence, this was perhaps his moment of most spontaneous feeling, at once identifying with and judging the city's wrongdoing. His evocation of Austin's disappointed expectations betrayed personal as well as political anxiety: "In the smoothest paths of fortune lurk the poisonous serpents of treachery; and when sailing before the fairest wind, with all our streamers spread, how often are we shipwrecked by the unforeseen and inevitable tempest."[63]

Pride, discord, and malice were ubiquitous in the careers and political intrigues of Federalist Boston. Society expected women to flee all overtly violent forms of discord but tempted men to be drawn in, even while condemning such behavior.

Four years after Mary and William suffered through the Austin family's crises, their own half brother Daniel Ripley would risk his life by challenging a Harvard classmate to duel over the trivial loss of a militia election. The code of honor and recrimination that fostered violence among youth lay just under the surface of adult politics as well, and increasingly William recoiled from it. With talk of war in the air, he wished he had been born among Quakers. "God preserve us, Mary, in this howling tempestuous world," he wrote at the end of 1807. "I have no heart for a happy new year, so black and portentous a cloud hangs over our country. One might almost as well be amidst the ruthless billows of the ocean, as to be overwhelmed by the floods of democracy." Mary, though personally in flight from society, may have had the more combative temperament of the two siblings, for at the same time William expressed his loathing of her "censures from the post office."[64] Men forced to struggle in the world did not expect further struggle with their sisters.

The Gates of Death

As the decade advanced, Mary rarely tasted the "new life" of freedom that she sought, but instead she balanced intellectual inquiry with the arduous female labor of nursing. By 1806 her sister Hannah, brother William, and nephew John Clarke were all battling without success against consumption. The following March Hannah died, with Mary and their friends in attendance; William visited during her last days, despite the eye and respiratory problems that signaled his own decline. A month later John succumbed as well. William and Ruth, having already borne the death of their firstborn Phebe in 1800, staggered under the grief of this loss. Such a rapid consumption, William wrote in despair of the science he loved, had allowed no time for the prescribed hot baths to provide a cure: "No state of no element on the surface of this miserable earth . . . could retain the connexion of this soul & body." Mary denied all grief. Called to Boston as she had just been to Newburyport, Mary entered the sickroom just fifty minutes before John's death. For her, as she stated briskly in her Almanack, "The loss of one whose constitution was like his was no subject of regret." Besides, John had died at seven "with more ideas of religion and more appearance of mind than many grown persons."[65] She habitually met the necessity of death by embracing it.

Over the next months, as William's letter lamented, the family's situation was further darkened by political storm clouds. That summer he and Ruth moved out of the old First Church parsonage, and while they occupied rented quarters, a grandly neoclassical church and parsonage rose on the site of the old house at Summer Street and Chauncy Place. But this sign of stature in an expanding Federal city seemed ill conceived, for by December 1807, Jefferson's embargo threatened a commercial standstill both in Boston and beyond. Now William faced direct animosity from a contingent of his church rather than the reconciliation held forth in his funeral sermon for Charles Austin. Whether bearing a grudge from 1806 or simply expressing political intransigence, Charles's father Benjamin penned an epigram that taunted William with financial overreaching:

> Farewell, Old Brick,—Old Brick, farewell:
> You bought your minister and sold your bell.[66]

Early in the new year, rumors of scandal added to the acrimony at First Church. Prominent parishioner Daniel Sargent confessed to William that a "natural daughter" of his youth, secretly supported and educated in Dorchester, had become a burden. The mother was dead, and as a pretty and intellectually precocious fourteen-year-old, the daughter was beginning to attract notice. What should he do? William proposed the Ripleys' Waterford home as the ideal solution, combining family charity with the oblivion of up-country wilderness. In later life Ann Sargent reconstructed the events of 1808: a relative mounted on an Arabian charger brought her in early February to William's waiting sleigh in Boston; William drove to meet his half brother Samuel Ripley, who completed the long journey to Waterford. Samuel, then a ministerial student of twenty-four, always remembered this "sorry business" and his sympathy for the trembling, tearful girl. Mary remembered the result at both ends of the journey: her childless sister and brother-in-law took in another child of Boston, now for the long term; and despite all efforts at secrecy William became the target of severe criticism by residents of Boston and Dorchester alike.[67] In his private and public projects, control was elusive.

Within weeks William was felled by a massive hemorrhage of the lungs while preparing for church and (in Buckminster's words) "brought down in an instant . . . to the very gates of death." Such bleeding was the sign of acute consumption, which he had apparently concealed before. Through the months of invalidity that followed, Mary stayed in Boston to help Ruth in sickroom and nursery. Debts accumulated. Of all the Boston ministers, only Channing visited, but Mary bristled at his "patronising and pastor like" air. In July William rose from bed to preach in the new church, choosing a text of reassurance: "My presence will go with thee, and I will give thee rest." Ruth saw ill omens instead: workmen left a long parlor mirror, a gift from the congregation, leaning against the front door of the parsonage, and when she and William entered "a grand crash was the result." Such signs must have seemed related to even worse realities. In these months of moving, illness, and division, it also became clear that the baby Robert Bulkeley, born just before John Clarke's death, was mentally retarded. He had seemed fine at birth, but now William declared, "This boy will never take care of himself."[68]

All crises had temporarily abated by the spring of 1809, at least enough that Mary's restlessness in the confines of Boston came again to the fore. Writing to Mary Van Schalkwyck White, Mary expressed appreciation for "the Bethlehem plan," which had lingered in their conversation through recent years. White, now wife, mother, and consumptive, was recommending to Mary the experiment in Moravian community that she could no longer consider herself. Mary felt "at loose ends in the world" but did not choose such a drastic move away from her family. Instead, that June she suddenly chose to visit her sisters in Waterford, and by October showed no signs of returning. William tried to resume the privilege of the previous year's crisis and define her domestic duty: "Come home, my good sister," he pleaded, "and help to alleviate the burdens of a minister of religion weighed down to the earth by a consciousness of incompetence to his awful function. . . . Come back, you wandering Christian. . . . My manor is still beautiful as Tirzah, and lacks nothing but the comely graces of a Moody to irradiate its walls."[69]

Mary was hardly wandering, either physically or mentally, only living with another sibling than William. Sister Rebecca, she reported back, was healthy but appeared "never for an hour to enjoy herself, . . . which is more than I can always account for from circumstances even the most adverse." The embargo had brought adversity in country as well as city, and Robert and Rebecca Haskins were suffering financially. Four years earlier, William had found Robert strong on credit and able to trade "swimmingly"; but from the start his store for city products in South Waterford had competed with another at the center of town, and now the farmers of Oxford County possessed no money for Boston imports from any vendor. Nor was Robert succeeding at buying and selling farm lots carved from the original proprietor's grant. Between 1804 and 1811 he acquired twelve such parcels of land, selling one to his brother Ralph and another to William. Acting as an agent for absentee investors in Massachusetts, however, won Robert no friends among Maine's independent farmers, who often appropriated the tillage and wood on such lots as their own. By 1809 this trade had dwindled, and he was becoming a small-scale farmer like his neighbors. Mary still felt determined to stay with the Haskinses, asking for her bed from the Boston house to supplement the meager two at Rebecca's.[70] If rural poverty did not make her sister happy, Mary chose it willingly over the strained affluence of William's "Tirzah."

Waterford spelled the highest freedom that Mary had known, and she stayed through the whole of 1810. With no desperate illnesses to care for, Mary could dine by herself when she wanted, explore the nearby hills, and read the "few books" on hand at the two family houses. At least jokingly, she even considered becoming the village schoolmistress. A new companion was the Ripleys' graceful, informally adopted young stepdaughter, "Ann Brewer," still using the assumed name that her Boston father Daniel Sargent had insisted upon. At sixteen Ann was a reader, thinker, and instructor to other children in the Ripleys' foster family. Looking back later, after decades in "the holy ground of friendship," Mary remembered that they had struck a mutual chord from their first conversation.[71]

She also enjoyed the time and space to renew her theological quest on ground physically and intellectually removed from William. As his epithet "wandering Christian" suggested, she was not content with Boston liberalism but sought to unite it with New Light intensity in her own way. He once questioned her attachment to the Baptists even before the flight to Maine; apparently she was experimenting in evangelical worship. Waterford's opportunities lay mainly on that side: Baptists and Methodists abounded, none of whom willingly paid taxes to support Lincoln Ripley's church. And wherever Mary chose to attend church, necessity or inclination steered her to books not talked about in liberal Boston. So, on a Sabbath near the end of 1810, she set down first thoughts upon reading Jonathan Edwards's *Freedom of the Will*, knowingly taking it up as a text from the Calvinist past to advance her deepest knowledge. "If there is any possible or established connection between means & ends, asking and finding," she wrote as though in invocation, "I'll ask that the dark cloud of ignorance be removed in a manner consistent with my condition & my hopes as a believer in a divine relation & agency."[72]

Edwards directly showed Mary a relation between means and ends. "In short," she recorded, "it seems that the will of a being with a moral capasity is nothing more than an instrument of the divine govt of the most misterious kind in bringing to issue the most stupendous schemes, according to Edwards' system." For her the paradox of personal agency and divine plan was so emotionally ingrained that she could not quite see his need for systematic argument. "For myself, I never remember to have met with that difficulty in the scriptures in a way to perplex. When the Eternal declares his sovereignty and electing conduct, I see and rejoice in the security of such a Governor." Yet her experience confirmed his argument; because there was such a divine Governor, she wrote, she could feel "beyond the possibility of doubt, *an agent*—one on whom he will pour the riches of his grace."[73]

Mary's desire for agency was writ large in all her life gestures, including the rebellion of staying in Maine and reading Edwards. Yet early "orphanship," female acculturation, and emotional fragility combined to require dependence on a divine parent and plan of redemption to achieve the capacity for self-affirmation. Her particular position between William's Arminianism and the extremes of Hopkinsianism came from her deepest needs, as well as from her genuine grasp of Edwards. Arguing for greater freedom than Edwards allowed, she insisted that humans need not be entirely self-determining to take action. But she still found freedom where Edwards found his:

> A glance at Edwards today, and the moral virtue of atonement appeared before me under his influence. . . . Ah wonderful & joyous condition of any created being whose destiny refers him to his Creator in the most absolute and unconditional dependence—that Creator the *first Cause* in the universe of every effect—the Alpha & Omega—the Origin of wisdom & goodness—how simple—how natural the reliance—the *branch* flourishes no longer than adhering to the *vine*.[74]

Mary's reading of Edwards stands in sharp contrast to William's intellectual project of these same months. Attempting to recover health in 1809 and 1810, William found time to advance the history of First Church that he had been planning for years. Combining anti-Jacobin and antienthusiastic principles in it, he portrayed two centuries of New England history as the repeated confrontation between forces of reason and disorder. Charles Chauncy was the hero of his eighteenth-century chapters. William barely mentioned Chauncy's theological antagonist Edwards but instead portrayed the fanatics led by George Whitefield and James Davenport, who had excited the people with "strong appeals to their imaginations and senses." In this company, William admitted, stood his own ancestors of York, Malden, and Concord. William declared that Chauncy had bravely opposed such disorders in *Seasonable Thoughts*, recommending the tract as a worthy indictment of "modern enthusiasts" as well.[75]

Like Chauncy himself, moreover, William began his history with New England's archetypal error of "imaginations and senses," the Antinomian controversy of the seventeenth century. Here the leader was a woman, the "female fanatick" Anne Hutchinson. Narrating at length the judicial process that finally condemned her, William named Peter Bulkeley among the moderators—this time without acknowledging his descent from the man. He quoted at length the magisterial words of Governor Winthrop, that by promoting her own opinions and maintaining meetings at her house Hutchinson had done a thing neither suitable to women nor "comely in the sight of God." He referred to Hutchinson's agile scriptural defenses but found them to contain "too much pertness and pride." All in all, William looked at Hutchinson as if from the bench. But he combined a Puritan patriarch's judgmentalism with tenderer sentiments, wondering at the intolerance of an age willing to forgo compassion. "We are ready to wonder," he commented, "that the private opinions of a woman, and even the parlor lectures, she was pleased to hold at her house, should excite so strongly the apprehensions of the most learned and powerful men in the state." William felt tolerant of opinions even by an "infatuated female," as long as she held no political power and stayed at home.[76]

Even as he wrote this history, William was crossing swords with the enthusiastic woman in his own family. He himself had limited her opinions to the home rather than encouraging her desire for public voice. Now she was choosing another home than his and from it once more lambasting him. Mary wrote from Waterford:

> You appear in fine health and spirits, and as usual are pleased to profess a devotion to the present world, and an ignorance of the future . . . Were you, my brother, placed in the Athens of the world . . . your predilection for this life would be less unaccountable. But when one considers your birth, your education which was nessecarily unfortunate, your profession, your lot in a Country struggling rather for means of subsistence than glory, in a crisis of the whole world too, when the Elijahs of the Chh are watching, in holy jealousy, for their alters, and looking for some amelioration of human misery, your fondness for the present is wonderfull![77]

Like her New Light ancestors, Mary opposed Antinomianism but still saw feeling as a means to knowledge and character. "You *will* talk of coolness and calmness in religion—," she expostulated. "Let Angels and burning Seraphs lie calm—let man struggle and agonize for truth, while any thing remains to be done or known relating to his salvation." In her view, even the possibility of delusion should not inhibit souls seeking self-improvement, for even "the darkest hallucinations of a religious imajanation are less pitiable than any species of atheism." Most of all, William needed such invigoration. Mary wrote pointedly:

> Ah, my dear brother, could [you] live with yourself—far away from those vain and ambitious objects w'h constantly press on the senses. . . . Could you commune with nature sublime and tranquil, contemplate dead men's bones—and take leave of the earth, hastening to revolutions—that light of genius, which your sultry air and diet have not yet extinguished, would rekindle, and aspire to the skies.[78]

William's demand for public order made Mary's intuitional faith seem a source of chaos, but to Mary intuition would alleviate chaos. In it she found the quality which her pseudonym claimed, "Constance."

Early in 1811 Mary returned to Massachusetts again to care for the sick. Nursing Sarah Ripley in Concord, she was summoned to William's side for the last time. He suspected that death was imminent, wondering how his wife would subsist and his children be educated. Once in Boston she despaired of him, too, especially if the old consumption had returned. But she joined in the contention of doctors over how to attempt a cure, urging "chocolate and milk" to strengthen his wasting form instead of the "beef tea, mutton and oysters" that others prescribed. William laughed at her cure, though it must have been the less nauseating alternative; every morning, he explained, his stomach felt "as tumultuous as the troubled sea." "Till he can journey, we can form no decided opinion," Mary wrote to Mary Van Schalkwyck White.[79] On the wisdom of traveling for health apparently she and the doctors agreed.

By mid-April they took William's tumultuous stomach directly to the tumultuous sea, brother and sister boarding a Portland-bound sloop that he described as "crowded with hunks, kettles, fish, women, and crying children." Mary wrote again to Mary Van Schalkwyck White, herself now bedridden, thinking only of William's approaching death. "How much better . . . than to outlive his mind, his exertions, his friends! Should it not be the prayer of every Christian that they may not survive any of these, but especially his *moral improvement*?" From long experience Mary knew how to welcome the inevitable. But now, about to lose her "protector" and sparring partner, she also made a rare admission of mortal sorrow. "An unaccountable heaviness weighs down my spirit,—pray for me that a visitation so painful and admonishing may be improved."[80]

Mary and William struggled back to Boston shortly before his death on May 12. Buckminster delivered the funeral sermon; the Ancient and Honorable Artillery Company, whose "piety and arms" had first brought William to Boston, led a procession of more than fifty coaches from Chauncy Place to King's Chapel burying ground. The man who described himself as living for the public and so "content to be buried wherever the publick shall please to dictate" received a splendid tribute. William died a man of science as well as ceremony. The results of postmortem examination, finding the cause of his death to be stomach cancer rather than consumption, were fully reported as a footnote in the printed edition of his funeral sermon: "The lower orifice of the stomach was almost entirely closed by a schirrhous tumor, or hard swelling, which on the inside was ulcerated. So completely was the passage of the pylorus obliterated, that a drop of water could hardly be pressed through it from the stomach, which was full."[81] The founder of Boston's Society for the Study of Natural Philosophy would have found satisfaction in such clinical precision.

Mary surely attended the funeral rituals, but she never alluded to any aspect of them. Instead, she always kept May 12 as a day for privately recalling the brother whom she had known—his ardor and "happy love of . . . doing justice to the merit of others," as well as his gloomy last years and "corrupted views of the gospel." She chose not to emphasize the mutual recriminations of their letters, instead recalling to Waldo more reconciling conversations during last days together. To both brother and sister transformation by grace had seemed a necessity, "not like the fanatic's—or antinomian's corruption." Both asked, "And where is the mystery—whence came the beauty & worth of the excited mind? And in higher wants why not richer gifts?" William the rationalist and Mary the enthusiast could come together in their "higher want" for immortality. "Yes I love to think of his future," she reflected, "of the vast variety spirits pass."[82]

Soon after William's death came a second closing in Mary's life with the death of Mary Van Schalkwyck White. Through the weeks of nursing William, Mary also kept track of her friend by mail, recommending air and sunshine as the best cure for consumption. But unlike William's gaunt appearance, Mary White's grace and fortitude amidst illness made the case seem less desperate than it was. Her husband Daniel stayed in Boston representing Federalist principles in the state senate, and Mary Emerson also postponed visiting. At the end of May, fire ravaged Newburyport, but the woman who had survived epidemic and insurrection declined to be taken from her sickbed unless the conflagration came within one house. The next morning Daniel arrived frantic from Boston to find his wife serene and unmoved. A cousin declared her already belonging to another world.[83]

The same language of spiritual transformation permeated the private and public eulogies about Mary Van Schalkwyck White at her death a month later. Ann Bromfield kept a journal of her last hours and closing words. The *Portfolio* of Philadelphia described her as a woman whose writing was inspired by the muse of piety, whose life had become a symbol of "purged sanctity." "Her eyes, beaming with that hallowed splendour which sometimes irradiates them before they are to close forever, seemed fixed on the smiles of her Saviour, and her soul bending at the footstool of her God. One would almost have thought her shadowy form that 'incorruptible body which is destined to be the soul's last covering.' "[84] Such a eulogy defines the radiant death that Mary Emerson, along with a generation of female contemporaries, had consciously aspired to. But instead, she faced the demands of ongoing life, without the friend and the brother who had played partner and opponent to her first phase as a writer.

6

Aunt Mary

> I doubt if the interior & spiritual history of New England could be truelier told than through the exhibition of family history such as this, the picture of this group of M.M.E. and the boys, mainly Charles.
>
> Ralph Waldo Emerson (*JMN* 7:446)

Before William Emerson died, his children came and stood by age around the bed for a last farewell: William the eldest at ten; Ralph Waldo, not quite eight; Edward Bliss, six; Robert Bulkeley, four; Charles Chauncy, two and a half. Behind the children stood Ruth, holding newborn Mary Caroline. Telling of the scene later to Charles, Mary saw in it a repetition of painful family history: "When my father left me I was within 6 months of the age you were at the loss of yours." Mary thought that Charles seemed "conscious of the scene" as father William gazed with particular regret upon him.[1] At least her own eye rested on this child, so like herself in vulnerability and precocious awareness.

With the two deaths of 1811, when Mary was thirty-six, a phase of her life closed. Never again would she admit aspiring to either intellectual mastery or spiritual perfection on earth, and defeated hope became a steady tone in her writing. She also rebounded to new objects of love, however, and William's children presented immediate needs. Ruth had agreed with William that the children should be kept together—perhaps they recalled Mary's separation and sought to avoid forcing any child to repeat it. But seeing no other means, Ruth and Mary mobilized relatives into supporting roles much as a previous generation had done. By mid-June they sent Bulkeley to live temporarily with the Waterford Ripleys; at four, as Ruth wrote apprehensively to Phebe, he was "utterly untutored" and destined for sorrow. Phebe confirmed that he never sat still, though he found delight in a pair of lambs from Lincoln. Meanwhile, the Concord Ripleys kept Edward, Waldo, and William by turns at the Manse that summer. "Ruthy sends her duty to you," wrote Mary to Ezra in July, "and thinks it may have a very good effect on Wm if you should be surprised with the unwelcome intelligence that he is not so good a schollar as he might be." Master Bigelow of Boston Latin had found young William to rank in only the second quarter of his class but thought him capable of rising to the first. "We also regret," Mary added, "that Wm has a notion of being a merchant—and we aim to direct his taste in a manner that he shall not feel his self will stimulated."[2]

Mary's pronoun "we" tells of a genuine parental partnership with Ruth—one formed to perpetuate Emersonian mind and spirit in the rising generation even against the attractions of business that Ruth's own family represented. But the letter to Ezra also reveals that Mary, less than two months after William's death, felt far from resigned to spending her future only in Boston with Ruth. Instead, Mary suggested, she might help at the Manse while Sarah Ripley accompanied Robert Haskins to Waterford; or she herself might return to Maine, though not particularly invited. Over the coming years Mary would give William and Ruth's children, as Elizabeth Peabody later wrote, "not merely the mental but the physical energies of the meridian of her life."[3] She did so, however, while sustaining a well-established habit of family visits and personal solitude. She had not acquiesced in William's desire to fix her residence with him while he lived, nor would she let his death call a halt to her travels.

Furthermore, she sought to direct young people more widely than just in Ruth's family. As friendship with women had made her own intellectual life possible, so now she offered herself as a mentor to aspiring girls. At seventeen, Louisa was the favorite among Hannah Farnham's six daughters, all of whom Mary had guided by letter and visit since their mother's death four years earlier. She also now took on the spiritual direction of Ann Brewer, that disowned daughter of Boston whose confidences had so moved her in Waterford. "It will always give me pleasure to remember you," Mary wrote in 1811, "because I hope you will make religion the chief business of your life."[4]

The same improving hopefulness took Mary within the year to visit another First Parish family, home of eighteen-year-old prodigy Sarah Alden Bradford. Sarah wrote to a friend at the time, "I have commenced an acquaintance with a Miss Emerson, a sister of our minister. . . . She was so kind as to make the first advances by calling on me, and from her I expect to derive the greatest advantages, she appears extremely interested in the religious improvement of the young." Thirty years later, Sarah's memory took a more biting tone: Mary "sought me out in my garret without any introduction," she recalled, "and though received at first with sufficient coldness, did not give up till she had enchained me entirely in her magic circle." At the time, however, Sarah sought to protect her place in that circle. Writing to Mary in Newburyport, Sarah half-jokingly confessed her jealousy of Louisa Farnham's prior claim: "I do not see how it is possible for Aunt Mary's young friends to love each other very cordially."[5] Mary often violated the rules of decorum surrounding both family and friendship, and she probably enjoyed wielding power in this limited realm. But she could also enlist passionate loyalty.

The Doctress

Mary's interest in raising children developed long before 1811. She had originally gone to Newburyport when sister Hannah first gave birth in 1791, and she lived with the Haskins family through the childhood of Rebecca's last daughter, born in 1822. That made, in all, thirty-five nieces and nephews in her immediate family—ten Farnhams, thirteen Haskinses, eight Emersons, and four adopted Ripleys. If she attended the actual birth of these children, not a single family letter says so; she may possibly have avoided this way of assisting the "ill-fated sex." But the prospect of fostering growth, even from infancy, kindled her most visionary language and feeling. "I trust," she wrote to William and Ruth in 1798 at the birth of their short-lived daughter Phebe, "we shall early discover in her those *languid* 'looks that deeply pierce the soul, where with the light of tho'tfull reason mixed, shines lively fancy and the feeling heart.' "[6]

Discovering signs of grace in children had long been among a Puritan woman's highest tasks. But Mary brought to it all her proto-Romantic assumptions about the innate power of the human mind: the words she applied to baby Phebe were from her beloved poem *The Seasons.* Two years after the prediction about Phebe, William took his second-born to Malden especially to "show John to the doctress." Mary was an expert—a woman doctor of both medicine and philosophy—in judging and nurturing children. "She gave high counsels," Waldo declared many years later in concluding his lecture "Amita." "It was the privilege of certain boys to have this immeasurably high standard indicated to their childhood; a blessing which nothing else in education could supply." Waldo unjustly narrowed her influence to a band of *boys* but truly described its quality. She had different expectations of the two sexes, in concession to the gender roles of her culture, but directed "high counsels" to both. "I expected a brother," she wrote to Mary Van Schalkwyck White's second baby girl, "but am agreeably disappointed, as I seem to think you will be more connected with me. There will be more interesting things to put into your little mind, than I could into your brother's."[7]

Though in the matter of gender Mary felt less connected to William and Ruth's six sons, she also had powerful reasons to make them a special province of her life. As an aunt, even before William's death, she had begun forming them toward a public greatness inaccessible to her personally. She always did so after her own light. No less demanding of John Clarke's mind and body than was William or Ruth, she also urged the value of active play. "He does his Mother honor by his manners," she reported from Waterford in 1806,

> but his bodily habits, to an observer, are defective. . . . He cuts a poor figure in walking & worse at running; and as to any thing so brave as swinging, he will not be courted, nor induced by my ridicule or example. But such habits belong to a Father. Any nursery Maid can teach a child to read but never will form to independance. Now how fine a plan, after the beams of the morning have extinguished the epictitan lamp of your husband, for him to expose

> himself & the boys to the cold air before their bodies are relaxed by artificial heat?[8]

Neither William nor Ruth was apparently so involved with their children, preferring austere directives to personal demonstrations. Nor were they so devoted as Mary to encouraging independence. As William instructed John to make his mother be strict with him, so Ruth wrote to Phebe that she must be watchful of his "desire to evade prompt obedience." A woman who spent her adolescence as the Emersons' ward remembered Ruth as a firm enforcer of household law, though "when it was necessary to correct the children, it was not done in anger." Mary hardly approved all of a child's natural instincts, as her resistance to young William's "self will" in the matter of a business career shows. But in her fostering of spiritual growth toward heaven she preferred nurture to correction. "I saw some little children the other day whose father was in the habit of singing and playing on the viol," she told Ruth in 1805, "and I *never* saw children whose minds were attuned to so much harmony."[9]

Rather than working through two intermediaries, advising Ruth what William might do with his boys, Mary became her nephews' female stepfather after William died. Ruth cast her in that role as much as Mary chose it. Confessing herself still "desolated and afflicted" in the third month of widowhood, Ruth sought for help that—despite a mother and sisters near at hand—only Mary could give. "You know not how important you are to my existence," she wrote that August when Mary had retreated to Concord. "This desolate habitation is rendered indescribably more desolate by your absence." Continuing the argument for Mary's residence in Boston that William had previously conducted, Ruth now claimed that Mary was William's substitute, possessing "traits of character that bear so strong a resemblance to my dear departed husband as render her peculiarly dear to me."[10]

Mary sought to protect her independence and fulfill family duty at once. She remained unimpressed by the extreme grief displayed by Ruth, whose life had seen mercies "throw'd with a liberal hand." Instead of sharing a household, she began by the summer of 1812 to find alternative ways of caring for her nephews. Choosing again to live in Concord, she took three-and-a-half-year-old Charles with her. "He knows no sorrow," she wrote to nephew William, "but when I am under the necessity of leaving him." Mary's wit with children—as well as her moral intensity and ability in the kitchen—are revealed in a letter to Charles himself soon after:

> My own dear boy,
>
> I send you a little cake, as a remembrance of our sweet friendship. And I would have it answer a nobler purpose. Let the milk, flour and eggs of which it's constituent parts are composed represent the solid virtues of your character, The sugar it's sweetness—the flavor of its fruit and the fragrance of it's spices be emblamatical of the ornaments and graces of your soul. But especially let the white encrustation be a type that the lovely veil of modesty will be a

cover even to your virtues. It is this which inhances the value of goodness itself, and renders it useful and dignified.

If Mother will permit you to go to school the first letter you write with your own hand will be rewarded by

MME.[11]

Though Ruth sent sweets to absent children, too—and the confection described here sounds very much like the "Plumb Cake" in her recipe book—Mary knew how to moralize from cake as well as make it. She could also forge bonds of friendship with the young, associating its pleasure with literacy through the promise of letter-writing. Thanking eleven-year-old William for a recent message, she hoped it would "commence a correspondence which may accompany us thro' life." Already favoring the middle name of nine-year-old Ralph, she urged, "Go on, my dear Waldo, and exert every nerve to gain the favor of God and the good will of the worthy part of society will follow. I sometimes antisapate the time when you shall be at man's estate, the Protector of your beloved Mother and Sister, with emotions of hope and pleasure. How delightfull the thought that your virtues shall honor the memory of your Father!"[12]

Later Waldo would write that he could not remember "any sentence or sentiment" of his father's repeated by mother or aunt.[13] In her letters Mary made no effort to expunge William's memory; early and late, she honored more than castigated him. But her words of inspiration were her own, not William's. She wanted this nephew to exert every nerve, not just to be bright; to find the goodwill of society, but only through the favor of God. These were themes that she had argued with her brother directly only two years before. By standing in his place she was already diverting the family heritage from his version to her own.

Ruth rose from her mourning to meet the family's need in more immediate ways, by sorting out financial disarray. Like his father before him, William had died intestate, but now the assessors listed household goods of a style and expense unthinkable at Concord's Revolutionary Manse. Mahogany furniture and China tea sets are testament to the imported luxury available from Boston's wharves, a telescope and 452 books to William's expensive intellectual life (valued together at a third of his $1,926 estate), the absence of animals and stored foods to the family's habit of buying from city merchants for their needs. Furthermore, William died with debts of $2,458, well above the estate's whole value and nearly twice his annual salary. Ruth suffered no immediate wants upon his death, but she faced an acute longer-range need. She could live in the elegant, three-year-old Chauncy Place parsonage only until a new minister arrived; and though First Parish generously continued William's full salary of $25 a week until 1812, it then settled with her for a promise of $125 a quarter over seven more years.[14]

Ruth's demands on Mary had as much to do with income as with the direct care of children. She first sold a portion of William's books and the land in Waterford. Next, while still enjoying the Chauncy Place house rent-free, she resorted to a time-honored means of income for widows and took in boarders.

With the rents, as well as her stipend from the church, she could begin to pay debts. Household labor was also doubled, however, and multiple servants an impossible luxury. So Mary joined her that winter and tried with difficulty to maintain children and boarders at once. In her Almanack Mary expressed appreciation of the quiet evening "after a day of crying babes—wasting perplexity," and a few days later added, " 'Another day is done' of activity so intense that every nerve throbs, yet the gloom of these little painfull labours could not be shook off."[15]

Mary's letters and Almanack do not in fact tell of unremitting toil. There was still time to attend a foreign mission lecture, hear Channing's moving sermon, or describe the solemn scene of Buckminster's funeral to Ann Brewer. She could share an occasional tea with Hannah Sawyer Lee, her elegant Newburyport friend, and most of all could grow in rapport with "modest learned Sarah [Bradford]." But the kind of mental and spiritual concentration that Mary desired was impossible amidst the combined stresses of labor and gentility. She appealed to Sarah as "soother of my dark life," asking her to brighten a path seeming almost unsupportable, and in her Almanack wrote that former hopes of improvement had lapsed, her mind weaker than it had been seven years before. "How strange too that after two years of much in every view to be lamented—somewhat to wonder at—more to loathe—defeated pursuit of knowledge &c. now to return to labour—to service of cares instead of ease & reading & sentiment & hope—ah rich is the provision of God."[16] Her sentence labors toward affirmation of God's plan but really tells of distress.

A week later, with or without Ruth's blessing, Mary had bolted to Waterford. She delighted in the snow, the midwinter air, even more "the scenery w'h opens on the soul in eternity." Such withdrawal was not complete. Mary's letters, full of inquiry and information about people, make this clear as the meditations of her Almanack do not. In Waterford, Bulkeley spent two nights with her and parted tearfully. Rebecca Haskins acted "more reserved than ever" toward her. From Boston, news of half brother Daniel Ripley's illness aroused concern, and Ruth's sister Betsy, Mary supposed, was "as much engaged in *publick* schemes of benefiting the world as ever." None of the Haskins sisters seems to have helped much with either the boardinghouse or the Emerson children. Mary in no way dismissed Ruth, but affirmed "how closely we have been united by the dead and by the living—how much we have conversed on the greatest of all subjects, the harmony and kindness so unbroken."[17]

Most of all, she continued her special vocation with the young. Charles went with her to Maine, and she made him a companion by day and night, supervising his precocious reading and feeling the tension of valuing both freedom and obedience. "I am always fearfull of too many restriction[s]," she had written to Ruth the previous year, "because I want to press those which are infinitely important, therefore in wishing him to fear no one, or rather, be under no one's govt but mine, he incroaches faster on me than I wish." Meanwhile, she expressed concern for Mary Caroline's temper tantrums, warning of the dire consequences "if she acquires base and selfish habits" but sanctioning Ruth's use of the rod only to "ingraft other and nobler fears." Having family in both Waterford and Boston offered an opportunity to exchange children in both directions. "Your manner will benefit her," Mary wrote of the Haskinses' daughter Rebecca, about to join Ruth's household for a term of school. "Never do I think was a journey and diffirent scenes more nessecary. . . . Let her be cheerfull and her mind expand to new objects. But of all virtues make her frank, open and ingenuously confident. Torpor and timidity, those foes to all that is great and pious, she is naturally inclined to, *there*, may all your instructions aim."[18] On balance Mary was more fearful of timidity than temper, in girls as well as boys.

Ruth wanted more from Mary than exhortation by letter. In late spring came a challenge to the first boarding arrangement: the new minister, bachelor John Abbot, would arrive within weeks, giving Ruth the options of providing him board or moving out. Ruth wanted the former, with Mary again as her assistant. Mary preferred the latter even for Ruth herself, arguing the merit of laying aside "every anxiety for yourself and your children to appear genteel" and finding a humbler house elsewhere. But Mary was adamant about her own choice: "You know it was what I always expected on my own account more than on Becca's to reside here chiefly."[19]

"I am astonished," Ruth wrote back, "to hear you speak so calmly of your plan of staying at Waterford." Unlike Phebe Bliss or Phebe Emerson in a simpler time and place, Ruth worried about the propriety of taking in a single man "without a female friend in the house." But Mary continued to resist. "Indeed my dear Ruthy," she responded, "I think it probable you love me better than any of my Sisters but I cannot think of returning, and beg you would not compliment me with the idea of my adding to your happiness, for I am very incredulous on that score with any of my friends."[20]

By the summer of 1813, Mary was purchasing a home in Waterford. Though Ruth would not consent to leaving the city, their mutual siblings Becca and Robert had become country people and, whether or not they would admit it, needed help. Accounts of their situation are thin. Mary wrote that Robert was suffering "outward troubles" and had fallen into the hands of a creditor; and Robert's usual supporter, his brother Ralph, wished only to be disentangled. In 1807, at the height of his dealing in land, Robert had sold Ralph a house and farm alongside Bear Pond in South Waterford, then rented it back as a place to live. Mary lived there with the Haskinses in 1809, telling of the farm's midsummer beauty and "luxuries of fruit and flowers in profusion." But now Ralph and his brother Thomas—who were expanding from rum to cotton and wool in the family's city workshop—wished to reclaim their capital from Robert. "Trading business in Boston," Ralph would comment at the end of his career, "is done in the most keen manner—so much so that a man must learn to live on air, & almost be a rogue from necessity, to hold his own or get ahead there."[21] The struggle gave him no space to subsidize a failing brother.

Mary, on the other hand, wanted to invest one thousand dollars, thereby pursuing both her own interest and Robert's freedom from creditors. She had used Thomas Haskins as a business agent since 1807, investing the money from her Malden property in plots of Massachusetts real estate that apparently yielded more money. Father Ripley disparaged all such ventures, advising her to buy bank stock. "She is wholly unqualified to deal in mortgages and land," he wrote to Ruth. But Mary paid no attention; however otherworldly her professions, she had been negotiating questions of property since youth, and she felt due respect for "money, that valuable commodity which so often provides wealth and ease." By July she had finalized the purchase from Ralph Haskins of the house and 150-acre farm, her major earthly estate and her sister and brother-in-law's as well. Wanting Robert to save face, she allowed the property to remain his in name. Even Rebecca and her children did not hear of the deal that they had struck, and Mary declared herself a boarder in their house.[22]

She called the farm "Elm Vale" and always thereafter datelined letters from Waterford with that title. From her front door, Mary could look out from the valley to lofty heights. Across a meadow dotted with elm trees and enclosing the village graveyard, Bear Pond reflected the sky's changing light and the granite cliffs of the adjacent mountain, while at a greater distance gentle hills rolled fifty miles southeast toward Portland. Standing by the pond, Mary could turn her eye to the more steeply ascending land westward, where thirty miles away Mount Washington reigned over the White Mountains. "Here," as Elizabeth Hoar said, "she read and wrote, and enjoyed poetic and spiritual raptures, in comparative seclusion from living intellectual companionship."[23]

Here also was a landscape to be shared with Charles, who remained with her through the rest of 1813. "Do you remember anything of this place?" she asked a decade later. "The grave yard (now one of the the most populous establishments) on the east, and the brook on the west, were the bounds of your freedom?" She taught him the substantial freedom that she deemed possible for a five-year-old child—and also her own passion for nature. "This morning was such as you love—," she continued. "I rode far on horseback. The mist rose from the waters & mingled with the blue haze of the mountains, and formed that soft atmosphere w'h invelopes the traveller in a new & complete solitude." Charles cherished his early childhood experience as well. "One thing I could not help remarking," he wrote to Mary in 1831, "how much the mind ran back to its earliest consciousness. . . . I thought of you—& my first walks under the blue Heaven & in the green woods—I thought of Waterford & all my Tunic days."[24]

Raising the Boys

Though Mary always preferred to live at Elm Vale, she had returned to Massachusetts by the time of taking ownership and did not return for another three years. The Emersons in Boston and the Ripleys in Concord vied for her time, and she again accommodated and avoided them by turns. She still wondered why Ruth would send for "so conceited a body as your friend and sister Moody often proves. . . . You can have no more of a cat than her skin, you know." By admitting to a feline, egocentric character she could win a modest space around herself. "I was never patient with the faults of the good," she later declared of her relation to Ruth.[25]

But Ruth and her children also pulled at Mary's genuine affection, and whether absent or present she provided one line in their supporting network of family and friends. Early in 1814 she arrived from Maine with both Charles and Bulkeley, so reuniting the family for the first time since William's death. Soon the band shrank again. Ruth had repeatedly written to Phebe in Waterford asking for Bulkeley back, wanting him not to forget his own family, but now that he was home she realized that the confinement of a city yard could not compare with the Ripleys' farm for this child of impetuous energy. By midsummer he returned to Waterford on one of the Haskins brothers' regular runs between city and country, and Ann Brewer took up the difficult task of schooling him. Meanwhile three-year-old Mary Caroline was suddenly swept away by the same kind of early childhood illness that had taken her sister twelve years before. Mary commented that Sarah Bradford was "the only Watcher we had & the only *friend* who remained for the following *nights*. No consideration would have tempted one of the Miss Haskins to hazard the danger." But all the Emersons, Haskinses, and Ripleys grieved that now no daughter would comfort Ruth's declining years, and the brothers felt sharp loss again. Decades later tears sprang to eldest brother William's eyes at the mention of Mary Caroline, and Waldo recalled her as "a fair little thing. Oh! Eyelashes, eyelashes!"[26]

By now Sarah Bradford visited the Boston house often enough to make an additional partner with Ruth and Mary in raising the boys, and as one biographer of Ralph Waldo Emerson wrote, his youth was presided over by "three Fates" or "maternal Parcae." Though Sarah's friendship with Mary had begun in 1811, she grew closer to all the Emersons upon Mary's return from Maine. As Mary reported to Ann Brewer, "She very often comes in from Charlestown (where they have lately removed to a most elegant Seat), sleeps with me, spends part of the eveg with Mrs E. & children, animates the boys to study, and becomes herself so animated that I hear her voice up chamber, and can hardly believe it she, who among the fashionable is silent and awkward." Sarah had received the education in languages and mathematics that Mary had not, and her gifts could animate the boys in many ways. Mary wrote to Ruth from Concord that five-year-old Charles had drawn a monument on his slate inscribed to "S. A. Bradford, the female Hero of Science."[27]

Mary herself was the female hero of religion amidst the Emersons' reduced circumstances. In a series of rented boardinghouses, amidst the political stress of the War of 1812, she exerted her most direct influence over the boys' early years. "Give us peace in our boarders," she wrote, intending to pray against the threatened British invasion of Boston. But when shown the misspelling she said "it would do as it was." During 1814 and 1815 she and Ruth moved four times, accepting the Ripleys' hospitality in Concord during the worst of the hostilities but returning to a borrowed house on Beacon Street. "We are surrounded by a Neighbourhood of the highest Class—," Mary wrote to Ann, "Otis, Dexter, Sulivan, Emery, Gore, Phillips, and Eliot; but if we should live here always we s[d] have no intercourse, never see them. . . . Ladies do not like to visit where are Boarders." Preferring the equality of heaven to the status-consciousness of Boston, Mary instead gazed out the window at the Granary Burial Ground. "You will not wonder that I dwell more on our Neighbours with whom we certainly are connected and with whom we shall one day mingle."[28]

These lines suggest the odd humor with which, according to Waldo, Mary played with the family's everyday incidents. So do they resonate with her visionary zeal. "In my childhood," Waldo remembered, "Aunt Mary wrote the prayers which first my brother William & when he went to college I read aloud morning & evening at the family devotions, & they still sound in my ear with their prophetic & apocalyptic ejaculations." Later Waldo recorded in his notebooks a few of the prayers that Mary wrote for the boys to recite: "Whether poverty, sickness, loss of senses, or disappointment awaits us in thy holy ordinations, *thy will be done*! Only foresake us not; and save us from meaness and pride and deceit which Thou abhorest and society despiseth." Her echoing of the Lord's Prayer would provide an ongoing litany in their adult imaginations. But the apocalyptic tone can better be heard in her letters and Almanack of 1814, just as William left for college, Waldo became the eldest, and Boston was directly threatened. "But so dark and misterious is the condition of man, ever since the apostacy, that [one] war raging, and one Country distroyed, is but an epitome of the whole earth," she wrote to sister Phebe that September. "How should the friends of Zion give themselves to prayer for the coming of His kingdom, whose reign will be peace & righteousness." To Sarah she actually imagined the earth's final moment: "It is past midnight— . . . Oh each echo of [the bell] warns us, as with an Angel's voice, to prepare for that period when the Herald of Omnipotence shall say *time shall be no more*! . . . Oh how grand are these events when viewed as contrould—nay, ordained by Him who rideth on the tempest of war and terror and saith peace to a contending world."[29]

Such visions of an end time were new in Mary's writing during these years of political and religious excitement. Earlier she had anticipated inward ascent to heavenly realms, but not public tempest. "Ah how I loathe my turtle shell," Mary now wrote, "at moments when I peep out & find the world in arms—the world of theology, science & literature in arms." She welcomed living in Boston because she wanted to know "what is doing." There was a wide stirring as New England's religious establishment rose to meet the crisis. Her Almanack tells of diverse occasions for prayer—a fast day on account of war, a Baptist prayer meeting, the gathering of a new female society. The pulpit orator who kindled her most ardent response was Buckminster's young successor at Brattle Street, Edward Everett. From him, as Mary wrote to Ann that September, "I have heard sermons of late so powerfull that all the vissisitudes of life lost their power—religion alone triumphed, and the glory of the resurrection morning appeared to open in visions of blessedness on the eye of faith." Later Mary reminded Charles that he had admired the book of Revelation upon first reading it at five, and that Waldo had shared this love. Charles was five and Waldo eleven in 1814, as amidst alarms of war she taught her nephews the love of St. John's "prophetic voice w'h embraces the consummation of all the nations." When bells and guns announced peace early in 1815, Mary saw a direct answer to prayer and an omen of such consummation.[30]

In this setting she also passed on the family tales derived from Aunt Ruth in Malden and Grandmother Phebe in Concord. As Waldo reflected later on the depth of "ancestral religion" bestowed by Mary, he thought first of tales about the moment of death, when one man called out to open the door for the passing angel, and another with speech failing held up his hand to witness Christ's presence. Mary's own death longing did not cease because she saw omens of the world's change: "Oh how I long," she wrote, "to put on my shroud to cuddle down in my coffin & be covered up." But she did not urge nephews to settle into their coffins. The pressure for transformation that drew her personally to death translated into lessons of active virtue for young, especially male, protégés. She told of ancestors departing this earth but also celebrated Samuel Moody's commanding holiness and profuse charity. Moody may have been the subject when Sarah Bradford once arrived to find the boys in high exaltation—they had given the last bread to a poor person and were staving off hunger by hearing Aunt Mary's stories of heroism.[31] If Mary's "genealogical extracts" to her brother William had castigated his efforts to build public order, now she could inspire a younger audience in a more enthusiastic time.

Nor were all the heroes ancestral. After evening hymns and prayers, they took turns reading Rollin's *Ancient History*, and the month of his eleventh birthday Waldo declared in verses to Sarah his love of the "Athens bravery" in those stories. He always remembered the sentences of Shakespeare, Milton, and Antoninus, he later said, as quoted by Mary Moody Emerson. Little matter that Mary had read Milton in a coverless copy, seized moments for Shakespeare amidst the domestic routine of Malden, and borrowed Antoninus from the Concord Charitable Library. Waldo, learning the ancient languages at Boston Latin School as Mary had not, nonetheless attributed knowledge of all books to his aunt. When Waldo told Elizabeth Peabody that he could spare Greece and Rome better than Mary's influence, he was speaking more than hyperbolically. Mary had been the source of a "little body of literature, divinity, & personal biography" that intertwined and competed with Greek and Roman wisdom. She directly compared the heroes of ancient and modern books with those of family memory—Cicero against William of Concord, the "spirit of derision" in Byron's *Don Juan* against "the alleged earnest & religious spirit of the puritans & especially the austere saints of Concord & Malden."[32]

Waldo later wrote of his boyhood with Mary in glowing terms, and she referred to him as her "child of old." But none of her writing from those years singled Waldo out among the brothers, except when she teased him at twelve for "tilting the chair & overhawling somthing at every sentence" during dinner. The few letters from nephew to aunt barely hint at the relationship he would see retrospectively. In 1813, while she remained in Waterford, he recited the schedule of a day, told how affected cousin Rebecca Haskins was at the news of her baby brother's death, and declared himself her "most dutiful Nephew." Three years later he could share learning with her—telling of Massillon's character from the encyclopedia—and gently mock her taste for poetic sublimity. "My dear Aunt," he began, "the sun has not yet illuminated the arch of Heaven nor begun to display his brilliant beams—this I suppose is the time to feel inspired and this the time I shall improve to write to you."[33] He was both responding to her desire for inspired thoughts and resisting it.

More frequently he shared witticism at the expense of Moody-esque inspiration with his closest companion, brother Edward: "By my date I see & by my feelings I know that warm weather is leaving us fast; and the cold frosts of Autumn are preparing the way for the dreary reign of Winter!!! Ah cold winter!" "Sentiment" was Mary's watchword for both the method and style of rhapsodic intuition, a style the younger generation tended to mock. Writing to Mary, Edward later invoked this "word which brings up your image and at which your nephews ignorantly smiled." By 1817 he, Waldo, and William were regularly exchanging letters "in the 'sentimental' line," gushing over the weather and season in a way that clearly parodied their aunt. Waldo hinted at the tension over gender buried within their jokes when he declared himself "*delighted* (a girl's word)" with Spenser's *Faerie Queene*.[34] Directed so authoritatively by bluestockings, he and his brothers had to keep bluestocking style at arm's length.

Among the trio of older brothers, neither William nor Edward seems to have felt the affinity with Mary's inspirations that was growing beneath Waldo's joking exterior. These two were hardly alike—William square, commonsensical, and perhaps most in competition with Aunt Mary for the honor of replacing his father at the family's helm; Edward outspoken and skeptical, with energy quickening in his gray eyes and red cheeks. But neither took to the ways of inward centering that she advocated, and both in her view were too worldly. Just as she had resisted William's preference for business, Mary warned of his "lack of possibility" and admitted ruefully when he left for Harvard that they both would be saved many quarrels. She was also repressive rather than indulgent toward Edward. Wanting to rule by persuading, she met only opposition and so would tell him, "If you contradict me, I can't reason with you." As Sarah recalled Edward's childhood, he was "always on tiptoe to speak, holding on to his chair to keep from interrupting, and at every pause springing up to say his say, but they kept him ironed out with a hot iron." Edward got along best with Mary when sick, as he frequently was by early adolescence. Then she would care for him "like old times," returning to the loving ways she had with little children.[35]

A decade later Mary reminded Waldo sardonically of the "pretty" theory that had formed him: "It seemed best to tell children how good they were." But Waldo told the fuller truth when he remembered how Mary responded to a neighbor's praise of the children's careful education: "My good friend, they were born to be educated." Her point was to emphasize their inborn gifts, including their goodness—such children could easily be educated. But she also saw education as destiny, giftedness as inviting and needing improvement. As Waldo wrote, she set an "immeasurably high standard." Having lost a father and a brother, having often met defeat in her own ambitions, she found little patience for boys who did not improve such privilege and potential. Often she censured angrily and wounded their feelings, though apologizing afterward. Mary wanted to befriend the young; Sarah animated rather than scolded the boys to study; and Ruth taught the precept "In things of moment, on thyself depend."[36] But there was more control than permission in this household, a divergence from father William's methods but certainly no reversal of his goals.

Bulkeley's limitations were especially poignant in such a family. This was not a severely retarded child—Aunt Phebe had set him to reading lessons on first arrival in Waterford at four, and the highest possible literacy continued to be every elder's goal in his education. Bulkeley was a "comely boy," Waldo later remembered; and he seems also to have possessed charm and verbal gifts. The first summer in Maine he played at "preaching and having a pulpit." He both participated in this churchly family and played his own games with its materials. "I lately married myself to a Miss Julie Sargent Parsons just my age!" Phebe wrote for him. "I asked to be her husband for the wedding cake"—and after a bow and curtsy ate the cake. But by 1815 Ruth was urging Phebe to have him do useful work on the Ripleys' farm rather than learn reading, and a year later Phebe admitted with sorrow her lack of progress in either education or discipline. That summer, though Ruth had wished "retirement" for him and Mary tried to negotiate another place in Waterford, he came back to the Boston household and began reciting lessons with Charles to Mary.[37]

Between the lines of the women's letters is an admission that by the age of nine Bulkeley's uncontrolled activity had become threatening, maybe even violent: whatever mental retardation he suffered was increasingly accompanied by mental disorder, not open to cure by any known approach to child rearing. Perhaps Bulkeley had inherited his condition genetically from the Moodies and Emersons. There is shadowy evidence that two members of the Haskins family suffered from mental problems as well: Ruth referred in her 1795 journal to an unidentified sister's "being disordered in mind," and Waldo's later reference to a "Dr. Haskins" at the Charlestown asylum probably referred to his mother's eldest brother, John.[38] The offspring of William and Ruth Haskins Emerson may have had a double predisposition toward such trouble. Now Ruth and Mary met it willingly but with few resources. One letter by young Bulkeley himself survives, dated in 1820, when he had progressed at the age of thirteen to studying at Boston Latin. His message to brother Edward was blotched and labored, the spelling imprecise, but only by high Emersonian standards would it have been considered illiterate. "I got to the first punick war in my viri Romae," he reported, desperately trying to keep up with the Latin language and heroism of his ingenious brothers.[39]

Mary found Bulkeley a trial, confessing that she loved him "notwithstanding his excentricities." She had too little patience for such a boy. Yet her single surviving letter to him is both witty and respectful of its reader's understanding, a parable based on her observation in 1818 while riding to Uncle Ripley's in Waterford on the old horse, whose slow pace provided time for beholding the beauties around her. The grasshoppers, she noted, were encroaching on the grain and filling the air with empty noise, just like "the more unhappy insects of the human kind." But the modest yellow butterfly, hanging on the purple thistle "without intruding on any prohibited land," provided a contrasting emblem of beauty and innocence.[40] The moral—that he should be content with his lot in life—was graceful and understated, genuinely expressing both Mary's conviction and Bulkeley's circumstance.

For Charles she reserved her most personal attention and unqualified love. The bond of their year in Waterford proved a potent magic in the family's ongoing mythology. None of the three eldest boys either visited there in childhood or enjoyed her undivided companionship; as an adult Edward wrote to Mary from Puerto Rico, still hoping to "see the 'Vale' and the mountains of Waterford and all that is blooming in nature & society thereabouts." There may also have been isolation in Charles's boyhood. Almost four years younger than Edward, he remained somewhat apart from the older trio; Waldo looked back on him as "Aunt Mary's boy, a pale little boy dressed in bottle green"—probably an odd garb of her own construction. Whether rambling in the Waterford woods or visiting Sarah on a cool morning in Charlestown, Mary took her boy along. She gave and received perhaps the most unalloyed affection she ever knew. "My joy and companion," she called him in letters; and he signed in return, "you and I forever," from "your affectionate and only son."[41]

Through Charles, Mary hoped to improve upon the past, to be a better aunt than Ruth had been to her, even to care for the unnurtured child within herself. She had struck out for independence amidst the abandonment of the older generation; with her nephew she wanted to give that liberty as a gift without the grievous experience. She spoke of these things with Sarah, who attributed her own fear of offending to early education. "Think you, want of candour or independance will ever be a defect in your boy's character?" Sarah asked Mary. "Can we look for the same results from systems so opposite as one of almost perfect freedom, and one where fear and deference to authority are long the governing principles of action?"[42]

Mary's plan for Charles was to "unfold his powers" by exposure to conversation, books, and new scenes. Having taught the child to read in Waterford, she kept him out of school after returning to Boston and directed his education herself. As she wrote to Ruth, "I do flatter myself that in no long time, wishes would always answer in the room of commands. And that almost every day, tho' it is never marked with any effort like the Systematisers, yet leaves him, with some little impression of humility, kindness & disinterestedness." Watching one of the "Systematisers," her second cousin Joseph, stuffing his young sons with history and geography some years later, she countered with stories of Charles's "unlearned childhood." She led Charles to books and often had him memorize long passages from the Bible and English classics. But, as Mary put it, she never "catechised," instead asking him every evening to "recollect what you read thro' the day or fix some valued subject on your mind."[43]

Sarah Bradford joined in the project of teaching Charles, adding to his freedom the rigor that Mary had always resisted. When he was five or six, the opening of his conversational powers seemed a sufficient goal. "We vied with each other in telling stories," Sarah recounted after he spent the night in Charlestown; "the little budget of learning and fancy was all emptied, nor were its contents so inconsiderable as Aunt would sometimes represent them." But two years later she concluded that he needed to become "initiated into the mysteries of hic, haec, hoc," Latin mysteries that no child would pursue without "emulation or fear[,] the moving springs of a public school." Mary cheerfully agreed, soon looking for certificates of his excellence in Latin and all other subjects.[44] Compared with the experience of her other nephews, Charles's freedom from system to the age of eight had been a significant accomplishment.

Mary may have realized that Charles by now needed independence from her more than through her. At least her planned return to Vale conflicted with the possibility of staying with her boy, since Ruth refused to send him again to Maine. Mary left Boston in the fall of 1817, and Ruth sent a reproachful account of how Charles's eyes glistened with tears at hearing her letter: "Whenever he feels any want he is for sending immediately to you—and thinks you will at once gratify all his wishes." But Mary did not therefore return, instead urging Charles not to cry and to continue their evening reviews of learning on his own. She knew how to deny the importance of her nephews when Ruth used them as a way of casting blame. "I know that however well we love children," Mary wrote when taking leave from Boston, "—yet how often inadequate thier society is to lessen care, and disapate the weariness of life's lone journey."[45]

This hard-hearted declaration expressed genuine inner loneliness, but it also took into account the approaching maturity of her nephews. That fall, Mary first wrote to Waldo as a "son of Harvard," her letter stammering in pretended awe at his majesty. By two years later Edward was ready to enter, while William had graduated and begun teaching school in Kennebunk to help cover his brothers' expenses. Only Charles remained to send and Bulkeley somehow to settle in life. Meanwhile, Mary was closing out her care of the older generation as well. In 1815 Samuel Waite had died in Malden. "I . . . laid his remains in the room where I was so often blest in my book," she wrote in her Almanack. "Could I have done better? Oh yes. . . . I did not do all about the afflicted Aunt I fear." Aunt Rebecca, despite her mental condition, had married Waite after sister Ruth died in 1808 and now remained the sole surviving Emerson in Malden. Mary sought to find help for her until she died a year later. At the same time, Mary regularly expected the death of mother Phebe in Concord, devoting weeks of every year to her care. Phebe laughed at the "philosophical survey" Mary was writing and thought her idea of sending Aunt Rebecca to Waterford insane, but at least this mother and daughter seem finally to have carried on real conversation.[46] Meanwhile Mary, having given her youth to old people and her meridian to children, was ready to continue journeying.

Protégées

New intellectual life had arisen amidst the grief and work of these years. By owning Elm Vale, even when not residing there physically, Mary located herself amidst the delight and revelation of nature. She came alive to politics as a theater for God's plan, balancing quietism with zeal for millennial change. And in a third respect her world was also changing. A French woman writer, Germaine de Staël, had emerged publicly—in political defiance of Napoleon—to celebrate Europe's Romantic revolution in literature and philosophy; from 1814 to the end of the decade, Mary kept de Staël's *Germany* and *The Influence of Literature upon Society* as close to her reading table as a life of shuttling among family houses allowed.

Mary's copies of both books survive among those cherished and handed on to friends, though hardly any detailed notes on either remain. One lengthy Almanack passage about *The Influence of Literature* shows Mary both drawn to de Staël's distinction among national literatures and resistant to it as an exclusive universal theory. As even Mary's briefer comments suggest, de Staël allowed her to revalue the intuitions that she and her bluestocking friends had taken as their province a decade before. "What do you think Madame De Stale means," Mary asked Sarah, "by saying no Genius has risen much above his times?" Reflecting on devotion as an instrument of God's redemptive plan, she concluded with de Staël, " 'Enthusiasm is God within us' the weak." De Staël spoke of "enthusiasm" as an authoritative knowledge embraced by Germany's philosophers, not just the religious transport that Mary had grown up affirming or even the sensibility embraced by Mary Van Schalkwyck. Likewise, the "Sentiment" that Mary espoused to her nephews in these years was not mere sentimentalism but what de Staël defined as "the primitive fact of mind" linking Plato and Kant.[47]

Major texts of European Romanticism, with their call for a new subjectivity in literature and philosophy, were coming into the purview of American readers, and Mary's long-standing Romantic mentality quickened anew. "At times," she wrote in 1815, "a humble flower creates thoughts too deep for tears to use the high language of W[ordsworth]." If she had read Wordsworth's *Lyrical Ballads* a decade earlier, by now she was incorporating the vision of glory and resignation from his "Immortality Ode" directly into her thoughts. She had probably already read as well his poem and manifesto of 1814, *The Excursion*, seeing in it a beauty and grandeur even beyond what she had known in *Night Thoughts*. Wordsworth's poem especially defined the loneliness and grandeur of Vale to her, perhaps even echoing in the name of her farm. "Oh that man [Wordsworth] reads well here," she wrote from her favorite terrain in later years. "I always think he had such a mount & lake in view as mine, when he described the peasant." The setting for Wordsworth's Solitary in *The Excursion* was "a little lowly vale . . . uplifted high / Among the mountains," with "a liquid pool that glittered in the sun, / And one bare dwelling." But even more, the Wanderer's opening speech in book four, which Mary recalled in old age, gave language to her devotion in this place:

How beautiful this dome of sky;
And the vast hills, in fluctuation fixed
At thy command, how awful! . . .
My lips, that may forget thee in the crowd,
Cannot forget thee here; where thou has built,
For thy own glory, in the wilderness![48]

By the decade's end, Mary could without further explanation name "the sublime Wordsworth" as her particular treasure. She made no breakthrough of personal vocation, became neither social critic nor poet-priest, as her favorite themes began to move toward recognition in literary America. Driven by a "mania for the pen,"[49] she still exercised it in the private literary forms of letter and diary—and through these the shaping of others' vocations.

Mary's first protégées amidst the decade's ferment of Romanticism were not her nephews, whose ages ranged from thirteen down to six in 1814, but the young women Ann Brewer and Sarah Bradford. Ann and Sarah had each in some sense been adopted by the extended Emerson-Ripley family, but neither generally used the title "Aunt Mary." At least in Ann's letters to her adoptive mother Phebe (those to Mary have been lost), she always named her respected senior friend "Miss Emerson." Sarah quickly stepped beyond such formality to the salutation "My dear Mary." For both, Mary was a mentor with twenty years' seniority and a formidably confrontational style of address, but they enjoyed very different relationships with her. Mary found the alter ego of her ambitions in Sarah, of her inhibitions in Ann. She took Sarah's intellectual life as a given, even a personal resource, while trying to bring the younger woman to share her faith, whereas she took Ann's faith as a given and tried to perfect it, while warning her off from intellectual life. She asked Sarah's view of de Staël and urged her to read *Corinne*, even while finding de Staël's fictional heroine "not sufficient to herself." But after recommending de Staël to Ann in 1814 she wrote again: "I mentioned a book called 'Germany,' but it is two [dollars] and not nessecary to your real improvement. I found it a different thing from what I first expected."[50] She felt no certainty that this European "Sentiment" encouraged faith rather than skepticism.

Eventually Mary would call Ann her "poet bro't up in the pure mountain air," but during the younger woman's adolescence in Waterford she offered no clear encouragement to seek either nature or poetry. "Where abouts in the journey of life, moral, intellectual & sublime art thou?" Mary asked the eighteen-year-old in 1812. "Does the rapidity of the planets which carry about your body mark the rapid growth of your mind[?] . . . Are your faculties concentered in the great & infinite subject of moral perfection?" She urged her own highest goal—one that she now felt unequal to—yet narrowed the field so as to exclude all other aspiration. When Ann sent a letter full of high-flown language, Mary (recalling none of her own early efforts) criticized its trifling. When Ann disparaged father Ripley's sectarian opponents in Waterford, Mary urged humility. Quite disingenuously, Mary claimed not to be personally inclined toward "metaphisical solutions nor even meditations"; describing Sarah Bradford's classical languages, she expressed contempt for mere acquisition of learning compared with the virtue of service. Ann hungered for knowledge, but Mary declared that its "sybil leaves" were "never destined to be unrolled to you or me."[51]

The relatively conventional female piety that Mary professed to Ann proved to be ground for warm friendship and prolific letter writing. Mary urged her to write with heart and put "the dear Waterford . . . into miniature," and in turn she sent some of her own most newsy letters about the family in Boston.[52] Whenever Ann expressed the pain of her fatherless, nameless state, Mary wrote back with acute sympathy. But the affinity between her own "orphanship" and Ann's was precisely why she encouraged humility; condemning her own pride as sinful resistance to the mysterious ways of Providence, she allowed no resistance in Ann.

As a result, for years Mary protected the patriarchal conspiracy of silence about Ann's origins. When Ann proposed attending a Boston school in 1816, Mary relayed Ruth's opinion that personal acknowledgment would "bring an implication . . . on the memory of her deceased husband." On occasion during her stays in Boston, Mary even saw Ann's father, Daniel Sargent, still a member of First Church. She met him and his legitimate daughter, Maria, at Louisa Farnham's wedding, describing the mysterious half sister to Ann as a "fair flower" robbed of her freshness by the thick atmosphere of society. "I longed to speake to him of another person," Mary concluded, "—but did not." Nor did she urge her friend to reveal her identity or spurn the hated, rootless name "Ann Brewer." When Ann objected, Mary advised the following explanation: "The name I bear is not my Fathers—I am not ashamed of his—but I have no right to publish the errors of his youthfull days of which he has repented. That illegitimate children should suffer some inconveniences in this life is the law of society, and a duty society owes to good morals. Were there none, what confusion and guilt would multiply!"[53] She countenanced no rebellion against the "law of society" protecting fathers at the expense of daughters.

When Ann resisted at least half of Mary's advice, however, Mary characteristically accepted the result and held fast to her friendship. In 1820 Leander Gage, the young Waterford doctor whom Ann had agreed to marry, traveled to Boston and introduced himself to Daniel Sargent; then Ann wrote informing her father that she planned to be married under her original name. The father offered no resistance, she followed her plan, and Mary soon was sending letters to "Mrs. Ann S. Gage." Mary approved heartily of the marriage—Gage was her own friend and physician—but offered characteristic advice to the new wife: "Beware, my young friend, how you go to keeping house on this ball of dust so as to lay up treasure in Heaven. However we theorise contemptuously of earth, it gets dominion & the grandure of the soul lies beneath rubbish. Pardon the caution."[54]

By the time she married, Ann had also found her way to a few terms of higher education. "Go on and the God of Ruth and of all the interesting Travellers on the face of this wide & lonesome world be with you and give you success," Mary offered in blessing to this plan. Starting in 1816, Ann attended two boarding schools in Maine, then in 1819 spent a term in Byfield, Massachusetts, at the newly founded girls' school of Mary's second cousin Joseph Emerson. To Ann's taste, all of these schools were evangelical and restrictive. Joseph had once believed in teaching women all the branches of science and philosophy, but the early death of his student-wife had convinced him to educate women instead "for usefulness in their appropriate sphere." As Ann wrote home from Byfield, he offered her "no end of suggestions" and objected when she did not comply. Mary enjoyed Joseph's company, writing that she was "almost a Catholic" when conversing with him on religious practice; the old pietism still lingered in her. Ann preferred Mary's visits from Boston as a break from Joseph's suggestions.[55]

A less humble, more rhapsodic message must have been audible in Mary's conversation, because despite herself she inculcated Romanticism in this protégée. Amidst Ann's surviving papers are several pieces of prose and verse datelined from Byfield, with the further notation "not submitted for inspection." At least by 1819 she had begun writing for her own pleasure, within Joseph Emerson's walls but not for his eyes. As she went home to Waterford and married, she associated her personal life with Wordsworth by naming the Gage house "Rydal Mount" after the poet's home in the Lake District. A son would later describe Ann as an "early admirer of Wordsworth," primarily through the influence of Mary Moody Emerson. By the time of Ann's marriage, Mary eased her cautionary warnings and found equal friendship. "You will please see to Germany—it is my darling," Mary later requested when absent from Waterford.[56] She had long since given up her worries about the influence of de Staël.

The modest literary vocation toward which Ann struggled, however, did not compare with Mary's high expectation for Sarah. Describing the latter protégée to the former, she warmed to these prospects even as she simultaneously discouraged imitation: "She is gaining in eclat. Society begins to find that we shall have an Elizabeth Smith." A recent edition of this British woman's writing had offered a model of knowledge in science, languages, and literature to readers of the younger generation, sustaining in a new decade the bluestocking tradition that Constance and Cornelia had earlier sought to imitate.[57]

At twenty Sarah appeared not only a potential Elizabeth Smith but also a fulfillment of Mary's prophecy that a woman's knowledge would adorn the temple of natural history. Sarah had been studying botany since the year she first met Mary, and in 1813, while the older friend enjoyed nature firsthand in Waterford, the younger reported by letter on a Boston lecture series about Linnaeus's study of plants. "What a world of wonders the vegetable creation unfolds to the enquiring eye!" Sarah exclaimed, going on to defend science for its illustration of divine wisdom. She also found aesthetic delight in nature's processes: "Some [seeds] confined in an elastic cone, when ripe burst their prison, and are propelled abroad with amazing force; others borne as it were in a light balloon cut the liquid air, or skim the surface of the wave." Five-year-old Charles called Sarah the "Female Hero of Science," but Mary herself addressed Sarah by such half-serious hyperboles as "scientific Oracle of Altitude" and "lady Mind."[58] Sarah was fulfilling an agenda that Mary yearned for herself.

Still Sarah's description of the botany lectures would have offered little relief to Mary's concerns about the younger woman's faith. Though Sarah sincerely sought out deistic wisdom in plant life, she had also been asking how Mary could care for a person "without the pale of Christianity." Sarah was at heart an empiricist and skeptic, disinclined either to biblical revelation or to discovering ideal realms beyond nature. Mary refused to accept her resistance as final, arguing that she could not be "so cold—so indifferent to religion." The intuition of divine presence and Christian grace appeared beyond doubt to Mary. Sarah tried to explain:

> Here I conceive lie the great obstacles to my reception of your views in religion, a dread of enthusiasm, of the mind's becoming enslaved to a system perhaps erroneous, and forever against the light of truth. What Hydras to an imagination that has been taught to consider speculative truth as the result of laborious investigation, that has ever been referred to the exercise of Christian affections, and the performance of Christian duties, for the evidences of an internal principle of religion.[59]

Mary the Arian-Christian pietist and Sarah the moralist and scientific investigator belonged at opposite ends of the Boston liberal community. In fundamental ways Sarah stood closer intellectually to her old minister, William Emerson, than to his sister Mary.

What brought the two women together was a mutual passion for philosophy and the pleasure of conversation about it, with their differences serving as grist to the intellectual mill as much as a barrier between them. "You will enjoy Butler's analogy with me," wrote Sarah about one of Mary's favorite old texts, but after summarizing its argument for the continuation of a "living principle" beyond death, she declared the actual witnessing of death a grievous challenge to belief in immortality. Such a turn on Butler's argument must have proved difficult to Mary, whose faith in eternal life was bedrock belief. But Mary could always learn from Sarah, and the older woman asked for outlines of anything that the younger had been studying: "Write me more. Ever you read Dante? Why is it that his infernal reigions are so much more interesting than his celestial? . . . But oh do write a portrait of *Edwards on will* and especially give me *Stewart* in short hand." If Sarah spent time on Edwards, Mary would have agreed with few of her conclusions. Sarah's summary of Dugald Stewart interested more, because she had already hinted that he offered a refutation of Locke on the origin of knowledge."[60] Stewart was himself a Lockean, leader of the Scottish Common Sense school; but if he was amending Locke's theory of knowledge by attributing more power to the human mind—and if her empiricist friend Sarah concurred with this development—Mary certainly wanted to hear.

Sarah shared Mary's decade of mounting Romanticism primarily as an antagonist and critic. She read de Staël's *Germany* for Kantian method rather than enthusiasm and never mentioned Wordsworth. The sublime largely eluded her. Mary felt frustration at this resistance but claimed her own vision against it the more vehemently, as she had against brother William's effort to contain her. Now, though, the hierarchy of authority was less clear and the dialogue one of uneasy equality—Mary enjoying the stature of age and faith, Sarah the confidence of youth and learning.

One weapon in Sarah's arsenal was humor, as she gave up apologizing for their difference and turned to mockery of "sentiment" as "the district within our enclosure as daughters of mother Eve." The boys who made similar jokes may have learned from her, but Sarah's satires were much more pointed than theirs. After a page of effusion about Mary's "magic influence" on the tedious day, she broke off, "This is the veriest raw material for epistle weaving." Though she genuinely valued Mary, she could also dismiss feminine excess. "The fair enthusiast finds a 'sacred fane in every grove,' a sentiment starts up from behind every bush, . . . and she believes there is in the nature of things a real analogy between morning and youth, sunshine and prosperity, clouds and disappointment." At last Sarah turned the satire directly on Mary's melancholic nature worship. "Why can't you be disinterested enough, after you have exhaled the fragrance of autumnal wild flowers to press some of them for me, Tucker's holy dying will be just the book to entomb withering beauty."[61]

Even as this letter deflated Mary, however, Mary's energetic fancy continued to influence its free flow of associations. "George stands waiting with his Homer," Sarah wrote, "Betsey teasing to know how the meat is to be dissected, the south wind blowing paper and books in every direction but 'cacoethes scribendi' I keep on." Her Latin phrase was common currency for the "writer's itch" that, as Mary and Sarah both knew, was seizing many an otherwise sane woman. Sarah argued persistently against Mary on an intellectual level but enjoyed her friend's soaring words and feelings. And if she drew absurd pictures of enthusiasm, she laughed equally at her own earth-bound science. Sarah's best portrait of both Mary the Romantic and herself the empirical botanist was written declining a visit to Waterford in the summer of 1818:

> I wish I were with you but I dare say you do not, nothing tends more directly to diminish the effect of the sublime than a companion of a certain grovelling cast. In the midst of a grove, the tall pines on every side bowing their heads with reverential whispers, mediatrix between the world of matter and world of spirits, priestess in great Nature's temple, 'at once the head, the heart, the tongue of all,' up springs fancy on triumphant wing forgetting a certain tie viz gravitation, now should a tall black figure, in stooping down to pick some dirty stone or claim kindred with some humble fungus, chance to twitch the string[,] woe to the *companion* if not the *toadstool.*[62]

In no surviving written text did Mary ever claim to be a "mediatrix" or "priestess" of nature, just its humble beholder as she looked for heaven. But spiritual *afflatus*—like the Romantic message to Ann Brewer—seems to have escaped confinement in her direct manner with Sarah.

Though Sarah turned away from enthusiasm, moreover, she persistently called Mary's effect on her "romantic." The word referred not to visions of nature or spirit but to Mary's sheer personal power. "I was bantered a little at tea about violent romantic atachments," Sarah wrote to Mary soon after their reunion in 1814. "My mother considers [our friendship] a delusion innocent as to its object, rather dangerous as to its effects, making me unsteady as she terms it. I too have sometimes believed it a phantom of imagination." Mrs. Bradford seems to have considered her daughter's intense friendship with an older woman threatening not to morality but to reason. Mary's response the same spring, however, implied that their friendship was being noticed as socially unconventional as well. "As to our walk to M[alden] it is a little curious that we may write within sight of each other, & visit ever so often, yet not fall under the wofull imputation of *romantic*, unless we inhale the pure air of the wide atmosphere." The conventions of nineteenth-century women's friendship allowed for professions of love, sharing of beds, and copious exchange of visits and letters; so would they have supported both women's belief that friendship united them "more fervidly to the Source of all Good." But walking independently through the open countryside—Mary's favorite setting for talk—disrupted the domestic routine out of which such friendships ordinarily grew. She and Sarah felt and displayed a dangerous freedom. "Dreamt of escaping with you last night from company through a back door," Sarah wrote a few years later.[63]

Sarah found freedom in Mary, but also a fearful and imprisoning strength. Charging in later life that she had been magically "enchained" by this friendship, Sarah called Mary's "power over the mind of her young people . . . almost despotic." A similar language of bondage had a less sinister cast in the early letters, and Mary used it as well as Sarah. "You are 'the Spring to me'— . . . And I at times query whether I should so fondly attach myself?" Mary wrote near the beginning of their friendship. Sarah answered, "You have entwined yourself about my heart with magic threads." Mary admitted feeling pulled away from herself in a way that she never had in previous friendships. "I told [brother Samuel Ripley]," she wrote from Vale in 1818, "I was alive, eat & slept without S. A. B.—that in truth I was glad to find myself capable of an individual existence, after so long merging myself and all that I know."[64]

The degree and quality of erotic "romance" implied in this charged language of magic and merging cannot be known; at least it signals the approach and avoidance of two women who valued their limited autonomy and felt it threatened by each other's power, as much as in a sexual relationship. "You—you only excite me," Mary wrote, "—I can love nothing so much above me tho' I do [you] more than any one—I believe." Sarah commented that she would have more often owned her love except for "the incredulous smile with which the expressions of affections were repulsed." In the summer of 1817, for unnamed reasons, Mary felt that Sarah was trying to end their friendship, and soon thereafter—perhaps in response—made her departure to Vale. "Never never will you find so fond an Admirer," she wrote self-pityingly that November. "I already antisapate—ever have my nonexistence in your heart." The separation was never complete. Even as she arrived in Waterford, Mary wrote of her travel experience, asking Sarah to send a list of books including *Germany*.[65] She tried without success to bring Sarah for a visit in Maine. But the years of highest ardor were ending.

Changes in Sarah's life made the decisive difference. With the death of her long-invalid mother in May 1817, she could begin at twenty-three to plan an adult future. A year later, Sarah wrote that the new Charlestown minister—rising Unitarian leader James Walker—well suited her fancy with his "vigorous and comprehensive mind, of independance bordering on obstinacy, in manners fresh from the hand of nature." She even hinted that the gossips rightly placed her first on his list of eligible young women. Mary wrote back in dismay, as if Sarah had already married the man. "Oh were you old enough to 'wish the hairy gown & mazy cell—how could you spell of stars & herbs,' " she paraphrased from Milton's "Il Penseroso." "I do hope you will not be prisoned in heart or soul." She had once written to Ann Brewer, "It is well to marry, and it is well not to marry."[66] Mary hardly opposed the institution—indeed, had more than once worked to arrange it—but she held out a single vocation of mental freedom for the splendid Sarah.

Then came a reversal for them both. "I am on the very eve of engaging myself to your brother," Sarah wrote in June 1818, "and now I believe you will be amused if a long epistle should ever reach you written a week since and lost in the street on its way to Boston—two days and as many words from my father have changed my mind entirely." Mary's half brother Samuel Ripley, now thirty-five and the minister in Waltham, probably appeared to father Bradford a better prospect for Sarah than uncommitted James Walker; and despite the views just aired in her lost letter, Sarah acquiesced. Mary could not have been entirely surprised. She herself had introduced Samuel to Sarah by asking him to carry a letter a few years earlier, and the Ripleys had long been acquainted with her. A favorite topic at the Manse on New Year's Day of 1817 was Sarah's "prominent figure." "We speculate on your career and think how splendid it may be," Mary wrote to her. A month later Sarah Ripley wrote to Mary of Samuel's progress in both building a house and choosing a wife: "Who that one will be I cannot say, tho I hope & often allow myself to expect that it may be one that you love."[67] The women of the Manse had correctly surmised Samuel's intent.

Neither Sarah Bradford nor Mary Emerson seems to have shared the Ripleys' pleasure in this engagement, however. Far from condemning her brother to her friend, Mary predicted that though "little acquainted" they would love each other better every year. She advised Sarah to be herself and stay uninvolved in Waltham parish business. But she did not rejoice in this union, did not return from Vale for the wedding, and no longer expected a new Elizabeth Smith in her friend. "Adieu Sarah Bradford—," Mary wrote, "I will not lose a moment in painfull recollections that the joys annexed to that name are no more."[68] Such a cruel wedding salutation reflected a personal loss of both vicarious authority and love.

But through the months of 1817 and 1818, amidst misunderstanding, separation, and disappointment, Mary was also defining her own authority in conversation with Sarah. Their letters and even more her Almanack reflect this newly declarative tone. Together in Boston, the two women once more went over the ground of Butler's analogy between nature and spirit, and upon returning home Mary exclaimed, "Oh nature, child & workmanship of God Himself, how lovely thy face, how exquisitely fair thy forms—and forever capable of discovering new beauties to thy most enthusiastic admirer!" Together she and Sarah went to visit a new friend, and after expressing disappointment in the woman's cold piety, Mary spun out a continuing series of Almanack entries on joy as "nature's first impulse" and hope as the source of "moral grandeur." "Oh where [the grandeur of hope] is wanting—the will of God must be submitted to—but give me that oh God—it is holy independance—it is honor & immortality—dearer than friends wealth and influence. . . . I bless thee for giving me to see the advantage of loneliness."[69]

Then Mary's thinking about her "holy independance" connected with new reading in a volume borrowed from Sarah, Dugald Stewart's *Dissertation First: Exhibiting a General View of the Progress of Metaphysical, Ethical, and Political Philosophy*. This book went with Mary to Maine, and amidst their exchange of thoughts about friendship and marriage, Sarah also took part in Mary's debate with the Scotsman, getting a tangle of questions and opinions in response. But Mary had already recorded her clearest rendering of the debate in her Almanack during the summer and fall of 1817. There she discovered and embraced a new series of Continental philosophers whom Stewart described—but did not endorse—as opponents to Locke. Defending imagination as a gift of heaven, Mary argued, "It may be the receptacle of knowledge—what Leibni[z] means when he speaks of the soul being a living mirror of the universe, containing the seeds of that knowledge w'h is unfolded by the use of its faculties." Stewart himself, she added, had found Leibniz's theory "another impotent attempt to explain a mystery unfathomable by human reason." But Mary agreed with Leibniz—along with Malebranche, who found "every perception illumined by God's immediate agency," and Descartes, who assumed "the cardinal truth . . . that the senses are not the only sources of human knowledge." She was especially impressed with Descartes's argument from his own consciousness to God's existence, and she proclaimed with him, "Know thy intellectual self is the experimental philosophy of the human mind."[70]

"Is it worth while to read Locke on understanding?" Mary asked Sarah. She did not take advantage of Stewart's history to learn more of Locke, knowing only enough to dismiss him as "probably the source of much materialism and the mean stuff which attaches to it." But, along with de Staël's *Germany*, the *Dissertation* allowed her to assemble a wide range of English, American, and Continental philosophers in defense of intuition, adding Descartes and his contemporaries to previous knowledge of Edwards, Clarke, and Price. She made no use of Kant, balking at his complexity and pervasive doubt. "For my weakness, forebear to speak of the German," she requested. But then Stewart also dismissed the Germans, asking if there was anything in them beyond Cudworth's Platonism in "deep neological disguise."[71] By 1818 Mary had assembled a varied and impressive set of philosophical resources for arguing around Locke and his "mean stuff."

The energy of her letters and Almanacks came from her play of philosophy with personal writing, whether a barb for Sarah or a report of rapturous experience in nature. Between entries about Stewart on Descartes, she recorded the pleasure of a day at church with friends from Fryeburg. "What an enchanting day this," she went on:

> I rode and walked home a little. The trees lose their beauty—but it is renewed for them—the stream is afresh supplied, and bubbles with new pomp. The very straw w'h floats on its hoary surface is carried no one cares whither, but lodged in a warmer nest springs in some lovely lilly and is painted by the hand of the supreme Artist. Oh who wd not cast his load of mortal cares, and hear the voice of nature if it respond to providence & grace. Blessed God I am passing away with the cloud—I am flying with the gale of Autumn—with the waves and winds. On all I trace "the bright impression of thy Hand," tho never permitted to read one page of the great volumn of nature with the eye of science.[72]

Mary returned to the argument from consciousness to divine existence on the strength of her own "passing away with the cloud" much more than Descartes's austere "cogito ergo sum." Sarah resisted and mocked such flights, though conceding, "There is no bottom to dame Nature's coffers and either fancy's or science's key will fit."[73] Mary's nephews would soon be her more responsive partners in exploring the ways of fancy.

Oil and crayon portraits of Reverend Daniel Bliss and Phebe Walker Bliss, leaders of the Great Awakening in Concord and grandparents of Mary Moody Emerson. By permission of the Ralph Waldo Emerson Memorial Association.

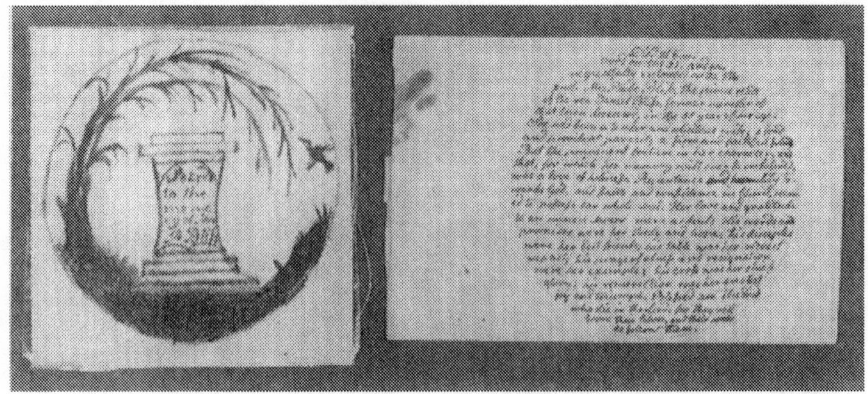

Memorial to Mrs. Phebe Bliss on paper and silk, 1797, probably by Elizabeth Haskins. Reproduced by permission of the Houghton Library, Harvard University.

Case clock and Queen Anne chairs from the mid-eighteenth century, Old Manse. Mary Moody Emerson wrote of the clock as an emblem of time's slow passage. Photo by Patrick F. Padden Jr.

Sampler of the alphabet by Phebe Bliss, mother of Mary Moody Emerson, when she was "aged 8 y." Photo courtesy of the Concord Museum, Concord, Massachusetts.

Wax miniature of Reverend William Emerson of Concord, Mary Moody Emerson's father. Reproduced by permission of the Concord Free Public Library.

William Emerson's farewell to the Manse in 1776, as painted by his great-grandson Edward Waldo Emerson a century later. Painting owned by the Old Manse, Concord; photo by Patrick F. Padden Jr.

Silhouette of Mary Moody Emerson as a young woman, which she later called her "pilgrim profile."

Reverend Ezra Ripley, Mary Moody Emerson's stepfather and minister in Concord from 1778 to 1842.

Reverend William Emerson of Boston, brother of Mary Moody Emerson and father of Ralph Waldo Emerson. Waldo found the character of this engraving "not so alive as he."

Bookplate of Reverend William Emerson, showing the family's heraldic shield and motto, "I will serve the faith." Mary Moody Emerson added her own signature in a copy of Ann Radcliffe's *Mysteries of Udolpho*. Reproduced by permission of the Beinecke Library, Yale University.

Ruth Haskins Emerson soon after her marriage to Reverend William Emerson.

Manuscript passage from the 1804 Almanack of Mary Moody Emerson, in which she reports dancing to her own "imajanation" and pictures a female genius of Christianity. Reproduced by permission of the Houghton Library, Harvard University.

Silhouette of Mary Wilder Von Schalkwyck White, "Cornelia" to Mary's "Constance."

Sarah Alden Bradford Ripley, crayon portrait by Seth Wells Cheney c. 1846. Photo by permission of the Concord Free Public Library.

Ralph Waldo and Ellen Tucker Emerson, from miniatures by Sarah Goodridge, 1829. By permission of the Ralph Waldo Emerson Memorial Association.

Medallion portrait of Charles Chauncy Emerson by Sophia Peabody, 1840. By permission of the Ralph Waldo Emerson Memorial Association.

Elizabeth Hoar about the time of her engagement to Charles Chauncy Emerson. Photo by permission of *Studies in the American Renaissance.*

The Basins, near Waterford, Maine, scene of Ann Sargent Gage's sonnet.
Photo by permission of the Waterford Historical Society.

Stagecoach at Lake House, Calvin Farrar's water cure establishment in Waterford. Photo by permission of the Waterford Historical Society.

Lidian Jackson Emerson with her son Edward about 1847.
Photo by permission of the Concord Free Public Library.

Edith and Ellen Emerson in the late 1850s. Photo by permission of the Houghton Library, Harvard University.

The Haskins family of Williamsburg, Mary Moody Emerson's nieces and nephew, c. 1875: Hannah, Samuel Moody, Charlotte, Sarah, and Phebe. Photo by permission of E. William Chamberlain.

Gravestone of Mary Moody Emerson, Sleepy Hollow Cemetery.
Photo by Nancy Craig Simmons.

III

THE MOVEMENT

7

Secret Oracles

> We love nature—to individuate ourselves in her wildest moods; to partake of her extension, & glow with her coulers & fly on her winds; but we love better to cast her off and rely on that only which is imperishable.
>
> Mary to Waldo, 1821
> (*Letters of MME*, p. 139)

Looking back from the end of his career, Ralph Waldo Emerson believed that the year 1820 had seen new opposition between the Establishment and the Movement in New England intellectual circles. "The key to the period appeared to be that the mind had become aware of itself. . . . The young men were born with knives in their brain, a tendency to introversion, self-dissection, anatomizing of motives."[1] Waldo described the origins of Transcendentalism in terms that put his own kind at the center of larger change—he had been a sixteen-year-old Harvard sophomore when 1820 began. However, his history failed to make room for a middle-aged, self-educated female introvert who had by that date recorded in her journal, "Know thy intellectual self is the experimental philosophy of the human mind."

Mary Moody Emerson belonged more fully to the Movement than the Establishment. Though often defending old ways, she persistently sought out new. In 1820 Mary had contact with every form of thought that Waldo later called an originating force of Transcendentalism. One of its signs, Waldo said, was the "genius and character of Channing": that year she had returned to Boston and was attending his vestry conferences. Others included a new dissemination of scientific knowledge and Nathaniel Frothingham's new sermons on German biblical criticism: Mary responded to both in her Almanack and letters. Early in 1821 she looked forward to reading the article on astronomy in a recent *North American Review*, but she exclaimed in pleasure upon also finding there a history of Greek art by Edward Everett. "Can any thing be more poetical and sublime than the figure of Minerva in the supposed grave of Achilles?" she asked. "I want, in vain, to form an idea of the genius which can give *soul* to marble!"

Waldo chose 1820 to date the Movement's initiation because Edward Everett returned then from five years' European study, teaching Harvard students about the most advanced criticism of ancient art and literature. Mary shared this interest through the public media and relied on her nephews for closer reports. "How does Everett?" she asked. "May his progress be rapid to new hieghts of fame."[2]

Waldo suppressed the extent of Mary's interest in new thought, but even more the depth of her influence as a new thinker on him. His most important action of 1820 was to begin writing a regular journal, his vehicle for recording self-awareness over the next half century. Mary sat nearby as he did so, the place not Harvard College but the Emersons' latest boardinghouse on Essex Street, where William kept a school for girls by day and conversation filled the parlor by night. On vacation from college that January, Waldo started by elaborately invoking magical assistance. "O ye witches assist me!" he exclaimed, apologizing to Queen Mab's realm of fancy for seeking out darker powers than hers. "There is probably one in the chamber who maliciously influenced me to what is irrevocable." Mary seems to be that creatively witchlike influence, herself a model of journal writing and spinner of dark fancies. Certainly she took a major role in teaching Waldo to value the kindred faculty of mind under whose rule he planned to continue the journal. "I do hereby nominate & appoint 'Imagination' the generallissimo & chief marshall of all the luckless raggamuffin Ideas which may be collected & imprisoned hereafter in these pages (signed) Junio."[3] Channing, Frothingham, and Everett had not championed the imagination to this young man, but Mary often had and would continue to do so.

Mary influenced Waldo as other writers did, through her written words. A year after Waldo began his journal, Mary sent a letter quoting and rhapsodizing upon de Staël's *Germany*. He found immediate use for it, copying sentences by both de Staël and Mary (only the former with attribution) into his senior essay on "The Present State of Ethical Philosophy." He won second prize. But Mary's letter would have a longer and more pervasive influence as well, for Waldo transcribed it whole into his journal, along with others like it, as the writing of "Tnamurya." This signature was not only his anagram for "Aunt Mary" but also his pseudo-Asian, oracular name for access to the divine. "All tends to the mysterious east," he had quoted from Edward Everett's introductory lecture on Greece.[4] While Waldo learned the record of past mysteries from Everett's lectures, however, he was receiving and storing Mary's live responses to mystery.

If I Were a Poet

Mary consciously assumed the role of mentor to Waldo, and she did so with an urgency arising from her own displaced vocational need. "I want influence—agency—," she had burst out in her Almanack as recently as 1817, "this this is glory virtue wisdom! . . . I know not what to do oftentimes—offer my every sense & faculty to God—trusting him for their disposal, waiting for His sending for me." Disappointed desire was again her theme a few years later at the Concord Manse: "Why, o why . . . am I never to reach the goal of perfection here? Never to pick a bone of metaphysics,—sweeter than the marrow of social life with Dr. Reason and his sickly daughter." These sardonic names referred to her stepfather and half sister Ripley, with whom she had shared the Sabbath. " 'Government of God' at church," she added. "I could not stand it, nor pray." She wanted to feed directly on metaphysics, if not mount the pulpit and preach instead of "Dr. Reason." Waldo was a vehicle for Mary's own hopes in the face of that frustration. Even as her fiercest ambition for Sarah Bradford closed, her aspirations for him rose. "I remember no hour of our solitude so pleasantly as the last sab. eve.," she wrote to the young teenager. "The Justice of your theological views was noticeable for your age and *non*-application—that is there are *some* books you have not read. But some serious questions were inferred which I did not put. You will. To know one's duty is a great step."[5] Such language mixed admiration with wry insistence on her own greater knowledge and authority.

Rather than shadowing her nephew's progress through Harvard from 1817 to 1821, Mary was becoming more willful and solitary than ever. Arguments with Rebecca and Robert prompted her to leave Vale in 1818; a year later she announced the "whim" to "suspend all human connections & Waldo's correspondence[,] not as that he was faulty in the least for complaining of my manners—but that I have nothing to communicate & nothing to sympathise about." She soon repented and called him a "dear play Mate," but still left Boston in February 1821 for months of traveling among Connecticut Valley towns, boarding first with cousins and then with strangers. As she told Ruth, the goal was to find a secluded place to rest the infirmities of age; her old impulse to flee criticism was finding new extremity of expression, as was the oddity of manners provoking criticism. From now on, Mary would often buy room and board rather than depend on relatives. "I had rather live a wandering life & die a beggar, . . . than drag down to active littleness," she wrote. "The Pilgrim, the itinerant, how often we envy their poetic leisure & their religious enthusiasm!" It was amidst a welter of contradictory feelings that Mary shared her most precious thoughts with Waldo. "I am too much beguiled by you & your imajanation to wish to see you much—," she explained in 1821. "Other ways demand me."[6]

Simultaneously, whether close at hand or wandering, Mary was calling forth the power of mind that so beguiled her. From Waldo's first autumn in college, even while arguing for enthusiasm with Sarah Bradford, Mary had begun in extravagant, seriocomic style to encourage her nephew in the vocation of poetry. "What dull Prosaic Muse would venture from the humble dell of an unlettered district, to address a son of Harvard?" she opened a letter from Vale. But Harvard impressed her less than the series of terms she pretended to stammer after it: "Son of — — of — — poetry — — of genius—ah were it so—and I destined to stand in near consanguinity to this magical possession." Mary cast herself only as a mediator to the poet's work; she spoke in the subjunctive mood of what Waldo might do. "If I were a Poet this night would inspire me," she wrote, but then gave hints about how to describe the glorious moon shining over a graveyard. Mary must have used such a turn of phrase often, for Waldo parodied it to William on New Year's Day of 1818: "If I were aunt Mary, I should tell you how auspicious an omen it was to your future happiness in the . . . mind-expanding air, & piety-inspiring regions of Kennebunk."[7] The nephews' jokes at Mary's expense continued.

How genuinely Waldo listened to Mary is clear from his journal, however, where he quoted from "Tnamurya" both the suggestion for a poetry of moonlight and her fuller counsel on poetic vocation in 1818. In the latter, Mary parodied the mythological allusions of her beloved poets to tell Waldo what awaited if he could fly like a muse to Vale: "You might . . . hear the songs of the grove echoed by the little tritons of Neptune, who is suspected of holding a smale court in the neighboring Lake. . . . If not, you could people a sylvan scene with Nymphs or Faries; and Queen Mab might send her followers after moon beams." Out of such joking about fairies and Queen Mab probably arose the language of his journal dedication in 1820. Here, however, Mary moved on to urge seriously that Waldo seek retirement and its power to inspire divine poetry. Again she recalled the English poets, now quoting Akenside's visionary response to the beauties of nature:

All declare
For what the Eternal Maker has ordained
The powers of man. He tells the heart
He meant, He made us to behold and love
What He beholds and loves, the general orb
Of life and being; to be great like Him,
Beneficent and active.[8]

At least since Waldo's infancy, Mary had known such affirmations of the human capacity to hear in nature a word from God about affinity to God. In 1818, however, these words offered a vocation that neither aunt nor nephew could fulfill. Waldo had been versifying for several years, but loved wordplay more than sacred chants. Mary held out such greatness as possible for him with effort and sacrifice: "The lowly vale of penitence and humility must be passed, before the mount of vision—the heights of virtue are gained." Mary herself knew the travails of humility firsthand, but she had never claimed the mount of vision except as a heavenly prospect. The vocation of transcendent, post-Miltonic poetry, she implied, was for men, who like Akenside's ideal man could imitate the creative power of God. She also promoted a male-centered tradition of imagining the poetic process, urging Waldo to resist the "seductions of the vagrant flower-clad Muse" for vision from the holy Muse. "May yours if she should continue and preene her wings, be sanctified by piety and I shall not blush to decorate my age with a sprig from your garland."[9] Mary has often been called Waldo's "muse," and certainly this letter enacts the female role of inspiring the male. But she never claimed to *be* any muse but a "dull, prosaic" one. In more exalted moods she invoked for the young man a goddess-partner explicitly separate from herself, claiming only a souvenir from the poetic garland as her own right.

Naming Waldo as a potential poet did not wholly replace Mary's interest in the clerical calling of her ancestors; she offered reassurance that if he did not "swell the literature of the age" he might serve the religion of Jesus as a minister. But her priority remained with the written word and the power of fancy. By his senior year she could even ask, "How is thy soul? Not that of which Paul speaks—but thy poetic?" A month later she weighed Shakespeare's self-taught strength against his regrettable sensuality, then added, "It is for a still brighter era to erase his deformities and possibly set a mightier Magician over the witcheries of fancy."[10] She was urging Waldo to become that magician of the spirit.

In these same letters of his senior year, Waldo found language and ideas to incorporate into his essay "The Present State of Ethical Philosophy." He solicited Mary's partnership by asking questions about both the ancients' natural religion and the historical outline in Dugald Stewart's *Dissertation.* Mary declined to share her Almanack notes on Stewart, protesting that they offered no history, only metaphysical comments "boldly interspersed with my objections & queries." Instead, she consulted with Sarah Bradford Ripley on Stewart. Two years earlier, teaching at the newly married Ripleys' school in Waltham, Waldo had rejoiced in gaining an aunt who could both make puddings and read great books. "As to her knowledge talk on what you will she can always give you a new idea," he told William, "—ask her any philosophical question, she will always enlighten you by her answer." Now his two philosophical aunts joined in his support. Sarah relayed to Mary the news that President Kirkland had read Waldo's junior-year essay on Socrates and asked, "Why not a better Locke, Stuart & Pal[ey] scholar?"[11]

But Mary's views rather than Sarah's—or Locke's—filled these letters. In her own dense, semidecipherable style, she claimed both Price-Platonism and Staël-Romanticism as central to moral philosophy. Describing morality as "coeval with existence" rather than a product of history, she appropriated Price's language: "*Right* and *wrong* have had claims prior to all rites—immutable & eternal in their nature." Quoting de Staël, she offered the Germans' two approaches to reading nature: "one that the universe is made after the model of the human soul; the other that the analogy of every part of the universe, with it's *whole*, is so close that the same idea is constantly reflected from the whole in every part & from every part in the whole." With the Germans—but alluding also to Swedenborg and echoing her old reading of Butler on analogies—Mary hazarded the possibility that "the phisical world [is] the basso-releivo of the moral."[12]

Mary was presenting to Waldo an idealism and a Romantic theory of correspondence far beyond what he was receiving at Harvard. He incorporated these ideas into his essay only within the boundaries of the curriculum. Levi Frisbie's moral philosophy course had presented Price and encouraged a critical attitude toward Locke, while the Common Sense philosophers current at Harvard, including Stewart, found conscience innate to the human mind. Now Waldo affirmed the intuitionist-idealist side of what he had learned, omitting Locke, calling Price the representative modern philosopher, and espousing Cudworth's "Immutable Morality"—a Christian Platonism known to him through Price's quotations. All of this was shared ground with Mary as well. But he valued the Common Sense school more highly than she did, endorsed Stewart and Reid as a basis for future philosophical labors, and did not mention the Germans.[13]

Waldo was cautious even in his momentary plagiarism from Mary. Surveying the history of ethics, he quoted de Staël, as Mary had, on the "intimate relations between Man & Nature" enjoyed by the ancients in "the mysteries of Eleusis, the religion of Egypt, the system of emanations of the Hindoo, the Persian adoration of the elements, the harmony of the Py[thagorean] numbers." Slightly revising Mary's words, he also pointed out the kindred, even greater, attraction of modern minds to nature: "More fortunate is our condition; we recognize, with scientific delight, these attractions; they are material, still they are the agency of Deity, and we value them as subservient to the great relations we seek and pant after, in moral affinities and intellectual attractions, from his moral influence."[14] In essence the sentence was affirming the modern enterprise of reading nature scientifically and philosophically as a sign and analogy of God.

Waldo's larger argument, however, did not pursue any such relation to the divine. He spoke of nature worship as pre-Socratic history and, despite the quick aside, did not return to any analogous mode of thought in his own era. Mary's source letter, on the other hand, quoted de Staël amidst her own autobiographical reports. "The spirits of inspiration are abroad tonight," she began. "I have rode only to go out & see the wonderous aspect of nature." The appropriated sentence about nature as a sign of God introduced a second personal declaration: "We love nature—to individuate ourselves in her wildest moods; to partake of her extension, & glow with her coulers & fly on her winds, but we better love to cast her off and rely on that only which is imperishable." The words that Waldo did not take anticipated his later individuation of soul—at once an embrace and an apocalyptic casting off of nature—more than the sentence that he took. Waldo was not only deferring to the authority of his professors but also moving in another direction from Mary's. The boldest aspect of his senior essay was an expression of interest in Hume, who went beyond Locke to "gloomy uncertainty" of all knowledge. But even in 1821, recording the whole passage of thought by "Tnamurya" in his journal, he was gathering fragments toward an affirmation that would eventually counter that uncertainty.[15]

Out of a "whim engendered of *Solitude*," Mary refused to attend the Harvard exhibition that spring where Waldo read his poem "Indian Superstition," an early and ambivalent expression of interest in Hindu mythology; she did join Ruth and the Emerson boys, however, at Waldo's commencement in August. The autumn of 1821 fulfilled the hopes of neither nephew nor aunt. Waldo began teaching at William's school for girls. Mary took Bulkeley to board in Malden after a mental breakdown that at first, as she wrote to Ruth, had threatened "frightful [idiocy] or complete distraction."[16] Bulkeley would suffer periodic derangement from this time on and always require special care. But amidst Waldo's teaching and Mary's nursing, their conversation continued.

Sometimes it was immediate. In January 1822 she wrote to Ann Sargent Gage at a table alongside Waldo, declaring both his genius and her affection for him. As he read theology and philosophy, their talk supported his inquiry, for several of the passages from Stewart, Clarke, and Leibniz that he recorded in his journal overlapped with those noted by her four years earlier. The reading was not always so arduous. After Waldo read Charles Maturin's gothic romance *Fatal Revenge*, she recorded their dialogue in her Almanack. "He asked me, how I loved Nature so well, if &c." Mary had no patience to fill out the etcetera: this tale of blighted hopes and bloody deaths was all too familiar in revealing the world's destructive force. But she recorded her succinct defense of nature: "I said that it afforded emblems of death and resurrection."[17]

Letters exchanged in periods of separation left the more substantial record of such exchange. Two from Mary offered Waldo early seeds of Orientalism. Unexpectedly detoured from a trip to Waterford in the parsonage of Byfield minister Elijah Parish, she told of a visitor from India who had been showing "representations of the incarnation of Vishnoo" and telling about the conversion of "*Rheumas* (I *think*) a learned Hindu, to xianity from his own researches." The convert in fact was named Rammohun Roy, and his discovery of likeness between the Vedas and Western Unitarianism had interested the Boston press. "I am curious to read your Hindu mythologies," Waldo responded, even though his poem of the previous year shows him already to have dabbled in the subject. But the single text central to Mary and Waldo's early interest in Brahmin wisdom is a portion of the "Hymn to Narayena," as translated by Sir William Jones, with which Mary ended her letter a month later:

> My soul absorbed one only Being knows
> Of all perceptions one abundant source,
> Hence every object every moment flows;
> Suns hence desire their force,
> Hence planets learn their course
> But sun and fading worlds I view no more
> God only I percieve God only I adore![18]

Waldo copied Mary's own thoughts from this letter, calling it a monument to her affection; but he separated the "fine pagan strains" of "Narayena" for separate use, under the heading "IDEALISM," with no attribution to Mary.[19]

In fact the idealism came largely from Mary. In this single letter she encapsulated not only her love but also all of the philosophy and vicarious poetic vocation that she had been directing toward him since 1817. Fearing the muse of "sensation rather than sentiment," she urged his aspiration to a celestial poetry based on Plato and Plotinus, which in its wild form might offer a source of vital freedom. "We are not slaves to sense any more than to political usurpers," Mary wrote, making of opposition to Lockean sense epistemology a figurative American Revolution as well as an ideal inwardness. She ended, as in her 1821 letter on nature, by moving toward an apocalypse of consciousness, now by citing Eichhorn's commentary on Revelations and leaping ahead to the "morsel of Hindu poetry." Hinduism, Mary noted finally, "is as it respects matter the same as Berkliasm you know."[20]

Mary knew the extent of her influence on Waldo but referred to it only in a cryptic language of denial. Writing a full letter to his muse—that deity explicitly not herself—Mary protested that Waldo owed her nothing, for she had followed "no habit of dictation" and received life-giving responses back from him. Actually Mary dictated in this very letter, requiring that the muse provide "sterner & holier" gifts, determining that she herself could meet Waldo on no ground but her own, "about those relations which unite us to a common Center."[21]

Meanwhile, Mary reflected in her Almanack on the losses and gains of serving as the source of another's thinking. On the one hand, to give away an idea was "to lose that portion of one's soul—that all of existence—and none say how that soul lived & felt." On the other, a freely given idea might "go into another state—become a germ of future ideas." "Think of a De Stael treasuring up sentiments & ideas for a Son—abandoning her own publick existence that he might be 'decked with unfading honors—!' " In fact, as Mary went on to acknowledge, de Staël had never sacrificed a public career for her son and so represented mere genius unilluminated by Christian humility. At least in part, Mary justified her influence on Waldo as a calling holier than that of the age's most eminent public woman. She sent this Almanack entry to him, and a few years later, urging further generosity, he recalled the point that de Staël had "thought for her son."[22] He had both misread Mary's sense of de Staël and overlooked the fear of losing a portion of soul.

Waldo liked being cast as the son of de Staël and accepted Mary's gifts freely. Unlike Sarah Bradford a few years earlier, he did not fear imprisonment by her will. He did, however, perceive a priestly power in his aunt for above the lay sanctity of Protestant tradition. Just after receiving the 1821 letter that would find its way into his senior essay, Waldo first recorded a journal entry *about* Mary, expressing awe at a religion so deep and independent. "She is the Weird-woman of her religion," Waldo concluded, "& conceives herself always bound to walk in narrow but exalted paths which lead onward to interminable regions of rapturous & sublime glory."[23] This language repressed half of the truth—both her broad, explicitly philosophical reflection and his own present debt to it. However, the title "Weird-woman" cut deep into the power that Mary held for Waldo, naming no mere strangeness but a power to read the fates and pronounce omens.

Over the next months, Waldo composed two fantasy romances, interspersed in the same journal with his notes on ethical philosophy and transcripts of Mary's letters, about men who were the son or follower of a "Weird-woman." These half-formed fictions internalized the meanings of "Tnamurya" even as Waldo was recording her prophecies. In "The Magician"—a name that Mary had earlier hinted might be Waldo's own—the woman Uilsa declares herself "queen of the woods" and welcomes a questing youth to her cave, where a power of divination descended from Odin and his daughters promises to open the future's secrets to him. Instead, she meets her death in the coils of a gigantic serpent, leaving the youth to relate her end; whether he receives her power is left unsaid. In the second fiction, however, the New England founder Foxcroft is facing his own death and openly proclaims the part of his mother Elspeth in spurring on his life's work. "She instructed me in the signs & omens. . . . And had she never taught me, I must have been blind indeed to the doings of fate. . . . But I saw my life was devoted by Providence to promote this great design and immediately obeyed my weird."[24] The character of Uilsa resembled Mary in avoidance of human society and association with nature's forces, but Elspeth was much more openly an extension of the aunt who had told the visions and heroic deaths of ancestors to her nephews. Waldo's story transformed Mary, narrator of the New England past, into the visionary guide of its mission.

His most frequent naming of Mary's guidance, however, came from neither Norse legend nor Puritan history but from the Romantic classicism so pervasive in their conversation about the ways of imagination. Warned by her of the potentially blighting circumstance of teaching in a school for girls, Waldo protested that the company of women would not shadow his inspiration. "Will the Nine be shamed by the company of their sex? Did they shun Corinna and abhor de Stael[?]." Unlike Mary, Waldo freely associated from his aunt to the nine muses, the French author, and her oracular Roman character Corinne. The prophetic figure of Cassandra summed up these visionary possibilities; Waldo both associated her explicitly with Mary and hoped for her "second sight" to reveal his future. "Your letter is as Cassandra's should be," he commented, "dark, and not entirely intelligible." In return, Mary asked to be considered only "a dead Cassandra—not prophesying, but praying for thy welfare"; she claimed only the more Christian ground of saintly, postmortem blessing, not second sight. Indeed, she turned the tables and charged that *his* "oracular page" had held no clear meaning, having to be read "like a sybiline leaf."[25] From this year onward, however, Waldo would persist in highflown, only partially humorous, characterizations of Mary as a Greek oracle, sibyl, or prophetess.

Though Waldo's metaphorical names attributed power to Mary, he also fantasized in his journal about godlike males capable of effacing female powers. In March 1822 he described a paradise where nature had her throne. As much as its scene of mountains and forests was Mary's, both literally in Waterford and figuratively in the story of Uilsa, he now placed a solitary male at the center, both the "worshipping enthusiast" of female Nature and the witness to its sudden destruction at the hand of a fiery male deity in the skies. In this collapse of Genesis into Revelation, Waldo was appropriating both Mary's love of nature and her eagerness for apocalypse, absorbing her gender into nature and naming all power and perception as male. The experiment seemed silly before it was finished: "An exceedingly noisy vision!" he wrote in breaking it off. Dedicating the sixth volume of his journal that April, however, Waldo imagined a young male giant with dominion over his American continent and "communication with his mother—Nature." This son was able to perform a rite in his mother's presence—in a golden cave never before "polluted . . . with [man's] tools of art"—so interpreting future destiny. As well as embodying a naively Oedipal fantasy, this fiction again claimed powers of divination previously attributed to Mary and her figurative kin. Now the archetypal American male needed no Elspeth but had become his own weird woman. Though the prophecy that he divined was apocalyptic—"A thousand years, A thousand years, and the Hand shall come, and tear the Veil for all"—now Waldo reinterpreted the millennium as a "mighty progress of improvement & civilization . . . which shall reveal Nature to Man."[26] The empire of the male was secure.

On any level but fantasy, Waldo came nowhere near being a young giant of nature. Six weeks after penning his dedication to nature's mysteries, he and William spent a week in the country near Northborough, thirty miles west of Boston. Waldo at least insisted on fishing; William declared himself too squeamish for such "murderous designs." But most of all Waldo sought the breakthrough to vision and poetry that Mary had been promising: "Who could suddenly find himself alone in the green fields where the whole firmament meets the eye at once, and the pomp of woods & clouds and hills is poured upon the mind," he asked his journal, "—without an unearthly animation?" Writing to Mary the next day, however, he confessed that he had experienced only a little of the intoxication that she had predicted. "Perhaps in the Autumn, which I hold to be the finest season in the year, and in a longer abode the mind might, as you term it, return upon itself; but for a year, without books it would become intolerable."[27]

Waldo's terms for framing his encounter were Mary's, that although nature could delight, only the solitary mind itself, once able to "return upon itself," would break through to heaven. Mary reasserted these terms by analyzing his failure: "You should have gone seperately. Other sprites than Egerian haunt the solitude of perfect retirement."[28] Since Egeria in Roman legend was a nymph and female adviser, these were peculiarly self-condemnatory terms of advice: she was urging him to avoid not only company but also effeminacy. Mary herself was aiding in his subordination of all female figures.

Neither aunt nor nephew was really the magician that each sought in the other. Desiring a male alter ego in Waldo, Mary acted from her own perceived failures. Waldo continued to find in Mary a power that eluded his grasp. By the spring of 1823, he and his family had moved out of Boston to Roxbury, rural countryside though still only a few miles' walk from their city schoolroom. "I am seeking to put myself on a footing of old acquaintance with Nature, as a poet should," Waldo wrote to a Harvard classmate, but he confessed that so far such aspirations were unfulfilled. His next sentences made clear where these had arisen:

> My aunt (of whom I think you have heard before & who is alone among women,) has spent a great part of her life in the country, is an idolater of Nature, & counts but a small number who merit the privilege of dwelling among the mountains. The coarse thrifty cit profanes the grove by his presence—and she was anxious that her nephew might hold high & reverential

notions regarding it as the temple where God & the Mind are to be studied & adored & where the fiery soul can begin a premature communication with other worlds.[29]

Even more than his earlier account of Mary as "the weird woman of her religion," this portrait delineated the figure from whom Waldo hoped for assistance. In his mind, Mary could worship nature and find there the direct sight of God usually reserved for life after death. Nowhere in her own writing did she personally claim an opening of heaven to her earthly eye. Even when an eclipse or an autumn wind brought ecstasy, it was only in hope of coming transformation. And such moments came rarely in the acquiescent, wandering mode of these years. As she wrote at Byfield in 1822, her only goal was to "keep in a waiting posture" and "conquer the long habit of reaching after the notions which float in poetic heads and philosophical." Her highest moments instead rose along the *via negativa* of emptiness and self-surrender. Scattering seashells amidst a Newburyport garden later that summer, she took pleasure in assisting the Creator's role of aiding growth, then declared her own exemption from the coming harvest: "The corn reaches the apple trees in stately growth; every morning I behold an increase,—the apple blushes more deeply,—the trees bend over the shooting spindles with heavier, stiller look,—while I alone remain the same ignorant, useless being,—withering, without dying. These days of high summer, no wind disturbs the field, and the shade so dark that its beauty thrills through a vacant soul."[30]

Division and Skepticism

The same spring that Waldo called Mary an "idolater of Nature," he and William became members of First Church Boston. Mary's quest for holiness in nature coexisted with a vehement defense of the church establishment, and she insisted that they join it only from real conviction. "In less liberal days it was the right of the meanest member to inquire the motives of the Noviciate," she challenged Waldo. "*What mean you by this rite*? Is it a monument rendered sacred by ages, by holy martyrs who have sealed their faith by blood, at its alters to the *history* of its Founder?"[31] Mary valued Christianity in all its long history and most spirited forms, but her ancestors' awakened church from the previous century, with its strenuous limits on membership, offered her highest standard. The possibility that William and Waldo might join as a mere matter of course boded well for neither them nor the church.

Indeed, Mary knew that her nephews joined as potential ministers, and she interrogated as well as fostered that ambition. Their pastor Nathaniel Frothingham believed William "ignorant of the difficulties of a clerical profession," she warned, and Frothingham's own career pointed these out. By preaching from a knowledge of German biblical criticism he was trying to sustain the church, stripping it of irrational doctrine and discovering core belief. Waldo later remembered Frothingham's sermons as a harbinger of Transcendentalism, however, because their inherent skepticism was a centrifugal force moving listeners away from churches and pulpits. As a woman, Mary suffered exclusion from ministerial power, but she also enjoyed the freedom to use or dismiss the arguments of Frothingham and his colleagues. Having joined the church at twenty, she would remain a member for life but seek God at will in or out of it.[32] Ministers, on the other hand, bound themselves to the institution in exchange for their authority. Mary hoped for her nephews to assume that station only if they were believers and reformers of sufficient power to resist the forces of skepticism.

It was an irreparably divided church, furthermore, that Mary upheld to her nephews in 1823. Just four years earlier, William Ellery Channing had definitively named the liberal wing in his sermon "Unitarian Christianity"; now individual Massachusetts towns were widely and rapidly splitting into separate orthodox and Unitarian congregations. From Waltham, Sarah Bradford Ripley reported a "rout" as early as 1820, when the mill workers in one quarter of town rebelled against Samuel's Unitarian leadership. Meanwhile, an orthodox seminary had been founded in Andover—the descendants of Daniel and Hannah Emerson among its supporters—and Harvard was forming its own divinity school at the urgent recommendation of Channing.[33]

As the Massachusetts church split, Mary seems to have devoted herself with new intensity to both of its cultures, as though holding them together through her own physical and intellectual sojourns. "What sermons!" she exclaimed from Boston in 1822 after hearing Channing. Her primary allegiance would continue to be to his liberal pietism. In these years, however, she also traveled in the Connecticut Valley for the first time, visited Professor Moses Stuart at Andover, and took up several months' residence at the parsonage of Elijah Parish in Byfield. She did not represent herself as orthodox in these strongholds of Calvinism. When Parish criticized the "levity and coldness" of Unitarians, Mary faulted "the mischiefs which result from the long faces & cant" of the orthodox. But she actively sought news of the pamphlet war between Andover and Harvard, seeing truth in both parties. When Waldo too quickly dismissed Calvinism, she charged that he knew only "a few bug bear words" from its complex theology, quoting to him the most important tenet from Calvin's *Institutes*, "the end for w'h all men are born & live to know God."[34]

In Maine the division fell differently, but with equal ill will. Mary addressed her questions about church membership to Waldo as she returned there, datelining her letter from "Space & time" en route. Newly reconciled with the Haskins family, she at last settled for the long term, returning to Massachusetts only for visits over the next decade.[35] But Waterford was not a temple of nature apart from New England church politics. Just as Mary expressed anxiety about her Boston nephews' future as ministers, she was returning to a town where her brother-in-law Lincoln Ripley had recently lost his ministry amidst competition from Methodists and Baptists.

Lincoln's dismissal cannot have been a secret within the family, but it was suppressed in the lofty rhetoric of Mary's letters. New turmoil had come in 1820 when Maine voted for independence from Massachusetts and separation of church and state. Now no taxes would be collected in any town to support the Congregational establishment. Lincoln's position had never been secure, and he was especially unsuited for competition with other sects. A timid man, short in stature and given as a preacher to calm reasoning from Scripture, he foresaw the reign of Antichrist in their victory. Despite moderately orthodox views influenced by an education at Dartmouth, he was associated by family and political principle with the Massachusetts establishment. In 1818, just as Mary left Waterford, Methodists had built a chapel along the road near her house; suitably, the place was called "Mutiny Corner." By 1819 sectarians so controlled town meeting that no money was raised for Lincoln's salary at all. So when a new state constitution allowed for only voluntary support of churches, his fate was sealed. Lincoln resigned in exchange for a year's salary and a promise of freedom from taxes on his own land.[36]

When Mary returned in 1823, the Ripleys had gone to Greenfield, Massachusetts, where Lincoln stayed with a brother while looking for new ministerial prospects. Ann Sargent Gage expressed pleasure that her adoptive mother Phebe felt no longer obliged to "do good to the obstinately ungrateful." Despite this animosity, however, the Ripleys soon returned to live out their lives as farmers in Waterford. Lincoln would raise the finest sheep and apple trees in town, offer impromptu exhortations from the pew of his successor's church, and join the pious young doctor Leander Gage in organizing benevolent societies. Rebecca Haskins joined her husband as a member of the church only now that her brother-in-law had left the pulpit. The Haskins and Ripley families do not seem to have stood united in church politics. Mary's loyalties are unclear. When Charles visited the Ripleys several years later, he heard stories of her "calling to the people round about the Meeting House."[37] Possibly she too, like Lincoln, did some lay exhorting. But she did not share such matters with her protégés in Massachusetts.

To these young people Mary spoke in bookish rather than local terms, issuing invitations to rural retirement that would uplift the mind and spirit. In 1823 Sarah Bradford Ripley parodied such language by contrasting Mary's sublimity with her own domestic fatigue: "My correspondent, who, with nerves braced by the pure breath of heaven as it descends to rest on Elm Vale, and an imagination excited by its wild scenery, will probably have but little sympathy with the stupidity of one whose head has been in an oven the greater part of the day." Sarah had gained a reputation for bluestocking conversation in the Boston area, but while she was caring for a burgeoning school, a divided parish, and four children—including three-year-old daughter Mary Emerson Ripley—she could not think of visiting Maine. Waldo made his first pilgrimage to Vale the following summer, both he and Mary holding forth expectations of vision that could only be disappointed. She wrote afterward that Charles had rightly stayed home, for Waldo had taken solitary walks and spoken little. "Tis a dull place," she concluded of her country home, "—A parc[el] of dolts who dont distinguish a Genius." But Charles did visit soon thereafter, and the despite the "dolts" of Waterford, its landscape became embedded in both nephews' memories.[38]

From the country, moreover, Mary responded to the wrestling of her young intellectual kin with the age's leading forms of skepticism. As she arrived in 1823, William was planning to follow Frothingham's model of ministry by studying biblical history under Eichhorn in Germany. She answered this news with unhesitating pleasure and kindred scholarly devotion: "I have thought of you often the past week, in which I have gone thro' the 1t vol. of Michaelis' 'Introduction to N.T.' I beg when you come to antient MMS—to latin versions, and above all, to the history of the Syrian antient [version], you would write to me. What fields of knowledge, as well as labour, lie before you! . . . Repay me by one single learned letter."[39]

Though Mary lacked the languages required for this new biblical scholarship, she knew its chief issues both from books in English and from sermons. Listening in 1817 to Frothingham's speculations "that the old bible is not inspired," she had at first responded self-confidently: "Take from the modern preachers the inspiration of the holy scriptures—but leave me the omnipresence, the constant agency of god." But then a second thought arose: if the Bible had no higher status than "heathen records," she might lose the certitude of redemption that enabled her to recognize God's agency. Mary remained divided and curious on these questions, asking Sarah for more news of Frothingham even while disparaging Eichhorn. Now five years later, with William setting out to study under Eichhorn, she felt confident that the scholars were validating key portions of Scripture, as well as dismissing the rest. Identifying with the position of a "bible theist" that fall, she told Waldo that "all we have to do with rev.[elation] is its miracles as they are the foundation of our faith." As long as the unique miracles of Christian resurrection and redemption survived, the mind would be enabled to experience "omnipresence."[40]

Waldo rather than William continued the talk about knowledge and revelation with Mary. While the older nephew never responded to her request for an intellectually stimulating letter, the younger beguiled her from silence with one after another. He sent a "catalogue of curious questions" that had accumulated in her absence, confessing, "I ramble among doubts to which my reason offers no solution." He had seemingly declared a moratorium on the pursuit of visionary power in nature. Just the Sunday before, Dr. Channing had compared the lights of revelation and nature to show that the latter was insufficient alone. Now Waldo was delving into that insufficiency: his current reading was "the Scotch Goliath" Hume, before whom no one could easily prove the existence of either God or the universe. Waldo had expressed respect for Hume even in his senior essay at Harvard but now wrestled with radical empiricism in a new way. As he wrote in his journal the week of his letter to Mary, Hume assumed that nothing could be known apart from experience, but denied the mind's capacity to connect events and construct a sense-based knowledge.[41] On Locke's ground he was denying Locke's solidly founded universe.

Mary knew Hume at least by reputation, for she had once jestingly compared her friend Sarah to him and now accused Waldo of feigning respect for a shallow philosophy. But by January 1824, Mary herself had wrestled with Hume's essays and could throw back objections in earnest. "That this Out law, who finds every thing unconnected uncertain & illusory, and 'the effect totally different from the cause,' should cast such a mist that we cant get hold of his sofistry is irritating," she began. Still her letter offered an extended statement of the proofs of God's existence that she had learned in youth from her master Samuel Clarke. If even one of nature's phenomena lay beyond human power, did there not need to be a superior being? "If we find a bird's nest we know there was a builder—and we know by the same way there was an Artist to the world." Even more centrally, she argued for God's existence in the "apriori ways w'h Hume very consistently detests." Was it not proof of an eternal being "that the mind is so formed as to be unable to get rid of the ideas of immensity & eternity?" Was it not the mind's very nature to step from present experience to future?[42] Mental life was her *indubitandum* and source of relationship with both the world and God.

Not fundamentally skeptical of either nature or divinity, Mary quickened to skepticism. Between knowledge and ignorance, she argued, lay enigma, which could "do no hurt" because it told "no bad tales of any operations of nature illusory or contradictory. Is it not wholly sattisfactory to reason, that all it discovers and *knows* indicate design & good ends?" Some mysteries remained hurtful, however. In response to Waldo's point-blank question about the origin of evil, as represented by the fate of the "poor slave," she asked in return about the greater mystery that human beings capable of loving God could torment slaves. "Would it be folly or manicheanism to suppose there was something of evil in the nature of things, or laws w'h God is rather controuling than distroying?" Even while subscribing to the idea that human virtue proceeded from love of "being universal," she was not sure that the slave owner's evil could be explained without some comparable anti-being to pervert love.[43] She did not hesitate to return her own "curious questions" in response to his.

As Waldo approached the ministry amidst division and skepticism, Mary urged resistance to "the times." How, she asked early in 1824, did he differ from the new breed of ministers whose faith was a natural by-product of "enervating literature, luxury & ambition"? Whereas nine months before she had recalled the sacred traditions of the church to oppose such conformity, now she held up the possibility of a faith with no church at all. "In intire solitude," she wrote, "minds become oblivious to care & find in the uniform & constant miracle of nature, revelation alter & priest." Never had she so bluntly claimed so much for the individual mind, allowing it to replace the biblical word and all its rites and ministers. Why, she boldly went on, should those disloyal to the church not say so? "One would like to have them desert openly and form a novel religion. Why cannot some of them have ingenuity to recall the antient philosophy of the Hindoos?" Mary was playing defender of the faith and antiestablishment innovator at once in these sentences. Given a dwindling collective religious life, where could one find truth but from the mind's own communion with nature? Though not instructing Waldo to found a new religion, she clearly preferred Hinduism to soulless modernity. But then she took a step back and surveyed the more immediate scene, predicting that Christian faith would return and swell the Calvinist party—"w'h will make some demands on our resignation, who are attached to unitarianism."[44] Her volatile mind took in multiple possibilities, and she offered them all without constraint to Waldo.

More centrally than either Calvinist or Hindu belief, Mary looked to the tradition of English poet-priests for validation of the individualism that she proposed as worship. When Waldo complained that science had robbed the landscape of sacredness, she affirmed that Milton's mind and spirit "wove their own place & came when he called them in the solitude of darkness":

> Solitude w'h to people, not talented to deviate from the beaten track (w'h is the safe gaurd of mediocrity) without offending, is to learning & talents the only sure labyrinth (tho' sometimes gloomy) to form the eagle wings w'h will bear one farther than suns and stars. Byron & Wordsworth have there best and only intensely burnished their pens. Would to Providence your unfoldings might be there—that it were not a wild & fruitless wish, that you could be united from travelling with the souls of other men, of living & breathing, reading & writing with one vital time fated idea *their opinions*. . . . Could a mind return to its first fortunate seclusion, when it opened with its own peculiar coulers & spread them out on its own rhymy palette, with its added stock, and spread them beneathe the cross, what a mercy to the age.[45]

Within this awkward prose lay a fully Romantic recasting of Milton's *Paradise Lost*, the poem that Mary had long ago pored over without knowing the author or title. Conflating the poet's blindness with Satan's determination to make his mind "its own place," she imagined the solitary soul soaring to heaven in a "fortunate seclusion" that was both resurrection and regaining of paradise. This passage made a demonstrable impact on Waldo, in part reappearing in his essay "Culture" more than three decades later as the counsel of a "wise instructor" to a "young soul."[46] He was referring to his own soul's formation.

In 1824 he was not prepared to adopt this post-Miltonic myth of the self. Mary affirmed the likeness between her ideal solitude and that of Wordsworth and Byron, but Waldo held qualified views of both poets. He had dutifully summarized *The Excursion* three years earlier but expressed no love for Wordsworth either then or since. Both Waldo and Mary intensely admired Byron's *Child Harold's Pilgrimage*; she had even accused him of imitating this dark poet in his prose fictions. But when Byron died soon after Mary's "fortunate seclusion" letter, Waldo's respect for his genius fought against moral judgment of blasphemy and sensual excess. Finding Byron an "archangel ruined," like Milton's Satan in fallenness rather than solitude, Waldo pointed out the Christian lesson to Mary: "He might have added one more wonder to his life its own redemption." Mary condemned less strongly: "Virtues were gathering around his vices," and none but Byron "could so call the voice of nature from her dreadest heights or deepest caverns." Later, in the lecture "Amita," Waldo recalled Mary's amusingly old-fashioned judgment that Byron's mind would never have been attracted to Unitarianism, only the depths and elections of Calvinism. He was recalling her words outside the context of 1824, where *he* had sought conversion for the fallen poet, and where her critique of Unitarianism could take Calvinist and pagan forms by turn. "But it is melancholy to have your well dry up," he wrote to Mary when Byron died, "your fountain stopped from whence you were wont to look for an unfailing supply."[47] She was more a Romantic than he.

She was also the more enthusiastic advocate for Plato and the philosophical idealism that he represented. Both Mary and Waldo seem to have known Plato's dialogues in 1824 only through secondary comments and quotations, but Plato was already becoming a dramatic personage in their play of ancient ideas and mythology. In retrospect, Mary called Plato Waldo's "early patron," but Waldo attributed the envisioning of this philosopher to Mary: "She described the world of Plato . . . & all the ghosts, as if she had been mesmerized, & saw them objectively."[48] Probably both memories began from the same moment—when Waldo wrote a letter to Plato and Mary answered on Plato's behalf.

Far from addressing Plato as a patron, Waldo spoke first in brash resistance, preferring his own language, political system, and religion to the philosopher's dubious pre-Christian wisdom. Even as Waldo described the subsequent unfolding of history to this imagined Plato, however, he reached curiously contradictory conclusions. The practical ethics and inspired truth of Christianity had swept away Greek philosophy, Waldo claimed; yet he pronounced his own choice of reason over revelation, condemned the depraved and enchaining Calvinist dogmas that had grown from Christianity, and admitted the difficulty of finding "connexion & order in events" by any means. Opening the door to skepticism, he was undermining all rationale for judging a modern worldview preferable to Plato's. Yet in his last paragraph, rather than reaching equality with the Greek in ignorance, he leaped back to declaring Plato "unawakened by the thunders of the Church eternal."[49] He seems to have been speaking in two unreconciled voices, one a doubting empiricist and the other a traditional son of nineteenth-century Protestantism.

In response, Mary imagined Plato turning aside from heavenly conversation to rebuke the young man's familiarity. Declaring himself now outside history, Plato still reminded Waldo of the modern world's failings, its condoning of slavery and neglect of nations outside Christian revelation. Furthermore, he blasted Hume as a font of modern skepticism and defended his own ideas by contrast:

> What *did* he *know* or *prove* to vanquish my universals—my innate ideas independent on *perception*. . . . I exulted that my ideas—my existence, had been one of the divine ideas. . . . My Demiurgus—the stars inhabited by Genii—could *you then* have imajined better? In my theology, was [there] not the unity—the

> absolute perfection of the first Cause? . . . In my Republick (apart from the woman kind and the neglect of the ignorant) what can you object?[50]

Mary could find fault in Plato's elitism of gender and social class. At the same time, however, she was knowledgeably endorsing an idealism that transcended history, conceiving of creation as divine energy, and bringing divine and human consciousness into one primal reality.

Mary had no desire in this defense of Plato to surrender her commitment to Christian revelation. Very much in the tradition of Christian Platonism since the Renaissance, but with her own graphic way of imagining the unimaginable, she had Plato tell Waldo of a personal journey in heaven to acceptance of Christ's incarnation and redemption. Yet heaven itself, in Mary's vision, was an augmentation of Plato's own ideas and images: a sundial with dimensions beyond human reckoning, its pointers or "gnomons" casting a shadow beyond themselves to ever-greater realities, its energy whirling ever outward, its reality to offer growth to all freed souls. "Silence thou lisping Inquisitor—," Mary's transformed Plato thundered at Waldo. "Know . . . that pagan Plato whom thou darest to pity is found nearer the Head of principalities . . . than many of those who have assumed [Christ's] name and ministered at his alters."[51]

Waldo found this a "prodigiously fine letter."[52] Mary had countered the unorthodox skepticism of his thinking with an equally unorthodox faith. In all these letters, while holding on with one hand to New England's religious tradition in the midst of the Unitarian-Calvinist controversy, she was reaching with the other toward an enthusiasm of the solitary soul that was universalist, idealist, and eclectic. Saving Puritan piety from "the times" meant infusing it with energies not its own. As she spoke in the guise of counselor to a young man preparing for the ministry, Mary herself was generating major themes and languages for a new Romantic vision.

Amidst wide reading of his own, Waldo listened, recorded, and wanted more. About to begin divinity studies that April, he dedicated his talents to the church, aspiring in particular to the eloquence of Dr. Channing, whose Dudleian Lecture of 1821 had proceeded from "a sort of moral imagination . . . akin to the higher flights of fancy." Channing was genuinely Waldo's model preacher, but Mary his active source. Channing's lecture had expounded the evidences for revealed religion in a manner which, to Waldo, embodied "moral imagination," but Mary offered experiential report in the explicit name of imagination, as Channing had nowhere even intimated. Likewise, Channing had offered Waldo a reading list and a few encouragements, but Mary was regularly writing prodigious letters. Waldo's journal entry of self-dedication came just three weeks after an equally important letter to Mary: as he set out to learn the world's wisdom, he asked, would she kindly not withhold her pen? "I please myself that if my gross body outlive you, you will bequeath me the legacy of all your recorded thot."[53]

Waldo's breathtakingly bold proposal was that he be allowed to appropriate from and in a sense to complete his aunt's thought. He offered a winsome case for doing so. As a "docile child" in the world's library, he had discovered that books often borrowed from each other and reached few conclusions. "I am therefore curious to know what living wit (not perverted by the vulgar rage of writing a book) has suggested or concluded, upon the dark sayings & sphinx riddles of philosophy & life." Because Mary had been unwilling or unable to publish, her words did not to him count as written text, but occupied the category of "living wit," like conversation, protected by no authorial right. By implication, he rated this wit at the highest level of genius, asking whether she planned to burn her books like Prospero, calling her "too proud to expose the mind's wealth to the vulgar voice of fame (as De Stael has done)."[54] Mary was at least figuratively kin to the Shakespearian magician and the celebrated woman author. But, unlike de Staël, she had kept her power secret, so she could contribute most to the world through generosity to him.

Mary offered no direct reply to Waldo's petition but answered another part of his letter by offering her meditation on Miltonic solitude. She was providing the "living wit" that Waldo requested. Though the energy of her writing suggests a real sense of agency, moreover, Mary never articulated the rewards and stresses of such collaboration even to herself. "I have read some of W[aldo]'s MMS," she wrote in her Almanack as he visited in Waterford. "No I never shall get on—there is no kind of prospect that I shall be more heavenly minded—abstracted—nor so much . . . I love to feel how much better & brighter others."[55] Even while contributing to his accumulated legacy, which also included a Harvard education and a growing assumption of authority in the world, she compared and found herself wanting.

She did not therefore withhold her disputatious voice as Waldo enrolled at Harvard Divinity School near the end of 1824. He had been hasty, she warned, in rejecting the thought of studying under Stuart at Andover, but at least should have stayed "under the wing of Channing—w'h was never preened at Cambridge. . . . True they use the name Christo—but that venerable institution it is thought has become but a feeble ornamented arch in the great tempel w'h the [Christ]ian world maintains to the honor of his name." Mary was not choosing between Calvinist and Unitarian doctrine, but opposing the easy answers offered by Harvard's collective tutelage. Most of all, she counseled inner direction: "For yourself, were you a stranger, I could with more confidence intreat you to gather up yourself in solitude with the scriptures—to forget the world and that profession w'h is to connect you to its duties before you enter Cambridge."[56]

The Spirit Now Abroad

Meanwhile the world was stirring Mary's solitude. Early in 1824 a stranger had given her the news account of Daniel Webster's maiden speech in Congress on "The Revolution in Greece," and she shared her response with fifteen-year-old Charles: "Nothing else but Webster & the Greeks—the Greeks & Webster filled my head all night. I had to put out the lamp—open the window—and look out on other worlds to get rid of an excitement so useless." Mary disowned political excitement even in the midst of expressing it; her preference for heavenly realms silently acknowledged the world's refusal of a political role for her sex. As she realized, even Plato had generally excluded women from authority in the state. The exception, explicitly noted in her Almanack, was that "old maids may realize the publick spirit of Plato's republick" by having "no private attachment." Separated from the husbands defining them as property, Plato had proposed, they might be trained to join the guardian class.[57] As an "old maid" in the American Republic, Mary intimated such a possibility for herself, but she did not act upon it or even approach the scenes of public power.

So on her fiftieth birthday, August 25 of that year, she was present only vicariously at Harvard commencement, when her nephew Edward shared the platform as first scholar with visiting Revolutionary hero Lafayette. "Well it has been a proud period for our country and not much otherwise for a certain name," she wrote to Waldo afterward. "If you will not think it demeaned send Edward's oration." A year later she was still remembering that her half-century anniversary had been a day of national glory, and upon meeting Lafayette in Portland told him of her early moment "in arms at the Concord fight." All of these turns of phrase juxtaposed her existence in time or space with great events, but claimed no part in any of them. In the privacy of her Almanack the political world hardly existed: she recorded her fiftieth birthday without any reference to events in Cambridge, but lamented a life of "weakness" and "miscalculation." A one-eyed animal seen from horseback "bro't to mind . . . that I am, compared to some, like one born blind."[58]

Even more than with poetry or theology, Mary developed a political voice in the 1820s only for and with her nephews. A self-celebrating age of oratory had come to New England, the world was demanding freedom, and the nation rapidly approached its own fiftieth anniversary. In these heady times, she kindled to the prospect of male Emersons playing a role. As she foresaw erudition for William and poetic genius for Waldo, she expected political leadership from Edward and Charles.

Mary communicated with Edward primarily through his brothers. Since the days when she and Ruth "kept him ironed out," their quarrel had deepened, each accusing the other of neglect. Charles wrote that she had exiled Edward from correspondence for joking about "sentiment," but then Mary offended him with an ill-tempered comment that seemed to slight his mother. Even while attempting reconciliation after her return to Waterford, they spoke no word of the more fundamental issues between them. As a Harvard student, Edward drove himself to make a mark on the world, repudiating Mary's counsels to inwardness and battling familiar symptoms of consumption. All that Mary had opposed in her brother reappeared in him. Though in the months after graduation she repeatedly asked for a copy of his oration "The Advancement of the Age," none of the brothers seems to have sent one. Waldo loved Edward and his address, but he probably knew that its endorsement of secular American progress would not please his aunt.[59]

Meanwhile, Mary joined in criticizing Edward's mentor, Professor Everett, whose rhetoric had expanded from describing ancient Greek liberty to endorsing its legacy in the American political order. Mary had once loved Edward Everett's sermons and had thrilled with her nephews in his first revelations of Greek lore. But by the early months of 1823, Mary, Waldo, Charles, and Sarah Bradford Ripley concurred that he offered only an "eloquence of display." The display, it seemed obvious, was for personal gain. Charles observed the highly visible professor amidst the office seekers that fall at the Brighton cattle show: "I kept walking round Mr. Everett in order to hear him make a common place remark—but no—he only remained as cold, and dignified as ever, & answered yes-sir, no-sir, as if the statuary were already at work. It is strange that in the pulpit he can so kindle up the soul—but the flint can strike the fire, by which it is not affected." To Mary, Everett's masking of ambition behind a profession of liberality represented the times in their most facile, debilitating form. "I am glad," she admitted to Waldo, "that his notice has fallen on Edward, who will be for flinging his light on a civil profession, [rather] than on another destiny."[60]

This was a brutally unsympathetic judgment of Edward's aspiration to the law, but it anticipated a true joining of interests that August at commencement. Edward's student oration on progress was followed a day later by Everett's Phi Beta Kappa address, which so overwhelmed its audience that he was immediately nominated for Congress. Following his election that November, Everett did not forget a high-achieving son of Harvard, but urged Daniel Webster to take on Edward as his law student.[61] A new political establishment was building in Boston, and the Emersons' star pupil was in training to join it.

Instead of attempting any further to influence Edward, however, Mary directed her more God-centered vision of American political liberty toward Charles. Probably as he entered Harvard that fall, she sent a "Lafayette letter" (now lost), which Waldo remembered as equal in brilliance to his own from Plato. She also offered her youngest nephew a critique of Everett's Phi Beta Kappa address, questioning the claim, based on analogy to Athens' s Golden Age, that an American literature would naturally follow from its republican experiment. Even liberty could not explain all literary and religious genius, Mary argued: had Jewish poetry ever been loftier than in Babylonian captivity? But more, what had Everett urged beyond "the accustomed name of Providence" for the spiritual liberty of America and the world? Having noted that her own allusions and metaphors somewhat resembled the professor's, she rose in the cadences of formal rhetoric to her own American jeremiad:

> The Spirit that goes now abroad on the earth asks not only for political freedom—but for immortality— . . . and in some forms looks for the completion of that glorious scheme which will consolidate all the nations and all their honors into one perfect fabrick. . . . But think—our nation had her nativity cast beneathe the influence of the cross as no other nation—and . . . if she wander (as some of her sons) into the havenless and heavenless chaos of deism, the graves of our sainted fathers and their sons will be trodden by despots & slaves—if there be no worse retribution.[62]

In this private oration, Mary both expressed hope in the redemptive force of American liberty and warned against apostasy. Webster's speech on the Greeks kept her awake all night because it supported Christians against their Turkish oppressors. Though the congressman proposed only sending an American commissioner to Greece, she expressed sympathy with those who would "throw the 'brand into the Porte' and perish in the flames" to aid the struggle for freedom. But she did not, like Webster and his friend Everett, glory without reservation in ancient Greek ideals. "The miseries & cruelties suffered by their slaves," she reminded Charles, "disgrace their government & names." Already by the mid-1820s, Mary was speculating that the only politics worthy of a nation "cast beneathe the influence of the cross" was an antislavery cause. Amidst her praise of Webster she also held up England's William Wilberforce as a model of the Christian orator. When Wilberforce originally argued against the slave trade, she had tried to defend him in a *Monthly Anthology* article; and in 1814 her blunt counsel to Sarah Bradford had been, "*Read Wilberforce.*" Now this Briton had taken up the battle for complete emancipation, and Mary set him above the men of New England in giving the age an "imperishable lustre."[63]

Mary's most passionate ideal of liberating oratory, however, was her father, who came to new life in memory as the fiftieth anniversary of his patriotic service approached. The moment electrified her all the more amidst the movements to free Greeks and slaves, the emergence of Everett and Webster on the political stage, and her nephews' vocational readiness. In April 1825 Everett continued his ascendant oratorical career at the anniversary of Concord's historic battle; focusing on Paul Revere and the military, he did not even mention William Emerson. "Alas," Mary lamented to Waldo, that he had never known "the character of your Ancestor."[64]

William Emerson of Concord appeared rather differently in her counsels to Waldo and to Charles. She urged divinity student Waldo to be a "pharos" or beacon to his country, implicitly recalling the character of his Ancestor in Revolutionary times. To Charles, more directly and insistently, she pressed his grandfather's model of political oratory in the holy cause of freedom. As early as 1822, Mary told the thirteen-year-old how moved she had been by a recent address, for the speaker "reminded me of other Orators—of my prize-getting boy—of that patriot so enthusiastic who was sacrificed by the events of 76." Reminding Charles that their respective fathers had left both of them in infancy, Mary collapsed family history so as to make Charles in effect the son of her own father. That same lineage—with herself merely as witness to patriarchal succession—structured the closing of her incandescent letter on Webster and Greek liberty:

> And when one thinks of our own great Land—of those whose principles & virtues gave it existence, and of those who redeemed it at the Revolution, how infinitely dearer than all Grecian & Roman fame is our glory! Of this Country, should you, my ever loved Boy, become an ornament—the idea of it would in death endear it to me, as in life has the memory of one, whose

love of liberty & honor is escutechoned in more desirable characters than the earth could ingrave.[65]

Mary insisted that she valued the memory of her father only as heaven had preserved it. When, in the aftermath of April 19, 1825, the town of Concord planned a monument to William, she threw herself simultaneously into proposals and protests of indifference. "I shall never cease to think of my Father," she wrote to half sister Sarah Ripley, "—but as to his name or memorial it can be of no importance to any but his grandsons." Having yielded responsibility for the epitaph to the young men, however, she expressed pleasure that Sarah had not liked Waldo's proposal. Mary's own version placed "enthusiasm" first among her father's virtues. "Our Sisters dont like enthusiasm," she noted, "—but you will & it is true & [a] good quality. Without it dear Sarah what [are] all our hopes in [the] future?" In the end, her interpretation of the patriarchal legacy prevailed: the motto in bronze, though shortened by nephew William, began "Enthusiastic eloquent affectionate and pious."[66]

A dream that Mary recounted at the time dramatized both her preservation of the legacy and her marginality within it. The four nephews, all advanced in age, arrived together at the Concord monument accompanied by a woman married ambiguously to any or all of them. Reading the inscription, she observed severely that "the quiet office of priest in an Army" did not necessarily imply sacrifice of life. "But you assured her," Mary wrote to nephew William, "that his constitution was such, that he little expected to return. She appeared sattisfied—was silent at least—read it again—looked at the little boy beside her[,] thought of those who absent were entering an Everett's career, and seemed more curious to learn the character of thier Ancestor." This dream scene concerned a descent of political mission from fathers to sons. Yet the mission's sustainers were women, for now Mary herself intervened to tell the wife what she needed to know about her son's Ancestor: how generous William had been and how he had risen above Concord's party enmities.[67] In entirety this was also a woman's dream, of course, one which Mary begged her nephew to show to his brothers.

Charles believed most wholly in Mary's dream, writing from college his intent to "exert an influence on the affairs of the nation, . . . aid the distressed, & support the weak, defend truth, & vanquish error." Waldo responded with greater resistance. As the year of grandfather William's jubilee began, he confessed to his journal a personal "humor to despise pedigree." "I was educated to prize it. The kind Aunt whose cares instructed my youth (& whom may God reward) told me oft the virtues of her & mine ancestors. They have been clergymen for many generations & the piety of all & the eloquence of many is yet praised in the Churches. But the dead sleep in their moonless night; my business is with the living." Waldo was especially separating himself from his aunt's idealized Ancestor William. She had not urged similar imitation of his more worldly father William. "Were you gratified with the mention of your father?" she had asked after Harvard commencement four months earlier. "It might be as well, as it is a protestant Country, to let the dead slumber." Waldo echoed her language in leaving all the dead to "sleep in their moonless night."[68] The implication of this journal entry was to refuse her replacement of father with grandfather as the true patriarch, declaring himself fatherless and therefore free to seek his own vocation.

Springs of Wonder

Waldo's declaration of January 1825 might seem to have put Mary behind him as well as the ancestors. Though she did not yet sleep with the dead, she held a diminished importance in this journal passage: Waldo represented her instruction in family virtue as an aspect of childhood, not a live presence. Despite this moment of repudiation, however, Mary's part in the conversation was far from over; Waldo turned to her language and ideas repeatedly in the years immediately following. Later he asserted that "in her prime" Mary had been "the best writer . . . in Massachusetts, not even excepting Dr. Channing or Daniel Webster." This prime must have come after Webster's emergence in 1824. Clearly it had not ended when he implored her to define poetry in the summer of 1826: "If the spirit of him who paced the academe . . . or ye laurelled lovers of ye British muse harp in hand sit on your misty mount or soothe their majesties by the margin of your lakes, conjure them I beseech you to announce this secret that the wit of humanity has been so long in vain toiling to unriddle."[69] Waldo now imagined hyperbolically that Plato and the British poets kept her company on the Parnassian heights of western Maine. Mere orators like Webster and Channing could hardly have competed with such a figure of genius, for either height of feeling or gnomic sentences revealing hidden wisdom.

Preparing for approbation to preach in August 1826, Waldo invoked this mythic and poetic wisdom explicitly to support his future ministry. "Can you not," he asked Mary, "suggest the secret oracles which such a commission needs; the lofty truths that are keys & indexes to all other truth, and to all action on society? . . . The letters I get from the Vale prove this purpose better than any other compositions, so I beseech you to forgive the importunity of your nephew."[70] Since first coining the name "Tnamurya," Waldo had not so pointedly called Mary an oracle and Vale her Delphi. He was even willing to sweep away all "other compositions"—books and sermons, as well as other letters—in praise of her divinations.

Waldo's gestures of dismissing and beseeching Mary constituted two sides of a single intellectual and emotional relationship. To be sure, the journal entry of 1825 had turned away from her advocacy of ancestors, while the letters of 1826 sought after her Platonic-Romantic mysticism. The dynamic of these passages, however, was more fundamentally to express paradoxical autonomy and need, as Waldo would go on to do with many of his most potent sources. As a young man he could not fully acknowledge indebtedness to an aunt, and so relegated it to childhood, declared it an influence "from within," or bantered her with comic exaggeration. The metaphors for his "importunity" are nonetheless strong:

he claimed to suffer from poverty in the face of prodigious expense, from hunger too savage to be resisted. "I am whole Cormorant," he confessed when she sent an incomplete letter. Such confession, like his praise of her, was a strategy of appropriation. "Flattery I love it," Mary wrote on the back of this letter.[71] She responded with disbelief and self-protective irony when he asked too much, but continued to feel his need as her own.

The need was genuine, for over the months between these reflections Waldo suffered a crisis of health that threatened to end all hopes in his future. Shortly after embracing "the living," he withdrew from formal study of divinity, his sight too impaired for regular reading and writing. Mary felt personally afflicted by this crisis, perhaps even suffering a sympathetic condition of her own eyes. Their medical situations differed substantially. Waldo's visual dysfunction was a symptom of tuberculosis, probably the same that his father had experienced in 1807, and the disease itself continued to pursue him after two operations cured his eyes by wintertime. Mary treated her merely "sore" eyes topically and never became consumptive. Her condition probably resulted from the inflammatory infection erysipelas, which would return to her eyes and face in later years. The letters of 1825, however, told of her own condition while asking about Waldo's, as if she too had suffered his dreadful and mysterious blow.[72]

Mary confronted the mystery, however, by assuring Waldo that there were "no accidents" outside the providential destiny of the universe. "To learn the nature of man & the origin & nature of evil the liberal school is not sufficient," she argued, "—the weakest part of their system appears then." Instead of seeking reality in science, she urged the Bible's simple account: "*As by means of Adam sin entered and death so by means of a divine man death & sin are destroyed*! Ah, my dear Waldo, prepare (sight or no sight) to preach this divine medicine to a thoughtless ambitious world."[73] Theologically Waldo could not have agreed with this old-fashioned typology. But her evocation of a blind—implicitly Miltonic—preacher sustained belief in his future.

Their dialogue was one line in a network of letters among the brothers and Mary in the fall of 1825, offering news and counsel amidst accumulating troubles. As Charles reported in mid-September, William was due home from Germany; Edward, weak with tuberculosis, had resigned from Webster's office to take a European voyage; and he found his own moments of confidence overwhelmed by hours of melancholy. In turn, Waldo told of his declining vision and Bulkeley's lapse into derangement, and by the end of the month Mary somehow knew that William had come home resolved not to enter the ministry. Even while assuring Waldo that no events were accidental, she inquired anxiously into all of these difficulties. But she could still advise resignation when answering Charles soon thereafter. Amidst the world's many shipwrecks, she wrote, he should decline to pursue greatness and instead adopt a "constitutive superority to trifles in fame & self love—what the stoics called a generous surrender of ones self to the order of events."[74] Classical as well as biblical wisdom counseled self-surrender amidst crisis.

William returned from Europe just five days before Edward embarked, allowing the brothers a hasty conference. At first Mary's inquiries about William's experience met no response, perhaps because of another conspiracy of silence by the nephews. Finally William sent a letter at Ruth's urging but gave impressions of ocean voyaging rather than inner experience. Mary thanked him for the eloquence and homed in on the real questions: "I want to know of the German literature—how connected with theology and morals? What impulse your character heart & mind recieved from letters society & the grander scenes of nature. What is most of all—your change of profession. The roman women were fond of calling themselves Mothers to the youth—Think I have no smack of their patriotism—no right to call you to account?"[75]

Finally William answered these confrontational questions, though his letter does not survive. Probably he told Mary, as he had Waldo, how on the voyage home he had realized his inability to follow Goethe's advice and simply disguise personal skepticism. Even more, her next letter shows that he had laid responsibility for loss of belief upon Johann Eichhorn and his dissection of biblical authority. Far from condemning, Mary sought information for herself. Did the original, uncorrupted gospel that Eichhorn posited offer any proof of Jesus' miracles, mission, or even spiritual life apart from matter? "Yet again I beseech you tell me of what athority E.[ichhorn] esteems this mutalated gospel?"[76]

Likewise, she wanted to hear what remained of William's faith: "You must go all lenghts to compleat your generosity—and tell me not only what you dont believe—but what you do. I respect heartily your renouncement of ministry. It is a proof that those who leave it for doubts—have doubts that it may be true—and fear to have preached what they did not believe." Disappointed at losing a minister from the Emerson lineage, she still rejoiced that William could confess his ignorance without sophistry. "It must be a bold sailor on the abyss of infidelity that can do that. . . . God, in whom I believe, take you in the arms of his mercy, prays fervently MME."[77] More than her nephews apparently expected, her response was not resistance, but the "generous surrender" that, as in her counsel to Charles, was itself a form of faith.

As Waldo absorbed William's experience in the winter and spring of 1826, the abyss of infidelity yawned beneath his letters, too. But sharpened skepticism produced a play of thought with Mary rather than his brother's reticence. In January Waldo wrote "To Tnamurya," as his journal transcription headed the entry, linking Hume's empiricism to the German theology currently challenging the evidences of Christianity. "For me I hold fast to my old faith," he wrote, "that to each soul is a solitary law a several universe." If eyes saw red and green differently, each mind also perceived innocence and guilt on its own, and each era affirmed faith for itself only. As he added a month later, his generation might anticipate a time "when the majestic vision that has for ages kept a commanding check on the dangerous passions of men . . . shall roll away and let in the ghastly reality of things." Had eighteen hundred years of Christianity—"the chivalry of the universe"—become ridiculous? So far no form of internal authority had emerged to replace the old verities and lift his soul from isolation, just a hope for sight to study these puzzles and a request that Mary share her views.[78]

Mary's ability to see was equally partial. "This is the first moment of eyes [for] writing," she responded, "since your letter (the sight of w'h raised an interest I hardly tho't lived in my old heart)." But she turned the crisis of vision into a figure for his epistemological quandary, asking that he turn his eye within to its "native and great objects." Solitude did not necessarily lead to solipsism or Humian doubt but to intuition of the soul's source. Later in the spring she struck on the Miltonic figure that most clearly bespoke this inward grounding. "Oh I do rejoice," she wrote, "that you have been kept from launching till your anchor is stronger than I suspect it is—till the tide w'h you imajine is sweeping away old beliefs will ebb & return with full bearings of truth—if you prefer society to the solitude of an Abdiel."[79] Earlier she had incorporated Satan's "own place" into her evocation of solitude, but now recalled the archangel in *Paradise Lost* who, amidst defection in heaven, had consciously opposed Satan and declared loyalty to God.

In the course of the spring, while Waldo began to regain health and vocation, Mary offered response and guidance. As defender of the faith, she offered more than an attack on skepticism or a simple spiritual illumination. Her allusions brought the scriptures of past and present to bear on their intimate, shared moment, while she mustered all her strength as a lay theologian to grapple with the enemy. That April, having used her own strengthened eyes to reread Hume, she offered a more complete counter to Waldo's doubts from the winter. On the infamous case against miracles, she argued that minds were themselves made to "receive & love" them. Though not meeting Hume's objection on its own ground, she was constructively proposing the mind's own constitution as an opening on the divine. So she responded to Eichhorn's attack on biblical miracles by affirming what remained undamaged,—the report of Christ's ascension and the prophecies of his mission. When young, she wrote, she had collected the Gospels' "harmonies" in an effort to make their story cohere. "But since I learned that the revelation, tho' divine was cast into human circumstances . . . I dont want any more natural account of the event than terrified men & women running back & forth would give."[80]

The best of her letters in 1826 meditated upon the accumulation of reports from three nephews since the year's beginning. A letter from Waldo on "divination" prompted Mary to write on June 13, but her response also expostulated against his worldliness in two April letters and returned to thoughts on evidence and solitude from January. Meanwhile, just as William's crisis of belief was playing into this sequence, so Charles had prompted their thoughts on "divination." The previous December he had asked her aid in preparing a Harvard prize essay on "the Nature of the Grecian Oracles," repeating Waldo's conceit that she was herself an oracle and he a suppliant. Responding to Charles, she called these priestly women a means by which, in the absence of revelation, "the terrific and lovely forms of nature unfolded the instincts of immortality & imaged to [man] the authors of his destiny." But she also found such wisdom inferior to the Hebrew, its priestess the victim of her masters, and the name "oracle" an unkind joke upon herself. "Pardon the whim if such it be, to ask you not to compare me to any weird woman. I . . . pray you to spare my age & vocation."[81]

Now in her darting, by turns sarcastic and lofty, rejoinder to Waldo, Mary denied attaching any great importance to the "Pythoness" or Delphic oracle. Picking up the thread of her earlier letter to Charles, she insisted on the unique inspiration of the Hebrew prophets and their fulfillment in Christ. But divination, in the broader sense of communication with the divine, continued to be her theme. Against Waldo's speculation that heaven, like earth, would require social acquaintance and education, Mary claimed for the lover of virtue an immediate ability "to imbibe knowledge of the Great Spirit as naturally as the bodily senses do their elements." So, she affirmed, might the soul still struggling against earthly constraints know God "within." After countering Waldo's concern about mental isolation by affirming the uniformity of law, Mary leaped beyond her previous argument with a quotation: "The priests of God, says De Stale, should be able to tell us what they suffer and what they hope; how they have modified their characters by certain thoughts, in a word we expect from them the secret memoirs of the soul in it's relation with the Deity."[82] Now she was claiming the soul's capacity to perceive not only a universe of uniform design but also its own live partnership with divinity.

Waldo showed no confidence in his ability to write such "secret memoirs." He was still a reluctant Romantic in the summer of 1826. But he looked for Mary to voice unrealized possibilities, continuing the conversation by asking about the poet as diviner. She had slighted poetry in comparison with revelation, calling it merely a "delightfull vision" of the moment; and in return he asked for a full essay-letter on the subject. Waldo laid out his own schematic history of English poetry, with Shakespeare and Milton as the "great precursors" and Wordsworth their failed follower. Knowing well that he was addressing an admirer in Mary, Waldo listed all of Wordsworth's faults: failure of contact with the boisterous world, composition by theory rather than inherent vision, and foolish inquisitiveness into the metaphysics of his beloved woods and rivers.[83] This was a provocative letter.

In response, Mary bypassed Waldo's charges to rhapsodize about the poet's quest. Heaping the images of Romantic classicism, she described poetry as a treasure to be sought, a Proteus, a Minotaur in a labyrinth, a scattering of sybilline leaves. Though also capable of public and triumphant themes, poetry in the guise that most interested her was a "celestial Guest" coming to meet the male seeker, a female form of nature "decked with the humblest flowers w'h grow wild in the mountains—often with the staff of the wanderer—sometimes in rainbows & the loftiest gifts of nature . . . to concentrate around her alter the *souls* of men." Here was the Wordsworthian scene, and Mary left no doubt that it would also prove the site of sacred revelation:

> [Poetry] has constituted her priest—and he alone of poets, since Milton, deserves to be called *a hermit in the fields of thought*— . . . she has enticed him into the sanctom santorium of nature—where there is a perpetual millennium—

> yet she has her festivals and arrays herself in magical vestments—when the seer & yellow leaf of Autumn lies motionless—when the aged trees lift their naked arms to the dun & mellow clouds—when the sun seems to tarry in the Heavens & take no note of earth—marks no sign on the dial—gives no form to the [shadow] of man—then . . .[84]

In this fragmentary form the letter ended—leaving its recipient, as he wrote back, "whole Cormorant," still wanting the completion of vision that Mary would not offer.[85] Nonetheless, she was articulating her fullest vision of the holiness at nature's heart, a "perpetual millennium" of perception rather than an apocalypse at the end of earth's history. Such a breakthrough culminated more than two decades of Mary's seeking analogies between nature and divinity, quoting Young and Thomson, telling Waldo what she would write if she were a poet. She did not explicitly assign that status to either of them now but by implication granted visionary power to both. Waldo might directly follow the Wordsworthian model of poetic quest. But Mary strongly identified with the figure of nature, its mountain flowers and wanderer's staff, and she owned great power here as well. Not only did this female figure sanctify the priest and lead him to her mysteries, but also enjoyed her own autumnal festival, so like Mary's life of stillness. The meditation had to break off because its discordant elements were impossible to complete: Mary could not pursue a marriage with Waldo even figuratively, could not provide his vision, could not continue a near self-portrait of female power in identity with nature.

"The eye sees not its own lustre," Mary wrote in introducing her thoughts on poetry. She might have been describing her own visionary power, which in all these meditations cloaked itself in a rhetoric of modesty. In the letter on divination she admitted to Waldo that she was phrasing as questions thoughts that were really positive propositions, "but indeed I feel a diffidence in shaping my tho'ts to you."[86] As she described poetry she ignored the oracular power that Waldo, like Charles, had attributed to her in his request, and she constrained herself from rising to such visionary power only by breaking off her rush of words. These letters, including the aphoristic sentence about the eye, epitomize the nascent Transcendentalism that was her gift to Waldo. He could look back on her as the "best writer in Massachusetts" because, quite simply, she was most fully articulating these themes amidst all the writers associated with the fledgling "Movement." And she was articulating them to him.

Waldo's full response would take another decade, but its growth began in the extraordinary series of self-affirmations that he wrote to Mary in the summer and fall of 1826, as, despite continued sickness and fear of death, he projected future health and accomplishment. Even as she wrote her mid-June letter about the power to know God within, he met her thought by stating that he knew himself made by another and so could "welcome the Coming on of my untried Being." He offered his own "secret memoir" that August:

> There are, I take it, in each man's history insignificant passages which he feels to be to him not insignificant; little coincidences in little things, which touch

> all the springs of wonder, and startle the sleeper conscience in the deepest cell of his repose; the Mind standing forth in alarm with all her faculties, suspicious of a Presence which it behoves her deeply to respect—touched not more with awe than with curiosity, if perhaps some secret revelation is not about to be vouchsafed.[87]

This passage, often quoted for its quietly eloquent thrill of self-discovery, directly answered Mary's rhapsodic letter on the poet's revelation, and it led directly to his asking for more letters from his oracle at the Vale. Her active partnership in his growth has gone too long unrecognized.

Least known has been the conscious and complex intellectualism of the Romantic enthusiasm that Mary transmitted to Waldo. "Is it not true," he wrote to her that September, "that modern philosophy has got to be very conversant with feelings? Bare reason, cold as a cucumber, was all that was tolerated in aforetime, till men grew disgusted at the skeleton & have now given him in ward into the hands of his sister, blushing shining changing Sentiment."[88] He knew that he was acknowledging conversion to a philosophical method and vision that she had long held. Not only was Sentiment for her a transmutation of New Light piety from the past; she had conceived its value among bluestocking, poetry-reading friends in her nephew's infancy, rediscovered it as the starting point of a revolution in de Staël's *Germany*, and developed its defense by reading post-Lockean philosophy over two decades. Waldo's metaphors captured the choice of Sentiment over Reason with a wit and delicacy that was his own. But he personified as female the Sentiment that he owned, and he did so from deep association of that inner wellspring with her.

Mary encapsulated her synthesis of traditions, her mission to heal and empower, and her refusal of personal authority in a "horoscope" that she wrote for Waldo's twenty-third birthday on May 25, 1826. Picking up directly from her Plato letter of two years before, she imagined a new conversation in heaven concerning Waldo. In this fantasy, however, Plato does not rebuke the young inquisitor but declares an interest in his future greatness. And though once again shown as a Christian convert, "bearing a palm among the order of [the] elected," he now keeps company with a "son of light & truth" simply named "Ancestor." In this year of the nation's fiftieth anniversary, Plato's partner in conversation was grandfather William Emerson.

Mary expressed her hope for Waldo primarily in the voice of the Greek philosopher rather than the patriot minister. Explaining that his predictions arise from consulting not the stars but the certainties of cause and effect, Plato tells Ancestor, "I have had a favorite (for years called a seer) among your descendants." Ancestor, too, has clearly been following Waldo's path, for he acknowledges the young man's illness: "How then if he remains[?]—you see me not rid of earth—I own I'd have him live." In response, Plato prognosticates not only Waldo's but also Mary's future: Waldo will not die, but "the genius of the peculiarly good will translate one whom the order of things has connected with him."

"Is it one whom your former coterie or mine will admit?" asks Ancestor.

"Both both—[she has] a natural taste for what is fine in spiritualism & what is infinite in [Christ]ian practice."

Ancestor responds with interest: "Would she could go on with your boy."

"No better not," Plato answers, "—a mind not well balanced thrown between antagonist objects & affections is like the ocean in a tempest where sun & winds contend—her place is not found on earth I hope."

"But the youth—will he stand firm in mind & virtue?"

"Yes! He will in both if I can read the cypher . . . —yes he will come out of all manner of eclipses & illusions & 'his age be as the noon day & remember his ills no more.' "[89]

Just as in the dream that Mary recounted to nephew William, her horoscope embodied a patriarchal tradition. Only males speak in it, and her own father has no apparent knowledge that she exists until Plato informs him. Though Plato praises her taste for Greek and Christian knowledge, anticipating a genuine place for her in heaven, he also finds her unbalanced, anomalous, certainly not an active source of her young man's future greatness. While diminishing her own character in this fantasy, however, Mary was coming perilously close to acting out the part of a Delphic oracle by composing it. Only insofar as she projected herself in these male figures could she be said to share in the horoscope's prophecy of victory. Whether for Waldo or for herself through him, however, it was a victory entirely characteristic of her ways of thought: that the family descended from William Emerson contained a "seer," that the darkness of eclipse and illusion would pass and bring this power of vision to noonday light.

8

God Within Us

> I touch eternity—let me do nothing small. Yet my whole life has consisted of noughts. Well a single figure at their head, put down by another, makes them immense. Been nothing? Done nothing? Let me hide myself more completely in thy omnipresence oh father of the universe! Absorb me in thyself—let my consciousness remain—& it will!
>
> Almanack, December 30, 1826

The Manse

The Concord Manse and its inhabitants had become aged by the mid-1820s. Mother Phebe died at eighty-three, just three months short of the battle jubilee in 1825; Mary was present to hear her deathbed complaint about Ezra Ripley's squeaky boots but did not soften old judgments of a habitually delicate mother. She had already concluded that Phebe and her daughter Sarah were "accomplished invalids," overly critical of the casual housekeeping she offered and too long attentive to society's opinion. "My mother's education has been impressed on all her children," Mary wrote to Ruth, "—and Providence has either removed or disciplined them to obviate the effect." She felt that her own discipline had lasted long enough, asking if it would be improper to remind Ezra that she had never received the interest on her portion of father William's estate. Soon thereafter, Ezra purchased Phebe's third of the estate by paying each of her living children and grandchildren fifty dollars.[1] It is unlikely that Mary felt adequately compensated.

She was not without sympathy, however, for the Manse's beleaguered patriarch. Later in the spring of 1825, Ezra and Sarah learned that their youngest son and brother, Daniel, had died in Alabama, where he had settled nine years earlier to practice law. Since his youthful days of dueling, Daniel had never found his way in life but had sadly fallen into illness and conflict with southern in-laws. Over the next year, Ezra's griefs compounded: his daughter and closest companion, Sarah, was dying too; at the same time, the once-peaceful Concord parish divided into separate orthodox and Unitarian churches. Relenting from old animosity, Mary signed her letters as Ezra's "affectionate friend," as well as "dutiful daughter." To her, the loss of religious fanatics seemed a blessing on the church; and, though admitting herself "peculiar in not estimating life," she hoped that Sarah would live for his sake. Having stayed with the Ripleys in the summer and fall of 1826, she mistook the pace of Sarah's decline and returned to Waterford before the actual death in November. Then Mary admitted how keenly she too would miss her "only sister in single blessedness."[2]

With the deaths of Phebe and Sarah the Manse had no mistress, but the extended family of Ripleys and Emersons remained close to it. Only Samuel survived of the three Ripley children, but he lived nearby in Waltham and could often visit along with his wife, Sarah Bradford, and their children. Daniel's widow, Susan Fitts Ripley, left her own kin in Alabama through most of 1826 to acquaint herself and her small son with Concord. Of William and Phebe Emerson's descendants, the Farnhams still remained in touch from Newburyport and Boston, and all of the Waterford kin, whether related to Ezra directly or indirectly, often returned to Concord. Ruth Emerson and her sons had never stopped viewing the Manse as a home amidst many rented quarters; Edward and Waldo inscribed their names beneath their father's on the wall of the "Prophet's Chamber," claiming its lineage as their own. Now Ruth came to live there, caring for Ezra's gout as well as finding a place of retreat for the still-ailing Edward. At the end of 1826, Ezra's oddly assorted family circle consisted of Ruth and Edward; Susan Fitts Ripley and son; and "little Sarah," the nine-year-old daughter of Robert and Rebecca Haskins, who, as Sarah Ripley's namesake, had been raised by her at the Manse for the past five years.[3] This family still offered hospitality and expected service in the manner of the eighteenth century.

Such a family group was again on hand eighteen months later to witness Edward's lapse into mental illness. Thirteen-year-old Hannah Haskins had replaced her younger sister in the household, doubtless as the more skilled domestic worker, and her memory long retained the horrifying scene. One morning Edward came down to breakfast making fun of Grandfather Ripley instead of addressing him with the customary veneration. Ruth and Ezra were both stunned to silence, but Hannah, with a child's response to disrupted decorum, burst out laughing. Later that day she hid under the bed upstairs to overhear Edward praying that God would restore his mother's and grandfather's reason.[4]

Edward recovered briefly, but at the end of June 1828, Ruth summoned Waldo to help convey his brother to Charlestown Asylum. Edward had been deranged for a full week, shifting between wild joking and violence. "He would throw down every thing in the room & throw his clothes &c out of the window," Waldo wrote to William with unblinking honesty; "then perhaps on being restrained wd. follow a paroxysm of perfect frenzy & he wd. roll & twist on the floor with his eyes shut for half an hour." Waldo joined two Concord physicians in a borrowed hack for the drive into Charlestown, then picked up Sarah Bradford Ripley in Waltham, since Ruth had "no woman to lean upon or comfort her." The asylum now had enough family members in it to pose a problem for the superintendent: Bulkeley was there, too, suffering one of his periodic bouts of mania, as well as the "Dr. Haskins" who was probably Ruth's eldest brother. Waldo recounted all these calamities—along with the crowning irony of Charles's simultaneous Bowdoin prize at Harvard—upon returning to Cambridge "from Concord from a desolate house."[5] His phrase described the family as well as their gathering place.

Mary's place in the house of Emerson is epitomized by her location and response during the crisis. She was absent from both Concord and Waterford, having retreated to the frontier town of Andover, Maine, where a young protégé named Thomas Treadwell Stone had become minister of the fledgling church. A few months before, Ezra had chided her for leaving the land of her nativity to hear "the screaming of loons, the hooting of owls, & the howling of wolves." In return, Mary asked whether one place in Maine's interior was really wilder than another, even while describing her horseback ride through drifted snow to reach Andover. But her extreme gestures of individualism coexisted with clannishness as fierce as Ezra's. Having heard of Edward's breakdown, she composed multiple letters of comfort to Ruth, offered immediate help, and beseeched Waldo and Charles for information about treatment in a modern asylum. "Suppose the patient alone & reason returning—my God how frightfull the conviction of such a place. . . . Oh how gladly would I spend the rest of weary wasted life in watching in his cell—in seeing there was no severity used by Nurses—or whatever they have."[6]

In addition to offering care to Edward, both Mary and Waldo responded by defending self and family. Mary first claimed that insanity could not be inherited, then insisted that her cousins' and aunt's "embicillity" did not amount to real madness. She was suppressing as well as acknowledging the record of past generations. Waldo explained that "silliness" guarded him against the family's "constitutional calamity . . . which in its falling on Edward has buried at once so many towering hopes." Later in the year, his former disinterest in ancestors now forgotten, Waldo began a journal entitled "Genealogy," consulted a professional researcher to ascertain his descent from Peter Bulkeley, and affirmed the value of "good blood." His sidestepping of Mary as a source of ancestral information may suggest doubt of her sanity, too. Even before the demise of Edward, Waldo had charged that a lack of "adjustment between reason and feeling" permanently affected her mind; and during the weeks of Edward's stay at the asylum, Waldo described her to Sarah Bradford Ripley as a "she-Isaiah" who "quotes as wildly as she talks."[7] Mary was defending herself as well as Edward by arguing away a troublesome heritage.

Her offer to join in care for him began a renewal of ties. When the family silently declined her services and extended no invitation to Charles's commencement, she protested "how tame" she had become. Soon thereafter, she returned to Waterford and began exchanging letters with Edward, who after long rebellion against Mary insisted on an exaggerated version of her piety, repudiated worldly ambition, and wrote to her of repentance. In Waldo's estimation, Edward never fully recovered: "He was sane, able to attend to his work, but the spring was broken. . . . The eagerness, the freedom, was all gone." Mary doubtless welcomed more self-doubt than Waldo, declaring to Edward that the world was a hospital and its devotees the truly insane, asking with Antoninus "if it be of importance whether a good action is performed by you or another." But she also offered the Pauline motto "Rejoice always," encouraging no self-mortification. By the following summer, Mary was back at the Manse with Edward, telling Waldo that she had been "wonderfully favored with cautions" from the convalescent. "But some questions he answers with great interest about my speculations. The interior of his mind is good not strange."[8]

The dialogue that Mary and Waldo conducted throughout these years was uniquely speculative but not isolated from the larger family group. Characteristically, Mary could apply her concept of the mind's interior power equally in affirming de Staël's view of priesthood and judging the extent of Edward's recovery. Nor was the group, as Waldo later imagined it, really limited to "M.M.E. and the boys," but included diverse others. Mary and Edward exchanged talk at the Manse, but she also joined her kinswomen Ruth and Hannah in the kitchen. Writing to Charles, she quoted from a "most antient housekeeper's buttery" the homely wisdom "As runs the glass / Man's life doth pass." To her eyes, she confessed, the Manse was always mourning its first residents. But she could acknowledge a grudging affection for its current master Ezra, somewhat, she said, as in "the case of old Catharine when she was converted to love Wolsey."[9] Both his needs and his austere kindness drew the family back to Concord.

Ezra was not a cardinal of the church, like Wolsey in Shakespeare's *Henry VIII*, but in the countryside west of Boston he possessed authority. In the fall of 1828, after losses to family and congregation alike, he still celebrated his fiftieth anniversary of ordination with a grand review of social and theological history. Ezra's *Half Century Discourse* articulated common ground with stepdaughter Mary, but more than enough differences to keep their love a matter of negotiated settlement. Defining doctrine for Concord Unitarians, he declared his opposition to a tripartite God but also his belief in humanity's fall and regeneration through the Messiah. He wished to be considered "Evangelical" if not "Calvinistic," having never departed from the doctrine of grace through twenty-five hundred sermons. But for Ezra, grace did not translate into a foretaste of heaven or inner knowledge of God, only a spur to the "good and godly life" within church discipline. Unlike the Moodies, Emersons, and Blisses, whose New Light pietism had descended to Mary, Ezra found nothing positive to say about "religious excitement."[10]

Furthermore, his memorial sermon gave no hint of the difficulties and aspirations that Mary and her nephews were entertaining under his roof at the Manse. Ezra conceded that infidelity, imported from Europe in the writings of Voltaire and Hume, had gripped the learned class in post-Revolutionary times, but he declared this climate now changed in favor of Sabbath schools, charities, and inventions. If this summation of progress showed none of Mary's doubt of institutions or flight to solitude, neither did his faith in biblical authority show any response to recent challenges. "The great current of mind sets strongly to the divine authority of the Bible, and bends to the doctrines and sceptre of Jesus Christ," he proclaimed, as if stepgrandson William had not recently lost his faith to German higher criticism. The discontents that Waldo would later call a Movement were beyond his ken. Mary tactfully reminded Ezra of their common adherence to the "good school of Sam. Clarke" but privately found him "easily satisfied with one's theology (if not calvin)." Apart from any particular point of doctrine, he was simply not a speculator.[11]

By 1828 the extended family of the Manse had produced two epic accounts of religious life, Ezra's sermons and Mary's letters and diary. They were separated by generation, gender, public authority, and fundamental belief about the individual self in relation to God. Ezra declined to dwell on himself at all. He had, in fact, begun a diary the week of his ordination in 1778 with ten resolutions detailing his intended walk with God, then returned to it periodically to record the anniversary of his vows. By 1824, the forty-sixth year of his ministry, he reached the seventeenth page of the manuscript and noted having written more than he first intended. He felt none of the diarist's impulse to confess and preserve personal experience. Attempting self-examination in 1811, he broke off after registering "serious objections to the keeping of a Diary, to be inspected after Death, even if it would be kept with *exactness* and *truth.*" Even abbreviated record keeping ended after Sarah's death. "I have made up my mind," he recorded, "to write for inspection no more of my religious views, feelings, and resolutions. . . . So many and great have been my trials the past two years, and at this time, that I am liable to note things under the influence of feeling rather than understanding. I prefer silence, when there is not a certainty of uttering truth."[12]

Mary did not hesitate to record either emotion or understanding. While her letters of the middle and late 1820s were a daring affirmation in the face of infidelity, expressing visionary possibilities to young correspondents, her Almanack also explored this ground on her own terms, with first-person voice and identity firmly at the center. Even in its surviving, partial form, the Almanack is an expansive record of inner life, not thinking vicariously for others but presenting her flawed, regal self directly to divine presence. In its pages Waldo appeared only occasionally: she called him her "better genius" and hoped for illumination from the "uraka's" (eurekas) that his best letters contained. Ezra, the Waterford sisters, Ruth, and the other nephews were mentioned even less often. Mary responded to news of her sister Sarah's death by overcoming regret at not being present, vowing to imitate her virtue of sympathy, and pressing on to "what is great & future." "Good God!" she exclaimed. "To individuate myself with thy presence is all—oh how rich!"[13]

The hunger to preserve identity, always driving Mary's religious quest, found perhaps its most extreme expression in her Almanacks of the late 1820s. She expressed the redeemed state in extravagant metaphor, as a mathematical miracle transforming her "life of noughts" to immensity. Seeking absorption in God, she assured herself that consciousness would remain, individuality be rendered eternal and not obliterated by such meeting. From Waterford she reflected, "I, that I call I, have had no one to wake me"; on her retreat in Andover, she mused about memory as a "strange power within." Even in heaven there might be "higher conditioned spirits [who] look away from me—," she conceded, "those who in my circumstances, belittled as they have been, would have done better than I have—felt larger presence." Then she resigned herself and admitted, "I ... can indeed form no idea of things out of my experience." She also defined a capacity for sympathy quite different from her sister Sarah's: "I have had no one to sympathize with—tho' I sympathize in general benevolence from the President to the Cat. Should it be so always I can be happy.... My life I would occupy only in the study of it's wonders—in arranging my ideas of it's real character."[14]

Mary's Almanack expressed a Puritan sensibility in language refracted through diverse literary lenses and given quirky, often brilliant form. She never lapsed into incoherence but often used language "wildly," for better or worse. Sometimes her high style bombastically echoed Shakespeare and Milton, as on New Year's Day in 1827: "Howl winds—roar tempest—shake from thy preened wings the hoary sleet. Thou carriest us on—dim & dolefull as thou art—to other scenes where the unbodied spirit will defy thee." More characteristically, she had moved beyond the exclamations of her earliest Almanack to greater understatement and invention. "Rich sky and air—," she noted. "The wheel w'h revolves death & change & hope to others touch not the orbit I move upon—so circular—yet *that* goes forward—connected with the great center of other orbs." The hands of clocks, or "gnomons"—often misspelled as "gnomes"—especially symbolized the slow passage of time: "The old gnome points towards 11. My glasses downstairs—yet these stars shining thro' these naked trees on a misty atmosphere is so like Heaven beaming comfort on poor man that I can't go to bed."[15]

The Almanack continued to envision the soul's ascent to heaven in Platonic terms, here again with new vehemence and idiosyncrasy. "The imajanation," she concluded in July 1826, the week of her letter on poetry to Waldo, "was given for more lasting uses [than] to paint the caprices of dame Luck—it was to scale the skies— ... to hold high converse in walks of boundless thought." Such impulses toward free motion and language, however, were continually balked by the limits that Mary attributed to material form:

> Channing ... can get no better than the old orientalists who so early said [matter] was an emanation of Deity.... But after all ... matter in its most splendid forms is only a dumb Betty. And we, I surely, are slaves to it whether it wings in excitement or fetters in clay.... Oh I am impatient to burst my prison—but this repressed fire may burn brighter for confinement, in other states.[16]

As a written text, the Almanack was enriched by Mary's failure to ascend; instead, her "repressed fire" habitually returned to earth. Though she had looked for imminent death since the 1790s, only now did a fully macabre sensibility overtake her writing: "If one could choose, and without crime be gibbeted, were it not altogether better than the long drop[p]ing away by age without mentality or devotion[?] The vulture & crow would craw—craw—and unconscious of any deformity in the mutilated body, would relish their meal—and make grimace of affected sympathy—nor suffer no real compassion." As Waldo commented to Sarah Bradford Ripley, Mary was "alive to the comedy" of such language. "I sing te Deum over my pale face & sunk eyes," she wrote, "and would more heartily, if the worm were at the door w'h would crawl in & crawl out."[17]

Just as characteristically, however, the earth drew her loving attention as a sign of God's immanence. She often identified with animals. The family cat received her contemplative benevolence, and the cricket that she was "too superstitious to kill" held its place in the divine scheme. Expressing the human potential for awakening, she found an organic metaphor in Maine's slow springtime: "Mankind may be frozen & subdued like the snake by discipline, but thaw it &———!" Her analogies often surprise. In one of her annual memorials to brother William, she lamented their religious differences and her coldness on the day of his death. But then without transition came a discovery of likeness: "This morning I have been playing with the goslings—how astonishing is nature! They have no parents—yet discover a strange instinct for each others society, tho' there is no protection from it."[18]

Waldo eventually transcribed the passage on William and the goslings into his "MME" notebook and marveled at the wit of such writing: "M.M.E.'s style is that of letters—an immense advantage—admits of all the force of colloquial domestic words, & breaks, & parenthesis, & petulance—has the luck & inspirations of that,—has humor, affection, & a range from the rapture of prayer down to details of farm & barn & *help*."[19] He could sometimes stand in judgment of this "she-Isaiah," but equally admired her.

By 1828, as Ezra reviewed fifty years in the ministry, Mary had produced one of the longest and most refractory diaries in the Puritan tradition, by turns angry and loving, narcissistic and sympathetic, humble and learned, and always self-dramatizing. Reading a review of Stewart by Alexander Everett not long after, she raised the "darker problem" of evil that Everett had not confronted, then drew back to repudiate her own struggle of thought: "But these discussions seldom enter my head. Everett has done nobly and I withdraw my head in happy silence into its shell, w'h his spear drew out in admiration. And I take my own proper shapeless ignorance, and will put some crumbs on this tree for birds." Identifying her female being with the small creatures of nature rather than the spear-carrying males of intellectual debate, she seemed to abandon the realm of mind altogether. "Yet I cannot but add—," she began the next sentence—and launched a new thought. "The future only can unriddle the web. . . . Happy are they who are involved in its far-reaching threads, w'h connect them to the first Cause."[20] Surely she was counting herself among these happy people, able to reach even in these sentences from her tree of birds to the first Cause.

Thy Will Be Done

Meanwhile, a new preacher had declared himself within the Emerson-Ripley clan. In October 1826, Waldo delivered his probationary sermon, first to the Middlesex association of ministers and then to Samuel Ripley's church in Waltham. Mary, already present in Massachusetts to attend her sister Sarah's illness, was in the congregation. She heard a sermon much closer to her own vein of pietism than to the sturdy moral teachings of Ezra and his son Samuel. Waldo had written pieces of it since the summer, before and after his plea for "oracles" and his declaration of the mind's capacity to awaken before divinity. Instead of "Sentiment," he now named this mental power "Conscience, God's vicegerent, enthroned within." Choosing the text "Pray without ceasing," he drew his listeners to consider prayer as a perpetual exercise of consciousness—and an exercise met with response from the spiritual world. "All prayers are granted," he declared.[21]

By the following January, Mary had returned to Maine, and Waldo had journeyed to Florida in search of health; but by letter she told how often she relived "the day at Waltham—the enthuseasm of Mrs. Ripley—the admiration she felt." If Waldo could impress Sarah Bradford Ripley, he had met a standard beyond what the association demanded. Soon thereafter, Mary wrote to Sarah in response to a darkly skeptical letter; when Waldo returned from the South and preached again in Waltham, he copied this hyperbolic defense of faith into his journal. " 'Can't believe,' " Mary exploded. "Commit a crime—form an intrigue such as Queens & great outlaws do; blot the fair fabric of your fame quench the torch which has been light for others & you will have faith enough. Conscience will do an office which reason seems slow in doing."[22] He and Mary shared a confidence in all the powers of mind that Sarah, despite her praise for the October sermon, did not easily affirm.

But contention had not ceased between Mary and Waldo. Though he began his preaching career by concurring with her on intuitive consciousness as the core of religious experience, they now began to diverge on the nature and role of Christ. Even as she praised the manner of his first sermon, she also asked, "But where [was] the miracle power of the name of the Savior? The athority of the Founder? The wonders he performed? The self devotion—the contempt of honor—the tenderness of benevolence?" That winter he expressed a hope to go beyond Paschal or Young in describing a man with "nothing between his head & ye infinite heavens," but also responded to her questions with his own blunt account of Christ's role in human history: "Men were so ignorant & besotted they cd. not see the perfection of morals. Jesus Christ was sent to remove ye blindness from their minds. They are now able to see the majestic proportions & the sufficiency of the first Law. And it needs no corroboration."[23]

At this point Mary and Waldo were only affirming varieties of Arian belief, both seeing Jesus as a savior but not a person of God. They even used similar metaphors of sight in articulating these beliefs. Mary had written in her Almanack the spring before that virtue was like a power of vision that, once lapsed from its first condition, needed the lens of revelation. Both Mary and Waldo posited an inability to see divine light that was the particular Emersonian "fall." While Waldo saw all blindness as removed by Christ's past intervention, however, Mary needed the constant assistance of a lens. Still she felt Waldo's possibility of unaided vision strongly enough to admit it as a temptation. "When so harmonised with God & his existence," she commented in her Almanack, "I forget the means of the Xian rev.[elation] w'h has drawn me so close—then I dwell on the natural & moral attributes as tho' I had not forfeited so often this natural inheritance." Rereading Mary's Almanack years later, Waldo rightly detected a "polite and courtly homage to the name and dignity of Jesus" that veiled more fundamental dislike of "any interference . . . between her and the Author of her being."[24]

Mary was prepared for no such ambiguities, however, as she wrote to Waldo in his first year of preaching. Sharply aware of his role as a public teacher, she stood for the tradition and so represented the divide between them as wider than it really was. When he had been following Hume from the senses into skepticism, she had been willing to assert the power of intuition in terms orthodox or pagan. Now that he was seeing intuition as a power to do without Christ, she insisted on scriptural truths alone. "It is worse than idle to ridicule the fall," she wrote to him in 1827. "The apple may be allegorical—but if it were real it answered for a sign (an arbitrary one, be sure) of a government diciplinary & p[ro]spective." If evil existed, it could only be remedied by a "suffering Messiah," not a mere martyr or teacher; and that remedy should be celebrated in the communion supper, whose authority both the gospel and St. Paul had established.[25]

By contrast, Waldo, was increasingly preoccupied with the figure of Jesus as man rather than Messiah, desiring even before the trip south to consider his "personal character & influence & . . . death." Writing from Florida of an ongoing health crisis, he echoed words from the Lord's Prayer, "Thy will be done," which Mary had expanded so eloquently in the prayers of his childhood. This petition, as a human stance of Stoic-Christian resignation, now focused his interest in Jesus. One of the new sermons he preached repeatedly through 1827 reflected on Paul's words "We preach Christ crucified." In fact, he dwelled on the story of crucifixion in a way that Mary never had. An Almanack entry from the year before explained her avoidance of Jesus' agonies as a focus of devotion: "It may be owing to my difficulty of geting room that I enjoy nothing w'h costs anybody or even myself any pains." Waldo, however, had just written to Mary of the wisdom resulting from being shown the "house of Pain," and he found in Jesus a character and teacher of heroic transcendence.[26]

His letters to Mary sounded further possibilities as well. At the end of 1827, Waldo stated his new fundamental principle—a radical incorporation of the human figure of Christ that might soon replace traditional Christianity. "Connexion between God & ye Soul,—what is religion but this Connexion. . . . Is not this unutterably beautiful & grand this life within life this literal Emanuel God with us[?]" Mary responded without shock, indeed with a certain recognition. Waldo's new philosophy seemed "frigid." "Yet it meets in it's extreme," she wrote to him, "the extreme of [Christ]ian faith."[27]

Personal events punctuated the growth of Waldo's new faith. He preached more widely, substituting for Frothingham at First Church and taking on missionary lectures in the Connecticut Valley. "Waldo is the most popular preacher among the candidates," Samuel Ripley wrote to Mary near the beginning of 1828, "and all he wants is health to be fixed at once in Boston." The threat of consumption was fading from his life, and in proportion his self-confidence rose. By the time of Samuel's report, Waldo had additional reasons to look favorably on life. Preaching in Concord, New Hampshire, he had just met seventeen-year-old Ellen Tucker and was already planning further acquaintance. Meanwhile, his brothers, always an extension of himself, were succeeding in their various plans, with William settled as a lawyer in New York City and Charles at the top of his class at Harvard. Such optimism proved premature, however: later months of 1828 found the family struggling to understand Edward's demise. Waldo reviewed these circumstances to Mary and commented, "Nemesis keeps watch to overthrow the high. . . . The way to be safe is to be thankful. I cannot find in ye world without or within any antidote any bulwark against this fear like this, the frank acknowledgement of unbounded dependance."[28] His "literal Emanuel" was not a mere exercise of human will or self-confidence, but a residing of the self in God.

By the time of this letter, Waldo was both engaged to Ellen and entertaining an attractive offer to settle as Henry Ware Jr.'s colleague at the Second Church of Boston. Waldo wrote to ask Mary, who had followed his "straitened" walk to manhood, for meditations upon this new fortune. He might have appreciated an updated horoscope from Plato and Ancestor, but instead her response was in a "porcupine humor." Mary reminded Waldo that he exaggerated both his former poverty and his newborn success; and she accused him of vaporing about changes as though he were the fisherman of Galilee, with the world about to bear the permanent marks of his destiny. He seemed to be taking over the gospel rather than submitting himself to it. But she also admitted her personal spleen—that *she*, unlike her nephews, was promised no change, "and the utmost delight ever known has been in bounding on without any thing." Waldo's acquiescence was strategic, as if sure to produce power and success; Mary's was necessitated by persistent absence of opportunity. Claiming sympathy with "those whose golden spoke the white fates have turned up," she still felt suspicious of good fortune.[29]

Despite Mary's mockery, her own most passionate desires for Waldo were reaching fulfillment. All the pride that she refused to offer directly went to his fiancée the same week, as she inculcated the traditional role of ministerial helpmeet: "The man that God has blest you with is devoted to the highest & most urgent office. Lean not on him for resources—but urge him on to aid in the work of moral improvement which is going on for Heaven. Be yourself a ministering angel to him and society." Slipping into her favorite role of guide to youth, she recommended a reading list, from Law's *Serious Call* and Young's *Night Thoughts* to de Staël's *Corinne*. "I hope you dont paint nor talk french," she added. "Hope you'll be a unique. And *love* poetry—that musick of the soul." This was close to self-parody, as she recognized in a postscript to Waldo on her admirable directing of Ellen's education: "Fudge you'll say." Meanwhile her passion for his thoughts had not really abated, as she declared, "The sermons I want."[30]

Mary was not present for Waldo's ordination at Second Church on March 11, 1829. Whether by her own or others' choice, she stayed in Maine while the family-dominated ceremony took place. Uncle Samuel Ripley preached, and the charge was delivered by two clerical fathers, Ezra Ripley and Nathaniel Frothingham; Ruth, Edward, Charles, Ellen, and Ellen's mother were all in attendance. Charles wrote his description of events to Mary, and in response she applauded the Pauline text of Waldo's first sermon, "I am not ashamed of the gospel of Christ." Edward Everett, she recalled, had preached from the same text when he began at Brattle Street, and she had then told eleven-year-old Waldo that "truly there is nothing to be ashamed of in this gospel." Now she did not ask what he had presented from this text, and probably would not have liked his promise to apply the gospel's greatness in a freely innovative spirit. Instead she wove her own meditation: "the gospel of Christ" led her, quite unlike Waldo, to reflect on Jesus as "an individual—sent of God—His son—as no other being." She conceded that this view (essentially the same Arianism that she had voiced in the *Monthly Anthology* of 1804) was an "old exploded faith w'h florished in the augustan age of the Chh."[31]

Theologically as well as personally, she and Waldo were going separate ways, and never again would they exchange letters with the intensity of the past decade. She continued, however, to influence his ministerial thoughts and words indirectly through her Almanack. As she now wanted "the sermons," he sought to read her diary of inner faith, to which he had not had frequent access in the past. He wrote as though the Almanack were part of his capital: "I grow more avaricious of this kind of property like other misers with age, and like expecting heirs would be glad to put my fingers into the chest of 'old almanacks' before they are a legacy." This request came simultaneously with his critique of a minister who was "all of clay & not of tuneable metal," who plagiarized from the common stock of knowledge instead of creating anew.[32] Once more his desires to declare originality and to appropriate coincided.

Mary resisted, claiming that the diary offered nothing new, but was her own, unsharable. Still she began sending sections. "Return these—or a blank in my Al[manack]," she instructed the first time. "And it is strange but the same feelings return not. However feeble they are a part of ourselves." Waldo felt no hurry to return her manuscripts, but kept them from one year to the next while transcribing passages for himself. "Never was time more lost than [by] RWE's retaining my MMS and extracting my extracts," she wrote. In June 1830 came the explosion: "I send you an Almanack? 'Catch me!'—Soberly—I will not till you return the others. They are my *home*—the only images of having existed." This was not quite the ultimatum it appeared, since a month later she was lending one last Almanack with the proviso that he not read the pages folded over within it.[33] But she seems to have lent him no others for years after 1830.

In the meantime, however, Waldo absorbed as much of Mary's diary as he could. "I have read with something more of profit than you mt. approve, the Almanacs," he wrote at the end of July 1829. "Before you charged me not to transcribe I had copied off thus much which I send." He did not explain his motive but jokingly described the day's work: "I am striving hard to establish the sovereignty & self-existent excellence of ye moral law in popular argument, & slay ye utility swine & so must run." Waldo referred especially to a sermon for the Sunday following on a theme close to Mary's heart, "the *beauty* of virtue apart from its *utility*," but her spell was on all of this month's preaching. The previous week he had spoken on the biblical Mary's choice of the "good part" that conscientious Martha had neglected; and whether or not he privately alluded to his own kinswoman Mary, he twice echoed her words to his childhood: "Despise trifles."[34] Preaching an especially self-defining sermon in early July, moreover, he had actually quoted the Almanack to evoke his sense of "God in the soul."

In this earliest sermon Waldo preached on a text embodying the central theme linking his and his aunt's faiths: "In him we live, and breathe, and have our being." He began by affirming life in God as the shared heritage of Calvinists and Unitarians, so embracing the church's past and urging an end to liberal complacency. Meanwhile, however, he was also staking a claim on the edge of liberal thought moving toward Transcendentalism. Christianity of any sectarian label, he argued, was "only the Interpreter of Natural Religion," and the human mind had lived in God both before and after the Christian revelation.[35]

Mary was his ally in both aspects of this argument, in her respect for Calvinism and her internal natural religion. The Almanack that Waldo had borrowed also called Christianity "an Interpreter of natural religion"; and though such similarity of phrasing might reveal only affinity rather than direct debt, the rest of the sermon moved even closer to Mary. Having told of nature, human history, and especially the "individual experience" as sites of God's revelation, Waldo recalled Christ as a model for life in the "Omnipresent Soul": solitary and unsupported, the man of sorrows was able to say, "Father not my will but thine be done." Then in closing Waldo addressed the congregation directly about a power of relationship to God possible even in "the ruins of fortune," presenting the devout words of one who had, after a youth transported by hope, found peace with God in old age. Though disguised by masculine pronouns, this was Mary in her November 1828 Almanack: "Scathed and mildewed by age without one illusion of hope left, I unite myself to this first of Beings. Luxury or comfort I do not ask—cold, hungry, sick, I can praise him; the faster the days go by, the more I praise him, waiting till it shall please him in his high will, to remand my dust to dust, release my spirit into the Communion with him for which it aspires."[36]

Using Mary's words in his own context, Waldo also changed their significance. He found in Mary a Christlike attitude translated into universally accessible human experience. What linked Christ and Mary was not saving power but acquiescence—the surrender of will resulting from life in God. Such relationship, Waldo concluded, was the "literal Emmanuel God within us." This phrase mined the language of his previous letter to Mary, while he expressed the virtue of God-reliance by her example. But she would have had none of Waldo's transformations, if indeed she ever saw his sermon. He was continuing to present Christ as a model of character rather than a messiah—using her character and words to do so. As he wrote to her several years later, the "excellent Teacher . . . cannot exist to me as he did to John. My brothers my mother my companions must be much more to me in all respects of friendship than he can be."[37] For Mary the glorification of any human individual, most certainly herself, was idolatrous.

Despite Waldo's limited access to Mary's Almanack, it echoed intermittently through his preaching career at Second Church. He read some sections that no longer survive—for instance, a record of her months in Andover, Maine. But a few examples suggest the kind of language that he sought. As he described the believer to desire "a little virtue at the bottom of the heart," so she had written, "Oh how I love a little virtue at my heart's core, come how it will." Surprisingly, when he preached in defense of companionship, "It is the voice of active intellectual society which the recluse hears," he was appropriating her words upon returning from solitude in Andover to society in Waterford.[38]

He especially loved her language of relationship to the divine, though moderating its more grotesque and self-pitying tones. Waldo described contemplation of Jesus' perfection as an opportunity to "hang on his attributes," whereas Mary had phrased a similar sentiment more personally and darkly: "Yet the heart still beats with the idea of God. . . . I do not think of dear Edward, I think of what a poor silly narrow being I am—yet there's none so mean but has a right to hang & writhe on the divine attributes." With only minor editing, Waldo could also take whole sentences from her, as in describing a faith of exclusive attachment to God:

> Then it comforts the wretched, it unchains the slave, it is father mother, friend, house, and home to them who are destitute of all. . . . Can the favoured child of his election love him so well or cling to his will with the submission of the shrunken sufferer pinched by poverty and sensitive to the touch of error and shame? No, an angel knows not the height and depth and breadth of resignation like him who, stript of all and satisfied that in him is no strength, yet exults in all that is good and fair; he has a property in all through his relation to God.[39]

Waldo turned to these passages less for ideas than for their voice. Though he preached Mary's words without attribution, so for the most part did he use quotations from Young and Wordsworth. Her letters, to which Waldo had much greater access, less often contributed language to the sermons. From a description of Ruth Emerson he picked up Mary's phrase "the faults of the good," from the letter amidst his worst illness of 1825 her biblically worded declaration "An enemy hath sown tares." Perhaps most significantly, he adopted her quotation from de Staël about the priests of God, which he had transcribed separately into his journal.[40] But none of the letters that he had transcribed and attributed to "Tnamurya" went into his preaching. He seems to have held this "oracular" voice in reserve. Indeed, from both letters and Almanack Waldo took only certain strains, her stoicism and Puritan/Pauline dependence on God. His sermon series in July 1829 quoted Samuel Hopkins and defended the Calvinist tradition even as it quoted Mary; and both of the extended passages on faith from her Almanack were accompanied by references to Paul and Silas praying at midnight in prison.[41]

Whether responding to her recent conservatism or wishing to reserve innovation for himself, Waldo quoted less directly when his message anticipated early Transcendentalism. Though he had learned powerfully of natural religion and contemplative solitude from her, his frequent evocation of these themes shared only broad affinity with Mary rather than specific words. When he found his topic in external nature, as he did only a few times, Waldo spoke a language of seasonal and astronomic cycles, sublimity, and omnipresence, but without Mary's strong imprint. Preaching on a solar eclipse, he said with Young, "The undevout astronomer is mad," and with Mary, "The God of nature and the God of the Bible are affirmed to be the same."[42] Her influence was deeply assimilated amidst other sources. Most of all, he did not make any use of the suggestions in her letters or Almanack that a momentary apocalypse of perception might lift the observer beyond nature to divinity. He echoed none of her language of imagination or the flight that it allowed. He never quoted her explicit judgments of literature or philosophy, instead quoting directly from sources that he knew through her. He drew upon Mary in her destitution and God-reliance rather than her empowerment.

Eve and Philosophy

Waldo's early spending of his "legacy" from Mary might have drawn their relationship to a close, but changes in the wider culture brought new energy to both aunt and nephew during the first years of his ministry. Just prior to Waldo's ordination, Mary had been struggling with the new boldness of her friend William Ellery Channing. His influential sermon at Providence, "Likeness to God," affirmed a religion of intuitive knowledge with strong affinity to her own. "The creation is a birth and shining forth of the Divine Mind," he preached, "a work through which his spirit breathes. In proportion as we receive this spirit, we possess within ourselves the explanation of what we see." Mary fundamentally agreed with Sarah Bradford Ripley, however, that Channing had gone "clean out of his reckoning." Here was no Scripture and no saving Christ. Insofar as Channing maintained his old caution, it was to warn against the "extravagance" of religious excitement and solitude. Mary pursued these very extremities, but only within the frame that she saw Channing repudiating, "old fashioned unitarianism, such as Paul preached." "Never was more glorious sermon," she wrote to Charles, now her main partner in thought, "tho' his view of human nature is too bright for truth."[43] Mary answered the undisputed leader of liberal thought, as well as her nephew, when she settled in to defend revelation.

If Channing trusted too much in the power of intuition, however, the German philosophers claimed too little for it. During the summer of 1829, as Waldo transcribed Almanack extracts, Mary recorded her first real encounter with Kant and Fichte. She had presumably known of both since reading *Germany*—and two years earlier, even while writing positively about de Staël, had referred to Kant as "a name now done with." But in August, browsing at the Concord bookstore, she found an issue of the *Edinburgh Review* that reintroduced German thought. Though declaring the anonymous author a "no God man" to Waldo, she entered both lengthy extracts and resistant responses in her Almanack. She never noted, if eventually she realized, that Kant's defender was Thomas Carlyle.[44]

Mary learned that Kant had surpassed all the English and Scottish philosophers by beginning "within," finding proof of God and the soul "in obscure but ineffaceable characters within our inmost being." "This last I jump with heartily," Mary wrote, "—but why do the Ger[man]s deny universal persuasions & instincts, when they come at lenght to the same thing, tho' under new terms[?]" This new philosophy sounded less solid in its certainties than her own Platonic idealism. "We consider the grand characteristic of Kant to be the distinction beween understanding & reason," she recorded; the latter, higher faculty could discern a "region where logic & argument does not reach," where poetry and virtue abide in a "sea of light at once the fountain & the termination of all true knowledge."[45]

Though twenty-five years earlier Mary had reached beyond argument by the power of imagination, she withheld more than she granted to this new spiritual philosophy. "Now I grow suspicious," she responded. "Do not the Ger[man]s mean atheism, in a modified sense, by 'true knowledge'[?] Because the Review applauds Fichte, and quotes his 'Divine idea' pervading the visible universe: w'h universe is but its symbol & sensible manifestation having in itself no meaning or independent true existence to it." The "divine idea," she feared, was merely a projection of human reason, leaving inner mind and outward deity disconnected. Mary saw with an explicitness never matched in Waldo's reflections on Kantian reason the erosive skepticism at the heart of the new philosophy, and she met it with sarcastic dismissal. "How wonderfull is the mechanism of that hypothesis w'h in recognizing a divine idea—a God within—banishes the only God who self-exists—in whom we live and move."[46]

Indeed, she denied most of Carlyle's new views as well, including his celebration of "literary men" as "a perpetual priesthood, dispensers and living types of God's everlasting wisdom." "Blessed be our revelation," she answered, "we can have ideas of God without literary men." Behind this apparent orthodoxy was a Protestant laywoman's suspicion of all priests, in the cloth or on the printed page. Why pause to note the inconsistency that she had long been urging her nephews to just such literary priesthood? When it came to discerning God for herself, the Bible gave her more personal latitude than the *Edinburgh Review*. "David's rapturous aspirations, whoever or whatever this David was, have sanctioned mine," she noted two days later. "And the baseless fabrick of German idealism vanishes."[47]

Coleridge was another matter. Mary read his newly available treatises through the winter and spring of 1830, and her mind quickened. The vocabulary was baffling, but she saluted his interest in the Bible and redemption, then found her "old face all in smiles" at the idea of basing morality on identity, the personal "I am." Most of all, Coleridge took the Kantian word "reason" as an ally of faith:

> Nothing that God has made is more intelligible than the emotions—instincts, or rather to use Cole.[ridge]'s phrase reason itself may be the power which perceives—communes with the divine omnipresence. . . . I feel that where the agency—power—contrivance of God is, there he is—and it is according to Kantian deffinition, reason w'h persuades—reposes me on the omnipresence in the fullest sense.[48]

Coleridge allowed Mary to accept Kant by seeing reason as an "agency" of God, rather than God as a creation of reason. Given this possibility, reason became the powerful final term in a series that had engaged Mary for decades, from "passion" and "imagination" to "sentiment," always affirming the inward and intuitive over the discursive and mechanical.

She soon put this new vocabulary to work in comprehending her intractable friend Sarah Bradford Ripley. Urging Charles that June to adopt Coleridge's distinction of understanding and reason, she went on to ask, "Is it not possible that [Sarah's] talents are of the former? Baconian? Paleyian? She is not so superficial a scholar as to lose her faith in religion—in immortality from German scepticism, were there no constitutional defect in those qualities w'h seek a spiritual existence??"[49] In Mary's estimation, Sarah had moved from British empiricism to Kantian skepticism rather than Coleridge's "Spiritual Religion": instead of fixing her eyes on the toadstools at her feet, she had turned inward to the processes of thought, but still without finding in that thought a channel to God.

Through Coleridge, Mary felt an influx of self-confidence that counterbalanced her recent scriptural conservatism. As much as she defended the Bible against German higher criticism, there now seemed no absolute need for its revelation: "But will the barbarian innovators take away the divine athority of my bible? Were it possible my reason my nature—this divine identity—this incomprehensible I remains—and God an infinite contriver—Adapter remains—and I will pray pray with more frequency, importunity, till I die with exhaustion and lose every fear." Mary and Waldo read Coleridge simultaneously in these months, but her affirmation of Coleridgean reason as a "divine identity" amounts to the earliest use by any Emerson of this fundamental term of Transcendentalist philosophy.[50]

Aunt and nephew did their new reading separately. Since the previous November, she had been on pilgrimage in the Connecticut Valley, eventually with Coleridge in hand. Correspondence, once her favorite way of talking with Waldo, now faltered; bound to the regular production of sermons, he had little time to explicate the delightful knowledge that, he hinted to Mary, opened like a "green lane" in front of him. Even more, he was absorbed in Ellen, his wife since September 1829, and he associated the spiritual world with this young, consumptive, poetry-writing woman. As he wrote to Charles in the midst of their engagement, "Ellen has an angel's soul & tho very skeptical about the length of her own life hath a faith as clear & strong as those do that have God's kingdom within them."[51] To Waldo, Mary exemplified the "literal Emanuel" in the God-dependence of her age and poverty, but Ellen brought heaven itself into view.

Mary saw Waldo once—and met Ellen for the first time—when their paths crossed that March in Hartford. Waldo and Ellen were traveling for her health; Mary was "wandering" amidst cousins and boardinghouses. In fact, she had gone there, bidding her nephews "adieu at last," just as the young couple took up housekeeping together. Possibly, hearing of the young lady's refinement, she wanted to avoid disgracing Waldo in his new beatitude. Both Mary and Ellen seem to have felt nervous about meeting. Mary had been full of instructions at first, but kept her distance and spoke of Ellen only as a "beau ideal" of imagination. Ellen, in turn, worried about the judgments of this formidable aunt, whose reputation preceded her. "I have heard from many tongues of Aunt Mary from as many more of 'Mary Emerson,'" Ellen wrote after a few months of marriage, "—yet have at every mention of you made some alteration in my ideal Aunt Mary."[52]

The actual meeting was easier on both sides than expected. Mary found Ellen "not so beautifull—but more attractive than expected." Ellen told a similar story in verse:

Aunt Mary's eyes her niece did scan
Compared it with her previous plan,
The building was not half so fine
Nor did the painted windows shine
As her fond fancy nurse his lies,
But hard enough to like she tries
To faults determined closed her eyes
And wouldn't mind them—[53]

Soon after, Ellen proposed that Mary come stay with them in Boston, and amidst reluctance to bore the young lady, Mary felt relief at the undisturbed acceptance of her "oddities."[54]

Possibly Ellen was so attracted to Mary because, already approaching death, she saw the older woman as a priestess of the afterlife. Certainly Ellen's quoting to her a passage from Doddridge on heavenly communion implies the theme of their conversation in Hartford; and all of Ellen's references to Mary after the visit spoke of her as an angelic presence—dreamlike and of a nature between heaven and earth. A poem that Ellen wrote about Mary in 1830 remained in

Waldo's mind long after as a double memorial to the younger and older women of spirit:

> She will dwell upon our mind,
> Flesh and blood so well refined
> That one questions whether death,
> Wasted form, or loss of breath
> Will be in her path to heaven,—
> All her spirit seems to glow
> With her spirit's action so.[55]

This was as much Ellen's epitaph as it was a portrait of Mary; Ellen, not Mary, was following a path to heaven by way of troubled breathing. In fact, such a death by spiritual refinement was the ideal that Mary had long desired and failed to achieve.

The meeting in Hartford again allowed Mary to hear Waldo preach, a rare opportunity since his first sermon in Waltham. He offered three sermons; Mary may have had the third in mind when she wrote to Charles that Waldo's preaching had been "an era" to her, moving head and heart. Beginning from a potentially moralistic text, "We should live soberly, righteously, and *godly*, in this present world," Waldo had argued that godly living meant exercising the noblest part of human nature, "sentiment, or feeling, or affection, by whatever name we call it, this principle which . . . leaps to duty and goodness." He was encapsulating their family heritage and recent conversation alike. "On every comparison with clergymen [I] like you better," she wrote to the preacher himself.[56]

Renewal of conversation was limited, however. Though Ellen took part in Waldo's and Mary's spiritual religion, she could not discuss theological ideas of the spirit. She had read Doddridge, the Bible, and the English poets, but no philosophy or history; when Waldo suggested that she study Hume's *History of England*, which he had once assigned to Boston schoolgirls, he cautioned that it might prove dry. Especially with the universal attention to Ellen's comfort and health, there must have been few moments for talk of Coleridge and the Germans. "In truth," as Mary put it, "what time or incli.[nation] for speculation when the heart is full?" Nor was she able to get back into their old conversation by letter after the visit. When Waldo sent her Ellen's poetry instead of his own thoughts, Mary withheld a previously written letter about *Aids to Reflection*. "The theology is designed for comments," she observed, "and you favor me with none since you wedded." Her challenges later in the summer had an even sharper edge: "I want to know what is going on in the sanctorum of your brain. . . . Your Eve and Eden . . . spoil philosophy."[57]

Meanwhile, Mary had again fled quarrels with Robert Haskins, wondered if there was any prospect for a return to Vale, and felt at loose ends. She thought of going to see her father's grave in Vermont and unsuccessfully sought to board with the minister in Springfield. Wandering seemed less poetic now than it had a decade before, and her Almanack recorded unsuccessful attempts at resignation. A month after the meeting with Waldo and Ellen, she envied Madame Roland, imprisoned during the Reign of Terror, who declared, "I fortify my heart against adversity by deserving happiness and thus I avenge myself on that fortune that refuses to grant it." Her diary entries grew reckless: "Past into the frying pan at Hartford Stage Hotel," and a few weeks later, "I charge the great Provider with my lodging."[58]

But Mary's intellectual vocation in 1830—no matter if precipitated by homelessness—could be defined as exploring Coleridgian reason in New Light territory. Visiting Springfield intermittently over several months, she meditated upon the birthplace and prophetic zeal of her grandfather Daniel Bliss. Although she respected the God that early Calvinism represented, she continued to criticize its modern transformations. In Wethersfield, soliciting the views of her cousin Joseph Emerson, Mary discovered with chagrin that this evangelical educator meditated an approaching earthly millennium and felt himself to be "carrying on the plan rather individually." Such comfortable defining of oneself at the heart of God's unfolding history smacked, she felt, of a "pride and dogma" directly counter to the profoundly humble Calvinist tradition. Cousin Joseph's educational methods, furthermore, had produced a seven-year-old son who merely parroted knowledge, and she countered by telling how Charles's "unlearned childhood" had given him the head of a philosopher.[59]

She described this conversation with Joseph Emerson to Charles himself, even as she also analyzed Sarah Bradford Ripley according to the distinction of reason and understanding. Neither her friend's science nor her cousin's millennial plan led to God as would the vitality of inner life. Coleridge knew this, she told Charles: "Now Cole.[ridge] is an egotist & I like it the better—not *him*—but the exampel to shelter ones own private character of ego. And this fullness of existence in one's self, however ridiculous it may appear here, where appearances are all in all[,] yet prophesies well for a full partaking of existence hereafter."[60] Coleridge's conscious existence was the fulfillment of Daniel Bliss's fire that she could herself live out—and (even without a prophetic mantle) recommend to others.

Despite her insistence on Christian grace and a real, personal God, Mary's defense of egotism in 1830 was closer to the nascent spirit of Transcendentalism than to institutional religion of either the liberal or orthodox variety. Back in Waterford the following year, having worked out yet another fragile living arrangement with the Haskinses, she wrote to Charles about her—as opposed to their—way of finding God:

> O could you be here this afternoon—not a creature but the dog & me—we don't go to four-days-meeting. There's been one at the methodists', closing today, & such a rush from the other society. But such a day! Here's one balm-of-gilead tree—but a few leaves left, as though on purpose to catch the eye to see them play in the wind day after day,—& the deserted nest. Ah where the anxious parents & their loved brood? Dead? Where the mysterious principle of life?[61]

The mischievous tone of the opening sentence did not acknowledge that "the other society" had been her brother-in-law's until the Methodists undermined his ministry, that now even her own kin had been wooed by the revivalists. But she and the dog were detached from such sectarian squabbles, home alone to catch glimpses of sacred mystery in two signs of immortality, the balm of Gilead tree and the young birds' flight from their nest.

Mary's evocation of the birds' flight was only one symbol for the grievous mystery of 1831, the death of Ellen. Ellen took a conscious part with Waldo, Charles, Ruth, and Mary in the ritual of her own death and spiritual victory. The gradual disease of consumption enforced leisure, attenuated the body, and gave its sufferer ample opportunity to anticipate the inevitable. Ellen drew two families around her to share this passage, with Mary—in the terms of the earlier poem—a spiritual participant and guide. She briefly appeared at Ellen's bedside in December to give her blessing. Ellen did not expect to live through the winter and died six weeks later, wishing in her last days for a letter from Aunt Mary.[62]

"My angel is gone to heaven this morning & I am alone in the world," Waldo wrote to Mary two hours after the death. "Her lungs shall no more be torn nor her head scalded by her blood nor her whole life suffer from the warfare between the force & delicacy of her soul & the weakness of her frame." Though he first spoke of her "presence" as withdrawn, however, five days later he claimed that her dying words had "infused such comfort into my soul as never entered it before & I trust will never escape out of it."[63] Waldo was now making of Ellen's spirit a holy ghost within himself, an actual realization of the "literal Emanuel" that he had claimed in intellectual terms for several years. The experience of losing Ellen and gaining her spirit would be a cornerstone of his new philosophy.

Simultaneously he also shared with Mary a preoccupation with Ellen's new life in a more traditional heaven. It was Mary who put into words the vision of her entry there, a new saint met by an elder guardian spirit and conducted to meet the Messiah and her own sister. Less inclined to understand Ellen's angelic mission as the comforting of his soul, Mary imagined Ellen's heavenly guardian to foresee "a time when she would also lose earthly love." Perhaps under Mary's influence, Ellen herself had written a more tongue-in-cheek verse to Waldo about heaven as a place where "our earthly marriage / will be vain as a song": her strong angelic wings would take her out to tea whenever she wanted. Both Mary and Ellen entertained ideas of heaven focusing on the soul's own strength, pleasure, and self-development. When Waldo imagined that he might receive an actual sign from Ellen's spirit, Mary found the possibility "strange indeed." Stopping short of declaring marriage irrelevant to heaven, she still offered sensible advice for living on earth: "A sight—a sound—the very musick of Ellen's voice is not so certain—so elevating as the ever living faith which oversteps a few years & rejoins divided hearts for ever. . . . Go forward with her sainted character enshrined in your heart and gather round new objects of love & friendship w'h shall inlarge your capasity to bless & be blessed here and forever."[64] Mary's belief in the world of spirit did not tempt her to consort with spirits on earth.

Her own interest in Ellen had its peculiarities, however. Bleeding lungs and "raising blood" had been the symptoms of Ellen's tubercular state since before her marriage to Waldo. So when Mary, on her last visit, asked Ellen's mother to buy her material for a dress "red as blood," she seems to have identified with the disease. Ellen even joined in the fantasy, giving a progress report on Mary's red dress while reporting that Mother herself had now "raised blood." "A drop of vermeil should be the family coat of arms," she concluded. Were they both imagining that Mary was to wear the Tucker coat of arms? Mary would certainly have been happy to follow where Ellen led. Ellen, she wrote to Charles, was their "synosure" or north star; and after death she became an "amaranthine," the eternal blossom that Mary had always hoped her own life would be. That July, sick for ten days, she was disappointed when her cold once again failed to settle into consumption.[65] Clearly she envied Ellen's escape to the realm of spiritual progress, even if the way was indicated by the color of blood.

In the spring and summer of 1831 Waldo felt a burst of confidence in the God within, one he recorded in alternating journal passages about divine presence and the spirit of Ellen. Without doubt his love of Ellen had enabled him experientially to overcome reserve and *feel* as he long wanted to do. But if Ellen was the angel of this presence within, Mary was its oracle. Before, during, and after his romance with Ellen, she had urged a life and faith of feeling, even urged the deprivation of earthly goods and loves as the means to receiving faith. Her own experience of mourning led the way for his. Two women enabled him to discover the doctrine of a God within, one its precursor and the other its symbol, one a mourner and the other the mourned.

Parricide

That September Mary wrote again "in the old loose strain," answering Waldo's letter of 1829 since she had received no new ones. When Waldo wrote back pages of his new philosophy, however, she tore up the letter in rage and lamentation. "This is the bitterest moment of my life," Mary told him. "You I cannot think of—you are above human sympathies."[66] In all their correspondence, there is no comparable attack in either direction.

The attack fell not on specific ideas but on his ability to philosophize without considering Mary herself. Consumption continued to scourge the family: Edward, though for a short time settled in New York with William to practice law, had been forced to seek a warmer climate in Puerto Rico at the end of 1830; and now the following autumn she had just heard that Charles's symptoms would require the same treatment. She foresaw the death of another alter ego, this one a "protector" for her own old age. Charles looked after Mary in an affectionate, everyday sense that Waldo did not, and now Waldo was so caught up in his own ideas as to relate them without speaking first of the danger to Charles or the consequence for Mary. A day later she could finish her letter in another mood, declaring Waldo "dear & priceless" and assuring them both that Charles would be fine. Still she put her finger on a self-sufficiency in Waldo unlike her own: "Your philosophy [is] natural to one who has lost all before & can lose all now."[67] She, too, had lost all, but her grieving would never end short of heaven. It was beyond her to incorporate the absent loved one as an internal "comfort," a holy spirit beatifying the mourner on earth.

What Waldo may have communicated in the torn-up letter was the rush of self-confidence expressed the same summer in his poem "Gnothi Seauton," "Know Thyself," justly known as a landmark of his new thinking:

> Then take this fact unto thy soul—
> God dwells in thee.—
> It is no metaphor nor parable
> It is unknown to thousands & to thee
> Yet there is God.[68]

Coleridge provided the Greek expression in *The Friend*, but Mary had known the precept since 1817 and bound Waldo to its wisdom.[69] She could not acknowledge the debt, however, for all her energy was now devoted to slowing the pace of his heresy. From now on—when she got a hearing at all—she would argue for revealed religion over natural and the "Platonic" reality of God over the "German" deification of humanity.

Waldo resisted these messages but continued to draw upon Mary from the wells of memory and manuscript. At the end of 1831 he preached the sermon describing inner faith, in words from her Almanack, as "father mother friend house and home when destitute of all." It also made a strong statement of his new affinity with Coleridge and Carlyle, extending religious experience from the inherent human pleasures of admiration and devotion to their final object in God. Even amidst a growing rebellion against institutional religion, Waldo claimed continuity with the past. Mary would have embraced his Old Testament text: "Choose ye this day whom ye will serve: as for me and my house, we will serve the Lord."[70] Less than two months later, Waldo confided to her that he was considering resignation from the ministry.

His letter does not survive, but her response has long been known—and misread as only reactionary. Sheer family pride drove her passionate argument for Waldo's continuation in the church. "And is it possible," she began without salutation, "that one nurtured by the happiest institutions[—]whose rich seeds have been bedewed by them—should be parrisidical?" Mary was accusing him of ruining the very house he had pledged to serve. She admitted her hope that

> an old venerable pastor in the most delightfull spot, you could point to your grand children that within a few miles reposed the ashes of your pious ancestors—who preached the gospel—and that the very place w'h gave you birth & contains your father should wittness your last aspirations after the sovereign Good. It may be that the short lives of those most dear to me have given couler to the hopes of one minister remaining to be enrolled with [the] Mathers & Sewalls of that venerable City.[71]

This defense of the Emerson patriarchy was entirely of a piece with her glorification of "Ancestor" to Waldo and Charles and her dream of tombstone inscriptions to William. Rarely, however, had she been so explicit about her own stake in preserving lineage, that she had lost in succession the father and brother who would have established her own vicarious place amidst the Mathers and Sewalls, and now she was about to lose one last opportunity. A woman who had devoted her life to religious thinking and writing in the tradition of her male ancestors, but ascended no pulpit with them, now faced the prospect of having no protégé there either.

But Mary did not flatly insist on Waldo's staying in the ministry; instead, she found it "a problem" that "love of truth . . . leads you to sin against what is believed by the highest men to be truth." She continued to respect that love and inquired after his state of mind with diffidence: "On what footing you are to treat with [your Creator] excites the deepest curiosity. But I take not the liberty to inquire. What you commit to me is enough." Meanwhile, she suspected "the 'senses' writers" (not the Germans) as the source of his skepticism, preferring Descartes, Malebranche, and Clarke for their study of "the Cause" and fearing his loss of a personal God. She described this divinity, however, in words that Waldo himself—as well as their joint teacher Coleridge—could have composed: "God within the heart but not the heart."[72]

Opposing the "withering Lucifer doctrine of pantheism," Mary had little to say about the narrower issue over which Waldo at length resigned, whether or not Jesus had meant to institute the celebration of communion. In May, Charles declared Waldo "extravagant," willing to "shake the yoke of Institutions & venerable forms"; Mary responded, "I respect your respect for our hallowed institutions & the ties w'h bind selfish man to man—tho' I admire the extravagance of Waldo and the truth of that excess." Despite her earlier strictures against his abandoning the church, another side of her went with him; after all, she had urged him in adolescence toward poetry rather than the pulpit. Her more fundamental objection was theological rather than institutional: "But the truth w'h lies in such visions of virtue & freedom can only find strong hold in the [Christ]ian plan whose outlines are alone so grand as to give foretaste of this perfect liberty and transcendant virtue." When pushed for an opinion of the communion rite by Ezra Ripley that summer, she gave only a measured allegiance. "That it is abused by protestants sometimes for a cloak and by others for a test of [Christ]ianity is no argument against its' importance if considered only as a invaluable evidence of the historical kind."[73]

At best she could claim no sacramental value to bread and wine and no personal spiritual experience through it, only "evidence" of Jesus' historical mission. Against the three reports of taking communion in the half century of her Almanack are scores of occasions when she was "fed" by books and transporting natural scenes. "In imitation of the 'banquet language' the Heavens & earth mingled in the pure embraces of love," she wrote at Vale the year before Waldo's resignation.[74] The holy feast was all about her.

Mary's reverence for the clergymen of her own family, furthermore, had always coexisted with a strong vein of anticlericalism. She not only found "banquet language" in a Maine landscape but also could explicitly compare the holiness of nature and church to the disadvantage of the latter. "Halleluia," she ended an entry in 1829. "How can I quit this hour for the lagging worship of the priest?" Immediately after came the qualification: "Noon. But the priest was good & devotion rose." This postscript only refined her point: since 1804, when she danced to the music of her own imagination during Mr. Green's sermon in Malden, she had valued church for its effect on her own soul and more often than not had found the minister worldly or cold. "Last night heard Gannett—," she reported of Channing's young colleague, "the thin partition of life moved—or rather, the Divine presence was felt."[75] She would not have valued Waldo's preaching career if his sermons had not been in an equally spiritual vein.

In the last week of June 1832, after writing a statement of his doubts about the communion rite and receiving acknowledgment from Second Church, Waldo left Boston in the company of Charles, who had recently returned from Puerto Rico. Despite their relative silence in recent months, he planned to visit Mary while crossing through his "hour of decision" about the wisdom of resigning the ministry.[76] He sought distance from the city—and also a kindred, if critical, listener.

For a week the brothers joined Mary and the Haskinses at Vale. Waldo wrote nothing in this time, but Charles reported that they enjoyed "sweet air, green earth, rustic diet &c." Members of the Haskins family, especially Uncle Robert, had come through Boston and Concord often enough, but Waldo had hardly ever seen them on their own ground. Now he promised to send books to seventeen-year-old cousin Hannah and must have spoken with nineteen-year-old Samuel Moody, about to leave home for Union College. But this year most of the family was immersed in another round of "four-day meetings" at the Methodist Chapel. It is hard to imagine a conversation between them and the doubt-ridden young minister. In addition, Charles had come to search the land records of Oxford County and see who—Robert or Mary—was the genuine owner of Vale. She wrote later that he had found the farm "mine as justly as my shoes."[77] Conversation within the house must, as always, have been constrained.

They met more congenial responses from Mary's Waterford protégé Thomas T. Stone, who two years before, after embracing liberal views, had resigned his Calvinist pulpit in Andover, Maine. Now principal of nearby Bridgton Academy, he promised Waldo his account of McIntosh's *Ethics* and so began an acquaintance that would continue. Mary privately called Stone a superficial philosopher, knowing "nothing but what I tell him." While accusing Waldo of "overrating" others, she was also acknowledging her intellectual stature in this up-country region. Later that year Mary expressed what she herself thought of McIntosh in a letter to Sarah Bradford Ripley: that he affirmed the universality of conscience too timidly, opening the door to light "like a child who fears a spirit and hopes some grown person will come & finish the business by opening it wide."[78]

Houses and books were not the only concerns of Mary and her two nephews during this trip; its more fundamental goal was precisely the retreat into nature that she had always counseled. Mary may have guided them, on foot or horseback, along her favorite creek and up the slopes of Bear Mountain. None of the three kept a journal of these days together. Much later in life, however, Waldo returned to Waterford as to Mecca: once he found the creek flowing white over its granite floor and felt that his life would last twenty more years if spent here; another time he passed several hours at "his" flume and regretted that he could no longer climb Bear Mountain. Such were probably the central scenes of 1832. The landscape that Waldo associated with Mary and their "grave relatives" was one of his most powerful symbols: a "Thebais" or "Mt. Athos," as he put it in 1841, a place "to bewail my innocency & to recover it, & with it the power to commune again with these sharers of a more sacred idea."[79]

Perhaps disinclined to intrude on solitude, Mary left her nephews to journey to the White Mountains in the second week of their stay. She boarded in Fryeburg while Waldo and Charles went over the New Hampshire border to Conway. Then Charles returned to Boston, leaving Waldo alone "under the brow and shaggy lid" of the Presidential range; and Mary went to join him and ride north to Crawford Notch, at the foot of Mount Washington, on July 13. There they stayed at the public house of Ethan Allen Crawford, who had cut a path up Mount Clinton and—through five miles of rocky terrain above tree line—across to the top of Mount Washington. "The good of going into the mountains," Waldo wrote a day later, "is that life is reconsidered." Mary argued against his determination actually to make the climb: the weather seemed threatening, and Wordsworth had found the infinite equally well in a stone or a flower.[80]

Before the day was over, however, Waldo remained alone again with his decisions about the mountain and the larger future; his combative partner had bolted, leaving a hasty apology before returning to Fryeburg. Mary's note, though cryptic, is the closest account of their actual conversation at the Notch. "I have done wrong," she admitted, "to speake as tho' it were possible [that] in your present state of opinion & 'aversion' you could . . . break that emblem of life & nurture." She had argued the importance of using his authority to maintain, not dismantle, the life of the church, but now conceded that the larger institution did not rise or fall with his decision of conscience. "I was dazzled by your presence—," she added, "degraded by the love of your office & situation." Though hoping that time would return him to Jesus, she would await new vision by their next meeting. Even as she dissented from Waldo, she allegorized the landscape that they loved in common: "My solitude opens far distant views—& would see you climbing the h[ei]ghts of salvation thro' the lonely roads of what appears to you truth & duty."[81]

In the weeks following this visit, Mary blessed Waldo's decision more than she resisted it. "I am grieved by the step he has taken—," she wrote to Ezra Ripley six weeks later, "tho' I respect, in no common measure, the fidelity to his conscience which induced it." Conscience—as indeed her strictures on McIntosh made clear—deserved a wide-open door. "Others," she wrote to Charles, "may be led to prize more the symbols of an everlasting feast—may learn to disrobe the institution of remaining corruptions w'h prevail among the ignorant.

And he himself free from ties to forms & instruction may find the Angel who can best unite him to the Infinite—may find in the religion of a solitary imajanation that nearer to the heart without bating but adding to the respect of his reason." She saw clearly, and could only accept, the extravagance of his coming vision. In the meantime, she quieted her emotions by going to the Methodist chapel in the woods near Vale, and that September awaited final revelation in her own way: "Oh these mystic scenes of autumn, when her solemn stole encircles us, it seems but a moment when the veil will be raised."[82]

Heresy and Antislavery

> Have you curiosity about the issue of this freethinking on all subjects, political, philosophical, religious? . . . It would seem as if the human mind were undergoing a change like that which sometimes alters the climate of a country.
>
> Charles to Mary, July 26, 1834

Mary and Waldo kept their distance in the year after his resignation from the ministry. In the physical sense his journey to Europe separated them, but correspondence also fell away. Each looked for letters from the other, but none from Mary and only one from Waldo survive. His single, fond and reflective message came from Rome, a scene he called reminiscent of Mary herself, "for the spiritual affinities transcend the limits of space and a soul so Roman should have its honor here." Mary's soul seemed Roman most of all through the lens of European Romanticism; Waldo quoted Byron to her—"Here is matter for all feeling"—and alluded to a fictional counterpart in de Staël's Corinne, whom Rome had honored in public ceremony. He continued privately to reflect on Mary's place among these sources of inspiration. Confessing that he searched in vain for new "instructors," he rebuked himself in her imagined voice for such arrogance: "Son of man, . . . all giving and receiving is reciprocal; you entertain angels unawares." After this single letter, however, Waldo did not tell Mary of new discoveries that would have stirred her as well—the inadequacy of Coleridge and Wordsworth when met in person, the exhilaration of talk with Carlyle, the awareness of "strange sympathies" with all natural forms at Paris's Jardin des Plantes.[1] He was charting territory for himself in Europe.

Charles rather than Waldo now became Mary's chief partner in thought, giver and receiver of copious letters. She often asked for word of Waldo: "Tell him . . . that I dont see a star in the nightly Heavens with out often thinking he is standing on deck & reading their fates." Sometimes Waldo's lack of traditional faith made her feel that she had "lost" him; and when Charles called him a reformer, Mary shot back, "A reformer! . . . Who on earth with his genius is less able to cope with opposition? Who with his good sense [has] less *force* of mind—and while it invents new universes is lost in the surrounding halo of his own imajanation[?]" In more optimistic moods, however, she predicted a different outcome. A dense, six-page letter to Charles defending her Arian theology honored Waldo with a place in the spectrum of alternatives. While Channing's humanitarianism gave "no consummation of this passing world," only the waxen wings of high-flown language, she attributed a loftier error to her own nephew: "Waldo with his poetic eye sees nothing but the race immortal here—[as] tho' stars have vanished."[2] This oblique description found Waldo to have claimed the "consummation" completed, immortality already achieved on earth.

While Mary still admired Waldo's eye, however, she directed her ideas and guidance to Charles, now at twenty-four completing a legal apprenticeship in Daniel Webster's office. The impassioned interest of her theological letter was how Arian belief in Jesus could motivate the career that Charles saw before him: "*A bible lawyer*! What a gift to your age dear Charles." The strictures on Channing made clear what Charles might do better. "Humanitarianism—," she asked, "what has it done to lessen slavery—to convince the obdurate persecutors of man—to promote publick good & lofty private virtue? . . . The only eagle wing is that pruned & strenghtened in the divine Sun." The "bible lawyer" she spoke of was a reformer, as in her view Channing and Waldo could not be, especially a reformer of American slavery.[3] As Mary awaited the result of Waldo's vision, she looked for this alternative Emersonian heroism in Charles.

None of Us Live Dissevered

Such thinking continued the dialogue that Mary and Charles had pursued since the mid-twenties, when she faulted Everett as a model of oratory and praised Wilberforce and Webster. Hoping at first that Charles might preach, she had soon felt assured that a law career could serve God equally by influencing a nation and world in the throes of self-liberation. The autumn of Waldo's resignation she opposed Channing's peace principles, declaring war "better than oppression."[4] Far from advocating any actual military exploit, however, she anticipated wars of conscience that Christian citizens might join.

The particular public evil of slavery had often been on Mary's and her nephews' minds even before the 1830s. Waldo's "curious question" to her in 1823 about the suffering of slaves implied ongoing conversation; and Mary's Almanack entry four years later, while identifying with the excitement of Columbus's exploration, added, "May his selling of the first slaves be forgiven." Self-identification as a childhood "slave" no doubt intensified her sympathy with those legally in bonds. As she wrote in 1830—and Waldo rewrote in his sermon a year later—"the faith" above all "shelters the wretched—unbinds the slave and converts the bloody persecutor."[5] Unbinding slaves was for her religion, politics, and personal rage.

Charles took Mary's diffuse hunger for freedom into the abolitionist era. From

Webster's office he watched in 1831 as the American Colonization Society, supported by pillars of society like the senator himself, encountered William Lloyd Garrison's new, Boston-based movement for immediate emancipation. Since 1817, the older organization had proposed freeing slaves by purchase and transporting them to Africa; Garrison called the ownership of slaves sin, offered no payment, and accepted no resettlement. By August, Charles's account to Mary of the recent Nat Turner uprising suggested sympathy for the more radical alternative:

> The politics of the day have been my cud for the last few weeks— . . . The poor blacks have roused in Virginia, have murdered a few families of their hereditary oppressors, & are now to be hunted down in the swamps & killed like wild beasts—Who is it has made them such? If all the consequences of wrong actions, in another state, glare upon the consciousness of the original transgressor, what must be the hell of the first slave-dealer?

This was dangerous doctrine from a young man in favor with the powerful. "Settle!" Webster had said of him. "Let him settle anywhere. Let him settle in the midst of the backwoods of Maine, the clients will throng after him."[6] Charles probably expressed his views more quietly at the law office than in letters to an aunt residing in those backwoods.

Within six months after this letter to Mary, Charles could observe slavery as well as speculate about it, for he joined Edward in San Juan, Puerto Rico, to guard his lungs from the New England winter. In this generation the Caribbean was an education for many New Englanders of quick conscience and tubercular health. Channing had crossed paths with Edward a year earlier on Santa Cruz, and both responded to the omnipresence of slavery with discomfort. Edward remarked on the tense atmosphere of a society protected by offshore gunboats and believed masters more damaged by dependence than slaves by harsh labor. His concern for the slaves themselves was limited. Hearing of the American insurrections just before Charles arrived, he hoped for "some greater than Franklin who will divert the electric fluid before it accumulates with fatal and consuming force." By now clerk to the American consul in San Juan, he thought of the nation's safety rather than wrongs done to the oppressed. On the other hand, Charles soon wrote home reports of conscience. It made no difference, he told William, if the slaves were "neither over-worked, nor ill-fed. Still a slave is a slave, & is made to feel it." Their generation would have to take action against this wrong: "What my dear brother is to be done before you & I sleep with our Fathers, with the great question of Slavery? . . . The country where slavery is tolerated, has sewed up in one sack with its national being, a living viper. Will the day arrive, soon, for a public & fearless canvassing . . . —ought not you, & I, & all of us, to be meditating deeply[?]"[7]

Unlike Edward, Charles had come to Puerto Rico with indignation fed by Mary's longtime encouragements and the newly charged rhetoric of 1832. Channing's recent sermons on the moral degradation of slavery, product of his own

Caribbean experience, had joined the swelling argument. Now the brothers ranged through the new forms of thought with characteristic Emersonian intensity. Reading *Germany* together, they passed one day considering the merits of German infidelity and concluded against it because of "the desperate condition of humanity." Charles must have expressed actual as well as theoretical interest in the slaves who served his daily life; as he left in April, Edward wrote that "the bondswomen as well as the free seem to love him." Edward was left, as one slave commented, "solito con Dios," and Charles returned to a Boston alive with controversy. Though none of the Emersons hastened to join Garrison, Charles's 1833 Lyceum lecture on Puerto Rico made a tentative critique of slavery as a corruption for master and slave alike, on that foreign island if not yet closer to home.[8]

Charles's attention to antislavery issues provided a strong counter to Waldo's crisis of individual conscience in these years. When Charles declared Waldo's individualism "extravagant," he was not merely upholding tradition but voicing a collective ethic of his own. "Come out of your individual shell," his 1828 commencement address had urged. "Give your thoughts to the interests of your race." In the year of Nat Turner, he admitted to Mary, "I am sick to death of talking & thinking of myself," and simultaneously reported on a recent gathering of the Massachusetts Bible Society. The nascent empire of American benevolence, which never really interested Waldo, called with considerably more power to Charles. As he wrote in response to her theological letter, he sought a scheme beyond humanitarianism to serve humanity's deepest needs: "I love Christianity for something more than its perfect morality—I love it for . . . the medicine it pours into the broken and contrite heart where no proud philosophy can enter."[9]

Mary contained the contradiction between Waldo and Charles. She understood Waldo's individualism, his inclination to abrogate and incorporate all institutions within the self; she herself had been a major source of that impulse. What she lacked from Waldo she got in Charles, explicit Christianity and the social justice that it promised. She had no intellectual disputes with the younger nephew comparable to those with the older.

Instead, the problems in their letters were temperamental, and Mary's role was more often nurturing than antagonistic. Charles had graduated with the applause of his fellows as well as academic honors: one classmate remembered him as "well-proportioned and straight as an arrow," with clear blue eyes, fair complexion, and handsome features; another added that people would turn to look at him as he passed in Harvard Yard. Much more than Waldo, Charles enjoyed society. But in the midst of achievement, he suffered deeply from self-doubt. Starting the summer of his graduation and Edward's mental breakdown, Charles confessed to Mary that he felt "seared" with overwork and almost desperate at the distance between himself and his goals. She responded by blaming society and shallow theology, urging patience while his latent fire kindled. In fact, discontent might be a positive sign: "Your complaints are a mystic music—

betokening that your horoscope is cast for better scenes."[10] To her, contempt of worldly things was not incompatible with energetic pursuit of one's vocation in the world.

Troubling signs increased after he unexpectedly developed symptoms of tuberculosis. At the first word of "pills and blisters" in November 1830, Mary asked in alarm what was the matter. Even worse than the health crisis itself was Charles's attraction to death. "For a week or two I thought myself in a consumption," he wrote a year later, "—I looked on on through a long narrow passage, & at the end I saw a white couch & a peaceful sleeper. . . . *Spiritually* I felt entirely resigned to die."[11] Charles spoke in terms eerily like Mary's own of "better scenes"; but he was imagining neither a completion nor an alternative to accomplishment on earth, only rest and respite on a heavenly couch.

Mary staggered at the thought of early death for Charles, thinking always of his potential greatness on earth. Probably an inherited tendency to depression—the complement to Edward's mania—underlay Charles's moodiness, but Mary's expectations seem to have increased it. "I thought God was removing me," he wrote, "because He saw that I had not strength of mind to fill up in action the outline which my own principles & hopes had sketched for me, & I felt grateful that I was to be spared the unequal contest." Amidst such feelings of inability to fulfill their shared goal of national service, Charles turned to antislavery politics, almost propelling himself into a whirl of news that might give him new life. In the meantime, as Charles put it, "Waldo is very well—speculates on—on—happy he!"[12] Waldo seemed to be neither racked by self-doubt nor so troubled by the suffering that Nat Turner's uprising revealed. Charles was drawn to both kinds of darkness.

The problem was doubt of a personal center, exactly the "reason" that Mary, Waldo, and the new European prophets all celebrated. Charles could survive the grinding daily work of the law on the level of understanding, he claimed, but for greatness he needed a capacity from outside himself. Thus he assented too eagerly to Mary's theme of Christian self-loss, devoted himself to high causes, and depended on Mary herself. "I cry you to the rescue," he wrote, and yearned to "sit by you again, the boy you called yours." He identified with female passivity, wishing to be a Delphic oracle seized by the god and made to utter prophecies. His favorite author was de Staël, especially her heroine Corinne, and he identified with Ellen's verse about a "restless spirit" unable to break from the dark earth. Vacillating between a softer Romanticism than Mary's and a Ciceronian devotion to society, he doubted Mary's own affirmation of the ego. "None of us live dissevered & alone," he told his lonely aunt.[13] At least he was sure that he could not. What might have been a constructive counter to Emersonian solitude was marred by powerful lack of self-trust.

The center of Charles's and Mary's letters from 1831 to 1834 was his own vocational crisis more than his brother's. Charles put up no force to argue against like Waldo's intellectual negations, just persisted with his "devil of dreamy unbelief" despite all right thinking philosophically. Instead of feeling depleted by her charge or lamenting that she had lost him, she felt anxiety for his survival.

At some point Mary wrote a "Plato letter" to Charles as she formerly had to Waldo, but he remembered that it "intimated some insuperable defect" of constitution. Meanwhile, she admitted her dependence on him for companionship and advice about life's daily business.[14] Each felt need as well as love for the other.

Back to Concord

Mary hardly clung to Charles, however. She hoped instead that he would find "some gifted Ellen" who would stand in her place as a female inspirer and instructor. Though Mary could doubt the advantage of marriage in a woman's life, she had no qualms about seeking the blessing of a wife for a beloved male kinsman. Especially was a pious woman imperative to save the statesman from moral compromise. Had "the genius of deStale . . . or the piety of a Rowe" shed light on Edward Everett, she declared in 1831, he might have been saved from his meager worldly success. Charles agreed, damning Everett as "a weather-watching, tide-waiting man-serving temper— . . . a trimmer of words to village politicians": "Pity Pity he married so far beneath him—a better wife would have been his 'good angel.' "[15]

Charles wished fervently to follow this script, to find a wife and so attain virtue above that known to the men leading Massachusetts. He also knew how to resist Mary when her fantasies got carried away. In the spring of 1833 she was encouraging further acquaintance with Elizabeth Peabody, a new correspondent in Boston, but Charles wrote back that he required "a certain measure of fine taste & delicate manners . . . in a woman in order to be attracted." A woman four years his senior, to whom Mary was drawn for her gifted mind and plans to become "an Authoress," was not the sort of angel he could entertain.[16]

He pleased everyone, most of all himself, by becoming engaged to Elizabeth Hoar of Concord in the summer of 1833. Charles had hinted to his brothers of developing romance but had not confided in an overly eager aunt. Mary wrote on August 13 that his last letter seemed so sociable she dreamed he was falling in love. Just a day later came his news of the engagement, and Mary responded on the instant, thrilled as both an aunt and a promoter of family interest. Marriage to the daughter of Concord's Squire Samuel Hoar would ally the Emersons' patriotic history with present social position and power: "Her family! Roger Sherman a signer! Her father so good & influential—Her mother excellent pious & charitable & sincere. Herself beautiful & what is incomparably better *ardent*." Mary had known Samuel Hoar and his family through all her Concord days. Now he was Concord's most eminent lawyer and judge, an invaluable potential mentor to Charles; Sarah Sherman Hoar a daughter of the Connecticut elite and officer in the Female Charitable Society; Elizabeth at nineteen a graduate of Concord Academy, learned in Greek but, unlike Peabody, free of independent ambitions.[17]

Compared with her earlier self-introduction to Ellen Tucker, Mary approached Elizabeth with circumspection. The excitement was too intense, she explained to Charles, for her to write without congratulating his new fiancée; and she remembered an earlier occasion when Elizabeth had preferred the nurturing friendship of Ruth to her own difficult temper. Mary's explanation backfired, for Elizabeth soon discovered this letter. "If I had time & room here," Charles told his offended fiancée, "I could paint you out as on canvass her entire state of feeling as she wrote, looking backward, looking forwards, & you would allow & forgive the whole."[18] So a long year passed after the engagement before Mary met Elizabeth as a new member of the family circle. During that time, Mary was often ill with erysipelas, which disfigured her eyes and mouth with painful red lesions. She may also have wanted to keep her distance from a relationship going well without her. Mary recognized that Charles's letters had for the most part taken on a more buoyant tone, as he became established as a practicing attorney in Boston and exchanged almost daily correspondence with Elizabeth.

Powerful forces were needed finally to draw Mary from Maine to Massachusetts in the course of 1834. On the negative side, the bargaining with Robert Haskins and his sons over ownership of Vale wore against Mary both financially and personally. She had spent most of 1833 boarding in Maine towns and returned to Vale only with her lapse of health that winter. Now Concord and Boston beckoned; for on the positive side, the metropolis seemed afire with new ideas, and her own circle of family and friends belonged among the kindling spirits. Waldo, back from Europe, had won financial security with Ellen's estate and was now lecturing in Boston on natural history. Charles called himself one of Waldo's "Natural-historical associates" but also scrutinized the development of Garrison's antislavery movement. Reading the literature of abolition and colonization side by side in July, he resolved that truth was with the former. A change was in the winds, as Charles declared: "What abundance of speculation now a days! What restlessness under old opinions & forms!" Inquiring into Mary's curiosity about this freethinking, he told her, "The Slavery questions appear hastening toward an issue. God help the right & guide us therein!" Though sick, eyes shaded, unable to read or write at length, Mary promised to make the journey in September.[19]

Charles described the arrival of his "Lady of the Lake" with a mixture of affection and chagrin. "Know then," he wrote from Boston to Elizabeth, "that the Aunt, even the Aunt Mary, hath been here since Monday." Other literary heroines than Scott's came to mind as he described Mary's flouting of manners at the Haskins house. "She is galled by the lightest harness of 'accomodation'—yea were the traces, like Queen Mab's, 'of smallest spider's web,—the collar—of moonshine's watry beams.' Poor Aunt Betsey & the rest were dismayed at even the transient visit of this lawless Undine." Charles was serving notice in Concord of what to expect: Mary had left "rags & tea slops & all kinds of litter about her room," yet was vain enough of her own appearance to postpone seeing Elizabeth until her mouth and eyes looked better. "The very infinite of whim is in her, & I can only lay the troublesome sprite by a strong diversion towards the regions of sentiment & moral speculation."[20]

Fortunately, life abounded in those regions. Just four days later Charles could tell Elizabeth without comic irony of the three-way Socratic conversation renewed at Ruth Emerson's rented house in Newton:

> Aunt Mary & Waldo & I have been measuring over again the old grounds of religious speculation. Why could not you be at our Symposium[?] The lady in the beginning mourns at the latitude we allow to our faith—& will have it that the faith is naught. But presently as she or we persist & from words pierce to things, we have shot the gulf that divided us, & are guiding our course by the same pole-star, or are moored by the same rock.[21]

Soon the conversation shifted to Concord. Ruth had been invited to the Manse for the winter, and Waldo decided to join her. Charles was still living near his work in Court Street, Boston, but Elizabeth Hoar drew him frequently to Concord. In everyone's mind Mary had to be there, too, but "whim" or defensiveness made her want no longer to reside with the family. So they promised to find a boardinghouse or, as she called it, "a rooftree for the 'youthful traveller.' " Finally Mary was too impatient to wait for Ruth and Waldo. Bolting back to Boston for two days with Charles, she met her friend Elizabeth Peabody, received a visit from Dr. Channing, then took the coach for Concord a week ahead of the others. In the move to Concord that would found a center for new thought, Ezra Ripley's hospitality and Elizabeth Hoar's love were the motivating forces, but Mary managed to be once again in the advance guard. Presumably Elizabeth met her and arranged the "rooftree" at Persis Woodward's house, next door to her own gracious home on Main Street. "Write to me," Charles requested, "and tell me what new marvels or mines you explore in the terra incognita of Aunt Mary."[22]

Mary herself, though making a fresh start in Almanack writing, first found in Concord a voice of nature telling of age and defeat:

> Ah, as I walked there just now, so sad was wearied Nature that I felt her wesper, "even these leaves (you used to think my better emblems,) have lost their charm on me too, and I weary of my own pilgrimage—tired that I must again be clothed in the grandeurs of winter and anon be bedizened in flowers and cascades. . . . Oh for transformation—I am not infinite . . . cannot aid the creatures w'h seem my progeny—myself!"[23]

Before Mary had even been joined by her progeny, she felt that her time to influence them had passed.

When the family did gather, they found their primary bond in mourning. William wrote the news to Charles that Edward had died in Puerto Rico on the first of October, and Charles arrived in person to tell both mother and aunt. Ruth dwelt on the loneliness of her son's death and burial but took comfort in his soul, "beautiful unblameable ardent" despite all trials. Mary, though strongly agitated at the news, soon quieted her nerves and chided herself for feeling loss. The two elder women consoled each other, their shared mourning an ancient bond, and quickly Elizabeth joined with them. Thanking her for wearing mourning clothes and so "adopting another family," Mary finally wrote the welcome to Elizabeth that she had postponed for a year. "You dear Girl will comfort the Mother for a most valued Son—You do—& will help us to regret not always the sainted Ellen."[24]

Mary was often agitated amidst the combined griefs and stimulations of 1834. She went to see Dr. James Jackson in Boston about her erysipelas but lost his written instructions on the chaise ride home, protesting that he had offered no useful advice anyway. She refused to visit Sarah in Waltham, apparently wanting to spare herself the sight of an old protégée in philosophical chaos. She arrived at the Manse, Waldo wrote to William, driving a shabby horse and chaise commandeered from a man at the store where she had been shopping. "The man I suppose demurred;—so she told him 'that she was his own townswoman, born within a mile of him' & finally she says when she left him *in the gig*, he told her 'not to hurry.' "[25]

Waldo used this incident to illustrate the "transcendental way of living" that their aunt practiced daily. He referred jokingly to Mary's lack of touch with common courtesy or reality but also acknowledged her involvement in the new spiritual ways of Concord. Charles, echoing Waldo's old habit, persisted in naming her their Delphic oracle. Admitting to Elizabeth that Mary "certainly behaved not very prettily Sunday night," he went on to defend her. "But she is one of the persons to whom I can forgive almost everything, a sort of Cassandra-Pythoness. The god rushes, & She speaks." Two months later, with Elizabeth and Aunt Mary once more friends, Charles described her as a book to read:

> As by seeing a high tragedy, reading a true Poem, or novel like Corinne, so by society with her one feels the mind electrified & purged. She is no statute-book of practical commandments—nor orderly Digest of any system of Philosophy divine or human; but a Bible—miscellaneous in its parts but one in its spirit—wherein are sentences of condemnation, chapters of Prophecy, promises & covenants of love, that make foolish the wisdom of this world with the power of God.[26]

Allying Mary to the conscious breakdown of philosophy into aphoristic inspiration, Charles was placing her utterance close to the heart of Transcendentalism.

Since they conducted their "symposium" directly rather than by letter now, it left fewer recoverable traces than in previous years. Waldo, living at the Manse and beginning to write, still benefited from conversation with Mary. In December she recorded recent talk by the "literatie" about the nature of God. She had insisted that Jesus was a more primary embodiment of God than either a flower or a great man like Martin Luther, one of the subjects of Waldo's new biography lectures. But when Waldo quoted Coleridge on the possibility of praying to the eternal reason, Mary had the decisive word. "I . . . only answered that we were so distinct from this universal Reason, as to need prayer, so intimate with it as to be heard and answered. W[aldo] praised the remark." He also recorded it in his journal.[27]

Waldo reflected on his relationship with Mary amidst the journal record of his own new creative life. Individuals without ability to act directly in public, he wrote, could serve an indirect good through their friends. "How serves the Aunt M? How but by bearing most intelligible testimony which is felt where it is not comprehended." Considering his need for a listener to new ideas, he concluded, "A good aunt is more to the young poet than a patron." Whether as testifier or audience, she could still energize. A gesture of unmediated originality began his writing career that fall: "Henceforth I design not to utter any speech, poem, or book that is not entirely & peculiarly my work." Not only did he make this vow within a journal entry paradoxically saluting his fathers' "quiet fields" as the site of new labor. In addition, the Emersonian "father" who mattered most, Aunt Mary, was a present voice rather than a bygone ancestor, one even now mediating the blessing that he sought upon this work.[28]

Mary's Almanack bears witness to this creative current in her admitting—albeit in fleeting phrases—the extent of their power over each other. "Waldo (so strange, so captivating) first came that evening," she began one entry, and in another called him "dear taking (of the imajanation) W[aldo]." Waldo's "taking" had been a half-articulated theme in her writing since 1821, when Mary first realized the sense of loss as well as indirect power that resulted from giving ideas. She had responded in self-defense during his years of preaching, when he borrowed Almanacks and wrote nothing back. Now, with mentor and protégé in one neighborhood on the eve of literary revolution, Mary made no effort to resist the taking: Waldo's superior power went unchallenged, and Mary felt pleasure when he praised her remark. Instead, she lamented loss of control over the object of her influence, criticizing him for giving wing to fancy without thinking as systematically as either Calvinists or Unitarians: "The fault lies not in his head, . . . but in his tastes—his feelings go not as yet to the Center of all things."[29]

A Court of Our Own

In the early months of 1835 a new community began to appear in Concord. Samuel Hoar had been elected to Congress in December, and Waldo rightly surmised at once that Hoar would ask Charles to take charge of his law office. Even before that offer was firm, Waldo wrote on January 24 to Lydia Jackson of Plymouth, whom he had met while lecturing there, and without preamble proposed marriage. Charles rather than Waldo put into words the possibility of a family seat that these two developments made possible. "We should be mutually helpful many ways, & should collect about us a society, & hold a Court of our own. The removal of the Plymouth Penates once effected, I do not think it would be hard to reconcile them to the new home. . . . Mrs. Ripley will come one day & live in Concord, & Aunt Mary is likely to make it her 'Capital Seat' if they warn her off from the Vale."[30]

Charles's reference to Lydia Jackson as a movable household deity suggests the family's skepticism of Waldo's sudden domestic plan; all of them would have preferred Ellen to return. But he spoke of Sarah Bradford Ripley from recent rediscovery of her mental and emotional depths. Lecturing to the Waltham Lyceum in mid-January, Charles had gone home with Sarah to long and searching conversation, and never before had he so fully perceived the woman who had taken part in his early education. "It is good to find the contrariest fortune fused as it were by the genius of the individual," he wrote to Elizabeth, "and the 'Deus in nobis' asserted & returned unto, after clouded days & years. The woman is a believer." Charles did not explain how he defined belief, but at least he was welcoming Sarah into the new Concord symposium, eagerly imagining her taking possession of the Manse with husband Samuel, son Christopher Gore, and daughters—Mary the family's domestic "Fairy" and Elizabeth the seeker of solitude.[31]

Most of all, however, Charles's plan focused on the bond between himself and Waldo, which had never been stronger. Somewhat separated by age and upbringing as children, they had become close friends since Waldo's return from Europe. Waldo had opened the subject of their relationship nine months earlier, claiming that Charles seemed only to tolerate him. In fact, as Charles confessed to Elizabeth, he acted with reserve because he felt himself Waldo's "pupil" and loved to the point of idolatry. By 1834 Charles had come around to considering the Lord's Supper an abridgement of his freedom, and the "Everlasting Yea" of Carlyle's *Sartor Resartus* thrilled him as it did Waldo. But Charles was also discovering his own strengths alongside the supposed teacher's. Only that year did he share with Waldo his plan to "go to congress one of these days," and he believed that he could have delivered Waldo's Phi Beta Kappa poem at Harvard more effectively than the poet himself.[32]

Then, too, Charles was a naturalist as Waldo had only aspired to be since his epiphany at the Jardin des Plantes in Paris. Having spent so much of his childhood with Mary, he had grown up directly responsive to the forms of nature. Among his papers, unlike Waldo's, are a Harvard exhibition problem in astronomy and a list of birds sighted in 1833. The following year, as Waldo lectured with his brother's approval on "The Naturalist," Charles noted to Elizabeth the signs of spring in a warm hollow of the Roxbury hills: "The robin, the blue bird, yea a moist Frog with green uniform & gold-enamelled eye—were my companions. . . . I found the Saxifrage sometimes bloom out, sometimes just urging through moss & leaves its little 'ear' of buds." Charles easily found religious inspiration as well as scientific lore in nature. He took flowers home to his Boston Sunday school class but could also spend Sunday in "God's first Temples," with wind for choir and organ, praying for "that balm which is in Gilead for the wounds & weaknesses that ignorance & sin have wrought in the soul." "Here from my window toward the East," he wrote later in the year, "I shall presently peruse at length large-limbed Orion, my shining chronicler of many a winter.

God be thanked who set the stars in the sky! planted their bright watch along the infinite deep & ordained such fine intelligence betwixt us & them."[33]

Waldo valued this responsiveness in Charles, although he did not often pause to acknowledge it in his journal. That March, the month after his brother proposed a "mutually helpful" community in Concord, Waldo wrote a passage that would prove one of the beginnings of *Nature*:

> As I walked in the woods I felt what I often feel that nothing can befal me in life, no calamity, no disgrace, (leaving me my eyes) to which Nature will not offer a sweet consolation. Standing on the bare ground with my head bathed by the blithe air, & uplifted into the infinite space, I become happy in my universal relations. The name of the nearest friend sounds then foreign & accidental. I am the heir of uncontained beauty & power. And if then I walk with a companion, he should speak from his Reason to my Reason; that is, both from God. To be brothers, to be acquaintances, master or servant, is then a trifle too insignificant for remembrance.[34]

Though mere fraternity appeared insignificant, Waldo suggests that a companion, probably Charles, shared this transport in Concord's springtime woods.

Mary may also have joined the woodland walks when her health permitted, and certainly she continued to take part in the society of talkers. Concerning an energetic but crude new acquaintance of Waldo's, she set the standard of judgment, asking "if a star could be any thing to him & Herschel's mighty facts." She received bulletins from Elizabeth Peabody in Boston on the ideas in Waldo's biography lectures, then finally read the manuscript of "Michelangelo" and responded in writing to its likening of the sculptor to Christ. Waldo entered this "merry critique" in his journal with pleasure.[35]

At just this moment of community-gathering, however, Mary seems consciously or unconsciously to have provoked a fight with everyone. Early in February, just the week after Charles proposed a family community in Concord, she was refusing all conversation with him. He had to ask Hannah Haskins by letter to Waterford, "Tell me if you can what I have done to be so frowned away from court? & by virtue of what charm I can restore myself to my envied post of favorite?" Nor was her critique of Waldo always merry. Sometime during March, as she recalled to him a year later, "I told a truth about my opinion & taste opposed to yours—and I felt sure that our intercourse must end." She also referred to such quarrels at the time: "To live to give pain rather than pleasure (the latter so delicious) seems the spider like necessity of my being on earth and I have gone on my queer way with joy saying shall the clay interrogate?" Love and antagonism always lingered near each other in her irascible temperament. "Here is MME," Waldo wrote in his journal, "always fighting in conversation against the very principles which have governed and govern her."[36] He described not only her temperament but also her relationship to ideas that she had helped establish for at least a decade and a half.

As in early meetings with Elizabeth, Mary behaved "not very prettily" to Lydia Jackson, now already referred to by the Emersons as "Lidian." The two women met in Boston even before Lidian first visited Concord, and Mary disparaged the bride-to-be to Waldo after only fleeting impressions. The result was an unpleasant exchange of letters between Waldo and Lidian, which he then had to retract with apologies. When Lidian actually visited Concord, first in mid-March and then again in May, she more substantially won over the notoriously difficult kinswoman. "In Aunt Mary I have found a congenial soul," Lidian confided to her sister Lucy, "—one who understands and says she likes with all her heart every thing I tell her." Mary in turn called Lidian "*her other half* there in Plymouth." In fact, there were substantial grounds for religious communion between Mary and Lidian: both, though professed Unitarians, believed in Christian grace and the mystic communion with God that it enabled; both had come to such intensity through childhood experiences of bereavement. "She has my own faith and nerves," Mary summarized to Sarah, now restored to friendly terms. "I would live and die with her—but her connection of one kind I can not see why or wherefore. Only that such a strange multitude of things are hurrying on together without apparent direction or order."[37]

Their relationship continued as combat hedged with professions of love. That June Mary decided to make a personal visit to Plymouth. "I know Lidian will be glad to take care of me," she wrote to Sarah when Dr. Bartlett urged travel for her health. Lidian and Lucy received a substantial lesson in Mary's most whimsical behavior. Mary informed Lucy upon arrival that "fresh fish was a great luxury to her," but after Lucy put aside the beef already ordered and acquired fish, Mary declined even to taste it. Later she explained that she had imagined there was nothing but fish to eat on the seacoast and intended to ease her hostess's mind, but then lost her resolve at the dinner table.[38] Surely Mary, so often a resident of Boston and Newburyport, was affecting inland naïveté in a perverse test of her new niece.

Mary also recognized in Lidian a possible partner in antagonistic manners. When the Unitarian minister of Plymouth came paying his respects to the sister of a late colleague, Mary walked out of the parlor and invited Lidian to do the same: "Come, my dear, leave him, and come take a walk with me." Lidian refused but looked upon Mary with amusement as well as indignation. Lidian's daughter Ellen later described the two women's relationship as "diamond cut diamond," Lidian soon learning the weapon of laughter against Mary's barbed words. "Father and Grandma trembled when mother answered her back and enjoyed the combat; and were astonished and most thankful to find that it was pure pleasure to Aunt Mary to find a foeman worthy of her steel." Mary's decree from the Plymouth trip was a mixed endorsement. Telling Waldo that his fiancée suffered from "certain epicurean diseases," she also promised Elizabeth a fine future with Lidian. "She is intellectual and poetic as I did not suspect at Concord. The everyday cares will arrange and balance her mind."[39]

In August Waldo found a setting for his new domestic life, purchasing what Charles called a "naked white establishment" along the Middlesex Turnpike near town. Large enough to include a room especially for Ruth, it could also be expanded from an L-shape to square, so making new space for Charles and

Elizabeth. Mary, though reconciled with her nephews, continued in her boardinghouse at a safe distance. But she was present to witness the great events of September, first Waldo's delivery of the bicentennial address on Concord, including a spirited recital of their mutual ancestors' contributions, then his departure to a Plymouth wedding and return with Lidian.[40] Spirits of the past and the future must have seemed for the moment all favorable.

Mary's desire to stay in Concord society despite painful temper had a strong additional motive. Among the events falling hurriedly into these months of wedding plans and nature walks had also been a new local campaign against slavery, and she was wholly committed. In late January, just as Waldo was proposing to Lidian, British abolitionist George Thompson had arrived in town to address the first meeting of the Middlesex Anti-Slavery Society at the Unitarian church. Directly sponsored by Garrison, this populist orator cleaved sharply between abolition and colonization, leaving the two local newspapers at odds and the ministers scrambling to define their positions. Mary wrote her excited report just as she also heard news of Waldo's engagement: she declared herself "zealous in Thompson's cause," gravitated toward the stronger commitment of the Trinitarian minister John Wilder over Ripley's assistant Hersey Goodwin, and concentrated her own slanted prose on bringing a young friend to the "great goal" before them.[41]

Two months later, Mary renewed the intention to convert others by turning directly to her nephews and their fiancées. With Charles as escort she went in late March to hear Charles Burleigh, a young agent of the Massachusetts Anti-Slavery Society. Mr. Wilder was now the host, but Ezra Ripley sat fully in front of the pulpit, his gaze riveted on the speaker. Charles declared the event exhausting to himself and rapturous to Mary. In fact. she was so stimulated that near "the high noon of night," unable to sleep, she wrote both an Almanack entry and a letter to Lidian about the event. "I was carried to the top of my being this eve," she wrote to her new acquaintance—and from that height saw the prospect of Waldo, under Lidian's influence, lecturing on abolition instead of "Great Men." "He has done enough for the great this winter," she pronounced, "—has *cause* & genius—invite him to leave the higher Muses to their Elysian repose and with the higher genius of humanity enter those of living degraded misery and take the gauge of slavery."[42]

Abolition was giving Mary, at almost sixty, a new cause and a new critique of Waldo's ideas. What she had the temerity to lay in Lidian's lap was the possibility of diverting his pursuit of spiritual beauty to her own ethics of resistance. Now she had a new edge for her religion of biblical redemption and high feeling. In an Almanack entry that night, Mary spelled out these implications, contrasting the elevation granted by the young orator for emancipation with the "torpor" she had suffered in church all day. "God bless him—he gives hope of it—shows the way—vindicates the bible. All the lectures w'h Waldo gives on biography seemed like the fleeting flowers of a summer day compared to this zeal in humanity." In this context she acknowledged the urgency of her efforts to work through nephews: "Let him and C. C. lecture on this subject with zeal

& I will rejoice like Simeon of old."[43] Then, like the old man finally witnessing the Messiah, she could finally "depart in peace."

The antislavery agent was impressed by Mary, too. A few days later, in a letter to his colleague Samuel May, Burleigh offered a portrait of Mary Moody Emerson at this juncture in her life:

> She is an elderly lady—say sixty—unmarried I think. Her name is Mary Emerson, and she . . . has been very much prejudiced . . . against Abolitionists & especially Garrison. . . . I answered all Miss Emerson's questions as well as I could, & do believe I removed some of her prejudices. She seems to be a good-hearted woman, easily excited, inclined too hastily to take up wrong opinions, but willing to abandon them as soon as the error is clearly pointed out to her.[44]

Burleigh underestimated his elderly follower, taking her suspicions of Garrison as a sign of simplicity. Mary could no more be taken straight in this conversation than on the occasion when she chose fish over beef; her own writing shows a much longer development of allegiance to the antislavery cause than she revealed that evening. Still he clarified the nature of her excitement as a last removal of doubt about Garrison's religious absolutism. As Burleigh defended him "her countenance brightened . . . , & . . . she exclaimed 'he ought to be *canonized.*' She said she had written to her friends in Maine, to have nothing to do with Garrison's paper, but says she 'I must write again, & tell them better.' "[45] Clearly her new mission to convert others to the cause extended far beyond Waldo and Charles. Without transgressing the traditional boundaries of private influence, she was taking on a public and communal cause for the first time in her life.

Soon she had a representative to speak in public. Charles, though exhausted at the Burleigh lecture and lapsing once more into consumption, delivered an antislavery address in Concord less than a month later. It was a lawyer's speech, aimed at producing action by the nation's professional classes. Starting with a well-researched presentation of facts about the legal institution of slavery in the United States, Charles declared that he was exercising forbearance in not detailing the "cruelty and debauchery" that it produced. He directly addressed the slaveholders' fears of impoverishment and violence. But there were no concessions on either ground, as Charles dismissed all colonization and gradualist schemes as encouragement for the very "prejudices against the Blacks which keep them out of their rights."[46]

Such a style did not entirely square with Mary's zeal for the cause: Charles never alluded to the Bible, nor did he, like Garrison, urge emancipation for overtly religious reasons. Instead, Harriet Martineau's tract *Demerara* had offered a model with its endorsement of West Indian emancipation for reasons of "political economy." He did quote Mary's early hero Wilberforce on the "wrong and sin" of slavery and echoed his own 1831 letter from Puerto Rico in a rare figurative flourish: "What should we do in the case of any other evil which we saw nestling in the bosom of the people? be silent, tread softly, for fear of waking the sleepers round whom the snake had wound his coil?" Charles was at least as independent in acting upon Mary's inspirations as Waldo the minister had ever been. His oration showed genuine power, and though it may not have made Mary feel like Simeon beholding Christ, she later spoke warmly of its success.[47]

Mary's own favorite forum, conversation, flourished at reform-minded houses. She heard Charles hold forth one Sabbath in the Concord parlor of Mary Rice, who was becoming self-appointed caretaker of the grave in Hill Cemetery where Tory Daniel Bliss had memorialized John Jack's slavery. She cemented a long-term friendship with Mary Merrick Brooks, founder of the Concord Female Anti-Slavery Society, and no doubt attended some of its earliest meetings. On her way to Plymouth in June, she stayed at a Boston boardinghouse with the Peabodies and Alcotts so as to meet the antislavery vanguard. Abby Alcott was Samuel May's sister, and although May could not introduce her to Garrison and Lydia Maria Child, he came to breakfast and offered encouraging news of the cause. In this setting Mary also for the first time sized up Bronson Alcott, who "talked of the infinite with much ease" and took his four-year-old to have a tooth pulled without informing her in advance. "I objected," Mary told Elizabeth Hoar. The objections took theological form as well. Immediately she argued for Samuel Clarke's Enlightenment faith against this new-school spiritualism—and by fall was sending an "antidote" of Unitarian thought to Alcott, now visiting his new friend Waldo Emerson in Concord.[48]

Two social events especially brought Mary into the swell of abolitionism. Sarah Bradford Ripley invited her to the first, a party for Harriet Martineau at the parsonage in Waltham after Harvard commencement. The British reformer had just arrived in New England on her tour of the United States, and at the Ripleys she gathered Unitarian dissenters both of Waldo Emerson's stamp, like Henry Hedge and Convers Francis, and of abolitionist conviction, like Charles and Eliza Follen. Nephew Charles and Elizabeth came, too, so Mary enjoyed companionship as well as a glimpse of the great lady. She and Charles agreed, however, that Martineau seemed worldly—"not a Madame de Staël."[49] Though Charles had learned from her tracts, he felt only a measured interest in a woman who could not claim the soul as her primary ground.

Mary herself engineered a second gathering at the new home of Waldo and Lidian shortly after their marriage in September. Seeing May and Thompson at an Acton antislavery meeting on October 9, she probably wished to repeat her casual and inspiring breakfast conversation at the Alcotts in Boston, so invited both men for the very next day. "So he comes & Mr. T.[hompson] before 8 o'k expecting to breakfast at 8," she wrote to Lidian. "Have I done you a favor? It would do me one if *you* could see the subject w'h agitates the Country as some do." Lidian would gladly have declined the favor, accustomed as she was to the formalities of Plymouth society and not yet fully settled in her house. Late that evening she ended her letter to Lucy with an impatient postscript on the "put-out" involved.[50] Both sisters had already discovered Mary's presumption on the visit to Plymouth.

Whatever distress Lidian experienced at eight the next morning, however, was repaid by the intensity of talk. Waldo reported in his journal that George Thompson seemed unable to hear any opinion but his own. Still, this was a moment for Waldo to articulate the idea that a cause so sacred needed facts and principles above personal feeling. "As Josiah Quincy said in the eve of Revolution," Waldo went on to himself, if not to Thompson, " 'the time for declamation is now over; here is something too serious for aught but simplest words & acts.' " Waldo had so far given no sign of interest in the active movement for abolition but now began growing toward commitment. Charles, already convinced, reported the breakfast meeting to William with pleasure: "I rejoice that this question is set afoot in the United States." Furthermore, Lidian responded as Mary hoped she would. Before the year ended, she had made the Female Anti-Slavery Society and Mary Merrick Brooks central to her life in Concord, guaranteeing that this reform would continue to cross her husband's reform over the breakfast table.[51]

The Emersons met Thompson, as it turned out, in his last week of public appearance in America. Already he had been targeted as a special enemy of the fifteen hundred "respectable gentlemen" who gathered in Boston's Faneuil Hall that August to declare war on abolitionists, and by mid-October he went into hiding to protect his life. When the newspapers announced falsely that he would appear before the Boston Female Anti-Slavery Society on October 21, placards appeared around the city offering a reward for delivering Thompson to be tarred and feathered. The resulting mob failed to find Thompson but instead seized Garrison and nearly hanged him.[52]

In the aftermath of this explosion of forces, Charles faced public hostility as an advocate of the cause. The Boston Female Anti-Slavery Society reconvened four weeks after the attack on Garrison, and Harriet Martineau rose to declare her full agreement with abolitionist principles. For so doing, Boston society ostracized her almost universally, and the press launched a scurrilous attack. As Martineau herself later remembered, Charles "stood alone in a large company in defence of the right of free thought and speech, and declared that he had rather see Boston in ashes than that I, or anybody, should be debarred in any way from perfectly free speech."[53]

Free speech was the issue of the day, a natural outcome of the suppressions that Martineau and the Anti-Slavery Society were suffering. Charles not only defended his British acquaintance personally but also offered an address to the Lyceums of Concord, Cambridge, Waltham, and Boston on "Freedom of Opinion." Even though it made no direct reference to recent events, instead recounting a history of toleration and censorship since the Inquisition, its references to popular ignorance and newspapers were sufficiently pointed. "I fell foul of the mobs & convent rioters," Charles wrote afterward to a Harvard classmate. But among his own Boston friends—Maria Lowell, James Jackson, Ellen Sturgis, Mary Channing—he could talk "heresy & antislavery & anti-formalism & man-worship" to full satisfaction.[54] By his own route, Charles, like Waldo, was becoming a leader of the free thought that he had announced to Mary fifteen months earlier.

Mary responded to these events in light of her highly personalized American history. "Boston had a respectable mob to rout the females of anti-sl.[avery]," she wrote in her Almanack. "Oh were I to bring forth a child I would fly to English ground. Could I take the dust of my father from the Green Mountains I would. I would send it to a tomb where there were there [no] slaves."[55] She hardly stood alone in likening slavery to the tyranny which the Revolutionary patriots had resisted or in now embracing England as a land of liberty. Still, Mary wrote from her particular obsession with the martyr William Emerson and her inner need to fly from all prisons.

At moments when her father's enthusiasm seemed again to be infusing politics, she could seek action instead of escape. Early in 1836, as antislavery leaders defended abolitionist rights before the Massachusetts legislature, Mary read and listened to signs of change. Sending William Goodel's speech to Lidian as a statement of religious faith, she expounded her vision of the dawning American millennium:

> The subjects w'h this "Report" includes are *deep & high* as an interest in God—practical—indispensable to that part of our nature—that moral constitution w'h our divine Saviour directed all his ministry—and for the fullfillment of w'h the present times seem preparing. Only think that the revolutions of only half a century concentrate the great idea of man's greatness *as a man*—That the old Countries w'h have literally breathed the air impregnated with the ashes of the Aristocratic oppressor and the oppressed are about to be purged—that the *Heavens will hear the earth*—and man shall not thrive on the miseries of his brother! These are the broad & deep things, my dear Mrs. Emerson, to w'h I would hail your devotion—to w'h I would (as fellow traveller) consecrate your growing influence in a place sacred to the memory of Ancestors eminently spiritualised.[56]

Ten years after her ironic celebration of the nation's fiftieth anniversary, she now had a quickening of hope in both public and private affairs—including hope that the Emerson family might again exert influence. Furthermore, Mary now wrote herself and her new niece into the communal drama, speaking with excitement of the work to be accomplished as a "fellow-traveller" among antislavery women. She felt confidence in Lidian's own influence, not just through Waldo. Likewise, she prayed for Sarah's conversion to the cause and asked that Elizabeth Peabody, staying with the Emersons, read this letter, "for it is on the abolition principle & she is not a convert I fear." An offering of love went to Mary Brooks, Concord's antislavery leader, in the same breath with family salutations.[57] The abolition principle created its own family.

Even in this heady year of awakening, however, Mary had only moments of hope for connection with others. "I love to dwell in the secret sorrow that I am appointed to endure—," Mary wrote in her Almanack a month before her antislavery letter to Lidian, "while others are 'instruments of the invisible operations of the spirit of God—minds that go forth from their privacy to act with strong moral power upon multitudes of other minds. . . .' Oh I ask no influence—but ask peace, sober pious obscurity." She had always wished for influence even as she repudiated interest in it, but the presence of it in others prompted her desire, in words that she then canceled, "for the dark uninterrupted solitude of Vale." Or else for heaven: "I would forget self . . . till I can go & make speech with Him I seek to know—to learn his character & connection with God & man."[58] Self-forgetting and silence were only provisional, knowledge and speech the goal.

Mary was more than ever in a hurry to reach the goal. "Shake not thy bald head at me," she addressed time itself. "I defy thee to go too fast. Am I puny in sight—altered by age—marred by climate—I wander beyond thee—I pass with the comet into space w'h mocks thy gnomons." Such cosmic defiance was a vein of expression that Waldo cherished in his aunt; part of this particular passage would eventually be woven into the rhymed couplets of his poem "The Nun's Aspiration."[59] He never acknowledged, if he knew, that his own new ability to "go forth" and influence society sharpened the disappointment that made her defiant.

He and everyone else seeing Mary daily in Concord knew, however, how difficult she had become. "I love to be a 'vessel' of cumbersomeness to society," she wrote in February, wandering on opaquely about "familiar trials" and the advisability of the "brick house." Her boarding arrangement with Persis Woodward had ended, and soon she wrote from the Manse, where Ezra would take her in when all else failed.[60] But she had grown too irascible to tolerate or be tolerated by her Concord family.

At some point in this winter of declining relations, with lack of a home shortening her temper, she had a decisive quarrel over dinner at Waldo's house. In part she argued with Waldo over philosophical principles, renewing the disagreement of a year earlier. In part she hurt Lidian's feelings; Mary later regretted "two or three jokes," especially a "hit at Jackson extravagance." Charles, too, was embroiled in the dispute, censuring Mary's comments on Lidian. Whatever the balance among aggravations, the resulting vow was clear to Mary even five years later: "Did I not promise—say that I wd never spend an hour in your house, except brought there on a lit[t]er, w'h I shall never suffer[?]" By the end of February Mary had abandoned Concord and the company of her influential nephews, staying in Waltham with Sarah, the very friend whom she had refused to visit eighteen months before.[61] She wrote her socially committed letter to Lidian, extending family greetings even to Mary Brooks, while in flight from all the people she named.

Charles and *Nature*

Mary's sojourn in newly transcendental Concord was punctuated by death at both ends. The family had reunited in 1834 to mourn Edward's death; now in 1836 she left just before Charles's final, precipitous decline and so played only a peripheral role during his last illness. It was a dreadful piece of timing, though no one realized how close to death he was coming. In Waltham, Mary's primary attention went to Sarah, whose own crisis of health, as Mary put it, tested one of her "last holds on friendship." Charles wrote to wish Sarah well, asking if Mary's pen had lost favor with him; and Mary denied all ill feelings: " 'Out of favor,' dear Charles! In sober truth I cannot recall a look—or word like it . . . —with smiles I sustained the sarcasm—pleased as in your boyhood, to illicit your wit & humour your nature." By the beginning of April Mary knew that Charles was again sick, but she fretted over his "dull giddy head ache" rather than his life.[62]

Three weeks later she went to Concord, learned the extent of his illness, and witnessed Elizabeth's anxiety. Elizabeth was near despair: measuring a space for her piano in the new Emerson parlor that month, she stopped and cried out to Lidian, "It is of no use. It *never* will be." Elizabeth knew more than the medical advisors. Charles had been to see Dr. Jackson in Boston and, told he had a "catarrh" (though still no lung disease), stayed in the city expecting to visit William and Ruth in New York while cold weather lasted.[63]

In Boston, probably just a day later, Mary saw Charles for the last time. Finding his brother too weak to travel alone, Waldo postponed his Salem lectures to offer company. Mary and Elizabeth were both on the scene as well, Mary at her least helpful. Later she wrote of the bitterness of parting coldly, on "a dark day . . . like a dream in w'h we say nothing we want to." As so often in the past, she finally said what she wanted by letter after Charles had left: "His hand is over & under & about you & I say hail to your course." Charles received this message in New York two days before his death on May 9.[64]

The stunning news took Mary back to Concord just briefly. Dr. Bartlett, upon hearing the news from Lidian, drove to Waltham and sympathetically offered Mary a ride. She did not stay long, perhaps leaving before Waldo, Ruth, and Elizabeth even returned from New York. Elizabeth wrote to her on June 7 that Ruth was "sorry continually that you have gone from us so that you and she cannot bear this affliction together as you have so many before." But Mary received that letter at Vale: in the shock of Charles's death, she had at last to seek out solitude and so made her way back through Newburyport and Portland.[65] Under such circumstances, the Haskins family had to forget their grievances.

Waldo wrote a day after the funeral with a first expression of the losses that he felt "to Elizabeth, to Mother, to you and to me." He dwelt on his own emptiness. "In him I have lost all my society. I sought no other and formed my habits to live with him. . . . I see well I shall never cease grieving as long as I am in the earth [that he has] left it." The truncation of hopes that they all had shared found expression in Waldo's mourning "for the Commonwealth which has lost, before yet it had learned his name, the promise of his eloquence and rare public gifts." In return Mary had more capacity to offer comfort than to tell her own story of loss. "Your loss is unspeakable—," she wrote back, "& I see it's shadow over the longest path you may tread—tis over all your books & pens—but it must not retard the spirit." As for herself, she turned down Lidian's invitation once again to visit: "I am designed to be alone."[66]

The emotional channels were more open in response to Elizabeth, and from this point she, rather than either Waldo or Lidian, became Mary's chief correspondent in Concord. Elizabeth knew how to be direct. "But if you are absent from us, you must not separate yourself from us but write write of yourself, of Charles." Mary answered, "Here I am thinking of no one but him—reading his letters when 12 & 13—and wishing you could see them." She admitted her long hope that he would someday speak openly of his childhood with her—"that however I might linger, the voice of his fame would penetrate my cell. A man losing himself in setting forth some great pri[n]ciple—getting under some publick evil had always much hold on my ambition . . . and I am sad at the loss—at the disappointment of my own hopes w'h grew—w'h formed my co[nnec]tion."[67] Here rather than directly Mary responded to Waldo's grief "for the Commonwealth."

Waldo, too, grieved by reading and remembering. He invited Elizabeth to come home with himself and Lidian after the funeral, explaining to William that she had "a property so large in Charles's drawer of papers" that she should sit over it. He also read the papers that she brought along, Charles's letters to her. In the first few days of resuming his journal, amidst "helpless mourning," he transcribed six pages of quotations from them. Within three weeks he recorded new thinking about transcendence of death, prompted by conversation with Elizabeth: "We are no longer permitted to think that the presence or absence of friends is material to our highest states of mind." His way of emerging from the paralysis of grief was to deny the value of all merely personal relationships compared with the "absolute life" of relationship with God. "In that communion our dearest friends are strangers. There is no personëity in it."[68]

Mary was right that Charles's death would shadow Waldo's writing but not "retard the spirit." Out of his transformation of loss to divine communion in the summer of 1836 came the completion of *Nature*, published the following September. As when Ellen died, Waldo was flooded by a beatitude of spirit in mourning, but this time denied angel presences in favor of "absolute life." In *Nature* he represented the experience of mourning, as well as the woodland vision of spring 1835, by incorporating Charles's consciousness into his own communion with divinity. In the actual process of composition, death interrupted and then gave new impetus to the movement toward apocalypse of mind at the center of his new vision in *Nature*, and at the end of the chapter entitled "Discipline," he indirectly bade Charles farewell before moving on to "Idealism." Considering the process of a soul's growth, he paid tribute to friends "who, like skies and waters, are coextensive with our idea," beyond all capacity of analysis. But the key to such friendship was impermanence in any but internal form:

> When much intercourse with a friend has supplied us with a standard of excellence, and has increased our respect for the resources of God who thus

> sends a real person to outgo our ideal; when he has, moreover, become an object of thought, and, whilst his character retains all its unconscious effect, is converted in the mind into solid and sweet wisdom,—it is a sign to us that his office is closing, and he is commonly withdrawn from our sight in a short time.[69]

Charles was the "withdrawn" friend, and his conversion to wisdom is discernible at moments throughout *Nature*. "The eye is closed that was to see Nature for me, & give me leave to see," Waldo wrote in his journal upon returning from his brother's funeral. Now Charles's seeing remained within Waldo's in the description of woodland ecstasy, but augmented into a setting for omniscient, God-perceiving vision as a "transparent eyeball." When Waldo wanted to dramatize true solitude, he thought of a man alone with the stars; and later in the essay he summoned up Charles's favorite constellation, Orion, the description of which he had transcribed into his own journal. The journal entries on Charles reveal other affinities and appropriations too. As a preacher Waldo had often echoed Jesus' phrase "Thy will be done," but in the journal he quoted Charles's sense of it, along with the attendant gesture of bent head and folded hands, as the essence of a Christian philosophy of suffering. Now he cited this phrase as the culmination of a child's growth in power and portrayed nature itself as standing with bent head like Jesus in prayer. Distinguishing between the soul and nature as "me" and "not-me," Waldo was echoing Carlyle's words in *Sartor Resartus*, but also Charles's use of these terms. Twice Waldo wrote down Charles's comment on nature as a symbol of the mind: "Yes there sits the Sphynx by the road-side, & every fine genius that goes by has a crack with her." With only minor changes in wording, this sentence was fitted directly into the essay.[70]

Only part of Charles's expression found a place in Waldo's journal or *Nature*. Though acknowledging his brother's acute political judgments, Waldo transcribed no antislavery sentiments, lectures on social issues, or expressions of interest in corporate life. With surprise he acknowledged the "bitter strain of penitence & deprecation" present in Charles's journals. Charles must not have confessed his crippling doubts to Waldo as he had to Mary and Elizabeth, and Waldo repeated very little self-doubt and no death longing even now. Still the elements held in common were of surpassing importance to Waldo. As he commented in his journal, "An occult hereditary sympathy underlies all our intercourse & extends further than we know."[71]

That hereditary sympathy led straight back to Mary, who had formed and shared more aspects of Charles's thoughts than had Waldo. When he wrote "C.C.E." at the head of his specially dedicated 1837 journal, Waldo penciled in "M.M.E." just above it; four years later, reconsidering the possibility of a memoir to Charles, he conceived a more promising version exhibiting "M.M.E. and the boys, mainly Charles" as an emblematic center of New England's history. Most of all, Mary as well as Charles remained in Waldo's thoughts during the summer of 1836, as *Nature* moved toward completion. His "Discipline" chapter was more than a farewell to Charles and incorporated friends other than those withdrawn by death. Indeed, its movement of ideas contained an abbreviated family autobiography, starting with the growing soul's education by "debt, grinding debt, whose iron face the widow, the orphan, and the sons of genius fear and hate." Waldo claimed human individuals rather than material nature as the crowning resource of education. As he wrote in the paragraph immediately before his salute to withdrawn friends,

> In fact the eye,—the mind,—is always accompanied by these forms, male and female; and these are incomparably the richest informations of the power and order that lie at the heart of things. Unfortunately every one of them bears the mark as of some injury; is marred and superficially defective. Nevertheless, far different from the deaf and dumb nature around them, these all rest like fountain pipes on the unfathomed sea of thought and virtue whereto they alone, of all organizations, are the entrances.[72]

Interpreters of *Nature* have never paused over this abstract, rather awkward language. The "forms" to which Waldo attributes such power are both plural and (amidst many masculine word choices) explicitly of two genders; furthermore, their common attribute is not having withdrawn or died but rather possessing "some injury" that incapacitates them from fully articulating their genuine access to thought and virtue. As well as Charles, such a description encompasses Edward, Waldo's once most admired brother who had never truly recovered from mental illness; Ellen, his spiritually gifted and physically racked adolescent wife; even severely incapacitated Bulkeley. But most of all it describes Mary, Waldo's contentious oracle and provider of living wit.

Though echoing none of her particular phrases as he occasionally had in his sermons, Waldo incorporated more of what he had learned from Mary in *Nature* than in any other single published work of his career. He had received her messages directly in letters during college and ministerial training, then delved into the devotional mentality of her Almanack in his preaching years, and finally discovered a new transmutation through the talk and writing of Charles. All of these layers of influence, as well as her personal presence during most of the period of composition, are felt in his manifesto of Transcendentalism. Charles "saw Nature" for Waldo, but Mary was in a sense nature, which he figured as nurturing and female, though finally to be rejected in favor of a divinity perceptible through it. Even more, Mary provided a model for this apocalypse of perception itself. In the year of his resignation from the ministry he wrote, "My aunt had an eye that went through and through you like a needle. 'She was endowed,' she said, 'with the fatal gift of penetration.' She disgusted every body because she knew them too well."[73] This joint statement by Waldo and Mary defines both her power and her "injury." Perpetually alienating and alienated from others, more capable of giving pain than pleasure, she could also see through appearance to reality. It was a "fatal gift" in being uncomfortable, even deadly, but also in its ability to read the fates.

In *Nature*, Mary's enthusiasm for ancestral faith and resignation to the divine will echoed in the shared family litany "Thy will be done," which had been her ejaculatory prayer in family devotions before Charles and Waldo adopted it as their watchword. Now at the center, however, was the active espousal of imagination that Waldo had recorded from "Tnamurya" and left untouched during his Unitarian ministry. The radical solitude of the essay's opening invitation, figured as presence before the stars, had been the gesture of Mary the nighttime sky-watcher long before it belonged to Charles; and it was also the substance of her counsel to Waldo through years of letter writing. Though "Reason" rather than "Imagination" provided the key term of mental vision, Waldo, like Mary—and after years of shared usage in conversation—moved easily from one to the other. When he wrote of nature as a "symbol of spirit," he was embracing Swedenborg's version of the analogies and correspondences that Mary had learned from Price and Butler in Waldo's infancy. "Man is an analogist, and . . . a ray of relation passes from every other being to him," Waldo wrote.[74] This derived from his perception of relationship at the Jardin des Plantes but also descended directly from her transmission of de Staël's correspondential theory in 1821. And even if Waldo never read Mary's essays as Constance from 1804, she had there established the principle—regularly affirmed ever since—that mind might progress by analogy from the humblest shrub to infinite wisdom.

Most of all, Mary influenced Waldo's philosophical idealism, the focus of his crucial chapter following "Discipline" and his fundamental orientation toward knowledge. Here Waldo quoted Plato (whom Mary had established as his "patron"), paired Berkeley and Viasa (as she had cited British idealism and Hindu scripture in 1822), and flouted nature with reference to the Manicheans and Plotinus (both of whom she had taken as allies in attempting to transcend matter). Exemplifying the poet's capacity to transfigure material objects by imagination, he turned to the case he found readiest at hand, Prospero from Shakespeare's *Tempest*—who had stood for the magical power of poetry in his correspondence with Mary since 1821. Once bidding the White Mountains "farewell," Mary had herself echoed Prospero's prophecy that humanity would behold " 'the great globe itself vanish like the baseless fabrick of a vision.' " "Old age sits sternly beneath the mountain scenery," she had pronounced, "and asks if this be all." In *Nature* Waldo celebrated a mental apocalypse, "the reverential withdrawing of nature before its God." So had Mary, though a seeker of symbols in nature, expected it to be obliterated in the presence of divinity. Mary had urged that Waldo "cast [nature] off," and Waldo now declared matter "an outcast corpse."[75]

So, too, he brilliantly fused elements of their long conversation by attributing this transformative power to an opening "eye of Reason." The metaphors of sight, enlightenment, and healed blindness that structure his essay *Nature* had been on their tongues and written pages for even more years than their use of Coleridge's term for the transcendent faculty of mind. Mary had never imagined becoming an omniscient "transparent eyeball," but she would certainly endorse Waldo's proviso in dismissing calamities: "leaving me my eyes." Sight and blindness had long been Miltonic in Mary's language of aspiration for Waldo, and he transmuted both aunt and poet in closing his essay, making the eye a means of restoring paradise and entering heaven: "The kingdom of man over nature, which cometh not with observation,—a dominion such as now is beyond his dreams of God,—he shall enter without more wonder than the blind man feels who is gradually restored to perfect sight."[76]

Of course Mary would not have advanced that claim for herself, nor would she have accepted it for any mortal outside the context of an objectively real deity, made known through a saving Christ. She could neither embrace *Nature* fully nor own her part in its long evolution. Far from spurning Waldo's manifesto, however, she responded with a witty critique of kindred spirit when he sent a copy that fall. "Some of it is invaluable to the lover of nature—," she wrote to Lidian, who had enclosed a note with the book. "Yet the solitary admirer of the Author's youngest pen little thought that when his plumes were grown he would like some other classical kind set fire to his gentle nest." Instinctively resuming her own vocabulary of solitude and nature worship even here, she was calling Waldo a phoenix burning its earthly nest in self-propelled ascent toward heaven. She herself, she went on, planned not to "burn a straw of the eyrie," but rather to maintain the old terms of faith for the remaining steps of life. She expressed little confidence in "the creations of ideal beauty w'h belong to the imajanation." Yet in the next breath she invited Lidian and Waldo to visit Waterford: "You (who have so much imajanation) would have been in extacies one morning last week (monday) at the beauty w'h burst from the skies—the breaking light on the rich blue mist of the mountains and the stars riding high to crown them."[77] To her such beauty, if not heaven itself, was a powerful foretaste to the eye and soul.

Her own mourning for Charles continued unabated, but it took forms recognizable to Waldo. She invited Elizabeth to come to Vale and "see the place where Charles first saw nature in her wilderness of beauty," then described the moon hanging over her lake and an emblematic flower rising from its waters to "become an amaranthine" in heaven. On her birthday that summer, she compared her solitude with the constant visiting and conversation of the previous, but declared the present way of living nearer to invisible realms. "I look at the darkest events of the winter and spring. I hug them closely and say I have lost nothing . . . for I am passing on to the divine attributes. The cause of my existence was to know and love God!"[78] Mary and Waldo alike responded to loss by uniting themselves with the divinity beyond loss.

To Mary's eye, however, nature never became transparent or quietly withdrew before its God; her essential position, rather than standing "uplifted into infinite space," was to seek apocalypse on the winds blowing toward winter and death. In September 1837, she encapsulated her own farewell to Charles, flight beyond nature, and Hindu rejection of illusion in an address to the autumnal trees:

> How richly cast up these intrenchments of beauty! Here would the spirit dwell in consort with those powers, that are thus emblemized. No, 'twould enervate at length, fall leaves with all thy exquisite charms, which are already reclining like the beautiful youth who bowed to the dust his head, but his soul rose to

> higher purposes. The trees begin to fade, & bear us on & on! One glimpse of reason's nature & office & origin worth all the phantasies painted by dumb Nature's wand. Siren-like, she talks of illusions. . . . Hence! "God only I perceive."[79]

Though written the year after Waldo's *Nature*, this owed nothing to it but drew from the same store (even the "Hymn to Narayena") that had proved formative to him. When at length he read the passage in her Almanack, he transcribed it as one of her best.

IV

LAST THINGS

10

Vale

> Events of publick guilt in government there are enow to make one tempted to suicide— . . . the very beauty of the skies becomes eclipsed and the foliage so exquisitely rich this season murmurs of oppression.
>
> Mary to Lidian, July 13, 1841
> (*Letters of MME*, p. 433)

With the death of Charles and the "losing" of Waldo, Mary came to the end of her hope in the male Emerson lineage that she had so long loved and railed against. About 1838 she listed the thirty-one ancestors and relatives who had graduated from Harvard and admired the "poetry" of their Latin names. But it was the catalogue of a past ambition. Beside "1761 Gulielmus" she wrote "my father"; beside "1789 Gulielmus," "my brother." The end of the list expressed bereavement where once she had hoped would come compensating new life:

1819 Gulielmus my nephew . . .

1821 *Radulphus Waldo* nephew and friend . . .

1824 *Eduardus Bliss* nephew & loved

1828 *Carolus Chauncy*!! All all gone[1]

Still all was not gone. Throughout life Mary had retrieved identity and purpose from loss, and this greatest loss was no exception. Her friendship with nephew Waldo continued to produce brilliant, if sporadic and often biting, commentary on both sides. Moreover, in coming back to Vale Mary recovered her natural world and friendships with women, and despite aging and illness she launched into another fifteen active years of reading, talking, and millennial expectation. Though invited, Waldo never visited Waterford during his prime years as a writer, but Lidian, Ruth, Sarah Bradford Ripley, Elizabeth Hoar, and Elizabeth Peabody all did. Now in her sixties, Mary lived and corresponded with women more wholly than at any time since early adulthood.

She heard news of Transcendentalism primarily through the chronicles of Elizabeth Hoar, her "sweet Iris,"[2] who also arranged boarding places for occasional Concord visits. (Mary kept her vow not to stay at Waldo's house.) In Waterford her closest friends, the Haskins nieces and Ann Sargent Gage, in turn befriended the Concordians, so that a network of women grew up around Mary to protect her health, hear her wisdom, and comment among each other about her outrages to sense. Both the Maine and the Massachusetts members of this circle counted themselves among the followers of Ralph Waldo Emerson, but they conversed more often with each other than with him.

A Maine Woman's Transcendentalism

To do so was not to retreat from books and politics, for by the late 1830s American women had begun making their way into public culture. Elizabeth Peabody now proposed a correspondence in the midst of her career as teacher and critic. Of the four women present when the Transcendental Club first gathered at the Emerson house in 1837, Mary was exchanging letters with three—Lidian, Sarah Bradford Ripley, and Elizabeth Hoar. Through them she soon heard of the fourth, Margaret Fuller, whom Elizabeth herself had helped draw into Concord's "circle of enchantments" the summer after Mary's departure. "Tell me . . . of Miss Fuller's visit," Mary requested in her first letter to Elizabeth from Vale, and when Elizabeth obliged she responded in enthusiasm to this "wonder of a woman."[3]

The bluestocking ambitions of Mary's generation were vindicated and transformed by Margaret Fuller and hers. Elizabeth described Fuller as a catalytic force in her own life:

> Her wit, her insight into characters, such that she seems to read them aloud to you as if they were printed books, her wide range of thought & cultivation, the rapidity with which she appropriates all knowledge, joined with habits of severe & exact mental discipline, (so *very* rare in women,). . . . All these things keep me filled with pleased admiration & (true to the nature of genius) constantly inspire me with new life new hope in my own powers, new desires to fulfil the possible in myself.[4]

Mary objected only to the prospect of increasing one's moral power "at any human shrine."[5] She would not attribute godlike power to genius in women any more than men.

Yet within her own more traditional religious belief Mary herself had long played a kindred role of provoking other minds. In conversation about the promising women they knew, Elizabeth had recently told Waldo that she "never knew a woman excepting M. M. E. who gave high counsels." When Elizabeth sent a transcript of the Conversations that Margaret was conducting in the winter of 1841, Mary not only thanked the courier but told how the record had inspired Hannah Haskins. By June, Mary was passing the Conversations on to

Ann Sargent Gage and her daughters as well, in effect serving as Fuller's country agent in developing the minds of women.[6]

Though keeping her distance from Massachusetts, Mary believed its advanced ideas to be needed in Maine. Abolitionism preoccupied her at least as much as Transcendentalism in these years. At first she relied primarily on male authorities and voices to extend antislavery influence, asking Elizabeth to send Charles's speech so that she could have it read publicly by Dr. Gage, Ann's husband and president of the Waterford Lyceum. By the end of 1836, however, she was reading Lydia Maria Child's *Appeal*, as well as Channing's *Slavery*, for light on emancipation. Women's voices were beginning to be heard, both through local organizations like Concord's and on the national level, and Mary even began to promote the influence of her own writing. To Gage she sent not only Charles's speech but also her own manuscript on slavery, asking that he pass it on to the ministers of Waterford and Fryeburg. Lacking confidence as both author and social reformer, she admitted that she reread the manuscript with doubt, fearing that "the antidotes I wrote were by no means adequate." Still she could urge Gage to study slavery with religious devotion so as to enlighten the prejudiced: "Till influential people are engaged in missionizing we must blame any public teacher."[7] If not counting herself fully among the public teachers, she was at least their exhorter.

For Mary such missionizing sustained and vindicated the past tradition of piety, even while opening new doors to action. She expressed that continuity by allusion to her own most revered ancestor when writing in 1840 to Phebe Gage, Ann and Leander's eldest daughter and third-generation heir to the name of Grandmother Phebe Bliss. Her letter both blessed and instructed the young woman, about to become a teacher in Louisville, Kentucky: "*Phebe*, (a name almost sacred to my early remembrance from my Granmother Bliss whose saintly life will never be effaced from me). . . . If you do go—God will guard, guide & bless. And in that very land of slaves & slavery you may plant, thro' his agency, some of those seeds w'h are destined to cover our wretched land with the glory of their freedom."[8]

Her own planting of seeds began to produce growth the same year, and she sent word to Concord that the cause in Maine had begun to "see the light thro' ignorance & rusticity." Enough Waterford people were taking up the antislavery cause to support regular speakers, despite the inertia of more traditional country revivalism. For Mary the crowning moment came in the fall, when her own protégé Thomas T. Stone returned home from a new parish in East Machias to promote the cause. "The lectures presented novel & higher views than any I had seen," she wrote to Elizabeth, "—reason was prominent & fancy & poetic art were not wanting. . . . 'And there was light—' and there were tears of joy & conversion of the Gages completed."[9]

Thomas Stone's "conversion" of Ann and Leander Gage to abolitionism came after years of Mary's instructing all of these Maine protégés in the ideas of Massachusetts. She had guided Ann since adolescence and known Thomas since birth—his father was an early deacon of Lincoln Ripley's church. Ann may even have taught Thomas, seven years younger than herself, in her days of keeping school, for Ann and Mary together later considered him a "child of our love—our mutual interest." Mary had made a Platonist and a liberal of him by the time in 1832 that Waldo met him at Waterford. Already Stone had resigned his first ministry at Andover, Maine, because he was too liberal theologically for its frontier congregation, and in later years he would resign two more pastorates in gestures of conscience. Temperamentally a come-outer, he had seemed uncommunicative to Mary during their season together at Andover. Eventually, however, he like Waldo would write a tribute to Mary's influence.[10]

By the late 1830s, Stone had become committed to both the antislavery cause and his own variation on Transcendentalist themes. Mary conveyed a letter from him to Frederic Henry Hedge, another Maine resident with a strong Concord connection, who in turn forwarded it to Margaret Fuller for the *Dial*. The letter's appearance in the January 1841 issue encouraged Mary to send a second letter by Stone directly to Waldo, charging the Transcendentalists with ignoring the need for redemption from sin. It, too, was eventually printed. Coming home to Waterford for the funeral of his father in 1841, Stone preached from Lincoln Ripley's old pulpit and "battered the vulgar prejudices w'h regard 'tempels & priests & forms.' " As close as Mary stood to Stone's views, she could not agree with his rather Trinitarian formulation of Jesus' role. But the prayer by his father's graveside, as she told the Gages, was "transcendentalism in it's reality."[11]

Ann Sargent Gage and her family were predisposed by Mary to hear both Transcendentalist and antislavery messages from Stone. A versifier and reader of Wordsworth since adolescence, Ann had turned to raising eight children and supporting her husband's practical benevolence since marriage. Starting in 1830, however, Mary had "conjured her muse to awake" in more than one letter, as well as advocating independent, antiformalist religion. About 1839 Mary voiced regret that Ann had deemed "a philosophy, w'h has engaged the deepest thinkers in Germany . . . moon shine. . . . *What did you know of it*?? I alas spent too much time when in the very nest of Mass. scholars flouting it." Both the Concordians and Thomas Stone, she went on to say, believed her attached to an exclusive form of Christianity. "But dont you believe these suspicions of either of the parties but by writing often give me your views. . . . Wherever there is a good person there is a church— . . . Jesus is its Priest & altar & inspirer whether ever they take the *external* sacraments."[12]

Ann was already offering her own views in both verse and prose. Mary ended her 1839 letter by noting that she had sent a poem of Ann's to Samuel Ripley—a friend since first escorting the young girl to Maine—entitled "Transcendental Sentiment." Soon thereafter, Ann recorded her view of the struggle between Tradition and Spirit, her "diviner name" for Emerson's Soul. The Trinitarian Calvinists, she argued at length, had turned against their own most inward and "transcendental" truths:

> A system which used to create and sustain the most fervid enthusiasm, as is its nature, for it makes God all in all, leads in crusade against all even the

> purest enthusiasm. It fights for the letter of orthodoxy, for usage, for custom, for tradition, against the spirit as it breathes like healing air. . . . The Transcendentalists do not err in excess, but in defect, if I understand the case. They do not hold wild dreams for realities; the vision is deeper, broader, more spiritual than they have seen.[13]

It is important to hear Mary's conversation with these young Maine intellectuals because we have known only her remonstrances against Waldo's circle. She was quite capable of playing the game both ways. In the "nest of Mass. scholars" she flouted their ideas and defended a real and redemptive divinity, but in Maine she attacked orthodox rigidity by disseminating the Concord gospel. When Waldo sent a copy of his Divinity School Address in 1838, she gave the manuscript to Stone even before finishing it herself. As she explained, "I knew it's value to him & loved to please my favorite." As she asked for another copy, however, she offered responses even from partial reading. Mary's critique of Transcendentalist reform was not therefore hasty; she stated deep reservations with genuine power, allegorizing in the manner of her old horoscopes:

> And I lost my inquiries in thinking of the fabled [Uriel], who belonging to the coterie of Plato, was sent down by that high person (before he was initiated into the arcana of the last science) to reform a certain district and give it some utopian ornaments—but the bright ambassador found everything so slow in movement—so dully progressive so sober & stale that in his disgust he breathed a fire w'h consumed every old land mark—tore up the moss covered mounds[;] and the very alters w'h had been the refuge of the poor & sinfull & decripid instead of being better were almost demolished—and in the destruction it is said the wings of the spiritual vehicle were so scorched that he was forced to ask aid of a desciple of the old reforming Patriarch who was buried on some old loved spot, and he (tho' looked on as a very plodder) constructed a chariot of clouds w'h conveyed the messenger home to new fledge his wings.[14]

At least two years before Waldo recorded the opening lines of "Uriel," his poetic fable of the Divinity School heresy, this letter provided crucial hints toward it. Once again Mary pictured Plato's heaven and agents, but she also gave a Miltonic cast to the story, naming her "bright ambassador" like the archangel of the sun in *Paradise Lost* and echoing Milton's accompanying imagery of light and flight. But while Milton's Uriel only witnessed Satan's flight downward to corrupt the world, Mary conflated Uriel and Satan by having this archangel breathe destructive fire upon the earth.[15] She saw religious institutions as a necessary "refuge" and feared the consuming fire of reform. Herself perhaps the plodding old disciple of Plato, she at least claimed an ability to rescue the young reformer whose wings were scorched by his own flame.

Mary valued the Divinity School Address and (though she never owned the fact) had significantly brought into being both its natural religion and its critique of the church. But at the same time she spoke for the "poor," including herself, who might under its influence be left without resources. No longer did she argue with Waldo on theological grounds about the nature of Christ: she let his stunning humanization of Jesus in the 1838 address pass completely without notice. Instead, she criticized on the moral grounds of human limitation and suffering. Waldo's latest lectures, she commented the same year in her Almanack, were reminiscent of "Charles' Sphinx," with the author himself as the riddling beast: "But he [is] of etherial order—and as few will try to interpret, he will not kill himself. The lectures facinate the great & learned—to me their power neither diminishes nor adds to the weight w'h oppresses me." By departing from redemptive faith, she added eight months later, he was telling a tale "so utopian that the dwellers in the common vales of tears wish they could rid themselves of the voice of the oppressed & the sight of human woes w'h history & fact present."[16]

In the vale where she lived, "history and fact" could not be ignored. Though she could urge unsettling ideas upon Waterford neighbors Thomas Stone and Ann Gage, she told Waldo news of their own kin as evidence that a more trustworthy and healing divinity needed to be preached. His Aunt Phebe was dying, and cousin Rebecca Haskins Hamlin (long ago Ruth's household helper) grieving over the death of two young children. Mary apologized ironically for intruding these harsh facts: "Let us fancy that there is no disease—that the cauldron of woe & sin exists only in the morbid imajanations of ascetics. And it is grand in the unity of the Infinite Personality to lose every discordant fact—to live in a Utopian [world] of our own." To Samuel Ripley, more attuned to the trials of village life, she lamented Phebe's death in December 1839, after "long years of struggling with one kind of difficulty or other, & that of the malcontents the most bitter." Phebe had died without religious comfort after a life of rigidly pursued duty. Mary faulted her lack of poetry or intellect but later found a statement of "true devotedness" in her biblical epitaph at Elm Vale cemetery: "She hath done what she could."[16] This daughter of the Concord Manse had never found transcendence in her country life.

Increasingly Mary also identified personally with human woe, as ill health overtook her elder years. Despite claims of stoic acceptance, she became increasingly a trial to her family and physicians. The first winter back in Waterford, Mary developed a "fellen" on her thumb, a growth serious enough to require weeks in bed and threaten an amputation that would have ended writing. Though helpless physically, she still had her faculties of thinking and talking, so became—as she admitted—a "whimsical patient." She chose Dr. Gage as her physician and thoroughly enjoyed his visits, mostly for the opportunity to discuss religion. "I called myself a sufferer to bring out the virtues of others," she insisted innocently.[18] Most of the virtues were her niece Hannah's. But when Mary decided for once in her life to have a "watcher" stay by her bedside through the night, she found that she could not abide that traditional form of womanly care.

As Hannah told the story to Waldo and Lidian, Mary spent the previous day dispatching notes to the woman's house, advising her to prepare by sleeping in advance. Then when the neighbor arrived, Mary put her to bed and "watched her herself," but woke the woman when she began to snore shockingly. As daybreak approached and Mary realized that she was getting no service from her experiment, she roused the watcher and demanded that her bed be made—then dismissed her before daylight, "declaring she never would have a watcher again, she had passed the worst night she remembered." The neighbor vowed in return that under no circumstance would she ever watch Miss Emerson again.[19]

This story suggests how uncomfortably the aging woman (once Mary Wilder White's ideal "garde malade") fit into the female culture of illness and care. Mary's incapacity to be cared for caused great friction in her life; for beyond temporary distress over the "fellen," she and her often inimical sister Rebecca shared the lingering and infectious disease erysipelas, caused by streptococcal bacteria akin to those of the more lethal childbed fever. When the condition spread from skin to nerves and underlying organs, as was the case with Rebecca, it could have a fatal outcome, but meanwhile the symptoms were chronic, painful, and disfiguring.

In the 1830s, before the advent of an infectious theory of disease, no doctor could either prevent or cure erysipelas, but many confidently offered remedies. Those who led the profession believed that all disease arose from hypertension of the blood vessels. Seen only as signs of this deeper imbalance, skin eruptions were treated by the same "heroic" remedies as were used for other illness: lancing and leeching to release bad blood, blistering (creating second-degree burns) to draw disease to the skin's surface. By the decade's end, however, health reformers were contesting this orthodoxy with "natural" remedies, seeking to purify the body with herbal purgations, whole-grain diet, and water baths. Predictably eclectic, Mary seems to have tried all the doctors and all the remedies. From 1838 on, she periodically visited Sweden, Maine, to take the waters, and by 1844 was following Sylvester Graham's grain diet. At the same time, she often underwent a daily regime of "blistering the temple neck and arm by turns."[20]

Now in her mid-sixties, Mary neither reached the climactic illness that would be her desired apocalypse nor regained the health to ride freely and read strenuously that she had once enjoyed. Her red lesions, numbed forehead, headaches, and limited eyesight could not have added to an already limited capacity to mix in society. Moreover, simultaneous hunger for care and protestations of independence—the heart of a difficult temperament from childhood—must have intensified competition with her sister Rebecca for the attention of Hannah and Charlotte, the only Haskins daughters remaining at home. Mary would have liked to die elegantly in youth of consumption, which in its physical wasting could be interpreted as a triumph of spirit; instead, she only became grotesque.

The most frightening aspect of Mary's erysipelas, however, was the prospect that it might affect mind as well as body. The disease centered in her face, and doctors believed facial erysipelas the most lethal kind because it could spread to the brain, causing delirium and then death. Insanity was Mary's deepest fear. When in the winter of 1841 she suffered an "attack of insensibility," the doctor (presumably Gage) blamed a congestion of blood on her brain, and Mary hoped for quick release. "Never was prisoner more irked," she wrote to Elizabeth, "who in escaping his Cell & leaping over hill & dale with sky & ocean in view [was] dragged back." She also mused to her young confidante about the kindred fear: "Now why do I shrink at passing a few years insane? No responsibility—no desire to get rid of 'what we hate in this degraded state.' For how little has all this so cherished reason done for me?" But two days later in her Almanack, recording the same experience and fear, she answered her own question: "God will be with me, tho I shall not have the nameless delight of consciousness."[21] That delight had always been her channel to God's presence.

The medical establishment did its best to limit Mary's consciousness: a few years later, Dr. Warren of Boston warned her against the excitements of fiction and politics but absolutely forbade "deep thought." Mary commented to Elizabeth that she was naturally incapable of it anyway. Her Almanacks through these years, however, record many returns from illness to thought, given edge by reading and voice by writing. "Now I crawl towards Cousin again," she wrote after months without intellectual challenge. She had begun reading Victor Cousin's French Eclecticism many times since the spring of 1835 in Concord, but personal and family crises always intervened. With more decisive energy she rebounded into writing six weeks after the fearful loss of consciousness in 1841: "I rise this morning with new gust and health to get a thought—a single new thought of the infinite is motive—object—enough to fill the soul—(oh thousands of souls no bigger than mine)—throws lustre over every object and import to every sand w'h runs in my glass."[22]

Mary's next sentence launched into a favorite thought about Jonathan Edwards: "When Edwards says 'the end of creation was God's glory—to manifest himself—some may think this strange and misrepresenting the divine benevolence. Not a jot." Edwards was the presiding figure in an Almanack that Mary composed with particular care—in a covered book rather than on letter paper—through 1840 and 1841. Leaving behind the "vapory" Cousin and even Coleridge, she refocused depleted energy on her older masters and their clearly God-centered philosophy of mind. Mary spoke for all her Calvinist ancestors as she inscribed inside the back cover: "The meta.[physics] of Edwards demolished those of [his opponents] for the phi.[losophy] of Arminius can no more endure a rigid analysis than a citadel of rooks could sustain musketry."[23]

In this reading, however, Mary was not merely backtracking historically, but seeking a system of thought to reconcile opposite beliefs in the power and the limits of individual reason. "How often but never weary," she reflected, "have I written that the venerable Clark has talked so wisely of 'fitnesses' Hutcheson of being and Edwards on the love of being universally (the best of all) and even the utilitarians—all all unite and point to the Cause and origin . . . in God." "Being universally" (expressed as a verb, not a noun) was her way of finding the way from God-reliance to self-reliance, grounding fragile identity in something beyond itself. Edwards's universal being of course included herself. "Why," she wrote to Lidian, "is it not in God we love ourselves & prize more existence as individuated with the infinite?"[24]

The Edwardsian sense of a divine will working beneath human will harmonized for Mary with non-Christian ideas of "Necessity" met in a wide variety of sources. Cousin introduced her to the Hindu Bhagavad Gita, and from it she endorsed Krishna's advice to Arjuna:

> And another great view of a necessity sort (that friend to souls who have so eagerly longed for moral perfection & so awfully failed) when the Indian philosopher exclaims "keep thy eye on the eternal principle and remember that all thy actions [are] indifferent in their results—today you live—tomorrow return to what you were, yesterday a plant or a beam of light. The beauty & merit of an action consists in performing it with profound indifference as to its consequence. It is necessary to act but as if one acted not,—interiorly motionless, fixed on the absolute principle w'h alone exists with a true existence"![25]

Whether informed by Christian, Greek, or Hindu wisdom, this freedom in acquiescence found repeated expression in Mary's Almanack writing in the years after her return to Vale. It was a vision predicated upon failure, but received as blessing. "That my mind is not formed for a Plotinus, or Edwards, I never dared repine," she wrote, "only sought that awe that concentrating fervor, which is the boon of small ones."[26]

In the spring of 1841, struggling with a "sick head" to reflect on universal being, Mary received a packet from Concord containing both Elizabeth Hoar's record of Margaret Fuller's Conversations and Waldo's newly published *Essays, First Series*. To the Conversations she responded enthusiastically, but in the second half of the letter remonstrated against "Self-Reliance" in terms completely predictable from the course of her own recent writing: "Is this strange medly of atheism and false independence the real sane work of that man whom I idolized as a boy, so mild, candid modest obliging, before you were conscious of reason? . . . And is he to go down to posterity an enymy to that faith w'h has saved millions? Oh how glad that I seperated." "Self-Reliance" aroused her wrath more than either *Nature* or the Divinity School Address: withdrawing the divine ground of individualism was anathema as neither nature idealism nor antiecclesiastical protest would ever be. Mary felt indignant because she was so deeply implicated in Waldo's attitude: the word "*Whim*," which he now proclaimed he "would write on the lintels of the door-post," had always been used in family parlance to describe her. Writing to the idolized nephew himself a month later, Mary referred to her own prickly solitude as a "reliance on myself and One."[27] That was her significant—Edwardsian, Plotinian, Hindu—dissent from his individualism.

By the time of this letter, a new communication had sprung up between Mary and Waldo, even in the midst of her greatest despair for him. Probably Elizabeth showed him the outburst on "Self-Reliance," an angrier critique than anything Mary would have written directly to him. Aptly, Waldo began in late April to meditate deeply on his relation to his aunt. He dreamt twice of prophetic figures pouring power into him, the second a "sublime" woman who had shared "the moral sentiment" with him. He immersed himself in rereading her letters, then filled nine journal pages with thoughts on her genius and her role in the Emerson family. In the midst of these reflections he wrote directly to Mary, proposing a reunion after five uncommunicative years:

> I feel in every line I read of these prized MSS. the strictness of the tie that joins these two separated souls—yourself & me. In the multitude of my friends, if I read letter of yours I seem at once to be solitary; for you are the older & the native friend. I feel as if only you & such as you, (if such were,) would challenge many things that now sleep & perhaps die in me. Yet why must we live so severed? Is it your pleasure? It is not mine.[28]

In the aftermath of "Self-Reliance," this plea is fraught with paradox. Waldo the rhetorician of independence sought relationship with his "native friend"—a friend who allowed him access precisely to his own solitude. If Waldo had eliminated God-reliance from his essay, he apparently sought a human but equally inward reliance on Mary in its stead, not so much for the relationship itself (he offered little reciprocally) as for the resource she provided to his thought and writing. Indeed, Mary had never been "severed" from Waldo's thoughts, for he had both praised her genius and named her deficiencies in passage after passage of journal writing in these most productive years.[29] Now he was looking for renewal at the source.

Mary's responded by apologizing for her independence as the product of a personal "nature or fate," disowning all memory of past altercations, and repeating the promise never to spend an hour at Waldo's house. At heart, beneath the smoke screen of quarrels and vows, Mary was resisting relationship with Waldo under circumstances that rendered her powerless, dependent for accommodations and open to his "taking of the imajanation." For she did want to renew the friendship on her own ground, inviting Waldo to "make a party of wife, children, Elisbeth & some of the Ripleys & come here."[30]

This Transcendentalist family excursion never took place, despite Waldo's yearning for her rural "Mt. Athos" in his recent journal entry. Instead, he took up Mary's offer of a summer meeting in Portland, inviting her to join him and hear his lecture at Waterville College, "The Method of Nature." At the last moment William joined them there as well, and Mary had a joyous double reunion: she had not seen Waldo for the five years of his most intense work, nor William since 1829. Upon returning to Vale, she wrote, "I shall be glad to recall the tones of your voice & the mere movements of your frame in the desk. And the wide emotions my spirit tasted." She claimed to dismiss her own objections into "the old Limbo." "Yet I would place the 'extacies of nature' beside the dreams of wandering visitors to the said place."[31] Mary still had reservations about Waldo's merely human idealism.

Great Disappointments

Almost immediately events called her back again to Waldo's circle. In September Ezra Ripley died at ninety. The circumstances show how closely the Waterford and Concord branches of the family had always been knit: his final stroke came the night after brother Lincoln fortuitously arrived and spent an evening of talk, and his caretaker for several years had been Sarah Haskins, that daughter of Waterford whose early childhood had unfolded largely at the Manse. There was no practical reason for Mary to stay above the Maine border, as Waldo reminded her: "The fall of this oak makes some sensation in the forest, old & doomed as it was, and on many accounts I could wish you had come home with me to the old wigwam & burial mounds of the tribe." Whether or not in respect to Ezra, she did at last return before the fall ended, allowing Waldo and Ruth to fetch her from Newburyport. She stayed two full weeks, residing independently at Howe's Tavern.[32]

In Concord, Mary found new ways as well as old. At Waldo's house there were now two small children, and Lidian expected soon to deliver a third. Domesticity had arrived, with Elizabeth Hoar a devoted third partner in raising the children. Mary had never seen five-year-old Waldo before, in fact had written to Elizabeth in his infancy of her unwillingness to "hail his entrance on a stage of so much danger." Her reason was a lifetime's bereavement. "How often I had done it & the child had scarsly budded or the man promised before they were passed!" Now, though saying little in his praise, she heard the precocious words and saw the beautiful face that had so captivated all these celebrants of childhood.[33]

Even more, she found a new culture of Transcendentalism extending from Waldo's house. She had known the elder Thoreaus for decades and seen enough of Henry in 1836 to ask for news about her "man of the wilderness"; but now he was living in the house whose hospitality she refused, writing poems for the *Dial* and considering a move to more solitary life. Mary must have heard him weigh options, for the following spring she asked Elizabeth, "How and what doing HDT?" Waldo had also invited the Alcotts to share the house that year, but, to Lidian's relief, Abby Alcott refused. Still, they lived only a mile away, and Bronson visited often. Mary had already judged his "Orphic Sayings," printed in the *Dial*, to be "like 'plumb pudding hot & plumb pudding cold,' " the work of a man without a "sound Johnsonian mind."[34] Probably no productive conversation came from that quarter.

Her greater interest had been to meet Margaret Fuller, genius of the Conversations and editor of the now sixteen-month-old *Dial*, familiar primarily through Elizabeth's pen-portraits. Possibly Mary even sought an intellectual friendship that would place some of her own writing in the Transcendentalists' journal: its first issue had been like a family album, including pieces by Charles, Edward, and Ellen, as well as Waldo; and Samuel Ripley had written to Mary then, "I think you had better become a contributor."[35] No one had brought up that possibility since, but Mary requested its issues eagerly and took an indirect part by promoting Thomas Stone's letters.

Mary's only meeting with Fuller, however, was a catastrophe. It took place not in Concord but in Newburyport, where Hannah Sawyer Lee and her sister introduced Mary to their friends Caroline Sturgis and Fuller. Both women managed to be sick at the time, and Fuller never favored Mary with "one sparkel of her fine wit—one argument for her dissent." Instead, as Mary recalled, Fuller "laid all the day & eve. on [the] soffa & catechised me who told my literal 'traditions' like any old bob[b]in woman." Questions that might have betokened respect instead felt like consignment to the past. Fuller in turn wrote to Elizabeth Hoar that she had gotten nothing from meeting Mary but insight into Waldo. "Knowing such a person who so perpetually defaces the high by such strange mingling of the low, I can better conceive how the daily bread of life should seem to him gossip. . . . It is certainly not pleasant to hear of God & Miss Gage in a breath." Mary must have argued the merits of one of Ann Sargent Gage's daughters, and Fuller considered a young lady from rural Maine intrusive on high discourse. Interestingly, Waldo had already likened Mary and Margaret to each other for a reputed female inability to be "impersonal."[36]

Each of these women formed a quick, negative judgment of the other, but Fuller's was much more dismissive. "To me, this hasty attempt at skimming from the deeps of theosophy, is as unpleasant as the rude vanity of reformers," she wrote to Elizabeth. "Dear Beauty where where amid these morasses and pine barrens shall we make thee a temple[?] Where find a Greek to guard it!" Mary continued to think about Fuller, years later still regretting the "bigoted impression" she had made. She also remembered Fuller's "speaking of something evil in nature":[37] she agreed with Fuller, apart from Waldo, that evil needed to be met and overcome.

No matter how ill and irritable, Mary persisted in meeting the Transcendentalists. After an "intemperate supper" in Concord, she fled to Boston, where she debated whether a shabby cloak should keep her from going to church. She felt no hesitation, though, about visiting Peabody's bookshop on West Street or Channing's study. Though Channing had risen in her estimation by writing *Slavery*, she was "not warmed" by their long talk on the movement. "His personal expressions of interest could not do much when one is in search of other sources of thought & faith."[38]

Probably she found those sources in other conversation during her days in Boston, in contact with the community of abolitionist women, for back at Vale that December she wrote two letters intended for the "Post office at the Anti-Slavery Fair." This was a Christmas bazaar, originally Lydia Maria Child's project, held annually by the Boston Female Anti-Slavery Society to raise money, showcase free-labor products, and make converts to the cause. Mary's characteristically elliptical letters probably did little to fill the society's coffers, if ever they were offered at the fair, but they articulated her position amidst the decade's storms of opinion. One justified women's activism: writing "To Albert," Mary urged a husband to support his wife's reform work and not insist on the "tame moonshine" of exclusively domestic preoccupation. "No, it is those [women] who are on the wing of disinterested pursuits—of objects beyond the ken of the senses who support the toils of every day life with the most ease and capasity." Amidst an ongoing public debate over women's sphere, between the domestic ideologue Catharine Beecher and the public lecturers Sarah and Angelina Grimké, Mary clearly leaned toward the latter.[39] She was not urging full public voice or political equality but did open the door by taking in politics as an expression of spirit.

Indeed, the second letter claimed the need for a divine grounding before ethics or politics could come into being. "No wonder," she wrote to her anonymous, doubting reader, "you are at a loss on this subject if your principles are not fixed on those relations which connect you with the Creator of all beings and the obligations which naturally result." Mary was expounding the ethical implication of "being universally," the principle she had derived from Edwards just months before. If there were no "voice *within*" there would be no human rights, the slave "crushed into sordid ignorance & bestiality." Human affliction was "like the deformed Sphinx with her riddles, till solved by the radient Genius of the gospel."[40] Here the sphinx—that persistent Emerson family emblem—riddled about suffering and oppression, not nature's meaning; and the riddle's answer was human awareness made possible by Christian grace.

Writing was on Mary's mind in this year of sojourning in Massachusetts. She not only ended the year with new letters to the public but also was contemplating what to do with her old Almanack, the major work that had accumulated in her hands rather than being dispersed as letters. Mary asked Ann's aid to sort out the disconnected papers, hoping both to gratify her friend's taste and save Waldo from the need to sort through her "womanish whim." Into one trunk would go papers for Waldo and his female kin; the rest, she proposed to Ann, "you might like to throw . . . bye in your large house." Mary could not write of her long-prized diary without jocular dismissal, especially to Waldo: "I have put into a trunk your richest gifts (letters) with some old Almanacks [lest] they might be found undirected and might give anxiety to the orthodox. The last you may burn or if any of my female freinds wish may have a N[umber]."[41]

Mary was portioning out her Almanack manuscripts because, as she told Ann, she was "every night . . . preparing for a sudden departure." Long eager for death, she believed her apoplectic head a sign of its approach. Instead, 1842 brought the loss of others in every quarter of her life. At the end of January came Waldo's message, "My boy, my boy is gone." Little Waldo had died after three days of scarlatina; and Mary, who had seen him for the first time in November, now sent to Concord the words she had hoped to avoid, mourning another newly budded child: "Blessed God how severe is thy hand. This moment sad[d]est of many sad news my old ears have received, I read yours. 'Grieve' I more than grieve—could any ills of mine have saved him. . . . Mother Granmother Elisbeth what a heavy sweep off of the holiest sweetest joys. I know too well those—of loving boys whose looks are of the soul & create new prophecies."[42]

Her role as a priestess of mourning is nowhere more evident than in her separate notes to members of the household through the following months. To Waldo that May, answering a confession of having lost his center, Mary made a sweeping attack on his whole dream of nature:

> And art thou become like one of us? Does nature who seemed thy favored Angel to wait thy walkings & musings and be the servator of thy Muse look askance— . . . And you do not like the little grave she has dug so blindly that you cannot drop your plummet into its sad chasm. Right glad am I! Abandon her! . . . Pass her bye—go behind her stage decorations alike with her inquisitions and prostrate thy higher capasities of enjoyment before Him who for some time of inscrutable purposes weilds her secret forces.[43]

To the women she adopted a wholly different tone, reminding Ruth of their shared suffering, exchanging with Elizabeth impressions of the child's beauty, asking Lidian for an account of "feelings in the loss you have sustained."[44]

Lidian's account of her spiritual progress seemed so valuable that Mary shared it with Ann Gage and her daughters, for these closest Waterford neighbors had kindred sorrows in the death of fifty-year-old Leander Gage at the end of April. Earlier the miracle child had died instead of the aged aunt; now the doctor died instead of the patient. In a formal eulogy for newspaper publication, Mary praised Dr. Gage as a believer in the church and a promoter of morals and freedom. To Elizabeth she focused more sharply where this man stood on her scale of virtues—"he had force of character rather than intellect—was wide awake"—and lamented the loss to his household.[45] Ann, at forty-eight the mother of a large family, would now enter the struggles of widowhood.

Finally, the news of William Ellery Channing's death came to Mary that October amidst her salt-air cure in Portland. Surviving the death of a man nearly her equal in years was no triumph, but instead a closing of her proper era. The only compensation was to be able to recall all of his career in Boston. They had met in agreement over the savior and redemption, Mary recalled, but had long since parted company. She had always wished for "the youth . . . to imbibe his spirit," but believed he would also experience regret once transported to heaven. Finally, she confessed to Elizabeth, "That smile returns to me with irking." Waldo concurred in measuring his praise. "I wish you would write me," he asked Mary, "what you think after so long a perspective as his good days have afforded, of your old preacher." Even as he associated aunt and Unitarian founder, Waldo distinguished them as elders in his own life. From Channing he withheld the highest praise, judging him "the sublime of calculation, . . . the nearest that mechanism could get to the flowing of genius," whereas five months earlier he had found Mary to embody that very quality: "Genius always new, subtle, frolicsome, musical, unpredictable."[46]

These three deaths of 1842, touching in different ways to the heart of Mary's living circle of friends, drove her nearly mad with impatience to be gone. Heading for Newburyport in July 1843 to board in the same block with her "antiently formed acquaintance" Ann Bromfield Tracy, Mary seemed to enjoy the town's live advantages. Again Hannah Lee and her sister were there, along with the poet Hannah Gould, and Mary invited Elizabeth to come share Plum Island's sea air. A cold brought on her most severe attack of erysipelas to date, however, and Mary turned to courting death actively. "She says," Waldo reported when called to the scene by Ann Tracy, "she much desired to die here, & be laid beside her sister [Hannah], & seems to have stayed here to give her fate a greater room."[47]

Mary wanted not only to die but to stage her own death and burial. As well as proximity to a living friend and a dead sister, the right doctor was required. She dismissed the first "because she wanted to die in the presence of a superior & intelligent man," perhaps judging this one against the late Dr. Gage and his conversation. Dr. Spofford, called out second, gratified by declaring the disease terminal but then had the bad grace to cure her. She assured Waldo and Elizabeth that she would never employ such a physician again. They found Mary furious with Ann Tracy for divulging her condition, sitting up with her face covered in burdock bandages, and cheerfully meddling in all her caretakers' work.[48]

The pressures of illness and bereavement intensified Mary's death-wish, but she also responded to the culture around her. Death was Mary's solution to apocalyptic urgency, and that desire took many forms in the early 1840s. Writing to Ann on a fast day in 1843, she saw the times to foreshadow divine revolution. "And on the whole [I] hope more than fear," she added, "that God is revolving a crisis w'h will give nations to his praise thro' the glorious plan of redemption." Advent would be even better than death, Mary admitted by the end of the letter: "A sudden remove [from life] delivers from long suffering—yet I *wd* see & feel that joyous hour if permitted."[49]

Mary anticipated the hour of Christ's Second Coming much more literally than Waldo and his friends, who looked for millennial glory in their own humanity. Like the mainstream Protestant reformers around her, Mary saw the overcoming of social ills—slavery, drunkenness, pagan ignorance—as a direct means of reaching the kingdom. She felt skeptical, however, when cousin Joseph Emerson called simply for a millennium of benevolent societies and inventions: "Oh why does he want to see myriads of human beings if ever so happy multiplied on this cold earth?" She required the earth's transformation, not just its improvement, in this respect endorsing Anglican Isaac Taylor, whose *Saturday Evening* predicted an unfolding of the kingdom after a dark hour and a divine intervention.[50] Mary's personal yearning for apocalypse belonged within a rich, internally divided religious culture of expectation.

The more immediate antagonist to her belief in the kingdom was neither nephew Waldo's utopian scheme nor cousin Joseph's overly secular benevolence. At home in Waterford her housemates, the Haskinses, converted to Millerism and proclaimed 1843 the world's last year. Long immersed in a rural culture of revivals, Rebecca Haskins listened eagerly when Vermont farmer William Miller proclaimed his interpretation of the book of Daniel: adding together the numbers in King Nebuchadnezzar's dream of the latter days, Miller found that the coming could be expected *now*—without doubt between March 21, 1843, and March 21,

1844. Rebecca read all the Millerite papers, listened to the lecturers who circulated the news through western Maine, and grew "pretty full in it." Mary did not wholly object but told her sister that the prophecy was too good to be true. As she departed for Newburyport that summer, she packed a copy of Isaac Taylor's *Fanaticism*. The British rationalist, at once a believer in the kingdom and an anatomist of spurious religious claims, would provide ammunition against her sister.[51]

Mary had several reasons to resist the prospect of ascent from a burning earth. She read the Bible devoutly but with an ear tuned more to figurative language than to literal chronology of the future. She belonged socially as well as intellectually to Boston liberalism. "Has any of the respectable [or] the enlightened believed in the second advent?" she asked Elizabeth Hoar.[52] Adventist faith was both too common for her and unredeemed by the truth-telling of William Lloyd Garrison's rough social prophecies. Abolitionism promised liberation on earth and unity of classes and sects, whereas Millerism gave up the search for justice on earth.

When Mary returned to Vale in the fall of 1843 after the bout of erysipelas, she found Millerism to have overtaken both the family and their shared house. All eleven Haskins children but Hannah and Samuel had joined their parents' faith, and converts would not leave the unconverted in peace. When Rebecca's son Ralph brought home a Millerite lecturer, Mary warmed to see religious instinct in a nephew who had spent his thirty-five years without an intellectual glimmer. But she was mortified to find him missionizing among the neighbors, even more so when he tried converting her. "He was absent at supper," she reported to the Concord family, "& afterwards we heard a great deal of grieflike joy up garret & it was his emotions caused by having an answer to prayer for Hannah who was here, & poor me." Compared with this, she confessed, none of the Transcendentalists' excesses offended, neither Bronson Alcott's disassociated idealism nor Waldo's old admiration of Hume. "How we hate to see p[re]suming hands laid on the arks of our faith & visions substituted for reason."[53]

By early spring of 1844, with the last day of the prophecy nearly upon them, believers across the Northeast gave up all business, planted no crops, suspended even the publication of their own newspaper, and made white "ascension robes" for the coming event. The Haskinses brought "arrogant antinomian ignorant lecturers" to the house now in groups as well as singly; and as of March 3, when Mary reported to Lidian, their singing and preaching had rung through her closed chamber door for ten days straight. Sitting amidst the clamor reading Carlyle's *Past and Present*, with its painful indictment of England's social ills, Mary felt that she "might be willing the world should be burnt," then expressed her own more optimistic millennial faith instead. "I indulge the brightest hopes that the present commotions will end in glory to God. When this whole family (who are insane on this subject) insist on its destruction & expect it daily, I tell them of the multitudes of virtuous & happy ones, of the prosperity of their grandchildren."[54]

The world did not end that March, nor the following October as the faithful continued to hope, but Rebecca, Robert, and their converted children held fast even after the "Great Disappointment." In January 1845 Rebecca died of erysipelas, now settled in her lungs, and Mary regretted afresh her sister's refusal to abandon adventist illusions. Both of the eldest Haskins daughters, Rebecca Hamlin and Phebe Chamberlain, held meetings at their houses that winter and spring; and Charlotte, Sarah, and the Hamlins all received "second baptism" in Mutiny Brook. "I dont like to indulge the sense of the ludicrous about them," Mary told Waldo, "but yesterday they—two or 3 men strangers Sarah 'lotte & Hamlins[—] walked up to Chamberlain's for a meeting, as they [were] passing a good genteel house they fell on their hands & knees ('to humble themselves') and crept along, the sturdy farmer took a hoop & went to beating one of the preachers w'h presented as farcical a scene as could have been in our wilderness." Phebe and Rebecca stayed longest with the new transmutations of Millerism: the Chamberlains left Waterford for Battle Creek, Michigan, apparently to join in founding the Seventh-Day Adventist movement, and Rebecca and Mary Hamlin, like many other Millerites, became Shakers.[55]

Though condemning this heaven-bent pietism as delusion, Mary too felt urgency to speed the passage of time. Like the Millerites, she had often experienced the "Great Disappointment." During the very last month of Millerite expectation, October 1844, Mary was first reported in the garb that has constituted her major fame—a death shroud. Without doubt, early and late, Mary ordinarily wore dresses, often requesting kinswomen's help to find a "gown of grave beauty" to become her complexion. But in the spring of that year she asked for thin flannel to wear in her final illness, in May separated the lining from the outside of a robe and wore the lining daily, and in October appeared unexpectedly at the Waltham parsonage, as Sarah Bradford Ripley reported to her future son-in-law, "dressed in a white robe."[56] Reveling in the winds of her favorite season, feeling acutely her own hunger for heaven, Mary could don the heavenly garment in Massachusetts that she rejected in Maine.

This strange act must be understood against the background of Mary's personal desire for transformation and her millennial culture, as a visual sign of the coming change, neither comedy nor mere derangement, though surely acted out in moments when despair or excitement overcame conventional control. Eight years later, Mary made her most spectacular such appearance: staying at the Abiel Wheeler house in Concord, as the Wheelers recalled long after, she "astonished the neighborhood by crawling out an upper window and sitting in her ascension robes on the roof of the small entrance hall, to be ready for her translation."[57] Their phrase "ascension robes" reveals how the Wheelers and the town of Concord interpreted this behavior—as Millerite delusion.

Women of the 1840s

Such appearances were isolated, but the strains of erysipelas, grief, and religious excitement rendered Mary a highly unpredictable human being. Starting in 1841, moreover, she no longer hid herself above the Maine border, as she had for five years after Charles's death, but visited Massachusetts almost annually. The new railroad speeded her travels and added to their pleasure. Once, proceeding down the coast, she was hailed by Mary Wilder White's granddaughter and invited to the Ladies' Saloon for conversation all the way into East Boston.[58] Concord had become easily accessible, and as a result her visible oddities of behavior were recorded as incidental color in the memoirs of Transcendentalism. This was the eccentric, aged Mary of legend.

Even the anecdotes, however, made of Mary more than a reactionary force amidst innovation. The white robe was only one detail in Sarah Bradford Ripley's portrait of an impetuous, intellectual, oddly youthful figure, who "came at evening when we did not expect her at all" and picked up conversation where it had left off years before:

> She is seventy years old and still retains all the oddities and enthusiasms of her youth. A person at war with society as to all its decorums, eats and drinks what others do not and when they do not, dresses in a white robe such days as these, enters in to conversation with every body and talks on every subject, is sharp as a razor in her satire, and sees you through and through in a moment. She has read all her life in the most miscellaneous way and her appetite for metaphysicks is insatiable. Alas for the victim in whose intellect she sees any promise. Descartes and his vortices, Leibnitz and his monads, Spinoza and his Unica Substantia will prove it to the very core. Good Lord deliver us will be your prayer no doubt.[59]

Sarah drew a revealing portrait of Mary, but also an angry and denying one. "I owe her much," Sarah concluded, "but she is a person I could never love." Sarah's many professions of love in earlier letters stand as evidence against that judgment. Whatever the emotional dynamics of their loving feud over the years, the two women could surely agree on nothing intellectually. In 1838 Sarah had at last visited Vale, but instead of responding to sublime nature had ruminated about the chasm between the finite and infinite.[60] Probably in 1844 Mary was still trying to argue and convert. But Sarah's description focuses on Mary's presumption in coming to do so unannounced, interrupting an already exhausting routine of work in house and school. Though visibly anticipating the grave, Mary had never grown up to adult tact or respect for routine—so in the reformist forties seemed closer to the younger generation's impatience with decorum than to her fifty-year-old protégée Sarah.

Elizabeth Peabody managed a better balance between admiring and chastising this unconventionality when, a year later, Mary fell afoul of Horace and Mary Peabody Mann. Visiting at the Manns' home, she found letters on the parlor table and assumed that they were open for all to read, as would have been the case at Vale. Unfortunately, her eye lit upon some unfavorable comment about herself, and a quarrel erupted. Elizabeth Peabody made a lesson in comparative ethics of the event. "If I should tell *Mr. Alcott* that you read a letter in the above circumstances," she wrote to Mary, "*he* would consider it the evidence of a pure and exalted mind, which had entered into the *Universal*. But if I were to tell *Mr. Mann* the same thing, *he* would tell me to take care of my purse." Elizabeth herself found Mary's behavior neither exalted nor thieving, but typical of her willfulness, thirst for knowledge, and disregard for the mere "righteousness" of modern Unitarians. Whereas Elizabeth's own generation had grown up overly afraid of any misstep,

> you lived before that day, and do not exhibit any of this death-in-life which I complain of, but coquette with life like a girl of fifteen, who knows herself sovereign and can afford to play with *All*. You remind me of Mr. Emerson's saying in his first essays,—something of this kind—that if a person acts consistently according to their constitution *they are justified*. This is subjective transcendentalism I think I must acknowledge, but it is very exciting to see it done. I confess it makes my blood dance and is altogether more entertaining than the conscientious niceness of some people. Is it the Satan in me that is conciliated and tickled? or is it the freedom wherewith Christ doth make us free? *I am really in doubt.*[61]

Even if she doubted whether Transcendentalism came from Christ or Satan, Elizabeth Peabody placed Mary among its adherents.

Moreover, Mary had not ceased reading and responding to the newest publications. Throughout the forties, her strongest interest was to follow those reconstructing Christian theology on the base of German thought, Hedge, Brownson, and Peabody. Everything that Brownson's review of Schleiermacher gave her, Mary commented, she had herself thought out in her own "day book of '40 & '41 . . . after pouring over I[saac]. Taylor's review of Edwards on Will." With increasing interest in mid-decade, she followed Elizabeth Peabody's changing theological views, which she received in personal letters, as well as from periodicals. While defining life according to German philosophy as a dynamic process, Elizabeth urged Mary to reconsider orthodoxy for its understanding that sin was inherent in the "organic self." Nor was Mary interested only in theologically conservative parts of the movement. She regularly read the *Dial* and regretted its demise in 1844. That October—just after visiting Waltham—she went to see her friends George and Sophia Ripley at their utopian community Brook Farm. Amidst laments about Millerite zeal in the spring of 1845, she also asked Waldo, "Have you Fuller's 'Woman'[?] I am longing to see it, & Brownson's review of it."[62]

Mary's eventual response to *Woman in the Nineteenth Century* does not survive. Her view of Fuller is clear, however, from passing comments over the next several years, as Mary took pleasure in *Summer on the Lakes*, expressed astonishment at Fuller's death by drowning in 1850, and finally read the *Memoir* that Waldo and other friends prepared in her honor. Mary condemned Fuller for "monsterous" temperament, feverish imagination, and false theology. "Her opinion of our divine Saviour," Mary summed up in an ungrammatical but observant sentence, "prevented any advance to the Infinite but thro instinct, paganism & being unhappily steeped in Goetheism." But Fuller also received from Mary the awe that she accorded only to the great geniuses, whether or not of her own mind. "Had she been a [Christ]ian! What a spirit!" Mary looked ahead to the perfecting of that spirit—like Plato's and Byron's—in its immortal form, and even, recalling their ill-starred conversation of 1841, hoped herself to get nearer Fuller in heaven. "I may possibly in long ages of education be permitted to see & hear the eminent."[63]

Meanwhile, the antislavery movement rather than Transcendentalism gave Mary her fullest view of new roles for women. The high point of her 1845 trip to Boston was neither conversation with Peabody nor reading of Fuller, but direct witness of a protest meeting against the annexation of Texas at Faneuil Hall. Writing to her "Abolition friends" the Gage women that night, she found the event to sum up a sacred history and a millennial future: from the walls the portraits of Founding Fathers seemed to smile as the onrolling wheels of Providence were bringing Christ's kingdom to the needy world. At such a moment, women needed to participate. "And you will have time," she urged Ann's recently married daughter Irene, "to attend the great questions w'h agitate the world and loosen the holds w'h selfish & family interests cling too."[64]

With less caution than in her letter to the Anti-Slavery Fair in 1841, she now claimed the wider world as women's sphere. Mary had glimpsed the possibility of an American Republic to include women in her youth, "when freedom was alive," and now she followed the movements of younger women with enthusiasm. In Concord, Mary Merrick Brooks devoted her energies to petition drives and speeches, sent messages to Mary by way of Elizabeth, and herself wrote that Waldo had become a "no-government man."[65] Lydia Maria Child had emerged as a national editor and columnist; her *National Antislavery Standard* (rather than Garrison's *Liberator*) was Mary's constant reference for following the cause, though she tended to read only Child's pieces rather than the coverage of factional disputes among abolitionists. "She has a noble ingenuousness of bringing her beautiful self forward," Mary wrote to Waldo of the wide-ranging essays that Child would publish as *Letters from New York*; "I worship egotism in practice your poor ears are witnesses." Later preparing his notebooks of Mary's writing, Waldo wrote a note reminding himself to record Mary's views of Child among the "excellent pages" of her 1845–46 Almanack. The only American woman writer eventually to merit equal honor was Harriet Beecher Stowe, whose "primer-sized book" *Uncle Tom's Cabin* came to Mary early in 1853. "Is it not a gem?" she asked Elizabeth.[66] Child offered political virtue and a beautiful self, but Stowe made the sufferings of slaves and the virtue of women keys to the kingdom, giving influential form to themes long submerged in Mary's writing.

So could Mary warm to a range of women's benevolent activity. She read the memoir of Ann H. Judson's mission to Burma and asked Lidian, "Is there any American biography of woman equal?" She revealed her awareness of America's new Catholic order for women by calling Elizabeth Hoar her own "Sister of Charity." "Have you learnt the death or rather translation of Elis.[abeth] Fry?" Mary wrote to Ann when the British Quaker reformer died. "What a light from the prisons—what an alleviator of human woes & converter from guilt has departed!" But she endorsed only more tepidly a biography of cousin Joseph Emerson's onetime student Mary Lyons, "efficient and most devoted of pious & publick souls";[67] the planning of lockstep academic programs at Mount Holyoke did not, like Fry's light from the prisons, justify spiritual translation.

In the face of a newly constrictive culture of domesticity for American women, Mary returned to another theme of her youth, criticizing marriage and defending "single blessedness." Her earliest surviving will, recorded in 1832, had dedicated a small sum of money to begin "an institution such as the English have for women who are unable to afford to board"; her own desire for freedom from family dependence clearly extended to others as well. A decade later she often expressed her views of marriage. To Elizabeth Hoar, with whom she shared a special bond of single life, she imagined a debate between the respective claims of Celibacy and Hymen. The marriage claim won, but Diana's single daughters pursued their "lofty way" undaunted. When Hannah Haskins announced wedding plans a year later, Mary commented drily to Elizabeth, "Much as I say against matrimony—that I find no one better or happier and that probably a majority wish to be unyoked—folks will marry. And thus they lose great feelings & pursuits in individuals *sometimes*."[68]

Mary addressed the fiancées and wives themselves almost as bluntly. In 1850 she commented to Ann Gage's daughter Frances on the eve of her marriage that Swedish novelist Fredericka Bremer had portrayed childish bride-heroines devoid of the "individual reliance" alone guaranteeing marital happiness: "I really wish Bremer had been married tho', for her sorrowfull disappointment has left a strange predilection for mating." Soon reporting to Lidian on Frances's actual wedding, Mary wrote with apprehension, "If ever a happy girl is to be pitied it is the first year of leaving a good home & mother." Lidian wrote back defending a true husband as better than father or mother, but she agreed with vehemence to the rejection of unfit marriage, declaring it "more galling and degrading than that of the Negro Slave."[69] Both Emerson women, though declining active involvement in the nascent movement for women's rights, were making important claims to freedom in their private lives and letters.

Women writing for publication out of religious, especially reforming, zeal won Mary's respect; they extended her own being and vocation. But those who appeared in print for any lesser end incurred sharpest displeasure. Even religiosity offered no excuse if it served sentimental views of life; as Mary had written of Felicia Hemans, "We love devotion too well to have it *named* too often." In particular, she resisted the growing number of women in the 1840s offering their devotion for the worldly ends of fame or profit. Hannah Sawyer Lee of Newburyport had done modestly well as a writer of pious fiction, and through her Mary also knew Hannah Flagg Gould, a writer of verses for the periodicals. She took the former with a grain of salt and stood in round judgment of the latter. Lee appeared guilty of "egotism of a refined & proud kind"; Gould, deluging Mary with chatter of her Philadelphia and Boston publishers, seemed a "mori memento of literary fame." "I have at some moments," she admitted to Elizabeth, "yearned to be interested by some specific object—absorbed in a poem or novel—and it was good to fathom at once the narrow limits of capasity & knowledge—may be nothing excites more complete submission?"[70] Admitting with rare frankness her own potential interest in a writing career, Mary condemned the "submission"—both worldliness and dependence—demanded of the profit-making woman writer.

Close to Mary as well, however, were two younger women who in different ways followed out her idea of the woman writer's vocation, Elizabeth Peabody and Ann Sargent Gage. Both, in fact, needed money as much as Hannah Gould in the 1840s, Elizabeth as a single woman supporting herself and her parents, Ann as a widow still raising children. Ann found the more conventional solution, taking boarders into her genteel house and depending on the older children to make money. For her, writing poetry was a private and domestic act, though Mary always took her seriously as a "pen woman." Peabody had long supported herself by bookselling and teaching. Though by the midforties the store on West Street no longer made profits, she too did not see writing for the press as a solution;[71] her essays were too strenuously intellectual to win favor with Gould's publishers. So for two different reasons Mary could not only sanction, but bless and encourage, these two women as writers.

Not that her relations with either were easy. In the summer of 1846, Elizabeth Peabody took a rare vacation to see Mary's world of lakes and mountains, and Mary brought her Boston and Waterford friends together. Unfortunately, she responded to the stress of the visit in her most irritable and demanding humor, and Elizabeth and Ann met each other in dismay over Mary rather than in the threesome that all might have expected. Having waited sixteen years to see Waterford, Elizabeth wanted to "mount the mountains and ride the roads" rather than rest at home with her elderly hostess. So Elizabeth bathed in the lake with Hannah and walked with the Gages; and Mary, "restless like the eel" with the itching of erysipelas, felt excluded from their new intimacy. Elizabeth offered to stay in and read Channing on self-denial to Mary, thinking its lessons of value, but when she paused too often to invite conversation, Mary walked out. "Thus," as Elizabeth recounted the day's events to Frances Gage, "I was permitted an hour and a half of woodland life and the sight of a great many new pictures (though Miss Emerson insists that there is but *one landscape* in Waterford from all the standpoints.)" Mary had unaccountably insisted, "You are not to go upon the mountain however long you may stay."[72]

Each of these self-defensive women used the opportunity of their quarrel to dissect the other's character. Mary wrote to Elizabeth Hoar that Peabody had appeared completely different from what she had previously believed, indifferent to Mary's old-style Unitarianism, self-important with her "large machine of letters from the great and good," and inquisitive about Mary's personal dealings with Hannah and the Gages. Elizabeth Peabody, while recoiling from Mary's "*ugly sincerities* as she calls them," put her finger on Mary's flaws with surgical precision. The older woman had been wholly unwilling to listen to Peabody's religious views, to keep personality out of intellectual conversation, or even to leave her guest alone in nature. Every one of Mary's allegiances—to freedom, Christian humility, and solitude—was belied by contrary behavior. "If she were thirty years younger," Peabody wrote to the Gages, "I should certainly have asked her if she would tell me in what the principle that prompted this petty piece of tyranny differed from the principle of slaveholders, and I could not but be amased that a person who had lived in the light of Christs character so many years should *be left thus*. . . . Oh wad some Power the Gift gie us, etc."[73]

Peabody could describe Mary brilliantly, but finally neither woman had a great deal of Burns's gift to see themselves "as others see us." While discovering "so much wounded and unsatisfied affection" in Mary, Elizabeth admitted no difficulty herself: "I love her though she does stick hard things into all tender places. . . . I am surprised to think how little pain I felt."[74] Two single women, often devalued by others, were unable to keep from wounding each other. Their long correspondence broke off, ill feeling stood between Mary and Ann Gage as well, and Mary recalled the incident with penitence and indignation for another ten years.

Still Mary did not wholly let go of these women after their rupture. As a result of the painful vacation trip, Elizabeth Peabody got to know Ann Gage's poems; and when she published *Aesthetic Papers* in 1849, she included Ann's poem at the death of Leander. Mary hardly felt gracious about the new publication, telling Elizabeth Hoar that she wanted no copy and had "other fish to fry." A garbled sentence even may say that Peabody had turned down some "monidies" by Mary herself. But a month later, having after all gotten a copy of *Aesthetic Papers*, she found Ann's poems "mostly as good as when read at first" and Peabody's essay "The Dorian Measure" to be "original in it's design as [well as] ingeniously & learned[ly] written."[75] Its sympathetic interpretation of the Grecian Feast of Apollo for heirs of the Puritans met her own thoughts after all, and with characteristic generosity Mary extended the recognition she had denied at Waterford.

Likewise, though feeling her ancient friendship with Ann healed only in part, Mary proceeded to advocate her for honors among American women poets. She showed the verses in *Aesthetic Papers* to Waldo, and he liked them so much that he quoted several lines in a letter of condolence to Thomas Carlyle when his wife, Jane, died. Mary's favorite among Ann's poems, however, was a blank verse sonnet about "the Basins," a scene of river and forest near Waterford:

In God's true temples the whole heart cries out
For transformation, harmony with truth,
With all true forms, the vast and the minute.
The holy service needs not human speech.
The tall old Hierarchs from out their cores
Dispense the healing word, the Gilead balm,
The Balsam for torn hearts by discord rent.
The orchestra pours forth from inmost throat
A rich mellifluence of sacred song;
And the large blessing waits for ready hearts.

True Word of Life, distilling as the dew,
Sweet soothing Power, so softly breathing love,
Distill on us, attune our jarring strings,
And join our song in unison with thine.[76]

It was a good, if not strongly original, poem, Emersonian by way of both Mary and Waldo. The image of nature's balm of Gilead had perhaps been transmitted from Mary's 1832 letter, to Charles's of 1833, to Waldo's Divinity School Address of 1838, and now to Ann's poem. Mary never spoke of such origins, however, but instead held up Ann against Felicia Hemans and called her the "poet bro't up in the pure mountain air who exceeded all." She liked to carry a copy of Ann's lines with her to try the taste of those she met, in 1851 finding grim satisfaction that Hannah Gould of Newburyport "could not enter into the situation of their author."[77]

Milton's Old Room

Meanwhile, though identifying with women as artists and reformers through the 1840s, Mary never relinquished the right to judge, admire, and instruct her increasingly famous nephew. Showing him Ann's poem was a test of its merit, but she also regularly received and commented on his speaking and writing. In August 1844 came the news that he was delivering an oration on West Indian emancipation, and she expressed pleasure at the descent of his muse to such "humble ground." This oration really began Waldo's work on behalf of the cause that Mary and Charles had first set forth as a family commitment. Now, most of all, she was "impatient for the *essays*—if they predict any thing of an Abdiel flight from fallen Angels to the clear throne." Referring to the forthcoming *Essays, Second series*, she continued her personal allegory of the Miltonic archangels. In her view, as expressed over the years, Waldo had been a sprightly Ariel, a fiery Uriel, or Lucifer himself, but she hoped that he might at last become the angel to express his individualism in loyalty to God.[78]

When Mary received the *Essays* in December, however, she did not say whether they followed Abdiel's example. Instead, her response took the noncommittal form of quoting back to Waldo her "Mountain Rustics notes w'h crowd the margins." Once more she had lent out the book to a Waterford devotee of Transcendentalism, probably a young neighbor named Calvin Farrar. By quoting Farrar's marginal responses she identified herself with his enthusiasm: "So here RWE is one of the holy ones—," she quoted, "a Seer Poet divine yet human." These titles were precisely what she had urged upon Waldo since adolescence. Yet in the next sentence she undercut such attributions of visionary power: "If such be the effect of your writing, dearest Waldo, on many youth—there seems danger in their state of mental irreverence."[79]

Mary must have found him still a fallen angel, for two months later she wrote another allegory of rebellious Uriel. Waldo had proposed the metaphysical idea that there was "no straight line in nature," only curves returning ultimately to the perceiver; in his later poem "Uriel," this was the idea deemed treasonous by the "stern war-gods" of heaven. Mary extended the idea by imagining a heavenly conversation that Uriel's "assault on facts of sense" had prompted among all the philosophers and bards gathered in Plato's ongoing symposium—Leibniz, Berkeley, Kant, Clarke, Milton, and Goethe among them. Their particular opinions were opaque even by Mary's standards, but she still managed to dramatize philosophy in a manner that Waldo enjoyed intensely. The question of Mary's influence on the poem "Uriel" cannot be precisely pinpointed, since Waldo did not date his first full draft either before or after this February 1845 letter.[80] Once more, however, the mythmaking shared by aunt and nephew had provided raw material for finished literary form: the final poem "Uriel" seems to draw upon both the rebelliousness of her first characterization and the heretical talk dramatized in the second. Even when Mary took the opportunity to comment on Waldo's work, he found live wit to incorporate into further work.

Through the years she returned as well to find sustenance in their shared words and ideas. For several years Mary focused her intellectual energy on a new consolidation of idealist philosophy, rereading Price, finally exploring Cudworth and Plotinus through direct immersion in their works. Meanwhile, her Almanack entries considered the possibility of illusion that idealism brought with it, affirming that in any case "the Creator gives the vision immediately." Then at the end of 1849 she reappropriated from Waldo the text which showed his deepest debts to her and the tradition that she had taught: "But never shall discover an attribute [of nature], I believe, which will explain or reveal idealism in the sense of dear Waldo's splendid chapter in Nature which excited me last eve. This wonderfull universe w'h astonishes the profoundest thinking phi.[losopher] is a reservoir of means.—And these afford no belief in anything like deception." From the chapter "Idealism" in Waldo's *Nature* she could read, in response to the "noble doubt" whether nature actually existed, that through such appearance "God will teach a human mind."[81] She felt confirmed by this as though it had not been her own thought first.

Whether faulting or praising Waldo's achievement, she continued to measure him against the Miltonic model. When in the summer of 1847 he announced a plan to lecture in England for a year, Mary wished him to "go commissioned with thundering terrors to that government about these slavery plans to supply the west indies!" But her response to reading his recent work went to the heart of another shared passion: "I wish that you could get into Miltons old room & blind yourself to all but real poetry w'h would lead to the Center of all truth just, almost, as in the revelations, not as the Poet viewed them." In her view, Milton was too materialistic and his poetry sometimes wearisome, but Mary still wished for Waldo to be "blind" in the Miltonic sense: "Blind I mean shut up in yourself & alone with that Muse who like Plato smiled high promise on your dawn." In a sentence she had encapsulated the aspiration of decades. Three years later another, more gnomic word of praise to Waldo represented her continued demand for an epic from his eyes and mind: "When I saw how much light you used I tho't of the birds who become blind you know on snow mountains."[82] Mary was wresting her own, nature-worshiping but antimaterialistic vision out of Milton and Plato: she granted Waldo the status of a Miltonic poet, blind from excess of light, but also imagined him "using" the light like a bird amidst frozen, vacant mountains, lost to any vision but an intense, white concentration within.

Leaving Vale

The central scene of Mary's diverse imaginative sympathies—her "poor rich nest"—was a double front room upstairs in the Waterford house. The farm had become "desolate Vale" in 1841 when Robert took advantage of her absence to cut down most of the elms, so improving the land for use but rendering it less beautiful. Still from this room Mary could watch a star "shining thro the naked branches of the great tree—& disdain[ing] not its withered arms," or hear "many a groan from [the] bursting Lake which might be imajined some imprisoned giant or Prometheus."[83]

She valued her nest's interior equally. Able to purchase wood on her own contract, Mary kept the place warm as late at night as she wished. A valued possession was her bed, perhaps the same one first requested from Ruth in 1809, now covered with blankets made by Hannah. Her own bureau, carpets, chairs, and writing table had long since been added as well.[84] But the room's heart was her bookcase, both a locked depository of papers and a museum of memories. When absent from Vale, Mary longed to return to the books on its shelf, including Radcliffe's *Mysteries of Udolpho* (her brother William's bookplate in it), de Staël's *Literature and Society* and *Germany* (the latter inscribed to Waldo), Wordsworth's poems (dedicated to Ann and Frances Gage), all of Waldo's publications as they appeared, and a shifting assortment of periodicals and books on loan from Massachusetts. Her treasury of letters and remaining Almanacks were stored there as well. On top of the case was Sophia Peabody's medallion of Charles, veiled so as to be "hidden from all eyes but mine," as well as a silhouette from Elizabeth, which she wreathed in forest leaves. Alongside these stood silhouettes of John Clarke and Edward as children and a miniature of Waldo. She wanted a matching one of William. Nearby hung portraits of her Bliss grandparents, a picture of Dante's "wizard form" brought by Edward from Rome, and a memorial to "Mrs. Warren," probably the Revolutionary historian Mercy Otis Warren.[85] Her bookcase and wall symbolized the way private and public, female and male culture had converged in her life.

After Rebecca's death in 1845, the Haskinses' domestic economy underwent major changes, but at first they secured rather than threatened Mary's tenure at Vale. Whether by her insistence or by some other circumstance, "the world of Waterford" discovered that she, not Robert, was the owner of Vale. By the end of the year, Mary's agents, Levi Brown in Waterford and the Waltham Ripleys' son Gore in Massachusetts, recovered again the legal papers that Charles had seen in 1832, proving that the farm was hers. Mary deeded an adjoining "cottage" and twenty-five acres around it to Robert, buying Vale and its larger number of acres for one dollar from him so as to settle ownership unequivocally. She took a mortgage with Waldo, so that his name appeared as co-owner. Though she had long felt cheated by the Haskins men, claiming that a "vein of fraud" ran through them all, in the end she provided for her difficult brother-in-law, as well as claiming her own investment.[86]

Her plan was to provide for the Haskins children as well; as she wrote several years later, "I shall never be at peace with life or even dear Death unless I am sattisfied that they have reason to be." She alluded primarily to the Haskins daughters, however, rather than the five sons who had originally expected to be their father's heirs; in particular, she wanted to keep the land for Hannah and her farmer-husband Augustus Parsons, hoping eventually to divide it between Hannah and Charlotte.[87] Such a settlement would provide both care for herself and a family base for all of the Haskins children, but under the title of women rather than men.

For a while this arrangement worked out, at least to Mary's satisfaction. Augustus farmed the Elm Vale land as his own; Hannah did the cooking and housekeeping at both Vale and her father's house. Elizabeth Peabody visited and criticized the household in this form, finding Mary's long-boasted "solitude" really the worst of temptations for a character with "lust of power over others." Mary once confessed to Ann the same weakness, admitting that at home and especially with Hannah she would sometimes "give way to ease & a *sort* of dictation." Hannah could tolerate the petulance that had driven both her own mother and the neighborly watcher away, and Peabody found her to have an "angel temper."[88]

Larger forces than irascible temperament, however, weighed against the permanence of this new family group at Vale. Farming in the hills of Maine was a failing operation, and the children of Waterford's first settlers looked for lives elsewhere. By the fall of 1847, Augustus Parsons had sold his farm and was planning to migrate from Waterford to follow his original training in trade. Nor was farming easier for women: running two houses and farms, Mary realized, had "injured Hannah."[89] By the end of October, her caretakers had left Maine for good, with Mary's blessing but no clear plan where to settle.

Hannah and Augustus came through Concord by train in time to see Samuel and Sarah's last day together at the Manse, just two years after the Ripleys had retired from Waltham to take over the family home. All sat around the table in the old kitchen preparing Thanksgiving dinner, Hannah and Augustus helping Sarah pare apples as the Ripley children began gathering. But the Parsonses needed to move on, so Samuel drove them to the station the morning before the holiday. Later that day, he suddenly collapsed in his carriage and died. Elizabeth Hoar chronicled these family events to Waldo in England, and amidst all the losses she focused on Aunt Mary, now without either her last sibling or her chief supporters in Waterford. "The house there is empty," she wrote, "& she has lived alone there for two or three weeks."[90]

Amidst her meditations on idealist philosophy, Mary also wrote of feeling adrift in this new, unsupported solitude: "Can't succeed in geting a place to keep soul & body together for the winter. And here Hannah has gone—here am I almost naked & not a hand to serve me." Early in November she was in South Paris—having journeyed by open wagon, she told Elizabeth, as heroically as Victoria to foreign continents—eager to hear what sort of boarding arrangement could be made in Concord. Though the Gages continued to offer legal and financial advice, probably her friendship with Ann had at this inopportune moment reached a low ebb. By spring she was traveling again, feeling "sadly clut[t]ered" at yet another boardinghouse.[91]

Help came from another Waterford follower of Transcendentalism, who was attempting to establish a resource for city people in Maine's hills just as the country people departed. Calvin Farrar, the "Mountain Rustic" so worshipful of Waldo's essays, had recently opened a water cure house in town. Like Thomas Stone and very much following his footsteps, Farrar had rejected orthodox dogma for "things Platonica," talked earnestly with Mary, and borrowed her books. Soon after Mary quoted his words to Waldo, Farrar went to work in Boston and visited Concord; and two years later, converted at the Brattleboro Hydropathic Institute to the cause of natural health cure through water baths, he returned to Waterford to bring his visionary ideas to reality.[92]

Farrar was a reformer as much as the abolitionist and temperance agitators, whose causes he also supported. But he chose health as his particular field, writing to Waldo about his cure at Brattleboro as a fulfillment of the Emersonian vision. "Truth and Cold Water are mighty agents," he claimed, "& will yet revolutionize and redeem the world." Waldo did not agree; Mary assumed that he would visit Waterford only "without being ducked."[93]

For herself and her women friends, however, Farrar's reform appeared a great gift. Hydropathic medicine promised to heal Mary's erysipelas, as well as cure Elizabeth Hoar's migraines and Lidian's nervous distress. It also brought society to Waterford and (she did not hesitate to note) might even enhance real estate values. Steamers arrived from Lake Sebago through Long Lake to Harrison, just four miles south of the establishment in Waterford; having arrived, guests could eat Grahamite food (with meat optional), bowl for exercise, walk to the mineral springs, and submit their bodies to the German-based regimen of sweating, soaking, and wrapping in wet sheets. As Elizabeth Peabody wrote to the *Christian Register* in praise of the venture, the sheer beauty of Waterford's lakes and mountains was healing, reason to choose it over Brattleboro. Peabody had been visiting Ann Gage during the summer of 1847, while Mary entertained Elizabeth Hoar and Lidian.[94] Whether or not the two houses communicated fully with each other, both presumably tried the waters.

The next year Farrar's water cure house became Mary's latest home. Abby May Alcott encountered her there while serving for two months as matron. Actually Farrar, hoping to give his establishment a unique base in Transcendental philosophy, had invited Bronson Alcott as well to serve as preacher and teacher, but despite the offer of a rent-free cottage, Bronson felt "no clear call" to work beyond himself. So Abby arrived without him to meet the mammoth task of supervising the cooking and housekeeping for all of Farrar's guests. Among these she found "Miss Emerson," established not only in her own room but also in Farrar's study. "I wait upon her," Abby wrote in her first letter home to the family, "& give everything a slight touch of a la mode, to please the dear old body, who is dreadfully whimsical; we have rare bits of satire from her. We can bear her sharpness, she is so honest & sincere." A month later, writing to her brother Samuel May, Abby's patience had waned: "She is much too pungent a dose to take every day. . . . Her teeth & temper have been set on edge—at her time of life 75—*sweetness* is not easily recovered."[95]

Mary's estimation of Abby Alcott declined just as precipitously. "Is not her cheerfull independent spirit in so dependant a position noble?" she asked Lidian at first. "*Is it religious*? . . . What does Mr. A. for aid to her? Has he genius? How employed?" That was before she wearied of Abby's and Farrar's boastful talk against churches and Bibles. Farrar's institution was a failure, Mary declared splenetically: "The new forms of infidelity affect weak minds as intoxication does the [un]initiated." But then Abby returned to Concord, the institution did not close, and by the end of the summer Mary could enjoy a Sabbath there, doubly blessed by the preaching of Thomas Stone and "the absence of Mrs. A."[96]

Meanwhile, another imperfect dwelling place opened for Mary. Hannah and Augustus Parsons had continued their migration beyond Massachusetts to Williamsburg, the village in Brooklyn, New York, where her brother Samuel Moody Haskins had become an Episcopal rector. Samuel's self-financed education at New York's Union College, high church denomination, and urban location all suggest a strong rejection of the immediate family past; yet the Haskins family were following his lead and regathering on this unfamiliar terrain. Charlotte had moved to Williamsburg at least a year earlier to keep school and help in the rectory; then Hannah and Augustus joined them, Sarah moved nearby, and enfeebled father Robert came to end his days as well. In a few short years, Mary's nieces and nephew from Vale—both advocates and opposers of Millerite zeal—had joined forces in the New York metropolis toward the simple end of survival. By the end of 1849, as Hannah wrote to Elizabeth Hoar, she was mistress of the rectory, stepmother of widowed Samuel's son, caretaker of her father, and organizer of an otherwise unorganized circle to sew for the urban poor. She felt resigned but not happy; revisiting Maine earlier in 1849, she had stolen glances at the mountains and brook but did not trust her feelings enough to walk to them.[97]

In the same letter Hannah told her concern about Mary, whose loneliness she had recognized on the trip back to Waterford. Mary's months at the water cure house had ended, and once more she lived at Vale, now with tenants who seemed offended by her presence. "It seemed far worse than I expected, looking at it from this distance her solitude seemed grand & in harmony with her character but . . . she is not surrounded by beings cast in finest mould." Hannah hoped that Mary would succeed in selling Vale and come live in Williamsburg, where nearby nieces "would esteem it a privilige as well as pleasure to minister to her comfort." In this sentiment Elizabeth—and everyone in Concord—concurred. The only dissenter was Mary, who had visited New York in 1845 and felt that she could not bear city life.[98]

Mary had been trying to sell her farm since 1847, however, and now finally she succeeded. The purchasers were John Howe, his wife, and seven children, a family from the nearby town of Norway. The deal was closed by Gore Ripley in a parlor at the water cure house, with Mary tactfully removed from the room. Though she fully supported the sale, it signaled a great loss to her. As she reflected on the change, she also wrote a farewell to her longtime "Visitor . . . Imajanation." "True, thou touchest the core of my diseased age—," she wrote, "but I still spurn thy aid—w'h never could assume the forms of science or art in literature or progress in the supernal world."[99] She seemed to be disclaiming her major means of conscious life along with the setting that had so often supported it.

Rather than moving to dependence in Concord or Williamsburg, Mary planned to board with the Howes and remain in Waterford. This arrangement lasted scarcely a month, however, before Mary concluded that "mammon was their idol." The husband and older children were trying to run a hotel for workingmen instead of maintaining the farm; the wife accepted Mary's loan of her bed and then took it over; and the cooking was so unskillful that Mary had to fend for herself in the kitchen.[100]

While this arrangement lasted in some form into 1851, Mary seems to have spent as much time boarding elsewhere as she did living at Vale. In 1850 she was back at Calvin Farrar's, though by now disenchanted about the curative powers of water, and she found a last Waterford home for intervals with the Monroe family. She later referred to Betsey Monroe by the Bunyanesque name "Mrs. Whole Heart," but her hostess apparently remembered her with less pleasure. As a daughter of the family reminisced fifty years later, "O yes, I know that Aunt Mary Emerson was a noted woman with talent, all she did was to write read and study, and she thought every one else should. She found a great deal of fault with mother because she did her housework and sewing so well. . . . She always had one of mother's tables, the largest one, filled full of papers and books, never would allow mother to pick it up for she could not find anything if she did."[101]

Mary must have been trying to replicate the conditions of her own chamber at Vale, but in Monroe family memory the resulting invasion of domestic space was disastrous. Common decency also eluded her. "She never dressed like any-one, . . . used to wear her nightgown over into the village." This must have been the "shroud," though interpreted now as merely slovenly rather than funereal. But even worse were her bathing habits, as she would "commence with her feet and wash her face the last thing in the same water." Mary's bed and picture ended their days with the Monroes, and in 1902 the Monroes' daughter concluded, "I should be glad to get rid of the old bedstead."[102] She did not give equal attention to the picture; if it was the one of Dante's "wizard form," she did not know or care. Mary's positive values were beyond the ken of the Monroes and the Howes, and without that compatibility her way of life was insupportable.

Finally, in the summer of 1851, Mary left Waterford, a full half century after first coming. "Mrs. Howe & I lived & parted goodies," she wrote to Ann, glad to preserve decency after all. Deeper thoughts about the place went into her Almanack:

> This is the last sabbath I shall ever spend in a house no longer mine. . . . On the whole the MMS or almanacks have reminded me of hours surpassing all it ever fell to my meagre capacity to enjoy or think in any other place. And the forenoon was as full of gratitude as it could [be] with small space. The scene w'h seems a part of self, its sole companion so long, [I] shall know no more— . . . What a bird dancing on that gracefull limb. Had I any but this iron pen how could I give praise for every bird & tree w'h have met my responding senses in this tranquil & beautiful vale.[103]

For her Waterford had been a landscape for imagination and language-making, and if she described it only in fragments and with an iron pen, she had also given away the imagination and the language generously.

11

Skeleton Mind

What matters it by whom the good is done,—by yourself or another?

Marcus Aurelius Antoninus, quoted by Mary, quoted by Waldo in "Greatness" (*Works* 8: 312)

Concord 1851

While they were still partners in raising boys, Mary proposed to Ruth Emerson that they someday retire to Waterford and converse from their respective "paryletic beds." In 1851 her grim joke approached truth, but without the resource of Vale. Mary reached Concord in July just in time to hear that Ruth had fallen from bed and broken her hip; at eighty-two, Ruth would never recover, but in the course of the summer would lose memory as well as mobility. Mary found the news a sad omen—the dependent old age so long feared was upon her as well. "I cant but speake what crowds me—," she wrote to Waldo the day after her seventy-seventh birthday, "I don't like either to outlive my sole cotempor.[ary] in any way."[1]

Still she insisted on finding her own "Providential home," near kin but not with them, cheap enough to board on her annuity and profits from selling Vale. Two Haskins daughters had moved to Waldo's vicinity, bringing Mary's primary families within reach. Charlotte had come from Williamsburg to Concord that year as nurse to Lidian's chronic ailments, redoubling her efforts after Ruth's accident. Mary was pleased to find the country girl a "favorite" with the sophisticated Hoars and Ripleys. But her thoughts that July went also to eldest niece Rebecca Haskins Hamlin, now living with her daughter Mary at the Harvard Shaker settlement. By the end of the month, Mary was boarding nearby, visiting Shaker relatives in the very town where her brother had once been so plagued by New Lights.[2]

Mary left no account of Rebecca's religious community except a single enigmatic sentence. Explaining in September why she had moved on from Harvard to Stow and Bolton, she wrote to Concord friend Martha Bartlett, "In the first [town] the kind Angels of death hastened me." At this point the Shakers, probably including her Millerite niece, were immersed in spiritualistic communication, and Mary had long opposed such mixing of earth and heaven. Determined to undergo the discipline of waiting, she may have had to leave a place where angels urged haste. "What a boon to be clear in head," she wrote that October in nearby Lancaster, "& then the affections kindle & I would build a tabernacle forever & let ages renew their cycles till some revolution changes the style of the universe."[3]

For the next eight months, leaving these Worcester County towns, Mary once again boarded in Concord. Here head and heart were directly challenged by the political turmoil following the Fugitive Slave Bill of 1850. "Why have you not written to me anathemizing the odious *Bill* for returning the poor slave?" Mary had written to Lidian the previous October. "Are you all silent & acquiesent in Concord?!" Far from acquiescent, both Lidian and Waldo, as well as Mary Merrick Brooks and the Thoreaus, were taking their most direct action to date. In February, Mary Brooks sheltered the runaway Shadrach after abolitionists snatched him from Boston marshals; by October the Thoreaus joined in direct work for the Underground Railroad as well. Waldo's letter to Mary Brooks declaring his support for the cause appeared in the March *Liberator*; and after fugitive Thomas Sims was escorted to a southbound ship by three hundred policemen in April, Waldo delivered the most outraged and partisan address of his career, "The Fugitive Slave Law." Mary came back to a Massachusetts simmering with controversy, and she thrived on it. "I like a conscience war as did our kindred," Mary wrote to Waldo during the winter, and soon after added to her New York nephews, "While deeply interested in Hungary and all the oppressed by despotism, I am more affected by the unhappy state of our beloved Country on whom a corrupt govt encourages the blackest crime of slavery."[4]

In the "conscience war" raging around her, however, Mary offered no easy partisanship. At this late point in life she wrote two more pieces for the press, both conservative in temper. Reformer Daniel Foster came to Concord lecturing in November; and though Mary knew that he had been "noble on the warf when poor Simms was carried off," she could not approve his attack on the institution of the Sabbath. Her response appeared in the *Middlesex Freeman*, reminding the community that on the Sabbath the poor and the privileged could meet equally. Jesus had resanctified the day with his resurrection, she insisted; and even pre-Christian Socrates, Plato, Plotinus, and Marcus Antoninus had understood the need for "self-culture in ardent, self-denying, solitary, painful inspection." Writing about this article to her old friend Daniel Appleton White, she claimed proudly that the piece had met the approval of Barzillai Frost and Samuel Hoar, Concord's leaders of church and state, respectively.[5]

A month later, Mary made her most direct response to the new women's movement, which was prompting discussion on all sides. Waldo had declined to address the second Women's Rights Convention in Worcester on the ground that he was writing Margaret Fuller's *Memoir* instead. On December 2 he spoke on Fuller at the Concord Lyceum, and the last day of the year Elizabeth Oakes Smith gave a lecture on "Womanhood" to the same audience. Mary was present at both events, her eager applause for Smith winning the notice of others. As Mary explained, "I was amused & my young Townswoman said I was for 'the rights,' of which I desired to be rid of the notion." So she wrote out her views, submitting them again to the *Freeman* and then through White to the *Christian Register*. At last only a paragraph from her draft was printed in the *Register* as a letter (from "An Octogenarian"), but even in truncated and revised form it shows how Mary wanted to distinguish herself from the women's rights advocates:

> More than seventy years ago, I was present at a wedding, and I well remember the address of the minister of the time. . . . Among other things, he said, "The woman was not taken from the man's feet, to be trampled upon; she was not taken from his head, to lord it over him; but she was taken from his side, to be a faithful, bosom companion, truly a helpmeet, to be blessed and blessing, with mutual love and kindness." Such old-fashioned preaching might be useful at the present day, when there is much controversy about the rights and duties of both women and men. It might, figuratively, teach the true and proper rights and duties of women, and the sacred obligations of men, to treat them with care, respect and tenderness, so that the husband and the wife, in a proper, rational sense, may be considered as *one*, and the benevolent design of the creator be fulfilled who, in His love and wisdom, created man, male and female, for their good comfort and happiness.[6]

Recalling a moment from her Malden childhood and turning "old-fashioned preacher" herself, Mary enunciated the Puritan ideology of man and woman as equal partners, in marriage as in creation. What she suppressed, of course, was that she herself had avoided marriage, sometimes advised younger women against it, and hazarded the thought that "a majority wish to be unyoked." She offered here no right of revolution if the contract failed. The freedom she so fervently claimed for "all the oppressed by despotism" did not lead, as with Fuller, Smith, and Lidian Emerson, to an equal claim for women.

Though the conservatism of both essays was genuine, however, it hardly comprised this octogenarian's whole view in the winter of 1851–52. Writing to Lidian that December, Mary commented that she would go hear Mr. Frost preach on a weekday but reserved the Sabbath for solitude. "Pulpits & all the wonders dark & light of nature are but *means*—not the *end* of existing—that is for *God*!" She had defended the Sabbath but not its traditional observance at church. In the same letter she made room in heaven for the burning spirit of Margaret Fuller, a woman whose value could certainly not be equated with her wifehood. For all women Mary saw solutions primarily in their present and future relation to God. Telling Ann about the women's rights speaker, she commented in a single grammatically foreshortened sentence: "I am & think women have more than they improve."[7] What women could improve was the divine relationship leading to rights by apocalyptic justice.

This season of debate about women came just after Henry Thoreau pronounced Mary both a female genius and a misogynist. Passing a November evening at her boardinghouse, Thoreau found Mary "singular, among women at least, in being really and perseveringly interested to know what thinkers think." Her eminence was an ability to follow and draw out *him*:

> It is perhaps her greatest praise and peculiarity that she, more surely than any other woman, gives her companion occasion to utter his best thought. In spite of her own biases, she can entertain a large thought with hospitality, and is not prevented by any intellectuality in it, as women commonly are. In short, she is a genius, as woman seldom is, reminding you less often of her sex than any woman whom I know.[8]

Thoreau took away a great deal more than he gave in these sentences—granting Mary's ability to recognize a thinker rather than be one, meanwhile condemning the rest of womankind. But finally Thoreau enlisted Mary to support his own view: "Miss Emerson expressed to-night a singular want of respect for her own sex, saying that they were frivolous almost without exception, that woman was the weaker vessel, etc.: that into whatever family she might go, she depended more upon the 'clown' for society than upon the lady of the house. Men are more likely to have opinions of their own."[9]

Again this description revealed only part of Mary's mind. She had always wanted to hear "genius" rather than to prove her own, as Fuller had expected her to do a decade earlier; having reveled in Thoreau's intellectualism, she might well have dismissed her own sex. But Mary did not avoid the conversation of women, either through a lifetime or in 1851. "Tell of . . . my dear sisterhood the T[horeau]'s," Mary had requested of a Concord friend earlier that year, and once before had explicitly declined "the childish worldly desire to see & hear the men talk" for the company of Mary Brooks. Mary wanted both sisterhood and men's talk. Indeed, with Brooks and with Henry's sister Sophia Thoreau, both serving on the executive committee of the Middlesex Anti-Slavery Society, she was not declining all of her deepest thoughts when she chose to sit with the women.[10]

In the meantime, Mary's part in the men's talk of Concord was of real substance. She not only allowed Thoreau to voice ideas but also read or heard him read from his writing. In December she could allude to "Henry's 'scuttle of dirt' " in a letter to Waldo, assuming shared knowledge of the journal from which that phrase had come. In February she asked Thoreau why he had not visited her solitude. "Why not bring me the Plymouth lecture? . . . Age loves the old fashion of catechising the young." Thoreau's lecture in Plymouth on February 22 was a chapter from *Walden*, the fourth draft of which he had begun that January after two years' interruption.[11] These meager references point to the reason for Thoreau's high praise of Mary: the "best thought" she elicited from him foreshadowed *Walden*.

We can only speculate on the range of conversation that Mary Emerson and Henry Thoreau might have enjoyed at this crucial juncture. The year's antislavery politics were on both minds, but they also admired each other's solitude and devotion to natural history. Both had made experiments in independent living. They had Maine and its mountains in common: Thoreau had already published "Ktaadn and the Maine Woods." Unlike Mary's protégée Sarah Bradford Ripley, Thoreau the naturalist did not shrink from sublimity as he read the progress of seasons or the flight of birds. On December 31 he witnessed the thawing clay bank by the Walden railroad cut and recorded the journal passage that propelled him back into *Walden*. Mary would have urged him to a seasonal thaw ending in the "amaranthine" bloom of heaven, but she (old seeker of analogy and design) would also have kindled to his account of these "fancy sketches and designs of the artist" of the world. Together they also followed an interest in Asian quietism and Romantic philosophy. "Love to Henry T.," she wrote a year later, "do tell me of his phenom[en]al existence."[12] The joke assumes earlier conversation about his noumenal self as well.

With Waldo her conversation concerned "The Conduct of Life," which he had given as a partial lecture series in Pittsburgh that March, then presented fully in Boston the following December and January. Even before returning to Massachusetts, when she heard that one of the new lectures concerned "Wealth," Mary had raised her hackles: "You who have steadily stood for the *rights* of the slave are riveting his chains & pursuing the fugitive with increasing the rage the mania for wealth." Yet in December she expressed longing to see these new lectures, which Sarah Bradford Ripley had told her were in readiness. "I mean to remain (God permitting w'h is glorious as a decree[,] free will in all duress) in this place for one of the stirring motives w'h bro't me, till I *read some lectures*!"[13]

Her sentence of explanation had lost grammatical control, but at the same time coined a phrase for the theme that Waldo and Mary alike were pursuing: "free will in all duress." The first lecture of his December series was "Fate," newly composed that fall while Mary lived nearby in Concord. She wanted to read his manuscript on the subject, but he also wanted to read hers. "If RWE will send his Fate works it will *oblige*," she wrote. "Alas your covetousness in this way increased my zeal for the places I sought in other Towns. . . . I have written a sort of draft of my notions or dream of *fate*, But will not show it before yours—And you or the very nearness to you locally always stops pen like the beaver whose architecture always subsides before men."[14] Mary's metaphors defined their relationship as artists with brilliant irony. Waldo was a man (civilized, transcendent) and she a mere creature of nature (silent, instinctual). In proximity to him and his "covetousness," she the beaver-architect could do nothing. She did not wish to give over her work; as she had written before, it was her home.

The sort of thoughts that Waldo looked for are scattered throughout her Almanacks over the decades, as Mary struggled with "duress" and tried to convert it to a divine "decree" both protecting her and allowing for freedom. For her this was the oldest paradox, the center of Edwardsian faith, though she had also found it in Greek tragedies and Indian religions. Within the past five years she had read at least the reviews of scientific books about the constraints of nature on human freedom, some of the same works influencing Waldo at this point. Even though he had known Robert Chambers's *Vestiges of Creation* longer than Mary, he eventually transcribed her meditation on it into his notebook of Almanack excerpts.[15]

Possibly Mary's "dream of fate," however, was a comment written onto his lecture manuscript "Fate" that winter. Several years later, in his notebook "MME 3," Waldo quoted it on a page facing the 1851 letter about his "covetousness." In murky prose Mary offered the latest in her series of dream compositions, her own horoscopes of fate, to nephew Waldo. She imagined a creature oddly compounded of Chambers's prehistoric animals and Milton's rebel angels, going straight from hearing Waldo's lecture to meeting the ultimate powers of the universe, especially "the umbration which is called Fate." This figure

> was about to decorate [Fate's] wings, . . . when lo! one of the seven select spirits that attended the vision of the inspired Prophet, flew like lightning from the Source Eternal of light, & snatched the wreath from the vacillating image whose shadow represented Fate. But he left it not for scorn,—rather ornamented with flowers such as fascinate young fancies,—its feet & limbs, tho' shape had none, but on the semblance of wings, he confined immaterial but adamantine chains. He left thus a subject of poetry—of female dreams and old men's omens.[16]

Mary was imperfectly representing the victory of Christian faith (the prophet John with his seven guardian spirits) over the Necessity of material creation. This victory did not banish Necessity, but tamed it, confined its wings and adorned it to create "a subject of poetry" rather than a terror. This poetry was offered specifically for "female dreams" (her own imaginings) and "old men's omens" (her nephew's treatment of a subject fitting the aged).

The last phrase alone may have attracted Waldo enough to record this strange passage, but its large movement from acknowledgment to taming of fate complemented his own thinking in 1851. As he began compiling thoughts and quotations about fate in a specially designated notebook, he did not immediately turn to Mary, with whom he had shared a language of fatalism since youth. He had by now, however, already compiled a notebook of transcriptions from her letters, perhaps planning the family history remaining on his mind since 1841. Most of all, cross-references into his own journals show his intention to use these passages in current work as well.[17] His last attempt to consolidate Mary's unruly prose—both to acknowledge its power and to tap into it anew himself—was well under way when he first asked for her "dream of Fate."

The Angel of Death

Despite Mary's genuine involvement in the literature and politics of 1851, she appeared old and odd. The legend of her eccentricity flowered, and she called forth many descriptions. Susan Loring, a twelve-year-old friend of Waldo and Lidian's daughter Edith, later remembered seeing Mary, no taller than herself, standing near the pulpit of the old meetinghouse dressed in a "white woolen shroud" and a black "cottage bonnet," with a black veil drawn to one side and fastened in a large knob on top of her head. Other sightings of Mary in the 1850s confirm such an incongruous picture. Harriet Hanson Robinson remembered the hat as a "fearsome bonnet," Frank Sanborn as a "black band and a mob cap" covering her still-yellow hair. Waldo noted that Elizabeth Hoar had become the unwilling accomplice to such effects, searching "from Dan to Beersheba" to find a nonconforming bonnet for Mary.[18]

Though the bonnet was merely unfashionable, evidence that Mary belonged to another age, the shroud signaled her belonging to eternity. Waldo's testimony that Mary wore a shroud all her life has been taken too literally, but by these years her letters spoke casually of wearing a "woolen habit" or "white flannel." In 1847 Waldo had recorded, "M.M.E. went out to ride horseback in her shroud"; by the spring of 1852 she not only wore her shroud to church but also climbed out on the landlord's roof in an "ascension robe"; and in the course of the decade she took to the fancy of making her bed "in the form of a coffin."[19] Earlier self-control, always maintained with difficulty, had slipped significantly toward despair, delusion, or manic excitement.

In these elder years, however, Mary was simply enacting a drama of preparation for death that had once remained internal or verbal. She had genuinely practiced an *ars moriendi* through much of her life, evoking the shroud and coffin as figures of speech long before they became literal accoutrements of life. Informing Ann of "favored omens" in 1841, she added, "But when one lives with their shadow & shroud so long as I have such things do not excite." Such a way of living both derived from the New England past and belonged to her own generation. Historian David E. Stannard ends his study of Puritan death customs by disowning the case of Mary Moody Emerson, finding her death obsession "a product—a quite extreme product, to be sure—of the romanticization and sentimentalization of death that emerged full-blown in America with the dawning of the nineteenth century."[20] But this sentimentalization had grown from native soil, and Mary's own words trace the continuity.

Ancestral memory had been her earliest source of a mythology of death. From elder Emersons and Blisses she heard

> tales of the pale stranger who at the time her grandfather lay on his death bed tapped at the window & asked to come in. The dying man said, "Open the door"; but the timid family did not; & immediately he breathed his last, & they said one to another It was the angel of death. Another of her ancestors when near his end had lost the power of speech & his minister came to him & said, "If the Lord Christ is with you, hold up your hand"; and he stretched up both hands & died.[21]

Surrounded in childhood by sickness and death, she turned from fear to certainty that the afterlife would bring happiness; witnessing the death of both grandmothers, she found in their deaths a model for her life. Mary embraced the vision of salvation that the "watchers" could witness at the end of a saint's life but eventually rejected Calvinist anxiety about salvation. Recalling her early reading of the Puritans' central devotional text on the afterlife, Baxter's *Saints Rest*, she declared in 1838, "I am not able at this time to conceive of godlike benevolence occupied in its future heaven & believe in the orthodox damnation of others."[22] Originally the question of damnation had been quite real.

Preparing a coffin or shroud might have been an appropriate Puritan practice if the omens of death were really present, after a lifetime of recognizing life's fragility and repudiating the world's goods. In extreme cases these symbols of death might even have preoccupied the mind earlier in life: Mary's ancestor "S. E.," probably the uncle Samuel whose childish sayings had so impressed his father, is reputed to have kept a coffin in his house as a "constant memento that the world is subject to change."[23] For him this would have been an emblem of fear and prospective dissolution, not the hope and haven that Mary found in coffins. And he was the only Moody or Emerson or Bliss remembered for such practices. But Mary could hold up the tales of her ancestors' assurance when meeting death, cut away their sobering doubts and fears, and celebrate the grave as a utopian alternative to her limited life.

She discovered the Romantic glories of death from a new culture of mourning and consolation in early adulthood. When Phebe Bliss died and her young female protégées exchanged urn-and-willow memorials, when Ruth comforted herself after the death of her firstborn by imagining the child as a flower "transplanted to a richer garden," the question of salvation and damnation had already receded before a celebration of life in death for all the deceased. This new imagining of death primarily benefited mourners, assuring them that loved ones had moved beyond pain and sorrow. Mary's lifelong mourning followed such a pattern, but in addition she appropriated as her own best prospect the transformation facing the deceased. Young's *Night Thoughts* centrally provided this inspiration, with its wide popular appeal to the "urn-and willow" generation and offering of hope for transcendence above the sublunary world of death. Mary never tired of Young but wished in the late 1840s that she could blot out all memory of *Night Thoughts* and read the poem as if for the first time. "Nobody can read her manuscript, or recall the conversation of old-school people," Waldo wrote, "without seeing that Milton and Young had a religious authority in their mind, and nowise the slight, merely entertaining quality of modern bards."[24] He was referring to the "old school" of Mary's youth at the century's opening.

Mary's famed death obsession was in fact a life obsession, a hunger for fulfillment perceived as impossible on earth. "I never dreamt of showing skeletons & palls to your deep blue eyes," she told Elizabeth Hoar when charged with morbidity. "The most complete existence is when you long to enter a state for w'h you were designed—then the deepest solitude & stillest midnight give you the happiest & clearest reasonings & feelings." "Would I could die today," she habitually cried out, but then continued, "that this aching sense of immortality might be sattisfied or cease to ache."[25]

She claimed no prophetic vision of immortality but often turned her pen to "imajanings" about the journey ahead. Its scene was a Christian heaven, but with Christ only the abstract "mercy seat" to which Plato repaired after exploring the ultimate realities. On the other hand, when her brother William arrived, as Mary imagined to Waldo, he would form "some intimacies with a platonick Angel," his tutelary and guide. Greek and Christian would harmonize in this heaven, as the duty-charged keepers of orthodoxy would be released to "rejoice with the humbled & disciplined pretenders to natural religion who vainly imagined they saw God in everything." Even the natural religionists whom Christian Americans thought pagan would be embraced by this future life of spirit. Mary once accused Boston missionaries of underestimating the worshippers of Pele who danced in the flames of Hawaii's volcanoes—such "ideas of terror," after all, had arisen from a genuinely terrifying nature. "One is tempted to say, if the natives who live over that burning furnace are so mild—let them alone, [Christ]ian Nabobs. Their dust will soon mingle with the lava, & their souls to God."[26]

In imagining a heaven of continued growth for all souls, Mary joined some of her favorite theologians, from Channing to Isaac Taylor, who had led in a new vision of the afterlife as motion and progress. Mary called herself a "Restorationist": like one group of Universalists, she believed in salvation for all souls, but only after growth through the opportunities afforded by heaven. In her fullest account of eternal life, published by the *Christian Register* in 1846, a newcomer was chilled to see "a dark ugly worm" near the heart of a former acquaintance, otherwise honored with a splendid robe and a part in the mystic dance. This, explained the already initiated friend, was an emblem of his distortions of truth in an otherwise virtuous life; but such blemishes would in time be eradicated. Mary sometimes named explicitly the sorts of amendments her own relatives would need in this reinvented *purgatorio*, brother William regaining the "glowing generous traits of his character," Waldo called to a special realm for "intellects alone without affections."[27] About herself she ventured no particulars but always saw long remediation ahead.

She anticipated eternity, furthermore, as an opportunity to "enlighten and cement" friendship after all misunderstanding. "Ever your first of friends and hereafter where friends meet to part no more," she signed one letter to Ann. In this prospect of social pleasure she agreed with mainstream Victorian America: the cult of consolation imagined most of all the reunion between bereaved and deceased. But Mary held back explicitly from the materialism and domesticity that sentimentalists attributed to heaven, projecting no family circle around her, no direct communication of the dead and the living, and no heavenly marriage. She urged Waldo to "avoid the 'dull heaven' and silly loves" of Swedenborg: "When new worlds of new & undreamt of sciences open on regenerated minds—touch with new raptures every law of existence[—]where will be any material vestige?"[28] Friendship with chosen others was the ideal society for sharing knowledge and rapture, but the rest of earthly arrangements would fade.

Most of all the body would be left behind—its smallness, irritability, illness, and sex. Mary's heaven was androgynous and spiritual, the outcome of a Plotinian dualism valuing "minds purified from sense." There would be no resurrection of the body in the orthodox Christian sense, nor did she express interest in any modern heavenly scheme replicating the conditions of earth. Instead Mary foresaw that "naked spirit" would "as naturally mingle with the Infinite consciousness as the lungs inhale the vast air." The result of that divine air would be "individuation" before the source, at once self-loss and perpetual self-discovery.[29]

If there was great denial in this abstraction from earthly existence, there was also transcendence and empowerment. Mary did not consistently efface hierarchies in heaven, and she sometimes saw herself merely listening to the high dialogue. But more often she was "permitted to mingle" with the whole line of patriarchal philosophers with whom she had struggled on earth with inadequate intellectual training. Mary's paradise sounds too much like Harvard to have a wide appeal, but it was the school that she never entered. She conversed with the philosophers not only to make intellectual progress but also to explain her dissents:

> Some dear image has now & then passed over me of being in grace & beauty, taking sketches of the long & wearied barren & briery roads of life. Should Spinoza meet me, I'd tell him how often I tho't of him while in those arid scenes—that I had sought one idea—not his w'h requires no other; . . . not his original substance comprehending all matter & mind . . . ; not his God whose all-embracing being contains in his sole substance, tho't, extension, spirit & matter.[30]

In this scene, Mary conceived the conversation topic of heaven to be life on earth. Memory would be exercised not only (as in her published essay) to recall personal faults but also to make self-justifying autobiographical "sketches" through eternity, and the experience of having lived would lend any soul sufficient authority to take on the austere fathers of philosophy. The substance of Mary's dissent from Spinoza, furthermore, is central to her imagining of the scene: if "all matter and mind" were one substance, as the pantheist Spinoza had claimed, there would have been no disengagement possible for Mary, therefore no possibility of the free and empowered heaven allowing this conversation. She left matter behind in this scene but retained her own identity in all its briery particulars.

Mary's heaven encompassed all the goals of her pietistic and philosophical search. On the one hand, its goal was mystic gnosis. She recorded Plotinus's words in her Almanack as the clearest representation she had seen of this ecstasy: "a certain invisible thing, . . . a *knowledge* of the fountain & principle of things." To nephew William she told of "places where interpretation shall take [the] place of symbols and the realities of philosophy for many of it's dreams." On the other hand, she required the biblical language of ethical justice, that along with knowledge would come redress of grievances. "Ah how often in suffering & ignorance of nature's extended laws have I said, am I & the poor slave swept on through the sternest ordinations w'h *slay*? Yet I'll *trust*. Give me but the God I love and all will be restored."[31]

Mary's Almanack entries, her chief expression of these theological mysteries, thinned and finally fell silent in the course of the 1850s. Occasional passages still stormed the heights of fate and freedom, death and immortality, the daunting questions still centrally on her mind; and the best, like her imagined conversation with Spinoza, raced in Mary's nervous style directly from the particulars of her life to the most abstruse principles of the universe. Her 1855 summation of personal history started with "trouble" and proceeded to early knowledge of God's restoring benevolence, then recast this earthly suffering as "fate" and argued God's plan to be as necessary as the evil it overcame:

> Amid our darkness & fears & poor efforts after holiness, & the heavy problems w'h writers fail to solve, we find the faith in necessity while mingled with sorrow & penitence, adhering to & enlightening our confidence & joy in the perfect holiness & goodness of God. But we repose in the [Christ]ian plan as sufficient to quiet all fears and close our remarks with asking only a mind humble & lowly to insure our peace.[32]

Mary never truly closed her remarks. The last dated Almanack entry, written at eighty-four in 1858, is followed by another date for a thought that went unrecorded. But this entry shows unabated both her desire for transformation and her identification with the powerless:

> The 3rd year and the same infirm frail hungry skeleton mind. Yet I pray with earnestness that God would end this divine gift of loving Him this richest this only true gift of love to Him . . . if I am deluded & not regenerated to love Him with heart & mind that is the spark of reason. . . . I pass Angels & seraphs and seek a vivid aprehension of thee—without this what were existence to one so helpless, so frail so incapable of virtue & happiness. And the help thou laid on one mighty to save—to sympathize with human life what a world of treasure [it] is for man. Oh let the Chhs partake this day of his influence. Blessed Jesus make haste to come & reign in this confused guilty world. . . . God of mercy whose purposes are wise & perfect tho eclipsed look on thy coloured people. Behold their sufferings. Deliver me with thine own hand![33]

Wandering

Just as Mary's shroud began as a metaphor of desire and became increasingly literal, so her wish to "live a wandering life and die a beggar" threatened to come true. Previously she had always maintained a home from which to wander; now left without a home, her aim was to settle. By June 1852, she had left Concord again, returning to a series of Maine towns for the summer and dating one more Almanack entry from Mrs. Monroe's house in Waterford. She apparently found no satisfaction in this fleeting return and still left most of her earthly goods behind, trusted to the keeping of neighbors. The Howes and Monroes had her furniture, but her anxiety was for the "treasures" stored at Ann Gage's house: her trunk of papers, favorite blankets, portraits, medallion of Charles, and shelf of books.[34]

A new possibility for gathering family and goods arose, however, when Charlotte Haskins married a young Episcopal minister named Charles Cleveland in the fall of 1852. Charlotte had met him during her months in New York, but Cleveland now found a parish much more to Mary's liking, in Ashfield, Massachusetts, a country town west of the Connecticut River. By early spring, having settled with a kind landlady near the Clevelands, Mary expected to send for the "books & blankets & etcs" when warm weather returned. Charlotte and Charles gave her kind attention, Mary wrote, and "the certainty that they will take my last cares is a source of ease." But this precarious peace ended with the sudden death of the landlady. Mary tried without success to find another house in Ashfield, migrated twenty miles west to Charlemont, and went with Elizabeth Hoar to spend a month with William's family in Staten Island. By the fall of 1854 she was relying for advice on second cousins and finding the hope of permanence in a boardinghouse elusive.[35]

Still Mary refused two standing offers: having visited Hannah's Williamsburg, she declared its noise insupportable to nerves feeling "rather naked"; and she so wanted to avoid Concord that she would not send letters there until already established elsewhere. Since the age of twenty-three, she commented, there had always been "an intire satisfaction (to say the least) when a week was before me." So for three more years, until the end of 1857, Mary stayed in the Connecticut Valley, returning to Maine no more and making only a few trips to eastern Massachusetts. Twice, with the Clevelands' help, she found places to stay for substantial periods in Ashfield; in any case, Charlotte and her husband were the nearest resource as she moved restlessly from Deerfield to Cummington to South Adams. She seems never to have gotten her portraits, medallion, or blankets from Waterford, even after Ann Gage moved from town and had to parcel out the treasures among neighbors.[36]

She did manage to make western Massachusetts a significant location for thought and feeling. When William visited Mary in Ashfield, he complained that she was "bereft of books" in a place without any tie but Charlotte. He underestimated Mary's resourcefulness and failed to recognize the drawing power of a region that, over the years, she had visited many times for its associations with her cousin Joseph, uncle John, and revered Bliss grandparents. Here she could board cheaply (for the three dollars per week she was willing to pay) and find a quiet akin to Vale. She enjoyed some eminence, she admitted to Waldo, as "the Aunt of yourself." Her definition of a "desert" was Savoy, which sustained neither an antislavery society nor a church; elsewhere she found both, the churches varying from Cleveland's Episcopalianism to the traditional orthodoxy of the Connecticut Valley.[37] These she could both enjoy and resist more freely than Waldo's domain.

She also found books, including some of a different stamp from Concord's. Edwards was available in many of the households she visited; one of his volumes served "as a table to write on by the fire" as she quoted from it to Waldo on justification by faith. But Edwards's intellectual descendants also interested her. Slowly reading the "meta[physica]l chapter" of Horace Bushnell's *God in Christ*, she reflected that the Hartford theologian "rather disturbs my old *intuition* of the *Absolute necessary Being* whose idea is an *element of the soul*." Mary wanted to claim, unlike Bushnell, that the mind knew God in part even without Christ: "Dearer than all meta[physic]s it is natural theology, the ground & preparation for the glorious rich charter of revelation by Jesus Christ, the *arian* high scheme." Yet she also recognized that the old divisiveness between liberal and Calvinist was softening: "[Bushnell] is *meeting* it *seems* the unitarians who are also meeting bible orthodoxy." This was a shrewd judgment by a long mediator between the two traditions. Reading a copy of Channing's *Memoirs*, she commented that there "never was a more apostolic view of Christ" than in his charge to ministers working with the poor.[38]

Mary recorded these theological views in one of many letters to Ann, her chief correspondent in serious thought. Ann now lived with her children in Gorham, Maine, and both women needed the sympathy and intellectual stimulation they could give each other. With the Peabody quarrel largely over, their exchange of letters once more flowered, even as Mary's Almanack entries and letters to Waldo and Elizabeth dwindled. With Ann, Mary could go over the theological ground that most interested her, follow the career and publications of Thomas Stone, and recall Ann's accomplishments in writing verse. Repeatedly Mary found her a "poet bro't up in the pure mountain air."[39]

Warming to the new liberalism of the Calvinist Valley and exchanging letters with a woman poet, Mary crossed through Emily Dickinson's Amherst in the fall of 1854. There is no evidence that the two women met, but possibly they heard some of the same sermons in the Amherst meetinghouse. That November the twenty-four-year-old Dickinson heard a minister preach on the coming judgment and commented, "The subject of perdition seemed to please him, somehow." Dickinson was rapidly moving away from the orthodoxy she had encountered at Mount Holyoke from Joseph Emerson's onetime student Mary Lyons. Instead, she sent a poem to her friend Susan Gilbert about a bird flown to a "truer land," a "lingering emblem of the Heaven I once dreamed." From across the meetinghouse Dickinson's curiosity may have been aroused by the sight of a white-shrouded woman and the news that this strange visitor was Ralph Waldo Emerson's aunt. But two solitaries could not easily meet to share their dissent from the sermon and exaltation in the flight of birds. Mary commented to Ann from Amherst in a vein that would hardly have encouraged conversation; she found the landlady "smattered with books" and deplored the "partial dash of literature" among modern women.[40]

Back in Concord a year and a half later, Mary gave Thoreau the attention across generations that she had no way of giving Dickinson. Once more he recorded the event in his journal. "Talking with Miss Mary Emerson this evening, she said, 'It was not the fashion to be so original when I was young.' She is readier to take my view—look through my eyes for the time—than any young person that I know in the town." Mary endorsed his high valuing of simplicity, even at the expense of his own mother. Holding court at the "Deacon Brown" house the same year, she shut her eyes while conversing with her old friend Cynthia Thoreau in protest against the long yellow ribbons on her cap. "I did not wish to look upon those ribbons of yours," she explained, "so unsuitable at your time of life and to a person of your serious character."[41] Perhaps others in the room challenged her to defend the more "original" oddities of her own apparel.

Despite such high-handed judgments, Mary returned to Concord in 1856 because the resources for independence in western Massachusetts were exhausted. She had heard at a distance about the deaths of others—Ruth Emerson, Rebecca Hamlin, Robert Haskins, Ann Tracy—and though she expressed no regret at the news of Robert, she gave up a real portion of herself with each of the others. Wider and wider circles of friends were enlisted in the search for places to board. That year she inquired again for a place in Calvin Farrar's Waterford cure house and asked Lydia Maria Child for leads in Wayland, Massachusetts. Farrar asked guidance of Waldo before encouraging her; Child commented, "I marvel at your enterprise in going about as you do," but counseled her to stay in Concord. Back in the Valley for all of 1857, Mary was increasingly helpless, finally inviting Elizabeth Hoar to come rescue her, stranded in Savoy and "destituet." Somehow she had lost twenty-five dollars out of her trunk. This letter openly acknowledged weariness: "I have spent most of my life in running, from Concord when unimployed or boarding from Newbury the best of sisters from Elm Vale when [unconsidered?] from Malden *itself* when my dear Uncle became broken."[42]

Mary had almost stopped running. "Come this time, & try to stay," Waldo wrote, "and domesticate yourself for good with this dull household of ours. . . . Elizabeth, of course, is on the lookout for a boarding place, but do you come & stay here, with your own, & let the strangers alone." She came, accompanied by Charlotte and Charles Cleveland, but stayed with the Emersons only until Elizabeth had settled her again at the nearby Deacon Brown house.[43]

Some last moments of dialogue with the Emersons and their friends were still possible through the summer and fall of 1858. Twenty-one-year-old Ellen befriended her, coming to visit daily for stories about grandmother Bliss's character or brother William's rearing of sons. They also exchanged views on the current *Christian Register*. "An interesting note from Dr. Gannet about the telegraph," Mary wrote as she sent an issue up the road to Ellen. "But I want to ask him if it will tend to the benefit of 3 millions *of our fellow men*?" The "telegraph" in question was the newly arrived transatlantic cable—and the fellow men America's slaves, whom Mary saw as betrayed by England and the United States alike. It would be better, she wrote, to question Gannet "on the divine Telegraph who descended 18 centuries since to preach *truth Justice* and *charity*. . . . And tis hoped & believed by such as Taylor, he is coming!"[44]

By now Mary presented herself to Waldo as a seeker of favors rather than a critic. His speech on Kansas seemed the voice of truth, and after his trip to the Adirondacks she asked to see poems "fed from the magic of lakes & wizard mountains." Still she put into language her own interpretation of the mountains—"where no voice of science, oratory or civil law intrudes its proses, or human mists obscure the open vision." One message seemed so characteristic that Waldo later inserted its small manuscript intact into his notebook as "one of the last notes received from her when in Concord": "Dear W: If you are not engaged long in the use of your valuable opticks & it dont rain & &c cant you give me an hour? & oblige a pilgrim. At what hour & moment? MME."[45] She had not relinquished either her interest in Waldo's "opticks"—a favorite term for his eyes—or her own self-styled role of pilgrim.

A longer letter written on her eighty-fourth birthday, moreover, suggests that Mary and Waldo had again conversed about the material growing into his *Conduct of Life*. In cryptic, semireadable language she expressed the fear of illusion, seeing herself as one who did not know "whether her existence is noted by any communion with reality—or only a kind of painting an influx of images of delight to eye & ear." And she affirmed, despite the existence of "odious reptiles" in the world, "the sublime idea of *nessesity* w'h gives our existance to be connected by *it's nature* to the only Source of life and joy & virtue!"[46]

Only the immediacy of conversation now brought out Mary's fullest verbal power. Bronson Alcott, who had won enough of Mary's confidence to attract her to his public conversations, offered dinner and an afternoon's talk in early September. She appeared witty and incisive, regaling the company with stories about Waldo's childhood and forebears. The two Platonists finally pursued their common ground as well: Alcott declared her "metaphysical in her tendencies and a match for any theologian," favoring Dr. Price and his school.[47]

Their reconciliation came just in time for Mary to make her justly famous last stand in Concord a defense of Bronson Alcott. Waldo was out of town lecturing the evening of Alcott's conversation on "Private Life" in the Emersons' parlor; but those present, in addition to Mary, included Henry Thoreau and his sister Sophia, Ellery Channing, Franklin Sanborn, Lidian Emerson, Mary Brooks and her son George, Sarah Ripley's daughter Elizabeth, "others of our townfolk," and from out of town Sam Ward and Henry James Sr. Alcott's list of guests amounts to a group photograph of a Concord cultural event, rather easily blending genders and generations, writers and their neighbors. But Sanborn's report of the evening brings the photograph to life. James did not understand Alcottian conversation and took charge, so that neither Alcott nor Thoreau could "check the flow of the semi-Hibernian rhetoric." Even worse, James's point was to exonerate criminals from their crimes and charge society instead. Such moral relativism appealed to no Concordian. But Mary, amidst the men's consternation, grappled with the enemy directly. When James "spoke repeatedly and scornfully of the Moral Law," she burst forth to the whole group.

> Rising from her chair at the west side of the room, and turning her oddly-garnished head toward the south side, where the offender smilingly sat, she clasped her little wrinkled hands and raised them toward the black band over her left temple (a habit she had when deeply moved), and began her answer

> to these doctrines of Satan, as she thought them. She expressed her amazement that any man should denounce the Moral Law,—the only tie of society, except religion, to which, she saw, the speaker made no claim. She referred him to his Bible and to Dr. Adam Clarke (one of her great authorities from childhood) and she denounced him personally in the most racy terms. She did not cross the room and shake him, as some author, not an eye-witness, has fancied,—but she retained her position, sat down quietly when she had finished, and was complimented by the smiling James, who then perhaps for the first time had felt the force of her untaught rhetoric.[48]

Sanborn's account of Mary's gestures and style of speech is unparalleled among all of her chroniclers, but he did not fully grasp the issues at stake in this encounter. Mistaken in the name of Mary's philosopher (it was Dr. *Samuel* Clarke), he knew even less about the eighteenth-century school to which Clarke, along with Price, belonged. In fact, moral law was the center of Enlightenment ethics, allowing for an affirmation at once of the mind's intuition and of God's universal truths. The "fitness" between those two realities had been the formative discovery of Mary's youth and the basis of her first argument with Alcott in 1834. Now it was her bond to the Transcendentalists, despite their replacement of Clarke with Kant: Waldo had written in 1841 that he and Mary could meet across generations "where truly we are one in our perception of one Law in our adoration of the Moral Sentiment."[49] All of the inhabitants and visitors at the Emerson house except James wanted to affirm the individual's intuition of moral right as one with a "higher law."

Sanborn seriously underestimated Mary as well in calling the speech a piece of "untaught rhetoric," as though it were the natural effusion of her soul rather than the result of long and difficult self-education. James himself was guilty of much greater condescension in his description of Mary several years later. He had not really been upset at "that confabulation at Mr Emerson's," James recalled, when " 'shamefully treated' by the old Lady from Maine." "The old lady had the flavour to me of primitive woods wherein the wolf howls, and the owl has never been dislodged; and I enjoyed the novelty of her apparition in those days too much to mind the few scratches I got in making her better acquaintance."[50] Leaving Clarke and the issues of universal ethics wholly behind, he jovially dismissed his critic by lowering her to a backwoods animality beneath mental life.

In truth her response to James was a triumphant ending to Mary's years of intellectual exchange in Concord, at once a recollection of her reading as a young woman at the Manse and a major defense of her vexatious allies the Transcendentalists. Alcott recorded that she won "the admiration of the party and thanks of everyone present." Then, after a Thanksgiving including all the Emersons and Ripleys, she was gone, finally assenting to Hannah Parsons's request that she come live in Williamsburg. Lidian and Ellen put in several hours packing her worldly goods and papers at the Brown house (she had either gotten them from Maine or collected more); Waldo accompanied her by train through

Hartford, where they stayed in a hotel that was an "old lady's paradise"; William and his wife welcomed her for dinner at their Manhattan townhouse on December 15.[51] At the age of eighty-four, Mary became a New Yorker.

Williamsburg

Williamsburg was a dense and alien urban world, as Mary's previous refusal of it implied. Three years earlier, in 1855, the village had consolidated with three others into the new city of Brooklyn, holding a collective population bigger than Boston's. From the Parsonses' house on South Fourth Street extended blocks of recently built row houses, the work of developers making living space for the working and professional classes. Brooklyn called itself the "City of Churches," and developers encouraged that title by granting land to a church from which a neighborhood might grow. At St. Mark's Episcopal, two blocks from Hannah's house, her brother Samuel Moody Haskins had already overseen twenty years of such growth. In 1839 the young minister had taken over a fourteen-family parish surrounded by cornfields, but before the end of his ministry he would look back at an urban congregation whose members had of necessity, with the "fluctuations of trade, labor, and rent," changed "almost entirely every decade."[52]

The reason for that expansion and fluctuation was visible from Hannah's house in 1858. Three hundred yards away lay the East River, where workers unloaded raw Caribbean sugar to be refined—or distilled into alcohol—in mammoth factories for national markets. This "Eastern District" of Brooklyn, three miles from the established residences of Brooklyn Heights, had both space for industrial growth and proximity to Manhattan's business district. From South Seventh Street, three blocks from the Parsonses' house, ferries connected directly to Manhattan, and the city fathers boasted of their gaslit streets and new running water. At the enlarged *Brooklyn Daily Times* office by Williamsburg ferry, editor Walt Whitman that year was promoting the cause of city water and castigating local churches for barring antislavery speakers.[53] This was Whitman's world of the "en masse," chaotic in growth and defensive in politics. The steady flow of people into Brooklyn followed less design than the supply of water. Immigrants from Ireland, Germany, and eastern Europe crowded the streets; by 1860 the Jews who would eventually make Brooklyn their largest urban community worldwide had built a first synagogue in Williamsburg. Both free blacks and Jews were sometimes the target of street violence by native whites.[54]

Most of the American natives had also emigated from elsewhere, including the Haskins siblings and their Aunt Mary. Sarah had married and remained in New York, and Charlotte and Charles Cleveland would soon return from Ashfield, Massachusetts. The staunchest onetime Millerites also regathered: Rebecca Hamlin's daughter Mary had left the Harvard Shaker community to marry, finally joining her aunts and their families; while Phebe Chamberlain and her family came back east after an interval of uncertain length with Seventh-Day Adventists in the Midwest. All seem to have secured a niche in the middle class after rural lives of financial insecurity. Sarah and Charlotte taught school; Hannah's husband was variously listed by the city as a post office clerk and "collector"; Phebe's husband and son became superintendents in turn of a new rural-styled cemetery in eastern Brooklyn.[55]

The major success story and center to the family group was Samuel Moody Haskins, who, after Waldo's resignation from the pulpit, had become the sole ministerial grandson of Concord's William Emerson. His career flourished as an ecclesiastical institution-builder; amidst the chaotic growth of Williamsburg, he established not only a thriving parish but also an adjunct parochial school and separate church for blacks. The Episcopalianism that he advocated was high and ceremonial. As Millerite enthusiasm swept up his parents and siblings in Maine, Samuel was erecting the first Gothic stone church in the whole New York City area, prominently displaying the cross and insisting upon "the more devout worship and the more frequent communions" of the Oxford Movement. Seven members seceded in protest against "Romanizers." It was an ironic accomplishment by this kinsman of Mary's and Waldo's who went by the name "Moody": his ancestor Samuel Moody, who had cut down the papist cross at Louisburg a century earlier, would hardly have blessed his enterprise. Moody's Grandfather Haskins had been Episcopalian, but no discernible institutions or traditions conveyed that style of worship to Waterford, so his conservatism disrupted the heritage at least as much as did the free thought of Mary and Waldo. Mary regarded Moody as her antagonist in disputes over Vale and spoke acidly of his ambition, claiming that success had "plumed his natural vanity so he expects no doubt a bishopship."[56]

Despite all migrations and divergences of view, however, these descendants of the Concord Manse functioned as a traditional family group in each other's mutual support. Women were the mediators. Hannah, Sarah, and Charlotte, all at last Episcopalian New Yorkers like their brother, had also spent long periods of time as domestic providers in Concord; all prided themselves on kinship to Ralph Waldo Emerson and enjoyed intimate friendships with Ruth, Lidian, and Elizabeth. Mary Moody Emerson had lived in transit among these family branches, no doubt strengthening their bond, and at last relied on their working together to care for her dependent old age. By coming to Williamsburg, though leaving behind rural New England and exposing her nerves to city noise, she was still within a New England family community.[57]

As a result Mary could move back into the old domestic habits of Vale with Hannah. "Her zeal in indulging me in my disorderly habits of sitting late & eating alone never fails," Mary wrote to Lidian. The Concord women sent gifts of clothing, but Mary explained that she needed few: "I seldom walk further than the garden w'h [is] ample for City." Waldo exchanged regular messages with William about her welfare and finances; they took boarding costs from her funds but supplemented them from their own in acknowledgment of Hannah's difficult task, as well as relief at their own distance from it. Waldo was brutally frank in finding Mary untrustworthy with money and "only a wreck" mentally.[58] When she wrote letters, they went to women of the family circle.

For the first few years these letters, produced in her most lucid moments, were not a "wreck" but still addressed the events of private and public worlds. Writing to Ellen after the death of Bulkeley in 1859, Mary recalled both his childhood spirit and Aunt Phebe's care after his father's death. But Mary's mind was on present as well as past realities. She urged Ellen not to be "indifferent to public evil" and by the year's end rose to full ardor over John Brown and Harpers Ferry. "Have you seen the verses of our favored M. Childs on the Martyr Brown kissing a coulered infant when going to death[?]" she asked Lidian. "Do thank her for me in giving to print that most delightfull characteristic of the man."[59]

No longer walking from home, Mary still established contact with the city, as she had with New England towns, by finding its best ministers and doctors. She ventured no opinion of Moody but went to hear two other ministers whose creed she must have preferred. One of them, "rather advanced," visited her in illness, and she asked him to pray "*for the slaves* nothing personal as to disease." Meanwhile, she found a physician whose chief virtue was owning Bushnell's *Nature and the Supernatural.* She asked for no cure but sought at least enough health to discover Bushnell's views of "dreams, premonitions &c &c." A year later, at the beginning of 1861, Ellen traveled to New York with her father, visiting Williamsburg and enjoying hearing more such tales of doctors and ministers—as told by Mary and corrected by Hannah.[60]

Ellen's visit was perhaps the chief event of Mary's years at the Parsonses' house, or at least Ellen's telling of it illuminates the working of a female clan around Mary. Staying at her uncle William's townhouse in Manhattan, Ellen spent most days with Mary in Brooklyn. Finally, when Mary felt the accommodations good enough for one "more tender than the True Princess," she allowed Ellen to stay overnight. Mary prepared carefully for Ellen's arrival, dressing all in black and arranging herself with the utmost dignity. "When she called me," Ellen wrote, "I went right up, and heard Aunt constantly crying 'Here—here!' "[61]

Their chief business was to hand on family memory, building on the conversations and letters that these two Emerson historians had already shared. Showing Eilen pictures and daguerreotypes the first day, Mary moved by the fourth to "story after story, all new, about the Ancestors," stories which Ellen later recorded from memory. Soon Hannah joined in, bringing out the "old-fashioned worked case" of William Emerson's letters to Phebe; Hannah had gotten these from her Aunt Phebe and now gave them to Ellen, along with an animated memory of Grandmother Phebe tearfully telling her children about their father. At Charlotte's house, Ellen got yet another pile of family papers, including Daniel Bliss's conversion narrative from Springfield.[62] All these manuscripts had survived in the keeping of daughters and granddaughters, migrating with them to Maine and New York before now returning with Ellen to Concord. They were coming back to Waldo's branch of the family, but for Ellen's continued custodianship and delectation more than her father's.

Now, too, came the final ingathering of Mary's Almanacks from their various keepers. These were more particularly for Waldo after long years of his asking for them. Elizabeth Hoar had written to Mary that he recently "seized" a cache of journals entrusted to her. Ellen wrote, "I ventured to ask [Aunt Mary] whether she had any more, and being answered kindly in the affirmative, I thought it would do to go one step further and ask where they were. To my joy she said, 'Here, in that chest,' and 'mirabile dictu' she trotted up to it and said she wanted me to look over her papers, and I might have all I liked!!! So I went away full of glee at such an opportunity, at such a triumph." Charlotte provided yet another pile of Almanacks, and Ellen went home weighed down with manuscripts.[63]

Memorabilia of the Sibyl

Waldo delighted in Ellen's ancestral stories as father and daughter traveled back to Concord. "They were new to him," she wrote, "so that when we had reached home, and had adjourned to the parlor after tea, he called for one and another, that Mother and Edith might hear them." Waldo had occasionally recorded Mary's family memories himself; but at a different stage of her life and in the presence of a young woman, new currents of memory had come forth. In addition, his own recollection of Mary's words was imperfect. Several years later, characterizing memory itself, he asked whether it was not more a visitor than a resident in the mind. "Is it some old aunt who goes in and out of the house, and occasionally recites anecdotes of old times and persons which I recognize as having heard before, and she being gone again I search in vain for any trace of the anecdotes?"[64]

Waldo came alive to his aunt's stories and papers in 1861 because he had spent a great deal of the past two years trying to get the memory of her into usable written form. Neither the new Almanack manuscripts nor even those seized from Elizabeth were the first he had transcribed. Just a month after delivering Mary to Hannah Parsons's house two years before, he had begun a notebook, "MME 2," inscribing on the first page, "January of 1859 though it be, I must quote from these bewildering Almanacks of M.M.E. a few scraps." This three-hundred-page transcription followed nine or more years after "MME 1," a shorter notebook of excerpts from letters to himself and his brothers. But the new notebook of 1859 was shortly followed by two more, all of Almanack excerpts: "MME 3" directly after, "MME 4" begun by son Edward in 1860 and completed by Waldo, quite possibly from the new accessions brought home by Ellen, sometime before 1863.[65]

These four notebooks were much more than a preparatory exercise for his 1869 lecture on Mary. Over a thousand pages altogether, they were at last the enactment of Waldo's "covetousness," the tribute to and appropriation from Mary that he had anticipated most of his adult life. Even as Waldo at fifty-six distanced himself from Mary's live presence, he claimed her legacy. He did so for his own work, at a time when inspiration had lapsed: through 1859, as he noted, he wrote almost nothing in his own journal, feeling life "quite at an end" and his thoughts scattered. But that year he did versify passages of the Almanack directly from "MME 2" into the opening lines of his poem "The Nun's Aspiration." One response to inner poverty of thought, now in these later years as in his youthful crisis of vocation, was identification with Mary's empowering acquiescence:

> The yesterday doth never smile,
> Today goes drudging through the while,
> Yet, in the name of Godhead, I
> The Morrow front, & can defy:
> Though I am weak, yet God, when prayed,
> Cannot withhold his conquering aid.
> Ah me! It was my childhood's thought,
> If he should make my web a blot
> On life's fair picture of delight,
> My heart's content would find it right.[66]

Waldo also sought to draw upon Mary's resources directly by traveling to Waterford with Ellen that June. They went briefly in search of a family house to rent for six weeks later in the summer, but even the short trip, as Ellen described it, put Waldo in touch with the power of the Maine landscape. As they approached, at the first sight of "water still as glass with the sky and clouds reflected in it and satisfying mountains beyond," he said, "Let's never go home any more." Then they found Mutiny Brook in South Waterford, with water that Lidian had described to Ellen as "white," flowing over granite with no mud or sand. "It was the most beautiful water that ever was seen and Father kept wanting to camp down and to sell Bush and buy this brook, and desired that 20 years might be added to his life that he might spend them here." This was his "Mount Athos," as he had written in 1841, a place to "bewail . . . innocency & to recover it, & with it the power to commune again with these sharers of a more sacred idea." Mary's writing and her wilderness, inextricably bound together, were for him the sacred idea itself, needed now more than ever. But he wanted to recover them without her involvement or knowledge, warning William not to speak of the planned trip to Mary or "those who will tell her."[67] He wanted her idea without the wreck of anxiety that she had become.

The plan to vacation in South Waterford did not work out because Waldo had to nurse a sprained foot at home through the remainder of the year. But his larger project of transcribing Mary's words went on, and the notebooks contributed in particular to the composition of his last major work, *The Conduct of Life*, the same series that he and Mary had discussed at its inception early in the decade. In 1858, before taking Mary to New York or beginning to transcribe the Almanack, Waldo had written to William, "I am trying to publish my 'Conduct of Life,' this autumn or winter; but it is not yet ready." Two full years would pass before its publication; Waldo asked William to convey a copy to Mary in the last month of 1860, adding, "I am ashamed to think what a relief is the delivery from this so little book."[68]

Both the labor of composition and the interweaving of Mary into it are evident in Waldo's elaborate cross-referencing. He indexed all of the "MME" notebooks topically, as he had always done in his journals so as to have access for use. "MME 2" included over a hundred headings, alphabetically arranged from "Atheism" to "Young Dr," including such foundational shared themes as "Genius," "Imagination," "Immortality," and "Solitude." Under "Necessity" he specified two Almanack passages, one from 1842 coming especially close to his essay "Fate" as it would emerge in *The Conduct of Life*:

> Nature should have taken the terrifying with the grand & beautiful forms, her frightful caverns, her cannibals & hideous reptiles. Necessity! We wonder & adore in silence. . . . Connected with the absolute existence, how grand & mystical! Personify it—weaving a web whose warp extends through unnumbered ages, whose woof human agency throws the shuttle & fills, and have we not some instinct of human condition, of that revealed economy which unites but never designates the line between human & divine agency?[69]

This meditation, turning the destructive forces of the created world into a object of worship, was joined in "MME 3" by both Mary's 1851 note about Waldo's "covetousness" for ideas of fate and the passage written on his blank lecture page. The index now referred to these under the topic "Fate." Recording her 1830 meditation that translated Daniel Bliss's enthusiasm to spiritual quietude, Waldo commented, "This is good Buddhism." Both notebooks, what is more, began with the same unattributed epigraph, which Mary had quoted in her 1837 Almanack while mourning for Charles, then again in her letter to Waldo after his son's death. It was Mary's capsule summation of faith in divine necessity amidst the disaster of loss:

> A richer boon his purpose knows,
> A holier gift his love bestows,
> In the ark of his decree
> Abides the Paradise for me.[70]

Meanwhile, before and during this period of recording Mary's words, Waldo also inscribed her influence in two topical notebooks laying out material for his book, "EO Fate" and "XO Reality & Illusion." The first recorded the Chambers-influenced language of snakes and coils that Mary and Waldo shared, as well as reflections on fate from Greek tragedy, Buddhist religion, and classic Stoicism. He quoted the line from Marcus Antoninus that she had taught to his childhood: "If the picture is good, who cares who made it?" And, in the midst of such reflections, Waldo inserted a letter of unspecified date to Mary, telling of his struggles to "state the doctrine of Fate for the printer" by finding the "Unity which inspires all, but disdains words, & passes understanding." In "XO Reality & Illusion," a topic that Waldo had not previously linked explicitly to Mary, he now quoted her by name on the abstraction of spirit from body achieved by Plato and Plotinus; repeated the line from Antoninus with its second half, "What matters it by whom the good is done,—by yourself or another?"; and cross-referenced to notebook "MME 2" Mary's posing of the problem of "the illusion of knowing." He also quoted her pithy solution to the problem that would underlie his essay "Illusions" in *The Conduct of Life*: "Illusion, yet M.M.E. says, 'Heaven, which never beguiles.' " Amidst the disorientation and failure of contact with the world that threatened him as an idealist, he followed her in trusting that the illusions of the universe were God's, therefore at last no illusions at all. Beyond all failure lay victory through association with divine law. "Face the worst enemy," he echoed her early words to him, "knowing you are guarded by the omnipotence of Destiny." "One can't but laugh," he quoted directly from "MME 2," "to read of painters, or any high artist of the quill spoken of as defeated. Pho! immortal, & defeated here!"[71]

Still another layer in this process of reflection and composition came in Waldo's primary journal, resumed in 1859 after months of silence. Here, too, was cross-reference to "MME 2" but also new thinking about her, beginning notes for his lecture "Amita." On the same pages he interspersed passages for *The Conduct of Life*, in several instances reflections on Mary in relation to the themes of that slowly unfolding book. Waldo considered her writing as a case of creative "fanaticism," the strong and fervid performance that alone would do the world's work, but he also weighed the negative aspect of her "force," its failure to be persuaded by any external fact or opinion. At the same time he considered afresh the power of the world's "oracles," including Mary along with Alcott and Charles King Newcomb, as those whose intellects equaled the ancients in pronouncing an "omen or fatum" with their apparently chance words.[72]

Waldo's word "Fate," title of his 1851 lecture and 1860 chapter, really derived from this oracular "fatum" or pronouncement, whether a prediction of future events or a decisive insight into character. In a quotation reiterated from his much earlier journal, he newly associated Mary with that power. " 'I had received,' said Mary, 'the fatal gift of penetration' "; owners of such a gift, Waldo went on to say, were Cassandras, Delphic oracles, realists able to see through the masquerades and pretenders around them.[73] He had first recorded Mary's pronouncement the year of his resignation from the ministry, and its force had lasted through a writing career, from *Nature* to "Fate."

Mary remained present in the published version of *The Conduct of Life*. In the chapters most indebted to her, the opening "Fate" and closing "Illusions," she was less an active source than an internalized voice in the affirmations toward which each of these dark essays turns. Surprisingly, the more explicit echoes of her voice and sources occurred in chapters less deeply characteristic of Mary's thinking. Her particular quotations from Roman Stoic Marcus Antoninus supported Waldo's argument at junctures where other elements ran counter to her views: summing up a new "Worship" purged of Christian dogma, he used a line that she had quoted to him in 1850: "It is pleasant to die, if there be gods; and sad to live, if there be none." He even conflated her language with the Stoic's:

urging the advice to "open your Marcus Antoninus" in "Culture," he echoed Mary's words to her nephews, that a great man "scorned to shine," as well as her self-description of herself as a vessel "dismantled and unrigged" before the ocean's wind and waves. He also used her words directly, though naming his source only by the human type that she represented. Turning in "Behavior" from surface manners to the powers beneath, he affirmed as he had in his journal the vision of the "sad realist": " 'I had received,' said a sibyl, 'I had received at birth the fatal gift of penetration';—and these Cassandras are always born."[74]

The moment in *The Conduct of Life* most directly paying homage to Mary, however, occurred in the chapter "Culture" after several pages of his acknowledging the power of cities and travel, means of self-development about which she had little enthusiasm. Then Waldo recognized the limit of these and defended retirement as a means of culture, the means known to Wordsworth and Pythagoras. "The wise instructor," Waldo asserted, "will press this point of securing to the young soul in the disposition of time and the arrangements of living, periods and habits of solitude." In the concrete terms of personal history, Mary had been that instructor and he that young soul; and now he appropriated her own words of 1824, transcribed in "MME 1," about "Solitude" as "the stern friend [of genius], the cold, obscure shelter where moult the wings which will bear it farther than suns and stars." She had originally associated such solitude with Milton and Wordsworth; now he omitted the literary allusion from her thought, but included both poets in his accompanying list of heroic solitaries: "Plato, Plotinus, Archimedes, Hermes, Newton, Milton, Wordsworth."[75] Both her words and her endorsement of others' words had fed Waldo's creativity through four decades.

There is poignancy in Waldo's return to explicit reliance on Mary, as he both drew from old texts and tried to wring more from her failing resources in the 1850s. Implicitly revealing the power of her wisdom, he continued to appropriate as well. But Mary had instructed him in these ways herself, defending egotism as the foundation of knowledge, urging genius to "sculpture the event & never name it." Waldo transcribed these very words from "MME 1" to his journal even in the midst of "sculpturing" her presence into *The Conduct of Life*. Mary felt keenly her lack of public influence but also asked with Marcus Antoninus, "What matters it by whom the good is done, by yourself or another?" She used this line so often in the family that Ellen called it "Aunt Mary's view" without knowing its ultimate origin. Waldo quoted and requoted the words, and they finally emerged in his late essay "Greatness"—attributed to Antoninus but not to Mary.[76]

Mary read at least a few pages of *The Conduct of Life* the spring after Ellen's visit but remained silent about its affinities to her own thinking. She only commented of Waldo's latest work, "It semed there was no other world than this [one]." Meanwhile, she continued to speak her own language of fate and freedom, asking Sarah Bradford Ripley whether all of their differences would not be erased in the light of heaven: "That great and boundless truth of the *nessissty* of the Infinite Existence will be unfolded forever, in all its relations to all beings

& histories?"[77] Less able than ever to spell the word, she continued to discover a principle of positive recovery in universal necessity.

In the few months after Ellen's visit in 1861, Mary found another burst of energy for letter writing. The doctors had pleased her by detecting "sure signs of death by a conjestion of blood on the brain," and she had practical business to transact, whether arranging yet another will with William or getting Lidian's word that she could be buried at Sleepy Hollow in Concord. The "times" and the history unfolding through it meanwhile lifted her from self-preoccupation. If the Emersons had no place for her in their cemetery plot, she assured Lidian in March, she would gladly go to the Old Hill burying ground, adding without transition or explanation, "I believe there is no dust of a friend to slavery on that Hill." She no doubt recalled Uncle Daniel Bliss's epitaph to John Jack, which had made antislavery territory of the Hill since Revolutionary days. Less than a month later, civil war began with the firing on Fort Sumter, and Mary wrote again with thanks to Providence if the slaves would be freed. Waldo answered these letters rather than Lidian, in an invitation to Sleepy Hollow and a rousing celebration of holy war:

> My dear Aunt,
>
> Lidian is very uneasy that she has written no reply to one or two poetic messages, which you have directly or indirectly sent her, and I who never write a letter except of necessity, must eagerly volunteer. If Death the Deliverer should not come to you with actual translation, as, the holy legends say, has sometimes befallen saints, but some bodily remainder should be found to bury,—be assured, that our little nook in Sleepy Hollow, in your native town, will be ready to receive & guard such deposit with all tender & honoring rites, & with what sympathy of stars & elements may be divined;—certainly, with a heed & pride of memory, in all the living who shall lay the dust there, & revisit it. It does not now look probable that the foot of any slave-owner or slave-catcher will pollute the ground. Let us hope that the very South wind will come to us cleaner & purer of that taint, until it is sweet as the air of Maine Mountains. What a relief in the political convulsions, you must feel with us. The shame of living seems taken away, & to mature & old age the love of life will return, as we did not anticipate.
>
> Ever your affectionate & deeply obliged nephew.[78]

As an expression of sympathy both personal and political, this was a powerful last word in the fifty-year correspondence of aunt and nephew.

Mary's own last surviving letters, however, set to rest the vexations of friendship with Sarah Bradford Ripley, now widowed mistress of the Old Manse: "My long loved Friend & Sister, tho' I never used the last dear word. Avoided it for I had no such claims tho' my brother was estimable to me. I was old and you young I was unlearned & you learned, known, & prized by friends and strangers. How vanished all these distinctions when your life was endangered!" Mary still wrote in hope that Sarah would receive faith in immortality. But when Sarah wrote back that she could not believe in an afterlife, Mary responded regardlessly by hoping, "May the God of love & wisdom draw you so near to communion with Him that you may long remain to bless your gifts of children." In both letters she took pleasure in thinking of Sarah and Elizabeth as friends in Concord, hoping that they would "sometimes mention one who loves you both."[79] Over the decades, her most fervent language of love had been for these two women.

In March or April, Mary received one more visit from Elizabeth but was not well enough to enjoy it. Now in her eighty-seventh year, her mental life closed down at last. William conveyed to Waldo the report from Hannah "that all the morning she is out of her head, but recovers herself about noon." She still did not stop writing letters during this decline; Waldo reported that she had been inquiring of a Concord doctor for help arranging board for the winter, and William wrote back that she was writing to her old friend George Ripley asking to come see him. "Aunt Mary's case is a very painful one," William added. "Her mind is much shattered, & it is a very hard duty for Mrs Parsons to take care of her, & yet nobody else can do it." By the next spring she was no longer making plans. "My capacity is gone," she told William in a characteristic moment of truth-telling. Those were her last recorded words, supplemented for family memory by the ambrotype that Hannah had a photographer take.[80]

Then another year passed, while Hannah continued the hard women's work of care for the dying. On New Year's Day of 1863, Lincoln's Emancipation Proclamation took effect, and possibly Mary could greet the freedom of slaves that she had so long anticipated. Only at the end of April did she lapse into a "state between dream and waking," as William reported after being called to her bedside by cousin Sarah. Recognizing an omen about which there would be no mistake, Waldo reflected in his journal on his aunt's death obsession as both the awesome defiance of a Muslim warrior and a cause for grim humor by her relatives:

> Saladin caused his shroud to be made & carried it to battle as his standard. Aunt Mary has done the like all her life, making up her shroud, & then thinking it a pity to let it lie, wears it as night-gown or day-gown until it is worn out; (for death, when asked, will not come;) then she has another made up, &, I believe, has worn out a great many. And now that her release seems to be really at hand, the event of her death has really something so comic in the eyes of everybody that her friends will fear they shall laugh at the funeral.[81]

He entered her actual death in his journal with entire gravity, however, as a moment of import for his own life record. "On Friday morning 1 May, at 3 o'clock, died Mary Moody Emerson, at Williamsburg, New York, aged 88 years, 8 months." Her moment of death allowed none of the triumphal gestures that she had admired in others; as Waldo put it, Hannah simply attended Mary and "closed her eyes." But he also felt that his aunt's own "Muse" of "Destitution and Death" had already embodied a preternatural consciousness. "We have said that her epitaph ought to be, 'Here lies the Angel of Death,' " he had recorded two years earlier. In Mary's own stories, as well as in centuries of Christian iconography, the angel of death was the "pale stranger" who appeared to lead away the soul, a figure of dread for the unprepared but for the saint a friend to be welcomed. Waldo's epitaph collapsed the dying person and the otherworldly messenger into one figure, as though Mary could defy death by summoning herself to it.[82]

Mary's anticipation of death had included explicit orders for her funeral: "No service of any kind should take place at Concord," she had repeatedly told Hannah and William. Samuel Haskins's friend "Mr. Clapp" (the clergyman who apparently received her last approval) read the funeral service in Williamsburg, and Hannah accompanied the body by train back to Concord for burial only. So Mary, having satisfied the need for ritual elsewhere, had a most unchurchly funeral in her native town. The casket was taken directly to a receiving tomb at Sleepy Hollow, never entering any Concord church or house. But the closest circle gathered around Hannah on Sunday evening at the Emerson house to hear her stories of Mary. Waldo, Sarah Bradford Ripley and her daughters, Elizabeth Hoar, and Elizabeth Peabody, as the last reported to Ann Sargent Gage, "discoursed of her individualities & her generalities—with many a laugh."[83]

Perhaps, then, they did not need to laugh the next day when, accompanied by Lidian and daughters, they met again at Concord's new garden cemetery, dedicated by Waldo only eight years earlier as "the palm of Nature's hand." The Emersons found the Ripleys and Elizabeth Hoar sitting in the summer-house and joined them in processing up the hill. Only Ruth had so far been buried in the new Emerson plot; Mary's grave was made in a line with hers. The day was misty, at the green height of New England's spring. Elizabeth Hoar commented that "it was just the day Aunt Mary would have chosen for her funeral, soft and pleasant, but with no sun." Waldo wanted Mary's own words heard, in conversation rather than ceremony. "I brought all our friends home with me, telling them I would produce all the memorabilia of the Sibyl, if they desired; They came, but did not ask for memories, and I reserved them."[84]

Others had different ways of memorializing. Ellen and Hannah soon proposed visiting the old family graves in Malden, leading Waldo on a rare pilgrimage to the family past. Elizabeth Hoar and Elizabeth Peabody both wrote down their memories—Hoar some years later, but Peabody almost immediately. Frank Sanborn (an outsider to all these proceedings) had written an obituary for the *Commonwealth* declaring Mary capable of "saying more disagreeable things in a half-hour than any person living"; Peabody thought the piece an injustice and assumed the responsibility of righting it. Waldo thanked her for this generosity, especially since she, like almost all of Mary's companions, "had something to forgive."[85]

The sibyl's papers continued to preoccupy him, however, especially the possibility of publishing them. "I see plainly," Waldo wrote to Elizabeth Peabody, "that I shall not probably rest until I have copied out some admirable letters & journals of the best days of this devoutest solitariest Muse, & tried whether these writings which I have found so poetic & so potent, will not speak to others as to me." The principle of his editing, he wrote confidently to William, would be to sift out and discard the "huge alloy of theology & metaphysics," leaving only the pure genius. But three years later, he had still found no easy way to do so.

"Read MME's mss. yesterday—many pages," he recorded. "They keep for me the old attraction; though, when I sometimes have tried passages on a stranger, I find something of fairy gold;—they need too much commentary, & are not incisive as on me."[86] At last his best audience and means of presentation, with minimal alloy of metaphysics, was the New England Women's Club and lecture "Amita" in 1869.

But even that reading neither contained nor exhausted Waldo's preoccupation with Mary. His quotation and borrowing from her continued as a significant element of his writing for another decade after her death, essentially the rest of his creative life. Taking up the topic "Quotation and Originality" in his journal, he thought of Mary's delight in the superiority of another mind as her "best gift from God." His principles of quoting were in significant measure justification for his own appropriations from her: "The quoter's selection honors & celebrates the author. . . . And originality, what is that? It is being; being somebody, being yourself, & reporting accurately what you see & are. If another's words describe your fact, use them as freely as you use the language & the alphabet, whose use does not impair your originality."[87]

In his journal he also made judgments of her stature far more audacious and explicit than anything claimed in "Amita." In 1867 she headed the list of his ten most influential "friends"; a year later he included her among "great men of the American past" along with John Adams, Channing, Washington, and the authors of the *Federalist Papers*. He focused more accurately on the gender and kind of her accomplishment, however, when he proposed in 1870, "I believe our soil yields as good women, too, as England or France, though we have not a book from them to compare with [de Staël's] 'Allemagne.' Yet M.M.E.'s journals shine with genius, & Margaret Fuller's Conversation did."[88] In his mind the woman of Romantic genius—the oracle—was her type, along with only one other American and the French prototype.

That year Waldo's thoughts returned with particularly luminous power to Mary. In August he found reading Mary to be "ever monitory & healthful as of old"; as he celebrated Mary's birthday with a dinner and reading for family and friends, Ellen handed him her photograph (probably the 1862 ambrotype) and he jumped with pleasure. Within a week he was headed for Waterford again, this time with son Edward for company. "I had been dreaming lately by day as well as by night," he explained, "of this old mountain town of my relatives,—near & in sight of Mount Washington, which promised me some informations that I wanted, & also, I hoped, some inspirations & some healthier tone." Probably it was the trip of 1832 with Mary and Charles that he was recapitulating; again he stayed at Crawford House and ascended Mount Washington, though this time in a carriage. But Edward's accounts make the visit to Vale the point of the pilgrimage. His father led the way to her farm, where they gazed at "the gleam of the lake and the fine mountain terrace and elms in the lowland," then "looked with eyes of old times at Aunt Mary's Window."[89] The window in question was almost certainly that opening from her room of books to the water and sky beyond.

Waldo associated inspiration with Mary's rural retirement from his first to last days as a journal-keeper. In 1872, dismayed and disoriented by the fire at his house, now seriously losing his memory and word capacity, he returned yet again to Vale with Ellen. But the complexity of Mary's presence in Waldo's mind is suggested by a journal passage just prior to the fire, when on his sixty-ninth birthday he rediscovered her in an urban landscape. Having just read her manuscripts to Frederic Henry Hedge and Cyrus Bartol, he turned the corner into Boston's Summer Street and found no trace of his boyhood home, then remembered the city as Aunt Mary had known it. "Aunt Mary . . . had such a keen perception of character, & taste for aristocracy," he wrote, "and I heard in my youth & manhood every name she knew." Now a hundred years after her birth, all the families familiar to her "as retail-merchants, milliners, tailors, distillers, as well as the ministers, lawyers, & doctors," were still notable. "She was a realist, & knew a great man or a 'whale-hearted woman,'—as she called one of her pets,—from a successful money maker."[90] As her life had extended from Maine wilderness to Boston urbanity, so did the "realism" of her eye extend from nature's phenomena to human character.

After the fire, Waldo's inscription of Mary, as well as his own writing, soon came to an end. Her Almanack manuscripts had been burned around the edges, probably the most seriously damaged of all the family papers; but a heroic salvage operation by neighbors and the sorting done by May and Louisa Alcott guaranteed that they, as well as the famous man's manuscripts and the ancestral papers, remained largely intact.[91] Possibly the 1862 photograph of Mary was lost; no portrait other than her silhouette has ever come to light.

The two Emerson children still living in Concord worked in the different ways defined by gender as their family's conservators. Both attended the deathbeds of their parents, Edward as a trained physician and Ellen as a traditional female caregiver, a "very Martha" in her own estimation. Edward edited his father's journals, wrote a book about his father's Concord, and painted an imaginary scene of his great-grandfather's farewell at the Manse. Ellen wrote a memoir of her mother and assisted James Elliot Cabot in preparing her father's manuscripts; some years after Lidian's death, when Samuel Moody Haskins had died in Williamsburg, she brought the widowed Hannah, Sarah, and Charlotte to end their days in her house. She contributed substantially to the official Emerson family genealogy, published in 1900, but included no entry for herself whatever.[92] Ellen shared little of either Mary's enthusiasm or her valuing of "dear self."

Edward and Ellen together chose designs for the family graves at Sleepy Hollow in 1892. Ellen wanted to decorate Mary's with "the regulation death's head & cross bones & hour-glass, and Memento Mori," but Edward prevailed with the Egyptian symbol of a winged sun. There was a logic in either choice, Puritan death or eastern resurrection. They did not engrave the stone with their father's fancied epitaph, "Here lies the Angel of Death," instead using words that Elizabeth Hoar had first spoken and Waldo adopted in his lecture on Mary: "She gave high counsels. It was the privilege of certain boys to have this immeasurably high standard indicated to their childhood; a blessing which nothing else in education could supply."[93]

Theirs was a significant memorial, though not Mary's choice. Characteristically, she had tried to anticipate the design of her own grave. Long before the family assured her of welcome at Sleepy Hollow, she had first asked to be buried at Elm Vale Cemetery without any stone or epitaph. She would have had her death encompassed simply by the mountains and sky of Maine, where "Natures wildest pebbles & sleet & wa[r]ing winds are welcome."[94]

Notes

Abbreviations and Short Titles Used in Notes

Names

AB, ASG	Ann [Brewer] Sargent Gage 1794–1876
CCE	Charles Chauncy Emerson 1808–36
DB_1	Daniel Bliss 1714–64
DB_2	Daniel Bliss 1739–1805
EBE	Edward Bliss Emerson 1805–34
EH	Elizabeth Hoar 1814–78
EPP	Elizabeth Palmer Peabody 1804–94
ER	Ezra Ripley 1751–1841
ETE_1	Ellen Tucker Emerson 1811?–31
ETE_2	Ellen Tucker Emerson 1839–1909
EWE	Edward Waldo Emerson 1844–1930
HH, HHP	Hannah Haskins Parsons 1814–[?]
HSM	Hannah Sewall Moody [?]–1728
JCE	John Clarke Emerson 1799–1807
JE_1	Joseph Emerson 1700–1767
JE_2	Joseph Emerson 1724–75
JM	Joseph Moody 1700–1753
LJE	Lidian Jackson Emerson 1802–92
LR	Lincoln Ripley 1761–1858
MME	Mary Moody Emerson 1774–1863
MME(g)	Mary Moody Emerson 1702–79
MWS, MWW	Mary Wilder Van Schalkwyck White 1780–1811
PB, PBE_1, $PBER_1$	Phebe Bliss Emerson Ripley 1741–1825

PBE_2, $PBER_2$	Phebe Bliss Emerson Ripley 1772–1839
PWB	Phebe Walker Bliss 1713–97
RBE	Robert Bulkeley Emerson 1807–59
REH	Rebecca Emerson Haskins 1776–1845
RH, RHE	Ruth Haskins Emerson 1767–1853
RWE	Ralph Waldo Emerson 1803–82
SAB, SABR	Sarah Alden Bradford Ripley 1793–1867
SamR	Samuel Ripley 1783–1847
SarR	Sarah Ripley 1781–1826
SM	Samuel Moody 1676–1747
WE_1	William Emerson 1743–76
WE_2	William Emerson 1769–1811
WE_3	William Emerson 1801–68

Sources and Locations: Abbreviations and Short Titles

AAS	American Antiquarian Society
A-H	Andover-Harvard Theological Library
Almanack	Mary Moody Emerson, "Almanack" (ms. Houghton)
CFPL	Concord Free Public Library
Collected Works	*The Collected Works of Ralph Waldo Emerson.* Vols. 1–5. Ed. Alfred E. Ferguson et al. Cambridge: Harvard University Press, 1971– .
Diaries and Letters of WE	*Diaries and Letters of William Emerson, 1743–1776.* Ed. Amelia Forbes Emerson. Boston: Privately printed, 1972.
"Father"	Ellen Tucker Emerson. "What I Remember About Father" (ms. Houghton)
Handkerchief Moody	*Handkerchief Moody: The Diary and the Man.* Trans. and ed. Philip McIntire Woodwell. Portland, Maine: Colonial Offset Printing, 1981.
Harvard Graduates	*Sibley's Harvard Graduates.* Vols. 1–3. Ed. John Langdon Sibley. Cambridge: Charles William Sever, 1873–78. Vols. 4–17. Ed. Clifford K. Shipton. Boston: Massachusetts Historical Society, 1937–75.
History of Concord	Lemuel Shattuck. *A History of the Town of Concord.* Boston: Russell, Odiorne, and Company, 1835.
History of Malden	Deloraine P. Corey. *The History of Malden, Massachusetts, 1633–1785.* Malden: Privately published, 1899.
History of Waterford	Henry P. Warren et al. *The History of Waterford, Oxford County, Maine.* Portland: Hoyt, Fogg and Donham, 1879.
Houghton	Houghton Library, Harvard University.
Ipswich Emersons	Benjamin Kendall Emerson. *The Ipswich Emersons.* Boston: D. Clapp, 1900.
JCB 1, JCB 2	William $Emerson_2$. "Journal and Commonplace Book," vols. 1 and 2 (mss. Houghton)
JMN	Ralph Waldo Emerson. *The Journals and Miscellaneous Notebooks of Ralph Waldo Emerson.* 16 vols. Ed. William H. Gilman et al. Cambridge: Harvard University Press, 1960–82.
"Letters of EH"	"Elizabeth of Concord: Selected Letters of Elizabeth Sherman Hoar to the Emersons, Family, and the Emerson Cir-

cle." 3 parts. Ed. Elizabeth Maxfield-Miller. *Studies in the American Renaissance 1984–86.* Charlottesville: University of Virginia Press, 1984–86.

Letters of ETE Ellen Tucker Emerson. *The Letters of Ellen Tucker Emerson.* 2 vols. Ed. Edith E. W. Gregg. Kent, Ohio: Kent State University Press, 1982.

Letters of LJE Lidian Jackson Emerson. *The Selected Letters of Lidian Jackson Emerson.* Ed. Delores Bird Carpenter. Columbia: University of Missouri Press, 1987.

Letters of MME Mary Moody Emerson. *The Selected Letters of Mary Moody Emerson.* Ed. Nancy Craig Simmons. Athens: University of Georgia Press, 1993.

Letters of RWE Ralph Waldo Emerson. *The Letters of Ralph Waldo Emerson.* Vols. 1–6. Ed. Ralph L. Rusk. New York: Columbia University Press, 1939. Vols. 7–10. Ed. Eleanor M. Tilton. New York: Columbia University Press, 1990–95.

Life of LJE Ellen Tucker Emerson. *The Life of Lidian Jackson Emerson.* Ed. Delores Bird Carpenter. Boston: Twayne, 1980.

Mary Wilder White Elizabeth Amelia Dwight. *Memorials of Mary Wilder White: A Century Ago in New England.* Boston: Everett, 1903.

Maternal Ancestors David Greene Haskins. *Ralph Waldo Emerson: His Maternal Ancestors.* Boston: Cupples, Upham, and Co., 1887.

MHS Massachusetts Historical Society

"MME 1-MME 4" Ralph Waldo Emerson. Notebooks "MME 1–4" (ms. Houghton)

MPL Malden Public Library

Moody Family Charles C. P. Moody. *Biographical Sketches of the Moody Family.* Boston: Samuel G. Drake, 1847.

NYPL New York Public Library

RMHS *Register of the Malden Historical Society*

Rusk Ralph L. Rusk, *The Life of Ralph Waldo Emerson* (New York: Scribner's, 1949).

SAR *Studies in the American Renaissance: An Annual.* Ed. Joel Myerson. Boston: Twayne, 1977–82; Charlottesville: University of Virginia Press, 1983–96.

Schlesinger Schlesinger Library, Radcliffe College

Sermons of RWE *The Complete Sermons of Ralph Waldo Emerson.* 4 vols. Ed. Albert J. von Frank et al. Columbia: University of Missouri Press, 1989–92.

"Stories of Our Ancestors" Ellen Tucker Emerson, "What I Can Remember of Stories of Our Ancestors Told Me by Aunt Mary Moody Emerson" (ms. Houghton)

"Tribute to MME" Elizabeth Palmer Peabody. "A Tribute to Mary Moody Emerson." In *Notes on the History of Waterford, Maine.* Ed. Thomas Hovey Gage. Worcester, Mass.: Privately printed, 1913. Reprinted from the *Boston Evening Transcript*, May 14, 1863.

Works Ralph Waldo Emerson. *The Complete Works of Ralph Waldo Emerson.* 11 vols. Centenary Edition. Ed. Edward Waldo Emerson. Boston: Houghton Mifflin, 1903–4.

Manuscript Sources

Most of the letter, journal, and sermon manuscripts on which my study depends are in the Emerson Family Papers at Houghton Library, Harvard University. The Emerson Family Papers fall into three major classifications; detailed finding lists are available at the library. Footnotes to manuscript sources refer to this collection unless otherwise specified. Individual Houghton call numbers are included only where clarification becomes necessary. Key documents and groups of texts are as follows.

b Ms Am 1280.226, Emerson Family Papers I (abbreviated in notes as 226):
- letters of CCE (items 25–151, each representing one letter)
- letters of EBE (170–259)
- letters of JE_1 (404–6)
- letters of LJE (534–85)
- letters of MME (620–1298)
- letters of RHE (2670–2762)
- letters of WE_1 (2812–32)
- letters of WE_2 (2833–2930)
- letters of WE_3 (2931–3049)
- individual letters by DB_2 (3137), PWB (3139), HSM and JM (3854), JM (3855)
- letters of SM (3856–60)
- letters of HHP (3912–14)
- letters of ER (2955–70)
- letters of $PBER_2$ (3977–91)
- letters of SABR (3997–98)

b Ms Am 1280.220, supplement to Emerson Family Papers I (abbreviated in notes as 220):
- letters of MME (items 70–78, each representing one correspondent)
- letter of RBE (25)
- diary, letters, papers of CCE (49–52, 118–126)
- letters of EH (92–95)
- MME, 1835 Will (135)
- Samuel May, "Reminiscences of CCE" (159)

b Ms Am 1280.235, Emerson Family Papers II (abbreviated in notes as 235):
- DB_1, Almanack with Diary, Relation, shorthand sermons (items 227–32, each representing one text)
- Memorial to PWB (233; cf. 463)
- CCE, "Journal of a Tour to Maine," lectures (267–314)
- EBE, notes and journal in Puerto Rico (349)
- ETE_2, "What I Can Remember of Stories of Our Ancestors by Aunt Mary Moody Emerson" (357)
- JE_1, diary, "Remarkables of Samuel Emerson" (363–64)
- MME, Almanack (385): fragile manuscript, must be viewed on microfilm. My notes specify folder number as well as explicit or reconstructed date. See also George Tolman's more legible if incomplete transcription (579) and, for passages that do not survive elsewhere, the "MME" notebooks (below).
- legal documents of MME (395)
- diaries and account books of RHE (396–405)

WE_1, diaries, real estate inventory, oration, sermons (409–35)
WE_2, "Receipts" (with RHE), commonplace books, papers (439–46)
ER, journal, sermons (513–18)
$PBER_1$, account of births, estate account (519–20)

Some important family manuscripts are separately classified at Houghton and other Harvard libraries. RWE's text for his lecture "Mary Moody Emerson" or "Amita" is Houghton b Ms Am 1280.211 [14], his four "MME" notebooks b Ms Am 1280H 146–49, and ETE_2's "What I Can Remember about Father" bMs Am 1280.227. Some of ER's sermons are listed under his own name at Houghton (bMS Am 1835 [11]), and an equally copious holding is available at Andover-Harvard Theological Library, Harvard Divinity School. The Phi Beta Kappa address of WE_2 and commencement oration of CCE are in Harvard University Archives.

Two collections at the Massachusetts Historical Society Library significantly supplement these manuscript resources. The library's recently catalogued Emerson Family Papers, formerly known to Emerson scholars as the "Wortis Collection," includes correspondence by and to WE_3; most is with his brothers, including RWE, and one letter is by MME. (My notes specify each WE_3 letter as belonging either to Massachusetts Historical or to Houghton.) The Farnham Family Papers provide a valuable glimpse of the family extending around MME's eldest sister, Hannah Bliss Emerson Farnham, and her husband, William Farnham; of particular value is the correspondence of both Farnhams with the Emersons and Ripleys, as well as the diary and letters of their son John Hay Farnham. In addition, the MHS owns the manuscript (shorthand) sermons of JE_1 and manuscript sermons and diaries of JE_2.

Constructing MME's place in a wider circle of relatives and friends depended upon many additional collections. The Egbert Starr Library, Middlebury College, and Ralph Waldo Emerson Collection, University of Virginia, each holds a small number of her letters. Letters of Samuel and Sarah Ripley, MME's half siblings, are available only through transcriptions made more than forty years ago by Joan W. Goodwin of now-lost Ames Family Papers from Duxbury, Massachusetts. All but a few of the letters of Sarah Alden Bradford Ripley are at the Schlesinger Library, Radcliffe College. The Foote Family Papers at Andover-Harvard Theological Library, Harvard Divinity School, include correspondence between MME and Mary Wilder Van Schalkwyck White. At the American Antiquarian Society Library, the Gage Family Additional Papers, 1785–1863, include the letters of Ann Sargent Gage to MME and Elizabeth Palmer Peabody to the Gages, as well as papers by and about ASG and her family; the Elizabeth Palmer Peabody Papers include a few letters from EPP to MME. Additional perspectives on MME can be gained from papers of the Peabody family in the Berg Collection, New York Public Library, and the Alcott Family Papers at Houghton.

Manuscript, archival, and material evidence is also available in towns where the Emerson family lived. Beatrice Parker of Pepperell, Massachusetts, owns the adolescent diary of her collateral ancestor JE_2; David Emerson, formerly of Concord, a manuscript by Josephine Hosmer about DB_2; Miriam Sylvester Monroe of Waterford, a family letter describing MME. In this field, written words are not all on paper. At the Old Manse the books, furniture, and even walls contain family inscriptions; but houses, churches, and cemeteries have provided "texts" in Malden, York, and Waterford, as well as Concord. Invaluable information has come from town and church records in these towns, in addition to the Registry of Deeds and Probate Records of Middlesex and Suffolk Counties, Massachusetts, and Oxford County, Maine.

Those seeking access to MME's letters beyond Nancy Craig Simmons's *Selected Letters of Mary Moody Emerson* should consult her detailed and complete guide, "A Calendar of the Letters of Mary Moody Emerson," *SAR* 1993, 1–41.

Introduction

1. Lecture ms. "Mary Moody Emerson," p. 9; it was published after RWE's death under this title rather than "Amita," first in the *Atlantic Monthly* 52 (1883), 733–45, and then in *Lectures and Biographical Sketches* (*Works* 10: 397–433). On RWE's late lecture career, see William Charvat, *Emerson's American Lecture Engagements: A Chronological List* (New York: NYPL, 1961), pp. 45ff.; he delivered many other lectures after this date, but few from newly prepared material.

2. *Works* 10: 399.

3. *Works* 10: 399–400, 407, 432. The lecture manuscript, though organized differently from the printed essay, contains all of these emphases in common with it.

4. *Works* 10: 408, 432, 402–3.

5. *Works* 10: 403–4, 411, 426, 400, 411.

6. Minutes, Members 1868–69 (New England Women's Club Records, Schlesinger). On the founding and significance of this organization, see Karen J. Blair, *The Clubwoman as Feminist* (New York: Holmes and Meier, 1979), ch. 4.

7. Harriet Hanson Robinson, diary, March 1, 2, 1869 (Papers of Harriet Hanson Robinson and Jane Hanson Robinson, Schlesinger).

8. Peabody quoted by Robinson, diary, March 9, 1869.

9. "Tribute to MME," pp. 54–57.

10. Waldo's speech reported by *Boston Daily Advertiser*, May 27, 1869; cf. "Woman" in *Works* 11: 337–56 for the full text of a similar, earlier message.

11. Virginia Woolf, "Emerson's Journals," in *Books and Portraits*, ed. Mary Lyon (London: Hogarth, 1977), p. 67; Tillie Olsen, *Silences* (New York: Delacorte Press, 1978), p. 17. Olsen lectured on Mary Moody Emerson in the period of her work on *Silences*, but these papers remain unpublished.

12. Ralph Waldo Emerson's first biographers all valued genealogy as a source of character and so included Mary in their portraits of him. James Elliott Cabot, in *A Memoir of Ralph Waldo Emerson*, vol. 1 (Boston: Houghton Mifflin, 1887), used Waldo's manuscript journals in characterizing her, as well as mining the lecture "Amita." For other early statements of their relationship, cf. Moncure Daniel Conway, *Emerson at Home and Abroad* (Boston: James Osgood, 1882), and Oliver Wendell Holmes, *Ralph Waldo Emerson* (Boston: Houghton Mifflin, 1885). The last such genealogical reflection was Oscar Firkins's *Ralph Waldo Emerson* (Boston: Houghton Mifflin, 1915). Meanwhile Franklin Sanborn printed his own reminiscences of MME in several memoirs, the chief of which is "A Concord Note-Book," no. 6, "The Women of Concord," *The Critic* 48 (Feb. 1906), 154–60; and George Tolman, having transcribed most of MME's manuscripts at the request of Emerson descendants, presented a fresh interpretation to the Concord Antiquarian Society in 1902, eventually published as *Mary Moody Emerson* (privately printed, 1929). But no new context for valuing her character or work replaced that of the genealogists; and Mary became merely the colorful character of Van Wyck Brooks's "Cassandra of New England," a portrait fabricated from previous printed sources with increasing condescension (*Scribner's Magazine* 81 [Feb. 1927], pp. 125–29, rpt. in *The Life of Emerson* [New York: E. P. Dutton, 1932], ch. 1).

In the professional scholarship of the 1940s that has given shape to Emerson studies ever since, Mary was included as a pious influence on Waldo's childhood and—though herself considered staunchly "Calvinist"—the recipient of some of his crucially defining letters of intellectual rebellion. Ralph Rusk was the first biographer since Cabot to read family correspondence in manuscript, for his *Life of Ralph Waldo Emerson* (New York: Scribner's, 1949), but he limited the implication of Mary's own letters to documentary purposes within traditional boundaries of interpretation. F. O. Matthiessen and Perry Miller—the two most powerful shapers of the field—had even less room for an eccentric aunt; the former omitted her structurally from literary study by focusing on the language of primary texts rather than "surfaces of the milieu," and the latter traced a history of "ideas" as conveyed by the male-dominated culture of pulpit and university. See Matthiessen, *American Renaissance* (London: Oxford University Press, 1941), p. xvii, and Miller, "From Edwards to Emerson," in *Errand into the Wilderness* (Cambridge: Harvard University Press, 1956), p. 184.

Since the late 1970s, both the availability of Waldo's full journals and the deconstructionists' skepticism of apparently authoritative texts have allowed for rethinking of his relationship to Mary. See, for instance, Joel Porte, *Representative Man: Ralph Waldo Emerson in His Time* (New York: Oxford University Press, 1979), pp. 128–29; Eric Cheyfitz, *The Trans-Parent: Sexual Politics in the Language of Emerson* (Baltimore: Johns Hopkins University Press, 1981), p. 47; David R. Williams, "The Wilderness Rapture of Mary Moody Emerson: One Calvinist Link to Transcendentalism," SAR, 1986, pp. 1–16; Alan D. Hodder, *Emerson's Rhetoric of Revelation: Nature, the Reader, and the Apocalypse Within* (University Park: Pennsylvania State University Press, 1989), pp. 45–47, 52–53, and passim; Lawrence Rosenwald, *Emerson and the Art of the Diary* (New York: Oxford University Press, 1988), pp. 34–36 and passim; and Robert D. Richardson Jr., *Emerson: The Mind on Fire* (Berkeley: University of California Press, 1995), especially ch. 5. Williams and Richardson have both made use of the transcriptions of Mary in "MME 1–4" but not of her own manuscript record.

13. Studies directly interpreting Mary's manuscripts include Evelyn Barish, "Emerson and 'The Magician': An Early Prose Fantasy," *American Transcendental Quarterly* 31 (Summer 1976), 13–18, and *Emerson: The Roots of Prophecy* (Princeton: Princeton University Press, 1989), chs. 2 and 7; Phyllis Cole, "The Advantage of Loneliness: Mary Moody Emerson's Almanacks, 1802–55," in *Emerson: Prospect and Retrospect*, Harvard English Studies 10, ed. Joel Porte (Cambridge: Harvard University Press, 1982), pp. 1–32, and "From the Edwardses to the Emersons," *CEA Critic* 49 (Winter 1986–Summer 1987), 70–78; and Nancy Craig Simmons, ed., *Selected Letters of Mary Moody Emerson* (Athens: University of Georgia Press, 1993).

14. Almanack, March 17, 1829 (f. 10).

15. Rosenwald (*Emerson and the Art of the Diary*, p. 35) characterizes Mary as a spiritual diarist and, as such, the "*genius loci* of the Emersonian journal." He is unaware, however, of the extent to which the Almanack is also a commonplace book of reading in theology and literature, holding out that synthesis of spiritual and intellectual reflection as the achievement of Waldo's own journal. On the diary as an autobiographical form, see Felicity A. Nussbaum, "Toward Conceptualizing Diary," in *Studies in Autobiography*, ed. James Olney (New York: Oxford University Press, 1988), pp. 128–40. Cinthia Gannett, in *Gender and the Journal* (Albany: State University of New York Press, 1992), both lists and synthesizes recent scholarship on women's diaries.

16. *Letters of MME*, pp. 287, 432; Almanack, April 28, 1829 (f. 10). On the final gathering of Mary's papers, cf. *Letters of ETE* 1: 223–24.

17. Almanack, [Aug.?] 27, [1801?] (f. 16); Oct. 17 and [29?], 1817 (f. 7). Sandra M. Gilbert and Susan Gubar define the "anxiety of authorship" as a dilemma shared by women of the early nineteenth century in *The Madwoman in the Attic: The Woman Writer and the Nineteenth-*

century Literary Imagination (New Haven: Yale University Press, 1979), ch. 2. Cf. the gestures of modesty required for public success by the twelve literary women studied by Mary Kelley in *Private Woman, Public Stage: Literary Domesticity in Nineteenth-century America* (New York: Oxford University Press, 1984).

18. *Monthly Anthology* 1 (Aug. 1804), 453; MME-EH, ca. 1840 (226.1210).

19. Cf. Alan Richardson, "Romanticism and the Colonization of the Feminine," in *Romanticism and Feminism*, ed. Anne K. Mellor (Bloomington: Indiana University Press, 1988), pp. 13–25.

20. "Tnamurya" entries are in *JMN* 1–2, the years 1821–24; cf. *Letters of RWE* 7: 125, 183. The four "MME" notebooks are available only in manuscript.

21. *JMN* 5: 385.

22. *Works* 6: 155–56; *Letters of MME*, 182; *JMN* 2: 380–81; "MME 1," 139.

23. "Stories of Our Ancestors"; cf. *Letters of ETE* 1: 221–26.

24. *Stowe: Three Novels*, ed. Kathryn Kish Sklar (New York: Viking, 1982), p. 1074; Almanack, a. 1837 (f. 21).

25. *JMN* 5: 323–34; 7: 446.

26. *Works* 1: 3; *JMN* 2: 316; *JMN* 3: 349–58.

27. "Stories of Our Ancestors"; *Letters of ETE* 1: 224.

28. Charvat, *Emerson's American Lecture Engagements*, p. 47; *Letters of ETE* 1: 654; F. O. Matthiessen, *The James Family* (New York: Knopf, 1947), p. 444. Cf. also Annie Fields, *Authors and Friends* (Boston: Houghton Mifflin, 1896), pp. 86, 199.

Chapter One

1. *Ipswich Emersons*, passim; Waldo Lincoln, *Genealogy of the Waldo Family* (Worcester, Mass.: Charles Hamilton, 1902), 1: 12, 41; John Homer Bliss, *Genealogy of the Bliss Family in America* (Boston: Privately printed, 1881), pp. 53, 81.

2. Four generations of male Emersons, however, tried consciously to establish their descent from Peter Bulkeley. During his days of ministerial apprenticeship, Ralph Waldo Emerson wrote three separate letters to a genealogist to ascertain "what I have to do with the Bulkeleys whose blood, I have always understood is within me for good or evil." Beginning his "Historical Discourse in Concord" seven years later, he casually and affirmatively referred to himself as the "blood" of Bulkeley. A generation earlier, his father, William, had written Uncle John Emerson asking about the early family, and John sent back *his* father's (Joseph's) "pedigree of the Bulkeleys" back "beyond ye times of good old Luther & Calvin." This preoccupation across generations (and recurrent use of the name Bulkeley) makes Mary's silence about Bulkeley ancestry appear all the more deliberate. Her brother William mentioned Peter Bulkeley among the moderators of a synod opposed to Anne Hutchinson in his history of First Church Boston, but otherwise none of these later family recollections includes any sense of his conservative theological or social positions. See *Letters of RWE* 1: 242–43, 247–48, 250–51; "The Historical Discourse in Concord" (*Works* 11: 30); John Emerson-WE_2, April 3, 1807, in *Ipswich Emersons*, pp. 432–34; WE_2, *Historical Sketch of First Church in Boston* (Boston: Munroe and Francis, 1812), p. 44.

3. Cf. 2 Kings 2: 9–15. *Letters of MME*, pp. 292–93; MME-CCE, Jan. 22, 1833.

4. For a summary of major events and themes in the Great Awakening, see Sydney E. Ahlstrom, *A Religious History of the American People* (New York: Doubleday, 1975), 1: ch. 18.

5. WE_2, *Historical Sketch*, pp. 41, 186, 190; WE_2-MME, Nov. 11, 1807. Cf. Joseph Conforti, "Edwardsians, Unitarians, and the Memory of the Great Awakening, 1800–1840," in *Amer-*

ican Unitarianism, 1805–1865, ed. Conrad Edick Wright (Boston: Massachusetts Historical Society and Northeastern University Press, 1989), pp. 31–50.

6. Miller, introduction to "From Edwards to Emerson," p. 184.

7. *JMN* 7: 443–44.

8. "An Account of the Late Assembly of Pastors . . . to Bear Their Testimony to the Wondrous Work of His Power and Grace in the Late Revival of Religion," in *The Christian History . . . for the Year 1743* (Boston: Kneeland and Green, 1744), pp. 165–66. Endorsements in Jonathan Edwards, *An Account of the Life of the Late Reverend Mr. David Brainerd* (Boston: Henchman, 1749); *A Careful and Strict Inquiry into . . . Freedom of the Will* (Boston: Kneeland, 1754); *The Great Christian Doctrine of Original Sin Defended* (Boston: Kneeland, 1758). None of the family's copies of Jonathan Edwards's works descended directly through the generations. WE_2, Waldo's father, owned a copy of *Freedom of the Will*, perhaps his father's and grandfather's originally, but it was sold at auction along with other books following his death in 1811. *Catalogue of Books Composing the Library of the Late Rev. William Emerson* (Boston: Whitwell and Bond, [1811]).

9. JE_2, "A Journal, Book 2" (ms. privately owned by Beatrice Parker, Pepperell, Mass.), Sept. 1740; Samuel A. Green, ed., *Diary Kept by the Rev. Joseph Emerson of Pepperell, Mass, August 1, 1748–April 9, 1749* (Cambridge, Mass.: John Wilson and Son, 1911), p. 8; see also *Ipswich Emersons*, pp. 115–21. Harry F. Stout lists young Joseph among the itinerants of 1741–42 in *The New England Soul: Preaching and Religious Culture in Colonial New England* (New York: Oxford University Press, 1986), pp. 200, 360n.

10. SM, *The Vain Youth Summoned to Appear at Christ's Bar*, 2d ed. (Boston: Timothy Green, 1707), p. 36; JE_1, *The Important Duty of a Timely Seeking of God Urged* (Boston: Kneeland and Green, 1727), pp. 4, 7. See Stout, *New England Soul*, esp. pp. 155–57 and 179–80, for discussion of pre-Awakening revivalism, including both Cotton Mather and Samuel Moody. Stout's quantitative study of 420 Congregational clergymen at the time of the First Awakening ("The Great Awakening in New England Reconsidered: The New England Clergy," *Journal of Social History* 8 [1974], 24) shows that, of ministers with "kinship ties to the clergy" by blood or marriage, almost 65 percent were foes of revival. This conclusion would put the Emersons and Moodies in a still-sizable 35 percent minority who were both dynastically connected and New Light.

11. SM, *The Vain Youth*, pp. 33, 60; JE_1, *The Important Duty*, pp. 18, 36, 23.

12. JE_1, *The Important Duty*, p. 3; SM-JE_1, June 9, 1727; *Boston Evening News-Letter*, March 20–28, 1735, p. 2.

13. *JMN* 5: 323; *Harvard Graduates* 4: 359; *Moody Family*, pp. 62–63.

14. *Harvard Graduates* 4: 361–62; Samuel Sewall, *Diary*, ed. M. Halsey Thomas (New York: Farrar, Straus and Giroux, 1973), 1: 563–64, 859.

15. SM, *The Children of the Covenant, Under the Promise of Divine Teachings* (Boston: John Allen, 1716), pp. 34, 37; *A Sermon Preached Before His Excellency Samuel Shute, Esq. . . . May 31, 1721* (Boston: Nicholas Boone, 1721), p. 12; Frederick Newberry, "The Biblical Veil: Sources and Typology in Hawthorne's 'The Minister's Black Veil,'" *Texas Studies in Literature and Language* 31 (1989), 174–76.

16. *JMN* 5: 323; *Moody Family*, pp. 64–65, 61–62; SM-JE_1, Oct. 25, 1725, Aug. 27, 1726.

17. *Handkerchief Moody*, pp. 107, 151, 153, 149.

18. *Handkerchief Moody*, pp. 195, 75, 99, 81 and passim, 87, 99.

19. *Handkerchief Moody*, pp. 59, 158–60. My sense of the Moody heritage of mental illness is influenced by Thomas C. Caramagno's study of similar intergenerational patterns in Virginia Woolf's family, *The Flight of the Mind: Virginia Woolf's Art and Manic-Depressive Illness* (Berkeley: University of California Press, 1992). Caramagno argues that literary and cul-

tural scholars need to amend Freudian models of their subjects' psyches in light of current medical insight into the biological basis of affective disorders.

20. *Handkerchief Moody*, pp. 118, 63, 79, 74–75, 81, 86. Puritan custom left ambiguous to what extent Joseph's preference should have been respected: marriage was considered a free, covenantal act with both partners exercising veto power; yet especially in the upper classes parents often engaged in long-term negotiation, both with each other and with their children. Daniel Scott Smith, "Parental Power in Massachusetts Marriage Patterns," in *Loving, Parenting, and Dying: The Family Cycle in England and America, Past and Present*, ed. Vivian C. Fox and Martin H. Quitt (New York: Psychohistory Press, 1980), pp. 147–58.

21. *Handkerchief Moody*, pp. 97, 103, 82. My interpretation of Joseph's lack of will and extreme deference to Samuel is influenced by Philip Greven, *The Protestant Temperament: Patterns of Child-Rearing, Religious Experience, and the Self in Early America* (New York: Knopf, 1977), pt 2.

22. Woodwell, "Joseph Moody: An Interpretation," in *Handkerchief Moody*, pp. 19ff.; JE$_2$, "A Journal, Book II," June 9, July 30, 1739; George Whitefield, *Journals* (London: Banner of Truth Trust, 1960), p. 467.

23. Newberry, "The Biblical Veil," p. 173; *Moody Family*, pp. 97–98.

24. Quoted in *Harvard Graduates* 4: 363; Whitefield, *Journals*, pp. 466–67, 519.

25. *The Christian History . . . for the Year 1743*, p. 157; *Moody Family*, p. 73. *Extract from a Late Sermon on the Death of the Rev. Samuel Moody* (Boston: Kneeland and Green, 1748), p. 9; *Harvard Graduates* 4: 360.

26. George Ernst, *New England Miniature: A History of York, Maine* (Freeport, Maine: Bond Wheelwright, 1961), pp. 61–68; *Moody Family*, pp. 77–78, 59.

27. *Moody Family*, pp. 99–100.

28. *JMN* 5: 4–5; MME-EH, July 12, 1842; MME-RWE, [Oct.?] 7, 1853.

29. Whitefield, *Journals*, p. 524; *Moody Family*, p. 93 (cf. Gen. 46: 4); Sereno Dwight Edwards, *The Life of President Edwards* (New York: Carvill, 1830), p. 284.

30. Cotton Mather, preface to JE$_1$, *The Important Duty*; Sewall, *Diary*, 2: 897; *Handkerchief Moody*, p. 84.

31. Cabot, *Memoir of RWE*, 1: 9; "Stories of Our Ancestors"; *Moody Family*, p. 69.

32. *History of Malden*, pp. 300, 500–519, 551.

33. *History of Malden*, pp. 500–19, 536; SM-JE$_1$, June 22, 1730. On the importance of meetinghouse controversies, see Michael Zuckerman, *Peaceable Kingdoms: New England Towns in the Eighteenth Century* (New York: Knopf, 1970), ch. 4.

34. *JMN* 10: 176.

35. *History of Malden*, p. 506; JE$_1$, *Meat Out of the Eater, and Sweetness Out of the Strong* (Boston: Kneeland and Green, 1735), pp. 4, 9.

36. JE$_1$, *Early Piety Encouraged: A Discourse Occasion'd by the Joyful and Triumphant Death of a Young Woman in Malden* (Boston: Draper, 1738), pp. 27, 11, 10, 13.

37. Whitefield, *Journals*, pp. 468, 533, 545; *Harvard Graduates* 6: 173; JE$_1$, *Exhortation to His People with Respect to Variety of Ministers* (Boston: Kneeland and Green, 1742), pp. 6, 10–11, 16.

38. Joseph Tracy, *A History of the Revival of Religion in the Time of Edwards and Whitefield* (Boston: Charles Tappan, 1845), pp. 241–48; JE$_1$, *Wisdom Is Justified of All Her Children* (Boston: Draper, 1742), p. 7, Appendix.

39. JE$_1$, *A Sermon Preach'd at the Ordination of the Rev. Mr. Joseph Emerson* (Boston: Kneeland and Green, 1747), p. 13.

40. JE$_1$, *Ordination of the Rev. Mr. Joseph Emerson*, pp. 10, 14, 16, 6.

41. *Ipswich Emersons*, pp. 74–78; *Moody Family*, p. 69; JE$_1$, Diary, Jan. 29, 1738.

42. *History of Malden*, pp. 481, 646n., 648–49n.; Cabot, *Memoir of RWE*, 1: 9; *JMN* 5: 323.

Examples of contact with the two richer brothers are JE_1, Diary, Nov. 25, 1837; Jan. 21, 1738; and JE_2, "Journal, Book 2," May 28, 1739; May 22, 1740. Cf. *Ipswich Emersons*, pp. 79, 122, 124, 125, on JE_1's brother Edward and his sons; Lincoln, *Waldo Family*, pp. 44, 48, on Edward's mentor and uncle Jonathan Waldo, whose estate was over £30,000. In JE_1's own will (Middlesex no. 6959), his major estate is land in New Hampshire, whose interest and eventual ownership go to the three merchant sons plus Samuel the schoolmaster; JE_2, William, and John get their portion in education and books. Brother John's will (*Ipswich Emersons*, pp. 81–82) shows him indeed to have more land to distribute and £240 for a son who has received an education as well. On land and patriarchy, see Philip J. Greven Jr., *Four Generations: Population, Land, and Family in Colonial Andover, Massachusetts, 1633–1785* (Ithaca, N.Y.: Cornell University Press, 1970), and Robert A. Gross, *The Minutemen and Their World* (New York: Hill and Wang, 1976), ch. 4.

43. *JMN* 10: 186–87; also quoted in his essay "Ezra Ripley," *Works* 10: 384–85.

44. Cabot, *Memoir of RWE*, 1: 9; JE_1, "Remarkables of Samuel Emerson."

45. JE_2, "A Journal, Book 2," May 1, 2, 4, 1739.

46. JE_2, "Journal of the Louisburg Expedition," *Proceedings of the Massachusetts Historical Society* 44 (1910–11), 72, 82–83; *Ipswich Emersons*, pp, 95, 117–18; JE_2, *The Fear of God an Antidote Against the Fear of Man* (Boston: Kneeland, 1758), p. 19.

47. Quoted in Gross, *Minutemen and Their World*, p. 21; *Letters of MME*, p. 263; "Stories of Our Ancestors."

48. *Letters of MME*, p. 526; *JMN* 9: 46–47.

49. "Stories of Our Ancestors"; *Works* 11: 66.

50. *Harvard Graduates* 9: 130–31; DB_1, "Relation of Daniel Bliss," 1730; Bliss, *Bliss Family*, pp. 23–24, 53, and passim.

51. C. C. Goen, *Revivalism and Separatism in New England, 1740–1800* (New Haven: Yale University Press, 1962), p. 20; *Harvard Graduates* 9: 130; *History of Concord*, p. 166.

52. *History of Concord*, pp. 167–68; DB_1, "Almanack with Diary," Sept. 17, 1740; Whitefield, *Journals*, p. 474; DB_1, "Almanack with Diary," Nov. [1], 1740.

53. *History of Concord*, pp. 168–69; Concord First Parish Records (microfilm CFPL), Aug. 6, 1742.

54. Chauncy quoted in *Harvard Graduates* 9: 133–34; Charles Chauncy, *Seasonable Thoughts on the State of Religion in New England* (Boston: Samuel Eliot, 1743).

55. *History of Concord*, pp. 169–73; *The Christian History . . . for the Year 1743*, pp. 159, 162–63.

56. *Boston Evening Post* quoted in *Harvard Graduates* 9: 132.

57. Bliss letter quoted in *Harvard Graduates* 9: 132.

58. *History of Concord*, p. 171; Joseph Hosmer, "Concord in Ye Olden Times," in Adams Tolman Scrapbook Collection, CFPL.

59. Concord First Parish Records, Aug. 6, 1742.

60. *Works* 11: 66–67; DB_1, *The Gospel Hidden from Them That Are Lost* (Boston: Kneeland and Green, 1755), pp. 10, 8–9, 42–43, 5.

61. *History of Concord*, pp. 175–79; Whitefield, *Journals*, pp. 533–34.

62. *Harvard Graduates* 9: 132; Concord First Parish Records, "Persons Received into Full Communion." Thomas Theodore Bliss owned the covenant in 1763 at the age of eighteen, but none of the other Bliss children are listed even in that capacity. Phebe joined fully in 1767 under her husband William Emerson's ministry, and her younger sister Martha in 1780 under Ezra Ripley.

63. Joseph Hosmer quoted in Josephine Hosmer, "For Mr. Edward Emerson" (ms., n.d., privately owned by David Emerson).

64. Hosmer, "For Mr. Edward Emerson."

65. *History of Concord*, pp. 183–84; diary of Joseph Lee quoted in *Diaries and Letters of WE*, p. 42.

66. Church documents quoted in Gross, *Minutemen and Their World*, p. 23; *Diaries and Letters of WE*, p. 20.

67. *Diaries and Letters of WE*, pp. 33, 84, 39; Ezra Stiles, *Extracts from the Itineraries* (New Haven: Yale University Press, 1916), p. 245.

68. WE_1, Sermons, July 6, 1765; Aug. 19, 1764.

69. WE_1, Sermon, Aug. 19, 1764. Cf. Daniel Walker Howe, "The Cambridge Platonists of Old England and the Cambridge Platonists of New England," in Wright, *American Unitarianism*, pp. 87–119, on the Harvard tradition of Platonism and its resulting liberal pietism, "a form of natural religion that looked inward toward human nature itself rather than outward toward the external world."

70. *Harvard Graduates* 4: 363; *History of Malden*, p. 642; WE_1, "On the Death of Mr. W[hitfiel]d who died on Sabbath Morning 6 O'Clock September 30th [1770]."

71. WE_1, "On the Death of Mr. W[hitefiel]d."

72. *Works* 11: 86; *JMN* 4: 335. In the "Historical Discourse" Waldo spoke of his discoveries in "a trunk of family papers," as well as his research in books (*Works* 11: 567n.)

Chapter Two

1. "Stories of Our Ancestors"; *Diaries and Letters of WE*, pp. 26, 33. Building of the Manse is dated in 1770 according to the land deed, April 16, 1770; see also *Diaries and Letters of WE*, pp. 50–52. The parish did not offer a ministry house for their use, as Malden had with William's parents, but instead sold a plot of "Ministerial land" and allowed him to use the proceeds toward buying this new land. It then became his property.

2. For references to the "old manse," see, for instance, CCE-WE_3, April 8–12, 1828 (Emerson Family Papers, MHS); MME-WE_3, Dec. 11, 1829; and especially WE_3-MME, July 28, 1842 (Emerson Family Papers, MHS): "The old manse . . . has undergone some changes, & having lost the old patriarch [Ezra Ripley] was waiting the arrival of the new tenants. What a history in those silent walls!" Cf. Hawthorne, "The Old Manse," Preface to *Mosses from an Old Manse, Centenary Edition of the Works of Nathaniel Hawthorne* (Columbus: Ohio State University Press, 1974), 10: 3–35; and *American Notebooks* (*Centenary Edition* 8: 323–26). Judgment of the Manse's uniqueness is made after consultation with the Society for the Preservation of New England Antiquities.

3. *Diaries and Letters of WE*, pp. 37–38; *Letters of MME*, p. 303.

4. My interpretation of the chairs' style, as well as the Manse's furnishings and household inventory, was made possible by conversation with staff members and especially Edward Cooke, former curator of the Concord Museum. Cf. Benno Forman, "Delaware Valley 'Crookt Foot' and Slat-Back Chairs," *Winterthur Portfolio* 15 (1980), 41.

5. Hawthorne, "The Old Manse" (*Centenary Edition* 10: 17); HSM-MME(g), July [31], 1727; PWB-PB, Aug. 26, 1762; Elizabeth Emerson Edwards–JE_1, May 10, 1766.

6. PB's sampler is owned by the Concord Museum. SM-JE_1, June 9, 1727; JE_1-Daniel Emerson, n.d. [April 1759?]; DB_2-WE_1, June 12, 1767; *Diaries and Letters of WE*, p. 24.

7. "Stories of Our Ancestors."

8. Early history of the house is in Ruth R. Wheeler, "Wheeler Houses" Collection, Concord Archives (CFPL). The house survives today, though relocated from the center of Concord. Its owner in 1985, Beth Ferber, generously showed me its large spaces and thick, fortresslike walls.

9. *Diaries and Letters of WE*, pp. 127–29.

10. *Diaries and Letters of WE*, pp. 119–20, 103, 127–29.

11. "Stories of Our Ancestors."

12. PWB-PB, Aug. 26, 1762; *Diaries and Letters of WE*, pp. 21–22; e.g. pp. 14, 46 for Hollis and Pepperell, 49 for Patty Bliss.

13. *Diaries and Letters of WE*, pp. 32, 44, 49.

14. "Stories of Our Ancestors"; *History of Malden*, pp. 649–50; Malden First Parish Records 1739–88 (ms. First Parish Universalist, Malden), March 14, 1768; Jan. 24, 1769; Feb. 1, 1770; Oct. 11, 1774.

15. JE_1, Will (Middlesex no.6959); *Diaries and Letters of WE*, p. 34; *History of Malden*, pp. 648–49n.; Mary Laurence Mann, "Some Notable Women in the Annals of Malden," *RMHS* 2 (1911–12), 56; Deloraine Corey, "Life in the Old Parsonage 1772–84: From the Diary of Rev. Peter Thacher," *RMHS* 1 (1910–11), 38–59 passim.

16. *History of Malden*, p. 406; *Diaries and Letters of WE*, p. 55.

17. On hiddenness and coverture, see Laurel Thacher Ulrich, *Good Wives: Image and Reality in the Lives of Women in Northern New England, 1650–1750* (New York: Oxford University Press, 1982), pp. 6–7; on the limited resources of widows, see Alexander Keyssar, "Widowhood in Eighteenth-Century Massachusetts," in Fox and Quitt, *Loving, Parenting, and Dying*, pp. 425–45. *Letters of MME*, p. 253.

18. Cf. the 1772 Malden church membership list: male and female members were listed separately, with two deacons leading the men's list and "Madam Mary Emerson" the women's. Madam Emerson was at this point the widow of the previous minister; Peter Thacher's wife was apparently not a member at all. *History of Malden*, pp. 659–60.

19. Joshua W. Wellman, "The Eccesiastical History of Malden," in *History of Middlesex County*, ed. D. Hamilton Hurd (Philadelphia: J. W. Lewis, 1890), 3: 496; Leonard I. Sweet, *The Minister's Wife: Her Role in Nineteenth-Century American Evangelicalism* (Philadelphia: Temple University Press, 1983), p. 18; Joseph Emerson of Byfield on his grandmother Hannah Emerson, quoted in *Ipswich Emersons*, p. 412.

20. WE_1, sermon for Communion Day, June 1776. Cf. Charles E. Hambrick-Stowe, *The Practice of Piety: Puritan Devotional Disciplines in Seventeenth-century New England* (Chapel Hill: University of North Carolina Press, 1982).

21. "Solemn Covenant Engagements . . . May 11, 1749" and "An Holy Covenant . . . July 11, 1776," First Parish Records (CFPL); cf. *Diaries and Letters of WE*, p. 100.

22. Gal. 3:28, 1 Cor. 14:34, 1 Tim. 2: 12–14; Increase Mather, *A Discourse Concerning the Subject of Baptisme* (Cambridge, Mass.: Samuel Green, 1675), pp. 45–46; Cotton Mather, *Ornaments for the Daughters of Zion*, ed. Pattie Cowell (Delmar, N.Y.: Scholar's Facsimiles, 1978; from 1741 edition), p. 29. I am indebted to George Huntston Williams for leads in tracing this definition of the covenant in Puritan literature.

23. "Solemn Covenant Engagements . . . 1749."

24. "Solemn Covenant Engagements . . . 1749." See, for instance, Deut. 10: 20 and Gen. 2: 24.

25. JE_1, *Early Piety Encouraged*, pp. 7, 21. On Puritan bridal theology and its special consonance with women's experience, see Amanda Porterfield, *Feminine Spirituality in America: From Sarah Edwards to Martha Graham* (Philadelphia: Temple University Press, 1980), ch. 2.

26. In 1739 the Concord congregation included forty-five women out of seventy-six, or 59 percent (First Parish Records, CFPL). No York church records survive from the eighteenth century, and none in Malden from Joseph Emerson's ministry. In 1772, however, the Malden congregation of eighty-four included forty-seven women, or 56 percent (*History of Malden*, pp. 659–60). The five-to-three estimate was made by Cedric B. Cowing in "Sex and Preaching in the Great Awakening," *American Quarterly* 20 (1968), 624–44; see also Mary Ma-

ples Dunn, "Saints and Sisters: Congregational and Quaker Women in the Early Colonial Period," *American Quarterly* 30 (1978), 583–601; and Richard D. Shiels, "The Feminization of American Congregationalism, 1730–1815," *American Quarterly* 33 (1981), 46–62.

27. *Handkerchief Moody*, e.g. pp. 92, 102, 124, 154; JE_1, Diary, Sept. 30, 1837.

28. Old Burying Ground, York.

29. Cf. Ulrich, *Good Wives*, p. 3. Bell Rock Cemetery, Malden; Hollis Cemetery.

30. Portrait of Phebe Bliss at Emerson House, Concord; of Daniel Bliss at First Parish Concord. DB_1 letter quoted in *Harvard Graduates* 9: 132; cf. Sweet, *Minister's Wife*, p. 5, on the "helpmeet" role, represented by Sarah Pierrepont Edwards and her daughter Esther Edwards Burr.

31. Middlesex Probate (no.1949); Phebe Walker Bliss Memorial (Houghton 235.233 and 463). The Concord Museum owns a silk pincushion in the shape of a beehive with the same inscription to Phebe Walker Bliss; probably all versions are the work of Elizabeth Haskins, sister of Ruth Haskins Emerson.

32. "Stories of Our Ancestors."

33. Almanack, [Nov.] 13, [1804], (f. 1); ms. Will, May 7, 1859 (Emerson Family Papers, Houghton); Almanack, June [27, 1841], (f. 22); RWE, ms. journal "Genealogy," p. 4 (cf. *JMN* 3: 349); MME–Phebe Gage, March 2, 1841 (Gage Family Additional Papers, AAS).

34. *Diaries and Letters of WE*, p. 8; *Works* 10: 414.

35. Cf. p. 19.

36. SM, *A Faithful Narrative of the Wicked Life and Remarkable Conversion of Patience Boston Alias Samson* (Boston: Kneeland and Green, 1738); "To the Candid Reader" (SM and JM), pp. 1–8, 29–31.

37. SM, *Patience Boston*, pp. 33–35. Cf. Jon Butler, *Awash in a Sea of Faith: Christianizing the American People* (Cambridge: Harvard University Press, 1990), pp. 172–73, on execution sermons as a means of evangelizing the wider public, warning about sin and holding out hope of salvation "to everyone, including the person about to die."

38. JE_1, *Early Piety Encouraged: A Discourse Occasion'd by the Joyful and Triumphant Death of a Young Woman of Malden*, pp. 27–29; cf. *History of Malden*, p. 638n.

39. JE_1 *Early Piety Encouraged*, pp. 22–23.

40. Jonathan Edwards, *A Faithful Narrative of the Surprising Work of God*, in *The Great Awakening*, ed. C. C. Goen, *Works of Jonathan Edwards* (New Haven: Yale University Press, 1972), 4: 191–99.

41. If in 1739 Concord's fully communing membership was 59 percent women, by the end of 1742 it was still 58 percent after the new conversion of two men and six women in 1739, six men and six women in 1740, 22 men and 27 women in 1741, and 28 men and 39 women in 1742. In only one of the remaining years of Bliss's ministry did more men than women join the church—and then just one more (Concord First Parish Records).

42. Edwards, *Works* 4: 331–41. On Sarah Edwards, see Porterfield, *Feminine Spirituality*, pp. 40–47; Sweet, *Minister's Wife*, pp. 20–23; and Sereno Dwight Edwards, *The Life of President Edwards* (New York: S. Converse, 1829), pp. 284–85.

43. Davenport quoted in Goen, *Revivalism and Separatism*, pp. 21, 30; Cutler in Edwin Scott Gaustad, *The Great Awakening in New England* (New York: Harper, 1957), pp. 31–32.

44. Amy Lang, *Prophetic Woman: Anne Hutchinson and the Problem of Dissent in the Literature of New England* (Berkeley: University of California Press, 1987), pp. 75–78.

45. *Concord Vital Records* list Hannah as born in 1746 to John and Hannah Melvin; and in Emily Wilder Leavitt, *John Melvin of Charlestown and Concord, Mass., and His Descendants* (Boston: David Clapp, 1901–5), pp. 252–53, she is the eldest of their eight children. Neither source names the date or place of her death. The 1749 North Book of Estates (Concord

Archives, CFPL) lists John Melvin in the bottom quarter of taxable property; in 1771 Hannah Melvin appears apart from her parents on the list of those receiving poor relief, so she must be on her own. In Concord First Parish Records, a name is blotted on the 1759 membership list, with the label "Excom." alongside it. Melvin quoted in Ezra Ripley, *Half-Century Discourse* (Concord: Herman Atwill, 1829), p. 39n.

46. "Acts and Votes of ye Chh in Concord," Feb. 23, 1775 (First Parish Records).

47. "Acts and Votes of ye Chh in Concord," May 15, 1791; Ripley, *Half-Century Discourse*, p. 39n.

48. Sereno Dwight Edwards, *President Edwards*, p. 127; *Moody Family*, pp. 61–62, 67–68.

49. "Stories of Our Ancestors."

50. *Diaries and Letters of WE*, pp. 28–29, 33, 45.

51. *Diaries and Letters of WE*, p. 36. Cf. pp. 39, 48; DB_2-WE_1, June 12, 1767.

52. "Memoir of the Life and Character of the Late Rev. William Emerson," *MHS Collections*, 2d ser. 1 (1838), 254.

53. "Stories of Our Ancestors."

Chapter Three

1. *Works* 10: 400;.Almanack, May 16, 1827 (f. 9).

2. Almanack, May 16, 1827 (f. 9); July 4, 1826 (f. 8). Mary's autobiography especially resonates with the national mythic language of filial freedom discussed in Jay Fliegelman, *Prodigals and Pilgrims: The American Revolution Against Patriarchal Authority, 1750–1800* (Cambridge: Cambridge University Press, 1982), where the "Hapless Orphan," once separated from parental tyranny, faces both a terrifying vulnerability and a potential for education into the new family of God's salvation.

3. *Diaries and Letters of WE*, pp. 56–57.

4. "Stories of Our Ancestors"; Gross, *The Minutemen and Their World*, pp. 47–49; Caleb Butler, *History of the Town of Groton, Including Pepperell and Shirley* (Boston: T. R. Marvin, 1848), p. 330.

5. "Stories of Our Ancestors." Women's part in the colony-wide boycotts is detailed in Linda Kerber, *Women of the Republic: Intellect and Ideology in Revolutionary America* (Chapel Hill: University of North Carolina Press, 1980), ch. 2, and in Mary Beth Norton, *Liberty's Daughters: The Revolutionary Experience of American Women* (Boston: Little, Brown, 1980), ch. 6.

6. Gross, *The Minutemen and Their World*, pp. 43–44; Membership Records, First Parish Concord (CFPL), Dec. 19, 1742; George Tolman, *John Jack, the Slave, and Daniel Bliss, the Tory* (Concord: Concord Antiquarian Society, 1902), pp. 5–6. See Bernard Bailyn, *The Ideological Origins of the American Revolution* (Cambridge: Harvard University Press, 1967), pp. 232–46, for the development of an American critique of chattel slavery out of the Whigs' rhetoric of slavery. For a full text and illustration of the epitaph, see Ruth R. Wheeler, *Concord: Climate for Freedom* (Concord: Concord Antiquarian Society, 1967), p. 87.

7. *Harvard Graduates* 14: 564; Bliss, *Bliss Family*, p. 81; Baptismal Records, First Parish Concord.

8. Josephine Hosmer, "For Mr. Edward Emerson."

9. Josephine Hosmer, "For Mr. Edward Emerson"; "Memoir of Joseph Hosmer," *The Centennial of the Social Circle in Concord* (Cambridge: Riverside, 1882), pp. 116–17.

10. *History of Concord*, p. 91; *Diaries and Letters of WE*, pp. 59–70; *Letters of MME*, p. 216; WE_1, Diary (ms.), Jan. 19, March 22, 1775.

11. *History of Malden*, pp. 738–43, includes the documents revealing Thacher's part in early Revolutionary politics. On his links to Dexter and to the Emersons, see also Corey,

"Life in the Old Parsonage," passim. *Diaries and Letters of WE*, pp. 59–60; cf. *Ipswich Emersons*, pp. 122–23, 125.

12. Gross, *The Minutemen and Their World*, p. 67; *Diaries and Letters of WE*, p. 60; "Acts and Votes of ye Chh in Concord," Feb. 23, 1775 (First Parish Records); *History of Concord*, pp. 94–95.

13. British reports are quoted in Allen French, *General Gage's Informers* (Ann Arbor: University of Michigan Press, 1932), pp. 11–13.

14. *History of Concord*, pp. 96, 94 (cf. Mic. 7: 5–6); "For Mr. Edward Emerson"; Wheeler, *Concord*, p. 109.

15. *Diaries and Letters of WE*, pp. 71–72; *Works* 11: 27–86 and 9: 158–59; EWE, "A Chaplain of the Revolution," *MHS Proceedings* 55 (1921), 8–29; *Diaries and Letters of WE*, pp. 73–74.

16. *Diaries and Letters of WE*, pp. 71, 91–92.

17. *Diaries and Letters of WE*, pp. 71–72; *History of Concord*, pp. 105–6; EWE, "Chaplain of the Revolution," p. 20.

18. *Diaries and Letters of WE*, pp. 72–73.

19. *Diaries and Letters of WE*, p. 91; Gross, *The Minutemen and Their World*, p. 122; Claudia Bushman, *A Good Poor Man's Wife* (Hanover, N.H.: University Press of New England, 1981), p. 65.

20. *Works* 9: 58–59; *Diaries and Letters of WE*, p. 94. Allen French examines all documents pertaining to William on April 19 in *The Day of Concord and Lexington* (Boston: Little, Brown, 1925), esp. pp. 165, 203–6.

21. ER, *A History of the Fight at Concord on the 19th of April* (Concord: Herman Atwill, 1832), p. 19; Chamberlain quoted in *Diaries and Letters of WE*, p. 73.

22. *Diaries and Letters of WE*, p. 92. See Norton, *Liberty's Daughters*, and Kerber, *Women of the Republic*, for accounts of women as refugees and preservers of family life in the wider Revolution.

23. *Works* 11: 77 (cf. Waldo's transcription of the battle narrative on pp. 567–69); *Letters of MME*, pp. 156, 519.

24. There are fifteen manuscript sermons, of which two bear directly on the Revolution and another three the circumstances of 1775–76. William's diaries for these years supplement the record, however, by regularly listing his sermon texts.

25. These interpretations are advanced respectively by Bailyn, *Ideological Origins*; Alan Heimert, *Religion and the American Mind: From the Awakening to the Revolution* (Cambridge: Harvard University Press, 1966); and Nathan O. Hatch, *The Sacred Cause of Liberty: Republican Thought and the Millennium in Revolutionary New England* (New Haven: Yale University Press, 1977).

26. *Diaries and Letters of WE*, p. 68.

27. *Diaries and Letters of WE*, pp. 69, 65–67; JE_2, *A Thanksgiving Sermon Preach'd at Pepperrell, July 24, 1766* (Boston: Edes and Gill, 1766), pp. 15, 19ff.

28. JE_2, *Thanksgiving Sermon*, p. 7; *Diaries and Letters of WE*, pp. 61, 66, 64.

29. *Diaries and Letters of WE*, pp. 63, 68, 70; Donald Weber, *Rhetoric and History in Revolutionary New England* (New York: Oxford University Press, 1988), p. 30.

30. *Diaries and Letters of WE*, pp. 75–77; *Ipswich Emersons*, p. 118; Almanack, n.d. (folder 9) on Thacher (cf. *History of Malden*, pp. 743–48); Samuel Langdon, *A Sermon Preached Before the Honorable Congress . . . the 31st Day of May, 1775* (Watertown, Mass.: Benjamin Edes, 1775), pp. 7–10.

31. *Diaries and Letters of WE*, pp. 79–80.

32. *Diaries and Letters of WE*, p. 81. Heimert argues for the significance of this 1775 Continental Fast as a high point of Revolutionary history (*Religion and the American Mind*, pp. 403–4).

33. *Diaries and Letters of WE*, pp. 83, 89, 87 (Gannett); ms. diary Jan. 21, 28, Feb. 11, April 7, 1776; *Harvard Graduates* 16: 239–40 on Thacher.

34. *History of Concord*, pp. 120, 125, on exiles still in Concord; *Diaries and Letters of WE*, pp. 95, 91, 94, 87 (Gannett); "Oration for the 19th of April 1776" (ms.).

35. *Diaries and Letters of WE*, pp. 91, 94–95.

36. *Diaries and Letters of WE*, pp. 96–97.

37. SM-JE_1, June 9, 1927.

38. WE_1, Sermon for Communion Day, June 1776.

39. WE_1, Sermon, Feb. 23, 1776. Other ms. sermons invoking social order are Nov. 4, 1771 (fast); Jan. 29, 1773 (funeral); Dec. 23, 1775.

40. "An Holy Covenant," Concord First Parish Records.

41. "Stories of Our Ancestors," pp. 7–8. On a child's bow of "duty" and the use of corporal punishment, see Lawrence Stone, *The Family, Sex, and Marriage in England 1500–1800* (New York: Harper and Row, 1979), pp. 171–72; on "breaking the will," see Greven, *Protestant Temperament*, pp. 32–43. Both use the Edwards family as an example.

42. *Diaries and Letters of WE*, pp. 102–3.

43. *Diaries and Letters of WE*, pp. 102–3, 110; cf. ms. letter WE_1-PBE_1, Aug. 16, 1776.

44. *Diaries and Letters of WE*, pp. 108–13; *JMN* 5: 13.

45. *Diaries and Letters of WE*, pp. 113–15; *JMN* 5: 13 on the pension.

46. *Letters of MME*, pp. 209–10, 521; Tolman, *Mary Moody Emerson*, p. 3.

47. *Letters of MME*, p. 519; *Diaries and Letters of WE*, pp. 120, 123; JCB 1, Feb. 8, 1795.

48. *Letters of MME*, pp. 101, 175.

49. *Works* 10: 400; *Diaries and Letters of WE*, p. 110; $PBER_1$ Estate, May 13, 1778 (Houghton 235.520).

50. *Diaries and Letters of WE*, p. 74, 97–101 passim, 59; "Stories of Our Ancestors."

51. A widow could not herself inherit her husband's estate according to Massachusetts law, but only hold it in trust for the true heirs, usually sons. If a man died intestate, as William did, his widow received a third of the estate's personal property forever and a third of the real property as a "life estate or dower." Characteristically, she was guaranteed a section of her son's house for life, and the full house while her son was a minor. Grandmother Mary Moody Emerson owned her house in full as a gift from her son Waldo; Phebe Bliss lived in hers until her sons Samuel and Joseph were ready for it. See Alexander Keyssar, "Widowhood in Eighteenth-Century Massachusetts," in Fox and Quitt, *Loving Parenting, and Dying*, pp. 425–45.

52. Concord Archives (CFPL), Nov. 4, 1776; Adams quoted by Kerber, *Women of the Republic*, p. 67.

53. Concord Archives, 1764; Caleb Gannet, ms. diary (Harvard Archives), Jan. 25 and Mar. 20, 1776; *Diaries and Letters of WE*, p. 103; E. A. Benians, ed., *A Journal by Thomas Hughes . . . 1778–79* (Cambridge, England: University Press, 1947), pp. 32–33.

54. DB_2, Agent (Middlesex Probate no.1947); DB_2 quoted in *Harvard Graduates* 14: 566; cf. *Diaries and Letters of WE*, pp. 87, 99 on communication with her sons.

55. WE_2-$PBER_1$, Mar. 2, 1807; estate accounts May 13, 1778 (Houghton ms.), Nov. 8, 1780 (Middlesex Probate). William referred to expecting Frank's arrival at Ticonderoga in two letters; family tradition is that "Grandfather liberated his slaves on his death bed," so possibly Frank was with him then (*Diaries and Letters of WE*, pp. 105, 113, 74).

56. This is an inherited oral tradition known to staff members at the Old Manse.

57. ER, *Half-Century Discourse*, p. 8.

58. The wallpapers in these spaces today are reproductions of those dated from 1780, which are believed to be Phebe and Ezra's from their first year of marriage.

59. *History of Malden*, pp. 439–40n., 580, 660; Malden Town Records, "Town Officers" and "Town Treasurer Records" (microfilm MPL); Malden First Parish Records (ms. First Church Universalist), July 2, 1756; Jacob Parker, Will (Middlesex Probate no.16595). Grandmother Mary did still have three living sons, the closest (Bulkeley) living in Newburyport; no family or legal papers suggest what sort of relationship they sustained.

60. *History of Malden*, pp. 439n., 631, 770n.

61. *History of Malden*, pp. 769–770n.; Gross, *Minutemen and Their World*, p. 144. Selectman Ezra Sargent (1729–1810) had been a member of the South Church since 1753 and a deacon since 1776; his father, grandfather, and great-uncle had all been among its supporters in earlier decades. In the 1770s Sargent became the first member of his family also to take town office, as selectman, member of the Committee of Correspondence, and finally representative to the General Court. *History of Malden*, pp. 533–34, 729; "Records of the Second Church of Malden 1747–92" (ms. New England Historic and Genealogical Society), pp. 157, 174; Malden Town Records, 1776; Aaron Sargent, *Genealogy of the Sargent Family* (Boston: S. G. Drake, 1858).

62. Mary Moody Emerson, Will (Middlesex Probate no.6968).

63. *History of Malden*, p. 779; John B. Blake, *Public Health in the Town of Boston, 1630–1822* (Cambridge: Harvard University Press, 1959), pp. 126–28; Malden Town Records, June 5, 1778 (MPL).

64. Jacob Parker, Will and appendages for Nov. 5, 1782, and Mar. 21, 1790 (Middlesex Probate no.16595); Corey, "Diary of Rev. Peter Thacher," *RMHS* 1 (1910–11), July 31, 1784.

65. See chapter 1 on Joseph Moody and his parents. *Harvard Graduates* 12:53–54; *Ipswich Emersons*, pp. 122, 133, 135; *Letters of MME*, p. 245.

66. MME-LJE, Dec. 31, 1859; *Malden Vital Records; History of Malden*, pp. 767–68, 826–27; Malden First Parish Records (ms. First Church Universalist), Dec. 6, 1770; Malden Town Records, Mar. 1, 1773 (MPL); Corey, "Diary of Rev. Peter Thacher," passim in year 1781; Middlesex Registry of Deeds, Feb. 17, 1783; April 25, 1787; *Works* 10: 400, 414.

67. *Works* 10: 401.

68. Cf. John Demos, "Developmental Perspectives on the History of Childhood," in *The Family in History: Interdisciplinary Essays*, ed. Theodore K. Rabb and Robert I. Rotberg (New York: Harper, 1973), esp. pp. 132–33, for an overview (influenced by Eriksonian identity-theory) of childhood stages in Puritan culture.

69. Almanack, Jan. 7, 1855 (f. 30); June [27, 1841] (f. 22).

70. Bell Rock Cemetery, Malden; MME-RHE, Sept. 27, [1825]; *Works* 10: 414.

71. Almanack, July 4, 1826 (f. 8); MME-LJE, Dec. 31, 1859; *Works* 10: 400.

72. Thacher, Diary (Peter Thacher II Collection, MHS), April 19, 1781; *Observations on the Present State of the Clergy of New-England* (Boston: Norman and White, 1783), p. 4; *Harvard Graduates* 16: 245.

73. *Letters of MME*, p. 326.

Chapter Four

1. *Works* 10: 404; Almanack, March 24, 1830 (f. 13).

2. Almanack, Jan. 7, 1855 (f. 30).

3. Franklin Sanborn, "The Women of Concord," 156–57; Sanborn, "Thoreau's Autumn and Mary Moody Emerson," in *Transcendental Writers and Heroes*, ed. Kenneth Walter Cameron (Hartford, Conn.: Transcendental Books, 1978), p. 97; "MME 1," 8.

4. MME-CCE, July 30, 1833. This letter reveals that the "profile" belonged first to

Mary Wilder White and then to the Farnham daughters before finally being given to Charles. Mary was pleased to have it displayed in his home.

5. Almanack, Oct. 2, [1813] (f. 37), Jan. 7, 1855 (f. 30).

6. Almanack, March 24, 1830 (f. 13) April 24, 1827 (f. 9), June 1, 1827 (f. 9); Aug. 27, [1835] (f. 18), March 1847 (f. 27).

7. In the words of Caramagno, "Manics rarely speak of mood spontaneously or examine it critically—rather, they live out their moods" (*Flight of the Mind*, p. 43). See Caramagno, ch. 2 for an account of manic-depressive behavior and pp. 103–4 for examples of "cyclothymic" or nonpsychotic mood swings in the childhood of Virginia Woolf's father, Leslie Stephen. Caramagno cites theory and clinical evidence that the genetic predisposition to manic-depressive illness can also manifest itself in a variety of milder forms within a family.

8. *Works* 10: 399; *Letters of MME*, p. 502. The Emerson property in Malden did include a barn, as well as six more acres out from the town center (*History of Malden*, pp. 648–49n.), but neither Mary nor Waldo speaks of Nathan Sargent's farming it as a source of income.

9. Almanack, [?] 28, [1828] (f. 10); *Harvard Graduates* 16: 242–43.

10. Joshua Wellman, *The Ecclesiastical History of Malden*, in *History of Middlesex County*, ed. D. Hamilton Hurd (Philadelphia: J. W. Lewis, 1890), 3: 497–98; cf. Joseph Haroutunian, *Piety vs. Moralism: The Passing of the New England Theology* (New York: Henry Holt, 1932), ch. 4.

11. *History of Malden*, pp. 648n., 631. Joseph Emerson's books had been divided among his ministerial sons, so any books remaining would have been leftovers from that process (*Diaries and Letters of WE*, p. 37).

12. MME-AB, Jan. 29 and 30, 1816 (Gage Family Additional Papers, b2 f2, AAS); Orlando Perry Dexter, *Dexter Genealogy 1642–1904* (New York: J. J. Little, 1904), pp. 46, 68–69; MME-RWE, Nov. 18, 1844.

13. *Letters of MME*, pp. 175, 221; *Maternal Ancestors*, p. 39; *Works* 10: 402.

14. *Letters of MME*, pp. 521–23; Almanack, May 12, [1827] (f. 9).

15. *Mary Wilder White*, p. 114; cf. *Works* 10: 411.

16. WE_2, "Almanac with Diary, Roxbury 1790."

17. MME-ASG, April 21, 1857 (Gage Family Additional Papers, b2 f2, AAS); Middlesex Registry of Deeds nos. 107/496 and 105/470; Middlesex Probate; ER–William Farnham, 1790 (Farnham Family Papers, MHS). William received all of his father's estate but the widow's third, but then sold it back to Ezra Ripley in 1791 for cash, thus keeping the Manse for the elder Ripleys. On October 15, 1795, Mary received her inheritance of $151.12.

18. On September 27, 1791, Nathan Sargeant bought two-sixths' interest in the house from his brothers-in-law Edward and Bulkeley for four hundred pounds, then resold them to Thacher for half that sum, kept the remaining money, and stayed in residence at the house. Thacher, though long gone from Malden, was continuing to serve as Nathan and Ruth's benefactor, as their own kin were not (Middlesex Registry of Deeds nos. 105/470, 471, 473). *Works* 10: 400; Waldo's sense (401) that Mary inherited the Malden property from Ruth, however, is contradicted by the legal records.

19. Bell Rock Cemetery, Malden; *Letters of MME*, pp. 326, 214; MME-EH, Nov. 10, 1857.

20. Almanack, Sept. 10, 1828 (f. 10).

21. Almanack, Jan. 17, 1832 (f. 15); JCB 2: 61, 53, 71, 59–60, 73.

22. *History of Malden*, p. 631; Norton, *Liberty's Daughters*, pp. 242–55, on redefinitions of women's role, 272–73, 280–82, on education, including Woodbridge.

23. "An Oration, delivered Sept. 5, 1789 . . . at the Request of the Phi Beta Kappa

Society," in *Phi Beta Kappa Register*, pp. 46–47 (ms. Harvard University Archives). William's own transcription of the address is included in JCB 2.

24. Benjamin W. Labaree, *Patriots and Partisans: The Merchants of Newburyport* (Cambridge: Harvard University Press, 1962), ch. 1; J. J. Currier, *History of Newburyport, Mass., 1764–1905* (Newburyport: Privately printed, 1906) 1: 472–74; WE_2-$PBER_1$, June 11, 1790; Newburyport Vital Records. Letters from Ezra Ripley to William Farnham also suggest a cordial and well-established family connection (1790; Nov. 28, 1790; Aug. 2, 1791 [Farnham Family Papers, MHS]).

25. Currier, *History of Newburyport*, 2: 229–32; declaration of William Farnham "collector of revenue over imported and domestic distilled spirits," June 15, 1791 (Farnham Family Papers, MHS). *Life in a New England Town: 1787, 1788: The Diary of John Quincy Adams* (Boston: Little, Brown, 1903), p. 108.

26. Almanack, June 16, [1842] (f. 23); Newburyport Vital Records; CCE-MME, Feb. 4, 1832; WE_2-$PBER_2$, May 14, 1807.

27. Currier, *History of Newburyport*, 2:230 on William Farnham's church membership and *Ipswich Emersons*, p. 124 on Bulkeley Emerson's; Sarah Ann Emery on Mary, Elizabeth, and Martha Emerson, quoted in *Ipswich Emersons*, pp. 173–74; *Letters of MME*, p. 580; MME-EH, Nov. 10, 1857.

28. *History of Concord*, pp. 129–32; First Parish Records, May 15, 1791 (CFPL); Ruth Wheeler, "Wheeler Houses Collection," Concord Archives (CFPL); Concord Vital Records.

29. *Letters of ETE* 1: 154; on mother Phebe's invalidism, "Rev. Samuel Ripley," *Christian Examiner* 44 (March 1848), 178, and *Letters of MME*, p. 11; *Letters of MME*, p. 506.

30. Sermon 751, Nov. 4, 1792 (Houghton, bMs Am 1835 [11]).

31. Sermon 1025, Feb. 17, 1799 (seventeenth sermon on social virtues).

32. *JMN* 14: 458; *Works* 10: 385; *JMN* 16: 175; MME quoted by Sanborn, *The Personality of Emerson* (Boston: Charles Goodspeed, 1903), p. 133.

33. WE_2-$PBER_1$, Feb. 3, 1802; June 11, 1790; *Letters of MME*, pp. 67–68; *Diaries and Letters of WE*, p. 120.

34. MME-CCE, [Nov.] 13, [1832] (226.719).

35. Almanack, July 15, [1853?], enclosed with MME-RWE, [6 Jan. 1857] (226.949); *Letters of MME* pp. 402, 9.

36. MME-WE_2, Dec. 20, 1793; *Letters of MME*, pp. 9–10; JCB 1, Feb 9, 11, 1795.

37. JCB 1 passim; *Letters of MME*, pp. 24–25; Sanborn, "Women of Concord," 155 (Mary Wilder) and 157 (Cynthia Dunbar Thoreau); Walter Harding, *The Days of Henry David Thoreau* (New York: Knopf, 1965), p. 9, for the Dunbars' arrival in Concord in 1798; *Mary Wilder White*, pp. 125, 28–29.

38. *Letters of MME*, pp. 15–16, 458, 459n.; Catalogue of Books (typescript, Old Manse), p. 1S4; JCB 1, passim 1795; MME-WE_2, March 17, 1795; MME-RH, Oct. 1795; WE_2-PBE_2, Oct. 13, 1795; *Ipswich Emersons*, pp. 176, 180.

39. MME-RHE, Sept. 27, [1825] (226.1036); WE_2-PBE_2, Oct. 13, 1795; *Letters of MME*, p. 16.

40. "Account of Books Lent from June 1795" (ms. Concord Free Public Library), information courtesy of Robert A. Gross. See his "Much Instruction from Little Reading: Books and Libraries in Thoreau's Concord," *Proceedings of the American Antiquarian Society* 97 (1987), 129–88.

41. *Works* 10: 402; Almanack, [Oct.] 20, 1840 (f. 22); MME-ER, April 6, 1830; MME-WE_3, [June 25, 1855] (220.75).

42. A book in the Manse's surviving library (its title page missing) is inscribed as a gift to Mary from Ezra and represents the kind of practical manual of devotion that he probably saw as most appropriate for her (Catalogue of Books, p. 2UH7). "Catalogue of

Concord Charitable Library Society, 1795–1800" (ms. CFPL); *Mary Wilder White*, p. 175. Cathy N. Davidson, in *Revolution and the Word: The Rise of the Novel in America* (New York: Oxford University Press, 1986), p. 42, discusses the shifting paradigm of authority from minister to book and its implications for women.

43. JCB 1, July 21, 1797. Mary's copy of Radcliffe is owned by Beineke Library, Yale University. Cf. Kenneth W. Cameron, "The Rev. R. Waldo Emerson and Aunt Mary's Books," *ESQ* 1 (4th Qu. 1955), 6–7.

44. *Mary Wilder White*, pp. 23–24; MME-EH, [Jan.] 24 and Feb. 4, [1847] (226.1167); *Letters of MME*, p. 344.

45. *Letters of MME*, p. 11.

46. *Letters of MME*, p. 12, 14.

47. MME-ASG [1835?] (Gage Family Additional Papers, b2 f2, AAS).

48. [MME], " 'The Woman'—A Reminiscence," *Christian Register* 31 (Jan. 24, 1852). See ch. 11 on Mary's composition of this essay. Cf. Lee Chambers-Schiller, *Liberty, A Better Husband: Single Women in America: The Generations of 1780–1840* (New Haven: Yale University Press, 1984).

49. RHE, Diary, April 23, 1795; Almanack, [Nov]. 19, 1849 (f. 28); [Oct.] 1834 (f. 17). On the bridal tradition, see Porterfield, *Feminine Spirituality*, ch. 2.

50. "Persons Admitted to the Church in Full," First Parish Concord (CFPL); *History of Concord*, p. 191; *Letters of MME*, pp. 14–16. Robert A. Gross discusses the change of membership practice in *The Making of Emerson's Concord* (New York: Hill and Wang, forthcoming 1998), ch. 1. In *Writing a Woman's Life* (New York: W. W. Norton, 1988), Carolyn Heilbrun distinguishes between marriage and quest plots (pp. 48, 42).

51. *Works* 10: 428; *Letters of MME*, p. 16. On women's religious memoirs, see Joanna Bowen Gillespie, " 'The Clear Leadings of Providence': Pious Memoirs and the Problems of Self-Realization for Women in the Early Nineteenth Century," *Journal of the Early Republic* 5 (Summer 1985), 197–221.

52. "Stories of Our Ancestors"; *Letters of MME*, p. 19. Julie Ellison outlines a tradition of female piety based upon Sarah Edwards's example (focusing on the term "indifference") in "The Sociology of 'Holy Indifference': Sarah Edwards' Narrative," *American Literature* 56 (1984), 479–95.

53. Phebe Bliss Memorial; MME-EH, Dec. 24, 1847. On the urn-and-willow design and sensibility, see Philippe Aries, *The Hour of Our Death*, trans. Helen Weaver (New York: Knopf, 1981), pp. 442–50.

54. JCB 1 passim; MME-WE_2, [Oct. 1797] (226.1052); Almanack, June 16, [1842] (f. 23), [July] 27, [1847] (f. 27).

55. Middlesex Registry of Deeds nos. 119/355–358, 124/100, 143/369; *History of Malden*, p. 648n.

56. *Letters of MME*, p. 22.

57. Almanack, [Jan?] 1838 (f. 20), Oct. 25, [1851] (f. 28); [Aug.?] 27, [1801?] (f. 16).

58. WE_2-ER, Aug. 2, 1805; *Works* 10: 417; RWE, "Mary Moody Emerson" (ms.), p. 69; Almanack, Jan. 30, 1807 (f. 3). On William Austin, see Timothy T. Sawyer, *Old Charlestown* (Boston: James H. West, 1902), p. 220, and Edith Austin Moore and William Allen Day, *The Descendants of Richard Austin of Charlestown, Massachusetts* (Privately printed, n.p., n.d.), pp. 38–39; on the Dexters, Orlando Perry Dexter, *Dexter Genealogy 1642–1904* (New York: J. J. Little, 1904), pp. 43–44, 68.

59. Almanack, April 23, 1807 (f. 3).

60. *Letters of MME*, p. 28.

61. Hurd, *History of Middlesex County*, 3: 499–501; "The Early Baptists of Malden," RMHS

5 (1917–18), 17–25; Ralph Emerson, *Life of Rev. Joseph Emerson* (Boston: Crocker and Brewster, 1834), pp. 40–45, 66. For these broader developments in New England church history, see Ahlstrom, *Religious History of the American People,* 1: chs. 24–26, and David Robinson, *The Unitarians and the Universalists* (Westport, Conn.: Greenwood Press, 1985), chs. 2 and 5.

62. Almanack, [Nov] 7, [1804] (f. 1).

63. Currier, *History of Newburyport,* 2: 230 on Farnham; Labaree, *Patriots and Partisans* p. 4; Minnie Atkinson, *A History of the First Religious Society in Newburyport* (Boston: Unitarian Historical Society, 1933), p. 38.

64. WE_2-ER, March 8, 1796; JCB 1, March 5, 1795, July 8, 1799; RHE, Account Book, Oct. 13, 1797. See Henry S. Nourse, *History of the Town of Harvard, Mass., 1732–1893* (Harvard: Privately printed, 1894), pp. 221–50 (for the evangelical sects), 253–67 (for the Shakers). Stephen A. Marini studies the Harvard village within the larger field of Shaker, Free Baptist, and Universalist history in *Radical Sects of Revolutionary New England* (Cambridge: Harvard University Press, 1982), esp. pp. 90–96.

65. *Letters of MME,* p. 20; Nourse, *History of . . . Harvard,* pp. 213–16. Jean M. Humez documents the innovative thinking of early Shaker women in *Mother's First-Born Daughters: Early Shaker Writings on Women and Religion* (Bloomington: Indiana University Press, 1993).

66. WE_2-SamR, Jan. 22, 1806; JCB 1, May 9, June 2–10, 1799.

67. JCB 1, June 1, 1797; Oct. 3, 1799 on Thacher; Aug. 28, Sept. 22–23, Oct. 20, 1799.

68. MME-RHE, [1799] (226.969); WE_2-RHE, Sept. 20 and Oct. 11, 1799.

69. JCB 1, Feb. 17 and Oct. 3, 1800; MME-RHE, August 4, [1800] (226.970); *Letters of MME,* p. 26.

70. *History of Waterford,* pp. 81–83; JCB 1, Feb. 16–17, 1800; CCE, "Journal of a Tour to Maine and New Hampshire," July 24, 1830; WE_2-ER, Aug. 25, 1800.

71. *History of Waterford,* pp. 79–80; Thomas Hovey Gage, "Rev. Lincoln Ripley," in *Notes on the History of Waterford, Maine* (Worcester, Mass.: Privately printed, 1913), p. 40; WE_2-ER, Aug. 25, 1800. On settlers from Harvard and the neighboring towns of Worcester and Middlesex Counties, see *History of Waterford,* pp. 227–309 passim, and Lincoln Ripley, "A Description and History of Waterford, in the County of York," in *Notes on the History of Waterford,* pp. 9–11.

72. The earliest evidence of Mary's residence in Waterford is a merchant's receipt dated "Waterford, Nov. 1, 1800" (Houghton ms. 235.395). *Maternal Ancestors,* pp. 6–8; David Greene Haskins, "Ralph Haskins," in *Memorial Biographies of the New England Historic Genealogical Society* (Boston: NEHGS, 1880), 1: 465, 467–71.

73. *History of Waterford,* p. 256; WE_2-REH, Nov. 2, 1801.

74. WE_2-REH, Nov. 2, 1801.

75. Almanack, [Nov.] 8, [1804] (f. 1). Cf. Chambers-Schiller, *Liberty: A Better Husband,* ch. 6, on single women's experience of conflict between the claims of vocation and family, and Christine Battersby, *Gender and Genius: Toward a Feminist Aesthetics* (London: Women's Press, 1989), on the masculine tradition of "genius" from ancient Greek to Renaissance and Romantic usage.

Chapter Five

1. See Gillespie, " 'Clear Leadings of Providence,' " 197–99, 211.

2. Almanack, [Nov.] 22, [1804] (f. 1) and passim; *JMN* 3: 98; WE_2-ER, April 18, 1811; *JMN* 14: 283–84.

3. Contributions by Cornelia appear in the *Monthly Anthology* 1 (July 1804), 393–95,

and 2 (Feb. 1805), 72–73; by Constance in 1 (Aug. 1804), 453–54 and 456–57; 1 (Dec. 1804), 646–47; 2 (Mar. 1805), 140–41; and 2 (July 1805), 342–44. The identities of Constance and Cornelia are revealed in *Mary Wilder White*, pp. 185–91; in M. A. DeWolfe Howe, ed., *Journal of the Proceedings of the Anthology Society* (Boston: Boston Atheneum, 1910), pieces under both names are attributed to "Miss Emerson." *Letters of RWE* 4: 179.

4. Almanack [1802?] (f. 16). Dating this folder in 1801–2 is based on the dateline "Aug. 30 Sab.," which fits either 1801 or 1807; the earlier is more likely since internal references place the writing in Malden, and a letter of August 1807 is addressed from Concord. In addition, there is no sign of the reading—especially of Price and Butler—that preoccupied Mary starting in 1804.

5. *Letters of MME*, p. 389; Almanack, July 15, [1853], in MME-RWE, Jan. 6, [1857]; Almanack, Oct. 18, [1847] (f. 27); *Ames Astronomical Diary for 1767* (WE_1's copy is in the Emerson Family Papers); Almanack [Dec.?] 23, [1801?] (f. 16). Butler discusses the Ames Almanack in relation to astrological thinking in *Awash in a Sea of Faith*, p. 49; Lawrence Rosenwald analyzes the almanac-diary in "Three Early American Diarists" (Ph.D. diss., Columbia University, 1979), ch. 3.

6. Almanack, Aug., 1828, quoted in "MME 2," 228. Almanack entries mentioning communion are [Sept. 1801?] (f. 16), Nov. 1826 (f. 8), and [Oct. 12?], 1834 (f. 17).

7. Almanack, [1801?] (f. 16).

8. Almanack, [1801?] (f. 16).

9. Almanack, [1801?] (f. 16), [Dec. 16?], 1806 (f. 2), [1801?] (f. 16).

10. *Night Thoughts* 3, line 57; *Letters of MME*, p. 513.

11. On Young's sense of the imagination, see Stephen Cornford, introduction to *Night Thoughts* (Cambridge: Cambridge University Press, 1989), pp. 9–13; for the larger intellectual history of the term, James Engell, *The Creative Imagination: Enlightenment to Romanticism* (Cambridge: Harvard University Press, 1981), especially ch. 4 on Akenside and his English contemporaries. Almanack, [Oct.] 18, 1806.

12. Almanack, Nov. 5, 1804 (f. 1). See Daniel Walker Howe, *The Unitarian Conscience: Harvard Moral Philosophy, 1805–61* (Cambridge: Harvard University Press, 1971), ch. 2, on the theological background of Boston liberal thinking.

13. Almanack, Oct. 2, [1825?], in "MME 3," 134.

14. Almanack [1801?] (f. 16).

15. *Letters of MME*, pp. 23–24; MME-RHE, [1802?] (226.973).

16. *Mary Wilder White*, pp. 111, 122, 175. Cf. Kerber, *Women of the Republic*, pp. 224–27, on contemporary ridicule of Wollstonecraft, and *St. Leon*, ch. 4, for the fictional portrait of Marguerite de Damville.

17. *Mary Wilder White*, pp. 25–97 passim.

18. *Mary Wilder White*, pp. 97–98, 39, 106–8.

19. *Mary Wilder White*, pp. 120–21, 128–29.

20. *Mary Wilder White*, pp. 128–30, 158–59, 186; *Monthly Anthology* 1 (July 1804), 393–94. Cf. Nina Baym, introduction to Judith Sargent Murray, *The Gleaner* (Schenectady, N.Y.: Union College Press, 1992).

21. *Monthly Anthology* 1 (July 1804), 394–95.

22. *Monthly Anthology* 1 (Aug. 1804), 453–54.

23. *Monthly Anthology* 1 (Aug. 1804), 456–57.

24. *Monthly Anthology* 1 (Dec. 1804), 646.

25. *Monthly Anthology* 1 (Dec. 1804), 646. For Waterhouse's authorship, see Lawrence Buell, "Identification of Contributors to the *Monthly Anthology and Boston Review*, 1804–1811," *ESQ* 23 (1977), 101.

26. *Monthly Anthology* 2 (March 1805), 140–41; 2 (Feb. 1805), 72–73; *Letters of MME*, p. 30; *Monthly Anthology* 2 (July 1805), 342–44.

27. See Lewis P. Simpson, introduction to *The Federalist Literary Mind: Selections from the Monthly Anthology and Boston Review, 1803–1811* (Baton Rouge: Louisiana State University Press, 1962), for the history of the Anthology Society. "To Sylva," Almanack, n.d. (Tolman transcript, folder 46); Sylva's remarks on Wilberforce were in *Monthly Anthology* 2 (March 1805), 131.

28. *Monthly Anthology* 5 (July 1808), 367–72; 5 (Aug. 1808), 416–19; 3 (June 1806), 285–88 (cf. Simpson's notes on these pieces in *The Federalist Literary Mind*, pp. 200, 216); WE_2-MME, May 18, 1806. In *New England Literary Culture: From Revolution to Renaissance* (Cambridge: Cambridge University Press, 1986), Lawrence Buell sees the *Anthology*'s youngest contributors (Andrews Norton and William Tudor) as part of the future establishment that would edge toward Romanticism, but he discovers no actual "American Neoclassical foreshadowings of Romanticism" in the *Anthology*'s pages beyond the Pope-Gray debate (pp. 31–32, 91–92). I see MME as a remarkable case to support Buell's larger view that the pre-Romantic phase of New England literary history closely coincided with its neoclassical phase (p. 92).

29. Pieces addressed to women in the *Monthly Anthology* include 2 (May 1805), 257–60; and 2 (Sept. 1805), 446–49. Rowson is reviewed in 1 (Nov. 1804), 611–12; Vickery in 2 (May 1805), 267–68 (cf. Davidson, *Revolution and the Word*, pp. 31–32, on the identity of this originally anonymous writer); de Staël in 6 (March 1809), 159–60, and 6 (April 1809), 241; Bluestocking Club described in 3 (Nov. 1806), 579–80. Hannah Adams in Howe, ed., *Journal of the Proceedings of the Anthology Society*, p. 209.

30. See Howe, ed., *Journal of The Proceedings of the Anthology Society*, passim, e.g., for a review by Hannah Adams and a few poems by Sarah Wentworth Morton; Lowell's review is in *Monthly Anthology* 6 (April 1809), 261–63. A second real exception to male neoclassicism is Eliza Townsend's early poem "Another 'Castle in the Air' " in *Monthly Anthology* 7 (Nov. 1809), 319–20. On Townsend, cf. Buell, *New England Literary Culture*, pp. 92, 129–31. I know of no relationship between this younger woman and Mary's group.

31. Hannah Adams in *Maternal Ancestors*, pp. 59–60, and *Letters of MME*, pp. 88, 308–9; Hannah Sawyer in *Letters of MME*, pp. 35–36, and Almanack, Nov. 1, 1806 (f. 2) (cf. Linda Mainiero, ed., *American Women Writers* [New York: Ungar, 1979–82], 2: 534–36, on the later career of Hannah Farnham Sawyer Lee); Ann Bromfield in *Mary Wilder White*, p. 99, *Letters of MME*, p. 580, and Almanack, Nov. 1, 1806 (f. 2).

32. *Mary Wilder White*, pp. 165, 166–68, 249, 244–45. Van Schalkwyck's excerpts from Mary's writings, along with their ms. correspondence, are in the Henry Wilder Foote Papers, A-H.

33. *Mary Wilder White*, pp. 209, 203; Elizabeth Palmer Peabody, *Reminiscences of Dr. Channing* (Boston: Roberts Brothers, 1880), pp. 86, 93; Eliza S. M. Quincy, *Memoir* (Boston: John Wilson and Son, 1861), pp. 122–23; Josiah P. Quincy, "Letters of Miss Anna Cabot Lowell," *MHS Proceedings* 18 (1904), 302; Almanack, Jan. 8, 1811 (f. 6). None of Lowell's manuscripts survive.

34. *Letters of MME*, pp. 41, 29; [Anne Grant], *Letters from the Mountains: Being the Real Correspondence of a Lady, Between the Years 1773 and 1803*, 2 vols. (Boston: Privately printed, 1809), passim; MWS-MME, Aug. 27, 1809 (Henry Wilder Foote Papers, A-H); *Mary Wilder White*, pp. 127, 138–39, 248, 175.

35. *Mary Wilder White*, pp. 100, 208–9, 211–12; Quincy, "Letters of Miss Anna Cabot Lowell," p. 310.

36. *Letters of MME*, p. 35; *Mary Wilder White*, p. 256; Almanack, Nov. 1, 1806 (f. 2), Feb. 13–March 27, 1807 (f. 3).

37. Almanack, Nov. 1, 1806 (f. 2); *Mary Wilder White*, pp. 242–55.

38. Almanack, Jan. 20, 1807; Feb. 13, 1807 (f. 3).

39. *Letters of MME*, p. 376; MME-CCE, Aug. 20, 1829.

40. Almanack, [June 16,] 17, 18, 1806 (f. 2).

41. WE_2-RHE, June 16, 1806; cf. Rusk, pp. 18, 20.

42. JCB 1, April 9, 1802 and passim; WE_2, *Piety and Arms: Artillery Election Sermon* (Boston: Manning and Loring, 1799), pp. 7–8; *Discourse Delivered Before the Roxbury Charitable Society Sept. 15, 1800* (Boston: Samuel Hall, 1800); *Discourse Delivered Before . . . the Boston Female Asylum, Sept. 20, 1805* (Boston: Russell and Cutler, 1805). *Maternal Ancestors*, pp. 59–60; WE_2 and RHE, "Receipts," p. 27.

43. *Letters of RWE* 4: 179; WE_2-$PBER_2$, May 14, 1807; WE_2-RHE, Aug. 12, 1796; WE_2-JCE, Dec. 13, 1805; WE_2-RHE, Mar. 4, 1799.

44. *Monthly Anthology* 1: i–iii (cf. Simpson, *Federalist Literary Mind*, pp. 139–40); WE_2-$PBER_1$, Jan. 11, 1810.

45. WE_2-RHE, May 25, 1805; WE_2-JCE, Oct. 3, 1805; May 17, 1806; *Letters of RWE* 4: 179.

46. *Catalogue of Books Comprising the Library of the Late William Emerson*; JCB 2, Oct. 21, 1800; *Monthly Anthology* 2 (May 1805), 257–60; RHE-$PBER_2$, Nov. 16, 1805; April 20, 1806; WE_2-RHE, Sept. 21 and Sept. 26, 1806. On the Locke-influenced custom of cold bathing as part of child rearing, see Randolph Trumbach, *The Rise of the Egalitarian Family: Aristocratic Kinship and Domestic Relations in Eighteenth-century England* (New York: Academic Press, 1978), p. 191.

47. Charles Lowell quoted in William B. Sprague, *Annals of the American Unitarian Pulpit* (New York: Robert Carter and Brothers, 1865), p. 244; Quincy in "Father," pp. 4–5; JCB 2, Jan. 1, 1800; Mar. 23, 1802; Sept. 6, 1803.

48. *Letters of MME*, p. 526; WE_2-MME, Nov. 11, 1807.

49. JCB 2, June 1, 1803; WE_2, *Right Hand of Fellowship for Joseph S. Buckminster Jan. 30, 1805* (Boston: Privately printed, 1805); WE_2-MME, May 18, 1806; *Letters of MME*, pp. 402, 523.

50. *Mary Wilder White*, pp. 200, 218.

51. C. Conrad Wright, *The Beginnings of Unitarianism* (Boston: Starr King Press, 1955), pp. 274–80; *Monthly Anthology* 2 (March 1805), 152ff. It is uncertain whether William wrote or only edited this unsigned review of Morse; his "Commonplace Book 2," however, is more than half drafts of letters and articles for the *Anthology*, including several expressing strong antagonism for Morse.

52. Constance, "To the Editor of the Monthly Anthology," *Monthly Anthology* 2 (March 1805), 141.

53. As C. C. Wright comments (*The Beginnings of Unitarianism*, p. 200), "There was no inevitable connection between Arminianism and anti-Trinitarianism." In the sermons and theological texts that he has studied, Arminianism was the crucial dividing issue from the First Awakening on, with the nature of God and Christ a secondary issue becoming focal only at the time of the Unitarian-Calvinist controversy. Mary's shift from Calvinist background to Arianism is surely less normative but hardly idiosyncratic.

54. Almanack, [1847] (f. 27). No Almanacks or letters survive to record the encounter with Price that clearly had gone on prior to July 1804. In 1827 (f. 9), she devoted ten pages of writing to a scrutiny of Price's *Four Dissertations*, calling him there the familiar names she characteristically gave her first intellectual mentors, "Father Price," "old friend," "venerated Author."

55. *Letters of MME*, pp. 523–24, 526; JCB 1, May 15, 1804 (cf. April 14, 1795 and Nov. 8, 1797).

56. Almanack, [1801?] (f. 16); [Nov.?] 25, 1806 (f. 2); [Dec.?] 1806 (f. 2); [1801?] (f. 16).

57. Almanack, [1801?] (f. 16); Dec. [1]8, 1806 (f. 2); Nov. 24, 1806 (f. 2). On Calvinist theories of atonement, see Haroutunian, *Piety vs. Moralism* ch. 7. Mary recorded little reading in Hopkinsian Calvinism in this period, though she was clearly aware of it; in 1809 she declared herself "altogether removed from condemning the Calvinist who reaches the pinnacle of Hopkinsianism. It is *possible* they may have discovered the *incognita* of man's condition" (1809, f. 4). Such an effort at sympathy it reveals her distance from contemporary Calvinism.

58. Almanack, [Oct.] 19, 1806 (f. 2); [Dec.] 26, 1806 (f. 2). Cf. Jerry Wayne Brown, *The Rise of Biblical Criticism in America, 1800–1870: The New England Scholars* (Middletown, Conn.: Wesleyan University Press, 1969), ch. 1 on Buckminster's early investigation of Lowth and Michaelis, before as well as after his trip to Europe. His articles appeared in *Monthly Anthology* 5 (Jan. 1808), 18–21; 10 (Feb. 1810), 107–14; and 10 (June 1811), 103–21.

59. WE_2-$PBER_1$, March 19, 1805; WE_2-MME, April 10, 1806.

60. JCB 2, July 22, Sept. 11, 1800; WE_2, *Piety and Arms*, pp. 17, 7, 18; *An Oration Pronounced July 5, 1802 at the Request of the Inhabitants of Boston, in Commemoration of the Anniversary of American Independence* (Boston: Manning and Loring, 1802), pp. 13, 6, 14, 16, 17. In his "Discourse Delivered at Harvard, July 4, 1794," on the other hand, William preached from a text that his father had loved—"Be ye not entangled again with the yoke of bondage"—and held up the Republic of France as a noble exception to Europe's absolute monarchies (Boston: Apollo Press, 1794). Ruth Bloch discusses this shift from Francophilia to Francophobia on the larger scale in American clerical thinking of the 1790s in *Visionary Republic: Millennial Themes in American Thought, 1756–1800* (Cambridge: Cambridge University Press, 1985), ch. 9.

61. Cabot, *Memoir of RWE*, 1: 7; Moore and Day, *Descendants of Richard Austin*, pp. 38–42; RWE, "Mary Moody Emerson" (ms.), p. 69.

62. *Letters of MME*, p. 175; *Literary Papers of William Austin*, ed. James W. Austin (Boston: Little, Brown, 1870); Peter Austin, *William Austin: The Creator of Peter Rugg* (Boston: Marshall Jones, 1925), pp. 39–43, 62–69.

63. Harold and James Kirker, *Bulfinch's Boston, 1787–1817* (New York: Oxford University Press, 1964), pp. 181–83; Moore and Day, *Descendants of Richard Austin*, pp. 41–42; WE_2, *Sermon on the Death of Mr. Charles Austin* (Boston: Emerald Press, 1806), pp. 13–16, 18–19, 5.

64. Daniel Ripley's duel is recounted in his cousin John Hay Farnham's letter to Mary B. Farnham, March 29, 1810 (Farnham Family Papers, MHS). WE_2-ER, June 18, 1808; WE_2-MME, Dec. 24, 1807.

65. The declining health of these three family members is variously described, for instance, in WE_2-RHE, Sept. 21 and 26, 1806; *Mary Wilder White*, pp. 237; and *Letters of MME*, pp. 37–38. WE_2-$PBER_2$, April 25, 1807; Almanack, May 2, 1807 (f. 3).

66. *Maternal Ancestors*, p. 45; "Father," p. 5; Cabot, *Memoir of RWE*, 1: 7.

67. ASG-Lucius M. Sargent, Jan. 15, 1852 (Gage Family Additional Papers, b1 f2, AAS), SamR and MME quoted in Mabel C. Gage, "The Story of Anne Sargent Gage" (Gage Family Additional Papers, AAS).

68. Joseph S. Buckminster, *Sermon at the Internment of the Rev. William Emerson* (Boston: Joseph T. Buckingham, 1811), p. 8; *Letters of MME*, p. 402; WE_2, *Historical Sketch of the First Church in Boston*, p. 245; "Father," pp. 6, 9 (cf. WE_2-MME, April 20, 1807).

69. *Letters of MME*, pp. 41–44 ; cf. MWW–MME, Nov. 12, 1805 (Henry Wilder Foote

Papers, A-H), and *Mary Wilder White*, pp. 97, 152, 210, and 269 on the Moravian plan. WE_2-MME, Oct. 23, 1809.

70. *Letters of MME*, p. 54; WE_2-RHE, Oct. 10, 1805; *History of Waterford*, pp. 200, 106, 124, 133, 112–14, 125–28; Oxford County Registry of Deeds, Box 2, p. 427; Ronald F. Banks, *Maine Becomes a State: The Movement to Separate Maine from Massachusetts* (Middletown, Conn.: Wesleyan University Press, 1970), pp. 6–10.

71. *Letters of MME*, pp. 58, 60; ASG–Lucius M. Sargent, Jan. 15, 1852 (Gage Family Additional Papers, b1 f2, AAS); MME-ASG, [April] 24, 1853 (Gage Family Additional Papers, b2 f2, AAS).

72. WE_2-MME, Dec. 24, 1807; WE_2-ER, Oct. 22, 1805 (cf. *History of Waterford*, pp. 93–100); WE_2-LR, Feb. 4, 1811; Almanack, Dec. 16, 1810 (f. 6). William's library included *Freedom of the Will*, but neither Mary nor William recorded any reading of it prior to 1810 (*Catalogue of Books*).

73. Almanack, Dec. 16, 1810 (f. 6).

74. Almanack, Jan. 4, 6, 1811 (f. 6).

75. *Historical Sketch of the First Church in Boston*, pp. 181, 187–91.

76. *Historical Sketch of the First Church in Boston*, pp. 191, 44, 50–52, 59. I am indebted to Amy Lang's analysis of William Emerson in *Prophetic Woman*, pp. 111–16.

77. *Letters of MME*, p. 54.

78. *Letters of MME*, pp. 54–55.

79. WE_2-MME, Feb. 26, 1811; WE_2-ER, April 18, 1811; WE_2-RHE, April 16, 1811; *Mary Wilder White*, p. 372.

80. WE_2-RHE, April 16, 1811; *Mary Wilder White*, p. 373.

81. WE_2-$PBER_1$, July 22, 1803; Buckminster, *Sermon at the Internment of the Rev. William Emerson*, p. 8n.

82. *Letters of MME*, pp. 73–74, 526.

83. *Mary Wilder White*, pp. 366–69, 375–78.

84. *Mary Wilder White*, pp. 379–81, 385–88.

Chapter Six

1. *Letters of MME*, p. 166.

2. RHE-CCE, Feb. 12, 1833; RHE-$PBER_2$, June 18, 1811; $PBER_2$-RHE, July 6, 1811; RBE [$PBER_2$]-RHE, Aug. 23, 1811; *Letters of MME*, p. 61.

3. *Letters of MME*, p. 61; "Tribute to MME," p. 56.

4. MME-AB, Jan. 29, 1811 (Gage Family Additional Papers, b2 f2, AAS). No letters between the Farnhams and MME have been recovered, but allusions in other correspondence make clear that close relations were maintained.

5. SAB–Abba Allyn [Winter 1811-12?]; SABR–George Simmons, Oct. 7, 1844; SAB-MME [c. 1814] (Sarah Alden Bradford Ripley Papers, Schlesinger). Most of SAB's letters are undated, so are assigned conjectural dates according to internal content. Joan Goodwin has generously shared the results of her research on Sarah Alden Bradford Ripley in this respect and others.

6. *Letters of MME*, p. 22.

7. JCB 1, Jan. 13, 1800; *Works* 10: 432; MME–Mary Elizabeth White, April 29, 1809 (Henry Wilder Foote Papers, A-H).

8. *Letters of MME*, p. 36.

9. RHE-$PBER_2$, Nov. 16, 1805; *Maternal Ancestors*, p. 64; MME-RHE, Dec. 30, [1805].

10. RHE, Diary, July 28, 1811; RHE-MME, Aug. 13, 1811; RHE-PBER$_2$, Jan. 27, 1812.

11. RHE-MME, Aug. 13, 1811; MME-WE$_3$, July 7, 1812 (Emerson Family Papers, MHS); *Letters of MME*, p. 66.

12. Ruth's recipe ("Receipts," n.p.) is as follows: "1 lb. Flour ¾ Sugar ¾ Butter 1 lb. Currants 7 eggs a piece of Sal Eratis as large as a nutmeg ½ oz. Mace ½ oz. Nutmeg 1 teacup Brandy." She also lists a frosting that may be like Mary's "white encrustation": "Whites 6 eggs 1 spoonful vinegar 1 Starch stir in loaf sugar till sufficiently thick—then spread over cake still warm from oven with a knife—wait a few minutes and do it over again." To modern taste, the resulting cake is inedibly dense. MME-WE$_3$, July 7, 1812 (Emerson Family Papers, MHS); *Letters of MME*, p. 65.

13. *Letters of RWE* 4: 179.

14. William Emerson Inventory, List of Debts (Suffolk Probate no. 23771); Rusk, p. 30.

15. William Emerson, Evidence . . . of Sale of Real Estate (Suffolk Probate no. 23771); *Catalogue of Books*; RHE, Notebook; Almanack, [Feb.] 23, 25, [1813] (f. 37).

16. *Letters of MME*, pp. 64, 69–70; Almanack, Nov. 1, 11, [1812]; Jan. 2, [Feb] 23, [1813] (f. 37)

17. Almanack, March 2–3, [1813] (f. 37); *Letters of MME*, pp. 71–75; MME-RHE, May 19, June 21, 1813.

18. MME-RHE, June 21, July 6, [1812] (226.989); *Letters of MME*, pp. 74, 71.

19. RHE-MME, June 11, 1813; *Letters of MME*, p. 74; MME-RHE, May 19, 1813.

20. RHE-MME, July 20, 1813; MME-RHE, Aug. 8, [1813] (226.990).

21. RHE-MME, Oct. 23, [1813]; MME-RHE, Aug. 8, [1813]; MME-RHE, Aug. 28, 29, [1813] (226.991); Oxford County Registry of Deeds no. 2/427 (Nov. 21, 1807); MME-RHE, July 10, 1810; David Greene Haskins, "Ralph Haskins," in *Memorial Biographies of the New England Historic and Genealogical Society* (Boston: NEHGS, 1880), 1:473–74.

22. MME-RHE, Aug. 28, 29, [1813]; Middlesex Registry of Deeds nos. 179/135, 201/204, 204/477; ER-RHE, Aug. 15, 1813; MME-RHE, July 10, 1810; Oxford County Registry of Deeds no. 10/229; MME-ASG, March 2, 1856 (Gage Family Additional Papers, b2 f2, AAS).

23. *Letters of MME*, p. 82n., for an early (Sept. 1814) use of the name "Elm Vale." Hoar quoted in *Mary Wilder White*, p. 116. My description of the landscape incorporates several by members of the family (*Works* 10: 410; CCE-MME, Jan. 23, 1825; MME-EBE, July 3, [1832] [Middlebury]; MME-EH, Aug. 16, 1836; *Letters of ETE* 1: 186ff.) and is also based on observation under the knowledgeable guidance of Margaret Sawyer of Waterford. The house at Elm Vale is no longer standing, but the cemetery bears that name.

24. *Letters of MME*, p. 172; CCE-MME, Oct. 27, 1831.

25. MME-RHE, [1814?] (226.995); *Letters of MME*, p. 175.

26. RHE-PBER$_2$, Jan. 27, 1814; PBER$_2$-RHE, July 30, 1814; *Letters of MME*, p. 83; PBER$_2$-RHE, May 17, 1814; "Father," p. 2.

27. Moncure Daniel Conway, *Emerson at Home and Abroad* (Boston: James Osgood, 1882), pp. 41, 43; *Letters of MME*, p. 82; MME-RHE, [1814?] (226.1000).

28. *JMN* 10: 168; *Letters of MME*, p. 93.

29. *JMN* 8: 391, 5: 323; prayer in "MME 3," 162; MME-RHE, Jan. 3, 1814; *Letters of MME*, pp. 79, 68.

30. Almanack, [March 1813?] and passim (f. 37); *Letters of MME*, pp. 82n., 333; Almanack, [Feb.] 14, [1815] (f. 35).

31. *JMN* 5: 323; Almanack, [June] 28, [1814] (f. 35); Rusk, p. 55.

32. *Letters of RWE* 7: 103, 1: 5; *JMN* 16: 80, 13: 413, 7: 443; "Tribute to MME," p. 56.

33. MME-ASG, Jan. 13, 1822 (Gage Family Additional Papers, b2 f2, AAS); MME-RHE, Jan. 9, [1816]; (226.1002); *Letters of RWE* 7: 102–4.

34. *Letters of RWE* 1: 45, 82 (cf. 1: 66 and EBE-RWE, Sept. 19, 1817); "Father," p. 9; EBE-MME, March 11, 1831.

35. "Father," pp. 9, 13; WE_3-RHE, Aug. 28, 1825 (Emerson Family Papers, MHS); MME-RHE, [1814?] (226.1000); CCE-RWE, Feb. 2, 1832; MME-RHE, Dec. 13, [1818] (226.1009); EBE-MME, Dec. 12, 1817; EBE-RHE, April 1819.

36. *Letters of MME*, p. 193; *JMN* 10: 385; *Works* 10: 432; MME-EBE, Jan. 1, 1818; RHE, "Precepts."

37. *Letters of RWE* 5: 149; $PBER_2$-RHE, July 6, 1811; June 30, 1816; RBE [$PBER_2$]-WE_3, Jan. 19, 1813; RHE-$PBER_2$, July 6, 1815; Oct. 5, 1815; June 18, 1816; July 12, 1816.

38. RHE, Diary, May 7, 1795; *Letters of RWE* 7: 173. Editor Eleanor M. Tilton states (173n.), "Dr. Haskins is clearly a patient and probably a collateral relation . . . , but cannot be identified." I conclude that the reference is to Ruth's brother John, who graduated from Harvard College in 1781 and practiced medicine, if only because the Haskins family letters and memoir are silent about him amidst specific news of all other siblings. One exception is Elizabeth Haskins's unelaborated note of July 10, 1798, to Ruth, "John must have painful . . . recollections upon his conduct" (226.3600). See also *Maternal Ancestors*, p. 147.

39. RBE-EBE, Jan. 17, 1820.

40. RHE-$PBER_2$, Jan. 27, 1814; *Letters of MME*, pp. 114–15.

41. EBE-MME, April 5, 1834; "Father," p. 9; CCE-RHE, Jan. 2, 1828; SABR-MME, [1814?] (Sarah Alden Bradford Ripley Papers, Schlesinger); MME-CCE, Jan. 1, 1818; CCE-MME, April 14, 1822.

42. SABR-MME, Nov. 9, 1814 (Sarah Alden Bradford Ripley Papers, Schlesinger).

43. MME-RHE, [1815?] (226.1001); *Letters of MME*, pp. 289, 224; MME-CCE, May 26, 1818.

44. SAB-MME, [1814], 1816 (Sarah Alden Bradford Ripley Papers, Schlesinger); MME-CCE, March 25, [1817?] (226.633).

45. RHE-MME, Jan. 20, 1818; March 12, 1818; MME-CCE, May 26, 1818; MME-RHE, March 31, [1817] (226.1004).

46. *Letters of MME*, pp. 104, 89–90; MME-RHE, Feb. 14, [1819] (226.1010); Almanack, Feb. 1, 1815 (f. 35); MME-RHE, Mar. 1, Mar. 9, [1816] (226.1005, 1006).

47. Cameron, "The Rev. R. Waldo Emerson and Aunt Mary's Books," 6–7; Almanack, [1814?] (f. 46), March 1815 (f. 35); *Letters of MME*, p. 87. Instances of Mary asking to have de Staël's books bought or sent include *Letters of MME*, pp. 84, 102, 117, 121. Cf. *Germany*, trans. from French, 2 vols. (Boston: Houghton Mifflin, 1859), 2: 118 on "sentiment," 2: 360 on "enthusiasm."

48. Almanack, [1815], (f. 35); *Letters of MME*, pp. 376, 484 (cf. 320); *The Excursion* 2, lines 331–33, 341–42, and 4, lines 34–42.

49. MME-WE_3, Nov. 1, [1819] (226.1066); *Letters of MME*, p. 98.

50. AB-$PBER_2$, July 5, 1817; Sept. 13, 1819 (Gage Family Additional Papers, b1 f1, AAS); *Letters of MME*, pp. 108, 84, 89.

51. *Letters of MME*, pp. 567, 61–63, 83–84; MME-AB, Oct. 18, 1812; June 28, [1814] (Gage Family Additional Papers, b2 f2, AAS).

52. MME-AB, Sept. 3, 1814 (Gage Family Additional Papers, b2 f2, AAS).

53. MME-AB, Dec. 25, [1816]; MME-AB [c. 1815] (Gage Family Additional Papers, b2 f2, AAS); *Letters of MME*, pp. 137, 96.

54. Mabel C. Gage, "The Story of Anne Sargent Gage" (Gage Family Additional Papers, AAS); *Letters of MME*, p. 137.

55. MME-AB, Dec. 25, [1816]; AB-$PBER_2$, July 5, 1817; Sept. 13, 1819 (Gage Family Additional Papers, b2 f2, AAS); Ralph Emerson, *Life of Joseph Emerson*, pp. 119, 140; *Letters of MME*, p. 134.

56. ASG, note in "Poems"; Thomas Hovey Gage, "Sketch" (Gage Family Additional Papers, b2 f2, AAS); MME-ASG, [1832?] (Gage Family Additional Papers, b2 f2, AAS).

57. *Letters of MME*, pp. 82, 84n.; cf. Sylvia Harcstark Myers, *The Bluestocking Circle* (Oxford: Oxford University Press, 1990), p. 293.

58. SAB-MME [May 1813] (Sarah Alden Bradford Ripley Papers, Schlesinger); *Letters of MME*, p. 108. See Joan Goodwin, "Sarah Alden Ripley, Another Concord Botanist," *The Concord Saunterer* 1 (Fall 1993), 77–86.

59. SAB-MME, [c. 1812] (Sarah Alden Bradford Ripley Papers, Schlesinger); *Letters of MME*, p. 75; MME-SAB, [1813?] (226.1261); SAB-MME, [1813?] (Sarah Alden Bradford Ripley Papers, Schlesinger).

60. SAB-MME, [1814?] (Sarah Alden Bradford Ripley Papers, Schlesinger) ; *Letters of MME*, pp. 86, 83; SAB-MME, [Jan. 1814?] (Sarah Alden Bradford Ripley Papers, Schlesinger).

61. SAB-MME, Sept. 5, [1816] (Sarah Alden Bradford Ripley Papers, Schlesinger).

62. SAB-MME, Sept. 5, [1816], Aug. 7, [1818] (Sarah Alden Bradford Ripley Papers, Schlesinger). Cf. Judith Fetterley on "cacoethes scribendi" in *Provisions: A Reader from Nineteenth-Century American Women* (Bloomington: Indiana University Press, 1985), p. 45.

63. SAB-MME, [Spring 1814] (Sarah Alden Bradford Ripley Papers, Schlesinger); *Letters of MME*, p. 78; SAB-MME, [Summer 1817] (Sarah Alden Bradford Ripley Papers, Schlesinger). Carroll Smith-Rosenberg includes the friendship of Mary and Sarah in "The Female World of Love and Ritual," *Disorderly Conduct: Visions of Gender in Victorian America* (New York: Knopf, 1985), pp. 72–73, rightly surmising the emotional and even "conspiratorial" quality of their messages to each other. See also Lillian Faderman, *Surpassing the Love of Men: Romantic Friendship and Love Between Women from the Renaissance to the Present* (New York: William Morrow, 1981), on the idealization of spiritual love and suppressed sexual instinct in the tradition of women's friendship (pp. 65–66, 80, 122).

64. SAB–George Simmons, Oct. 7, 1844 (Sarah Alden Bradford Ripley Papers, Schlesinger); MME-SAB, [1816?] (226.1262); SAB-MME, [1813?] (Sarah Alden Bradford Ripley Papers, Schlesinger); *Letters of MME*, pp. 87, 109.

65. *Letters of MME*, p. 100; SAB-MME, May 18, [1818] (Sarah Alden Bradford Ripley Papers, Schlesinger); MME-SAB, July 18, 1817; Nov. 4 and 20, [1817] (226.815); *Letters of MME*, pp. 101–2.

66. SAB-MME, May 11, [1818] (Sarah Alden Bradford Ripley Papers, Schlesinger); *Letters of MME*, pp. 111, 61. For the identification of James Walker, see Joan Goodwin, "Self-Culture and Skepticism: The Unitarian Odyssey of Sarah Alden Bradford Ripley," *Proceedings of the Unitarian Universalist Historical Society* 22 (1990–91), 39.

67. SAB-MME, June 12 [1818] (Sarah Alden Bradford Ripley Papers, Schlesinger); MME-SAB, [1816?] (226.1262); MME-RHE [1814?] (226.1000); *Letters of MME*, p. 99; SarR-MME, Feb. 1818 (Ames Papers, transcript owned by Joan Goodwin). See also *Letters of MME*, p. 117n., on the dating of Sarah's letter announcing her engagement.

68. *Letters of MME*, p. 116.

69. Almanack, [March] 12, [April] 22, 23, 27, [1817] (f. 7).

70. Almanack, [April] 27, [1817] (f. 7); SAB-MME, Aug. 7, [1818] (Sarah Alden Bradford Ripley Papers, Schlesinger); Almanack, [Aug., 1817], [Jan.?, 1818], [Oct.? 1817] (f. 7). Cf. *Letters of MME*, pp. 107–10 for letters to Sarah reflecting her reading in Stewart. The passages that Mary quotes from Leibniz, Malebranche, and Descartes are in *Dissertation Second*, originally published in 1815 and contained in *The Collected Works of Dugald Stewart*, ed. Sir William Hamilton (Edinburgh: Thomas Constable, 1854), 1: 147–48, 154, 117.

71. *Letters of MME*, p. 110; Stewart, *Dissertation Second*, 1: 85–87.

72. Almanack, [Oct.? 1817] (f. 7).

73. SAB-MME, Aug. 7, [1818] (Sarah Alden Bradford Ripley Papers, Schlesinger).

Chapter Seven

1. *Works* 10: 326, 329.

2. *Works* 10: 330–36; Almanack, April 23, [1817] (f. 7); *Letters of MME*, pp. 134, 141–42, 140.

3. *JMN* 1: 4–5; for the Emerson household in 1820, cf. *Letters of RWE* 1: 89–91 and *Letters of MME*, p. 134.

4. *Letters of MME*, pp. 139–40; "The Present State of Ethical Philosophy," reprinted in Kenneth W. Cameron, *Transcendental Climate* (Hartford, Conn.: Transcendental Books, 1963), 1: 11–20; *JMN* 1: 334–35, 12. The 1968 reprinting of *JMN* corrects its earlier attribution of Mary's letter to Waldo and notes Eleanor Tilton's recognition of the original letter text (1: 335n.). Cf. Barish, *Emerson*, pp. 99–101.

5. Almanack, [Oct.?] 17 and 29, 1817 (f. 7); Almanack, 1821 ("MME 4," 165–66); note to RWE in MME-RHE, Aug. 7, [1817?] (226.1015).

6. MME-SABR, [April 9, 1819?]; *Letters of MME*, p. 136; MME-RHE, [Aug. 17, 1820] (226.1007); Almanack, 1821 ("MME 4," 164); *Letters of MME*, p. 140.

7. *Letters of MME*, p. 104; *JMN* 1: 333; *Letters of RWE* 1: 54.

8. *Letters of MME*, pp. 112–13; cf. *JMN* 1: 333–34.

9. *Letters of MME*, p. 113.

10. *Letters of MME*, pp. 136, 139, 143.

11. *Letters of MME*, pp. 139, 143–44; *Letters of RWE* 1: 75. Waldo's two letters to Mary have not survived.

12. *Letters of MME*, pp. 139, 144, 143. Price derived from his explicitly anti-Lockean epistemology the "important corollary . . . that morality is *eternal and immutable*" (*Review of the Principal Questions in Morals*, ed. D. Daiches Raphael [Oxford: Oxford University Press, 1948], p. 50).

13. Rusk, pp. 81–82, on Frisbie and the Harvard curriculum; Cameron, *Transcendental Climate* 1: 14–16, 19 for Waldo's text, 1: 154–55, 165–66 on Waldo's knowledge of Price and Cudworth. For the Platonist strain in New England liberal thought, see also Howe, "The Cambridge Platonists of Old England and the Cambridge Platonists of New England," 87–121.

14. Cameron, *Transcendental Climate* 1: 12; cf. *Letters of MME*, p. 139.

15. *Letters of MME*, p. 139; Cameron, *Transcendental Climate* 1: 17–18. Cf. Barish, *Emerson*, ch. 5, for a reading of Waldo's essay that includes the borrowing from Mary and de Staël, but minimizes the importance of both in favor of Waldo's innovative Humian skepticism.

16. *Letters of RWE* 1: 100–103; MME-RHE, Sept. 14, [1821] (226.1027). Cf. Cameron, "Indian Superstition," in *Emerson Society Quarterly* 32 (1963), pt. 1, esp. pp. 49–54, and "Sources for Emerson's Early Orientalism," in *Young Emerson's Transcendental Vision* (Hartford: Transcendental Books, 1971), 578–83, for background on RWE's thinking about Asian mythology at this time.

17. MME-ASG, Jan. 13, 1822 (AAS); quotations in *JMN* 1: 377 (Clarke) and 1: 202 (Leibniz); Almanack, Jan. 19, 1822 ("MME 4," 198).

18. *Letters of MME*, pp. 152, 157.

19. *Letters of RWE* 1: 116n.; *JMN* 2: 373–76, 1: 153–54.

20. *Letters of MME*, pp. 155–57.

21. *Letters of MME*, pp. 157–59.

22. MME-RWE, [1821?] (226.822); *Letters of RWE* 1: 138.

23. *JMN* 1: 49.

24. *JMN* 1: 266–68, 284–86, 302–3, 337–39. Cf. Barish, *Emerson*, ch. 4, for an interpretation of these romances, especially "The Magician," in relation to Waldo's unresolved preoccupation with his father's death.

25. *Letters of RWE* 1: 104–5; *Letters of MME*, pp. 147–48.

26. *JMN* 1: 99–100, 115.

27. *JMN* 1: 138; *Letters of RWE* 1: 114–15.

28. MME-RWE, [June] 14, [1822] (226.827); cf. *JMN* 1: 199–200.

29. *Letters of RWE* 1: 133.

30. Almanack, June, Aug. 10, 1822 ("MME 4," 117–18, 150–51).

31. *Letters of MME*, pp. 170–71.

32. *Letters of MME*, p. 171. MME's church membership is relisted as of Jan. 1, 1815, the only Concord list surviving from her lifetime (Concord First Parish Records). Waterford lists do not include her.

33. Robinson, *The Unitarians and the Universalists*, ch. 3; Goodwin, "Self-Culture and Skepticism," p. 39; *Ipswich Emersons*, pp. 219–21, on Joseph and Ralph Emerson. Of all the descendants of Joseph and Mary Emerson of Malden, only those settled in Newburyport and Concord—Bulkeley Emerson's children and some of William Emerson's—definitely became Unitarians.

34. Almanack, Jan. 13, 1822 ("MME 4," 197); *Letters of MME*, pp. 136, 151; MME-RWE, [May] 13, [1824] (226.826).

35. *Letters of MME*, pp. 170, 172 (cf. 124, 274.)

36. *History of Waterford*, pp. 144–48, 92–93, 153.

37. ASG-PBER$_2$, [1823] (Gage Family Additional Papers, b1 f1, AAS); Thomas Hovey Gage, "Rev. Lincoln Ripley," pp. 40–41; Waterford Congregational Church Records; SarR-MME, Dec. 4, 1820 (226.3994); CCE, "Journal of a Tour to Maine and N.H.," [July 24], 1830.

38. SABR-MME, Nov. 19, 1823 (Sarah Alden Bradford Ripley Papers, Schlesinger); MME-RWE, Oct. 18, [1824]; MME-RWE and CCE, n.d. [Fall? 1824] (226.837); *Letters of RWE* 1: 160. Cf. Joan W. Goodwin, *An American Scholar: Sarah Alden Bradford Ripley* (Boston: Northeastern University Press, forthcoming 1998), ch. 2 on Sarah's growing family and reputation as an intellectual.

39. MME-WE$_3$, May 27, 1823.

40. Almanack, April 20, 23, 1817 (f. 7); MME-SABR, Nov. 4 and 20, 1817; *Letters of MME*, pp. 176–77. Cf. Barbara Packer on Waldo and William's thinking about the Bible in "Origin and Authority: Emerson and the Higher Criticism," in *Reconstructing American Literary History*, ed. Sacvan Bercovitch (Cambridge: Harvard University Press, 1986), pp. 67–92.

41. *Letters of RWE* 1: 137–38; *JMN* 2: 161.

42. *Letters of MME*, pp. 111, 177, 179. Waldo quoted Stewart on Clarke's proofs in *JMN* 1: 377; cf. Clarke, *A Demonstration of the Being and Attributes of God*, in *Works*, 2: 521–77.

43. *Letters of MME*, pp. 176–77 (cf. *JMN* 2: 376).

44. *Letters of MME*, p. 178.

45. *Letters of MME*, p. 182.

46. *Letters of MME*, p. 182; cf. *JMN* 2: 380–82 and *Works* 6: 155–56. See also my article "The Purity of Puritanism: Transcendentalist Readings of Milton," *Studies in Romanticism* 17 (1978), 139, which emphasizes this conflation of Milton and Satan but mistakes the writing as Waldo's rather than Mary's.

47. *JMN* 1: 271–72, 281–82, 165–67; *Letters of RWE* 1: 55, 7: 130; Almanack, 1819 ("MME 4," 113); *Letters of MME*, pp. 143, 191–92; *Works* 10: 403.

48. *Letters of RWE* 7: 117 and 117n.; *JMN* 2: 387; *Letters of MME*, p. 379; "MME 3," 266. Mary's 1821 Almanack includes several short quotations from Plato (f. 40). Cf. Richardson, *Emerson*, pp. 65–66, on stages in RWE's understanding of Plato.

49. *JMN* 2: 246–49, 250–52.

50. *Letters of MME*, pp. 185–86.

51. *Letters of MME*, pp. 187–88.

52. *Letters of RWE* 1: 160.

53. *JMN* 2: 237–38; Rusk, pp. 103–4; *Letters of RWE* 7: 125.

54. *Letters of RWE* 7: 125.

55. *Letters of MME*, pp. 182–83; Almanack, [May] 1824 (f. 34).

56. *Letters of MME*, pp. 192–94.

57. *Letters of MME*, pp. 180, 186; Almanack, [1821] (f. 40). Cf. Susan Moller Okin, *Women in Western Political Thought* (Princeton: Princeton University Press, 1979), chs. 1–3 on both Plato's misogyny and his radical proposal for abolishing the family and enfranchising women within the guardian class.

58. *Letters of MME*, pp. 189, 196; *Works* 10: 400; Almanack, Aug. 29, 31, 1824 (f. 34).

59. "Father," p. 13; CCE-MME, July 29, 1822; *Letters of MME*, pp. 174–75; MME-EBE, March 2, 1824; EBE, "The Advancement of the Age" (MHS).

60. CCE-MME, [Jan. 30 or Feb. 6, 1823] (226.30), Oct. 16, 1823; *Letters of RWE* 1: 128; *Letters of MME*, pp. 167, 178–79, 183.

61. Perry Miller, *The Transcendentalists: An Anthology* (Cambridge: Harvard University Press, 1950), p. 19; James W. Mathews, "Fallen Angel: Emerson and the Apostasy of Edward Everett," *SAR* 1990 (Charlottesville: University of Virginia Press, 1990), pp. 23–32; Rusk, p. 112.

62. *Letters of RWE* 1: 169–70; *Letters of MME*, pp. 190–91. Cf. Everett, "The Circumstances Favorable to the Progress of Literature in America," *Orations and Speeches on Various Occasions* (Boston: Little, Brown, 1850), 1: 10–44.

63. *Letters of MME*, pp. 180–81, 79; Almanack, n.d. [c. 1805] (Tolman transcript, 235.579, f. 46). Cf. "The Revolution in Greece, January 19, 1824," in *The Papers of Daniel Webster, Speeches and Formal Writings*, ed. Charles M. Wiltse (Hanover, N.H.: University Press of New England, 1986), 1: 83–111, and Wilberforce, *An Appeal to the Religion, Justice, and Humanity of the Inhabitants of the British Empire* (London: J. Hatchard and Son, 1823).

64. *Letters of MME*, p. 197. Cf. Edward Everett, "The First Battle of the Revolutionary War," *Orations and Speeches* 1: 73–100.

65. *Letters of MME*, pp. 193, 166, 181.

66. *Letters of MME*, pp. 209–11, 216.

67. *Letters of MME*, pp. 216–17.

68. CCE-MME, Jan. 30, 1826; *JMN* 2: 316; *Letters of MME*, p. 189.

69. Franklin B. Sanborn, *Sixty Years of Concord, 1855–1915*, ed. Kenneth W. Cameron (Hartford, Conn.: Transcendental Books, 1975), p. 48; *Letters of RWE* 7: 150.

70. *Letters of RWE* 1: 171.

71. *Letters of RWE* 1: 170–71 and 171n.

72. *Letters of MME*, pp. 196–98, 37–38. See Evelyn Barish, "The Moonless Night: Emerson's Crisis of Health, 1825–27," in *Emerson Centenary Essays* (Carbondale and Edwardsville: Ill.: Southern Illinois University Press, 1982), pp. 4–8, for an analysis of the medical evidence linking Waldo's eye problem with tuberculosis.

73. *Letters of MME*, pp. 198–99.

74. CCE-MME, Sept. 12, 1825; *Letters of RWE* 7: 139 (cf. 1: 164 on Bulkeley); *Letters of MME*, pp. 198–201.

75. WE$_3$-MME, Oct. 27, 1825 (MHS); EBE-RWE, [Oct. 1825] (226.193); *Letters of MME*, pp. 201–2.

76. "Father," pp. 15–16; *Letters of MME*, pp. 205–6. Just three months after beginning studies with Eichhorn, William had written to a friend, "My mind seems to have undergone a revolution which surprizes me" (Karen Kalinevitch, "Ralph Waldo Emerson's Older Brother: The Letters and Journals of William Emerson" [Ph.D. diss. 1982, University of Tennessee], p. 123). He seems to have shared little of this experience with his family until later.

77. *Letters of MME*, pp. 206, 212.

78. *Letters of RWE* 7: 140–42.

79. MME-RWE, Feb. 26 and March 22, 1826; *Letters of MME*, p. 213.

80. *Letters of MME*, pp. 208–9.

81. *Letters of MME*, pp. 214–15, 203–4; CCE-MME, Dec. 21, 1825; cf. *Letters of RWE* 1: 167–68, 7: 143–44.

82. *Letters of MME*, pp. 214–15.

83. *Letters of RWE* 7: 148–50.

84. *Letters of MME*, pp. 217–18.

85. *Letters of RWE* 1: 171.

86. *Letters of MME*, pp. 217, 215.

87. *Letters of RWE* 7: 148, 1: 170.

88. *Letters of RWE* 1: 174.

89. The manuscript is entitled "Waldo's birthday" and is included amidst loose papers in the Almanack (f. 42). Mary must have sent it to Waldo in 1826 or soon after. The folder also contains a transcription in Charles's hand, subtitled "a sort of horoscope imagined by her."

Chapter Eight

1. *Diaries and Letters of WE*, p. 120; MME-RHE, [Jan.?] 21, Feb. 8, March 19, 1823; Sept. 27 and Dec. 18, 1825; Middlesex Registry of Deeds, May 5, 1825.

2. *Letters of MME*, pp. 195–96, 218–19; ER–Henry Fitts, July 22, 1818; Sanborn, *Personality of Emerson*, p. 118; MME-WE$_3$, Aug. 16 and 28, [1826] (220.75).

3. *Letters of MME*, pp. 218, 220n.; Middlesex Registry of Deeds, May 5, 1825; *Diaries and Letters of WE*, p. 120.

4. "Father," pp. 26–27.

5. *Letters of RWE* 1: 236–37; 7: 172–74. Cf. ch. 6, n. 38 on Dr. Haskins.

6. *Letters of MME*, pp. 237–38, 238n., 244–45.

7. *Letters of MME*, pp. 245, 243; *JMN* 3: 351–53, 356–57; *Letters of RWE* 1: 242–43, 247–48, 250–51.

8. MME-RWE, Sept. 20, [1828] (226.859); *Letters of MME*, p. 249; "Father," pp. 27–28; MME-RWE, [Aug.? 1829] (226.860). Cf. Edward's journals as quoted by Rusk, p. 127.

9. MME-CCE, July 14, [1829] (226.671).

10. ER, *Half Century Discourse*, pp. 33–41 passim.

11. ER, *Half Century Discourse*, pp. 9–11; MME-ER, April 6, 1830; *Letters of MME*, p. 260.

12. ER, Journal and Notebook, Nov. 6, 1778; May 1, 1824; Nov. 11, 1811; Nov. 27, 1826.

13. Almanack, [June] 10, 1827 (f. 9); [Mar.?], 1830 (f. 13); [Nov.] 13, 1826 (f. 8).

14. Almanack, [Dec.] 30, 1826 (f. 8); June 1, 1827 (f. 9); Sept. 10, 1828 (f. 10); [June] 21, 1827 (f. 9).

15. Almanack, Jan. 1, 1827 (f. 8); Nov. 28, 1826 (f. 8); [Dec.] 29, 1829 (f. 12).

16. Almanack, [July] 22, 1826; [Dec.] 30, 1826; [Nov.] 26, 1826 (f. 8).

17. Almanack, [June] 24, 1826 (f. 8); [July] 15, 1827 (f. 9); *Letters of RWE* 1: 242.

18. Almanack, [June] 21, [Aug.] 17, [June] 27, 1827 (f. 9); May 12, 1828 ("MME2," 226–27).

19. "MME 3," 268.

20. Almanack, [March?] 1830 (f. 13).

21. *Sermons of RWE* 1: 55–62.

22. *Letters of MME*, p. 226; *JMN* 2: 391.

23. *Letters of MME*, p. 226; *Letters of RWE* 7: 157–58.

24. Almanack, [May] 26, 1826 (f. 8); [May] 30, 1829 (f. 10); *Works* 10: 427.

25. *Letters of MME*, pp. 229–30, 232–34.

26. *JMN* 3: 55; *Letters of RWE* 7: 158–60; *Sermons of RWE* 1: 85–92; Almanack, July 4, 1826 (f. 8). Cf. Wesley T. Mott, *"The Strains of Eloquence": Emerson and His Sermons* (University Park: Pennsylvania State University Press, 1989), ch. 1, on this sermon and its Christian Stoicism.

27. *Letters of RWE* 7: 168–69; *Letters of MME*, p. 245.

28. Cf. preaching record in *Sermons of RWE* 1: 45–48. SamR-MME, quoted in James B. Thayer, *Rev. Samuel Ripley of Waltham* (Cambridge: Privately printed, 1897), pp. 39–40; *Letters of RWE* 7: 176–77.

29. *Letters of RWE* 7: 176–77; *Letters of MME*, pp. 252–53.

30. *Letters of MME*, p. 251.

31. *Letters of MME*, pp. 258–60; *Sermons of RWE* 1: 231–37. Cf. Rusk, pp. 136–37, on the ordination itself.

32. *Letters of RWE* 1: 208.

33. *Letters of MME*, pp. 236, 287; MME-RWE, [Aug. 1829] (226.863); July 2, [1830] (226.877); Almanack, [Aug.] 19, 1829 (f. 11), [July 1830] (f. 13).

34. *Letters of RWE* 7: 183–84; *Sermons of RWE* 2: 31, 28, 19–24. Cf. *Works* 10: 406 for "trifles."

35. *Sermons of RWE* 2: 19–20.

36. *Sermons of RWE* 2: 23–24; Almanack, [Nov.] 30, [Nov.] 13, [Nov.] 18, 1828 (f. 10). Mary's version of these sentences: "Scathed and mildewed by age without one illusion of hope even for an easy & felt age I unite myself my very self to this first of Beings. 18. The little comforts—luxuries &c. I don't ask health—cold—hungry—dirty I can praise—the faster the days go tho' ever so torpid in mind & body the more I praise. . . ."

37. *Letters of MME* 1: 376.

38. *Letters of MME*, p. 287; *Sermons of RWE* 2: 48 (cf. Almanack, [May] 30, 1829 [f. 10]); 2: 82 (cf. Almanack, [Oct.] 1828 [f. 10]: "It is the voice of social intellectual society the recluse hears").

39. *Sermons of RWE* 3: 148–49 (cf. Almanack, [Nov.] 13, 1828 [f. 10]); 4: 34–35 (cf. Almanack, [Mar.] 24, 1830 [f. 13]). In the latter, Waldo's first sentence comes from two passages of Mary's: "The faith has been my father mother prized house and home when destitute of all to the purpose of literality. More—far more—it shelters the wretched—unbinds the slave and converts the bloody persecutor." I have not located the remainder of his quotation, but it is unmistakably from the Almanack as well.

40. *Sermons of RWE* 3: 92, 2: 34, 2: 195 (cf. *Letters of MME*, pp. 175, 199, 215; *JMN* 6: 176–77).

41. *Sermons of RWE* 2: 19, 33, 22; 4: 35.

42. *Sermons of RWE* 4: 157, 154 (cf. *Letters of MME*, p. 176).

43. Channing, *Works* 3: 230, 243–44; CCE-MME, Jan. 1, 1829; MME-EBE, Jan. 11, 1829 (Middlebury); *Letters of MME*, p. 255.

44. Almanack, May 8, 1827 (f. 9), Aug. 19, 1829 (f. 11); *Letters of MME*, p. 267, 268n. Cf. "The State of German Literature," *Edinburgh Review* 46 (June 1827), 304–51, and *Letters of*

RWE 1: 218, 218n.: Waldo had read this review two years before and written to William about the similarity of Aunt Mary's writing style to Richter's as it was there described. He did not respond to the review's presentation of Kantian ideas in his journal or letters.

45. Almanack, Aug. 19, 1829 (f. 11).

46. Almanack, Aug. 19, 1829 (f. 11).

47. Almanack, Aug. 19, 1829 (f. 11).

48. Almanack, Dec. 25, 1829, [Jan.] 1, 12, 1830 (f. 12); [May] 30, 1830, Feb. 3, 1830 (f. 13). Christian doctrine is more explicit in *Aids to Reflection* than *The Friend*; Mary eventually read both.

49. MME-CCE, June 19, [1830] (226.682).

50. Almanack, [June] 12, 1830 (f. 13). Mary wrote to Waldo on Nov. 10, 1829, that she wanted *Aids to Reflection* and had already seen *The Friend*; Waldo answered on Dec. 10 that he was "reading Coleridge's Friend with great interest" and saw him as "one new mind I never saw before." The latter is his first mention of familiarity with Coleridge. But his first use of the terms "reason" and "understanding," often cited as a turning point in the development of Transcendentalist views, came more than four years later in a letter to Edward. See *Letters of MME*, p. 267; *Letters of RWE* 7: 189, 1: 412–13.

51. *Letters of MME*, pp. 266–67; *Letters of RWE* 7: 186, 1: 272.

52. MME-RWE and CCE, [Oct. 1829]; *Letters of MME*, p. 267; *One First Love: The Letters of Ellen Louisa Tucker to Ralph Waldo Emerson*, ed. Edith W. Gregg (Cambridge: Harvard University Press, 1962), pp. 60, 112–13.

53. *Letters of MME*, p. 285; *One First Love*, pp. 116, 124–25.

54. *Letters of MME*, p. 295.

55. *One First Love*, p. 136; Henry Pommer, *Emerson's First Marriage* (Carbondale: Southern Illinois University Press, 1967), p. 37; for later quotations of this poem, cf. "MME 1," 1, and *Works* 10: 595n.

56. *One First Love*, p. 117; *Sermons of RWE* 2: 12, 1: 219–24; *Letters of MME*, p. 285; MME-RWE, Aug. 30, [1830] (226.878).

57. Pommer, *Emerson's First Marriage*, pp. 22–23, 39 (cf. Rusk, pp. 90–91); *Letters of MME*, p. 287; MME-RWE, July 2, Aug. 30, 1830. (226.877, 878).

58. MME-RWE, April 6, [1830] (226.874); Almanack, [April], April 7, May [1?], 1830 (f. 12).

59. Almanack, March 7, [1830] ("MME 2," 10–11); *Letters of MME*, pp. 293, 289; MME-RWE, April 6, 1830 (226.874).

60. *Letters of MME*, p. 290. Like Coleridge's American editor, James Marsh, who was of orthodox conviction, Mary sought in the British philosopher a new metaphysic to buttress the spiritual life and an unconditioned ground for the idea of God and God-redeemed humanity. Like him, too, she read Coleridge in line with the Cambridge Platonists, Leibniz, and Malebranche, all anti-Lockean philosophers of spirit. But she differed markedly in being a Unitarian and Wordsworthian, much more open to nature as revelation; in being a solitary enthusiast, not so scripturally or institutionally bound; and in being a laywoman. Cf. Peter Carafiol, *Transcendent Reason: James Marsh and the Forms of Romantic Thought* (Tallahassee: Florida State University Press, 1982), especially chs. 1 and 2.

61. Transcribed in *JMN* 7: 443.

62. *One First Love*, p. 136; CCE-MME, Feb. 6, 1831; *Letters of RWE* 1: 318.

63. *Letters of RWE* 1: 318; *JMN* 3: 227.

64. *Letters of MME*, pp. 304–5; *One First Love*, p. 157; MME-RWE, Dec. 1 and [2], [1831?] (226.885). Cf. Luke 20: 35.

65. *Letters of MME,* pp. 300, 304; *One First Love,* pp. 137–38; MME-RWE, [June 1831] (226.882); Almanack, [July] 17, 1831 (f. 15).

66. *Letters of MME,* p. 310; MME-RWE, Oct. 23 and [24], [1831] (226.884).

67. MME-RWE, Oct. 23 and [24], [1831] (226.884).

68. *JMN* 3: 290.

69. Cf. *The Friend* (ed. Barbara E. Rooke), 2: 509.

70. *Sermons of RWE* 4: 28–36.

71. *Letters of MME,* pp. 313–15.

72. *Letters of MME,* pp. 313–15. Cf. Waldo's definitive postresignation sermon of Sept. 2, 1832: "It is not our soul that is God but God is *in* our soul" (*Sermons* 4: 175); and *Aids to Reflection,* p. 208: "Reason is pre-eminently spiritual . . . through an effluence of the same grace by which we are privileged to say Our Father!" "There is . . . no *human* Reason."

73. *JMN* 4: 30; CCE-MME, May 30–31, 1832; *Letters of MME,* p. 316, 319.

74. Almanack, July 1, [1831] (f. 15). Cf. reports of communion in Almanack, [Sept. 1801?] (f. 16), Nov. 1826 (f. 8), and [Oct. 12?], 1834 (f. 17). In the last she speaks of attending the supper "after many months," so apparently has done so at least periodically, but neither recorded nor meditated upon it in her Almanack. Her Almanack for March 2, 1835 (f. 17), reports feeling "too disgusted with human modes" to take communion.

75. Almanack, Dec. 25, 1829 (f. 12); [April] 20, 1831 (f. 15).

76. *JMN* 4: 30.

77. CCE-WE, July 6, 1832 (Emerson Family Papers, MHS); *JMN* 4: 31; MME-CCE, Nov. 2 and [6], [1832] (226.718); *Letters of MME,* p. 321.

78. *Letters of RWE* 1: 355; MME-RWE, Aug. 26, [1832] (226.890); *Letters of MME,* p. 328.

79. *Letters of ETE* 1: 187–88, 689–90; *JMN* 7: 444.

80. CCE-WE, July 6, 1832 (Emerson Family Papers, MHS); *JMN* 4: 228–29; MME-CCE, July 14, [1832]. Information about Crawford Trail from the *Appalachian Mountain Club White Mountain Guide* (Boston: AMC, 1976), pp. 81–82.

81. *Letters of MME,* p. 318.

82. *Letters of MME,* pp. 319-21; Almanack, Sept. 12, 1832 ("MME 4," 110).

Chapter Nine

1. *Letters of RWE* 1: 375–76; *JMN* 4: 198–200. Cf. Richardson, *Emerson,* chs. 23–24.

2. *Letters of MME,* pp. 330–34.

3. George Frisbie Hoar, "Charles Chauncy Emerson" (1903), rpt. in *Emerson Society Quarterly* 16 (1959), 2; *Letters of MME,* p. 333.

4. MME-CCE, Jan. 11, 1829 (Middlebury); *Letters of MME,* p. 326.

5. *Letters of RWE* 1: 137; Almanack, May 13, 1827 (f. 9); Mar. 24, 1830 (f. 13); *Sermons of RWE* 4: 34. On the early signs of interest in slavery issues by RWE and others in his family, cf. Len Gougeon, *Virtue's Hero: Emerson, Antislavery, and Reform* (Athens: University of Georgia Press, 1990), ch. 2.

6. CCE-MME, Aug. 30, 1831; Hoar, "Charles Chauncy Emerson," p. 2.

7. EBE, "Porto Rico—notes and journal," Jan. 27, Feb. 26, Mar. 9, 1831; CCE-WE$_3$, Feb. 5, 1832 (Emerson Family Papers, MHS). Cf. Channing's views of 1831 in William Henry Channing, *The Life of William Ellery Channing, D. D.* (Boston: American Unitarian Association, 1880), pp. 521–27.

8. *Life of WEC,* pp. 527–28; EBE, "Porto Rico," Jan. 22, April 10, 1832; CCE, "Lecture on Porto Rico," n.p. [ca. 1833.]

9. CCE, "Public Opinion" (Commencement Oration, Aug. 27, 1828), Harvard University Archives; CCE-MME, May 7, March 7, 1833.

10. Hoar, "Charles Chauncy Emerson," p. 2; Samuel May, "Reminiscences of Charles Chauncy Emerson," 1895 (220.159); CCE-MME, July 20, 1828; MME-CCE, May 16, [1830] (226.681); *Letters of MME*, p. 295.

11. *Letters of MME*, p. 294; CCE-MME, Oct. 27, 1831.

12. CCE-MME, Oct. 27, 1831; CCE-MME, Aug. 15, 1831.

13. CCE-MME, Jan. 7, 1831; Mar. 20, 1833; July 26, 1834; July 7, 1834; June 29, 1830.

14. CCE-MME, April 30, 1832; CCE-RWE, July 7, 1834; *Letters of MME*, pp. 321–22 and passim. Charles was investigating the status of Mary's Waterford property, as well as consulting with brother William and Daniel Appleton White about an annuity for her.

15. *Letters of MME*, p. 265; MME-CCE, Feb. 9, 1828; Aug. 2 and 9, 1831; CCE-MME, June 22, 1833.

16. *Letters of MME*, pp. 336–37; CCE-MME, April 11–12, 1833.

17. MME-CCE Aug. 13, [1833] (226.733); *Letters of MME*, pp. 346–47. On the Hoars, see *Works* 10: 437–48; Robert A. Gross, "Squire Dickinson and Squire Hoar," *Proceedings of the Massachusetts Historical Society* 101 (1989), 1–23; Ruth R. Wheeler, *Concord: Climate for Freedom* (Concord, Mass.: Concord Antiquarian Society, 1967), p. 166; and "Letters of EH," pt. 1 (*SAR* 1984), 238–39.

18. *Letters of MME*, p. 346; CCE-EH, Aug. 29, 1833.

19. CCE-EH, Sept. 17, 1834; CCE-RWE, Feb. 12, 1835; CCE-EH, May 6, July 22, 1834; CCE-MME, July 26, 1834; CCE-EH, [Aug. 13, 1834] (f. 17).

20. CCE-EH, Aug. 27, Sept. 19, 1834.

21. CCE-EH, Sept. 21, 1834.

22. CCE-EH, Sept. 21, Oct. 1, Oct. 9, Oct. 13, 1834; EPP-Mary T. Peabody, Oct. 6–8, 1834 (Berg Collection, NYPL); CCE-RWE, Oct. 29, 1834. Cf. *Letters of MME*, p. 354 n. All references to Peabody Family correspondence are courtesy of Megan Marshall.

23. Almanack, [Oct. 1834] (f. 17).

24. CCE-WE_3, Oct. 20, 1834 (Emerson Family Papers, MHS); MME-EH [Oct. 19, 1834] (226.1086).

25. CCE-EH, Oct. 1, 1834; *Letters of RWE* 1: 423–24.

26. CCE-EH, Nov. 10, 1834; Jan. 20, 1835.

27. Almanack, [Dec.] 1834 (f. 17); *JMN* 4: 353.

28. *JMN* 4: 368, 371, 335.

29. Almanack, [Oct.] 14, Oct. 22, 1834 (f. 17).

30. *Letters of RWE* 1: 429, 7: 232–33; CCE-EH, Jan. 29, 1835; CCE-RWE, [Feb.] 1835 (226.127).

31. CCE-EH, Jan. 18, 1835.

32. CCE-EH, April 30, June 27, Aug. 27, Sept. 2, 1834; CCE-RWE, [Mar. 1834] (226.116).

33. CCE, "Astronomical Problems" (Harvard University Archives); "Catalogue of Birds"; CCE-EH, May 6, April 11, 1834; Nov. 10, 1833; *JMN* 5: 157–58.

34. *JMN* 5: 18–19.

35. *JMN* 5: 35–36, 80–81. EPP-Mary T. Peabody, Feb. 1, 1835 (Berg Collection, NYPL) reported writing to MME a summary of Waldo's "Tests of Great Men."

36. CCE-HH, Feb. 5, 1835; *Letters of MME*, p. 368; Almanack, Mar. 25, 1835 (f. 18); *JMN* 5: 64.

37. *Letters of LJE*, pp. 25, 27 (cf. EPP-Mary T. Peabody, Mar. 15, 1835 [Berg Collection, NYPL] for date); MME-SABR, June 22, [1835] (226.1285). For Lidian's religious views, cf. *Life of LJE*, especially pp. 41–42.

38. MME-SABR, June 22, [1835] (226.1285); *Life of LJE*, p. 50.

39. *Life of LJE*, pp. 50, 72–73; MME-RWE, [June 29? 1835] (226.893); *Letters of MME*, p. 362.

40. CCE–Joseph Lyman, July 24, 1835; *Life of LJE*, pp. 56–60; *Works* 11: 27–86; *Letters of RWE* 1: 454.

41. *Letters of MME*, pp. 355–56. Cf. *Concord Freeman*, Jan. 17, 31, Feb. 14, 1835; on Thompson, see Samuel J. May, *Some Recollections of Our Anti-Slavery Struggle* (Boston: Fields, Osgood, 1869), pp. 115–25.

42. CCE-EH, March 30, 1835; MME-LJE, [March 29, 1835] (226.770).

43. Almanack, [March] 29, 1835 (f. 18); cf. Luke 2: 25–32.

44. Quoted in Gougeon, *Virtue's Hero*, p. 25.

45. Quoted in Gougeon, *Virtue's Hero*, p. 25.

46. CCE, "Lecture on Slavery," *Emerson Society Quarterly* 16 (1959), 12–30. See also mss. "Notes on Slave Laws," "Fragment" (235.295), CCE–Joseph Lyman, April 20, 1835, and CCE-WE_3, April 29, 1835.

47. CCE, "Lecture on Slavery," pp. 14, 19, 20; MME-EH, Oct. [1837] (226.1103). Charles's manuscript is dated "Concord," and letters suggest that he also gave the lecture in Duxbury and Milton.

48. MME-EH, Oct. 22 and 23, [1836] (226.1094); George Tolman, "John Jack, the Slave, and Daniel Bliss, the Tory," p. 7 on Mary Rice; *Letters of MME*, pp. 367, 360–61; MME-ABA, Oct. 30, 1835, quoted in "Autobiography 1834 A. B. Alcott" (Alcott Family Papers, Houghton *59-M-306).

49. SABR-MME, [Aug. 1835]; MME-SABR, Nov. 11, [1835] (226.1287); CCE–Joseph Lyman, Sept. 4, 1835.

50. *Letters of MME*, p. 364; *Letters of LJE*, p. 43.

51. *JMN* 5: 90–91; CCE-WE_3, Oct. 10, 1835 (Emerson Family Papers, MHS); *Life of LJE*, pp. 64, 83–84. One letter survives to show the common allegiance of Lidian and Mary Brooks to the "spiritual kingdom" of women's reform (Mary Merrick Brooks–LJE, ca. 1857 [220.37]).

52. May, *Anti-Slavery Struggle*, pp. 124–25, 156.

53. May, *Anti-Slavery Struggle*, pp. 159–60; Martineau quoted by Gougeon, *Virtue's Hero*, p. 29.

54. CCE, "Toleration"; CCE–Joseph Lyman, Jan. 19, 1836; CCE-EH, Dec. 21–23, 1835.

55. Almanack, [Dec.] 20, 1835 (f. 18).

56. *Letters of MME*, p. 366.

57. *Letters of MME*, pp. 366–67.

58. Almanack, Feb. 8, Feb. 9, 1836 (Tolman transcript, f. 22).

59. Almanack, [March] 24, 1836 (f. 18); cf. *Works* 9: 253–4, 10: 397–98.

60. Almanack, [Feb.] 5, 1836 (f. 18), Feb. 6, 1836 (Tolman transcript. f. 22).

61. *Letters of MME*, pp. 367–69, 428–29.

62. Almanack, March 1, 1836 (f. 18); CCE-MME, March 5, [1836]; MME-CCE, March 8 and April 1, 1836.

63. Almanack, [April] 24, 1836 (f. 18); *Life of LJE*, p. 66; *Letters of LJE*, p. 44; *Letters of RWE* 2: 13–14.

64. *Letters of RWE* 2: 14, 18–19; MME-EH, June 28, [1836] (226.1092); WE_3-RWE, May 7, 1836; *Letters of MME*, p. 370.

65. MME-LJE, May 12 and [13], 1839 (Middlebury); "Letters of EH," pt. 2 (*SAR* 1985), 142; MME-EH, June 28, [1836] (226.1092).

66. *Letters of RWE* 7: 259–60; *Letters of MME*, pp. 370–71.

67. "Letters of EH," pt. 2, 142; MME-EH, June 28, [1836] (226.1092).

68. *Letters of RWE* 2: 21; *JMN* 5: 150–61, 170.

69. *Collected Works* 1: 28–29. My interpretation of *Nature* in light of Charles and Mary is especially influenced by B. L. Packer, *Emerson's Fall: A New Interpretation of the Major Essays* (New York: Continuum, 1982), ch. 2; and Alan D. Hodder, *Emerson's Rhetoric of Revelation: Nature, the Reader, and the Apocalypse Within* (University Park: Pennsylvania State University Press, 1989), ch. 2.

70. *Collected Works* 1: 10, 8, 29, 25, 37, 8, 22; *JMN* 5: 152, 157–58, 154, 153 (cf. 76); 6: 262, 266.

71. *JMN* 5: 151–52.

72. *JMN* 6: 255; 7: 445–46; *Collected Works* 1: 28.

73. *JMN* 4: 53.

74. *Collected Works* 1: 25, 17, 19.

75. *Collected Works* 1: 29–36; Almanack, n.d. (f. 30); cf. Waldo's transcription, "MME 2," 296–98. The reference in this entry to a "young companion"—probably Charles or Waldo—suggests a date of composition in the 1820s, possibly even 1832, the occasion of Mary's and Waldo's visit to the White Mountains; Mary loosely quotes Prospero in *The Tempest,* Act IV, scene i, lines 151–54. *Letters of MME,* p. 139.

76. *Collected Works* 1: 30, 10, 45.

77. *Letters of MME,* pp. 374–75; cf. *JMN* 5: 264.

78. *Letters of MME,* p. 371; Almanack, Aug. 25, 1836 (f. 18).

79. Almanack, Sept. 6, 1837 ("MME 3," 29–30).

Chapter Ten

1. Alamanack (f. 21).

2. *Letters of MME,* p. 441.

3. *Letters of MME,* pp. 385, 374; "Letters of EH," pt. 2, pp. 136n., 144; MME-EH, Sept. 26, 1837.

4. "Letters of EH," pt. 2, p. 153;

5. MME-EH, May 12, 1839.

6. *JMN* 5: 446; *Letters of MME,* p. 426; MME-EH, June 27, [1841] (226.1122). This transcript sent to Mary was probably identical to the one in the Elizabeth Palmer Peabody Papers of the AAS and edited by Nancy Craig Simmons ("Margaret Fuller's Boston Conversations: The 1839–40 Series," *SAR* 1994, pp. 195–226).

7. MME-EH, Oct. 22 and 23, [1836] (226.1094); SamR-MME, Sept. 29, 1836 (Ames Papers, transcript owned by Joan Goodwin); MME-EH, Jan. 22, 1837; MME–Leander Gage, [1836?] (Gage Family Additional Papers, AAS).

8. *Letters of MME,* p. 416.

9. MME-EH, Mar. 3, 1840; *Letters of MME,* p. 421. Stone's earliest published abolitionist tract was a tribute to Elijah Lovejoy, *The Martyr of Freedom* (Boston: Isaac Knapp, 1838); Mary's role in this statement of commitment to abolition is unclear.

10. *History of Waterford,* pp. 83, 293; George W. Cooke, *An Historical and Biographical Introduction to Accompany the Dial* (New York: Russell and Russell, 1901), pp. 87–93; *Letters of MME,* p. 558. Cooke states that Stone wrote a tribute to MME but does not identify it, nor have I been able to locate it.

11. Joel Myerson, *The Transcendentalists and the Dial* (Rutherford, N.J.: Fairleigh Dickinson University Press), pp. 204–5; *Letters of MME,* p. 436; MME-EH, Sept. 14, 1841.

12. Thomas Hovey Gage, "Sketch" (Gage Family Additional Papers, b9 f1, AAS); MME-ASG, [1839?] (Gage Family Additional Papers, b2 f2, AAS).

13. ASG, untitled ms. "The contest between the soul," n.d. (Gage Family Additional Papers, b7 f2, AAS).

14. *Letters of MME*, pp. 391–92.

15. Cf. *Paradise Lost* 3: 622–35. In *Letters of MME*, p. 392, Nancy Simmons reads the name of the ambassador as "Urah." But the handwriting of the manuscript is indistinct at this point, and I believe that the surrounding verbal echoes of Milton's Uriel are strong evidence of her intending this name. See also her clear reference to Uriel in 1845 (*Letters of MME*, p. 467). The earliest fragment of the poem "Uriel" is dated between 1840 and 1843 (*Poetry Notebooks of Ralph Waldo Emerson*, ed. Ralph H. Orth et al., [Columbia: University of Missouri Press, 1986], p. 956; cf. JMN 8: 463). On Waldo's later conflation of Satan and Uriel in the poem, see Kevin van Anglen, "Emerson, Milton, and the Fall of Uriel," *ESQ* 30 (1984), 147–48.

16. Almanack, Mar. 6, 1838 (f. 20); May 5, 1839 (f. 21).

17. *Letters of MME*, pp. 403–4, 593; Elm Vale Cemetery, Waterford; MME–SamR, Dec. 12, 1839.

18. MME-ASG [1837?] (Gage Family Additional Papers, b2 f2, AAS); MME-EH, Jan. 22, 1837.

19. *JMN* 5: 350–51.

20. *Letters of MME*, pp. 390, 457; Cecilia C. Mettler, *History of Medicine* (Philadelphia: Blakiston, 1947), pp. 474, 967 on erysipelas; Sarah Stage, *Female Complaints: Lydia Pinkham and the Business of Women's Medicine* (New York: Norton, 1979), ch. 2, for an overview of the schools of medical therapy.

21. Mettler, *History of Medicine*, p. 41; MME-EH, Feb. 17, 1841; Almanack, Feb. 19, 1841 (f. 22).

22. MME-EH, [Jan.] 24 and Feb. 4, [1847] (226.1167); Almanack, Feb. 11, [1837] ("MME 3," 38); Mar. 31, 1841 (f. 22).

23. Almanack, March 31, [1841?], March 1840 (f. 22).

24. Almanack, March 31, [1841?] (f. 22); MME-LJE, May 1, [1842] (226.786).

25. Almanack, [Dec.?] 16, [1838 or 1839] (f. 21). Mary was loosely quoting from Victor Cousin, *Introduction to the History of Philosophy*, trans. Henning Gottfried Linberg (Boston: Hilliard, 1832), pp. 72–73. I appreciate Alan Hodder's identification of this passage.

26. Almanack, July 17, 1837 ("MME 3," 44).

27. *Letters of MME*, pp. 426, 429; *Collected Works* 2:30. Cf. pp. 165, 168, 226–27, 254, 261, 277 in this volume for references to Mary's "whim."

28. *JMN* 7: 439, 449–50, 442–47; *Letters of RWE* 2: 396–97.

29. Waldo wrote about Mary seven times between 1836 and 1838: twice negatively in relation to female egotism and despondency (*JMN* 5: 190 and 410) and five times positively in relation to her "Greek" nature, "genius of ancestral religion," relation to him as "benefactor," model of journal-keeping, and ability to write sibylline "scripture" (*JMN* 5: 244, 323–24, 385, 409; 7: 22). Between 1838 and 1841 he occasionally quoted her and once called her letter evidence of the world's richness (*JMN* 7: 52, 148, 220), but he reflected much less upon her importance to him until the burst of renewed relationship that spring.

30. *Letters of MME*, pp. 428–29.

31. *Letters of MME*, p. 436; cf. WE_3-RWE, [Aug. 1841] (Emerson Family Papers, MHS), *Letters of RWE* 2: 433–34, 437, and *Letters of MME*, pp. 434–35. Nancy Craig Simmons has discussed the significance to Waldo of this meeting in her paper "Complex Configurations: Mary Moody Emerson, Ralph Waldo Emerson, and the 'Method of Nature' " (Northeast Modern Language Association, Boston, April 1995).

32. *Letters of RWE* 2: 451, 469.

33. MME-EH, Jan. 22, 1837; *Letters of MME*, p. 440.

34. MME-EH, Sept. 26, 1837; March 24, [1842] (226.1133); *Letters of MME*, p. 429. Cf. Walter Harding, *The Days of Henry David Thoreau* (New York: Knopf, 1965), pp. 126–31, and Madelon Bedell, *The Alcotts: Biography of a Family* (New York: Clarkson Potter, 1980), pp. 160–61.

35. SamR-MME, July 7, [1840] (Ames Papers, transcript owned by Joan Goodwin).

36. MME-SamR, Oct. 22, [1841] (226.1249); MME-EH, Oct. 15 and Dec. 9, [1846] (226.1162); *Letters of MME*, p. 523; *Letters of Margaret Fuller*, ed. Robert N. Hudspeth (Ithaca, N.Y.: Cornell University Press, 1983), 2: 246; JMN 5: 190. Fuller's printed description of Mary follows the version that Waldo prepared for the *Memoir*, naming the "low" young lady "Miss Biddeford." In his own transcription, however, Waldo crossed out "Miss Gage" and inserted the fictional name from the Maine seacoast town (*JMN* 11: 493).

37. *Letters of Margaret Fuller* 2: 246; MME-EH, Aug. 4 and 6, 1850; MME-LJE, [May 11, 1852] (226.785).

38. MME-EH, [Nov.? 1841] (226.1127 and 1131); *Letters of MME*, p. 438.

39. MME-"Albert," Dec. 9, 1841. On Anti-Slavery Fairs, see *Lydia Maria Child: Selected Letters, 1817–1880*, ed. Milton Meltzer and Patricia G. Holland (Amherst: University of Massachusetts Press, 1982), p. 58; on the Grimkés vs. Beecher, see Gerda Lerner, *The Grimké Sisters of South Carolina* (Boston: Houghton Mifflin, 1967), ch. 12.

40. MME–Anti-Slavery Fair, Dec. 8, 1841.

41. *Letters of MME*, p. 432; MME-RWE, Jan. 9, [1841] (226.909).

42. *Letters of RWE* 3: 7; *Letters of MME*, p. 439.

43. *Letters of MME*, pp. 442.

44. *Letters of MME*, pp. 439–40; MME-EH, Feb. 26, [1842] (226.1132); MME-LJE, May 1, [1842] (226.786).

45. MME-SamR, [April 25?, 1842] (226.1250); *Letters of MME*, p. 440–41.

46. *Letters of MME*, pp. 445–46; *Letters of RWE* 7: 513–14; *JMN* 7: 442.

47. MME-EH, Aug. 1, 1843; *Letters of RWE* 3: 208.

48. *Letters of RWE* 3: 209–10.

49. *Letters of MME*, pp. 450–51.

50. Almanack, [May] 11, 1842 (f. 23); MME-LJE, May 1, [1842]. (226.786). Cf. Joseph Emerson, *Lectures on the Millennium* (Boston: Samuel T. Armstrong, 1818): his classically postmillennial position is signaled by the claim that the "days of blood and horror" are giving way to universal peace, and that a "merely spiritual resurrection" will take place only at the end of an earthly millennium (pp. 35, 71). Isaac Taylor's position is not wholly different from this, also affirming the importance of missions, church union, and peace, but he speculates that suffering and trial will intervene before victory (*Saturday Evening* [Boston: Crocker and Brewster, 1832], ch. 13 "The Last Conflict of Great Principles"). Mary's fluctuation between postmillennial optimism and premillennial pessimism was hardly unique to her; James H. Moorhead, in "Between Progress and Apocalypse: A Reassessment of Millennialism in American Religious Thought," (*Journal of American History* 71 [Dec. 1984], 524–42) sees the tension between models of progress and overturning as characteristic of the mainstream ethos of revivals and reform.

51. MME-EH, June 1, 1843; Isaac Taylor, *Fanaticism* (Boston: Crocker and Brewster, 1834), p. i. See also *The Disappointed: Millerism and Millenarianism in the Nineteenth Century*, ed. Ronald L. Numbers and Jonathan M. Butler (Bloomington: Indiana University Press, 1987); and Ruth Alden Doan, *The Miller Heresy, Millennialism, and American Culture* (Philadelphia: Temple University Press, 1987).

52. MME-EH, June 1, 1843.

53. *Letters of MME*, pp. 453–54.

54. *Letters of MME*, pp. 457–58. For accounts of Millerite ascension robes, see Doan, "Millerism and Evangelical Culture," in Numbers and Butler, *The Disappointed*, p. 128, and Clara Endicott Sears, *Days of Delusion: A Strange Bit of History* (Boston: Houghton Mifflin, 1924), pp. 173–80 and passim.

55. *Letters of MME*, pp. 469–71. Waterford Congregational Church records list Phebe Chamberlain as "in absentia Battle Creek Michigan"; see chapter 11 for the Hamlins as Shakers. For these post-Millerite connections on the broader scale, cf. Lawrence Foster, "Had Prophecy Failed? Contrasting Perspective of the Millerites and Shakers," and Jonathan M. Butler, "The Making of a New Order: Millerism and the Origins of Seventh-day Adventism," in Numbers and Butler, *The Disappointed*, pp. 173–88 and 189–208.

56. On dresses, see for instance CCE-EH, March 29, 1835; MME-RWE, [1832?] ("MME 1," 42); and MME-ASG, Aug. 17, 1855 [AAS]. On the shroud, see *Letters of MME*, p. 458; MME-EH, May 25, 1844; SABR–George Simmons, Oct. 7, 1844 (Sarah Alden Bradford Ripley Papers, Schlesinger).

57. Blanche E. Wheeler Williams, *Mary C. Wheeler: Leader in Art and Education* (Boston: Marshall Jones, 1934), p. 39; cf. Mary R. Fenn, *Old Houses of Concord* (Old Concord Chapter D.A.R., 1974).

58. *Caleb and Mary Wilder Foote: Reminiscences and Letters*, ed. Mary Wilder Tileston (Boston and New York: Houghton Mifflin, 1918), p. 82.

59. SABR–George Simmons, Oct. 7, 1844 (Sarah Alden Bradford Ripley Papers, Schlesinger).

60. *Letters of RWE* 3: 262; Almanack, June 26, July 24, 1838 (f. 20).

61. EPP-MME, Oct. 7, 1845 (Elizabeth Palmer Peabody Papers, AAS).

62. *Letters of MME*, pp. 470–71 on Hedge, Brownson, Fuller; pp. 449 and 456 on Peabody; p. 458 on *Dial*; Almanack, [Nov.] 8, 1842 (f. 23), on Brownson's Schleiermacher; *Letters of Elizabeth Palmer Peabody, American Renaissance Woman*, ed. Bruce Ronda (Middletown, Conn.: Wesleyan University Press, 1984), pp. 263–66.

63. MME-EH, Oct. 19, 1847; Aug. 4 and 6, 1850; *Letters of MME*, p. 551; MME-LJE, [Dec. 2, 1851] (220.74).

64. *Letters of MME*, pp. 475–76.

65. MME-EH, [July/Aug.? 1845?] (226.1154); April 7, [1846] (226.1157). No letters between MME and Mary Merrick Brooks survive in either direction.

66. *Letters of MME*, p. 449; MME-RWE, Mar. 23, [1843] (226.913); "MME 4," 192; MME-EH, Feb. 17, 1853 (cf. *Letters of MME*, pp. 570, 595, on Stowe).

67. *Letters of MME*, pp. 366–67, 483; MME-ASG, Sept. 7, [1853] (Gage Family Additional Papers, b2 f2, AAS).

68. MME Will, April 2, 1832 (235.395); MME-EH, Jan. 11 and 21, [1841?] (226.1119); *Letters of MME*, p. 446.

69. *Letters of MME*, pp. 516, 518; *Letters of LJE*, p. 174.

70. Almanack, [May] 13, 1827 (f. 9); *Letters of MME*, pp. 577, 514, 480–81.

71. MME-ASG, [Mar. 27, 1846] (Gage Family Additional Papers, b2 f2, AAS); Louise Hall Tharp, *The Peabody Sisters of Salem* (Boston: Little, Brown, 1950), ch. 17, for EPP's moneymaking strategies of the 1840s.

72. MME-EH, Sept. 8, 1846; MME-EH, Aug. 14 and 15, [1846] (226.1160); *Letters of MME*, p. 490; EPP–Frances Gage, [Aug.] 26, [1846] (Gage Family Additional Papers, b2 f1, AAS).

73. EPP-ASG, [1846] (Gage Family Additional Papers, b2 f1, AAS).

74. EPP-ASG, [1846] (Gage Family Additional Papers, b2 f1, AAS).

75. MME-EH [May 14, 1849?] (226.1189), June 16, [1849] (226.1190).

76. *Letters of MME*, p. 580; Mabel Gage, "The Story of Ann Sargent Gage" (Gage Family Additional Papers, AAS); Ann Sargent Gage, "Visited the Basins in Albany Aug. 9th" (Gage Family Additional Papers, AAS).

77. *Letters of MME*, pp. 567, 531.

78. *Letters of MME*, pp. 460–61; cf. pp. 314–15, 392, and Almanack, Feb. 12, 1832 (f. 15), for the other angelic names. Gougeon discusses the significance of the West Indies Emancipation Address in *Virtue's Hero*, pp. 49–50.

79. *Letters of MME*, p. 466.

80. *Letters of MME*, pp. 467–69; *Poetry Notebooks*, p. 956; *JMN* 9: 170–71; *Works* 9: 13–15.

81. Almanack, [March 21?]-22, [May] 16, [May] 24, [July?] 23, Sept. 7, [Sept.] 23, 1847 (f. 27); [Dec.] 7, 1849 (f. 28); cf. *Collected Works* 1: 29.

82. *Letters of MME*, pp. 496, 527.

83. Almanack, Nov. 3, 1849 (f. 28); MME-SamR, Oct. 22, [1841] (226.1249); MME-EH, Oct. 19, 1847; MME–Martha Bartlett, Mar. 22, [1849] (226.622).

84. *Letters of MME*, p. 457, 555; MME-ASG, Sept. 26, 1851; [April?] 24, 1853; Jan. 15, 1854 (Gage Family Additional Papers, b2 f1, AAS); MME, Will, May 7, 1859 (235.395).

85. Cameron, "The Rev. R. Waldo Emerson and Aunt Mary's Books," 6–7; *Letters of MME*, p. 431; MME-EH, Sept. 8, Oct. 15, and Dec. 9, 1846; MME, Will, May 7, 1859.

86. *Letters of MME*, p. 533; MME-Christopher Gore Ripley, May 28, [1850]; Oxford Co. Registry of Deeds, nos. 73/88 (Jan. 8, 1846); 88/173 (Jan. 21, 1846); MME-CCE, Aug. 25, [1832] (226.712).

87. MME-RWE, Apr. 17, 1855; *Letters of MME*, p. 482 (cf. Simmons's account of the "Elm Vale Saga," pp. 412–15).

88. EPP-ASG, [1845], [Aug.] 26, [1846]; MME-ASG, [1841?] (Gage Family Additional Papers, b2 f1, AAS).

89. MME-EH, Oct. 19, 1847.

90. "Letters of EH," pt, 3, pp. 148–49.

91. Almanack, Oct. 18, 1847 (f. 27); *Letters of MME*, p. 502; MME-EH, Dec. 24 and 26, 1847; April 14 and 16, 1848.

92. Calvin Farrar–RWE, [March 1846]; May 1, 1845; Sept. 9, 1846; April 1847 (bMS Am 1280.943ff.).

93. Calvin Farrar–RWE, Sept. 9, 1846; *Letters of MME*, p. 518.

94. *Letters of MME*, pp. 495, 496; MME–Daniel Appleton White, Sept. 16, 1847 (A-H). Descriptions of Waterford Hydropathic Institute from "Way Down East" by "Nogg," clipping from the *Chronotype* in Alcott Family Letters, 1828–61 (Houghton), and from Elizabeth Palmer Peabody letter, *Christian Register*, May 1, 1847. For hydropathic theory and practice, see Harvey Green, *Fit for America: Health, Fitness, Sport and American Society* (New York: Pantheon, 1986), pp. 58–67.

95. Bronson Alcott quoted in Bedell, *The Alcotts* p. 268; Abby May Alcott–Family, May 27, 1848 (Memoir 1878, Houghton); Abby May Alcott–Samuel J. May, June 14, 1848 (Family Letters 1828–61, Houghton).

96. MME-LJE, [May] 18, 1848 (226.794); MME-EH, June 14, [1848] (226.1201); MME-LJE, Aug. 31, [1848] (226.797).

97. *Ipswich Emersons*, pp. 180–81; HHP-EH, Dec. 9, 1849 (226.3914).

98. HHP-EH, Dec. 9, 1849 (226.3914); MME-EH, Feb. 17, 1853.

99. *Letters of MME*, p. 528; Almanack, [Nov.] 19, 1849 (f. 28).

100. *Letters of MME*, p. 529; MME-ASG, Sept. 26, 1851 (Gage Family Additional Papers, b2 f2, AAS); MME–Martha Bartlett, Jan. 9, 1851.

101. *Letters of MME*, p. 527; MME-ASG, Aug. 17, 1855 (Gage Family Additional Papers, b2 f2, AAS); Eunice Monroe Glines–Ward Monroe, Sept. 19, 1902 (ms. owned by Miriam Sylvester Monroe, Waterford, Maine).

102. Eunice Monroe Glines-Ward Monroe, Sept. 19, 1902.

103. MME-ASG, Sept. 26, 1851 (Gage Family Additional Papers, b2 f2, AAS); Almanack, June 22, 1851 (f. 28).

Chapter Eleven

1. MME-RHE, May 24, 1822; MME-RWE, Aug. 26, [1851] (226.944).

2. MME-RWE, Aug. 26, 1851; MME-ASG, Sept. 26, 1851 (Gage Family Additional Papers, b2 f2, AAS); *Life of LJE*, p. 123. EH–Eliza Spurr, July 23 and Aug. 12, 1851, mentions accompanying MME's visit to the Shakers (transcripts by Elizabeth Maxfield-Miller, CFPL). Rebecca Hamlin visited the Concord Emersons at least twice; Waldo wrote to William that for her and her daughter "the plain fraternity at H.[arvard] seems a sunny asylum" (*Letters of RWE* 3: 335 and 4: 294).

3. *Letters of MME*, p. 536; Almanack, Oct. 25, 1851 (f. 28). The fullest impression of the Hamlins' Shaker community is ETE's in *Life of LJE*, pp. 131–34, telling of spiritualists who claimed contact with Rebecca's spirit after her death. Though Shakers saw the Second Coming in spiritual rather than earthly terms, they easily accommodated many Millerites into their communities and received new enthusiasm from them in return. See Foster in Numbers and Butler, *The Disappointed*, pp. 173–88.

4. *Letters of MME*, pp. 525, 538, 553; Harding, *Days of Thoreau*, pp. 314–15; Gougeon, *Virtue's Hero*, pp. 154–65; Richardson, *Emerson*, ch. 85.

5. *Letters of MME*, pp. 549–50; [MME], "The Sabbath," *The Middlesex Freeman*, Nov. 14, 1851.

6. *Letters of RWE* 4: 260–61; Charvat, *Emerson's American Lecture Engagements*, p. 26; MME-LJE, [Dec. 2, 1851] (220.74); *Letters of MME*, p. 550; "An Octogenarian" [MME], " 'The Woman'—A Reminiscence," *Christian Register* 31 (Jan. 24, 1852). The latter appears to be a substantially edited and shortened version of the letter that Mary submitted through White. Cf. Smith's account of the Concord lecture and Mary's positive response in *Selections from the Autobiography of Elizabeth Oakes Smith*, ed. Mary Alice Wyman (Lewiston, Maine: Lewiston Journal Co., 1924), p. 135.

7. MME-LJE, [Dec. 2, 1851] (220.74); MME-ASG, Jan. 1, 1852 (Gage Family Additional Papers, b2 f2, AAS).

8. *Journal of Henry David Thoreau*, ed. Robert Sattelmayer et al. (Princeton: Princeton University Press, 1981–), 4: 183–84.

9. *Journal of Thoreau* 4: 183–84.

10. MME–Martha Bartlett, Jan. 9, 1851; MME-EH, [1845?] (226.1154); Gougeon, *Virtue's Hero*, p. 154.

11. *Letters of MME*, pp. 538, 551; Harding, *Days of Thoreau*, p. 286. Nancy Craig Simmons discussed the " 'scuttle of dirt' " allusion in "Concord, 1851–52: Three Perspectives," paper at Emerson/Thoreau Societies, Concord, Mass., July 1991.

12. Robert D. Richardson Jr., *Henry Thoreau: A Life of the Mind* (Berkeley: University of California Press, 1986), p. 253; *Journal of Thoreau* 3: 164–66; MME–Martha Bartlett, Dec. 14, [1853] (226.629).

13. Charvat, *Emerson's American Lecture Engagements*, p. 26; *Letters of MME*, pp. 529, 538. She disliked "Economy" when Waldo read it to her later in the winter and declined to attend the lecture (*Letters of MME*, p. 552).

14. Charvat, *Emerson's American Lecture Engagements*, p. 26; *Letters of MME*, pp. 538–39.

15. "MME 2," 70–72 (cf. also 2, 111 on necessity; 2, 140 on faith rising "superior to fate"; 3, 57 on fate in the Odyssey.)

16. "MME 3," 141–42.

17. Cross-references in *JMN* 11: 265n., 315n.; cf. the family history plan in *JMN* 7: 446 and 9: 46. On Waldo's coding journal passages for use, see Rosenwald, *Emerson and the Art of the Diary*, pp. 34–35, 53–58, 140.

18. Susan Loring quoted in *Letters of MME*, p. 546; Harriet Hanson Robinson, Diary, March 1–2, 1869 (Papers of Harriet Hanson Robinson and Jane Hanson Robinson, Schlesinger); Sanborn, "The Women of Concord," 156–57; *JMN* 14: 67.

19. *JMN* 15: 343, 10: 65; MME-EH, [1858?] (226.1216); MME-LJE, Dec. 31, 1858; Williams, *Mary C. Wheeler*, pp. 38–39.

20. *Letters of MME*, p. 432; David E. Stannard, *The Puritan Way of Death: A Study in Religion, Culture, and Social Change* (New York: Oxford University Press, 1977), p. 167.

21. *JMN* 5: 323.

22. Almanack, [Aug.] 8, 1838 (f. 20).

23. *JMN* 3: 352n. (cf. ms. "Genealogy.")

24. Phebe Bliss Memorial (235.233); RHE, Diary [1800]; Almanack, Aug. 4, 1846 ("MME 2," 233); *Works* 10: 402.

25. MME-EH, Dec. 27, [1839] (226.1118); *Letters of MME*, 234.

26. *Letters of MME*, pp. 188, 526–27; Almanack, [Sept.] 20, [June] 11, 1827 (f. 9).

27. Colleen McDannell and Bernhard Lang, *Heaven: A History* (New Haven: Yale University Press, 1988), pp. 207–9, 277, 280–81; Robinson, *The Unitarians and the Universalists*, pp. 52–53, 56–57; *Letters of MME*, pp. 562, 402, 526–27; [MME], "The Meeting of Two Friends After Long Separation from Death," *Christian Register* 26 (Aug. 22, 1846). See *Letters of MME*, pp. 488–89, for Mary's publication of this "fragment of 1830" through Daniel Appleton White.

28. MME-WE_3, July 5, 1849 (220.75); *Letters of MME*, pp. 567, 527. She condemned the vogue of table-rapping and conversation with the dead, e.g. in MME–Martha Bartlett, Sept. 12, 1852, and *Letters of MME*, p. 587.

29. Almanack, 1824 (f. 34), May 24, [July?] 23, 1847 (f. 27).

30. Almanack, May 31, 1834 (f. 17).

31. Almanack, n.d. (Tolman transcript, f. 24); *Letters of MME*, p. 394; Almanack, Sept. 7, 1847 (f. 27).

32. Almanack, Jan. 7, 1855 (f. 30).

33. Almanack, Jan. 16, 1858 (f. 25).

34. Almanack, Oct. 16, 1852 (f. 28) for the dateline "Waterford Monroe's". Ann Sargent Gage's descendants still own the first American edition of Wordsworth's *Prelude* that Waldo inscribed to Mary in 1850 (private correspondence from William A. Wheeler III, Sept. 23, 1996).

35. *Letters of MME*, pp. 554–55, 564–66.

36. *Letters of MME*, p. 566; MME-ASG, Nov. 2, 1853 (Gage Family Additional Papers, b2 f2, AAS).

37. WE_3-RWE, Sept. 25, 1853 (Emerson Family Papers, MHS); MME-RWE, [Oct.?] 7, [1853] (226.947); MME-EH, Oct. 29, [1857] (226.1203).

38. *Letters of MME*, pp. 582, 566–67. My sense of Bushnell is indebted to Bruce M. Stephens, *The Mirror of Time and Eternity: The Person of Christ in American Protestant Thought from Jonathan Edwards to Horace Bushnell* (work in progress).

39. *Letters of MME*, pp. 565, 567.

40. *The Letters of Emily Dickinson*, ed. Thomas H. Johnson (Cambridge: Harvard University Press, 1958), 1: 309, 306; *Letters of MME*, p. 566.

41. *Journal of Thoreau* 8: 146; Sanborn, "The Women of Concord," p. 157 (cf. *Works* 10: 410).

42. MME–Calvin Farrar, June 17, 1856, enclosed in Calvin Farrar-RWE, June 19, 1856 (Houghton bMS Am 1280.948); Lydia Maria Child–MME, Jan. 6, 1857 (226.3275); MME-EH, Oct. 29, Nov. 10, 1857.

43. *Letters of RWE* 5: 106; *Letters of ETE* 1: 141–42.

44. *Letters of ETE* 1: 152, 154, 157; *Letters of MME*, pp. 589–90.

45. MME-RWE, Aug.[2?, 1857?] (Middlebury); *Letters of MME*, p. 592 (cf. "MME 3," 72–73).

46. *Letters of MME*, p. 588.

47. *Journals of Bronson Alcott*, ed. Odell Shepard (Boston: Little, Brown, 1938), p. 308.

48. *Journals of Bronson Alcott*, p. 308; Sanborn, "The Women of Concord," 158.

49. *Letters of RWE* 2: 397.

50. Henry James–Mrs. Carter, Jan. 27, 1862 (Knox College.), quoted in *Letters of MME*, p. 545.

51. *Journals of Bronson Alcott*, p. 310; *Letters of ETE* 1: 157–59; Jillian Smith, "A New Letter from Ralph Waldo Emerson to Edward A. Washburn," *New England Quarterly* 69 (1996), 629; *Letters of RWE* 5: 125–26.

52. *Lain's Brooklyn Directory* (Brooklyn: Lain and Healy, 1855); *Robinson's Atlas of the City of Brooklyn* (New York: E. Robinson, 1886), plate 10; Henry B. Stiles, *A History of the City of Brooklyn* (Brooklyn: By subscription, 1869), 2: 418–19; *Brooklyn USA: The Fourth Largest City in America*, ed. Ruth Seiden Miller (New York: Brooklyn College Press, 1979), p. 4; David W. McCullough, *Brooklyn . . . And How It Got That Way* (New York: Dial Press, 1983), p. 30; Samuel M. Haskins, D. D., *The Triple Semi-Centennial of St. Mark's Church* (Brooklyn: By request, 1890), pp. 15, 24.

53. Stiles, *History of the City of Brooklyn*, 2: 383, 419; Emory Holloway and Vernolian Schwarz, eds., *I Sit and Look Out: Editorials from the Brooklyn Daily Times by Walt Whitman* (New York: Columbia University Press, 1932), pp. 11–12, 15.

54. Samuel P. Abelow, *History of Brooklyn Jewry* (Brooklyn: Scheba, 1937), pp. 5, 9, 12; McCullough, *Brooklyn*, p. 32.

55. Haskins, *St. Mark's Church*, p. 14; HHP-EH, Dec. 9, 1849 (226.3914); *Letters of ETE* 1: 224–25; WE_3-RWE, Dec. 26, 1861 (Emerson Family Papers, MHS); *Lain's Brooklyn Directory*; private correspondence from E. William Chamberlain, Jan. 20 and Jan. 24, 1996, on the migration, employment, and religious affiliation of his ancestors John and Phebe Chamberlain.

56. Haskins, *St. Mark's Church*, pp. 14–17; *Maternal Ancestors*, pp. 10–13; *Letters of MME*, pp. 533–34; MME-WE_3, Sept. 6, [1851] (220.75).

57. HHP-EH, Dec. 9, 1849 (226.3914). Cf. *Life of LJE*, passim, for references to the three women's long-term involvement in Waldo and Lidian's household as well as the Manse.

58. MME-LJE, Dec. 31, 1858; *Letters of MME*, p. 594; WE_3-RWE, April 10, 1860 (Emerson Family Papers, MHS); *Letters of RWE* 5: 154, 326.

59. *Letters of MME*, pp. 593, 595; MME-LJE, Dec. 31, 1858.

60. *Letters of MME*, pp. 594–95; *Letters of ETE* 1: 223.

61. *Letters of ETE* 1: 222.

62. *Letters of ETE* 1: 223–5.

63. *Letters of ETE* 1: 223–5.

64. *Letters of ETE* 1: 226; *Works* 12: 97.

65. I date the four notebooks from cross-references in *JMN*, e.g., to "MME 1" in *JMN* 11: 315n. (1850), "MME 2" in *JMN* 14: 228 (1859), "MME 4" in *JMN* 15: 347 (1863), as well as from the dates specified in 1 and 4. "MME 3" includes no dates or references but seems to follow directly from 2 and to precede the September 1860 date that begins 4. Robert D. Richardson Jr., who has both consulted these notebooks and discussed their significance with me, suggests an earlier beginning date for "MME 1"—the early 1830s—because of its paper type. See *Emerson*, p. 25.

66. *Poetry Notebooks of Ralph Waldo Emerson*, ed. Ralph H. Orth et al. (Columbia: University of Missouri Press, 1986), pp. 470, 876–77. Cf. *Works* 9: 253–54, 10: 397–98.

67. *Letters of ETE* 1: 185–88; *JMN* 7: 444–45; *Letters of RWE* 5: 152.

68. *Letters of RWE* 5: 122, 233.

69. "MME 2," 111–12.

70. "MME 3," 140–42 for "fate; "MME 2," 12 for "Buddhism"; "MME 2," 1 and "MME 3," 1, 32, 35 for the poem (cf. *Letters of MME*, p. 443).

71. *The Topical Notebooks of Ralph Waldo Emerson*, ed. Ralph H. Orth et al. (Columbia: University of Missouri Press, 1990), 1: 77, 85, 242, 221, 248, 82, 251; *Letters of RWE* 8: 573–74. My reading of "Fate" in relation to MME complements Christina Zwarg's reading in relation to Margaret Fuller in *Feminist Conversations: Fuller, Emerson, and the Play of Reading* (Ithaca, N.Y.: Cornell University Press, 1995), ch. 9. Overlapping Emersonian themes of mourning, fatality, textual conversation, and assimilation of female minds deserve further study.

72. *JMN* 14: 228, 272–73, 283–84, 309, 297.

73. *JMN* 14: 280. Cf. *JMN* 4: 53 (1832), where the "fatal gift" is given the more negative connotation of her disgusting everybody "because she knew them too well."

74. *Works* 6: 240, 163, 188. On Antoninus, cf. *JMN* 16: 80: "Every one, too, remembers his friends by their favorite poetry or other reading, as I recall Shakespeare's 'Make mouths at the invisible event,' always from MME's lips, & so many of Antoninus's & Milton's sentences." This passage is used in the essay "Quotation and Originality" (*Works* 8: 194), with the MME allusion left out.

75. *Works* 6: 154–57; cf. *Letters of MME*, p. 182; *JMN* 2: 380–81; "MME 1," 139.

76. *JMN* 14: 286–87 and 348, with references to "MME 1," 50, 73. The Antoninus quotation appears in *Letters of MME*, pp. 249, 349; *Life of LJE*, p. 122; *Topical Notebook* 1: 221; and *Works* 8: 312.

77. *Letters of MME*, pp. 599, 598.

78. *Letters of MME*, pp. 599, 596–97; *Letters of RWE* 5: 249.

79. *Letters of MME*, pp. 598, 600.

80. *Letters of MME*, p. 600; WE$_3$-RWE, July 24, Nov. 24, 1861; March 16–17, 1862 (Emerson Family Papers, MHS); *Letters of RWE* 5: 257.

81. WE$_3$-RWE, April 26, 1863 (226.3047); *JMN* 15: 343.

82. *JMN* 15: 345, 92; cf. 5: 323. In *The Hour of Our Death* (New York: Knopf, 1981), Philippe Aries describes the "Angel of Death" in the late Middle Ages as a woman flying over the earth with a scythe, semibestial and diabolic with her batlike wings, but alternatively as the "good servant" of the will of God (p. 112).

83. WE$_3$-RWE, April 26, 1863 (226.3047); May 3–4, 1863 (Emerson Family Papers, MHS); *Letters of RWE* 5: 325–26; EPP-ASG, May 9, 1863 (Gage Family Additional Papers, b2 f1, AAS).

84. *Works* 11: 434; *Letters of ETE* 1: 310; *Letters of RWE* 5: 326.

85. WE$_3$-RWE and ETE$_2$, May 22–23, 1863 (Emerson Family Papers, MHS); EH quoted

in *Mary Wilder White*, pp. 114–17; EPP-ASG, May 9, 1863 (Gage Family Additional Papers, b2 f1, AAS); "Tribute to MME," pp. 54–57; *Letters of RWE* 9: 107.

86. *Letters of RWE* 9: 107, 5: 326; *JMN* 16: 15.

87. *JMN* 16: 79–80, 82. The latter passage was used in the essay "Quotation and Originality," *Works* 8: 201.

88. *JMN* 16: 66, 90, 259.

89. *JMN* 16: 194–95; *Letters of ETE* 1: 569; *Letters of RWE* 6: 131; EWE–Edith Emerson Forbes, Sept. 2–3, 1870.

90. *Letters of ETE* 1: 685–88; *Letters of RWE* 6: 217; *JMN* 16: 274.

91. *Letters of ETE* 1: 681.

92. *Letters of ETE* 2: 658; EWE, *Emerson in Concord: A Memoir* (Boston: Houghton Mifflin, 1888); *Life of LJE*, pp. xxxviii–xxxix; *Ipswich Emersons*, preface, p. 370.

93. *Letters of ETE* 2: 653; *JMN* 5: 446; *Works* 10: 432.

94. *Letters of MME*, p. 511.

Index

9 780195 039498

Printed in the United States
141687LV00002B/36/A

9 780195 152005